# MANAGEMENT:
# Theory and Practice

## G. A. COLE

MA, MBIM, MIPM

Research Fellow in Business Education
Continuing and Professional Education Area
University of Sussex

## 3rd Edition

DP Publications Ltd
Aldine Place
LONDON W12 8AW

1990

# ACKNOWLEDGEMENTS

*I am grateful to the following bodies for permission to reproduce past examination papers:*

    *Chartered Association of Certified Accountants*

    *Institute of Bankers*

    *Institute of Chartered Secretaries and Administrators*

    *Chartered Institute of Management Accountants*

    *Institute of Administrative Management*

    *Institute of Marketing*

*ISBN 1 870941 60 8*

A catalogue record for this book is available
from the British Library

Copyright  G A COLE © 1990

**First Edition 1983**
*Reprinted 1983*
*Reprinted 1984 (with additions to Chapter 40)*
**Second Edition 1986**
*Reprinted 1987*
*Reprinted 1988*
**Third Edition 1990**
*Reprinted 1992*

Printed in Great Britain by
    The Guernsey Press Co. Ltd.,
    Guernsey, Channel Islands.

Pageset by
    Kai, 21 Sycamore Rise,
    Cinderhill, Nottingham.

# CONTENTS

# PREFACE

## AIMS OF THE MANUAL

1.  The aims of the manual are as follows:
    *   To provide, in one concise volume, an introduction to the principal ideas and developments in the theory and practice of management.
    *   To set out these ideas and developments in terms that are relevant to business and accountancy students taking the examinations of the major examining bodies.
    *   To guide business and accountancy students in answering typical management studies questions as set in recent examinations.

## NEED

2.  Relatively few books on management are written specifically for business and accountancy students. Where such books are published, they do not usually develop the links between the subject-matter and the examinations of the major professional bodies. The purpose of this manual is to remedy this situation by:
    a.  Drawing up the text in the light of the relevant examinations set by the major professional institutions, and in particular the Association of Certified Accountants, the Institute of Chartered Secretaries and Administrators, the Institute of Bankers and the Institute of Cost and Management Accountants.
    b.  Providing discussion and practice-opportunities based on previous examination questions.

## APPROACH TAKEN

3.  The subject-matter of management is extensive, complex and frequently controversial. There are few 'right answers' to the issues it deals with. In order to minimise these difficulties, the material in the manual has been broken down into relatively short chapters which focus on the main aspects of each topic. There are frequent summaries and opportunities for reflecting on the contents by means of discussion points and examination questions.

4.  Like any other subject, management has its own range of technical terms, or jargon. A guide to these terms can be found in the Glossary immediately following this Preface. The manual avoids excessive use of jargon, but clearly some reference to technical terms and abbreviations is essential at times.

5.    The manual has been prepared mainly as a class text-book, but can be used equally well by independent students. In both cases the practice questions will be very useful for checking learning and assisting revision.

## LAYOUT

6.    The keystones of the manual are the individual chapters dealing with main aspects of each topic. Related groups of chapters are assembled into sections (eg Classical Theories), and, with a few exceptions, each section has its own summary, list of discussion – homework questions and previous examination questions.

7.    The Questions for Discussion – Homework are based on issues raised in the text and are designed to enable students and lecturers to check progress and understanding across a range of related topics.

8.    The Examination Questions (EQ's) at the section-ends are included to provide opportunities for testing knowledge and applying it to genuine examination questions. Their inclusion is intended to encourage students to think about examination technique in the planning and presentation of their answers. The EQ's are provided with brief commentaries and outline answers – in the form of key points – which may be found at Appendix 2. Students will gain most benefit if they consult the outline answers after they have made their own attempt at the question.

9.    In addition to the Examination Questions (EQ's) and their outline answers, a short selection of questions for additional practice appears at Appendix 3. These additional questions are supplied with suggested answers at Appendix 4.

10.   As an additional service to lecturers, a selected number of the more wide-ranging or more searching questions have been included at Appendix 5. These Further Examination Questions (FEQ's) are *not* provided with answers in this manual, but in a special supplement available only to lecturers adopting the book as a course text on application to the publishers. These further questions will enable lecturers to set work at which the students will have to rely on their own resources for the answer – as indeed they will have to in the examinations! In all, well over 70 questions are included.

11.   A Guide to Further Reading is included (Appendix 6) to enable students to follow up their own areas of interest at greater length, and to encourage them to take a wider look at the contribution to modern society made by the theorists and practitioners of management. All references made in the text of the manual are included in the Guide.

## USE OF THE MANUAL

12.  For most students it will be essential to read the first two introductory chapters before moving on. Subsequent reading must depend on the demands of the student's particular examination syllabus, but as related chapters have been grouped into sections, it would make sense to read through all the chapters in a section to get the right perspective.

13.  There are plenty of practice opportunities for testing knowledge and examination technique. By making use of such opportunities, students can increase their confidence considerably.

14.  The Appendices contain much useful information, including guidance in answering examination questions, and advice regarding further reading.

## SUGGESTIONS AND CRITICISMS

15.  The author welcomes constructive comments and suggestions from readers concerning the content and layout of the manual.

## PREFACE TO THIRD EDITION

1.  In response to comments from lecturers, some new chapters and additional materials have been included, and there has also been some updating, mainly in the final two chapters.

2.  There are new chapters on:-
   * Japanese approaches to Management (Chap. 10)
   * Types of Business Organization (Chap. 14)
   * Employee Performance Appraisal (Chap. 45)
   * Management Development (Chap. 46)

There is addition material on:
   * Management Information Systems (in Chap. 28)
   * Teams and team-building (in Chap. 27)

The main revisions and updating relate to:
   * Employee Relations (Chap. 48)
   * Employment Law (Chap. 49)

3.  The rest of the book retains most of the content and style of the earlier editions as these seem to have been useful to both students and lecturers.

# GLOSSARY OF MANAGEMENT TERMS

The following list provides a brief guide to some of the more common examples of management terminology in use in the United Kingdom today. It may be especially helpful for overseas students with little knowledge of British management practices. Most of the examples quoted are dealt with more fully elsewhere in the text of the Manual.

**ACAS** Advisory, Conciliation and Arbitration Service; set up by the Employment Protection Act, 1975, to promote the improvement of industrial relations and the extension of collective bargaining.

**Added Value** A measure of productivity, expressed in financial terms, which indicates the effects of the work-force on the sales revenue of the business; it is usually expressed as the value of sales less the cost of purchases.

**Arbitration** A device for settling disputes where the parties concerned fail to agree; the key feature is that the person (or persons) arbitrating takes the decision for the parties. (See also Conciliation and Mediation).

**Basic Pay** Pay which is guaranteed from one period to the next; it excludes bonus earnings, overtime etc.

**Behavioural Science** The study of the individual and the group in the working environment; subjects of study include motivation, communication, organization structure, decision-systems, and organizational change; as a science it is still in the development stage, relying considerably on the contributions of psychology and sociology.

**Benchmark Jobs** In job evaluation, these are the representative sample of jobs which are precisely written up and measured so as to provide a satisfactory range and standard of jobs upon which to base the evaluation of the remainder.

**Benefits** Items such as pensions, sickness payments, company cars etc, which are additional to earnings; sometimes known as 'fringe benefits'.

**BIM** The British Institute of Management.

**Blacking** The boycotting of goods or services by members of a trade union; a sanction used against employers by unions.

**Blue-collar Worker** A manual worker as opposed to a white-collar worker (clerical, administrative, managerial etc).

**Bonus** A payment in addition to basic pay; may be given for a variety of reasons, eg for attendance, for dirty conditions and for payment-by-results; can apply to managers as well as to employees.

**Bridlington Agreement** Refers to the TUC's own procedure for the avoidance of disputes between unions; its principal body is the Disputes Committee. (See also TUC).

**CBI** Confederation of British Industry. The principal employers confederation in the United Kingdom.

**Certified Trade Union** A trade union, which, under procedures originating from the Employment Protection Act, 1975, has been granted a certificate of independence by the Certification Officer.

**Change Agent** A third party, invariably a trained behavioural scientist, who acts as a catalyst in bringing about change by means of an organization development programme; usually an external consultant, but may be an internal specialist. (See also Organizational Development).

**Check-off** Arrangement whereby the employer deducts union dues from the wages of employees in the union, and pays them over to the union(s) concerned.

**Clocking on / Clocking off** Recording the times of arrival or departure of employees by means of a clock-operated franking machine; used mainly in manufacturing; clocking offences invariably invoke severe disciplinary action.

**Closed Shop** This refers to an agreement freely made between an employer and a union or unions that every employee shall become a member of the union(s) who are party to the agreement; non-compliance by an employee can lead to him being fairly dismissed, unless he objects on religious or conscientious grounds.

**Codes of Practice** Refers (i) to guidelines on employee relations matters issued by ACAS; and (ii) to guides issued by the appropriate Minister under the Health and Safety at Work etc Act, 1974 and others; they are not legally enforceable in their own right, but may be used in evidence at a court or tribunal.

**Collective Bargaining** The process of negotiating wages and other working conditions collectively between employers and trade unions, it enables the conditions of employees to be agreed as a whole group instead of individually.

**Collective Agreements** The results of collective bargaining are expressed in agreements; these are principally procedure agreements and substantive agreements; they are not legally enforceable in the UK. (See also Procedure Agreements and Substantive Agreements).

**Communications**   Essentially the process by which views and information are exchanged between individuals or groups; usually refers to the system of communication in use, but can also mean personal skills of communication.

**Conciliation**   Attempts by a third party to promote agreement between the original parties in dispute; unlike in arbitration, a conciliator does not aim to take any decision himself, but attempts to find common ground which may lead to a settlement between the parties themselves. (See also Arbitration and Mediation).

**Convenor**   A senior shop steward elected by fellow stewards to represent them at meetings with other unions or with management; may be full-time in a few establishments.

**Corporate Planning**   Company-wide planning process involving the setting or modification of objectives, and the short and long-term plans for achieving them.

**CRE**   Commission for Racial Equality; monitors effects of Race Relations Act, 1976.

**Delegation**   The process of assigning duties to subordinates to enable them to act within the authority granted to them; delegation does not take away the ultimate accountability of the senior person.

**Differentials**   Differences in earnings between groups of workers, usually based on skills, responsibility or custom and practice.

**Disciplinary Procedure**   A set of rules or guidelines for dealing with instances of bad behaviour or rule-breaking amongst employees; the most common sanctions are warnings, suspensions and dismissals.

**Discrimination**   Usually refers to unfair treatment of an individual or group on grounds of their sex or race.

**Dismissal**   The termination of an employee's contract of employment either by the employer, or by the employee himself in circumstances where the employer's conduct justifies such a step (constructive dismissal); dismissal may be with or without notice.

**Earnings**   The total monetary remuneration received by an employee, including overtime, commission, bonuses etc.

**EAT**   Employment Appeal Tribunal set up under the Employment Protection Act, 1975, to hear appeals from industrial tribunals; usually consists of a High Court Judge and two lay persons, experienced in industrial relations matters, from either the employers' or the trade unions' point of view.

**Employee Benefits**  Usually refers to pensions, sick pay schemes, company cars and other major additions to basic pay. (See also perks).

**Employers' Association**  An organization of employers set up for the purposes of collective bargaining and/or for advising and assisting members with industrial relations problems; some also deal with trading interests as in a 'trade association'.

**EOC**  Equal Opportunities Commission, set up under the Sex Discrimination Act, 1975, to monitor the whole field of sex discrimination.

**EPA**  Employment Protection Act, 1975.

**Flexitime**  Flexible working hours: A system enabling employees to vary their working hours in a particular period, provided they do attend during certain 'core hours', eg 1000 hours– 1600 hours.

**Foreman**  An employee who supervises the work of others, usually in a factory, but is not considered to be of managerial status. (See also Supervisor).

**Go-Slow**  Sanction imposed by trade union members which involves restrictions on work-output and productivity.

**Grapevine**  Refers to the informal and unofficial channels of communication in an organization.

**Grievance**  Complaint made by an employee about wages, conditions of employment, or the actions of management; most organizations have a special procedure for handling grievances.

**Hawthorne Effect**  Term used to describe changes in the productivity and morale of employees as a direct result of management interest in their problems; improvements may arise *before* management takes any action as such; the term originates from the famous studies in the United States in the 1920's at the Hawthorne works of the Western Electric Company.

**Hygiene Factor**  An element of work motivation concerned with the environment or context of the job, eg wages, status, security etc; to be distinguished from motivators eg achievement recognition etc, lack of attention to hygiene factors can lead to dissatisfaction with the job; based on a theory by F. Herzberg. (See also Motivators).

**Incentives**  Payments made to employees over and above their basic pay in order to encourage them to increase production; the payments are made on results achieved.

**Increment**  Refers to an increase within a pay scale, usually of a fixed amount and paid annually; incremental scales are especially common in the public services.

**Induction**  The process of introducing a new employee into his job with the aim of integrating the newcomer as quickly and effectively as possible.

**Industrial Democracy**  Term with a variety of meanings, but generally understood to mean any system at work that provides employees with opportunities for sharing in the major decision-making processes of the enterprise. (See also Worker Director Two-tier Board).

**Industrial Tribunals**  Tribunals set up under the Industrial Training Act, 1964, to hear appeals against training levies; their scope has increased considerably since 1971 and now includes unfair dismissal, sex discrimination etc.

**Job**  A set of tasks or responsibilities grouped together under a particular title.

**Job Description**  A statement of the overall purpose and scope of a job, together with details of its tasks and duties; the description is a product of job analysis.

**Job Enlargement**  The horizontal increasing of job responsibility, ie by the addition of tasks of a similar nature to be distinguished from job enrichment.

**Job Enrichment**  The process of vertically increasing the responsibilities of a job, by the addition of motivators, eg more discretion, improved job interest etc.

**Job Evaluation**  A technique for determining the size of one job compared with another, and the relationship between the two; job evaluation schemes can broadly be divided into analytical and non-analytical; the technique forms the basis for wage and salary administration.

**Key Result Area**  Term used especially in management by objectives; refers to those areas of a person's job that make the biggest impact on end-results. (See also Management by Objectives).

**Labour Turnover**   Percentage figure which indicates the rate at which employees move in and out of employment with the organization; usually expressed as follows:-

$$\frac{\text{Number of employees left during year}}{\text{Average number employed during year}} \times 100$$

**Line and Staff**   A reference to an organizational configuration which embraces line functions, which contribute directly to the provision of goods or services, and staff functions, which contribute indirectly by supporting the line functions; should be distinguished from Line and Functional organization structures, in which functional, ie staff specialist, managers can exercise considerable power over other managers, including line managers.

**Lock-out**   Situation where, as a result of industrial conflict, an employer closes down the business, or part of it, either temporarily or permanently.

**Long-range Planning**   Similar to corporate planning; depending on the industry concerned, long-range could mean two years or ten years; the technique is vital for highly capital-intensive industries. (See also Corporate Planning).

**Management by Objectives**   An approach to management which aims to integrate the organization's objectives with those of individuals; it involves the reduction of overall objectives into unit and individual objectives; in the UK the approach is associated with John Humble. (See also Key Result Area).

**Management Development**   A systematic process for ensuring that an organization meets its current and future needs for effective managers; typical features include manpower reviews, succession planning, performance appraisal and training.

**Manpower Planning**   A technique aimed at securing and improving an organization's human resources to meet present and future needs; three principal stages can be distinguished: evaluation of existing resources, forecast of future requirements and, finally, action plan.

**Marketing Mix**   The particular combination of marketing variables offered to a market at any point in time; the principal variables are usually grouped by reference to product, price, promotion and distribution.

**Matrix Management**   A system of management operating in a horizontal as well as vertical organization structure, where, typically, a manager reports to two superiors – one a departmental/line manager and the other a functional/project manager.

**Mediation** A process whereby a third party makes specific proposals to both sides in a dispute in order to promote a mutually acceptable solution; some-times regarded as a 'half-way house' between conciliation and arbitration. (See also Arbitration and Conciliation).

**Method Study** An aspect of Work Study; its object is to see whether a job is being performed in the most efficient and economical manner; it normally precedes work measurement. (See also Work Study).

**Motivators** Factors leading to job satisfaction and high employee morale; highlighted in F. Herzberg's theory of motivation; motivators are important in job enrichment programmes. (See also Hygiene Factors).

**Negotiations** Term used to describe the bargaining between employers and trade union representatives on the subject of terms and conditions of employment; the object of the negotiations is to obtain mutual agreement to improved conditions. (See also Collective Bargaining).

**Network Analysis** A set of techniques used to plan and control complex processes and activities on the basis of a network diagram; two commonest examples are CPM (Critical Path Method) and PERT (Programme Evaluation and Review Technique).

**O&M** Organization and Methods; a term used for the techniques employed in Method Study and Work Measurement when applied in an office situation for the purpose of improving clerical procedures.

**Operative** Manual worker, usually of a lesser skill than a trained craftsman.

**OR** Operational Research – a scientific method which uses models of a system to evaluate alternative courses of action with a view to improving decision-making.

**Organization Development** A systematic process aimed at improving organizational effectiveness and adaptiveness on the basis of behavioural science knowledge; typical stages in an OD programme include analysis, diagnosis, action plans and review, an external third party assists the process. (See also Change Agent).

**Overtime** A period of work, in excess of normal or standard hours, which is paid at an enhanced rate.

**Pay Policy**  Refers to Government intervention in collective bargaining by means of pay ceilings or other restraints on the negotiation of employment conditions.

**Performance Appraisal**  The process of assessing the performance of an employee in his job; appraisal can be used for salary reviews, training needs analysis and job improvement plans, for example.

**Perks**  Short for perquisites – incidental benefits allowed to an employee, eg tips, gifts from customers, use of telephone etc; not as formal nor as important as 'Employee Benefits'. (See also Employee Benefits).

**Picketing**  Trade union activity where groups of workers in dispute with their employers attend at their own place of work for the purpose of peacefully persuading other workers not to leave or enter the premises for work; the persons in attendance are the pickets, and the area they are picketing is called the picket line.

**Procedure Agreement**  A collective agreement setting out the procedures to be followed in the conduct of management – union relations with particular reference to negotiating rights, union representatives, disputes and grievance procedures. (See also Substantive Agreement).

**Quality Control**  An activity in manufacturing industries which aims to establish quality standards, check that they are being adhered to, take corrective action where necessary, and set improved standards where possible.

**Recognition Issue**  A situation where an employer and a trade union disagree about the extent to which the employer is prepared to recognise the union for the purposes of collective bargaining; unions may seek the help of ACAS, but employers are not obliged to grant recognition.  (See also ACAS).

**Redundancy**  The loss of a job on the grounds that it is no longer required or no longer available at a particular place of employment; it is regarded as a form of dismissal.

**Seven Point Plan**  A guide to selection interviewing, enabling interviewers to assess candidates under seven headings: physical make-up, attainments, general intelligence, special aptitudes, interests, disposition and domestic/family circumstances.

**Shop Steward**  A union member elected by his colleagues to represent them to management in their place of work; shop stewards are appointed under, and work within, their union rules; they are not full-time, nor are they paid for their union work. (See also Convenor).

**Substantive Agreement**   A collective agreement dealing with terms and conditions of employment, eg wages, hours of work, holidays etc. (See also Procedure Agreement).

**Supervisor**   A person who directly supervises the work of others, eg as a foreman (see above); a senior supervisor may in turn directly supervise the work of other supervisors, eg as a works superintendent; supervisors provide the main link between the organization's workgroups and the management.

**Synergy**   The extent to which investment of additional resources produces a return which is proportionally greater than the sum of the resources invested; sometimes known as the $2 + 2 = 5$ effect.

**T Group**   Training group – refers to training in interpersonal awareness or sensitivity training, where a group of people meet in an unstructured group situation and discuss the interplay of relationships between them.

**Theory X**   Theory about motivation, expounded by D. McGregor, which suggests that people are lazy, selfish, unambitious etc, and need to be treated accordingly; managers who act in accordance with this view may be dubbed 'Theory X Managers'; this theory contrasts with Theory Y – the optimistic view of people.

**Theory Z**   An expression coined by an American, W.G. Ouchi, as a result of studying Japanese success in manufacturing industry to denote a process of organizational adaptation in which the management of an enterprise concentrates on coordinating people, not technology in the pursuit of productivity.

**Trade Union**   An organization of employees whose principal purpose is to negotiate with employers about terms and conditions of employment and other matters affecting the members' interests at work. (See also Certified Trade Union).

**Training Needs Analysis**   A rational approach to assessing the training or development needs of groups of employees, aimed at clarifying the needs of the job and the needs of individuals in terms of training required.

**TUC**   Trades Union Congress – the principal national body for the co-ordination of trade union activities in the UK; its role is mainly political and economic lobbying on behalf of the trade unions as a whole; it has no direct power over individual unions. (See also Bridlington Agreement).

**TULRA**   Trade Union and Labour Relations Act, 1974.

**Two-tier Board**   Refers to the Continental practice of dividing the Board of a Company into a Supervisory Board, the senior body, and a Management Board, the executive body; contrasts with the unitary (i.e. single) Board, as in the UK.

**Unfair Dismissal**   A statutory definition of dismissal now part of the Employment Protection (Consolidation) Act, 1978; the Act states that every employee shall have the right not to be unfairly dismissed; remedies for unfair dismissal must be pursued via an industrial tribunal, which may award compensation or reinstatement or re-engagement.

**Value Analysis**   A term used to describe an analytical approach to the function and costs of every part of a product with a view to reducing costs whilst retaining the functional ability; sometimes known as value engineering.

**Worker Director**   An employee of a company who is elected to serve as a director on the Board; such directors are invariably non-executive and may also lack any representative capacity; where a two-tier Board exists, worker directors sit on the Supervisory Board; this form of worker participation has not yet taken root in the UK. (See also Two-Tier Board).

**Work Measurement**   A technique of Work Study designed to establish the time for a qualified worker to carry out a specified job at a defined level of performance. (See also Method Study and Work Study).

**Work Study**   A term describing several techniques for examining work in all its contexts, in particular those factors affecting economy and efficiency, with a view to making improvements; the two most common techniques of Work Study are Method Study and Work Measurement. (See also Method Study and Work Measurement).

# INTRODUCTION TO MANAGEMENT THEORY

The two chapters in this Section set the scene for the rest of the manual. Chapter 1 introduces the principal theoretical approaches to management theory that have appeared over the last fifty years. Chapter 2 deals with the leading interpretations that have been applied to the key concepts of 'management', 'organization' and 'administration'.

# 1
# BACKGROUND DEVELOPMENTS

## INTRODUCTION

1. The theorists who have contributed to our understanding of management have included practical managers as well as social scientists. The contribution of the practical managers has been to reflect on, and theorise about, their own experiences in management with the idea of producing a set of principles of management applicable in a wide variety of situations. In practice these theorists have applied their principles to the *structure* of organizations rather than to other aspects, such as people in organizations. The label which has been ascribed to these theorists is 'classical' or, in some cases, 'scientific managers'. Their approach has been described as prescriptive ie suggesting what is good for organizations.

2. The social scientists, by contrast, have been academics, whose starting point has been research into human behaviour with the intention of first describing, and subsequently predicting, behaviour in organizations. The earliest social scientists concentrated their attentions on the motivation and behaviour of individuals and groups in the work situation. They were particularly interested in social relationships and have been called the Human Relations movement. Their ideas were followed up by the so-called neo-Human Relations School, composed mainly of social psychologists. Modern theorists have taken a more *comprehensive* view of people in organizations. Their studies have looked at the various interactions between people and their environment with the aim of first diagnosing and subsequently predicting behaviour in given situations. This approach has been labelled the 'contingency' approach to management.

## CLASSICAL THEORIES

3. The classical approach to management was primarily concerned with the structure and activities of formal, or official, organization. Issues such as the division of work, the establishment of an hierarchy of authority, and the span of control were seen to be of the utmost importance in the achievement of an effective organization. The two greatest exponents of classical theories were undoubtedly Henri Fayol (1841–1925), and F. W. Taylor (1856–1915). Between them these two practising managers

laid the foundations of ideas about the organization of people at work and the organization of work itself. At first these ideas were developed separately. Fayol in France, and Taylor in the United States. By the 1930's their work was being promoted and developed by writers such as L.F. Urwick and E. F. L Brech on both sides of the Atlantic. The work of all these contributors is described in Chapters 3–5.

## BUREAUCRACY

4.    While Fayol and Taylor were grappling with the problems of management, a German Sociologist, Max Weber (1864–1924) was developing a theory of authority structures in which he identified a form of organization to which he gave the name 'bureaucracy'. The distinguishing features of a bureaucracy were a definition of roles within an hierarchy, where job-holders were appointed on merit, were subject to rules and were expected to behave impartially. Weber's ideas and their impact on modern organization theory are discussed in more detail in Chapter 6.

## HUMAN RELATIONS

5.    The fundamental idea behind the human relations approach to management is that *people's* needs are the decisive factor in achieving organizational effectiveness. The leading figure of human relations was Professor Elton Mayo, whose association with the so-called 'Hawthorne Studies' between 1927 and 1932 provided an enormous impetus to considerations of the human factor at work. A description of the Hawthorne Studies and their impact on industrial psychology is contained in Chapter 8.

6.    Many of the issues raised by Mayo and his colleagues were taken up in post-war years by American social psychologists. An early major influence here was Abraham Maslow's work on motivation based on an hierarchy of human needs, ranging from basic physiological needs (food, sleep etc) to higher psychological needs, such as self-fulfilment. Other important contributors included McGregor, Argyris, Likert and Herzberg. The work of these theorists and the results of their researches are covered in Chapter 9.

## SYSTEMS APPROACHES

7.    By the late 1960's another group of theories began to challenge the dominance of human relations and psychology. These were theories that viewed organizations as complex systems of people, tasks and technology. The early work on this approach was conducted by British researchers from the Tavistock Institute

of Human Relations, who, despite their title, recognized that human or social factors alone were not the most important consideration in achieving organizational effectiveness. They recognized that organizations were part of a larger environment with which they interacted and in particular were affected by technical and economic factors just as much as social ones. They coined the phrase 'open socio-technical system' to describe their concept of a business enterprise. An 'open' social system is one that interacts with its environment eg a commercial enterprise; a 'closed' social system is self-contained eg a strict monastic community. This approach is described in greater detail in Chapter 12.

8.    Arising out of the open systems approach is an essentially pragmatic 'theory' which argues that there is no one theory at present which can guarantee the effectiveness of an organization. Management has to select a mix of theories which seem to meet the needs of the organization and its internal and external pressures at a particular period in its life. This has been termed a contingency approach to management. Notable exponents of this approach are Pugh and colleagues in the United Kingdom, and Lawrence and Lorsch in the United States. A summary of their work appears in Chapter 13.

## CONCLUSION

9.    The task of management is carried out in the context of an organization. Over the past fifty years attempts to develop coherent theories to explain the behaviour of people in organizations have moved away from purely structural or human relations considerations to a more comprehensive systems view. The systems approach does not rule out ideas suggested by classical or human relations theorists, but emphasise that they must be evaluated in the context of the organization's need to adapt to change.

# 2
# DEFINITIONS AND INTERPRETATIONS

## INTRODUCTION

1.   Not unexpectedly, the variety of approaches to the theoretical background of management have produced their own versions of what is meant by such key words as 'management' and 'organization'. This chapter looks at the most typical variations in the interpretation of such words, and offers some explanations.

## THE MEANING OF MANAGEMENT

2.   There is no generally accepted definition of 'management' as an activity, although *the* classic definition is still held to be that of Henri Fayol. His general statement about management still remains valid after fifty years and has only been adapted by more recent writers, as shown below:

*'To manage is to forecast and plan, to organize, to command, to coordinate and to control.'*                           H FAYOL (1916)

*'Management is a social process ...... the process consists of ......: planning, control, coordination and motivation.'*

E F L BRECH (1957)

*'Managing is an operational process initially best dissected by analysing the managerial functions.'*

*'The five essential managerial functions (are): planning, organizing, staffing, directing and leading, and controlling.'*

KOONTZ and O'DONNELL (1976)

The changes made by Brech and the other two writers represent changes of emphasis rather than principle. Not surprisingly, in today's social climate, Fayol's 'command' is dropped in favour of 'motivation' (Brech), or 'directing and leading' (Koontz and O'Donnell).

3.   It has to be recognized that the above definitions are extremely broad. Basically what they are saying is that 'management' is a process which enables organizations to achieve their objectives by planning, organizing and controlling their resources, including gaining the commitment of their employees (motivation). Over the last decade, several writers have attempted to move away from this generalized approach to a more detailed,

behaviour-orientated analysis of what managers actually do in practice. The emphasis in this approach is primarily concerned with *what is a manager* rather than what is management. One such writer is Harold Mintzberg, who, on the basis of his studies of managers at work, has developed a list of roles which appear consistently in managerial jobs. A role is something wider than a mere job description, with its emphasis on duties and activities. A role also includes the behaviour that is expected of a person in fulfilling a job. In managerial jobs, in particular, there are likely to be several roles. Mintzberg sees the key roles as follows.

    a.  Entrepreneur ie planner and risk-taker.

    b.  Resource allocator ie organizer and coordinator.

    c.  Figurehead/Leader ie motivator and coordinator.

    d.  Liaison/Disseminator ie coordinator and communicator.

    e.  Monitor ie controller.

    f.  Spokesman/Negotiator ie motivator and communicator.

    g.  Disturbance-handler ie motivator and coordinator.

4.   In comparing Mintzberg's roles with the nearest equivalent expression available to Fayol, Brech, Koontz and O'Donnell, it can be seen that Mintzberg's list provides a finer analysis of what is involved in a managerial job, and is typical of the more analytical approaches to the study of management in practice.

## ADMINISTRATION

5.   At one time the words 'administration' and 'management' were more or less interchangeable. Fayol himself used the French word 'administration' to mean 'management' in his original treatise on the subject. Nowadays 'administration' tends to be understood as the narrower task of developing and maintaining procedures. That is to say it is seen primarily as an aspect of organizing. This interpretation of administration is even becoming accepted in the Civil Service, where at one time the word 'management' did not form part of the official vocabulary.

## ORGANIZATIONS

6.   Whatever view is preferred concerning the definition of management, it is clear that it can only be discussed realistically within the context of an organization. Brech once described organization as 'the framework of the management process'. However, that framework can be described in several different ways. The first distinction that must be made is between the use of the word 'organization' to describe the *process* of organizing, and

its use to describe the *social entity* formed by a group of people. Organization as a *process* is dealt with later in the Manual (Chapter 21 et seq). Organization as a *social entity* is what we are concerned with in this Chapter.

7.   As yet there is no widely accepted definition of an organization. Nevertheless, as the following quotations suggest, there are some commonly accepted features of organizations such as *purpose, people and structure.*

> *'Organizations are intricate human strategies designed to achieve certain objectives.'*                                    ARGYRIS (1960)

> *'Since organizations are systems of behaviour designed to enable humans and their machines to accomplish goals, organizational form must be a joint function of human characteristics and the nature of the task environment.'*                                    SIMON (1960)

> *'Organizations are systems of inter-dependent human beings.'*
>                                                        PUGH (1971)

8.   As in discussions about management theory, approaches to organization theory tend to follow the pattern of classical, human relations and systems perspectives. The classical approach concentrates attention on the organization structure and all that is required to sustain it (organization charts, procedures, communication channels etc).

Brech and Urwick are good examples of writers who see organizations in this way. The human relations approach says, in effect, that people *are* the organization. Therefore it is vital to give first consideration to issues of group and individual needs before such other issues as structure, authority levels, and decision-making, for example. Job enrichment is a typical example of a human relations approach to organizational design.

The systems approach, which is the one adopted by practically every modern theorist, aims to describe organizations in terms of open systems, responding to external and internal influences in developing, and ultimately achieving, their objectives. Key areas of attention for systems theorists include the relationship between formal and informal (or unofficial) organizations, the external environment, the question of boundaries, the organization's culture and the impact of technology.

## RELATIONSHIP BETWEEN MANAGEMENT AND ORGANIZATION THEORY

9.   Over the past twenty years the impact of the behavioural sciences on the study of mankind at work has led to the ascendancy of organization theory over purely management

theory. Management is no longer seen as *the* controlling factor in work organizations. Instead it is seen as a *function* of organizations. Its task is to enable the organization's purposes to be defined and fulfilled by adapting to change and by maintaining a suitable balance between the various, and frequently conflicting, pressures at work in the organization.

10.    Professor Handy, in his book 'Understanding Organizations', (Penguin, 1987), sums up the new relationship very neatly. In a discussion on the role of the manager, he suggests that the key variables a manager has to grapple with are:

 a.  People.
 b.  Work and structures.
 c.  Systems and procedures.

These variables cannot be dealt with in isolation but within the constraints of an environment in which Handy sees three crucial components.

 a.  The goals of the organization.
 b.  The technology available.
 c.  The culture of the organization (its values, beliefs etc).

All six factors, mentioned interact with each other, and change in one of them will inevitably lead to change in one or more others. To manage successfully is to balance these factors in a way that meets the needs of the organization at a particular period in time, which is essentially a contingency approach to management.

## SECTION SUMMARY – INTRODUCTION TO MANAGEMENT THEORY

1.    This Section has introduced the leading approaches to the study of management in the context of work organizations. It has given examples of the ideas propounded under each of the approaches: classical, human relations and systems/contingency.

2.    The Section has also outlined the relationship between management theory and organization theory, and drawn attention to the overriding influence of the latter in current thinking.

## QUESTIONS FOR DISCUSSION/HOMEWORK

*1.    What do you understand by the terms 'management' and 'organization'? Explain, using your own words.*

*2.    How would you describe the relationship between 'management' and 'organization' when the latter refers to a social entity?*

**3.** Broadly in what ways does a classical approach to organizations differ from a human relations approach?

**4.** What are the key variables that might confront a manager in a typical organization?

**5.** Why can it be of advantage to the student of management to consider managerial roles instead of managerial functions, i n analysing what management is?

## EXAMINATION QUESTIONS - INTRODUCTION TO MANAGEMENT THEORY

As this has been a introductory Section, most of the questions it raises occur with greater relevance in the next group of chapters. However one very general question on the role of management is listed below for practice purposes. An outline answer can be found in Appendix 2.

EQI Organizations employ various resources (eg finance, raw materials, people, plant and equipment) in order to achieve objectives. Discuss the role of management in an organization and assess the relative importance of management as a resource.

*(ICSA MPP)*

# CLASSICAL THEORIES

The four chapters grouped under this Section describe, and comment on, the main features of the ideas of the leading classical theorists.

Chapter 3 deals with the ideas put forward by Henri Fayol.

Chapter 4 looks at the contribution of F.W. Taylor and the so-called 'scientific managers'.

Chapter 5 describes how Lyndall F. Urwick and E.F.L. Brech adapted and extended classical ideas in the period after the Second World War.

Finally, chapter 6 deals with the major classical theory of organization/bureaucracy, and makes particular reference to the formative work of Max Weber.

# 3
# HENRI FAYOL

## INTRODUCTION
1.    This Chapter describes the most important of Fayol's ideas on management in organizations. Particular attention is paid to his General Principles of Management to enable them to be compared with similar principles proposed by other classical writers. The Chapter also includes some commentary on the impact of Fayol's ideas on the theory and practice of management over the last fifty years or so.

2.    Henri Fayol, (1841–1925) the celebrated French industrialist and theorist, began his working life as a young mining engineer at the age of nineteen. He spent his entire working life with the same company, rising to Managing Director at the age of 47 and only retiring after his seventy-seventh birthday! Under his leadership the Company grew and prospered despite its near-bankrupt state when he took over. His entrepreneurial successes won him considerable fame and popularity, and when, in 1916, he published his major work on management, he ensured himself a place in the annals of industrial history.

3.    The publication of 'Administration industrielle et generale' in 1916 brought to light the distillation of a lifetime's experience of managerial work. The best-known English translation is the one by Constance Storrs, published by Pitmans under the title of 'General and Industrial Management' in 1949. The foreword to this translation was provided by none other than L.F. Urwick (see Chapter 5). Urwick questioned the appropriateness of the title, in which the French 'administration' had been translated as 'management'. His fear was that with such a title Fayol's work would be seen as relevant only to *industry*, whereas in Urwick's view, it was just as applicable to central and local government as well. History has shown that he need not have worried – Fayol's ideas have been adopted in one way or another all over the world!

## FAYOL'S DEFINITION OF MANAGEMENT
4.    Fayol prefaces his famous definition of management ('to forecast and plan etc') by stating what he considers to be the key activities of any industrial undertaking. He outlines six such activities:
   a.   Technical activities eg production.
   b.   Commercial activities eg buying and selling.
   c.   Financial activities eg securing capital.

    d.   Security activities eg safeguarding property.
    e.   Accounting activities eg providing financial information.
    f.   Managerial activities eg planning and organizing.

Fayol accepts that the first five are already sufficiently well-known, but recognizes at the outset that the sixth group of activities will require further explanation for his readers. Whilst the other activities are all interdependent to some extent, there is no single one which is concerned with broad planning and resourcing. It is vitally necessary to isolate these last mentioned activities, says Fayol, and it is these to which he gives the name 'managerial'.

5.    To manage, says Fayol, is to forecast and plan, to organize, to command, to coordinate and to control. He sees forecasting and planning as looking to the future and drawing up a plan of action. Organizing is seen in structural terms. Commanding is described as 'maintaining activity among the personnel'. Coordinating is seen as essentially a unifying activity. Controlling means ensuring that things happen in accordance with established policies and practice. It is important to note that Fayol does not see managerial activities as exclusively belonging to *the* management. Such activities are part and parcel of the total activities of an undertaking. Having said this, it is equally important to point out that Fayol's general principles of management take a perspective which essentially looks at organizations from the top downwards. Nevertheless, they do have the merit of taking a comprehensive view of the role of management in organizations. Thus, Fayol's analysis has more far-reaching implications than F.W. Taylor's ideas on scientific management, which are centred on the shop floor.

## THE GENERAL PRINCIPLES OF MANAGEMENT

6.    In his book Fayol lists fourteen so-called 'principles of management'. These are the precepts which he applied the most frequently during his working life. He emphasises that these principles are not absolutes but are capable of adaptation according to need. He does not claim that his list is exhaustive, but only that it served him well in the past. The fourteen items listed below in Fig. 3.1 are given in the order set out by Fayol. The comments are a summary of his own:

**Fig. 3.1. Fayol's Principles of Management.**

| | |
|---|---|
| 1.   Division of work | Reduces the span of attention or effort for any one person or group. Develops practice and familiarity. |

| 2. | Authority | The right to give orders. Should not be considered without reference to responsibility. |
| 3. | Discipline | Outward marks of respect in accordance with formal or informal agreements between firm and its employees. |
| 4. | Unity of command | One man one superior! |
| 5. | Unity of direction | One head and one plan for a group of activities with the same objective. |
| 6. | Subordination of individual interests to the general interest | The interests of one individual or one group should not prevail over the general good. This is a difficult area of management. |
| 7. | Remuneration | Pay should be fair to both the employee and the firm. |
| 8. | Centralization | Is always present to a greater or lesser extent, depending on the size of company and quality of its managers. |
| 9. | Scalar chain | The line of authority from top to bottom of the organization. |
| 10. | Order | A place for everything and everything in its place; the right man in the right place. |
| 11. | Equity | A combination of kindliness and justice towards employees. |
| 12. | Stability of tenure of personnel | Employees need to be given time to settle into their jobs, even though this may be a lengthy period in the case of managers. |
| 13. | Initiative | Within the limits of authority and discipline, all levels of staff should be encouraged to show initiative. |
| 14. | Esprit de corps | Harmony is a great strength to an organization; teamwork should be encouraged. |

7. Fayol's General Principles have been adopted by later followers of the classical school such as Urwick and Brech. Present day theorists, however, would not find much of substance in these precepts. From our present day view point, the following general comments may be made.

a. The references to Division of work, Scalar chain, Unity of command and Centralization, for example, are descriptive of the kind of formal organization that has come to be known as bureaucracy. Fayol, in true classical fashion, is emphasising the structural nature of organizations.

b. Issues such as individual versus general interests, remuneration and equity, are considered very much from the point of view of a paternalistic management. Today, questions concerning fairness or the bona fide conflict of interests between groups, have to be worked out jointly between management and organized labour, often with third party involvement by the State.

c. Although emphasising the hierarchical aspects of the business enterprise, Fayol is well aware of the need to avoid an excessively mechanistic approach towards employees. Thus references to Initiative and Esprit de corps indicate his sensitivity to people's needs as individuals and as groups. Such issues are of major interest to theorists today, the key difference being that whereas Fayol saw these issues in the context of a rational organization structure, the modern organization development specialist sees them in terms of adapting structures and changing people's behaviour to achieve the best fit between the organization and its customers.

d. What Fayol did achieve was the first real attempt to produce a theory of management based on a number of principles which could be passed on to others. Many of these principles have been absorbed into modern organizations. Their effect on organizational effectiveness has been subject to increasing criticism over the last decade; mainly because such principles were not designed to cope with conditions of rapid change and with issues such as employee participation in the decision-making processes of organizations.

# 4

# F W TAYLOR AND THE SCIENTIFIC MANAGEMENT SCHOOL

## INTRODUCTION

1.   This chapter summarises the key ideas of the pioneers of 'Scientific Management' – especially F.W. Taylor, Frank and Lilian Gilbreth and H. Gantt – and comments on the main consequences of their work.

2.   Frederick Winslow Taylor (1856–1917), like Fayol, was one of the early practical manager-theorists. Born in Boston, Massachusetts, in 1856, he spent the greater part of his life working on the problems of achieving greater efficiency on the shop-floor. The solutions he came up with were based directly on his own experience at work, initially as a shop-floor worker himself and later as a manager. His career began as an apprentice in engineering. Having served his time, however, he moved to the Midvale Steel Company, where, in the course of eleven years, he rose from labourer to shop superintendent. It was during this time that Taylor's ideas of 'scientific management' were born. In 1889 he left Midvale to work for the Bethlehem Steel Company, where he consolidated his ideas and conducted some of his most famous experiments in improving labour productivity. Taylor was keen to pass on his ideas to others, which he achieved through his writings, most notably 'The Principles of Scientific Management' published in 1911. After his death, his major works were collected together and published as 'Scientific Management' in 1947. He did not meet Henri Fayol and it is possible that he did not know of Fayol's analysis of management.

## THE SETTING FOR SCIENTIFIC MANAGEMENT

3.   The last twenty years or so of the nineteenth century were a time for facing up to the often ugly realities of factory life. From the employers' point of view, efficiency of working methods was the dominant issue. The gathering pace of the industrial revolution in the Western world had given rise to new factories, new plant

15

and machinery; labour was plentiful. The problem was how to organize all these elements into efficient and profitable operations.

4.   It was against this background that Taylor developed his ideas. He was passionately interested in the efficiency of working methods. At an early stage he realised that the key to such problems lay in the systematic analysis of work. Experience, both as a worker and as a manager, had convinced him that few, if any, workers put more than the minimal effort into their daily work. He described this tendency as 'soldiering', which he sub-divided into 'natural' soldiering ie Man's natural tendency to take things easy, and 'systematic' soldiering ie the deliberate and organized restriction of the work-rate by the employees. The reasons for soldiering appeared to Taylor to arise from three issues:

a.   Fear of unemployment.

b.   Fluctuations in the earnings from piece-rate systems.

c.   Rule-of-thumb methods permitted by management.

Taylor's answers to these issues was to practise 'scientific management. '

## THE PRINCIPLES OF SCIENTIFIC MANAGEMENT

5.   Taylor recognized that what he was proposing would appear to be more than just a new method – it would be revolutionary! He stated at the outset that 'scientific management' would require a complete mental revolution on the part of both management *and* workers.

6.   In its application to *management*, the scientific approach required the following steps:

* Develop a science for each operation to replace opinion and rule-of-thumb.

* Determine accurately from the science the correct time and method for each job.

* Set up a suitable organization to take all responsibility from the workers except that of actual job performance.

* Select and train the workers.

* Accept that management itself be governed by the science developed for each operation and surrender its arbitrary power over the workers ie cooperate with them.

7.   Taylor saw that if changes were to take place at the shopfloor level, then *facts* would have to be substituted for opinion and guesswork. This would be done by studying the jobs of a sample of especially skilled workers, noting each operation and timing it

with a stop-watch. All unnecessary movements could then be eliminated in order to produce the best method of doing a job. This best method would become the standard to be used for all like jobs. This analytical approach has come to be known as Work Study, the series of techniques now utilised all over the world (see Chapter 40).

8.  In Taylor's time the most usual practice at the work organization level was for the management to leave working methods to the initiative of the workers – what Taylor called rule-of-thumb. His suggestion that managers should take over that role was certainly new. Not only that, it was controversial, for he was deliberately reducing the scope of an individual's job. Contemporaries said it turned people into automatons. Taylor argued that the average worker preferred to be given a definite task with clear-cut standards. The outcome for future generations was the separation of planning and controlling from the doing, or the fragmentation of work. McGregor's Theory X assumptions about people (see Chapter 9) are essentially a description of the managerial style produced by Taylor's ideas. In the last decade or so, ideas such as job enrichment and work design have been put into practice precisely to combat the fragmentation effects of years of Taylorism. Another comment of Taylorism is that the gradual de-skilling of work has been accompanied by a rise in educational standards, thus tending to increase worker-frustration even further.

9.  Taylor felt that everyone should benefit from scientific management – workers as well as managers. He disagreed with the way most piece-rate systems were operated in his day, as the practice was for management to reduce the rates if workers earnings went up beyond an acceptable level. Taylor's view was that, having *scientifically* measured the workers' jobs and set rates accordingly, then efficient workers should be rewarded for their productivity without limit. The difficulty for most managers was that they lacked Taylor's expertise in measuring times and had to resort to arbitrary reduction in rates where measurements had been loose.

10. So far as the *workers* were concerned, scientific management required them to:
- Stop worrying about the division of the fruits of production between wages and profits.
- Share in the prosperity of the firm by working in the correct way and receiving wage increases of between 30% – 100% according to the nature of the work.

- Give up their ideas of soldiering and cooperate with management in developing the science.
- Accept that management would be responsible, in accordance with the scientific approach, for determining what was to be done and how.
- Agree to be trained in new methods, where applicable.

11. One of Taylor's basic theses was that adoption of the scientific approach would lead to increased prosperity for all. It was, therefore, much more important to contribute to a bigger cake than to argue about the division of the existing cake. Needless to say this kind of approach did not receive much favour with the trade unions at the time. Taylor saw them as a decidedly restrictive influence on issues such as productivity. In his view wages could now be scientifically determined, and should not be affected by arbitrary factors such as union power or management whim. His own experience had shown how considerable were the increases in earnings achieved by workers adopting their part of the scientific approach.

12. In terms of work-organization, the workers were very much under the control of their management in Taylor's system. Taylor felt that this would be acceptable to them because management's actions would be based on the scientific study of the work and not on any arbitrary basis. It would also be acceptable, argued Taylor, because of the increased earnings available under the new system. He claimed that there were rarely any arguments arising between management and workers out of the introduction of the scientific approach. Modern experience has unfortunately shown Taylor's views to be considerably over-optimistic in this respect. The degree of trust and mutual cooperation, which Taylor felt to be such an important factor in the success of scientific management, has never been there when it mattered. As a result, although workers' attitudes towards Work Study have often been favourable, the ultimate success of work-studied incentive schemes has always been rather limited owing to workers' feelings that the management was attempting to 'pin them down' and to management's feelings that the workers had suceeded in 'pulling the wool over their eyes' concerning the timing of key jobs.

13. In support of his Principles, Taylor demonstrated the benefits of increased productivity and earnings which he had obtained at the Bethlehem Steel works. He described to his critics an experiment with two shovelers – 'first-class shovelers,' in his words – whose efforts were timed and studied. Each man had his own personal shovel, which he used regardless of the type of ore

or coal being shifted. At first the average shovel load was about 38 pounds and with this load each man handled about 25 tons of material a day. The shovel was then made smaller for each man, and the daily tonnage went up to 30. Eventually it was found that with smaller shovels, averaging about 21 pounds per load, the daily output rose even higher. As a result of this experiment, several different sizes of shovel were supplied to the workforce to enable each man to lift 21 pounds per load whether he was working with heavy ores or light coals. Labourers who showed themselves capable of achieving the standards set by the two 'first-class' shovelers were able to increase their wages by 60%. Those who were not able to reach the standard were given special training in the 'science of shoveling'. After a three-year period, Taylor and his colleagues reviewed the extent of their success at the Bethlehem Works. The results were impressive: the work of 400 – 600 men was being done by 140; handling costs per ton had been reduced by half, and as Taylor was quick to point out, that included the costs of the extra clerical work involved in studying jobs; and the labourers received an average of 60% more than their colleagues in neighbouring firms. All this was achieved without any kind of slave-driving, which was no part of scientific management, at least so far as Taylor was concerned.

## SCIENTIFIC MANAGEMENT AFTER TAYLOR

14. Three important followers of scientific management were Frank and Lilian Gilbreth together with Henry Gantt. All made significant contributions to the study of work, and these are summarised in the following paragraphs.

## THE GILBRETHS

15. The husband-and-wife team of Frank and Lilian Gilbreth, who were somewhat younger than the pioneering Taylor, were keenly interested in the idea of scientific management. In his now famous Testimony to the House of Representatives Committee in 1912, Taylor describes how he was first approached by Frank Gilbreth who asked if the principles of scientific management could be applied to bricklaying. Some three years later Gilbreth was able to inform Taylor that as a direct result of analysing, and subsequently re-designing, the working methods of typical bricklayers, he was able to reduce the number of movements in laying bricks from 18 per brick to 5 per brick. The study of task movements, or 'motion study' as it was known, was a development of Taylor's ideas and represented the Gilbreths major contribution to basic management techniques.

16.    A particular feature of the Gilbreths' work was its detailed content. 'Measurement' was their byword, and the Science of Management, as they put it, consisted of applying measurement to management, and of abiding by the results. They were convinced that it was possible to find the 'one best way' of doing things, and there is no doubt that they went a long way towards that ideal. As employers, the Gilbreths practised what they preached. They laid down systematic rules and procedures for the efficient operation of the work, and insisted that these be kept to. In return, the employees were paid well above competitors' rates, and, into the bargain were freed from unnecessary effort and fatigue. With this approach, the separation of the planning from the doing was complete. The employees had no discretion whatsoever once the scientific process had determined how the job should be done. Although these ideas were challenged at the time, they could not be ignored by the new industrial age and its obsession with ideas of efficiency. Whilst few people were prepared to undertake the sheer detail of the Gilbreths methods, the basic techniques caught on, and today (as Method Study) they represent one of the key measures used by managements to organize and control working methods in a wide range of industries.

17.    Two examples of the recording techniques used by the Gilbreths are 'therbligs' and process charting. Therbligs (Gilbreth spelt backwards, in effect) are the basic elements of on-the-job motions and provide a standardised basis for recording movements. They include such items as: search, find, grasp, assemble and inspect. A few items cover periods when no motion may be in evidence such as: wait-unavoidable, rest and plan. The most usual list of therbligs contains 18 items, and may be accompanied by appropriate symbols and colours to aid recording. Example of Therbligs are shown opposite in Figure 4.1.

Flow process charts were devised by the Gilbreths to enable whole operations or processes to be analysed. In these charts five symbols were utilised to cover Operation, Transportation, Inspection, Delay and Storage.

Flow chart symbols used in the flow process charts are shown opposite in Figure 4.2.

## HENRY GANTT

18.    Gantt was a contemporary and colleague of Taylor's at the Bethlehem Steel Company. Whilst accepting many of Taylor's ideas on scientific management, Gantt felt that the individual worker was not given enough consideration.

| Symbol | Name | Colour |
|--------|------|--------|
| 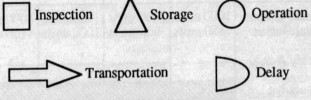 Search | | Black |
| Find | | Grey |
| Select | | Light Grey |
| Grasp | | Red |
| Hold | | Gold Ochre |

**Figure 4.1 Therblig symbols**

☐ Inspection    △ Storage    ○ Operation

⇒ Transportation    D Delay

**Figure 4.2 Flow chart symbols**

Although Taylor himself was not a slave-driver in any way, his methods were used by less scrupulous employers to squeeze as much production as possible out of their workforce. This was particularly true in respect of piece-rate systems. Gantt introduced a payment system where performance *below* that called for on the individual's instruction card still qualified the person for the day-rate, but performance of *all* the work allocated on the card qualified the individual for a handsome bonus. Gantt discovered that as soon as any one worker found that he could achieve the task, the rest quickly followed. Better use was made of the foremen, because they were sought after by individuals who needed further instruction or help with faulty machines. Thus supervision improved, breakdowns were minimised and delays avoided by all concerned. Eventually individual workers learned to cope on their own with routine problems. Gantt's bonus system also allowed for the men to challenge the time allocated for a particular task. This was permitted because Gantt, unlike the Gilbreths, did not believe that there was a 'one best way,' but only a way 'which seems to be best at the moment.' Gantt's approach to scientific management left some discretion and initiative to the workers, unlike those of his colleague, Taylor, and of his fellow theorists, the Gilbreths.

19.    Although it was his ideas on the rewards for labour that made Gantt a notable figure in his day, he is best remembered nowadays for his charts. The Gantt chart was originally set up to indicate graphically the extent to which tasks had been achieved. It was divided horizontally into hours, days or weeks with the task marked out in a straight line across the appropriate numbers of hours or days etc. The amount of the task achieved was shown by another straight line parallel to the original. It was easy from such a chart to assess actual from planned performance. There are many variations of the Gantt chart in use today, and an example is given below:

| Period | Week 1 | Week 2 | Week 3 | Week 4 |
|---|---|---|---|---|
| Planned Output | 1000 units | 1000 units | 1000 units | 1000 units |
| Actual Output | 850 units | 900 units | 1000 units | 1100 units |
| Weekly Actual | ———— | ———— | | — |
| Cumulative | ////////////////////////////////////////////// | | | |

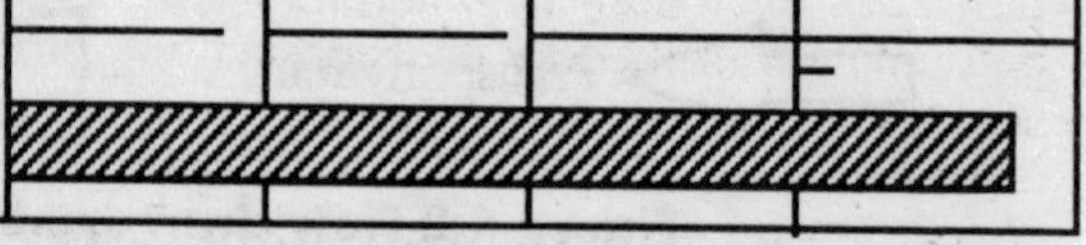

**Figure 4.3 Gantt Chart**

## COMMENTS ON THE SCIENTIFIC MANAGEMENT SCHOOL

20.    The *benefits* arising from scientific management can be summarised as follows:

Its rational approach to the organization of work enabled tasks and processes to be measured with a considerable degree of accuracy.

Measurement of tasks and processes provided useful information on which to base improvements in working methods, plant design etc.

By improving working methods it brought enormous increases in productivity.

It enabled employees to be paid by results and to take advantage of incentive payments.

It stimulated managements into adopting a more positive role in leadership at the shop-floor level.

It contributed to major improvements in physical working conditions for employees.

It provided the foundations on which modern work study and other quantitative techniques could be soundly based.

21.   The *drawbacks* to scientific management were principally the following:

It reduced the worker's role to that of a rigid adherence to methods and procedures over which he had no discretion.

It led to the fragmentation of work on account of its emphasis on the analysis and organization of individual tasks or operations.

It generated a 'carrot-and-stick' approach to the motivation of employees by enabling pay to be geared tightly to output.

It put the planning and control of workplace activities exclusively in the hands of the management.

It ruled out any realistic bargaining about wage-rates since every job was measured, timed and rated 'scientifically'.

22.   Whilst it is true that business and public organizations the world over have benefited from, and are continuing to utilise, techniques which have their origins in the Scientific Management movement, it is also a fact that, in the West at any rate, a reaction against the basic philosophy of the creed is taking place. Tasks and processes are being re-integrated, the individual is demanding participation in the key decision-making processes, management prerogatives are under challenge everywhere by individuals and organized groups alike. Yet, as Chapter 10 points out, Japanese companies in particular have taken up many of the beneficial aspects of scientific management and combined them with other approaches to produce a highly-successful production system.

23.   On balance, the most important outcome of scientific management was that it stimulated ideas and techniques for improving the systematic analysis of work *at the workplace*. It also undoubtedly provided a firm launch-pad for a wide variety of productivity improvements in a great range of industries and public services.

24.   Its major disadvantage was that it subordinated the worker to the work system, and so divorced  the 'doing' aspects of work from the planning and controlling aspects. This led to:

   a.  the creation of boring, repetitive jobs;
   b.  the introduction of systems for tight control over work; and
   c.  the alienation of shop-floor employees from their management.

23

# 5

# THE CONTRIBUTION OF
# URWICK AND BRECH

## INTRODUCTION

1.   This chapter describes the major contribution to the spreading of classical ideas made by L.F. Urwick and his colleague E.F.L. Brech, and comments on the significance of their efforts for the theory and practice of management.

## L F URWICK

2.   Lyndall F. Urwick has been an enthusiastic and prolific writer on the subject of administration and management. His experience covered industry, the Armed Forces and business consultancy. He was strongly influenced by the ideas of Henri Fayol, in particular. He was convinced that the only way that modern Man could control his social organizations was by applying principles, or universal rules, to them. In one of his best-known writings –'The Elements of Administration' published in 1947 – he set out numerous principles which, in his view, could be applied to organizations to enable them to achieve their objectives effectively. Like other classical writers, Urwick developed his 'principles' on the basis of his own interpretation of the common elements and processes which he identified in the structure and operation of organizations. On this basis, the principles represented a 'code of good practice', which, if adhered to should lead to success in administration, or management as we would call it today.

3.   In 1952 Urwick produced a consolidated list of ten principles, as follows.

   i.    The Principle of the Objective – the overall purpose or objective is the raison d'etre of every organization.

   ii.   The Principle of Specialization – one group, one function!

   iii.  The Principle of Coordination – the process of organizing is primarily to ensure coordination.

   iv.  The Principle of Authority – every group should have a supreme authority with a clear line of authority to other members of the group.

v.    The Principle of Responsibility – the superior is absolutely responsible for the acts of his subordinates.

vi.   The Principle of Definition – jobs, with their duties and relationships, should be clearly defined.

vii.  The Principle of Correspondence – authority should be commensurate with responsibility.

viii. The Span of Control – no one should be responsible for more than 5 or 6 direct subordinates whose work is interlocked .

ix.   The Principle of Balance – the various units of the organization should be kept in balance.

x.    The Principle of Continuity – the structure should provide for the continuation of activities.

4.    As a statement of classical organization theory, Urwick's list would be difficult to better, concentrating as it does on mainly *structural* issues. Compared with Fayol's Principles of Management, to which we referred in Chapter 3, Urwick's list is less concerned with issues such as pay and morale, for example. Its emphasis is very much on getting the organizational *mechanisms* right.

5.    There is no doubting the rational appeal of Urwick's 'principles', especially in relation to the internal environment of the organization. Organizations, however, do not operate in a vacuum. They have to interact with their external environment. That is to say they are open systems. Where modern studies have found weaknesses in Urwick's 'principles' is precisely on this point. The 'principles' tend to assume that it is possible to exert control over the issues mentioned, but many current trends in Western society, in particular, run directly counter to several of the 'principles'. For example, attitudes towards greater sharing of authority at work are likely to clash with the Principle of Authority and the Principle of Correspondence. Similarly, attitudes towards the reintegration or enrichment of jobs will conflict with the Principle of Specialization, the Principle of Definition and the Span of Control.

6.    Organizations are not self-contained. They have to respond to the pressures of an external environment – social, political and economic. Urwick's 'principles', therefore, are not capable of being introduced easily into modern organizations. They can be and are adopted with modification in several cases, but will always be suspect because they fall into the category of 'what ought to be'

rather than 'what actually is' in terms of the realities of organizations today.

7.    Urwick's ideas in general have been popular with business organizations on both sides of the Atlantic because of their commonsense appeal to managers in organizations. In the last decade, however, Urwick's emphasis on purpose and structure has not been able to provide answers to problems arising from social attitudes and rapidly changing technology. His ideas are now a little anachronistic. They prescribe part, but only part, of what is needed for organizational health. Nevertheless his influence on many modern businesses has been enormous.

## E F L BRECH

8.    E.F.L. Brech, has written widely on management and organization issues. Whilst sharing Urwick's concern with the development of principles, or general laws, of management, Brech is also concerned with the development of people within the organization. His approach is basically a classical one, but tempered to some extent by the prevailing human relations theories of the last twenty years. He sees management as a process, a *social* process, for planning and regulating the operations of the enterprise towards some agreed objective. This process is carried out within a framework, namely the organization structure. Key issues in the formation of the structure are:

   a. Defining the responsibilities of the management, supervisory and specialist staff.
   b. Determining how these responsibilities are to be delegated.
   c. Coordinating the execution of responsibilities and
   d. Maintaining high morale.

9.    Brech's own list of principles of organization overlaps considerably with the lists set out by Fayol and Urwick. It is less dogmatic in approach than the others, but is nevertheless concerned with the division of responsibilities, lines of communication, unity of command and the allocation of authority, to give just a few examples. Fundamentally, in his view, the principles exist to maintain a balance between the delegation of managerial responsibility throughout the organization and the need to ensure unity of action as well.

10.   In his latest writings (eg The Principles and Practice of Management, Third edition, 1975), Brech regrets that there is still no general agreement about a fundamental body of principles of management. Until such principles are developed, he argues, it will be impossible for management to gain recognition as a science

or indeed as a profession. He believes that such principles, or basic laws of management, could be deduced from an analysis of the nature of the management process, and this is what he himself has attempted in the footsteps of Fayol, Urwick and others. However he concedes that the development of principles will probably be acceptable only on the basis of first hand research into management practices – a view which would undoubtedly please researchers such as Rosemary Stewart, Henry Mintzberg and others who believe that it is primarily through research into managerial behaviour that a body of relevant knowledge or fundamental truths may emerge.

11. Brech's writings on principles are much more directed towards helping practising managers become more effective in their roles, than towards contributing to a general body of knowledge concerning the theory of management. In this respect his own contribution is that of a thoughtful management consultant aiming to improve management practice rather than that of an objective research worker seeking to test out hypotheses. Seen in this light, Brech's contribution has been considerably influential, especially in management training and development.

# 6
# THE CONCEPT OF BUREAUCRACY

## INTRODUCTION

1.  Bureaucracy is a term with several meanings, and this has led to genuine misconceptions about what it truly means. The most common meanings are as follows:
    a.  Bureaucracy is 'red tape' ie an excess of paperwork and rules leading to gross inefficiency. This is the pejorative sense of the word.
    b.  Bureaucracy is 'officialdom' ie all the apparatus of central and local government. This is a similar meaning to red tape.
    c.  Bureaucracy is an organizational form with certain dominant characteristics, such as an hierarchy of authority and a system of rules.

2.  In this chapter bureaucracy is interpreted as 1(c) above, that is to say as an organizational form. The object of the chapter is to describe and discuss this important and all-pervading form of organization, with particular reference to the fundamental work of Max Weber.

## MAX WEBER

3.  Max Weber (1864–1920) spanned the same period of history as those early pioneers of management thought, Fayol and Taylor, to whom we have already referred. Unlike them, however, Weber was an academic – a sociologist – and not a practising manager. His interest in organizations was from the point of view of their authority structures. He wanted to find out why people in organizations obeyed those in authority over them. The observations and conclusions from his studies were first published in translation from the original German in 1947. It was in this publication 'The Theory of Social & Economic Organization' that he gave the name 'bureaucracy' to describe a form of organization that exists to a greater or lesser extent in practically every business and public enterprise.

4.  In his analysis of organizations, Weber identified three basic types of legitimate authority: traditional, charismatic and rational-legal authority. Before describing these, it will be helpful to

understand what he meant by the expression 'legitimate authority'. Authority has to be distinguished from power. Power is a unilateral thing – it enables one person to *force* another to behave in a certain way, whether by means of strength or by rewards. Authority, on the other hand, implies acceptance of rule by those over whom it is to be exercised. It implies that power may only be exercised within limits agreeable to subordinates. It is this latter situation to which Weber refers when he talks about legitimate authority.

5.　The three types of legitimate authority described by him can be summarised as follows:

- Traditional authority – where acceptance of those in authority arises from tradition and custom.

- Charismatic authority – where acceptance arises from loyalty to, and confidence in, the personal qualities of the ruler.

- Rational-legal authority – where acceptance arises out of the office, or position, of the person in authority as bounded by the rules and procedures of the organization.

It is the last mentioned form which exists in most organizations today, and this is the form to which Weber ascribed the term 'bureaucracy'.

## BUREAUCRACY

6.　The main features of a bureaucracy, according to Weber, are as follows:

- A continuous organization of functions bound by rules.

- Specified spheres of competence ie the specialization of work, the degree of authority allocated and the rules governing the exercise of authority.

- An hierarchical arrangement of offices (jobs) ie where one level of jobs is subject to control by the next higher level.

- Appointment to offices made on grounds of technical competence.

- The separation of officials from the ownership of the organization.

- Official positions exist in their own right and the job holders have no rights to a particular position.

- Rules, decisions and actions are formulated and recorded in writing.

7.　The above features of bureaucratic organization enable the authority of officials to be subject to published rules and practices. Thus authority is legitimate, not arbitrary. It is this point more than any other which caused Weber to comment that bureaucratic organization was capable of attaining the highest degree of efficiency and was, in that sense, the most rational known means of carrying out 'imperative control over human beings'.

8.    Weber felt that bureaucracy was indispensable for the needs of large scale organization, and there is no doubt that this form of organization is the one adopted by practically every enterprise of any size the world over. The two most significant factors in the growth of bureaucratic forms of organization are undoubtedly *size* and *complexity*. *Size.* Once an organization begins to grow, the amount of specialization increases, which leads to an increase in job levels. New jobs are created and old jobs redefined. Recruitment from outside becomes more important. Relationships, authority-boundaries and discipline generally have to be regulated. Questions of control and coordination became all-important. Thus a small, relatively informal, family concern can suddenly grow into quite a different organization requiring new skills and new attitudes from its proprietors. *Complexity.* Although size almost inevitably implies complexity, there are also issues of complexity for smaller organizations. These can arise out of the requirements of sophisticated modern technology, for example. In such an environment specialized and up-to-date skills are required, the span of control has to be small, questions of quality control are vital, and last but by no means least, a keen eye needs to be kept on the competition. Add to all these points the rules and regulations of governments and supranational bodies such as the EEC, and the sum total is a highly complex environment, which can only be controlled in a systematic form of organization.

## BUREAUCRACY AFTER WEBER

9.    Weber's contribution to our understanding of formal organization structures has been a major one. No subsequent discussion or debate on this topic has been possible without reference to his basic analysis of bureaucratic organization. Nevertheless, without disputing the basic proposition that bureaucracy is the most efficient means of organizing for the achievement of *formal* goals, several researchers since Weber have established important weaknesses in the bureaucratic model. These researchers have identified a number of awkward side-effects or 'dysfunctions' of bureaucracy, in practice. These dysfunctions may be summarised as follows:

    a.  Rules, originally designed to serve organizational efficiency, have a tendency to become all-important in their own right;

b. Relationships between office-holders or roles are based on the rights and duties of each role ie they are depersonalized, and this leads to rigid behaviour (predictability);

c. Decision-making tends to be categorized ie choices are previously programmed and this discourages the search for further alternatives, another form of rigidity;

d. The effects of rigid behaviour are often very damaging for client or customer relations and also for management worker relationships; customers are unable to obtain tailor made services, but have to accept standardization; employees have to work within a framework of rules and controls which has been more or less imposed on them;

e. Standardization and routine procedures make change and adaptation difficult when circumstances change;

f. The exercise of 'control based on knowledge', as advocated by Weber, has led to the growth of experts, whose opinions and attitudes may frequently clash with those of the generalist managers and supervisors.

10. One particularly well-known follow-up to Weber's theories was conducted by an American sociologist, Alvin Gouldner.

He studied the effects of introducing a bureaucratic system into an organization which had been very informal and indulgent in its management style. The head office of a small gypsum company had appointed a new manager to make the plant more efficient. His new approach led to the replacement of informal methods of working by formalized procedures such as work study and production control. These changes were resented by the workforce and the eventual outcome was a *reduction,* rather than an increase in the efficiency of operations. In studying this situation Gouldner identified three different patterns of bureaucracy operating within the one organization. These were as follows.

i. **Mock Bureaucracy.** This was applied to situations where the rules and procedures were imposed by an outside body (eg Head Office) and where they were either ignored or were merely paid lipservice by the employees concerned. In practice a separate set of 'rules' was developed by these employees.

ii. **Representative Bureaucracy.** In this case the rules were followed in practice because both management *and* employees agreed on their value.

iii. **Punishment-centred Bureaucracy.** This description was applied to situations where either the management or the employees imposed their rules on the other. Disregard of the rules was seen as grounds for imposing sanctions. Each side considered its rules as legitimate, but there was no common acceptance.

11. Weber's thinking on bureaucracy was dominated by his view of how rational it was. Gouldner by contrast has helped to indicate that opinions and feelings are also a key ingredient in the success of a bureaucratic form of organization. Whereas Weber emphasized the structural aspects of organization, Gouldner emphasized behaviour. He saw that rules not only generated *anticipated* responses eg obedient behaviour, but also *unanticipated* responses eg minimum acceptable behaviour. Therefore, in any one organization, there will be a tendency to respond to the rules in any one of the three ways described above, depending on how and why the rules were introduced.

12. Professor Handy (Understanding Organizations, Penguin 1987- Chapter 7) describes bureaucracies as 'role cultures' based on logic and rationality. In the role culture, power comes from position power ie the authority of the office, as determined by rules and procedures. Such a culture offers security and predictability to its members, but can be frustrating for those who are ambitious and results-orientated. Handy sees bureaucracy as a Greek temple, based on the firm pillars of its speciality departments and ideally constructed for stability. This very stability is a drawback in times of change. The Greek temple is not designed for adaptability.

13. However one chooses to describe bureaucracy, there is little doubt that it is by far the most frequent form of organization in society, and the question that has to be asked is not so much 'is this organization a bureaucracy?' as 'to what extent *is* this organization bureaucratized?' The evidence seems to suggest that there is something of the Greek temple in every organization !

## SECTION SUMMARY – CLASSICAL THEORIES

1. This Section has looked at a selection of the most important ideas of the leading theorists of classical organization. These ideas have tended to focus on the structure of organizations and the management of structure. People and their needs have not been ignored by the classical theorists, but have been dealt with firmly against the background of some ideal structure.

2. Fayol, Taylor, Gantt and the Gilbreths, Urwick and Brech have endeavoured to find rational principles that can be applied to the development and management of organizations. These principles have concentrated on such issues as the division of labour, or

specialization, and the control of physical and human resources by means of hierarchical structures.

3.   Several of the principles put forward by these writers have been adopted by managements in practice. The scalar chain or management hierarchy, for example, is an integral part of most companies today. Similarly, issues such as authority matching responsibility and the clear definition of jobs and roles have also been absorbed into the thinking of many management teams. On the other hand, several of the principles advocated by Fayol and the others have not found favour in practice. Questions of unity of command, fair treatment of staff, remuneration and similar issues relating to leadership and motivation are not easy for modern managements to install on a unilateral basis. In the 1920's it was possible to conduct the management of people in a spirit of benevolent paternalism. Today that just is not possible. Increasingly, employees at all levels are demanding more participation in decision-making and more joint control of working conditions. In this kind of situation, classical theories stand little chance of success, without considerable modification.

4.   Whilst most attention has been given to the organization as a whole, the Scientific Managers, in particular, sought to apply rational methods to work itself. Their techniques have provided the foundation for the many forms of quantitative analysis of work in use today all over the world. The greatest benefits of the so-called 'scientific approach' have been in the productivity improvements gained by more efficient use of machines and manpower. The disadvantages have arisen mainly from the overspecialization of jobs, which has resulted in boredom and frustration for many employees, and (b) from the payments systems generated as a result of work study applications in the workplace. The implicit carrot and stick attitude at the heart of payments systems geared tightly to measured work has proved to be more of a stick than a carrot, and one that has been used by *both* sides of industry to beat the other!

5.   Most of the theorists referred to in this Section have been practising managers or consultants. The exception has been Max Weber, the sociologist. His analysis of, and subsequent enthusiasm tor, the bureaucratic form of organization demonstrates his position as a member of the classical school alongside Fayol, Taylor and the others. His concept of the efficiency of the structure and procedures embodied in a bureaucracy shares a considerable amount of common ground with the thinking of Fayol, Urwick and Brech. In particular, features such as the scalar chain, specialization, authority, and the definition of jobs, which were seen by these

writers as essential for successful management, are typical of a bureaucracy. There is also little doubt that Weber's ideas concerning specified spheres of competence and appointments based on technical competence would have had a considerable appeal for Taylor and the scientific managers.

## QUESTIONS FOR DISCUSSION/HOMEWORK

*1. What difficulties might confront a manager today, if he or she tried to implement Fayol's principles of management as they were originally stated ?*

*2. What common features do you see between Fayol's principles of management and Weber's description of bureaucracy ?*

*3. How would you summarize the principal effects of 'scientific management' on (a) managers, and (b) employees?*

*4. Why is it difficult to implement principles of management along the lines suggested by Fayol, Urwick and Brech, for example?*

*5. Discuss the main advantages and disadvantages of the ideal-type of bureaucracy, as described by Weber.*

## EXAMINATION QUESTIONS - CLASSICAL THEORIES

*The following list contains a typical cross-section of questions taken from the major examining bodies, and selected for their relevance to the subject-matter of this Section. Outline answers to these questions can be found at Appendix 2.*

*EQ 2. "Attempts to bring scientific methods into management merely show what an inexact art management really is." Discuss.*

*(ACCA)*

*EQ 3. Critically evaluate the contribution of the classical/ traditional school of management theorists to our understanding of organization.* *(CIMA)*

*EQ 4. Does the work of F.W. Taylor have any relevance to modern marketing management?* *(Inst. of Marketing)*

# HUMAN RELATIONS THEORY

Where the classical theorists were principally concerned with the structure and mechanics of organizations, the theorists of human relations were concerned with the human factor. Unlike the classical theorists, who were invariably practising managers, the human relations theorists have been academics – social scientists, or behavioural scientists, as they are now more commonly known. The focus of attention for the latter has been directed towards issues such as individual motivation, group behaviour and leadership. This Section introduces the leading theories of human relations. Chapter 7 looks at the meaning of 'motivation' and describes some of the assumptions about human behaviour that are implicit in our attitude towards other people's motives. Chapter 8 considers the impact of Elton Mayo on human relations with particular reference to the so-called Hawthorne Experiment. Chapter 9 describes the major theories of motivation which have been developed in the wake of the Hawthorne findings. Chapter 10 examines some Japanese approaches to motivation at work.

# 7

# MOTIVATION AND ASSUMPTIONS ABOUT PEOPLE

## INTRODUCTION

1. The purpose of this Chapter is to provide a basic understanding of the concept of motivation, and to discuss the relevance of assumptions about people that are implied in our attitude towards others, especially when the relationship is that of boss to subordinate. The best-known list of assumptions about people is Professor Schein's classification, and this has been chosen to illustrate the discussion here.

## MOTIVATION

2. Motivation is concerned with *why* people do (or refrain from doing!) things. A motive is a need or a driving force within a person. The process of motivation involves choosing between alternative forms of action in order to achieve some desired end or goal. As Figure 7.1 shows, goals can be tangible, such as higher earnings, or intangible, such as personal reputation.

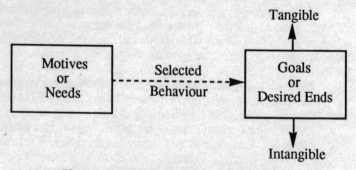

**Figure 7.1 Basic Model of Motivation**

3. Understanding human motivation is a complex matter. A person's motives may be clear to him but quite puzzling to others. On the other hand a person under stress may well not understand his own motives, even though these may be perfectly clear to a trained observer. On other occasions, both the person concerned and those around him understand what his motives are. It is

important for people in management and supervisory positions to understand such alternatives and adapt their leadership style accordingly.

4.    Not surprisingly, our understanding of another's motivation is influenced considerably by our own attitudes towards people. When a manager speaks of 'highly motivated staff' *he* is indicating that the staff are doing what he wants them to do. It could be that the staff concerned share his motives eg customer satisfaction, lively working environment etc, but equally they could be 'motivated' by fear of dismissal (the stick) or by greed for lavish bonuses (the carrot).

5.    If a manager assumes that younger employees are generally hardworking and ambitious as well, he will take the view that they can be motivated by means of demanding work, promotion opportunities and the exercise of responsibility. If, however, he assumes that younger people are lazy and unreliable, he will take the view that they must be given undemanding tasks to perform, and will want their supervisors to take responsibility in case things go wrong. In either of the above examples, if the manager has assumed *wrongly*, he will have de-motivated staff on his hands. The choices of viewpoint open to a manager are dealt with in Professor Schein's classification of peoples' assumptions about Man. These are considered now.

## MANAGEMENT'S ASSUMPTIONS ABOUT PEOPLE

6.    The American academic, Professor Edgar Schein, published, in 1965, a classification of the assumptions about people implicit in managerial ideas about what motivates employees. Following a broadly historical order, he identifies four sets of assumptions as follows:

   a.  **Rational-economic Man.** This view of Man has its roots in the economic theories of Adam Smith in 1770's. It states that the pursuit of self-interest and the maximisation of gain are the prime motivators of people. It lays stress on Man's rational calculation of self-interest, especially in relation to economic needs. Ultimately, according to Schein, this set of assumptions places human beings into two categories: (a) the untrustworthy, money-motivated, calculative mass, and (b) the trustworthy, more broadly motivated, moral elite who must organize and manage the mass. Schein sees these assumptions as being too black and white to provide any useful explanation of motivation. Nevertheless, in actual practice the rational-economic approach was clearly an important assumption in the minds of Taylor and the

Gilbreths, for example. It has also been an important assumption for the entrepreneurs of mass-production technology.

b. **Social Man.** In categorizing Social Man, Schein draws heavily on Mayo's conclusions from the Hawthorne Experiment, which is described more fully in the next chapter. This view of Man sees people as predominantly motivated by social needs, and finding their identity through relationships with others. Acceptance of this view by managers means more attention to people's needs and less to task needs; it means more attention to the role of groups within the organization; and it also implies a change of role for the manager from organizer and controller to guide and supporter. Research studies have shown that productivity and morale can be improved where management deliberately foster social relationships in order to improve cooperation and teamwork. It is unlikely, though, that this emphasis alone can improve these two factors, and the evidence for Social Man needs to be treated with some reservation.

c. **Self-actualizing Man.** The concept of Self-actualizing Man is based on Maslow's theory of human needs, described in Chapter 9. This view of human motivation sees not social needs but self-fulfilment needs as being the prime driving-force behind individuals. Self-actualizing Man needs challenge, responsibility and a sense of pride in his work. The managerial strategy which operates under this set of assumptions sets out to provide demanding, challenging work. It aims to maximise opportunities for real delegation of responsibility, or, to put it another way, it aims for greater autonomy at work. Research studies have indicated a considerable degree of support for the idea of Self-actualizing Man. This support appears to be particularly strong amongst professional and skilled grades of staff. However, it is less clear whether this model of motivation applies as strongly to lower-graded employees.

d. **Complex Man.** This view of human beings sees them as being altogether more complex and more variable than the other models described above. In this concept, the requirement for managers is that they should be intelligent, sensitive people able to diagnose the various motives which may be at work in their staff. These motives may vary with different tasks and different work-groups and different organizational climates. A consequence of this is that managers need also to be able to adapt and vary their own behaviour in accordance with the motivational needs of particular individuals and teams. Schein quotes several research studies which appear to support this view of Man, and this is an area where further studies are in progress. Schein himself sees motivation very much in terms of a 'psychological contract' based on the expectations that the employee and the organization have of each other, and the extent to which these are mutually fulfilled. Ultimately, the relationship between an individual and his organization is an interactive one. Therefore we shall only come to an understanding of motivation when we recognize this interdependence.

## SUMMARY

7.    This Chapter necessarily anticipates several aspects of the following two chapters. Our understanding of Social Man can only be put into perspective by assessing the impact of Elton Mayo and colleagues. Similarly, our understanding of Selfactualizing Man has to be seen in the context of the ideas of social psychologists such as Likert, McGregor, Herzberg and Argyris, whose contribution is examined in Chapter 9.

8.    The evidence for Rational-economic Man can be seen by reference back to the classical theorists, especially Taylor and the Scientific Managers. The concept of Complex Man begins to appear with some of the studies of the above-mentioned social psychologists, but becomes more apparent when considering the researches of those academics who take a more comprehensive view of human behaviour in organizations. This view can be described as a systems or contingency approach to motivation, and is discussed in the next group of chapters in the Section entitled Systems Approaches to Management Theory.

9.    Schein's classification, therefore helps us to relate all the major approaches of management theory to the concept of motivation. The basis of this concept is that human motives or needs are directed towards desired goals or ends, and that a person's behaviour is selected, consciously or unconsciously, towards the achievement of those ends. Different viewpoints have emerged concerning the key needs and ultimate goals of human beings at work. As a result differing proposals have been put forward by theorists to explain and predict human behaviour at work. The next chapter looks at one particularly significant development in the history of the behavioural sciences – the Hawthorne Studies.

# 8

# THE IMPACT OF ELTON MAYO

## INTRODUCTION

1.   The name of Professor Elton Mayo is most usually associated with what has come to be considered as the best known and most widely quoted piece of social research this century, namely the Hawthorne Studies, carried out at the Hawthorne plant of the Western Electric Company in Chicago, U. S .A., between 1927 and 1932.

2.   The emphasis in the Hawthorne Studies was on the worker rather than on work. Unlike Taylor and the Scientific Managers, the researchers at Hawthorne were primarily concerned with studying people, especially in terms of their social relationships at work. Their conclusions were that Man is a social animal at work as well as outside it, and that membership of a group is important to individuals. Group membership leads to establishment of informal groups within the official, formal, groupings as laid down in the organization structure.

3.   These conclusions gave rise to the idea of Social Man and to the importance of human relations. Elton Mayo has been described as the founder of the Human Relations movement, whose advocates have stressed the need for managerial strategies to ensure that concern for people at work is given the highest priority. This movement, if it can be described as such, spanned the period from the mid-1920's to the mid-1950's, after which there was a gradual trend away from Social Man and his close relation Self-actualizing Man towards the idea of Complex Man operating in a highly variable organizational environment.

## ELTON MAYO

4.   Elton Mayo (1880–1949) was an Australian by birth, a psychologist by training, and, according to some, a natural PR man by inclination. At the time of the Hawthorne Studies he was Professor of Industrial Research at the Harvard Graduate School of Business Administration. He was already involved in the study of issues such as fatigue, accidents and labour turnover, when he was approached by executives of the Western Electric Company for advice. The Company, which prided itself on its welfare facilities, had begun a number of studies into the effects of lighting on production and morale. They had discovered, to their surprise, that

the groups of workers who were the subject of study improved their productivity whether the lighting was improved or not. Clearly some human factor was at work, and the Company decided to call in the experts!

5.    Their decision was to bring considerable fame to Mayo, in particular. His popularization of the results and conclusions to be drawn from the Hawthorne Studies made an enormous impact at the time. The idea of Social Man was seen as a rebuttal of the ideas of scientific management, with its emphasis on the task and the control of work. Subsequent decades have also been greatly influenced by the findings at Hawthornes, and most of the credit has gone to Mayo.

## THE HAWTHORNE STUDIES

6.    The studies were carried out over several years in a number of different stages. These were as follows:

**First Stage** (1924–1927). This was conducted by the Company's own staff under the direction of Messrs. Pennock and Dickson. As mentioned above, this stage was concerned with the effects of lighting on output. Eventually two groups of comparable performance were isolated from the rest and located in separate parts of the plant. One group, the control group, had a consistent level of lighting; the other group, the experimental group, had its lighting varied. To the surprise of the researchers, the output of both groups increased. Even when the lighting for the experimental group was reduced to a very low level, they still produced more! At this point Pennock sought the help of Mayo and his Harvard colleagues.

7.    Stage Two (1927–1929). This stage became known as the Relay Assembly Test Room. The objective was to make a closer and more detailed study of the effects of differing physical conditions on productivity. At this stage there was no deliberate intention to analyse social relationships or employee attitudes. Six women workers in the relay assembly section were segregated from the rest in a room of their own. Over the course of the experiments the effects of numerous changes in working conditions were observed. Rest pauses were introduced and varied, lunch times were varied in timing and in length. Most of the changes were discussed with the women before being implemented. Productivity increased whether the conditions were made better or worse. Later studies included altering the working week. Once again output increased regardless of the changes. By the end of Stage Two the researchers realised they had not just

been studying the relationship between physical working conditions, fatigue, monotony and output, but had been entering into a study of employee *attitudes* and *values*. The women's reactions to the changes ie increased output regardless of whether conditions improved or worsened, has come to be known as 'the Hawthorne Effect'. That is to say the women were responding not so much to the changes as to the fact that they were the centre of attention – a special group.

8.    **Stage Three** (1928–1930). Before the Relay Assembly test had come to an end, the Company had decided to implement an interview programme designed to ascertain employee attitudes towards working conditions, their supervision and their jobs. The interviews were conducted by selected supervisors, initially on a half-hour, structured basis. Eventually the interview pattern became relatively unstructured and lasted for ninety minutes. Despite this, the numbers interviewed reached over 20,000 before the programme was suspended. The wealth of material gained was used to improve several aspects of working conditions and supervision. It also became clear from the responses that relationships with people were an important factor in the attitudes of employees.

9.    **Stage Four** (1932). This was known as the Bank Wiring Observation Room. In this study fourteen men on bank wiring were removed to a separate observation room, where, apart from a few differences, their principal working conditions were the same as those in the main wiring area. The aim was to observe a group working under more or less normal conditions over a period of six months or so. The group was soon developing its own rules and behaviour – it restricted production in accordance with its own norms; it short-circuited the company wage incentive scheme and in general protected its own sectional interests against those of the company. The supervisors concerned were powerless to prevent this situation. The group had clearly developed its own unofficial organization, run in such a way that it was able to protect itself from outside influences whilst controlling its internal life too.

10.    **Final Stage** (1936). This stage was commenced some four years after Stage Four because of the economic difficulties of the depression. This final stage was based on lessons learned from the earlier studies. Its focus was firmly on employee relations and took the form of Personnel Counselling. The counsellors encouraged employees to discuss their problems at work, and the results led to improvements in personal adjustment, employee-supervisor relations and employee management relations.

11.  The official account of the Hawthorne Studies was written not by Mayo, but by one of his Harvard colleagues and one Company researcher, namely Messrs. Roethlisberger and Dickson. Their detailed descriptions of the research did not appear until 1939 ('Management and the Worker'). In the meantime Mayo had already put the spotlight on the Studies in an influential work entitled 'The Human Problems of an Industrial Civilization' published in 1933.

12.  There have been many criticisms of the way the Hawthorne Studies have been interpreted. Mayo's references were included in writings which propounded *his* theories about Man and industrial society. As a result, his use of the Studies was biased towards his own interpretation of what was happening. For the official evidence one must look to Roethlisberger and Dickson. Modern researchers point out that their Hawthorne counterparts overlooked important factors in assessing their results. They also adopted some unreliable methods for testing the evidence in the first place. However, everyone is agreed that the Hawthorne Studies represented the first major attempt to undertake genuine social research. Important lessons were learned, and, perhaps even more importantly, many questions were raised by these studies.

## CONCLUSIONS

13.  The main conclusions to be drawn from the Hawthorne researches are:

  a.  Individual workers cannot be treated in isolation, but must be seen as members of a group.

  b.  The need to belong to a group and have status within it is more important than monetary incentives or good physical working conditions.

  c.  Informal (or unofficial) groups at work exercise a strong influence over the behaviour of workers.

  d.  Supervisors and managers need to be aware of these social needs and cater for them if workers are to collaborate with the official organization rather than work against it.

14.  The Hawthorne Experiment began as a study into *physical* conditions and productivity. It ended as a series of studies into *social* factors: membership of groups, relationships with supervision etc. Its most significant findings showed that social relations at work were every bit as important as monetary incentives and good physical working conditions. They also demonstrated the powerful influence of groups in determining behaviour at work.

15. By modern standards of social research, the Hawthorne Studies were relatively unsophisticated in their approach. Nevertheless, they represented a major step forward for the social sciences in their study of work organizations. Also, by their model of Social Man, they did much to further the humanization of work.

# 9

# MAJOR THEORIES OF
# HUMAN MOTIVATION

## INTRODUCTION
1.   The concept of Social Man dominated the thinking of social researchers and practising managers alike in the wake of the Hawthorne Studies. The emphasis on the employee's social or belonging needs, as opposed to the needs of the task, continued throughout the thirties and forties until the mid 1950's. At this point in time we move into what has usefully been described as the neo-Human Relations School. The writers referred to in this chapter may all be considered to belong to this school of thought. The emphasis is still on people as the most crucial factor in determining organizational effectiveness, but people who have considerably more than just physical and social needs. The dominant concept here is that of Self-actualizing Man.
2.   We begin by looking at the influential work of the American psychologist, Abraham Maslow, and go on to describe the best known theories of his fellow-Americans Douglas McGregor, Frederick Herzberg, Rensis Likert, Chris Argyris and D.C. McClelland. The chapter concludes with a short account of 'Expectancy Theory.'

## MASLOW'S HIERARCHY OF NEEDS
3.   Maslow's studies into human motivation led him to propose a theory of needs based on an hierarchical model with basic needs at the bottom and higher needs at the top, as in Figure 9.1 on the next page. The theory was first put forward in 1943 and has had considerable influence on developments in management theory.
4.   The starting point of Maslow's hierarchy theory is that most people are motivated by the desire to satisfy specific groups of needs. These needs are as follows.
    Physiological Needs – needs for food, sleep, sex etc.
    Safety Needs – needs for stable environment relatively free from threats.
    Love Needs – needs related to affectionate relations with others and status within a group.
    Esteem Needs – needs for self-respect, self-esteem and the esteem of others.
    Self-actualization Needs – the need for self-fulfilment.

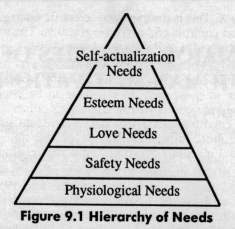

**Figure 9.1 Hierarchy of Needs**

5.    The second, and most central, point of Maslow's theory is that people tend to satisfy their needs systematically, starting with the basic physiological needs and then moving up the hierarchy. Until a particular group of needs is satisfied, a person's behaviour will be dominated by them. Thus, a hungry person is not going to be motivated by consideration of safety or affection, for example, until after his hunger has been satisfied. Maslow did modify this argument later (1968) by stating that there was an exception to the rule in respect of self-actualization needs. In this case satisfaction of need seems to give rise to further needs for realizing one's potential.

6.    What little research has been carried out on Maslow's hierarchy concept has proved somewhat inconclusive. Probably the most frequent criticism that has been made is that systematic movement up the hierarchy does not seem to be a consistent form of behaviour for many people. Nevertheless, Maslow's theory has provided a useful framework for the discussion of the variety of needs that people may experience at work, and the ways in which their motivation can be met by managers.

## D MCGREGOR – THEORY X AND THEORY Y

7.    Like Schein's classification of Man, McGregor's Theory X and Theory Y are essentially sets of assumptions about behaviour. In his book 'The Human Side of the Enterprise', McGregor specifically refers to the theoretical assumptions of management that underlie its behaviour. He sees two noticeably different sets of assumptions made by managers about their employees. The first set regards employees as being inherently lazy, requiring coercion and control, avoiding responsibility and only seeking security.

This is Theory X. This is the theory of scientific management, with its emphasis on controls and extrinsic rewards. Theory X is very similar to Schein's idea of Rational-economic man.

8.    The second set of assumptions sees Man in a more favourable light. In this case employees are seen as liking work, which is as natural as rest or play; they do not have to be controlled and coerced, if they are committed to the organization's objectives; under proper conditions they will not only accept but also seek responsibility; more rather than less people are able to exercise imagination and ingenuity at work. These are the assumptions of Theory Y. They are closely related to Schein's Self-actualizing Man.

9.    Theory X and Theory Y have made their major impact in the managerial world rather than in the academic world. The two labels have become part of the folklore of 'management style', which will be looked at in the chapter on leadership (Chapter 26). They do help to identify extreme forms of management style, but there is a danger that they may be seen only as an 'either/or' style. In real-life a blend of the two Theories may provide the best prescription for effective management.

## HERZBERG'S MOTIVATION-HYGIENE THEORY

10.   Herzberg's studies concentrated on satisfaction at work. In the initial research some two hundred engineers and accountants were asked to recall when they had experienced satisfactory and unsatisfactory feelings about their jobs. Following the interviews, Herzberg's team came to the conclusion that certain factors tended to lead to job satisfaction, while others led frequently to dissatisfaction (see Figure 9.2). The factors giving rise to satisfaction were called *motivators*. Those giving rise to dissatisfaction were called *hygiene factors*. These studies were later extended to include various groups in manual and clerical groups, where the results were claimed to be quite similar.

11.   The most important motivators to emerge were the following:
- Achievement.
- Recognition.
- Work Itself.
- Responsibility.
- Advancement.

Herzberg pointed out that these factors were intimately related to the *content* of work.

## FACTORS AFFECTING JOB ATTITUDES

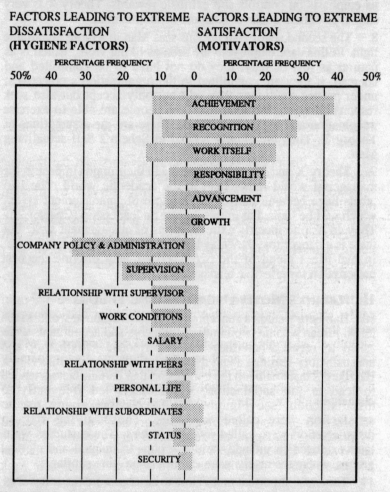

FACTORS LEADING TO EXTREME DISSATISFACTION (HYGIENE FACTORS)

FACTORS LEADING TO EXTREME SATISFACTION (MOTIVATORS)

PERCENTAGE FREQUENCY

50%  40  30  20  10  0  10  20  30  40  50%

ACHIEVEMENT
RECOGNITION
WORK ITSELF
RESPONSIBILITY
ADVANCEMENT
GROWTH
COMPANY POLICY & ADMINISTRATION
SUPERVISION
RELATIONSHIP WITH SUPERVISOR
WORK CONDITIONS
SALARY
RELATIONSHIP WITH PEERS
PERSONAL LIFE
RELATIONSHIP WITH SUBORDINATES
STATUS
SECURITY

Note: The le*ngth* of each 'box' denotes the frequency with which the factor occurred in the situations described by the respondents. The *depth* of each 'box' denotes the relative duration of the good or bad feelings about the job. The overlap of the boxes across the centre line indicates:

a) that motivators have their *negative* aspects eg Lack of achievement can lead to dissatisfaction; and

b) that hygiene factors have their *positive* aspects eg salary can be a source of satisfaction .

**Figure 9.2**

12. The most important hygiene factors, or dissatisfiers, were as follows:

- Company Policy and Administration.
- Supervision – the technical aspects.
- Salary.
- Interpersonal Relations – supervision.
- Working Conditions.

Herzberg noted that these factors were more related to the *context* or environment of work than to job content.

13. A key distinction between the motivators and the hygiene factors was that whereas motivators brought about positive satisfaction, the hygiene factors only served to prevent dissatisfaction. To put it another way, if motivators are absent from the job, the employee will experience real dissatisfaction. However, even if the hygiene factors are provided for, they will not in themselves bring about job satisfaction. Hygiene, in other words, does not positively promote good health, but can act to prevent ill-health. Figure 9.2.

14. If we apply Herzberg's theory to the ideas and assumptions of earlier theorists, it is possible to see that Taylor and colleagues were thinking very much in terms of hygiene factors (pay, incentives, adequate supervision and working conditions). Mayo, too, was placing his emphasis on a hygiene factor, namely interpersonal relations. It is only when we consider the ideas of the neo-Human Relations school that motivators appear as a key element in job satisfaction and worker productivity.

15. Herzberg's motivation-hygiene theory has been well received by practising managers and consultants for its relatively simple and vivid distinction between factors inducing positive satisfaction and those causing dissatisfaction. It has led to considerable work on so-called 'job enrichment' ie the design of jobs so that they contain the optimum number of motivators. The approach here is basically to counter the effects of years of Taylorism, which sought to break work down into its simplest components and to remove responsibility for planning and control.

Herzberg's ideas have been less well-received by fellow social scientists, mainly on grounds of doubt about (a) their applicability to non-professional groups and (b) his use of the concept of 'job satisfaction.'

## RENSIS LIKERT

16. Likert's contribution to the concept of motivation and its applicability to the world of work has come mainly from his work as Director of the Institute of Social Research at the University of Michigan, U.S.A. The Michigan Studies are described by Likert in his book 'New Patterns of Management', in which he theorises about high-producing managers. These are the managers (and supervisors) who achieve the highest productivity, the lowest costs and the highest levels of employee motivation, for example.

17. The researches indicated that the high-producing managers tended to build their success on interlocking and tightly-knit, groups of employees, whose cooperation had been obtained by thorough attention to a range of motivational forces. These included not only economic and security motives, but also ego and creativity motives (self-actualization, in Maslow's terminology). Another key feature noted by the Michigan researchers was that, although the high-producers utilized the tools of classical management – work study, budgeting etc – they did so in a way which recognized the aspirations of the employees, by encouraging participative approaches.

18. A dominant theme in Likert's discussion of these 'new patterns of management' is the importance of supportive relationships. Management can achieve high performance when employees see their membership of a work group to be 'supportive', that is to say when they experience a sense of personal worth and importance from belonging to it. High producing managers and supervisors tended to foster just such relationships with, and within, their groups.

19. The idea of supportive relationships is built into Likert's view of the ideal organization structure. Supportive relationships lead to effective work groups which can interact with other effective groups in an overlapping form of organization. In this form of structure certain key roles perform a 'linking pin' function. A head of a section, for example, is a member not only of his own group but also of his superior's group. His superior, in turn, is a member of a further group higher up the organizational hierarchy, and so on. Such an organization still has the basic shape of a classical organizational pyramid, but operates in practice on the basis of interlocking teams, instead of separate specialisms. This form is shown diagrammatically in Figure 9.3 opposite.

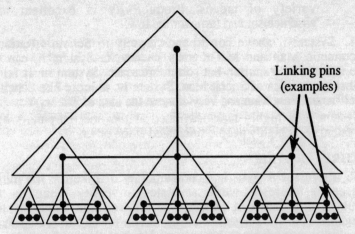

Linking pins
(examples)

**Figure 9.3 Overlapping Group Form of Organization**

20. In reviewing his work on motivation, leadership and organization structures, Likert has distinguished four separate systems, or styles, of management. These are founded on a number of differing assumptions about human behaviour and are useful to compare with Schein's classification of Man and McGregor's Theory X and Theory Y. The four systems are as follows:

   i.   **Exploitive-authoritative** where power and direction come from the top downwards, where threats and punishment are employed, where communication is poor and teamwork non-existent. Productivity is mediocre.

   ii.  **Benevolent-authoritative** is similar to the above but allows some upward opportunities for consultation and some delegation. Rewards may be available as well as threats. Productivity is fair to good but at cost of considerable absenteeism and turnover.

   iii. **Consultative** where goals are set or orders issued after discussion with subordinates, where communication is both upwards and downwards and where teamwork is encouraged, at least partially. Some involvement of employees as a motivator. Productivity is good with only moderate absenteeism etc.

   iv.  **Participative-group** is the ideal system. Under this system, the keynote is participation, leading to commitment to the organization's goals in a fully cooperative way. Communication is good both upwards, downwards and laterally. Motivation is obtained by a variety of means. Productivity is excellent and absenteeism and turnover are low.

21. System i. above corresponds closely to Schein's Rational economic Man and McGregor's Theory X. System ii. can be considered as a similar, but softer, approach. System iii. is fairly close to the idea of Social Man. System iv. is more like Schein's Self-actualizing Man and very close to the idea of Theory Y.

System i. is highly task-orientated at the one extreme, while System iv. is highly people-orientated at the other.

## CHRIS ARGYRIS

22. Professor Argyris is a contemporary of Likert's. His initial research interests, while at Yale University, were in the relationship between people's needs and the needs of the organization. He suggests that the reason for so much employee apathy is not so much because of laziness, but rather because people are being treated like children. This leads to his so-called Immaturity-Maturity Theory which suggests that the human personality develops from immaturity to maturity in a continuum, in which a number of key changes take place. These are as follows (Figure 9.4).

| Immaturity | ⟶ | Maturity |
|---|---|---|
| Passivity | - - - - - - - - - - - - - - - - | Activity |
| Dependence | - - - - - - - - - - - - · | Relative independence |
| Behave in few ways | - - - - - - - - - | Behave in many ways |
| Erratic, shallow interests | - - - - - - - - - · | Deeper interests |
| Short time perspective | - - - - - - - - | Long time perspective |
| Subordinate position | - - - - - - - · | Equal or superior position |
| Lack of awareness of self | - - - - - | Awareness and control of self |

**Figure 9.4 Immaturity-Maturity Theory**

23. Against the above model of maturity, Argyris sets the features of the typical classical organization: task specialization, chain of command, unity of direction and span of control. The impact of this type of organization on individuals is that they are expected to be passive, dependent and subordinate ie they are expected to behave immaturely! For individuals who are relatively mature, this

environment is a major source of frustration at work. This frustration leads to individuals seeking informal ways of minimising their difficulties such as creating informal organizations which work against the formal hierarchy.

24. The lessons for motivation are important. For the more we can understand human needs, the more it will be possible to integrate them with the needs of organizations. If the goals of the organization and the goals of individuals can be brought together, the resulting behaviour will be cooperative rather than defensive or downright antagonistic. Argyris's ideas, therefore, favour a self-actualization model of Man with some of the attributes of Complex Man too.

## ACHIEVEMENT MOTIVATION

25. Whilst many social psychologists have studied *common* factors in human motivation, others have focussed on *differences* between individuals. One such researcher, whose work is well known, is D.C. McClelland of Harvard University. He and his team have studied three basic needs in addition to physical needs. These are the need for achievement (n-Ach), the need for power (n-Pow) and the need for affiliation or belonging (n-Aff). In particular McClelland has isolated n-Ach as a key human motive, and one which is influenced strongly by personality and by environment.

26. Persons with a high need for achievement tend to have the the following characteristics:
   a. Their need for achievement is consistent.
   b. They seek tasks in which they can exercise personal responsibility.
   c. They prefer tasks which provide a challenge without being too difficult and which they see as within their mastery.
   d. They want feedback on their results.
   e. They are less concerned about their social or affiliation needs.

McClelland's view is that the need for achievement is developed more by childhood experiences and cultural background than by purely inherited factors. If this is correct, it has important implications for management and supervisory training. If the need for achievement is influenced primarily by environmental factors, then clearly it is possible to develop training programmes designed to increase the achievement motive in the employees concerned.

27. The major disadvantage of the person with high n-Ach is that, by definition, he is task-orientated and less concerned with relationships. These characteristics are not always suitable for those whose responsibility is to get work done through people ie managers and supervisors. This may not be a problem for an entrepreneurial figure in a small organization, but what of the high achiever working in a typical industrial or commercial bureaucracy? In the latter case high n-Ach can be frustrated by the constraints imposed by delegating responsibility. Nevertheless, McClelland's ideas are important as a contribution to our understanding of motivation at work, and how the concept of n-Ach might be applied in practice.

## EXPECTANCY THEORY

28. The theories referred to earlier in this chapter have tended to focus their attention on motives or needs. However, as we saw in the basic model of motivation in Figure 7.1, motives induce selected behaviour directed towards some desired end or goal. In themselves they are only part of the total motivational process. One set of ideas which does attempt to study the *process* of motivation has been named 'Expectancy Theory'. The development of this theory is mainly the result of the work of V.H. Vroom and E.E. Lawler in the United States during the 1960's. A key point in this approach is that an individual's behaviour is formed not on some sense of objective reality, but on his own perception of reality ie how he actually sees the world around him.

29. The core of the theory relates to how a person perceives the relationships between three things – effort, performance and rewards. The strength of the attraction of particular outcomes or rewards for an individual is termed 'valence'. The degree of belief that a particular act will produce a particular outcome is termed 'expectancy'. Valences and expectancies depend on the individual's own perception of a situation. For example, the prospect of promotion could be seen by a newly-appointed employee as an attractive prospect (valence), but his expectancy of gaining promotion could be low, if he perceives that promotion is attained primarily on length of service. In such a situation, performance does not lead to rewards, so effort in that direction is not seen as worthwhile. In any case, effort does not necessarily lead to effective performance, if the individual has insufficient knowledge and skills, or if his perception of his role does not equate with that of his superior, for example. The basic theory can be shown as follows:

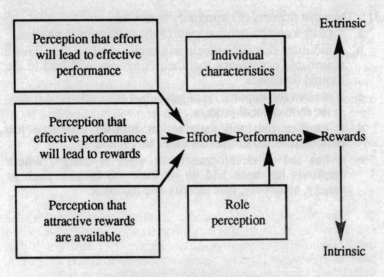

**Figure 9.5. Expectancy Theory**

30. Figure 9.5 can be elaborated as follows: Effort or motivated behaviour occurs when an individual perceives that the effort will lead to effective performance, which in turn will lead to rewards which are seen as attractive. However, effort alone may not necessarily lead to effective performance, as other factors are involved eg the individual's own characteristics (personality, knowledge and skills) and the way in which he perceives his role. Other environmental factors which are not shown may also affect performance eg constraints of the job, organization style etc. Effort, therefore, does not always result in effective performance. It is also true that effective performance may not always lead to the rewards anticipated by the individual. An individual's perception of rewards is a vital part of this theory. These rewards may be *intrinsic* or *extrinsic*. Intrinsic rewards are those which are derived from the fulfilment of the individual's personal needs, such as self-esteem and personal growth, and over which he can exercise personal control. Extrinsic rewards are those provided by the organization, and beyond the control of the individual, such as pay, promotion, good working conditions etc. Several research studies have suggested that the rewards associated with intrinsic factors are more likely to be perceived as producing job satisfaction. The extrinsic rewards are less likely to come up to the individual's expectations.

31. The main features of expectancy theory are:
    a. it takes a comprehensive view of the motivational process,
    b. it indicates that individuals will only act when they have a reasonable expectancy that their behaviour will lead to the desired outcomes.
    c. it stresses the importance of individual perceptions of reality in the motivational process.
    d. it implies that job satisfaction follows effective job performance rather than the other way round.
    e. it has led to developments in work re-design, where emphasis has been laid on intrinsic job factors, such as variety, autonomy, task identity and feedback.

# 10

# THEORY Z -
# THE JAPANESE APPROACH

## INTRODUCTION

1.   Over the course of the past decade considerable attention has been given to the success of Japanese manufacturing industries. One of the key factors in this success has been their approach to the management of their resources, especially people. An important American exponent of Japanese management style is W. Ouchi (1981) who has coined the phrase 'Theory Z' for attempts to adapt Japanese approaches to management in Western firms.

2.   The key features of Japanese industrial organizations, according to Ouchi are as follows:

- they offer lifetime employment (at least for their 'core' workers)
- they promote from within
- they insist on mandatory retirement of core workers at age 55
- they employ a large number of temporary employees, mostly women
- there is a high degree of mutual trust and loyalty between management and employees
- career paths are non-specialised with life-long job rotation as a central feature of career development
- decision-making is shared at all levels
- performance appraisal is long term (ie the first appraisal takes place 10 years after joining the company)
- there is a strong sense of collective responsibility for the success of the organization, and cooperative effort rather than individual achievement is encouraged
- industrial life is supported by a highly-competitive educational system
- industrial life is typified by groupings of large firms financed by major banks and supported by a host of satellite firms

3.   Although Ouchi recognises that many of the features of Japanese management could not be translated into Western

industrial society, he believes that certain features could be applied in a Western context. The move from the present hierarchical type of organization to a Theory Z type organization is a process which, says Ouchi:

> " ... has the objective of developing the ability of the organization to coordinate *people*, not technology,to achieve productivity."

In his view, this requires a 'new' philosophy of managing people based on a combination of the following features of Japanese management:

- Lifelong employment prospects
- shared forms of decision-making
- relationships between boss and subordinate based on mutual respect

4.   According to Ouchi, the introduction of Theory Z approaches into Western firms requires the following strategy:

   a.  The adoption of a 'Top-down' approach, based on a definition of the 'new' philosophy agreed and supported by the organization's top management.

   b.  The 'new' philosophy should embrace the ideas of security of employment, shared decision making, career development, team-spirit and acknowledgement of individual contribution within the team.

   c.  The implementation of the new approach should be carried through on the basis of consultation and communication with the workforce and with full training support to develop relevant skills for managers, supervisors and their teams.

5.   Much of Ouchi's analysis of Japanese industrial society is echoed by another commentator, C. J. McMillan (1985) who sees Japan's success as due to:

1. its culture and human relations
2. its use and adaptation of technology, especially micro-technology
3. its international outlook in relation to economic matters He concludes that:

> " ... if there is one quality which stands out in Japan, ... (it) is the recurrent theme in Japanese history of geographical and physical adversity ... ".

The basis of this adversity is principally, (a) the physical disadvantages of accommodating its population amongst a collection of mountainous and volcanic islands, and (b) its dependence on other nations for virtually all its raw materials, energy and foodstuffs. In such circumstances, says McMillan, it is not surprising that management attitudes are oriented towards such issues as energy conservation, technological innovation, quality control and human resource management. On the last point, in particular, he concludes that, precisely because of the pressures of population density, Japanese feel a great sense of their interdependence as communities, and this reflects itself in their work relationships.

## JAPANESE COMPANIES

6.   There are some fundamental differences between Japanese companies and British companies. Firstly, there is much less reliance on shareholders for the funding of business. Instead the major banks play the greater role in providing funds. One result of this is that the Board of directors is more powerful than the shareholders meeting. The Board determines the long-term strategy of the company, appointing an Executive Board made up of senior directors to concentrate on short-term, operational issues. Most Japanese directors have line responsibilities and this gives the Executive Board a strong production emphasis. However, this emphasis has to be seen against the background of Government fiscal and research-and-development policies aimed at encouraging long-term planning based on a close analysis of previous performance statistics.

7.   Secondly, the trade unions in Japan are company-wide rather than occupationally-based, as in Britain, or industry-based, as in West Germany. The company-wide approach to trade union organization is a reflection of a unitary attitude towards employee relations rather than the pluralistic attitude which typifies British employee relations (see Chapter 48). The aims of Japanese unions are primarily (a) to achieve lifetime job security for their members, and (b) to ensure, in collaboration with the management, the success and efficiency of the company, upon which they depend. This contrasts strongly with British trade unions, for example, where the emphasis is clearly on protecting and promoting the *members'* interests.

8.   Personnel policies in Japanese firms are based, so far as core workers are concerned, on the concept of employment for life. The implications of this are that, in exchange for labour flexibility, acceptance of new working practices and general loyalty to the organization, Japanese managers will place considerable emphasis

on providing job security, training, career development whilst at the same time reducing pay and status differentials.

9.    Thirdly, the organization structure of Japanese companies, whilst still hierarchical, is much less dependent on formal, bureaucratic, authority than on group consensus and individual expertise. Decision making processes in Japanese firms are focussed on defining questions or issues rather than on finding solutions. Thus, as all levels of the organization are involved in this process, so an overall consensus on problems and priorities emerges. This consensus approach tends to reinforce feelings of loyalty and commitment from all concerned.

10.    Fourthly, in Japan quality control has been seen as the responsibility of every employee not just supervisors or quality control specialists, for example. The widespread use of discussion groups called 'Quality Circles' in Japanese manufacturing firms enables employees at every level to participate in the achievement of high standards of quality. Training has been seen as a necessary ingredient in the task of bringing individual employees up to a state of readiness to influence quality in the workplace .

11.    A particular point of interest here is the Japanese use of key statistical data in discussions about quality and efficiency at shop-floor level, for this approach requires employees to understand what statistics are available and how they can be interpreted. Since most recruits to Japanese firms have to work their way up from the shop-floor level, there is a shared experience of life at this level for all managers and supervisors.

## THE INFLUENCE OF TAYLORISM

12.    The ideas of F W. Taylor (see Chap. 4) were taken up enthusiastically by the Japanese, but, in contrast to Western industrialised nations, they emphasised the importance of the human resource element in achieving production efficiency using Taylor's methods. In Japan today engineering is held in the highest esteem, and there is a marked production orientation in the workplace. The situation in Britain is rather different. Taylorism is seen as discredited on the grounds that it leads to the disintegration of work and loss of job satisfaction, and engineering has a low status compared with other professions. Robert Cole (1979) reported in a study entitled 'Work, Mobility and Participation' that in terms of specialist management functions, Japanese firms ranked production and personnel highest, whereas British firms chose accounting and finance.

13. The acceptance of Taylorist approaches to manufacturing has enabled the Japanese to capture an enviable place in world markets for their manufactured goods. It is not that the Japanese are particularly innovative, but they have found the secret of achieving a standard of production control which ensures a consistently excellent product. This standard has been achieved because of thorough attention to human resource issues as well as to questions of technology, quality and cost control. Backed by financial policies aimed at long-term growth rather than short-term profits, and a worldwide view of product marketing, Japanese manufacturing companies have set a high standard for their competitors to follow.

14. Critics of Japanese manufacturing companies point to the slow processes of decision-making, the lack of risk-taking, the reliance on a myriad of small firms and part-time employees, the docile nature of the trade unions, and the imprisoning effect of lifetime employment in one company. It is precisely because of such criticisms that Japanese management practices have to be adapted if they are to be employed successfully elsewhere. The whole point of Theory Z lies in the *adaptation* of Japanese approaches to Western production methods.

15. In a report published by the Work Research Unit –'Learning from Japan' (1984), the representative of Thorn EMI Ferguson, manufacturers of colour televisions and associated equipment in Britain, drew a number of conclusions about the relative situation of his company vis-a-vis the Japanese TV factories visited. He concluded that in production technology terms his company was unsurpassed by any of the Japanese companies visited. In labour flexibility terms, the Japanese were well ahead, principally because of their use of part-time employees (25–30% of the total workforce) and due to the high turnover of their predominantly female workforce. Very high volumes of colour televisions were produced in each of the Japanese factories, considerably in excess of the British company's output. It was also noticed that where the Japanese had a very limited range of models, the British firm had about two hundred in production. In terms of 'Personnel Policy' there were important differences. The Japanese policy was directed at maximising the contribution of each employee through exhortation, training, job rotation, use of quality circles and individual counselling. The emphasis on learning about, and being committed to, the company culture was striking. The British approach to Personnel Policy usually emphasised rewards and employee support mechanisms rather than employee attitudes and output.

16.  The Thorn representative concluded overall that:

> "If the Delegation came back with one single message, it would be that competing in design technology and production technology with the Japanese is not enough. To survive in the long term we must compete in the field of employee commitment."

Suggestions made by the representative, which might be said to be his version of Theory Z, were as follows:

1.  eliminate artificial status barriers (ie permit 'harmonisation')
2.  re-structure work as to allow individuals to undertake meaningful roles and thus offer the opportunity to contribute positively to company success
3.  develop training for management succession
4.  improve communications in each direction, especially on issues such as company performance, policies and future prospects
5.  encourage greater individual responsibility for work, quality and environment
6.  introduce major improvements in factory housekeeping

## CONCLUSION

17.  What is significant, in the context of British manufacturing, is that these ideas (Theory Z) are not new. Indeed many well-known firms have practised them for years. What has happened in Japan is that the will has existed to put them into practice *on a grand scale,* and therein lies the difference.

## SECTION SUMMARY – HUMAN RELATIONS THEORIES

1.  Chapters 7–10 have set out some of the leading ideas on the subject of the human factor at work. We commenced by looking at the concept of motivation, which underlies all the ideas and theories described in this Section. The basic model of motivation demonstrates that individual behaviour arises from the driving force of needs which are directed towards some desired goal or end.

2.  Our attitudes and behaviour towards other people are a reflection of the assumptions we make about our fellow Man. These assumptions have been examined by a number of people including the American social psychologists, Edgar Schein and Douglas McGregor. Schein sees four sets of assumptions about

people's behaviour. The first set depicts Rational economic Man – an individual whose chief motivation is reward and self-interest. Therefore rewards and threats form the basis on which he may be treated. Second comes Social Man, 'discovered', perhaps, by the Hawthorne Studies. Social Man needs people and satisfying relationships. These needs may be met by providing supportive groups with sympathetic supervisors and managers. Third is Self-actualizing Man who seeks challenge and self-fulfilment at work. These needs may be met by providing opportunities for greater autonomy in the job. Finally we have Complex Man. His needs are variable and he expects them to be met in terms of a psychological contract between him and his organization. Meeting these needs is a demanding task and requires considerable diagnostic skills on the part of managers.

3.     McGregor's Theory X and Theory Y assumptions correspond fairly close to Schein's ideas of Rational-economic Man and Self-actualizing Man respectively. McGregor's theories have been applied more to issues of leadership and management development than to broader issues of management and organization theory.

4.     The Hawthorne Studies are a major landmark in any discussion of human relations at work. Chapter 8 described the principal stages of these studies and indicated that the role of Elton Mayo was not so much that of active researcher as of influential writer and publicist. For their time the Hawthorne Studies were a major step forward for the social sciences, and although their methods and the results have been subject to various criticisms subsequently, they nevertheless paved the way for modern social psychology. The most significant lessons to be drawn from the Studies were that work is a social activity, where workers are part of a group rather than mere isolated individuals; that the need for, and rewards from, group membership are extremely important to individuals; and that informal groups at work exercise a powerful influence over the workforce, for better or for worse.

5.     The immediate influences arising out of the Hawthorne Studies were given the name 'Human Relations'. This label was given to distinguish the work of Mayo, Roethlisberger and others from the contemporary ideas of the Scientific Management theorists, whose efforts were directed at work and tasks rather than people. The exponents of human relations were predominantly interested in social needs and affiliation needs at work. In the period following the end of the Second World War, human relations gave way to social psychologists, whose focus was not only on social needs but a wide range of other motivators. These

have been described as the neo-human relations school, or Social Psychology School, and will be distinguished from the systems and contingency theorists who are dealt with in the next Section.

6.    One of the first major theorists of the neo-human relations school was Abraham Maslow His concept of an hierarchy of human needs made a considerable impact on his contemporaries, especially in relation to his higher needs – esteem and selfactualization needs. Until Maslow the emphasis in motivation had been on the basic needs – physiological and safety needs (Scientific Management approach), and love needs (the Human Relations approach). After him, it was possible for Herzberg, Likert and others to concentrate their researches on Man's capacity for self-awareness and self-fulfilment.

7.    Herzberg's Motivation-Hygiene theory drew particular attention to higher level needs in the motivation of professional (and subsequently other) groups of employees. A key factor in his theory was that these higher needs were related to the *content* of work and not to its context. This has led to our modern interest in job design and so-called job enrichment ie enriched with motivators (responsibility, recognition etc).

8.    The lower level needs of Herzberg's theory appeared to be associated with the *context* of work. Such needs included economic and social factors (pay, supervision etc) and were found to be a major source of dissatisfaction if they were not met). On the other hand where they were provided they did not necessarily produce a high degree of satisfaction. Herzberg's message to employers was a clear one: highly-motivated employees cannot be bought just with good pay and working conditions; they have to experience achievement, recognition and other motivators associated with the work they are required to perform.

9.    Rensis Likert took up this theme in his ideas on motivation. In particular he saw the leadership role of managers and supervisors as playing a crucial role in creating a motivational environment. Higher level needs can be met ensuring the development of 'supportive relationships' in work groups. Another key feature of successful organizations is that they are built up on inter-locking teams, in which team leader roles act as linking pins to hold the organization together. Likert, like Herzberg, acknowledged a range of factors which affect motivation and took the view that the optimum style of management ie participative group, has to utilise a variety of motivators.

10. Likert's identification of separate systems, or styles, of management is useful in distinguishing a range of alternative approaches which can be adopted in dealing with people and meeting their needs. Systems 1 and 2 identified a directive, task-centred approach to management, similar to Theory X and Rational-economic Man. System 3 identified an approach which is very similar to Social Man. System 4, the participative style, is closest to Theory Y and Self-actualizing Man.

11. Argyris saw motivation in terms of people's relative maturity and their need to become more mature eg more independent, with deeper interests and longer time perspectives. He saw a clash between people's needs and the needs of organizations. The typical classical or mechanistic type of structure demands behaviour that is dependent, subordinate and narrow (specialised). This requires people to act in what Argyris defined as an immature way. What effective organizations have to work towards is an approach which integrates organizational aims with those of individuals. This, according to Argyris, will only be achieved when management recognises the need for the average person to develop his or her personality, that is to say to become more mature.

12. The Chapter included a summary of McClelland's ideas concerning motivation. His somewhat different approach concentrated particularly on Man's need for achievement (n-Ach), which McClelland saw as being a key motivator. This need is developed mainly in response to upbringing and environment rather than by inherited factors. It is possible, therefore, to train people to acquire the need. McClelland's analysis is useful in its isolation of n-Ach and its description of the behaviour of the typical high achiever. The application of his ideas must be treated with some reserve, however, since one of the prime characteristics of the high achiever is low interest in relationships, and this conflicts with current views about the best management style. Today the ideal manager is considered to be a person who is high both on people and task. n-Ach may be developed (more suitably) in purely task-oriented jobs (salesmen etc).

13. The Chapter also included a brief account of the main features of Expectancy Theory, based mainly on the work of Vroom and Lawler. This theory lends itself less well to a 'management package' approach than most of the others described here. It concentrates on the individual's perception of the relationships between effort, performance and rewards, and is being applied in job design programmes.

The final chapter in this section examined Japanese efforts at gaining employee commitment and motivation through focussing on employee attitudes and company 'culture'.

14. This Section has presented the ideas of a number of the theorists who have contributed to the growth in understanding of the human factor at work. Most if not all of them have attempted to offer guidelines to practising managers to enable them to take appropriate actions to bring about high employee motivation and the consequential benefits of high productivity.

## QUESTIONS FOR DISCUSSION/HOMEWORK

*1.    What are the needs or motives most frequently referred to by the leading theorists of human relations? In what ways is it possible to group these needs?*

*2.    Give examples of tangible and intangible goals and suggest how a person might seek to achieve them.*

*3. What are the similarities between Schein's description of Rational-economic Man, McGregor's Theory X and Likert's System 1 (Exploitive-authoritative)?*

*4. What is the 'Hawthorne Effect'?*

*5.    Why were the Hawthorne Studies considered to be so important in their time?*

*6.    In what ways has Maslow's concept of self-actualization been taken up by other theorists?*

*7.    What are the essential differences between motivators and hygiene factors in Herzberg's theory of motivation?*

*8.    How can an understanding of the need for achievement be of use to managers in industry and commerce?*

*9.    In what respects is Expectancy Theory novel in the approach it adopts towards motivation at work?*

*10.    What is 'Theory Z', and to what extent could it be applied in non-Japanese companies?*

## EXAMINATION QUESTIONS – HUMAN RELATIONS THEORIES

The following are selected for their relevance to this Section, and, in some cases to the section on classical theories as well. Outline answers can be found in Appendix 1.

*EQ 5. Discuss the major features and significance of... the Hawthorne experience at Western Electric...*

*(ACCA–part of an either/or question)*

*EQ 6. Compare the approaches taken by the classical/traditional theorists with the human relations/resources theorists, in understanding the nature of organizations.* **(CIMA)**

*EQ 7. 'People only come to work for money.' Discuss.* **(IOB)**

*EQ 8. Motivation of subordinates is an important aspect of a manager's job.*

*a. What do you think motivates a person to work well?*

*b. What steps can a manager take to motivate his subordinates?*

**(ICSA MPP)**

# SYSTEMS APPROACHES TO MANAGEMENT THEORY

The dominance of first the Classical school and second the Human Relations/Human Resources schools has been overtaken by a more comprehensive approach to the study of management in organizations. This more recent approach views the organization as a system ie an interrelated set of activities which enables inputs to be converted into outputs. The approach, which is described in more detail below, enables theorists to study key elements of organization in terms of their interaction with one another and with their external environment. Whereas, in the past, the explanations were in terms of structures or people, now it is possible to identify theories which seek to explain or predict organizational behaviour in a multi-dimensional way by studying people *and* structure *and* technology *and* environment at one and the same time. The most recent formulations of systems theories tend to be labelled contingency theories' because they emphasise the need to take specific circumstances or contingencies into account when devising appropriate organizational and management systems. Chapter 11 introduces the concept of 'systems' as applied to organizations. Chapter 12 describes some of the major developments in the growth of systems theory, while Chapter 13 summarises developments in contingency theories.

# 11

# ORGANIZATIONS AS SYSTEMS

## INTRODUCTION

1.   This chapter defines the characteristics of open social systems and summarises the current theoretical position as a prelude to a discussion of the ideas of several outstanding theorists who have contributed to the growing understanding of organizations as systems (Chapters 12 & 13).

## DEFINITIONS AND CHARACTERISTICS

2.   Put at its simplest, a system is a collection of interrelated parts which form some whole. Typical systems are the solar system, the human body, communication networks and social systems. Systems may be 'closed' or 'open'. Closed systems are those, which, for all practical purposes, are completely selfsupporting, and thus do not interact with their environment. An example would be an astronaut's life-support pack. Open systems are those which *do* interact with their environment, on which they rely for obtaining essential inputs and for the discharge of their system-outputs. Social systems (eg organizations) are always open systems, as are biological systems and information systems. A basic model of an open system can be shown diagrammatically as follows:

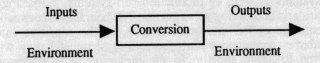

**Figure 11.1 Basic Model of an Open System**

3.   The three major characteristics of open systems are: a. they receive inputs or energy from their environment b. they convert these inputs into outputs and c. they discharge their outputs into their environment

In relation to an organization, the inputs include people, materials, information and finance. These inputs are organized and activated so as to convert human skills and raw materials into products, services and other outputs which are discharged into the environment, as shown in Figure 11.2.

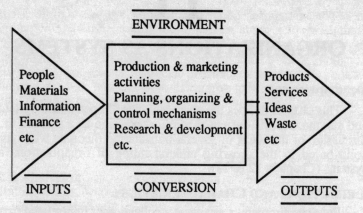

**Figure 11.2 The Organization as an Open System**

4.   A key feature of open systems is their inter-dependence on the environment, which may be relatively stable or relatively uncertain at a particular point in time. This feature is of considerable importance to business enterprises which need to adapt to the changing fortunes of the market place if they are to flourish. A classification of environments is given in Chapter 12 (paragraph 16).

5.   Most systems can be sub-divided into sub-systems. For example, the human body – the total system – encloses a number of major sub-systems, such as the central nervous system and the cardio-vascular system, to name but two. Organizations have their sub-systems as well, eg production sub-systems, marketing sub-systems and accounting sub-systems. The boundaries between sub-systems are called interfaces. These are the sensitive internal boundaries contained within the total system, and they will be referred to again shortly. In the meantime it is important to consider a few points about system boundaries. An organization's boundaries are defined as much by corporate strategy as by actual fact. This is not so for all systems. In physical or biological systems, the boundaries are there to be seen, and there is no problem distinguishing one motor-vehicle, or one human being, from another, for example. In such systems it is also easy to identify boundaries between the total system and its sub-systems. For example, the gearbox of a motor vehicle is a clearly recognizable sub-unit of the whole vehicle. In the same way the cardio-vascular system in the human body is a recognizable sub-system of the whole body. These boundaries are matters of fact. For organizations the issue is not quite so straightforward.

6.    The boundaries of an organization are not visible, for the boundaries of a social system are based on *relationships* and not on things. Thus while certain factual elements, such as physical location, do have some impact on an organization's boundaries, it is the results of management decisions ie *choices*, that really determine where the organization ends and the environment begins. Similarly, while the physical presence of machines may determine to a certain extent some of the internal boundaries of the organization, it is ultimately a matter of corporate or departmental strategy which decides where the production system, for example, begins and where it ends.

7.    In any organization, some employees work consistently at the *external* boundary. These are the people who have to deal with the inputs and the outputs to the system eg those responsible for raising capital, purchasing from suppliers, identifying customer requirements etc and those responsible for sales, distribution etc.

Other employees work consistently at the *internal* boundaries ie at the interfaces between the various sub-systems of the organization. These people may be responsible for the provision of services to others in the organization eg management accountants, personnel officers, office service managers etc. They may be responsible for integrating activities eg managers and supervisors. In fact, it is becoming increasingly recognized that 'boundary management' is of vital importance to the effectiveness of those in managerial and supervisory roles.

Boundary management in this context means establishing and maintaining effective relationships with colleagues working in neighbouring sub-systems.

8.    Whilst organizations are open social systems, taken as a whole, their sub systems may be either open or closed. Production sub-systems and accounting sub-systems tend to be closed systems ie they are relatively self-contained and are affected in ways which are usually predictable. Marketing and R & D (research and development) activities tend, on the other hand, to work best in open systems ie where they can be aware of, and adapt to, key influences in the external environment. In the main, closed systems are required for stability and consistency, whereas open systems are required for unstable and uncertain conditions. Closed systems are designed for efficiency, open systems for survival. The early Classical theorists were expounding a closed systems approach. Developments in Human Relations, by contrast, were biased towards open systems. The modern consensus appears to be that

both types are necessary for the maintenance and growth of successful organizations.

9.    One of the most useful attempts to summarise the complexities of organizations as open systems has been that of the two American academics, Katz and Kahn (1966). They identified the common characteristics of such open systems as follows:

a.    Importation of energy and stimulation eg people and material.

b.    Throughput or conversion eg the processing of materials and organizing of work activities.

c.    Output eg products or services.

d.    Cyclic nature eg the returns from marketing the output enable further inputs to be made to complete the cycle of production.

e.    Negative entropy. Entropy is the natural process by which all things tend to break down or die. Developing negative entropy means importing more energy etc than is required for output and storing it to enable survival in difficult times, eg firms building up their reserves.

f.    Feedback. Negative feedback, in particular, enables the system to correct deviations. Organizations tend to develop their own thermostats!

g.    Steady state. This refers to the balance to be maintained between inputs flowing in from the external environment and the corresponding outputs returning to it. An organization in steady state is not static, but in a dynamic form of equilibrium.

h.    Differentiation eg the tendency to greater specialization of functions and multiplicity of roles.

i.    Equifinality. This word was coined by an early systems theorist, Von Bertalanffy, in 1940. It means that open systems do not have to achieve their goals in one particular way. Similar ends can be achieved by different paths and from a different starting point.

10.    The Katz and Kahn summary utilizes a number of specialized systems terms (eg negative entropy and equifinality) which are beyond the scope of a general management text, and which candidates would not be expected to elaborate on in a Management Studies paper. What is important to grasp at this stage is that the input-conversion-output model, as shown in Figure 11.2, now needs to be expanded to take in the key factors of feedback and steady state. The result of including feedback from output to input

is to produce a so-called 'closed loop' system. A closed loop system is basically a self-regulating system, such as a thermostat in a heating system or, to take a business example, a budgetary control system in a departmental operating plan. In each case, information fed back to the input side of the system enables corrective changes to be made to keep the system on course ie in a steady state. The revised model of the organization as an open system can now be drawn as follows:

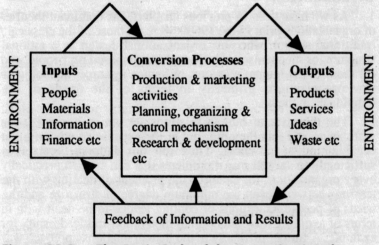

**Figure 11.3    The Basic Cycle of the Organizational System**

11.   The revised model shows the consequences of the outputs as information and results. The information can take many forms eg sales volumes, new orders, market share, customer complaints etc, and can be applied to control inputs and conversion processes, as appropriate. The results are the revenues and profits which are fed back into the organization to provide further inputs, and so ensure the survival and growth of the system. An adaptive system such as the one described above is sometimes referred to as a 'cybernetic' system. The term 'cybernetics' in this context means the study of control and communication in the animal and the machine. Cybernetics was made famous by Norbert Wiener in the late 1940's, but is still very much a developing science. The essence of a cybernetic system is self-regulation on the basis of feedback information to disclose a shortfall in performance against standards and to indicate corrective action.

# 12

## DEVELOPMENTS IN SYSTEMS THEORIES

### INTRODUCTION

1.    As we have seen in previous chapters, the dominant theories of organizations prior to the 1960's were (a) those of the classical / traditional school, who saw organizational design as a rational structure, or mechanism, which could be imposed on people, and (b) those of the human relations, or human resources school, who saw organizations primarily in terms of the needs of the individuals in them.

2.    The theorists of human relations set out to humanize the workplace, and this they did, but at the expense of studying the organization as a whole. They did not address themselves sufficiently to several major problems that can arise in practically every organization, for example the problem of dealing with the tensions between even the minimum degree of structure and the needs of people. Questions of conflict tended to be dealt with in terms of avoiding it by attention to motivation and leadership, for example. A further difficulty in the human relations approach was its emphasis on the practical application of ideas rather than on the conceptual development of organizational theory. This is not to deny the usefulness, to practising managers in particular, of the propositions of human relations, but it suggests the need to look elsewhere for a fuller explanation of behaviour in organizations.

3.    This is where we have to turn to theorists who see organizations as complex social systems, responsive to a number of interdependent and important variables. The key variables that are of greatest interest to those adopting a systems approach to organizations are as follows:

* People
* Technology
* Organization structure
* Environment

Whereas earlier theorists looked at individual variables in isolation, the theorists of systems study the relationship between two or more of them. Initially, the Tavistock researchers, for example, looked at the relationships between people and technology, and between structure and environment. More recent studies, such as those of Pugh and colleagues, have developed a more comprehensive and multi-dimensional approach, utilising all the above variables. The principal developments in systems theories of organization design are discussed in this and the following chapter.

4.    The researches, so far, have indicated that there is no one best way of designing organizations to meet their current objectives. On the contrary, the evidence seems to suggest that the variables are so volatile that only a 'contingency' approach can prove practicable. This suggests that organizations can only be made viable when steps are taken to adapt them to a particular set of prevailing conditions. Naturally, this approach appeals more to theorists than practising managers, who must feel daunted by the need to be eternally adaptive. Nevertheless, it offers the best prospect to date of achieving the optimum organization design. Before looking at contingency approaches which are outlined in Chapter 13, it is necessary to describe some of the earlier contributions to systems theory as applied to organizations.

## THE TAVISTOCK GROUP

5.    The Tavistock Institute of Human Relations in London has been engaged in various forms of social research for over forty years. Despite its title, the Institute has in fact made its reputation for its contribution to systems theory. In particular, Trist and Bamforth introduced the concept of 'socio-technical' systems (1951) and A.K. Rice and F.E. Emery promoted several important ideas relating to open-systems theory and types of environment.

6.    The Trist and Bamforth studies into changes in the method of extracting coal in British pits took place in the 1940's. The researchers were interested in the effects of mechanization on the social and work organization at the coal-face. Before mechanization the coal had been extracted by small, closely knit teams working as autonomous groups. They worked at their own pace, often isolated in the dark from other groups. Bonds established within groups became important outside work as well as during the shift. Conflicts between competing groups were frequent and sometimes violent, but were always contained. This was the system which operated before the coal-cutters and mechanical conveyors were introduced. It was called the short wall method.

7.    The mechanized coal-face was completely different. It consisted of a long wall which required not small groups, but

groups of between forty and fifty men plus their supervisors. These men could be spread out over 200 yards, and they worked in a three shift system. The new system, known as the longwall method, was essentially a mass-production system based on a high degree of job specialization. Whereas under the former shortwall method, each team had provided all the skills required, in the longwall arrangement the basic operations were separated between the shifts. So, for example, if the first shift cut the coal from the face, the second shift shovelled it into the conveyor, and the third shift advanced the coal-face along the seam. Even within each shift, there was a high degree of task specialization.

8.   The social consequences of the new method, arising from the breakdown of the previously closely-integrated social structure were: increased haggling over pay, inter-shift competition for the best jobs, the seeking of scape-goats in other shifts, and a noticeable increase in absenteeism. The results of the radical change in working methods and the miners' adverse response to them, led Trist and Bamforth to the conclusion that effective work was a function of the *inter*dependence of technology (equipment, physical layout and task requirements) and social needs (especially relationships within groups). It was not sufficient to regard the working environment as *either* a technological system *or* a social system. It was a combination of the two: a socio-technical system.

9.   Eventually a so-called 'composite longwall method' was developed which enabled the needs of the social system to be met, whilst at the same time utilising the benefits of the new mechanized equipment (the technical system). Tasks and working arrangements were altered so that the basic operations could be carried out by any one shift, and so that tasks within each group were allocated by the members. Payment was changed so as to incorporate a group bonus. The outcome of the composite method was increased productivity, reduced absenteeism and a lower accident rate.

10.   Alongside the coal-mining studies mentioned above, the reputation of the Tavistock group was also assured by A.K. Rice's studies into the calico mills at Ahmedabad, India. These were written up in a book entitled Productivity and Social Organization (1958) in which Rice elaborated on key aspects of systems theory as applied to organizations. Two features of this work are selected for inclusion in this chapter – Rice's concept of systems, and his views on work design.

11.   Rice saw any industrial system (ie a firm) as an open system, importing various items from its environment, converting them

into goods, services and waste materials, and then exporting them into the environment. Within the total system of the firm there exist two main systems: an operating system and a managing system. The operating system deals with the import, conversion and export of the product or service, while the managing system deals with the control, decision-making and communication aspects of the total system. Each system can have one or more sub-systems, which is why it is necessary to develop the managing system so as to coordinate the interaction of all the systems and sub-systems.

12. Rice's view of systems can be compared usefully with those of Handy, writing some twenty years later. Handy describes and comments on, not only the operating system, but also the adaptive, maintenance and information systems in activating the various parts of the total organization. It is these last three which come closest to making up the managing system formulated by Rice. On balance, the more modern analysis is the clearer of the two in helping to establish the prime focal points of the managing system.

13. The studies at Ahmedabad produced, among other things, some interesting conclusions about the design of work. These can be summarised as follows:

a. Effective performance of a primary task is an important source of satisfaction at *all* levels of work.

b. The capacity for voluntary cooperation is more extensive than is often expected.

c. There is great benefit in allowing individuals to complete a whole task.

d. Work groups of eight seem to have the best chance of success for achieving group tasks.

e. There is a clear relationship between work effectiveness and social relations.

f. Where group autonomy has been established, unnecessary interference by supervisors will be counter-productive.

14. The above findings have been incorporated into current ideas on the design and re-design of work so as to meet social and psychological needs of employees as well as the requirements of changing technology. They also share much common ground with Herzberg's ideas of motivation and job enrichment.

15. The final example of the work of the Tavistock Group relates to another key factor in systems theory – the nature of the environment. Emery and Trist ( 1965) were the first to produce a

classification of environments. They described four types of environment as follows.

i.    **Placid, randomized.** This represents a relatively unchanging and homogeneous environment, whose demands are randomly distributed.

ii.   **Placid, clustered.** This environment too, is relatively unchanging, but its threats and rewards are clustered. So, for example, in a monopoly situation an organization's failure or success depends on its continued hold over the market.

iii.  **Disturbed, reactive.** In this environment there is competition between organizations, and this may include hindering tactics.

iv.   **Turbulent field.** This describes a dynamic and rapidly changing environment, in which organizations must adapt frequently in order to survive.

16.  Emery and Trist have been particularly interested in the last type, the turbulent field. This is an area where existing formal or bureaucratized structures are ill-suited to deal with their environment. According to the writers, more and more environments are becoming turbulent, and yet organization structures are not becoming correspondingly flexible. This important point is referred to in the next chapter when dealing with the 'mechanistic-organic structures' concept introduced by Burns and Stalker in 1961.

17.  The field of management and organization theory has been poorly served, in general, by British writers and theorists. The outstanding exception to this situation has been the work of the Tavistock Group, whose contribution to our understanding of organizations as open social systems has been fundamental.

## KATZ & KAHN

18.  Reference was made to these two researchers in Chapter 11. In their book 'The Social Psychology of Organizations' (1966) the authors proposed an essentially systems view of organizations. This has had considerable influence on the developments of systems approaches to organization theory. Some of their principal ideas are summarised in the next few paragraphs.

19.  Katz and Kahn see social structures as essentially contrived systems, where the forces that hold them together are psychological rather than biological. Social systems are seen to be more variable than biological systems and are more difficult to study because they have no easily recognizable boundaries. They

have a structure, but it is a structure of events rather than of physical parts. Nevertheless Katz and Kahn set out to describe their view of social systems and their related sub-systems.

20. They follow similar lines to Rice in advocating an open system approach, in which they identify five sub-systems at work in organizations. These are as follows.

**Production or Technical sub-systems.** These are concerned with the accomplishment of the basic tasks of the organization (production of goods, provision of services etc).

**Supportive sub-systems.** These are the systems which procure the inputs and dispose of the outputs of the production sub-system. They also maintain the relationship between the organization as a whole and the external environment.

**Maintenance sub-systems.** These are concerned with the relative stability or predictability of the organization. They provide for the roles, the rules and the rewards applicable to those who work in the organization.

**Adaptive sub-systems.** The above systems serve the organization as it is. The adaptive sub-systems are concerned with what the organization might become. They deal with issues of change in the environment eg research and development, product research and long-range planning.

**Managerial sub-systems.** These comprise the controlling and coordinating activities of the total system. They deal with the coordination of substructures, the resolution of conflict, and the coordination of external requirements with the organization's resources. An important managerial sub-system is the authority structure which describes the way the managerial system is organized for the purposes of decision-making and decision-taking.

21. Other key features of social organizations, according to Katz and Kahn are roles, norms and values. Roles differentiate one position from another and require a standardized form of behaviour. The network of roles constitutes the formal structure of the organization, and the formalized role system. Roles limit the effects of the incumbent's personality on performance in the position. This idea is very much in line with Weber's view of the rational, and impersonal conduct of an office. In fact, Katz and Kahn describe bureaucratic structures as the clearest examples of their definition of social organization.

22. Whereas roles help to differentiate the activities of the organization, norms and values help to integrate behaviour. Norms or standards of behaviour, are closely associated with roles, because they specify role behaviour in terms of expected standards. For example, an office manager would be expected to conform to certain norms relating to dress, timekeeping and honesty, to name but three possibilities. Values are more generally held beliefs; they represent the ideology of the organization. Loyalty to the organization is an example of a value.

23. Katz and Kahn have provided us with a useful way of looking at organizations as systems. Their descriptions of the major sub-systems of organizations, together with the pattern of roles which are inextricably linked with them, represent an important step forward in understanding the complexities of the nature of organizations.

# 13

# CONTINGENCY APPROACHES TO MANAGEMENT

## INTRODUCTION

1.    There is no clear distinction between the systems approach and the contingency approach to the management of organizations. The latter has developed out of the findings of the former. A systems approach highlights the complexity of the interdependent components of organizations within equally complex environments. A contingency approach builds on the diagnostic qualities of the systems approach in order to determine the most appropriate organizational design and management style for a given set of circumstances. Essentially the contingency approach suggests that issues of design and style depend on choosing what is the best combination, in the light of prevailing (or forecast) conditions, of the following variables: (a) the external environment, (b) technological factors, and (c) human skills and motivation.

2.    The label 'contingency approach' was suggested by two American academics, Lawrence and Lorsch, in 1967. Their important contribution to this approach will be summarised shortly. Other writers referred to in this chapter, and who have adopted a contingency approach, are British: Joan Woodward is noted for her important studies into the effects of technology on structure and performance; Burns and Stalker introduced the concept of mechanistic and organic types of structure and discussed them in relation to the environment; finally, the so called Aston group (Pugh, Hickson et al.) have made some interesting studies into several of the technology-structure variables in organizations.

3.    Unlike the Classical and Human Relations approaches to the management of organizations, the contingency approach does not seek to produce universal prescriptions or principles of behaviour. It deals in relativities, not absolutes. It is essentially a situational approach to management. The contingency approach does not turn its face against earlier approaches, but adapts them as part of a 'mix' which could be applied to an organization in a particular set of circumstances. The following paragraphs look at several

important research studies which have dealt with two or more elements of this 'organizational mix'.

## LAWRENCE & LORSCH

4.    These two Harvard researchers set out to answer the question what kind of organization does it take to deal with various economic and market conditions. They were concerned, therefore, with structure and environment as the two key variables in their study. Initially Lawrence and his colleague studied the internal functioning of six plastics firms operating in a diverse and dynamic environment. The results in these six firms were then compared with two standardized container firms operating in a very stable environment, and two firms in the packaged food industry, where the rate of change was moderate.

5.    The major emphasis of their study was on the states of differentiation and integration in organizations. Differentiation was defined as more than mere division of labour or specialization. It also referred to the differences in attitude and behaviour of the managers concerned. These differences were looked at in terms of:

a.   their orientation towards particular goals eg issues of cost-reduction are more important to production managers than to sales or research managers.

b.   their time orientation eg sales and production managers have short-term orientations while research managers have long-term orientations.

c.   their interpersonal orientation eg production managers tend to be less relationship-orientated than sales managers.

d.   the relative formality of the structure of their functional units eg the highly formalized production departments with their many levels, narrow span of control and routine procedures as contrasted with the relatively informal and flat structures of the research departments.

6.    Integration was defined as the quality of the state of collaboration that exists among departments. It was seen to be more than a mere rational or mechanical process, as in the Classical approach. Integration was a question of inter-relationships, in the final analysis, said Lawrence and Lorsch. Inevitably the differences of attitude referred to in paragraph 5 above would lead to frequent conflicts about what direction to take. These conflicts were not catered for adequately in the Classical theories. A key interest of the two researchers, therefore, was to assess the way conflict was controlled in organizations.

7.  In approaching their studies, Lawrence and Lorsch took the view that there was probably no one best way to organize. What they could hope for was to provide a systematic understanding of what states of differentiation and integration are related to effective performance under different environmental conditions.

8.  Effective performance was judged in terms of the following criteria:

   a.  change in profits over the past five years,

   b.  change in sales volume over the same period,

   c.  new products introduced over the period as a percentage of current sales.

As it turned out, the firms selected for study encompassed a range of performance from high through medium to low performance when set against the chosen criteria.

9.  The main conclusions that Lawrence and Lorsch arrived at were as follows:

   a.  The more dynamic and diverse the environment, the higher the degree of both differentiation and integration required for successful organization.

   b.  Less changeable environments require a lesser degree of differentiation, but still require a high degree of integration.

   c.  The more differentiated an organization, the more difficult it is to resolve conflict.

   d.  High-performing organizations tend to develop better ways of resolving conflict than their less effective competitors. Improved ways of conflict resolution lead to states of differentiation and integration that are appropriate for the environment.

   e.  Where the environment is uncertain, the integrating functions tend to be carried out by middle and low-level managers; where the environment is stable, integration tends to be achieved at the top end of the management hierarchy.

10.  The research referred to above was based on a very small sample of firms, it relied on some rather subjective information, and several of the measures employed have been criticized as unreliable by subsequent researchers. Despite the criticisms, the Lawrence and Lorsch study represented a most important step forward in the search for a theory of organizations that could take account of the major variables affecting the structure of successful organizations.

## BURNS & STALKER

11. Another famous study of the environment-structure relationship was conducted by Burns and Stalker during the 1950's in Scotland and England. Some twenty firms in the electronics industry were studied from the point of view of how they adapted themselves to deal with changing market and technical conditions, having been organized to handle relatively stable conditions. The findings were written up in 'The Management of Innovation' published in 1961.

12. The researchers were particularly interested in how management systems might change in response to the demands of a rapidly changing external environment. As a result of their studies, they came up with two distinctive 'ideal types' of management system: *mechanistic* systems and *organic* systems. The key features of both systems are summarised below.

13. Mechanistic Systems. These are appropriate for conditions of stability. Their outstanding features are as follows:

    a. a specialized differentiation of tasks, pursued more or less in their own right,

    b. a precise definition of rights, obligations and technical methods of each functional role,

    c. an hierarchical structure of control, authority and communication,

    d. a tendency for vertical interaction between members of the concern,

    e. a tendency for operations and working behaviour to be dominated by superiors,

    f. an insistence on loyalty to the concern and obedience to superiors.

14. By contrast, organic systems are appropriate for conditions of change. Their outstanding features can be summarised as follows:

    a. individual tasks, which are relevant to the total situation of the concern, are adjusted and re-defined through interaction with others,

    b. a network structure of control, authority and communication, where knowledge of technical or commercial aspects of tasks may be located anywhere in the network,

    c. a lateral rather than vertical direction of communication through the organization,

d. communications consist of information and advice rather than instructions and decisions,
e. commitment to the organization's tasks seen to be more important than loyalty and obedience.

15. Burns and Stalker did not see the two systems as being complete opposites, but as polar positions between which intermediate forms could exist. They also acknowledged that firms could well move from one system to the other as external conditions changed, and that some concerns could operate with both systems at once. They stressed that they did not favour one or other system. What was important was to achieve the most appropriate system for a given set of circumstances – a perfect expression of the contingency approach!

16. The Burns and Stalker study was influential in the design of the Lawrence and Lorsch study mentioned earlier. Clearly, mechanistic systems are closely related to considerations of states of differentiation, and organic systems have much in common with the concept of integration. It is interesting to note, however, that whereas Burns and Stalker see organic systems as being more appropriate to changing conditions than mechanistic ones, their American counterparts see *both* systems as crucial to coping with diversity. The more dynamic and diverse the environment, the higher the degree of both differentiation and integration, say the Americans. Differentiation involves several of the features of the mechanistic systems, which Burns and Stalker see as being ill-adapted to conditions of change. This points to one of the major criticisms made against the mechanistic versus organic approach – it assumes that change can best be effected by organic types of structure, when this is not at all certain. Large organizations, however great their commitment to delegation, involvement and communication between groups, have to maintain a high degree of structure and formality, even when confronted by periods of change.

## JOAN WOODWARD

17. The Woodward studies, conducted by a small research team from the South East Essex College of Technology during the period 1953–1958, were initially aimed at assessing the extent to which classical management principles were being put into practice by manufacturing firms in the area, and with what success. Information on various aspects of formal organization was collected from 100 firms. About half the firms had made some conscious attempt to plan their organization, but there was little

uniformity. In terms of structure, for example, the number of levels of management varied between two and twelve, and spans of control (the number of persons directly supervised by one superior) ranged from ten to ninety for first-line supervisors. The conclusions drawn by the team were that there was little in common amongst the most successful firms studied, and there was certainly no indication that classical management principles were any more likely to lead to success than other forms of organization. At the time this was considered to be rather disconcerting, given the popularity of classical ideas.

18. Having had no positive conclusions from the first part of their studies, Woodward's team turned their attention to the technological data they had collected. The question they posed was as follows: is there any relationship between organizational characteristics and technology? In attempting to answer this question, the team made a lasting contribution to the theory of organizations by establishing the key role of technology as a major variable affecting organization structures.

19. Their first step was to find some suitable form of classification to distinguish between the different categories of technology employed by the firms concerned. Three main categories were eventually selected as follows:

    a. Unit and Small Batch Production. This included custom made products, the production of prototypes, large fabrications undertaken in stages, and the production of small batches.

    b. Large Batch and Mass Production. This encompassed the production of large batches, including assembly-line production, and mass production.

    c. Process Production. This included the intermittent production of chemicals in multi-purpose plant, as well as the continuous flow production of liquids, gases and crystalline substances.

20. When the firms in the study were allocated to their appropriate categories, and then compared by their organization and operations, some discernible patterns began to emerge. For example, it was seen that process industries tended to utilize more delegation and decentralization than large batch and mass-production industries. This was just one aspect of the link between technology and organization structure. Others included the following:

a. the more complex the process, the greater was the chain of command ie there were more levels of management in the process industries than in the other two categories.

b. the span of control of chief executives increased with technical complexity ie the number of people directly responsible to the chief executive was lowest in unit/ small-batch production firms and highest in process production.

c. by contrast with b., the span of middle management decreased with technical complexity ie fewer people reported to middle managers in process production than in large batch/mass production firms, who in turn had fewer people than in unit/small-batch production.

21. As well as the differences mentioned above, there were also some interesting similarities. For example:

a. the average number of workers controlled by first-line supervisors was similar for both unit/small batch and process production – and these were noticeably fewer in number than for mass production situations.

b. another similarity between unit/small batch and process production was that they both employed proportionately more skilled workers than mass production categories.

c. Woodward's team also found that firms at the extremes of the technical range tended to adopt organic systems of management, whereas firms in the middle of the range, notably the large batch/mass production firms, tended to adopt mechanistic systems.

22. Having established some definite links between organizational characteristics and technology, Woodward's team turned their attention to the relationship, if any, between these two factors and the degree of business success (profitability, growth, cost reductions achieved etc). What they found was that the successful firms in each category were those whose organizational characteristics tended to cluster around the median figures for their particular category. So, for example, a process production firm would be better served by a taller, narrower structure backed up by an organic system of management rather than by a flatter, broader structure operated mechanistically. On the other hand, a mass-production firm would appear to benefit from a flatter, broader structure, operated in a mechanistic way. Firms in either category which did not have their appropriate characteristics would tend to produce less than average results.

23. Woodward concluded that the predominance given to the Classical theorists, especially in respect of the application of their ideas in practice (span of control, unity of command, definition of duties etc), only made sense when seen in terms of large batch/mass production processes. Classical ideas did not seem appropriate for other categories of production. Her researches strongly suggested that not only was the system of production a key variable in determining structure, but that also there was a particular form of organization which was most suited to each system.

24. This contingency approach is very much in line with the conclusions reached by Lawrence and Lorsch. Woodward's conclusions also confirm the criticism of the Burns and Stalker study which has been made previously (see para. 16 above). From her studies it would seem that mass-production firms could not cope successfully with change if they adopted an organic system ie an inappropriate system, according to her evidence.

## THE ASTON GROUP

25. The so-called Aston group – Pugh, Hickson and others – now dispersed, but originally at the University of Aston, Birmingham, conducted a major study into various aspects of structure, technology and environment in the late 1960's. Unlike the earlier studies of Woodward and Trist and Bamforth, for example, which did not break technology down into more than one variable, the Aston study attempted to discern the basic elements of technology by gathering data on several possible dimensions. These included features such as operating variability, workflow integration and line control of the workflow. Many of the results of the Aston study did not accord with those of the Woodward studies. One explanation put forward was that the Woodward studies were conducted into mainly smaller firms, while. the Aston study had included several large companies. This was significant because Pugh and his colleagues had concluded that the impact of technology on organization structure must be related to size. In small organizations they said, technology will be critical to structure, but in large organizations other variables will tend to confine the impact of technology to the basic operating levels.

26. The importance of the Aston group is that they have adopted a multi-dimensional approach to organizational and contextual variables ie they have attempted to develop the idea of an 'organizational mix' which can be applied to an organization at a particular point in time in order to achieve successful results. This

essentially contingency approach has provided the basis for further research into what represents the ideal structure for an organization in the light of a particular grouping of circumstances.

27. The Aston study distinguished five primary variables of *structure* and considered them against a number of *contextual* variables. The structural variables were as follows:

  i.   Specialization (functional and role).
  ii.  Standardization (procedures and methods).
  iii. Formalization (rules).
  iv.  Centralization (concentration of authority).
  v.   Configuration (tall or flat structure).

These variables were considered in a number of different contexts including the following:

  i.   Size of organization.
  ii.  Technological features (in several dimensions).
  iii. Ownership, history etc.
  iv.  Location.
  v.   Market.

28. Among the conclusions reached by the Aston team was the relevance of size to the structural variables. As an organization grows beyond the stage at which it can be controlled by personal interaction, it has to be more explicitly structured. Larger size tends to lead to:

  a.  more specialization,
  b.  more standardization,
  c.  more formalization but
  d.  less centralization.

Overall, the conclusion of the researchers was that it was possible to predict fairly closely the structural profile of an organization on the basis of information obtained about the contextual variables.

## SECTION SUMMARY – SYSTEMS APPROACHES TO MANAGEMENT THEORY

1. Chapter 11 looked at organizations as systems. A system was defined as 'a collection of inter-related parts which form some whole'. Systems were seen to be 'closed' or 'open'. Closed systems were described as those which did not interact with their external environment ie they were practically self-contained. Open systems were described as those which relied on interaction with their environment for survival and growth. Biological systems and social systems were given as examples of open systems.

2. Open social systems were seen to have three major characteristics:

   i.   they received inputs (people, materials, finance etc) from their environment.

   ii.   they utilized these inputs to produce various outputs (goods, services etc).

   iii.   they discharged these outputs into the environment.

3. Reference was made to Katz and Kahn's summary of the common characteristics of open systems as applied to organizations. This summary added to the above three basic characteristics, mainly by including references to feedback into the system, and to the ability to store sufficient energy in the system to enable a steady state to be maintained, even in difficult times.

4. The issue of boundaries in systems was considered. Organizations, as social systems, did not have visible boundaries, since they were based on relationships rather than things. The organization's boundaries consisted of external boundaries with the environment, and internal boundaries between the total system and its sub-units or sub-systems. A major part of the work of managers and supervisors is to manage the boundaries between their own, and neighbouring sub-systems.

5. Chapter 12 provided a resume of some of the major developments in applying systems theory to organizations. Particular emphasis was given to the work of various members of the Tavistock Group, and to the work of Katz and Kahn.

6. The Tavistock Group contributed several important ideas to the systems concept, namely the following:

   a.   socio-technical systems ie the structuring of work activities depends not only on considerations of technology, but also on the needs of people, and both technical and social factors need to be seen as interrelated.

   b.   operating systems and management systems constitute the two main sub-systems of a firm; operating systems deal with the input, conversion and output activities of the system; management systems deal with the controlling, decision-making and communication aspects of the total system.

   c.   work should be designed so as to meet social and psychological needs as well as the demands of technology.

   d.   types of environment ie relatively placid or relatively disturbed affect the amount of adaptation required for the survival of the organization.

7.    Katz and Kahn viewed organizations as essentially contrived systems held together by psychological bonds. In adopting an open-systems approach to organizations, they distinguished five key sub-systems at work in them. These were as follows:

i.    Production or Technical sub-systems.

ii.   Supportive sub-systems.

iii.  Maintenance sub-systems.

iv.   Adaptive sub-systems.

v.    Managerial sub-systems.

8.    Katz and Kahn also concerned themselves with the significance of roles, norms and values. Roles were seen to require a standardized form of behaviour, and were important because they differentiated one position from another. By contrast, norms and values helped to integrate the activities of the organization. Norms specified role behaviour in terms of expected standards. Values were the generally held beliefs that represented the ideology of the organization.

9.    Chapter 13 described a number of systems approaches which have been labelled as 'contingency approaches' to organization. A contingency approach aimed to determine organization structure in the light of various related factors, such as environment and technology, at a particular point in time. The use of the word 'contingency' was first suggested by Lawrence and Lorsch in a major study of organizations in the United States.

10.   Lawrence and Lorsch's study was primarily concerned with the relative states of differentiation and integration within organizations. Differentiation was defined not only in terms of specialization of tasks, but also in terms of the different orientation of the job-holders concerned and of the formality of the structure. Integration was defined in terms of the quality of the state of collaboration that existed between departments.

11.   The researchers found that successful firms tended to develop states of differentiation and integration that enabled them to cope with the pressures of the environment. In particular, such firms were able to handle conflict in constructive ways.

12.   Other approaches mentioned in Chapter 13 were those of Burns and Stalker, Joan Woodward and the Aston group. Burns and Stalker were interested in how firms adapted to change in the electronics industry. Their studies indicated that there were two distinctive ideal types of management system, set along a

continuum. These were *mechanistic* systems, which appeared to be appropriate for conditions of relative stability, and *organic* systems which appeared to be appropriate for changing conditions. Mechanistic systems incorporated much of the apparatus of Classical organization design eg precise definition of roles, hierarchical structure and vertical interaction between members of the hierarchy. Organic systems were more flexible: roles were subject to re-definition in the light of circumstances, control and authority were exercised on a network basis, and interaction was lateral rather than vertical.

13. Woodward's study investigated the extent to which Classical principles were being applied in manufacturing concerns in South-West Essex. She found no evidence to suggest that such principles were an essential element of the organization of the successful firms. What the study did reveal, at least for the firms concerned, was a link between their structure and their production system (their technology).

14. Woodward identified three main categories of production – unit/small batch, large batch/mass production, and, finally, process production. Overall the study indicated that unit/small batch and process production firms benefitted from a more organic form of structure, whilst large batch/mass production firms gained more from a mechanistic structure. What was important for success was for firms to select a structure which was best suited to their production system.

15. The final contribution considered in this chapter was that of the so-called Aston group, who were originally at the University of Aston, Birmingham. The Aston researchers looked at various aspects of structure, technology *and* environment. In particular, they looked at the effects on a number of structural variables, of differences in organizational context. The structural variables were: specialization, standardization, formalization, centralization and configuration (shape). The contexts against which they were considered included size of organization, technology employed, location and markets.

16. The general conclusion reached by the group was that the structural profile of an organization could be estimated fairly well from information obtained about the different contextual variables.

17. Figure 13.1 below summarises the principal systems approaches to organization and management theory. The dates referred to are those of the publications which first mentioned the theory or study concerned.

| DATE | RESEARCH/THEORY | THEORIST(S) |
|------|-----------------|-------------|
| 1951 | Socio-technical systems | Trist & Bamforth |
| 1958 | Open systems/work design | A.K. Rice |
| 1961 | Mechanistic/Organic management systems. Environment and structure | Burns & Stalker |
| 1965 | Technology and structure | Woodward |
| 1965 | Types of environments | Emery & Trist |
| 1966 | Systems approach to organizations | Katz & Kahn |
| 1967 | Environment and structure. Contingency theory of organizations | Lawrence & Lorsch |
| 1968/9 | Environment, technology and structure – multi-dimensional approach | Pugh, Hickson and others |

**Figure 13.1. Developments in Systems Approaches**

## QUESTIONS FOR DISCUSSION/HOMEWORK

*1. What are the major differences, in each case, between the approach of the systems theorists and those of (a) the Classical theorists, and (b) the Human Relations theorists?*

*2. Why are 'open' systems so called?*

*3. What sub-systems do you see in the organization in which you work or study? Are these sub-systems open or closed?*

*4. What are the essential elements of a socio-technical system?*

*5. In what ways is the concept of 'integration' important for organizations?*

*6. How would you summarise the principal contributions to organization and management theory of:*

*a. Joan Woodward's Essex studies*

*and b. The Burns and Stalker studies?*

*7. In what ways could the Aston group's study be said to have furthered understanding about the analysis of organizations?*

## EXAMINATION QUESTIONS – SYSTEMS APPROACHES TO MANAGEMENT THEORY

*Questions relating to this Section appear to be growing increasingly popular with examiners. A representative sample across a wide range of examining bodies is included below. Outline answers may be found in Appendix 2.*

*EQ 9.* Discuss the major features and significance of ... the coal-mining research of the Tavistock Institute in the 1940's in Britain. *(ACCA—part of an either/or question)*

*EQ 10.* 'There is no one best way of designing an organization!' Discuss. *(IOB Nature of Management)*

*EQ 11.* Comment on the contingency approach to organization structures. *(IAM POC)*

*EQ 12.* Identify the principal factors that might influence the design of the structure of an organization. *(ICMA OMM)*

*EQ 13.* a. What are the main features of a bureaucratic organization?

b. How effectively do bureaucratic organizations respond to changing circumstances in the environment? *(ICSA MPP)*

# MANAGEMENT IN PRACTICE: INTRODUCTION

Previous chapters have dealt with the *theoretical* aspects of management and organizations. Now we turn to the *practice* of management. This short Section contains two chapters, dealing with

(1)  types of business, and

(2)  the process of management.

Subsequent chapters in the Sections which follow cover all the major areas of management practice.

# 14

# TYPES OF BUSINESS ORGANIZATION

## INTRODUCTION

1. The subject-matter of this manual is management. Many of the management issues touched upon are common to every kind of organization, be it business, state enterprise, public service, non-profit-making charity or private club. However, the full range of management theory and practice occurs mainly in, what we call 'business organizations', this chapter describes the main legal characteristics of such organizations.

2. A *Business* organization, in contrast to a public service organization or a charity, exists to provide goods or services at a profit. Making a profit may not necessarily be the sole aim of a business, but it is certainly what distinguishes it from a non-business organization. In Britain, business organizations are mainly to be found in the private sector of the economy, which has grown in recent years as a number of State-owned corporations have been privatised. The business organizations we are concerned with here range in size from the one-man business, or sole trader, through partnerships between two or more people working in collaboration, to large public limited companies (plc's) employing thousands of staff in a variety of locations. There are also cooperative enterprises notably in retail distribution, but also in manufacturing on a small scale.

3. The most common types of business organization are as follows:

- limited companies
- sole traders
- partnerships
- cooperatives

Society, through Parliament and the Courts, sets standards of behaviour tor all these types of business.

These standards are made public by means of legal requirements and judicial interpretations. The following paragraphs summarise the principal legal features of these businesses, together with the main advantages and disadvantages for the parties concerned.

## LIMITED COMPANIES

4.    When a limited company is formed, it is said to have become 'incorporated', ie endowed with a separate body, or person. The corporation so formed is treated in English law as a separate entity, independent of its members. The corporation, or 'company', as it is generally called, is capable of owning property, employing people, making contracts, and of suing or being sued. Another important feature of a company is that, unlike a sole trader or a partnership, it does have continuity of succession, as it is unaffected by the death or incapacity of one or more of its members.

5.    The key feature of a 'limited' company is that, if it fails it can only require its members (shareholders) to meet its debts up to the limit of the nominal value of their shares. The principle of legally limiting the financial liabilities of persons investing in business ventures was introduced by Parliament in the 1850's to encourage the wealthy to give financial support to the inventors, engineers and others who were at the forefront of Britain's Industrial Revolution. Without the protection of limited liability, an investor could find himself stripped of his home and other personal assets in order to meet debts arising from the failure of any company in which he had invested his money.

Since the turn of the century, various Company Acts have laid down the principles and procedures to be followed in the conduct of business organizations. Such legislation has been intended to minimise the risk to suppliers and customers as well as to shareholders, and to a lesser extent employees, arising from gross mis-management of, or deliberate restriction of information about a company. The legislation of recent decades has now been consolidated into one Principal Act – the Companies Act, 1985 – and three subsidiary pieces of legislation.

6.    Limited liability companies now fall into two categories – Public limited companies (plc's) and private limited companies. The Memorandum (see Para.7) of a plc must state that the company is a public company (ie its shares are available for purchase by the public) and the company name must end with the words 'Public limited company'. A private limited company by comparison may not offer its shares to the public, and is even restricted in the transfer of its shares between the private shareholders. The name of a private limited company must end

with the word 'Limited'. Both kinds of company must have at least two members and one director. Once registered under the Companies Act, a private company can begin trading without further formality. A public limited company has to obtain a certificate of trading from the Registrar of Companies. All limited companies have to fulfil certain procedures before they can be incorporated. These include the filing of two particularly important documents: (a) the Memorandum of Association and (b) the Articles of Association.

7.    The Memorandum of Association must supply the following information:

   a.  the company's name
   b.  the location of the registered office
   c.  the objects or purpose of the company
   d.  a statement that the liability of members is limited
   e.  the amount of share capital of the company, together with the numbers and class of shares
   f.  a declaration of association in which the initial members (subscribers) express their desire to form a company and to take up shares.

The details contained in the Memorandum are available for public inspection. Persons considering doing business with a company, or wishing to purchase shares in it, can therefore consult the register before deciding whether to take the risks involved.

8.    The Articles of Association are concerned with the internal affairs of the company and give details of the shareholders, directors, secretary and auditors. The directors of a company are, in law, its agents. They may also be senior employees of the enterprise. They are appointed by the shareholders to use their best endeavours to see that the company's objects are achieved. The main directors make up the Board of Directors, which in Britain acts as an executive management group as well as fulfilling the legal guardianship of the company. Company law requires that information about directors, including their interests in the company, be made available for the inspection of members and others.

9.    The ownership and control of a limited company are vested in the shareholders and the directors. The shareholders in general meeting have ultimate control over the company by virtue of their power to appoint or remove directors and to vary the constitution and regulations of the company. The directors of the company are entrusted with the day-to-day management of the business. Whilst

their responsibilities extend to ensuring that shareholders receive a satisfactory return on their investment, it is also expected nowadays that the interests of other stakeholders in the business will be considered. Thus employees, customers, creditors and suppliers all expect their needs to he given due weight by the directors. (For stakeholder theory of firm see Chap 18).

10. The main advantages of limited liability can be summarised as follows:
- in the event of failure of the business, shareholders are protected against the loss of more than the nominal value of their shareholding
- the separate legal person of the company exists independently of the members
- shares (in plc's) are readily transferable
- wider share-ownership is encouraged
- companies are required to submit annual returns to the Registrar, and these are available for public inspection

11. The disadvantages are primarily as follows:
- precisely because liability is limited, it may be difficult for small companies to borrow as extensively as desired, since banks and other financial institutions may be unable to recover their funds if the business fails.
- there are considerable legal procedures involved in setting up a company, as well as the procedures incurred in publishing the various financial accounts of the company.

## SOLE TRADERS

12. The sole trader is the simplest form of business organization – one person in business on his own. The legal requirements for setting up such a business are minimal, but the owner is fully liable for any debts incurred in running the business, since the owner literally *is* the business. Ownership and control are combined. All profits made by the sole trader are subject to income tax rather than the corporation tax levied on company profits. Apart from the need to maintain accounts for controlling the business and for dealing with the Inland Revenue, there are no formal accounts to be published.

13. The main advantages of operating as a sole trader are:
- the formalities for starting up are minimal
- complete autonomy to run the business as the individual wishes
- the profits of the business belong to the trader

- various business expenses are allowable against income tax
- no public disclosure of accounts (except to Inland Revenue)

14. The main disadvantages are as follows:
- the sole trader is entirely responsible for the debts of the business
- the individual as owner and manager has to be responsible for all aspects of the business (marketing, product development, sales, finance etc)

## PARTNERSHIPS

15. A partnership exists when at least two, and usually not more than twenty, persons agree to carry on a business together. The Partnership Act, 1890, defines a partnership as a relationship which 'subsists between persons carrying on a business in common with a view to profit'. The legalities required to set up a partnership are minimal, although it is advisable to have a formal Partnership agreement drawn up by a solicitor. Such an agreement can specify the rights and obligations of individual partners, and can make provision for changes brought about by death or retirement of partners. As with a sole trader, the members of a partnership are owners of its property and liable for its contracts. Therefore they are fully responsible for meeting their debts to third parties. Partners are not entitled to a salary for the services they provide for the partnership, but are entitled to their proper share of the profits of the business.

16. Many partnerships, and some sole traders, have been converted into limited companies because of the perceived benefits of incorporation. Most professional persons, and especially accountants and solicitors, maintain partnership as their form of business in order to preserve the principle of individual professional accountability towards the client.

17. The main advantages of partnership are:
- few formalities required for starting up
- sharing of partners' knowledge and skills
- sharing of management of business
- no obligation to publish accounts (except for Inland Revenue purposes)
- sharing of profits (or losses!) of business

18. The disadvantages are primarily these:
- each partner is liable for the debts of the partnership, even if caused by the actions of other partners

- risk that the partners may not be able to work together at a personal level
- the death or bankruptcy of one partner will automatically dissolve the partnership, unless otherwise provided for in a partnership agreement

## COOPERATIVE ENTERPRISES

19.  Small groups of people who wish to set up business along explicitly democratic lines and with the benefit of limited liability, can choose to establish a cooperative. This kind of business has been a feature of British commercial life for well over a hundred years, at least so far as distribution is concerned. These distribution cooperatives were essentially consumer-cooperatives in which the profits of the business were given back to consumers in dividends based on the amount of their purchases over a given period. The modern trend in cooperatives is towards producer-cooperatives in which individuals benefit not only as investors but as employees in the business. There are more than 700 such worker-cooperatives in Britain at the present time.

20.  The promotion of cooperatives has been encouraged by recent Governments in Britain, and a Cooperative Development Agency has been established since 1978 to provide advice and assistance to those considering setting up such a business.

21.  The legislation governing cooperative enterprises is the Industrial & Provident Societies Act, 1965, which requires that in lieu of Memorandum and Articles, every cooperative shall have a set of rules approved by the Registrar of Friendly Societies. The rules must embrace the following principles:

- each member must have equal control on the 'one person, one vote' principle
- members must benefit primarily from their participation in the business, ie as employees as well as investors
- interest on loan or share capital has to be limited
- surplus ('profit') must be shared between members in proportion to their contribution (for example, by number of hours worked or wage level), or must be retained in the business
- membership must be open to all who qualify

For the principle of limited liability to apply to the members, the cooperative must be registered, in which case a minimum of seven members is required.

22.  The main advantages of cooperative enterprise are:
- Provides opportunity for genuine pooling of capital between a group of people
- encourages active collaboration between all sections of the workforce
- enables decisions to be made democratically
- provides rewards on an equitable basis among those involved
- provides limited liability (if registered)

23.  The disadvantages are mainly:
- there is less likelihood of a level of profitability and growth that could be achieved by a limited company
- as with partnerships, relationships can deteriorate. especially when some members are seen to be making a smaller contribution than the rest
- democratic decision-making can lead to lengthy discussions before action is taken
- members who are not truly dedicated to the democratic ethos of the business, may find themselves at odds with the openness of communication and decision-making.

## CONCLUSIONS

24.  There are many kinds of organization in modern society. However apart from the smallest enterprises, it is the business organization in particular which makes use of the full range of management practices. This chapter has outlined the legal foundations of business organization in order to provide necessary background for many of the issues which occur later in the manual.

# 15

# THE PROCESS OF MANAGEMENT

## INTRODUCTION

1.   The systems approach to organizations, which we examined in earlier chapters, is based on the three major elements of inputs, throughputs/conversion, and outputs. The process of management is concerned with all three of these elements, and especially with the conversion processes of organizations. As Peter Drucker first put it, over twenty-five years ago, management is concerned with the 'systematic organization of economic resources' and its task is to make these resources productive (The Practice of Management, 1955). This chapter introduces the idea of management as a conversion process, describes its principal elements and emphasises that management is orientated towards results as well as towards action.

2.   Management is not an activity that exists in its own right. It is rather a description of a variety of activities carried out by those members of organizations whose role is that of a manager ie someone who has formal responsibility for the work of at least one other person in the organization. The activities carried out by managers have generally been grouped in terms of *planning, organizing, motivating*, and *controlling* activities. These groupings describe activities which indicate broadly what managers actually do. They are describing managers' jobs primarily in terms of their inputs.

3.   The groupings of management activities can be summarised as follows:

**Planning** – deciding the objectives or goals of the organization and preparing how to meet them.

**Organizing** – determining activities and allocating responsibilities for the achievement of plans; coordinating activities and responsibilities into an appropriate structure.

**Motivating** – meeting the social and psychological needs of employees in the fulfilment of organizational goals.

**Controlling** – monitoring and evaluating activities, and providing corrective mechanisms.

These traditional groupings – the POMC approach – are the ones chosen to represent the framework for the following chapters on management in practice. It is appreciated that they do not tell the whole story about what constitutes management, but they are a convenient way of describing most of the key aspects of the work of managers in practice.

4.   Before moving on to look at each of these groupings in detail, it will be useful to consider some of the shortcomings of the POMC approach, in order to make allowance for it in the chapters which follow. As stated above, the approach focuses on the *actions* (inputs) of managers rather than on *results* (outputs). It also ignores the role elements of a managerial job.

5.   Firstly, let us turn to the question of results. One particularly influential writer on the subject of managerial effectiveness, Professor Bill Reddin of the University of New Brunswick, considers it essential for the job of management to be judged on output rather than by input, and by achievements rather than by activities. In his book 'Managerial Effectiveness' (1970), he argues that we tend to confuse efficiency with effectiveness. Efficiency is the ratio of output to input. However, whilst 100% efficiency can be obtained by high output in relation to high input, the same result can be achieved where both output and input are *low*. Effectiveness, as Reddin defines it, is the extent to which a manager achieves the *output* requirements of his position. This assumes that the outputs have been identified and made measurable. Examples of differences between 'efficient' managers and 'effective' managers, according to Reddin, are that 'efficient' managers seek to solve problems and reduce costs, whereas 'effective' managers seek to produce creative alternatives and increase profits. On this basis the POMC approach is more concerned with efficiency than 'effectiveness'.

6.   The POMC approach is essentially a leader-centred approach to management. It does not take account of the *variety* of roles that managers can be called upon to play. We saw in Chapter 2 that Mintzberg's analysis of managerial roles identified seven key roles. These were:

Entrepreneur

Resource Allocator

Figurehead/Leader

Liaison/Disseminator

Monitor

Spokesman/Negotiator

Disturbance-handler

The roles clearly encompass more than just planning, organizing, motivating and controlling.

7.    Similar comments can be made about Schein's analysis of managerial roles based on the various assumptions about Man, which were described in Chapter 7. Schein's range of roles, in addition to the role of leader, include the following:

Counsellor and Intermediary

Catalyst and Facilitator

Diagnostician and Enquirer

These roles also suggest more than is implied by the POMC approach. Nevertheless so long as these criticisms are taken into consideration, the POMC approach has a great deal to commend it as a basic model for a discussion of the work of managers in practice.

## PLANNING

8.    Planning is an activity which involves decisions about ends (organizational aims/objectives), means (plans), conduct (policies), and results. It is an activity which must take place against the background of the organization's environment, and which must take account of the organization's internal strengths and weaknesses. Planning can be long-term, as in corporate planning, or short-term, as in production or sales planning. Long-term usually implies a time-horizon of about five years, although this may be ten or twenty years in certain industries. Short-term can be any period from the immediate future up to one year. Chapters 17–20 describe the major aspects of planning.

## ORGANIZING

9.    Plans have to be put into operation. This involves detailed organization and coordination of tasks and the human and material resources needed to carry them out. A key issue here is that of formal communications. Various aspects of organizing are dealt with in Chapters 21–25.

## MOTIVATING

10.  We have already considered some of the most significant theories of motivation in Chapters 7–10. The motivating activities of managers, however, are essentially practical in their intent. In setting plans and then executing them, managers have to gain the commitment of their employees. This is primarily a question of leadership, or style of management, and Chapter 26 outlines the principal options available to managers in practice.

## CONTROLLING

11. Controlling activities are concerned essentially with measuring progress and correcting deviations. The basic functions of control are:

  i.   to establish standards of performance.

  ii.  to measure actual performance against standards.

  iii. to take corrective actions where appropriate.

Control activities act as the feedback mechanism for all managerial activities. Their use is, therefore, crucial to the success of management. Key aspects of control are discussed in Chapters 28–30.

## QUESTIONS FOR DISCUSSION/HOMEWORK

*1.   What is the significance of limited liability to:*

*(a) shareholders?*

*(b) creditors?*

*(c) bankers?*

*2.   For what overall purpose are companies obliged to make public their constitution and activities?*

*3.   What is the principal distinction between a private limited company and a public limited company ?*

*4.   How would you describe the benefits of partnership over a sole tradership?*

*5.   Why do some people prefer to establish a registered cooperative enterprise rather than say a private limited company?*

*6.   What are the advantages and disadvantages of analysing 'Management' in terms of activities such as planning, organizing, motivating and controlling?*

## EXAMINATION QUESTION

*EQ 14. Describe and explain the recognised types of business enterprises. What are some of their advantages and disadvantages when seen from the viewpoint of a proprietor or manager?*

*(ACCA)*

# PLANNING

1.   This Section is about planning, its contents and ingredients. Planning is a decision-making process and this process is described and amplified in chapter 16. Planning is associated with the formulation of objectives as well as with their attainment, and so chapter 17 identifies key areas for organizational (or corporate) objectives and describes the major features of corporate planning as a means to achieving objectives. A brief discussion of the role of policies in the formulation and execution of plans is included in the same chapter. Chapter 18 deals with the topic of Management by Objectives, Chapter 19 looks at the principal features of manpower planning and Chapter 20 considers key aspects of work design.

2.   The major components of planning are set out in simplified form in Figure 16.1 below:

## Figure 16.1 Basic Planning Model

3.   The diagram shows that each planning stage constitutes a major decision-making exercise centred on the key issues of *ends*, *means* and *conduct* together with their associated results and feedback. Planning commences with a consideration of the ultimate aims and overall objectives of the organization ie ends. This is followed by a consideration of conduct, which results in the development of policies, or codes of conduct, to be applied to subsequent stages of planning. The next step is the drawing up of plans to achieve the organization's aims and objectives, which involves decisions about means. These decisions have to be made in the light of the organization's policies. Once plans have been implemented, their results are monitored and subsequently reviewed to provide feedback to all the previous stages of the process. Finally the diagram indicates the interdependence of the organization's ends and means on (a) its own internal resources, and (b) its external environment. The implications of this basic model of planning will be examined more closely in the chapter on Corporate Planning (chapter 17).

# 16

## DECISION MAKING

### INTRODUCTION

1. Decision-making is an accepted part of everyday human life. As individuals we may make decisions on the spur of the moment or after much thought and deliberation, or at some point between these two extremes. Our decisions may be influenced by emotions, by reasoning or by a combination of both. As members of groups we may find ourselves making decisions on a group basis, where our own views and feelings have to be tested and argued with the other members. In organizations, people with managerial roles are expected, among other things, to make decisions as an important part of their responsibilities. In this chapter we are concerned with managerial decision-making. That is to say we are concerned with behaviour that is designed to cause things to happen, or not to happen, as the case may be. Whilst it may be affected by feelings and interpersonal relationships, managerial decision-making tends to be rational in its approach. Considerable time and effort may be spent in assessing problems, developing alternative solutions and evaluating their consequences before arriving at an agreed decision. Certain types of decision-making can be made easier and faster by means of special techniques, some of which are referred to briefly later in the chapter.

### DECISION PROCESSES: A THEORETICAL MODEL

2. An analysis of the way decisions are made in organizations results in the sequence of events shown in Figure 16.2 opposite.

This sequence indicates a rational approach that can be applied to the business of reaching decisions in organizations. It commences by seeking to ask the right questions, continues by encouraging creative answers, and concludes by ensuring that the chosen solution is monitored and evaluated.

3. There are several important issues raised by a model such as the one we have described. These can be summarised as follows:

   i. The technical *quality* of the decision ie doing the right thing, has to be distinguished from the *acceptability* of the decision by the parties involved ie doing things right.

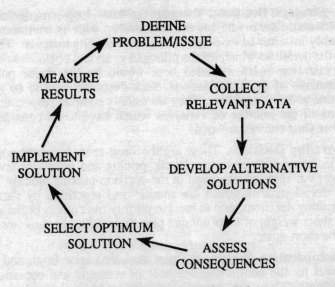

**Figure 16.2 Decision Model**

ii.    Both the development of alternatives and the selection of an optimum solution will be limited considerably by the organization's objectives and policies, and by the attitudes of managers and other employees.

iii.   The assessment of the possible consequences of proposed solutions is a step that is frequently given insufficient attention.

iv.    The model makes no allowance for the time factor. Clearly, however, it favours decision-making for the future rather than decision making for immediate problems.

## TYPES OF DECISIONS

4.    Decisions can range from those of a vital, once-for-all nature to those of a routine and relatively trivial nature. They can be immediate in their effect or they can be delayed. A decision to move a computer manufacturing enterprise out of mainframe computers into micro-computers is clearly a major long-term commitment of a strategic kind. H.I. Ansoff, in an article on the strategic theory of the firm (Business Strategy, 1969), sees management as having three principal decision-areas: strategic, operating and administrative. This seems to be a useful way of separating out the major categories of decisions, and the descriptions which follow adapt several of Ansoff's ideas.

5.    **Strategic Decisions.** These are the basic, long-term decisions which settle the organization's relationship with its environment, notably in terms of its product or service and its markets.  These are the decisions which set the principal goals and objectives of the organization. Also included here would be the major policy statements of the organizations. Such decisions tend to be non-routine and non-repetitive. They are usually complex, especially in terms of the number of variables which have to be considered before final choices are made.

**Operating Decisions.** These are the short-term decisions which settle issues such as output levels, pricing and inventory levels. Fewer variables are involved in the decision-making process, and the decisions themselves are routine and repetitive by nature. Operating decisions tend to receive priority over others because of the sheer weight of their volume plus their ability to show results in the short-term.

**Administrative Decisions.** These decisions arise from, and are subject to, the conflicting demands of strategic and operational problems. They are essentially concerned with settling the organization's structure eg by establishing lines of authority and communication. The use of 'administrative' in this context is narrower than the more usual meaning of the word, as defined in Chapter 2 (paragraph 5).

6.    A final distinction that can be made between types of decision concerns so-called programmable and non-programmable decisions. A programmable decision is one capable of being worked out by a computer ie the variables are quantifiable and the decision rules can be clearly stated. These criteria would certainly apply to numerous operating decisions. By contrast, a non-programmable decision is one which cannot be quantified in the same way, and where human judgements have to be made. This would be the case for all strategic decisions, for example.

## DECISION-MAKING TOOLS

7.    Figure 16.2 on the previous page showed the key steps that can be identified in the decision-making process. In recent years several techniques have been developed to aid the processes of problem-definition, of devising solution options and of evaluating their possible consequences. Since the majority of decisions have to be made in conditions of relative risks and uncertainty, any techniques which can help predict the future are worth having. In earlier centuries men of power looked to soothsayers, prophets or

gipsies for an indication of the future. Nowadays we can look to the combined efforts of mathematicians, statisticians and computer specialists to help us forecast possible outcomes.

8.    One of the most significant sets of tools now available for decision-makers is that of O.R. (Operational Research). This encompasses a collection of techniques which apply scientific methods to complex problems in organizations. In particular, O.R. involves the use of scientific models, or conceptual frameworks, to represent real situations. The models utilize mathematical and statistical terms to express the variables involved in a decision. Particular O.R. techniques include Network Analysis, Risk Analysis and Statistical Decision Theory. The chief benefits of such techniques are that they assist with the analysis of problems and the development of solutions.

9.    Whilst it is not necessary for detailed examples of O.R. techniques to be supplied in non-specialist examination papers in Management, it would be useful to outline the basic approach of such techniques. The procedure which follows is clearly influenced by general systems theory. The basic steps are:–

   i.    Formulate the problem in the context of the total system concerned.
   ii.   Construct a mathematical model of the system.
   iii.  Derive a solution from the model.
   iv.   Test the model.
   v.    Install a feedback mechanism.
   vi.   Implement the solution.

The principal advantage of such an approach is that it seeks to define and solve problems in their organizational context. It is important to appreciate that the approach is utilized to *assist* decision-making. O.R. techniques in themselves do not implement decisions. What they can do is to provide managers with information and options which can lead to qualitatively better decisions being taken.

10.   Another increasingly useful tool for management decision-makers is the so-called 'decision tree'. This is basically a conceptual map of possible decisions and outcomes in a particular situation. It is useful in cases where a manager is required to make a number sequential decisions ie where earlier decisions will affect later ones. A simple decision tree appears below:

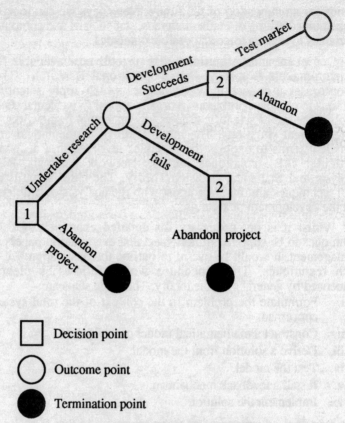

Decision point

Outcome point

Termination point

**Figure 16.3 R & D Decision Tree**

11. Such a diagram focusses attention on outcomes or consequences as well as decisions. These outcomes can be further elaborated in terms of their probability and their anticipated pay off. It is also possible to add a time dimension to the whole diagram, so that, for example, in Figure 16.3 the period from decision point 1 to decision point 2 could be one year. These additional features all help to make the use of decision trees a salutary exercise for managers.

## SUMMARY

12. Decision-making in organizations is becoming increasingly more complex. In particular the level of uncertainty in the organization's environment, and the degrees of risk involved, are key factors in this complexity.

13. The principal categories of decisions can be summarised as follows:
    i.   Strategic: Major, long-term non-routine and non-repetitive.
    ii.  Operating: Short-term, routine, repetitive and frequent.
    iii. Administrative: Coordinate structure of activities arising from implementation of strategic and operating decisions.

14. There are several aids available to managers to help them to cope with decision-making. These range from broad, rational approaches which set out a logical sequence of events commencing with problem definition and concluding by measuring results of chosen solutions, to highly quantifiable approaches, such as Operational Research, in which the skills of mathematicians, statisticians and computer specialists combine to produce information and evaluations as a basis for decisions.

# 17
# CORPORATE OBJECTIVES AND CORPORATE PLANNING

## INTRODUCTION

1. Planning, is an activity which involves decisions about ends as well as means and about conduct as well as results. Planning is a process which has to start at the top. Whatever else may be planned at operating and administrative levels, the first priority has to be given to the strategic goals (ends) of the organization. An organization that does not know where it is going and how, broadly, it will get there is, to put it mildly, at a considerable disadvantage compared with its competitors!

2. This is where corporate planning comes in. It has been described variously as a technique, as a style of management and as a process. It is probably best to think of it as a *process* within organizations – a process designed to ensure that an organization:

a. knows why it exists and what its principal objectives are,
b. knows what its own strengths and weaknesses are,
c. knows what opportunities and threats are posed by its external environment,
d. has a base for long-term (strategic) planning and for operational (tactical) planning,
e. can identify and establish appropriate standards of performance, and
f. has a set of rules of conduct (policies) to guide its employees in the pursuit of its objectives.

3. Corporate planning is not the same thing as long-range planning. The latter focuses on parts of an organization only but the former takes an organization-wide perspective. A further distinction is that long-range planning looks at the future selectively whereas corporate planning looks at it comprehensively. The basic stages of corporate planning are: set corporate objectives and policies, set strategic objectives, assess internal and external situation, evaluate alternative strategies and agree strategic plan.

4. This chapter outlines the corporate planning process, and aims to show the relationship between objectives, policies and plans. Since a good deal of confusion about terminology exists in this field, an effort has been made to clarify meanings and draw distinctions wherever possible.

## CORPORATE OBJECTIVES

5. A major part of corporate planning is the business of setting corporate objectives. Such objectives are usually of two kinds – those that state the overall objective or purpose of the organization, and those that set out the organization's long-term, strategic, aims. An example of an overall purpose for a business organization would be 'To obtain a return on the shareholders' capital'. A similar example for a public service would be 'To provide a service to the whole community'. Overall objectives are stated in general terms, and are intended to be relatively permanent. They are often accompanied by statements which declare how the organization intends to conduct itself in the pursuit of its purpose. These are the principal policy statements of the organization, and will be discussed shortly.

6. Strategic objectives or aims are set out in similar terms to the overall purpose. They focus on the fundamental purpose of particular parts of the organization eg marketing, personnel, finance etc. Their time horizon is usually at least five years, so inevitably such objectives have to be written up in fairly general terms. If they are specific and highly quantifiable they are not *strategic* objectives, but operational, or tactical, objectives. However, strategic objectives should be stated in such a way that it is possible to see whether they have been achieved or not. For example, a strategic objective for the Personnel function in an organization could be 'to ensure that the organization's needs for sufficient and suitable manpower are met over the next five years'. Such a statement says nothing about the different types of skills that may be needed, nor does it say anything about relative numbers. Nevertheless, it would be quite possible after the period concerned to assess whether Personnel had met their long-term aim. A marketing example could be 'to meet the organization's need for information and advice concerning (a) its markets (existing & potential); (b) its competitors and (c) its economic environment.' This kind of broad statement indicates one of the principal reasons why a Marketing Department exists, ie to provide market research and market intelligence for the organization.

7. Strategic objectives are normally set for all the major functions of the organization, and taken together they sum up what business the organization intends to be in during the foreseeable future. Such objectives cover areas such as markets (or community served), product or service development, and profitability or efficiency.

8. Strategic objectives will be influenced strongly by the views of the owners of the organization. The owners may decide that all such objectives shall be related firmly to the return on their capital. This has been called the shareholder theory of the firm. In the case of a business enterprise, the owners will be concerned with setting objectives relating to the return on shareholders' capital, earnings per share and profit, for example. In the case of a State-owned corporation, the emphasis will be more on providing an efficient service within the limitations of the funds allocated by Parliament. Another theory of the firm has been called the stakeholder theory. This suggests that the beneficiaries of the organization are not only the shareholders, but also the customers, suppliers, employees and the public at large. Where this theory is held, strategic objectives are set not only for the good of the business, but also for the good of these other groups as well. An example would be where a pharmaceutical company set objectives relating to the safety aspects of its products, both in relation to its own employees and to its consumers. Apart from small, owner-managed enterprises, most organizations tend to adopt the stakeholder theory, if only in response to external pressures.

## POLICIES

9. Once an organization has established its corporate objectives, it can begin to say in what manner it intends these to be achieved. Policy statements are made to indicate to those concerned just what the organization will, and will not, do in pursuance of its overall purpose. Such statements express the organization's culture and belief-system. Policies are not the same as objectives or plans, even though they are frequently confused with them. Objectives state an aim or goal ie they are *ends*; plans provide a framework within which action can take place to attain objectives ie they are *means*; policies, on the other hand, are neither ends nor means, they are *statements of conduct*. Policies cause managers to take actions in a certain way, but they are not actions in themselves.

10. A major factor affecting policy is the attitude of the organization's owners. Those taking the shareholder view will tend to adopt a narrower range of policies than those holding the stakeholder view. Organization policy is affected also by the attitudes of the society in which it operates. Thus national laws and local customs all play a part in determining an organization's policies. Examples of different kinds of policies are as follows:

a. A High-street retail chain will only sell goods under its own brand-name.

b. The same retail chain will concentrate its buying in British markets.

c. A shipping company will not permit its vessels to sail under a flag of convenience.

d. A newspaper group will not interfere with the freedom of its editors to decide what shall be included in their own papers, subject to the laws of libel and indecency, for example.

e. A manufacturing company will take account of its consumers' safety needs when using its products, regardless of whether or not legislation exists for health and safety.

Some of the above policies state what the organization will do, and some state what it will positively not do. Some policies relate to marketing issues, others relate much more to ethical and philosophical issues. The variety can be considerable, but the intention is the same: to guide the organization's managers in the conduct of its affairs. One important area for policy development is that of 'social responsibility', which we shall now consider.

## SOCIAL RESPONSIBILITY

11. Being 'socially responsible' implies playing more than just an economic role in society. Increasingly, firms are being expected by society to play a direct role in meeting community needs in the Arts and education, in health and environmental matters, and in social welfare, in addition to their roles as employers and producers. In response to the pressure to be 'socially responsible', many firms have developed their own social or community programmes. These are aimed at demonstrating that corporate organizations are just as capable as individuals of being 'good citizens'.

12. There are two ways of encouraging commercial enterprises to develop a sense of social responsibility:

1) they can be forced by law, or

2) they can be persuaded voluntarily.

In Britain, as in most other states, the law plays an important, though not dominant role, in regulating the relationships between firms and their various stakeholders. So, for example, there are laws designed to protect the community from less welcome effects of commercial activities, such as industrial pollution, unsightly building developments and hazardous products. However, when we are discussing 'social responsibility' we are generally referring to *voluntary* measures undertaken by firms as part of their wider role in society.

13. Most firms are likely to operate their social responsibility programmes from the point of view of enlightened self-interest. By contributing to those activities which, even in prosperous countries, are never sufficiently funded by the state, a firm can ensure that its reputation is maintained in society. In previous centuries, it was wealthy landowners and princes who patronised the arts and social welfare. Today such patronage is exercised by large business enterprises. As in previous times, patronage can bestow a number of benefits on the patron, notably the establishment of a high reputation for good works.

14. Individual company motives for engaging in social responsibility programmes range from the highest altruism to the most calculating self-interest. Historically, firms owned by Quakers (eg Rowntree, Cadbury) have pursued such programmes for altruistic reasons. Most firms generally do not aspire to such unselfish heights, but have a mixture of motives for patronising community activities.

15. An example of one entrepreneurial company's attitude towards social responsibility is provided by STC plc (formerly Standard Telephones & Cables) as follows:

Relations with the Community
- To be an economic, intellectual and social asset to the local community, the nation, the EEC, and the world as a whole.
- To respect the environment and to be sensitive to the interests of people living in the neighbourhoods in which we have plants.
- To encourage people to fulfil their personal sense of duty to the community as well as their objectives within the Company.
- To help in finding solutions to national problems by contributing knowledge and talent.
- To conduct the Company's affairs with honesty and integrity. People at every level will be expected to adhere to high standards of business ethics, and the Company will comply with the spirit as well as the letter of the law.
- To pursue a policy of equality of opportunity whereby all personnel actions will be administered regardless of race, colour, religion or sex.

(STC – THE BEST COMPANY BOOK, 1983)

16. In what way do statements such as the above get translated into action? At the present time, there are several types of

community activity that commercial enterprises support. The most typical of these are as follows:

- work creation schemes
- welfare programme
- support for educational institutions
- support for the arts
- contributions to overseas aid

Large companies tend to operate separate funding arrangements for those activities which are predominantly 'charitable' (altruistic) and those which are 'promotional' (enlightened self-interest). Charitable donations, usually to welfare and educational programmes, are made from distinct charitable funds or foundations. Promotional activities (see Chap. 33, para 31), mostly involving the arts or sport, are paid for out of the organization's operating budgets.

17. Specific examples of activities engaged in are:

- Work creation – London Enterprise Agency set up in 1979 to help small business start-ups. Funding and advice provided jointly by IBM, Marks & Spencer, Barclay's Bank, Midland Bank, BP, Shell and United Biscuits).
- Welfare – J. Sainsbury, the grocery firm, have established a 'Good Neighbour Scheme' whereby money from a central charitable fund is donated to local projects in support of a 'theme of the year' (eg Youth, Mentally Handicapped). Sainsbury's policy, as a High Street retailer is to give major support to local as well as to national activities. Other High Street firms have adopted a similar approach.
- Education – Support for specific universities eg Oxford (the Nuffield Foundation) and Nottingham (Boots). Support for specific forms of research, eg cancer, mental health.
- Arts – Financial subsidies to the Royal Philharmonic Orchestra by the Bankers Trust Company, the Woolwich Equitable Building Society and others.
  – £50m donation to the National Gallery, London, from the Paul Getty Foundation.
- Overseas Aid – Television programmes sponsored by the broadcasting media and a wide variety of others in support of particular appeals (eg Band-Aid appeal for Ethiopia).

## CORPORATE PLANS

18. Corporate planning commences with an examination of the organization's overall objectives and policies. The next stage is to move forward to a consideration of the key actions that need to be taken to achieve these overall objectives ie to develop a strategic,

or corporate, plan which will indicate the directions the organization must take over the next 5-10 years or so. In order to decide which strategies to adopt, the organization's planners have to consider two important issues: what is the organization's current performance? and what factors in the external environment might affect the organization's future? The answers to these questions are fundamental to the progress of a corporate plan.

19. The current performance of the organization is usually appraised under two main headings: *strengths* and *weaknesses*. Key performance areas such as sales volume, market share, production output, resourcing (financial, personnel etc) are considered in terms of their relative strengths and weaknesses. For example, sales volume may be increasing year by year – a strength – but most sales are in overseas markets with risky political situations – a possible weakness. Another example could be the continuing ability to recruit well-qualified staff for key functions – a strength – but the absence of a satisfactory career path for younger employees – a weakness.

20. The appraisal of the external environment follows a similar approach, except that here the two headings employed are *opportunities* and *threats*. In this case, the organization's planners are assessing the likely impact on organizational objectives of technological, economic, political and social trends together with the activities of competitors. Taking the last-mentioned factor first – the competition – supposing a firm has been the first in the field with a mass-production light-weight battery car for urban use, what opportunities does this lead give them and what threats might be posed by other manufacturers? One opportunity might be to offer competitors the possibility of producing the vehicle under licence, another might be to seek some joint production and marketing facility. A major threat could be the manufacture of cheaper varieties of such a car by overseas competitors with lower labour costs and/or the benefits of improved production technology. Another example, taking economic trends into consideration, could be the opportunities and threats posed by an organization's dependence on oil. In this situation there might be no opportunities other than seeking alternative forms of energy, whereas the threats could be fundamental to the future existence, let alone growth, of the organization.

21. In conducting what is often called a SWOT analysis (Strengths, Weaknesses, Opportunities and Threats), the organization's planners are concerned with *strategic* issues ie the relatively few, but crucial, issues within and external to the

organization which are considered to represent the major factors in relative success or failure over the next 5, 10 or even 20 years.

22. The next step in the corporate planning process is to develop a list of alternative corporate strategies which will form the basis for the final corporate plan. Organizations develop strategies along two lines: (a) those aimed at producing *actions* to fulfil objectives, and (b) those aimed at ensuring the *resources* to support these actions. Strategies therefore tend to be developed (a) in terms of products, services and markets where actions (or sometimes no actions!) will be required, and (b) in terms of size, structure, financing and staffing, for example, where resources are the issue. Typical corporate strategies could be as follows:

a. Expand into new markets with existing products (or services).
b. Continue to maintain market share in existing markets and with existing products ie a 'no change' strategy.
c. Add to product base/range of services by acquisition of related competitors.
d. Seek long-term, low-interest loans from European Bank/World Bank for re-development projects.
e. Reorganize company into separate profit-centres.

23. It can be seen that such strategies point the direction in which an organization is to move over a fairly lengthy period. They are sufficiently clear to be evaluated in terms of whether they have been achieved or not, but they are not so specific that they tie down the organization to meeting what could be impossible long-term targets in conditions of uncertainty. Specific targets can only be set for short-term purposes, say of up to one year. Such targets form part of the operational or tactical plans worked out by departments and divisions to meet the demands of the corporate plan. Examples of operational plans include marketing, production and manpower plans.

24. This leads us on to one of the final stages of corporate planning: the issue of key targets in a year-on-year format to the various departments and divisions of the organization. Some targets will be expressed in budget form, indicating, for example, sales revenue, direct and indirect costs, and trading profit. Others will be expressed in measures such as output per employee, percentage utilisation of machines, percentage increase in market share, cost levels and so on. Once these targets have been set, they are monitored and revised as necessary. If revisions are made the whole plan is rolled forward as a consequence. Thus the long-term perspective is maintained, but the entire plan is kept up-to-date.

## SUMMARY

25. Corporate planning is a continuing process by which the long-term objectives of an organization may be formulated and subsequently attained by means of long-term strategic actions designed to make their impact on the organization as a whole. Corporate planning also involves deciding the policy, or code of conduct, of the organization in pursuit of its objectives.

26. The corporate objectives and policies set for organizations are, in reality, the projections of the ideas of two groups: owners and managers. Where owners predominate, then objectives and policies will be related to achieving a satisfactory income from dividends and a satisfactory growth in share values. In large organizations, where the owners are remote from the decision-making arena, it is the managers who exercise the greater influence on objectives and policy. Managers tend to be less concerned with profitability as such, and more concerned with various monetary and non-monetary incentives. Managers tend also to be more concerned with the pressures exerted on them by outside interests, such as consumer groups and trade unions.

27. Most organizations tend to set long-term objectives in the following areas:

   i.    Profitability
   ii.   Market Share
   iii.  Sales Volume
   iv.  Production
   v.   Research & Development
   vi.  Stock/Inventory Levels
   vii. Resourcing (financial, manpower & physical)

28. In developing corporate plans, organizations appraise both the present performance of the organization and the environment in which it exists. This appraisal involves analysing internal strengths and weaknesses and external opportunities and threats (SWOT analysis).

29. The eventual outcome of a SWOT analysis is a strategic plan, which incorporates a set of decisions about the actions to be taken and the resources required to implement the organization's plan for the future. The strategic plan points the way ahead for the rest of the organization. From this plan flow the operational plans of the organization (market plan, manpower plan etc). The final stages of the corporate planning process are those concerned with monitoring progress and revising aspects of the plan where necessary.

30. An outline of the key stages in corporate planning is described in Figure 17.1 overleaf:

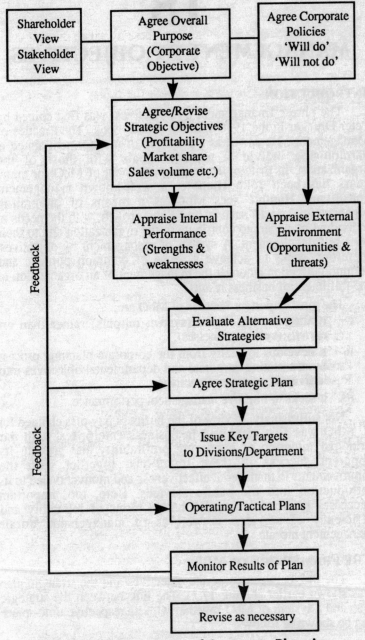

**Figure 17.1 The Stages of Corporate Planning**

# 18

# MANAGEMENT BY OBJECTIVES

## INTRODUCTION

1.    The phrase 'management by objectives' was first coined by Peter Drucker in the 1950's, in his classic book 'The Practice of Management'. He saw it as a principle of management aimed at harmonising individual manager goals with those of the organization. In Britain, the leading exponent of MbO for many years has been John Humble, a well-known management consultant. Humble sees MbO as a means of integrating organizational goals, such as profit and growth, with the needs of individual managers to contribute to the organization and to their own self-development. A system of management by objectives, therefore, seeks to achieve a sense of common purpose and common direction amongst the management of an organization in the fulfilment of business results.

2.    The most important features of MbO are:
   i.    it focusses on *results* (system outputs) rather than on *activity* (system processes).
   ii.   it develops logically from the corporate planning process by. translating corporate and departmental objectives into individual manager-objectives.
   iii.  it seeks to improve management performance.

3.    Not surprisingly, in view of the business pay-offs claimed for it, MbO was first employed in business enterprises, with the principal intention of improving profitability and growth. Its apparent success in these intentions, together with the improvements in managerial effectiveness and motivation led to its introduction into the public services. Here, too, important successes have been recorded but in terms of reliability and efficiency of services as well as of management morale management morale.

## THE FRAMEWORK OF MBO

4.    The link between corporate objectives and the strategic plan was shown earlier (Figure 17.1). The link between the strategic plan and a system of MbO together with its respective time-spans, can be shown as follows:

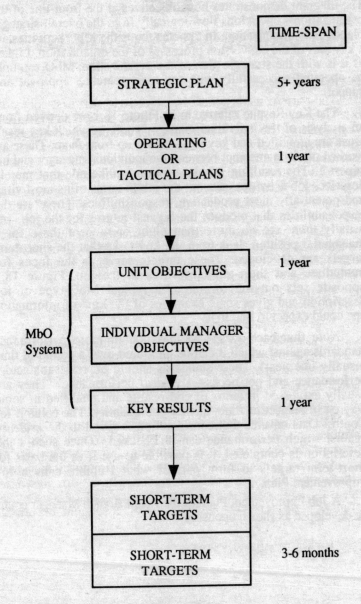

**Figure 18.1**

The diagram demonstrates how objectives at the front-line of the organization's operations flow logically from the overall strategic plan for the organization. In systems terms the MbO activities are a key part of the conversion processes of the organization. Linked as it is with the strategic plan of the organization, MbO can only be operated successfully with top management's approval and support.

5.    The Key Results referred to in Figure 18.1 are derived from an analysis of the individual manager's job, in which key result areas are identified and key tasks drawn up from them. These are worked out by agreement between the individual manager and his superior. The resulting job description, unlike one that merely describes job activities, sets out the job in terms of its most vital, and potentially most productive, responsibilities. These are the responsibilities that produce the biggest returns for the job, and usually there are no more than eight or nine of these for a managerial position. It is from the key tasks that the short-term targets are developed. These targets serve as the focus for immediate and short-term priorities in the job. Figure 18.2 opposite sets out the format of a typical MbO-type of job description and gives some examples of the kind of information one could expect to find in it.

6.    Note that each Key Task has one or more performance standards against which it can be measured over a period of time (usually one year). These standards should express satisfactory performance and not necessarily *ideal* performance.  They are usually expressed in terms of end-results and qualified in some way eg in respect of time, quality and quantity. The column for Control Data ensures that consideration is given to the *evidence* against which performance can be checked.  Once such a job description is completed, it is possible to use it as the basis for short-term targets to form part of what Humble calls a Job Improvement Plan.

7.    A Job Improvement Plan for the Retail Branch Manager could be developed as shown opposite.

*Job Title:* Branch Manager (Retail Chain)     *Date:* Jan 1989

*Reporting to:*  Area Manager

*Own staff:*  65 Full-time (incl. 12 Section Managers)
            45 Part-time

*Scope of Job:*  Annual Branch Revenue £x'000,000
                Average Sales per sq. ft. £x

*Overall Purpose of Job:*
To achieve Revenue targets in accordance with Area budget
by providing and maintaining an attractive and reliable retail
service that meets customer needs in the locality.

*Key Result Areas:*

| *Key Tasks:* | *Performance Standards* | *Control Data* |
|---|---|---|
| Prepare and gain acceptance for Branch revenue targets as contribution to Area budget | Targets accepted without major amendments | Area Budget |
| Set recruitment levels and standards for guidance of subordinate managers etc. etc. | (a) Branch fully staffed throughout year | Weekly staff report |
| | (b) Staff turnover not to exceed 20% per annum | Area Personnel Figures |

**Figure 18.2**

| Key Task | Actions Planned | Target Date | Notes |
|---|---|---|---|
| Branch revenue targets | Set up meeting with Area Manager to achieve improved checkout facilities at rear of store in light of major extension of public car-park | Within one month | Brief Checkout Manager beforehand |
| | Hold coaching sessions on revenue target-setting for all newly appointed Section Managers | By end of next quarter | |
| Recruitment levels/ Standards | Arrange meeting between Area Personnel Officer and all Section Managers on all the implementation of new staff induction procedures etc. etc. etc. | Within one month | |

**Figure 18.3 Job Improvement Plan for a quarterly period**

8.    The Job Improvement Plan is very much an *action* document. It sets out the actions which need to be taken in the short-term in order to ensure that the Key Tasks are fulfilled to the required standard. In each case the appropriate Key Task is identified and the priority actions are set alongside it together with a target date.

The time-scale of short-term actions is usually one month to one quarter, although some improvement plans may be spread over a six-month period. In fast-changing situations it may be better to set improvement plans at more frequent intervals than in situations of relative calm market activity.

9. One of the most attractive elements of MbO for top managements has been its emphasis on setting standards and specifying results for all managers at the operating level of the business. In the past only those in functions such as production and sales were subject to anything like measurable performance standards. Now, with MbO, it was possible to quantify, or at least *qualify*, the efforts of specialist managers as well. The performance standards, which are set as a measure of the degree of achievement of key tasks, are expressed in terms of quantity, where this is practical, or in terms of some agreed judgement of what could be reasonably expected ie some qualitative measure. Examples of the two broad categories of measurement are as follows:

| Quantitative | Qualitative |
|---|---|
| a. Increase sales of product X by 20% in next 12 months. | a. Vacancies for Branch Manager posts to be filled by internal promotion. |
| b. Staff turnover not to exceed 30% in any year. | b. Budget is to be accepted by the directors. |
| c. Stocks not to exceed budgetted levels. | c. All supervisors able to operate grievance procedure without incurring trade union complaints. |
| d. Previous month's Budget figures for actual against target results to be ready for distribution within two weeks of the start of the following month. | d. Conclude productivity agreements with the trade unions which realise genuine cost savings to the Company. |

10. An MbO system enables managers to see how well they are performing in the key areas of their jobs. It also provides a basis for realistic discussions between managers and their superiors concerning progress in these key areas. This brings us to another important aspect of MbO – appraisal and review. As the initial objectives-settings phase is hammered out jointly between the individual manager and his superior, so the results obtained are

jointly reviewed. The precise way the review is conducted by the superior will depend on the relationship he has with his subordinate and on his preferred management style. Some managers undoubtedly use the performance standards and improvement plans as sticks with which to beat their sub-ordinates. Others prefer a joint problem-solving approach where the emphasis is on how to make things better. Humble's opinion is that reviews should:

   a.  focus on *performance* rather than personality,

   b.  concentrate on *improvement for the future* rather than on criticism of the present, and

   c.  be genuinely *participative*.

11.  MbO allows for two types of review – Performance Review and Potential Review. The Performance Review is concerned with the individual manager's results in the key areas of his *present* job, as discussed in the preceding paragraph. The Potential Review is concerned with the manager's anticipated ability to succeed *in his next job*. This assumes, of course, that the organization concerned has a management development plan into which such a Potential Review can fit as part of management succession planning. For further information on the subject of management development, see Chapter 46.

12.  Reference was made in the previous paragraph to management succession planning and the contribution to it of the Potential Review. Management succession plans are drawn up to ensure that vacancies created by career moves, death, retirement and other reasons, are capable of being filled internally. Most plans provide for immediate temporary successors to certain key posts as well as identifying long-term successors to such posts. This is to ensure that a sudden death does not bring a particular function to a halt whilst a long-term successor is sought to replace the deceased member of staff.

13.  If the organization is intent on using MbO as a *system* of management rather than as a limited *technique* for improving manager-productivity, then it will indeed see training and development as a key factor in the total system. In fact, one of the great advantages claimed for MbO is that it provides an ideal basis for the analysis of managerial training needs. Once managerial jobs have been written up in terms of their key results and required standards of performance, it is clearly easier to identify those areas of the job, if any, where an existing job-holder is falling short of the required level of performance. It should then be possible to identify shortfalls due to gaps in the individual's knowledge and

skills, which hopefully can be overcome by suitable training. This particular subject will be dealt with later in Chapter 44 entitled Training & Development.

## SUMMARY OF CHAPTER

14.  Management by Objectives is best thought of as a system of management or an approach to management, rather than as a technique. It is a system which derives from the organization's need to achieve its corporate goals, and from individual managers' needs to contribute towards results and to find opportunities for personal growth in their work.

15.  MbO enables the management of an organization to concentrate their efforts on obtaining results from the key areas of the business. It provides an opportunity for managers and their superiors to collaborate in (a) identifying the key areas for results, and (b) establishing appropriate performance standards against which results can be measured. It also lays the foundation for a scheme of management development and management succession planning based on performance reviews which follow on from the setting of key tasks and performance standards.

16.  The principal stages of an MbO system can now be summarised as shown overleaf.

THE MbO CYCLE

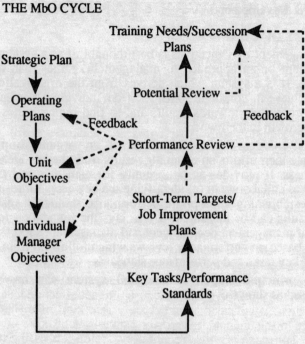

**Figure 18.4**

The cycle of events demonstrates the links between the organization's strategic plan, the objectives and key tasks of individual managers, and the vital review of performance which provides important feedback for other parts of the system. The Performance Review provides feedback to the operating system (plans and objectives), and to the training and development system (training needs and succession plans). The Potential Review feeds back to the training and development system.

# 19

## MANPOWER PLANNING

### INTRODUCTION

1.    Manpower planning, like any form of planning, is a means to an end. In this case the end is a secure supply of manpower able to undertake all the activities required to achieve the organization's corporate objectives. In organizations that have adopted corporate planning as the fundamental basis of the management process, the manpower situation with its strengths and weaknesses will have been assessed in general terms at the top management level. This assessment will have led, where necessary, to a number of long-term strategies for manpower aimed at securing sufficient and suitable employees for the achievement of the corporate plan as a whole. This represents the *ideal* context for the implementation of manpower planning.  Many organizations will not have adopted the comprehensive approach of corporate planning, but nevertheless will have been forced for economic and social reasons to consider the flow of manpower through their institutions.

2.    Whatever the nature of the organization, if it is of a size where changes in the workforce will have a significant effect on business results, then it will need to undertake some kind of manpower planning. In this manual, manpower planning is taken to mean a rational approach to the recruitment, retention, utilization, improvement and disposal of an organization's human resources. It is as concerned with quality as it is with quantity. Thus manpower planning is not just a numbers game.  If anything, *more* time should be spent on the qualitative aspects, in particular the different requirements for knowledge and skills.

3.    Before moving on to look at the various stages of manpower planning, it is worth considering the questions which manpower planning aims to answer. These can be summarised as follows:

    a.  What kinds of people does the organization require and in what numbers?
    b.  Over what time-span are these people required?
    c.  How many of them are employed by the organization currently?
    d.  How can the organization meet the shortfall between (a) and (c) from internal and external sources?
    e.  What changes are taking place in the external labour market which might affect the supply of manpower?

If these are the key questions, then manpower planning is essentially concerned with four major activities – analysing existing manpower situations, forecasting future demands for manpower, assessing the external labour market and forecasting the manpower supply, and, finally, establishing and implementing manpower plans. We shall now look at these major activities in more detail.

## THE MANPOWER PLANNING PROCESS

4.    Manpower planning can only make sense when seen in relation to business objectives. The basic demand for people springs from the organization's need to continue to supply goods or services to its customers. In this sense, the planning of manpower is a resourcing activity. However, it is also a fact that manpower resources in themselves can have a vital influence on organizational objectives. For example, a firm may be unable to pursue its expansion plans in a new market because it is unable to find enough suitably trained personnel to carry them through. So, information arising from the manpower planning process can produce feedback which causes other business plans to be cancelled or amended.

5.    In its simplest form, manpower planning can be depicted as follows:

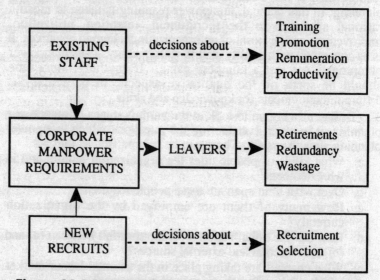

**Figure 19.1 Personnel decisions and the manpower flow**

Even this simple model of the process indicates the ramifications of manpower planning, and emphasises the qualitative aspects of it. Manpower planning is clearly not just concerned with numbers. Plans for training, for promotion and productivity all indicate the importance of getting the right kind of staff as well as the right numbers.

6.    Figure 19.1 shows the basic flow of people through the organization, and identifies some of the key actions that need to be taken at the operational level. This is the kind of model that almost every organization can utilize. However, larger or more complex organizations need a more strategic approach at the outset. Such an approach would incorporate the four major activities mentioned in paragraph 3 above. A more appropriate model for this situation would be as shown in Figure 19.2, shown overleaf.

7.    In the light of Figure 19.2 we can look at some of the key features of each of the major stages of the manpower planning cycle. Let us start with the demand for manpower. This is a more or less continuing demand in any organization. It has its short-term aspects ie the clearly-defined requirements for specific skills or positions which need to be filled in the context of existing budgets. This usually means periods of up to about 6 – 9 months. It also has medium-term (9 – 18 months) and long-term (18 months – 5 years) aspects, in line with the market and financial targets of the corporate plan. A longer-term view of manpower is essential for ensuring that the organization is supplied with skills which take time to be developed. Most professional jobs, for example, require a training period of three to five years before the trainee can claim even the basic competencies of the profession. If an organization decides to develop its own electronics engineers, it needs to look ahead for at least five years from the time the first apprentices are appointed. If the organization decides it will not train its own engineers, but buy them in from the market-place, then it has to be reasonably assured of the forecast availability of trained engineers at the time they will be required.

8.    This leads us on to the question of the manpower supply, which is the next major stage in the cycle of events. Any analysis of the supply of manpower must commence with the existing state of the organization's manpower. Answers need to be sought to such questions as What categories of staff do we have? What are the numbers in each category? What about age and sex distribution within the categories? What skills and qualifications exist? How many staff are suitable for promotion or re-deployment? How successful are we in recruiting particular categories of staff? These are important questions for both immediate and future needs.

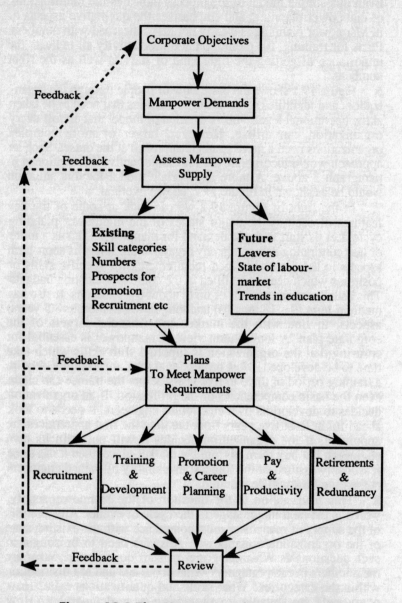

**Figure 19.2 The Manpower Planning Cycle**

If, for example, a contraction of the business was planned, it might be an advantage to have an ageing workforce. Equally, if *expansion* was planned in the same business, an ageing workforce would be a definite disadvantage, and the organization would need to draw heavily on the local labour-market.

9. When considering the existing supply of manpower available to an organization, we are not just considering the numbers and categories at a particular point in time. We are also considering (1) the organization's ability to continue to attract suitable recruits into its various operations, and (2) the rate at which employees are leaving the organization. Can the organization count on filling vacant posts satisfactorily when it goes into the market-place? Are some posts more difficult to fill than others, and can anything be done about this? What about leavers? Why are they moving out – retirements? seeking better opportunities elsewhere? pregnancy? dismissal? redundancy? Some organizations rely on a high fallout rate of employees to enable fresh recruits to be brought in at regular intervals. Other organizations expect a considerable degree of stability among their workforce, and build this expectation into their planning assumptions.

10. The analysis of the existing supply of manpower must also take account of the potentialities of existing staff to undertake other roles in the organization. There are considerable variances in the policies of organizations concerning career development. Some offer no real prospects for increased variety or responsibility at work. Others claim career development as the high-spot of their reputation as employers. Clearly firms that take the latter view can call on far greater internal resources for meeting change than those in the former category. As we saw in the chapter on Management by Objectives, an important part of management development is the succession plan that indicates the names of potential successors to a particular management post. This is very much a component of manpower planning.

11. Having considered the existing supply of manpower, an organization will know how far short are its requirements for the future. If we assume that the organization cannot meet its future manpower needs internally, then it must look to the external labour market. There are a number of important issues here. For example. What is the overall employment situation likely to be in the course of the next five years? How is this situation likely to affect our local labour market? What competition for manpower is likely? Are there any trends in the educational sector which might affect

our recruitment plans? Are there factors in our corporate plans which might speed up the voluntary leaving rate?

12. The answers to these questions will indicate the likely prospects of meeting future manpower needs from external sources. For example, until the recent slump in the world economy, labour – particularly skilled labour – was an extremely scarce resource in most advanced industrialised nations. Now the situation has changed dramatically with large-scale unemployment and even a surplus of some skills. These changes do not happen ovenight. Thus, firms that are planning ahead for their manpower requirements can offset some of the worst affects of acute shortages or surpluses of labour which may arise as a result of economic changes over which they have no control. Another example of the need to recruit externally is when changes in technology or production processes bring about subsequent changes in the numbers and types of employees required. Improved technology can lead to redundancies and/or more boring jobs for machine operators on the one hand, whilst leading to more jobs for skilled maintenance technicians on the other.

13. Once the organization has assessed its supply position in relation to its requirements, it can then draw up plans to meet these requirements. Since manpower is probably *the* most volatile resource available to the organization, the best plans will be those which have the greatest flexibility. Most man-power plans are developed on a rolling five year basis, which means that forecasts for next year and the succeeding years in the cycle are updated every year in the light of this year's out-turn. Detailed plans for securing sufficient and suitable employees for current needs are laid for a one-year period in line with current budgets. Less detailed plans are laid for the five year period, but at least major contingencies are prepared for in line with the organization's corporate strategy.

14. Whether long or short-term, the plans for securing the workforce will usually include consideration of the following:

**Recruitment:** How do we ensure our anticipated needs for replenishing or adding to our workforce? By increasing traineeships and apprenticeships? Or by recruiting trained and experienced people? How much provision should be made for recruiting part-timers and contract staff? What steps should be taken to promote the organization in schools, colleges and universities? What use, if any, should we make of recruitment consultants? What improvements could be made to our selection procedures?

**Training & Development:** What basic job and professional training needs to be provided to prepare new and existing staff to fulfill their roles satisfactorily? Should we concentrate on in-company or in-service training or should we send people on external courses? What special programmes need to be established to deal with re-training or up-dating? How can induction procedures be improved?

**Promotion & Career Planning:** How can internal pro-cedures be improved so as to facilitate the movement of staff to jobs where they can exercise greater, or different, responsibilities? What new succession plans need to be drawn up for key management and supervisory roles? How well is training linked to career development?

**Pay & Productivity:** What steps must be taken to ensure that pay scales and incentives are sufficient to attract, retain and encourage our workforce? What are the cost limits on pay? How can we accommodate high-cost groups of key employees? In what ways can labour costs be paid for out of improved output per employee or other productivity indicators? In what ways can individual departments be discouraged from over-manning? How much overtime, if any, needs to be worked to achieve production targets?

**Retirements & Redundancy:** What provision should be made for those reaching retirement age? What inducements may be needed to be provided to encourage non-essential employees over 55 to consider opting for early retirement? What arrangements should be made for dealing with planned redundancies? How should retirements and redundancies be phased over the course of the year? What are the estimated costs of these plans?

15. Manpower planning is essentially a corporate activity. It cuts across all the divisional and departmental boundaries of an organization. It is an activity which claims the attention of all managers. It is not the preserve of any one group of specialist managers (eg personnel), even though such specialists may well play a key coordinating role in the implementation and review of manpower plans. So, as we turn to the final stage of the manpower planning cycle – the review – we can see this as a responsibility in which all managers share. Major reviews of progress will usually take place once a year, when revisions may be made to the subsequent years of the five-year planning cycle. There will also be reviews carried out half-yearly or quarterly by the specialist coordinators in the organization. The principal vehicle of the monitoring process will be the monthly budget statements. These

may be expressed in terms of costs, headcounts or man-hours, for example. Costs will identify the total labour costs for each category of staff for the period concerned, and will also indicate the running totals to date. Current totals will be compared with budget targets and any variances noted. Headcounts are usually made against establishments, which are target manpower numbers fixed for a given period. This is probably the most popular method of controlling manpower. Man-hour methods are more likely to be used for employees whose work itself can be measured in this way. It is not very suitable for managerial-type work.

16. Manpower review activities are important for generating feedback information. This information tells the organization not only how well it is achieving its manpower plans, but also points the way to necessary changes in course that must be made at one or more points in the cycle. Some changes need only be made at the tactical level ie to amend next year's plans. Others may have to be made at the highest strategic level ie where plans for 5, or even 10, years ahead must be amended.

## SUMMARY

17. Manpower planning is a rational approach to the recruitment, retention, utilization, improvement and disposal of the human resources of an organization. Its purpose is to secure the organization's manpower in both the short and long-term in order to enable corporate plans to be carried through successfully. It involves line as well as specialist managers.

18. Manpower planning seeks to define what are the organization's needs for people, where they are to be found, and how they are to be obtained. It is concerned with the flow of people into, within and out of the organization. The major stages of the manpower planning cycle are:

    a. Define corporate objectives.

    b. Assess manpower requirements (demand).

    c. Assess manpower supply.
- internal/external
- current/future

    d. Plan to meet manpower requirements.
- recruitment
- training & development
- promotion & career plans
- pay & productivity
- retirements & redundancy

e. Review progress.
  - annually
  - half-yearly/quarterly
  - monthly
f. Revise plans as necessary.
  - short-term
  - long-term

# 20
# WORK DESIGN

## INTRODUCTION

1. The influence of 'scientific management' (see Chapter 4) on modern work practices in manufacturing has been enormous. One of its major legacies is that work has been designed to fit the technology available, rather than to meet the needs and aspirations of the people concerned. Thus the most important criteria for job design have been as follows:

- Maximise the degree of specialisation
- Minimise the time required to do the job
- Minimise the level of skill required
- Minimise learning time/training time
- Maximise the use of machines
- Minimise the degree of flexibility in the performance of the job.

2. Despite the theoretical arguments in favour of simplifying industrial jobs, it is clear that Britain and many other industrial nations have experienced far fewer benefits than expected. The principal reason seems to be that people nowadays are less willing than earlier to be subjugated to the needs of machines. This unwillingness to cooperate with what has been described as the 'engineering approach to job design' has manifested itself in high labour turnover, absenteeism, lateness and poor attention to quality.

3. The pressures on manufacturing organizations to reverse the trend towards work simplification have come from two main sources:

a. high manufacturing costs due to low productivity

b. demands for increased control over the pace and method of working by employees themselves.

A further pressure has also been applied by researchers and academics working in the field of social psychology. Studies into motivation and job satisfaction (see Chapters 7–9) have demonstrated vividly that employees at all levels seek some degree of self-control and self-direction at work.

## BOREDOM AT WORK

4.   If we are to be able to redesign jobs to adapt technology to meet the motivational needs of employees, then it is important to know what employees find demotivating about their work. Some useful evidence has been provided by Guest and colleagues (1978) in a study of boredom amongst three contrasting groups of employees: insurance workers, civil servants and manufacturing workers. The following factors were found to make a significant contribution to people's view of boredom:

a.   Constraints in the job – having to carry out certain tasks which the management saw as essential, but which employees found uninteresting (eg form-filling, figurework).

b.   Meaningless tasks – tasks which had to be done regardless of whether they were thought to be a waste of time by the employee.

c.   Lack of interest and challenge – clerical workers, in particular, found undemanding tasks such as filing and form-filling very boring.

d.   Repetition – repetitive tasks were seen as a major source of boredom for production workers.

e.   Never-ending nature of the job – the public-sector staff said that boredom arose from the lack of any sense of completion of the task; however much work was achieved in a day, there was always more to come.

5.   Boredom and lack of interest at work are not just caused by factors in the work itself. Two other factors, especially, play an important role:

1. individual differences;
2. compensatory activities.

Whilst some generalisations can be made about people's perception of boredom, researchers have found that individual viewpoints vary considerably. Differences in the physical, mental and emotional make-up of individuals lead to differing levels of need, differing abilities and differing responses to stress.

The extent to which individuals can offset boring factors in their work depends partly on what compensatory activities are available. These may be of a work or a non-work kind, such as having a different task to handle (work) or having a tea-break (non-work).

6.   Flexitime is one answer to this latter problem, as it enables employees to have greater control over the way they switch their

time between work and non-work activities. Typically, a flexitime system identifies a non-negotiable part of the working day called 'core time' and a negotiable part called 'flexible time'. Core time is usually between 1000–1200 and 1400–1600. The arrangement works well in situations where the employees can commence their work or break it off without disrupting the general workflow. The system is not normally suited to assembly line situations.

7. An organization which has made a particular study of work design is the Work Research Unit of the Department of Employment. In an occasional paper by R. Sell (1983), the Unit suggest that the following characteristics are crucial if a job is to satisfy human needs.

1. There should be some degree of autonomy over the way tasks are to be achieved.
2. Individuals should be responsible for their own work and for the resources they use (eg equipment).
3. An element of variety should be present in the job, so as to permit variations in task, pace and method, for example. Work cycles should be longer rather than shorter, and repetition should be reduced to a minimum.
4. There should be some arrangements for providing employees with feedback on their performance.
5. The job should enable the completion of a complete item, wherever practicable.
6. Some degree of social contact should be available to the jobholder.
7. Learning opportunities should be built into the job so as to provide an element of challenge as well as the opportunity to extend a person's repertoire of knowledge and skills.
8. The jobholder's role should be clear, so that he or she and others know what is expected from the job.
9. Every job should have some goals to aim for.

8. Currently, there are three main approaches to achieving increased job satisfaction at work through task restructuring. These are:

- job enrichment
- job enlargement
- autonomous work groups

Each of these approaches embodies several, if not all, of the characteristics referred to in the previous paragraph.

Note: There are, of course, other methods of enhancing employee job satisfaction, eg by improving consultation or permitting participation in decision-making (see Chaps. 24 & 48).

## JOB ENRICHMENT

9. The term 'job enrichment' is usually applied to the vertical extension of job responsibilities. It implies taking tasks from those both senior and junior to the jobholder in order to enable a jobholder to have more responsibility than before. Herzberg (see Chapter 9) saw job enrichment in terms of building motivators into a job. His view was that opportunities for achievement, recognition and responsibility need to be included in a person's job. For example, if a sewing machinist's job is expanded from being responsible for stitching one part of a garment, to the stitching of a whole garment with additional responsibility for the training of newcomers, then her job may be considered enriched.

10. One of the difficulties associated with job enrichment is that it will lead to changes throughout a job hierarchy. Some jobholders may find that their jobs are threatened by a job enrichment programme. Supervisors, in particular, may find that many of their duties have been handed down to members of their team. Any attempt at job enrichment must take account of such consequential changes on the overall structure of jobs.

11. The main benefits of job enrichment for individual employees are felt in terms of increased job satisfaction resulting from increased intrinsic rewards in the job (see Expectancy Theory, Chapter 9). Organizations tend to benefit by a reduction in overhead costs caused by absenteeism, lateness, lack of attention to quality and other negative features of poor morale.

## JOB ENLARGEMENT

12. Job enlargement, in contrast to job enrichment, is the horizontal extension of jobs, that is to add extra tasks of the same level as before. As someone put it 'to add one undemanding job to another!' To take the example of the sewing machinist again. Her job could be enlarged by giving her shirt collars to stitch as well as blouses. Job rotation (the switching from one undemanding job to another undemanding job) is a form of job enlargement. Such a step does increase job variety to a certain extent, and may create more meaningful tasks. What it does not achieve is any real increase in responsibility. The approach nevertheless has many supporters, not least because it often works in practice to bring about improved morale and/or productivity.

## AUTONOMOUS WORK GROUPS

13. The idea behind autonomous work groups is that job satisfaction and hence employee morale can be enhanced if employees work together in a group to achieve their production goals. An autonomous group is a self-organized work group which is held responsible for the rate and quality of its output. This approach to work design resulted from the efforts of the socio-technical systems theorists from the Tavistock Institute (see chapter 12). The first reported autonomous work groups were those established in the British coalmining industry under the 'composite longwall method'. Subsequent experiments in Norway and Sweden, especially the work at the Volvo car plant, have shown that such groups can improve quality and reduce overheads as well as providing greater job satisfaction for the employees concerned.

14. Autonomous group working may not prove effective over a period of years. For example, in a case-study reported by the Work Research Unit in 1982, a British clothing manufacturer, who introduced the practice of 'self-organized work groups' in 1973, found that after three or four years some of the machinists wanted to return to the original system of single working. By 1980 the self-organized groups had virtually disappeared! The reasons for the reversal of the autonomous group approach were seen to be as follows.

a. The women concerned were able to broaden and develop their skills, but some became noticeably more efficient than others in the group, and this caused frustrations to appear; efficient workers felt held back by the less efficient, while the latter felt the pressure on them from their workmates.

b. The group payment system did not meet the needs of the more efficient workers, in a manner that was possible with the earlier piecework system.

c. The group system carried the seeds of its own destruction, because it stimulated problem-solving, versatility and efficiency of working among all the members of the group, and once the best machinists were fully proficient, they no longer needed the group.

d. The technology involved in this case – individual sewing machines – did not require group working as a necessary element in the production process, unlike the assembly of a modern motorcar, for example.

15.   The above case demonstrates the importance of individual differences both in terms of ability and of need. Fortunately for the management concerned the improved versatility and efficiency of the women working on their own led to less work-in-progress and more styles of garment being worked on at any one time.

Productivity and quality did not suffer, and overall the outcome seems to be one of mutual satisfaction.

However, what started out as an experiment into autonomous group working ended up as an exercise in job enrichment!

## DIFFICULTIES IN WORK DESIGN

16.   Individual jobs are essentially a collection of tasks. The tasks are generated primarily by the needs of the organization, as made explicit by line managers who are confronted by a number of different pressures from marketing, financial and personnel colleagues.   To a manager at the operational end of the business, every job represents some sort of compromise between conflicting pressures, arising mainly from the following:

- the need to meet the customer's specification
- the need to meet financial targets
- the operating requirements of the machinery involved
- the nature of the production process
- the requirements for stocking materials
- the delivery arrangements
- the motivational needs of employees

17.   In the light of the above pressures, it is not surprising that job redesign is rarely considered by the majority of firms, on account of the complexity of the problems at precisely the point where the product is being manufactured (or the service delivered).

The approach taken by a typical production manager, for example, is to focus on the technical specification of the product and how it is to be met within the cost, time and quality  constraints imposed on him by his senior manager. Thus work is organized primarily to achieve accuracy, reliability, uninterrupted workflow, consistency of quality and the containment of costs. Only after  such considerations have been made is he likely to consider employee needs. The extent to which he may defer to demands for increased job satisfaction will depend as much on the relative bargaining power of the employees as on any magnanimity on his part!

18.   A further factor to be considered when looking at the above pressures is that the new technology (see Chapter 41) has all the

potential to deal comprehensively with the complexities of modern production systems, and to do so with very little need for an inter-face with human beings. Where people are working in a computerised set-up, they will tend to be integrated into the technical system rather than the other way round. Fewer operators, but with new skills will be the order of the day.

## CONCLUSION

19. Redesigning jobs is not easy. Changes in one part of a job hierarchy are bound to bring about changes elsewhere. Change may be welcome in one group, but not in another. This is likely to cause tensions between groups. Individuals may initially welcome change, but then feel less enthusiastic if related job conditions (pay, re-training etc) do not meet their needs. Once expectations are raised, there is no going back! Supervisory staff may feel particularly threatened by any form of job redesign, but will expect to benefit ultimately.

20. However, when work can be redesigned effectively, the rewards are twofold. For *individuals*, there is the opportunity to find personally challenging and satisfying work. For *firms*, there is the opportunity to achieve lower costs, better quality and improved productivity through a more effective match between the needs of people and the requirements of technology.

## SECTION SUMMARY – PLANNING

1.    Chapters 16 to 20 have looked at some key aspects of the planning function of management, which was seen as a decision-making process leading to the formulation of organization aims and objectives, and to the establishment of the means for fulfilling such aims and objectives. Planning also encompasses policy formulation, or the means by which the organization states how it intends to conduct itself in the pursuit of its aims and objectives. Planning must also include consideration of performance standards and of reviewing actual against target performance. The results of the review are fed back into the earlier stages of planning to complete the cycle of activities.

2.    Chapter 16 described a theoretical model of decision-making which implies that the really fundamental requirements of decision-making are firstly, to ask the right questions, secondly to seek creative answers, and thirdly to implement the best solutions in the circumstances. What are the best solutions will depend on a number of factors, including the sheer technical quality of the decision, the acceptability of the decision to those involved, and the likely consequences of the decision.

3.     The decisions an organization is likely to face can be put into three principal groups, as follows:

Strategic ie Long-term, complex, non-routine and non-repetitive.

Operating ie short-term, routine and repetitive.

Administrative ie establishing the organization necessary to carry through the other two.

4.     Another way of describing decisions is to see them as being *programmable* or *non-programmable*. The former have quantifiable variables and clear decision rules, and are thus capable of being worked out by computer. Non-programmable decisions are those in which the variables and the rules are not clear, and where the outcomes have to be the result of judgement. Operating decisions will often be programmable, and there are numerous techniques or tools available to assist with the identification and measurement of variables. The most important group of techniques currently available are those of Operational Research (Network Analysis etc). Strategic decisions are not programmable.

5.     Chapter 17 described the main features of corporate planning. In summary these were as follows:

i.     Set corporate objective(s) and policies.

ii.    Set strategic/long-term objectives.

iii.   Assess internal strengths and weaknesses.

iv.    Assess external opportunities and threats.

v.     Evaluate alternative strategies.

vi.    Agree and implement strategic plan.

These steps are conducted in terms of the organization *as a whole,* not merely for parts of the organization. Thus corporate planning can be distinguished from long-range planning, which applies a long-term perspective only to selected parts of an organization. Corporate planning is not only long-term (strategic), but also comprehensive.

6.     The main purpose why an organization exists has to be the subject of agreement at the highest level. For many business enterprises the main objective is to obtain a satisfactory return on the shareholders' capital. All subsequent objectives for marketing, finance, personnel etc have to serve that aim. This has been called the shareholder theory of the firm. For most organizations nowadays, whether they are business enterprises or public services, it is necessary to have more than one corporate purpose or objective. Return on capital alone does not meet the needs of other key groups with a stake in the organization eg employees,

customers, suppliers etc. Therefore other purposes will be included such as product safety, for example. This second theory of the firm has been called the stakeholder theory.

7.    The view of the firm which is taken by an organization is one of the factors which will influence the policies of that organization. Policies are broad statements of conduct. They state what the organization will or will not do in pursuance of its corporate and strategic objectives. Policies tend to reflect the dominant culture or ethos of an organization's top management. They represent one of the constraints on planning.

8.    In a business enterprise strategic objectives are usually set for the following areas of the organization:
  i.    Profitability
  ii.   Market share
  iii.  Sales volume
  iv.   Production
  v.    Research and development
  vi.   Stock/Inventory levels
  vii.  Resourcing (financial, physical & manpower)

The achievement of such objectives depends on the relative strengths and weaknesses of the various activities of the organization. It also depends on the opportunities and threats posed by changes in the external environment of the organization.

9.    In the light of the analysis of strengths, weaknesses, opportunities and threats (SWOT analysis), a number of alternative strategies can be developed into a final strategic or corporate plan. This plan reflects corporate strategies aimed at products or services and markets on the one hand, and at organization structure, size and staffing, for example, on the other. The objectives contained in the plan are stated in broad terms. Out of these broader objectives come the specific targets of the operating plans which are agreed for each division or department of the organization. Specific measures of performance are usually available for these operating plans, and it is these measures which provide the basis for the feedback of results which is the completion of the planning cycle (see Figure 17.2).

10.    Chapter 18 outlined the main features of management by objectives (MbO), as a system of management which seeks to integrate organizational objectives with the needs of the individual managers who are part of that organization. MbO is directly linked into strategic planning via the operating plans of the organization. The basis of the system is the identification of key results in each managerial job and the joint agreement between manager and

superior about short-term targets which need to be achieved in each key result area. MbO, therefore, encourages managers and superiors to focus attention on priority areas of the work and to assess results in terms of achievements not just activities.

11. The performance standards set for individual managers as part of their key results and targets are intended to be as measurable as possible. Such measures are either quantitative eg in terms of time, costs and quantity, or are qualitative ie where a judgement is made about what would constitute a satisfactory level of performance. These results are considered formally in a Performance Review, conducted by the manager's superior once a year. The Review not only acts as a feedback mechanism on results, but is also used to identify training and development needs. There is also provision for a review of potential performance in the MbO system, which is an important pre-requisite of management succession planning. Thus MbO can form the central feature of management development activities in the organization, rooted firmly in the business plans. (See Figure 18.5).

12. Chapter 19 dealt with the subject of manpower planning. This is an aspect of resource planning which is very popular with examiners. Manpower planning was defined as a rational approach to the recruitment, retention, utilization, improvement and disposal of the human resources in an organization. These activities are undertaken in pursuit of corporate objectives.

13. Arising from the objectives set out in the corporate plan, manpower planning is a process which attempts to assess manpower requirements, assess the manpower supply (internal and external), and then plan to meet requirements in the light of supply. This may mean making up a shortfall by means of recruitment, for example, or it could mean reducing staff by means of redundancy and other measures. Manpower plans contain contingencies for both the short-term (current year) and the long-term (five years or more). Such plans are therefore reviewed at a number of different intervals, ranging from one month to one year. Feedback from manpower plans can cause other plans to be changed, especially where a shortage of appropriate skills is identified.

14. The final chapter (Chap. 20) dealt with the topic of Work Design as a means of re-structuring jobs so as to achieve:

    a. improved productivity
    b. increased job satisfaction.

On balance, it is the former which takes precedence over the latter in most organizations.

## QUESTIONS FOR DISCUSSION/HOMEWORK

*1.   In your own words, describe the sequence of events which lead to successful decision-making.*

*2.   What are the benefits of corporate planning for an organization?*

*3.   What are policies, and why are they of importance to organizations?*

*4.   In what ways might the corporate objectives of a local authority differ from those of a merchant bank (or similar commercial enterprise)?*

*5.   Why may it be advantageous to consider Management by Objectives as a system of management rather than as a management technique?*

*6.   What is the part played by the following activities in manpower planning:*

> *a. recruitment?*
>
> *b. promotion?*

*7.   Why is manpower planning especially important to an organization in a period of change?*

*8.   How would you summarise the practical difficulties incurred in attempting to redesign jobs?*

## EXAMINATION QUESTIONS – PLANNING

*The questions selected below cover all the subject-matter of this Section. Outline answers can be found at Appendix 2.*

*EQ 15 What are the major steps in the decision-making process? Identify and explain the key considerations in each step.*

*(IOB NOM)*

*EQ 16 Why is it necessary for companies to establish and periodically review their objectives? What objectives should a business aim to achieve?        (Inst. of Mktg. Business Orgn.)*

*EQ 17 Describe what you understand by a system of management by objectives. What do you think are the advantages and disadvantages of such a system?        (IOB NOM)*

*EQ 18   Manpower planning is an important aspect of the work of a Personnel Manager.*

> *a. What is manpower planning?*
>
> *b. Why is it necessary?*

*(Inst. of Mktg. Business Orgn.)*

# ORGANIZING

1. If *planning* is considered as providing the route map for the journey, then *organizing* is the means by which you arrive at your chosen destination. Plans, as we saw in the previous Section, are statements of intent, of direction and of resourcing required. To put intentions into effect requires purposeful activity, and this is where the organizing function of management comes in. Organizing, above all, is concerned with *activities*. It is a process for:

    a. determining, grouping and structuring activities,

    b. devising and allocating roles arising from the grouping and structuring of activities,

    c. assigning accountability for results to both groups and individuals, and

    d. determining detailed rules and systems of working, including those for communication, decision-making and conflict-resolution.

2. It is important here to repeat a point made earlier in the Manual (Chapter 2 paragraph 6), and that is to make the distinction between 'organizing' and an 'organization'. The former, as we have just noted, is a *process*; the latter is a *social grouping*. The former, however, can only be explained in terms of the latter. If we take a systems view of an organization as an open social system receiving inputs from the environment, converting them and discharging certain outputs back into the environment, then *organizing* is essentially one of the conversion processes. It is one component of the total social system.

The next four chapters concentrate on key aspects of the *process* of organizing. In particular, chapter 21 deals with the structural aspects of organizations; chapter 22 highlights the issues of delegation, decentralization and control; chapter 23 looks at formal communication in organizations, and chapter 24 outlines some of the key issues involved in organizational change. The final chapter in this section deals with the management of time.

# 21

## ORGANIZATION STRUCTURES

### INTRODUCTION

1. The study of the structuring of work organizations is a developing field. It was of major interest to classical theorists such as Fayol, Urwick and Brech (see Chapters 3 & 5); it was the source of inspiration for Weber's theory of bureaucracy (Chapter 6), and it is now a major feature of the theorists of complex organization – the contingency school (Chapter 13). This chapter looks at the practical issues of structure facing modern organizations, and identifies the most important options that are currently available.

2. As Lawrence and Lorsch have pointed out (See Chapter 13), most organizations are in a state of tension as a result of the need to be both differentiated and integrated. Once an organization has grown beyond the point when the owners can exercise direct control, then some degree of differentiation, or specialization, is inevitable. Thus, most organizations have to face up to a number of crucial issues about the kind of structure that will best sustain the success of the enterprise. The most frequent issues are:

    a. to what extent should we encourage the specialization of roles?

    b. what degree of standardization should be imposed on behaviour and methods, or, to put it another way, what degree of discretion should be allowed to individual job-holders?

    c. how much formality should be encouraged?

    d. how many levels of authority should we establish?

    e. to what extent should decision-making be centralized or de-centralized?

There is no perfect answer to any of these questions, but there are a number of possible options, which, taken together can produce an optimum design for an organization. These will be considered shortly. First of all we shall look more closely at the key issues, commencing with the question of specialization.

### SPECIALIZATION

3. Specialization is concerned with the division of labour within an organization. It serves to break down the total mission of an organization into a number of subordinate objectives, which in turn give rise to tasks of various kinds. It is essentially a dis-

integrating process. This process acts initially by grouping key activities in the organization, and subsequently by allocating roles and tasks to individuals.

4.   Specialization by grouping of activities can be achieved in several different ways. The most frequent method is that of *functional specialization*. In this case, tasks are linked together on the basis of common functions. So, all production activities or all financial activities are grouped into a single function which undertakes all the tasks required of that function. A typical organization chart of a functional organization would appear as follows:

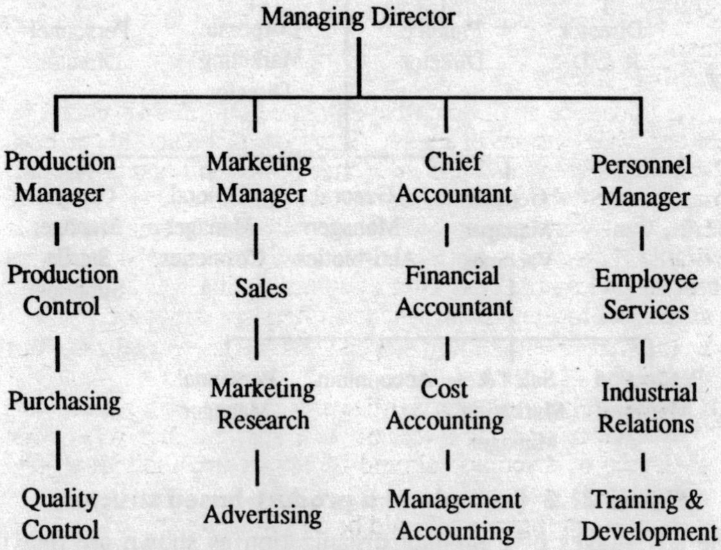

Managing Director

| Production Manager | Marketing Manager | Chief Accountant | Personnel Manager |
|---|---|---|---|
| Production Control | Sales | Financial Accountant | Employee Services |
| Purchasing | Marketing Research | Cost Accounting | Industrial Relations |
| Quality Control | Advertising | Management Accounting | Training & Development |

**Figure 21.1 Functional Organization Structure**

The main advantages of functional organization are that by grouping people together on the basis of their technical and specialist expertise, the organization can facilitate both their utilization and their coordination in the service of the whole enterprise. Functional grouping also provides better opportunities for promotion and career development. The disadvantages are primarily the growth of sectional interests which may conflict with the needs of the organization as a whole, and the difficulties of adapting this form of organization to meet issues such as product diversification or geographical dispersement.

5.     Another frequent form of grouping is by product. This is popular with large organizations having a wide range of products or services. In the National Health Service, for example, the key groups of employees – medical, nursing, para-medical and hotel services – are dispersed according to the service provided viz. maternity, orthopaedic, surgical, psychiatric and many others. By comparison, a large pharmaceutical company could be organized as follows:

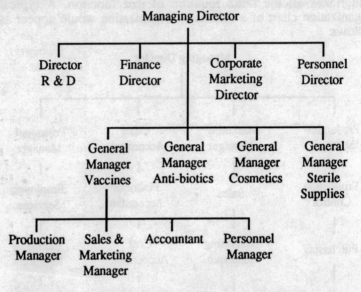

**Figure 21.2 Example of a product-based structure**

The advantages of a product organization as shown are that it enables diversification to take place, it can cope better with problems of technological change by grouping people with expertise and their specialized equipment in one major unit.

The main disadvantage is that each General Manager may promote his own product group in a way that creates problems with other parts of the company. This implies that top management must exercise careful controls, without at the same time robbing the product managers of their motivation to produce results.

6.     Another popular form of organization is grouped on a geographical basis. This is usually adopted where the realities of a national or international network of activities make some kind of regional structure essential for decision-making and control, in particular. An example of this form of organization is as follows:

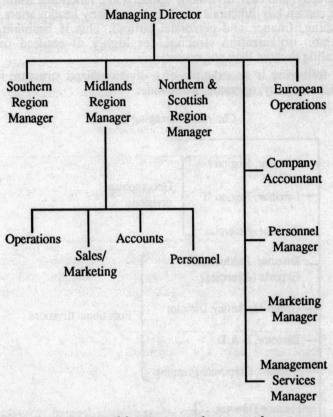

**Figure 21.3  Possible structure for a road transport company**

As in product organization, the de-centralized structure produced, causes additional problems of top-management control. Hence it is usual to find a group of senior functional managers located at headquarters in order to provide direction and guidance for the regional managers in the performance of their line role.

7.   With increasing complexity and size, many companies are opting for a mixed structure, which may combine the benefits of two or more of functional, product and geographical forms of organization. Two such mixed structures will be looked at briefly: divisionalized structures and matrix structures.

**Divisionalized structures.** In these cases, the organization is divided up into divisions on the basis of products and/or geography, and each division is operated in a functional form, but with certain key functions retained at company headquarters (eg planning, finance and personnel policy). This is becoming a common organization structure for highly diversified firms operating in more than one country.

The following is an example of a divisionalized structure in a British company, operating worldwide:

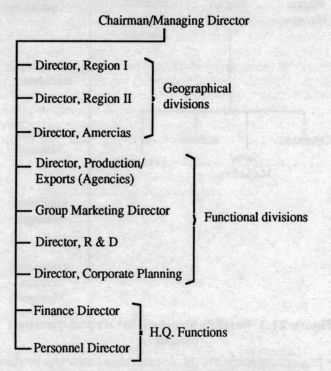

Chairman/Managing Director

— Director, Region I
— Director, Region II     } Geographical divisions
— Director, Amercias

— Director, Production/ Exports (Agencies)
— Group Marketing Director  } Functional divisions
— Director, R & D
— Director, Corporate Planning

— Finance Director
— Personnel Director     } H.Q. Functions

**Figure 21.4 Divisionalized structure**

In this example, the Regions act very much like self-standing companies in producing and marketing the products developed by the parent company. Standards are controlled worldwide via the functional divisions, and headquarters provides group policy in key areas such as finance and personnel.

A balance can, therefore, be maintained between necessary corporate control from the centre and desired divisional independence at the regional and functional levels.

**8. Matrix structures.** These are relatively new types of structure, which have come about as a result of coordination problems in highly complex industries such as aerospace, where the functional and product types of structure have not been able to meet the demands of the variety of activities and relationships created by the work. A matrix structure usually combines a functional form of structure with a project-based structure. Thus, for the purpose of a two-year project, for example, one project manager coordinates, and is accountable for, the work to be undertaken by the project team, and he is the person who deals with the client. However, although reporting to his own line manager, he is functionally involved with one or more functional managers, depending on the complexity of the project. The functional managers provide technical expertise and organizational stability. The project manager provides the leadership required to steer the project through during its relatively temporary lifetime. An example of a matrix structure is shown in Figure 21.5. below.

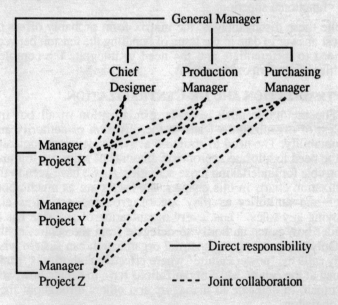

**Figure 21.5 Typical matrix structure (engineering industry)**

9. The main feature of a matrix structure is that it combines lateral with vertical lines of communication and authority. This has the important advantage of combining the relative stability and

efficiency of an hierarchical structure with the flexibility and informality of an organic form of structure. A matrix form focusses on the requirements of the project group, which is in direct contact with the client. It helps to clarify who is responsible for the success of the project. It encourages functional managers to understand their contributive role in the organization's productive efforts, and thus offsets one of the principal disadvantages of the purely functional form ie individual empire-building by the functional heads. However, like all organizational forms, matrix structures do have their disadvantages. The most important are:

a.  the potential conflicts that can arise concerning the allocation of resources and the division of authority as between project groups and functional specialists;

b.  the relative dilution of functional management responsibilities throughout the organization; and

c.  the possibility of divided loyalties on the part of members of project teams in relation to their own manager and their functional superiors.

Despite these disadvantages, the matrix form probably offers us the best answer to date to the issue of handling the tension between the need to differentiate and the need to integrate the complex activities of modern organizations.

## CENTRALIZATION AND DE-CENTRALIZATION

10.  The inevitable push towards specialization in all but the smallest of organizations leads to the diffusion of authority and accountability. The need to structure activities develops logically into the need to allocate appropriate amounts of authority to those responsible for undertaking those activities. As we have seen in the organization charts in this chapter, the issues are as much about power and authority as they are of grouping activities and deploying key roles. Thus, every organization of any size has to consider how much authority to delegate from the centre, or the top. Only the small entrepreneurial organization can sustain what Handy calls the 'power culture' where effective authority is firmly retained at the centre. Most organizations have to decide how, and how much, to delegate to managers and others throughout their total operation.

11.  The concept of centralization, as it is being considered here, is not referring to the *physical* dispersal of an organization, but to the dispersal of the *authority to commit the organization's resources*. The physical deployment of an organization may or may not reflect genuine power-sharing. In our definition, therefore, a highly

de-centralized organization is one in which the authority to commit men, money and materials is widely diffused throughout every level of the structure. Conversely, a highly centralized organization is one where little authority is exercised outside a key group of senior managers. In practice, some functions are more easily de-centralized than others. Production and marketing/sales functions are more amenable to extensive delegation than planning and R & D, for example. So, even highly de-centralized organizations usually reserve certain key functions to the centre. As well as planning and research, it is usually the finance and personnel functions that are least de-centralized.

12. The advantages of de-centralization are chiefly:
   a. it prevents top-management overload by freeing them from many operational decisions and enabling them to concentrate on their strategic responsibilities;
   b. it speeds up operational decisions by enabling line units to take local actions without reference back all the time;
   c. it enables local management to be flexible in their approach to decisions in the light of local conditions, and thus be more adaptable in situations of rapid change;
   d. it focuses attention on to important cost and profit-centres within the total organization, which sharpens management awareness of cost-effectiveness as well as revenue targets;
   e. it can contribute to staff motivation by enabling middle and junior management to get a taste of responsibility, and by generally encouraging the use of initiative by all employees.

13. The main disadvantages of de-centralization are:
   a. it requires an adequate control and communication system if major errors of judgement are to be avoided on the part of operational management;
   b. it requires greater coordination by senior management to ensure that individual units in the organization are not working against the interests of the whole;
   c. it can lead to inconsistency of treatment of customers, clients or public, especially in service industries;
   d. it may encourage parochial attitudes in subsidiary units, who may be inclined to look more to their own needs than to those of colleagues in the organization;
   e. it does require a plentiful supply of capable and well-motivated managers, able to respond to the increased responsibility which de-centralization brings about.

14. On balance, the advantages outweigh the disadvantages, but this is principally because of the enormous pressures on modern business organizations to concede more and more authority to staff

at executive and specialist levels, not to mention the pressures for shop-floor participation in the decision-making processes of the company. It is worth recalling at this point the University of Aston study's conclusion (see Chapter 13 paragraph 23) that large size tends to lead to less centralization, but relatively *more* specialization, *more* rules and *more* procedures.

## ORGANIZATION LEVELS

15. The emphasis so far in this chapter has been on vertical aspects of organization structures. Let us now turn to some of the horizontal aspects, and in particular to the question of how many levels are appropriate between the top and bottom layers of an organization. Organizations can be flat or tall in relation to their total size. The main features of flat and tall organizations are as follows.

**Flat organizations** tend to have:
  (a)  centralized authority;
  (b)  few authority levels;
  (c)  wide span of control;
as the following example shows.

Chief Executive

Department
Heads

Supervisors

Workforce

### Figure 21.6 Chart of a Flat Organization Structure

A structure as flat as the one shown above would apply, generally, only to a small organization, say of up to about 500 employees. Most organizations, whether business enterprises or public services, find that a flat structure produces a span of control that is unmanageable for most managers and supervisors. The span of control – the number of subordinates directly controlled by a superior – is dealt with in greater detail in the next chapter, but, clearly, wide spans of control create more opportunities for man mis-management than do narrow spans. On the other hand, a flat organization has fewer problems of communication and co-ordination, and does encourage delegation by the managers involved.

16.  **Tall organizations** tend to have:–
   (a)  de-centralized authority;
   (b)  many authority levels;
   (c)  narrow spans of control;
as the following example shows.

Chief Executive

|

Divisional Heads/Directors

|

Department Heads

|

Section Heads

|

Senior Supervisors

|

Supervisors

|

Operatives

**Figure 21.7 Chart of a Tall Organization Structure**

The above structure shows a typical number of levels for an organization of about 5000 employees. Research evidence tends to suggest that as organizations increase in size, so they appear to hold down the number of levels. An organization of 10,000 employees might still have seven levels, as in the above example, and certainly would not exceed eight. The advantages of tall structures arise mainly from the ability to sustain a very high degree of specialization of functions and roles. The principal disadvantages are connected with long lines of communication and decision-making. Thus tall structures seem to go hand in hand with formality and standardization, which may discourage initiative and risk-taking at operational levels.

17.   The major factors in determining the number of levels for any one organization are likely to be:
   a.   size of operation,
   b.   nature of operation, especially in relation to the complexity of production, and
   c.   management style.

As we have seen in the above discussion, size is one of the most important factors influencing organizations towards relatively flat or relatively tall structures. As a general rule, the smaller the organization, the more likely it is to have no more than three or four levels, and the larger it is, the more likely it is to have seven or eight levels. However, factors such as the technology employed can offset the influence of size alone. Woodward's studies, to which we referred in Chapter 13 (paras 13-20) suggested strongly that the type of production process had a direct impact on the span of control of managers at different levels. Mass production operations, for example, appeared to derive more benefit from a flatter structure, with wider spans of control, than from a taller, narrower structure. Management style also has a significant effect on structure. Organizations with a definite policy of increasing managerial responsibility for results will tend to adopt structures that consciously encourage decision-making and innovation at lower levels ie they will tend to adopt the flatter structure to minimise the length of the chain of command. Conversely, organizations that do not, or cannot, de-centralize decision-making, perhaps for safety reasons, will tend to settle for a taller structure with narrow spans of control.

## LINE & STAFF: FUNCTIONS & RELATIONSHIPS

18.   There is hardly a textbook on Management that does not refer to the confusion that exists between the terms 'line', 'staff' and 'functional' when these expressions are used to describe structural aspects of organization. One of the main reasons for this confusion undoubtedly stems from the attempt to promote classical 'principles' in complex organizational structures which are far from classical in themselves. For example, the classical concept of Unity of Command – one man, one boss – is just not practicable in organizations where the legal, financial, personnel and technological implications of the line processes can only be dealt with by diffusing authority *across* the management hierarchy as well as down it.

This is not to reject the classical view out of hand, but to say that it has to be considerably qualified in the light of modern organizational complexity.

19. The terms 'line' and 'staff' are usually understood in two senses: (a) as *functions* contributing to organization objectives, and (b) as *relationships* of authority. Taking these meanings in order, we can summarise the most frequent views that have been expressed about 'line' and 'staff'.

## Line and Staff as Functions

| Line | Staff |
|---|---|
| Functions contribute *directly* to the provision of goods and services to the customer. | Functions contribute *indirectly* to goods and services by supporting the line. |
| Typical line functions are **production** and **sales**. | Typical staff functions include **purchasing, accounts, legal** and **personnel**. |
| Seen as the *primary* functions of the organization. | Seen as the *secondary* functions of the organization. |
| Line functions *act*. | Staff functions *think*. |

## Line and Staff as Relationships of Authority

In terms of relationships of authority, 'line' and 'staff' can be more effectively distinguished if 'staff' is sub-divided into service and functional as depicted below:

| Line | Staff | |
|---|---|---|
| | Service | Functional |
| Direct authority over others. Part of the role of every manager and supervisor. Line authority is the essence of the chain of command. | Advisory only.<br><br>Seen as authority without responsibility. | Direct authority over others *in respect of specialist functions only*. |
| Line relationships *TELL* | Service relationships *SELL* | Functional relationships also *TELL*, but only *AS PRESCRIBED*. |
| Line authority is invariably qualified by functional authority. | | |

20. It makes more sense to consider line and staff in terms of authority relationships, where there are *real* differences, rather than in terms of functions, where it is highly arguable to state that some functions are primary and others secondary. The key point about functions is that every organization is a complex blend of functions that are dependent each on the other. Almost every comment made in the columns under *Functions* can be challenged. No wonder there is confusion! It is much more productive to concentrate attention on line and staff as an issue of differences of authority as between one manager and another.

21. Line authority is the simplest to understand as well as to agree about. It is the authority that every manager exercises in respect of his own subordinates. Thus specialist managers, such as chief accountants and personnel managers, exercise line authority over their own staff. In this role they are not different from so-called line managers, such as production managers and sales managers. Line authority, then, is not dependent on line *functions*. It is the central feature of the total chain of command throughout the entire organization structure.

22. Staff authority, as such, is a misleading concept altogether. It begins to make more sense when divided into two further concepts, those of 'service' and 'functional authority', as suggested above. Unlike the situation for line authority, the concept of staff authority *is* derived from the staff function, and this does relate it to the advisory and service functions of the internal structure of an organization. However, because of the very interdependence of all the key functions in a modern organization, one must distinguish between those aspects of the staff function that merely provide services (eg costing, recruitment, market research etc), and those that provide key standards of performance for all other sections of the organization (eg setting and monitoring company accounting procedures, installing and controlling industrial relations procedures etc). When looked at in this way, it is probably best to forget the term 'staff authority' altogether in favour 'functional authority', which is the former stripped of its servicing aspects, but made much more powerful in respect of standards in the particular function.

23. Functional authority, unlike line authority, is not exercised by every manager. It can only be exercised by managers of specialist functions, and it consists of the right to order others, including other managers, as to what to do, and how to do it, *in relation to agreed aspects of their own particular specialism*. So, for example, the Finance Director of a company is not only responsible (ie accountable) for the conduct of financial matters,

but also has the authority to insist that line managers and others shall adhere to the company's established financial procedures and policies. With the complexity of modern business, it would not be possible for senior line managers to be busy with their operational duties and to have the time to attend to the design and use of financial, personnel and other procedures. Thus the use of functional authority is a very real part of organizations today. Naturally, the existence of such authority detracts from the power of line managers to exercise their own discretion as widely as they would like, but, given the pressures imposed on organizations by their external environment, it is only by having strong specialist guidance that line managers can fulfill their responsibilities in the ways demanded by customers, employees, politicians and other groups. What has to be avoided is turning line managers into puppets, operated by functional masters at the centre.

24. Ironically, perhaps, the very power of functional specialists arises from the operation of another classical idea – that of the Principle of Correspondence (see Chapter 5 paragraph 3). This states that authority should be commensurate with responsibility. It will be useful to consider for a moment the differences between these two concepts.

**Authority** is the legitimate power to act in certain ways; it is rarely granted carte blanche; it can be delegated to sub-ordinates.

**Responsibility** is the obligation to perform certain functions on behalf of the organization; responsibility may range from the very specific to the very broad; it is commonly called accountability; unlike authority it cannot be delegated. Both of these can be distinguished from *power*, which is the ability to implement actions, regardless of considerations of authority and responsibility. For example, an unofficial strike leader may have no authority whatsoever to call a strike, and certainly will have nothing about such activities in his job description (!), but nevertheless has the power to lead his group into a strike situation. Managers in such a situation have the authority to prevent a strike, but do not necessarily have the power to do so.

## SUMMARY

25. This chapter has examined a number of key aspects of organization structure. It has, in fact, been looking at the consequences of many of the ideas promulgated by the theorists of management and organization discussed in the earlier part of this Manual. The chapter began with a discussion of the practical

implications of specialization, especially in terms of the grouping of activities. Five common forms of structure were identified.

These were:

i. Functional organization based on groupings of all the major functions eg production, marketing, finance, personnel etc.

ii. Production organization based on individual products or product ranges, where each grouping carries its own functional specialisms.

iii. Geographical organization centred around appropri- ate geographical features eg regions, nations and sub-continents.

iv. Divisionalized structure, usually based on products or geography or both, and with certain key functions such as planning and finance reserved for headquarters.

v. Matrix structures based on a combination of functional organization with project-based structures, and thereby combining vertical with lateral lines of communication and authority.

26. The issue of centralization versus de-centralization was considered next. This was defined as the extent to which authority to commit the organization's resources was dispersed throughout the organization. It was noted that certain functions such as production and sales were more readily de-centralized than others such as planning and R & D. Several advantages of de-centralization were mentioned, including the freeing of top management from operational-type decisions, the speeding up of the decision-making process and the improvement of management morale. The disadvantages were primarily the additional load on mechanisms for coordination and control, the greater possibility of inconsistencies arising and the development of parochial and sectional interests at the expense of organization-wide interests.

27. The chapter also looked at some of the issues relating to the shape of organizations, especially the alternatives of relatively flat or relatively tall structures. It was noted that flat structures resulted in centralized authority with few levels of authority but encouragement to delegate in circumstances where spans of control would tend to be large. Tall structures, by contrast, represented the decentralization of authority, although this was effected by means of numerous levels of management operating with narrow spans of control. The major factors affecting the number of levels were seen as the size of operations, their nature,

especially in respect of technology, and, finally, the management style of the organization.

28. The chapter ended with a discussion of line and staff functions and relationships. The term 'line function' was variously described, but was identified mainly as a function contributing directly to the provision of goods and services. A 'staff function' was seen mainly as a contributor to the line in the provision of goods and services. It was argued that it was not particularly helpful to discuss line and staff in terms of functions, but that it made more sense to discuss the issue in terms of relationships of authority. Line authority was defined as the direct authority exercised by every manager over his subordinate. Staff authority was seen as being a misleading concept, since it confused the provision of services (a passive role) with the setting and monitoring of key performance standards in the specialist areas. It was considered more useful to think of functional authority as the other main type of authority. Functional authority consisted in the right to order other people what to do only in respect of agreed aspects of the specialism concerned. The increasing use of functional power is a direct result of the increasing complexity of modern organizations, in which there is a high degree of interdependence between the line and the specialist functions.

29. The chapter concluded with a brief look at the distinctions between authority, responsibility and power. Authority was defined as legitimate power to act in certain ways. Responsibility was defined as the obligation to perform certain things for the organization. Power was defined as the ability to achieve things regardless of any authority and responsibility. Authority was contrasted with responsibility in one key respect: authority could be delegated, but responsibility could not be. Delegation will now be looked at in the next chapter.

# 22

# DELEGATION AND THE SPAN OF CONTROL

## INTRODUCTION

1.   As we saw in the previous chapter, one of the central issues of organization design is the question of how to create the best balance between control from the centre and delegation throughout the rest of the system. This chapter examines some of the factors surrounding delegation, including the question of the span of control. In the previous chapter, delegation was considered in organization-structure terms ie centralization and de-centralization. This was taken to mean the degree to which the authority to commit resources was diffused throughout the organization. This chapter considers delegation as from one individual to another ie as a *management* issue rather than an organizational one.

## DELEGATION

2.   Delegation is the process by which an individual manager or supervisor transfers part of his legitimate authority to a subordinate but without passing on the ultimate responsibility which has been entrusted to him by his own superior. The fulfilment of practically every task in an organization requires a certain amount of authority ie the right to act in a certain way. As numerous apprentices and trainees have discovered over the years, when you first start work you are hardly allowed to *touch* anything, let alone actually use it! The point is that to carry out the responsibilities of any job, the job-holder must have the rights that go with the job, and these include the rights to make certain decisions (authority) as well as the rights to adequate resources with which to complete the job. As the classical idea puts it, 'authority should be commensurate with responsibility'. In practice, it would be self-defeating if employees were assigned responsibilities, but given no rights to enable them to put their responsibilities into operation.

3.   The process of delegation is very much concerned with the amount of authority which should be delegated to a subordinate. It is important that this should be sufficient. It is equally as important to ensure that the amount of authority is defined or prescribed in an unequivocal way. For example, if a manager is to be appraised on the performance of his subordinates in work of a professional or

170

highly-skilled nature, then it would be reasonable to grant him the authority, subject to qualification if necessary, to select his own staff and to recommend their transfer to another unit, if unsuitable. This authority could be granted in several different ways, for example:

a. Complete authority to recruit staff within budget limits (costs and/or headcount).

b. Authority to recruit and select a shortlist of suitable candidates for *joint* final decision with his own superior.

c. Authority to select final candidates subject to approval by his superior.

d. Authority to appraise own staff within the scope of company procedures.

e. Authority to recommend the transfer, or possible dismissal, of employees who turn out to be unsuitable.

Few managers, however senior, have carte blanche in the exercise of authority. Modern organizations have developed countless policies and procedures to circumscribe the limits of authority at whatever level it may be granted.

4. The reasons for delegation are mainly practical, but a few are idealistic. Practical reasons are:

a. Senior managers can be relieved of less important or less immediate responsibilities in order to concentrate on more strategic duties;

b. Delegation enables decisions to be taken nearer to the point of impact and without delays caused by reference upwards;

c. Delegation gives managers the opportunity to experience decision-making and to live with the consequences of it;

d. Delegation enables organizations to meet changing conditions more flexibly at the boundaries of their system.

Idealistic reasons are those that suggest that delegation is a 'good thing' for individual growth at work, and/or that it contributes to staff morale. Undoubtedly, in recent years, it has become fashionable to favour a considerable degree of delegation in organizations as part of a total programme of humanizing work. Some practical guidelines for delegating tasks are given in Chapter 25 (Time Management).

## SPAN OF CONTROL

5. One of the major questions which has to be faced when considering the practical aspects of delegation is how many subordinates can be managed effectively by any one manager or

supervisor. This is the issue of the so-called 'span of control' ie the number of employees reporting directly to one person. In practice spans can vary between one and forty (or more) subordinates directly supervised, although the most likely range is between three and twenty. Smaller spans tend to be found among managerial, professional and technical groups. Here cost factors, the complexity of work and the need to deal adequately with the problems of people who are themselves managers of others, require a closer involvement by superiors in the total operation of their units. Towards the bottom end of the organizational hierarchy, where routine tasks are being carried out by employees who have no subordinates themselves, it is practicable to have much larger spans.

6.     Various writers and theorists have made proposals about the best span of control. The first of these was a French management consultant, V.A. Graicunas, who wrote a famous paper on this topic in 1933. Graicunas attempted to demonstrate mathematically the increase in the number of relationships arising from each increase in the number of subordinates reporting to the manager. For example with one subordinate, the total number of possible relationships was still one, but for two subordinates it rose to six relationships. By the time six subordinates were supervised, the total number of relationships rose to two hundred and twenty two! The formula which Graicunas developed to produce these figures was as follows:

$$R = n (2^{n-1}+n-1)$$

where R is the number of relationships and n is the number of subordinates.

7.     This concept of the span of control is a very theoretical one, of course, and bears no relationship to what happens in practice. The value of Graicunas's idea is that it does draw attention to the potentially rapid increase in the complexity of management and supervisory roles when the span of control rises beyond a certain point. Of others who have put forward views on the span of control, L.F. Urwick is among the most notable. Among his Principles of Management (see Chapter 5 paragraph 3) he included the span of control, which he believed should not exceed five or six subordinates *whose work interlocked*. The italics emphasise Urwick's thinking that it is the complexity of work that requires a smaller span. Where the work being undertaken by subordinates is discrete, then larger spans are possible.

8.     The whole question of spans of control is linked to top managements' views about the number of levels they should have

in their organization. If a flat organization is preferred, then larger spans are an inevitable consequence. If a tall structure is preferred, then spans can be smaller. Any final decision has to be a compromise between these opposing consequences. There are also several other important influences on the size of the spans in any single organization or sub-unit. These include the following:

a. the level of ability of management ie they are capable of producing results with spans of a certain number?

b. the level of knowledge and experience of the subordinates concerned eg well-trained and experienced staff require less supervision than those without training and experience;

c. the complexity of the work of the unit and the degree of change to which it is subject ie the more complex and more fast-changing the work, the more necessary it is to install narrow spans of control;

d. the costliness of possible mistakes by individuals in the unit;

e. the degree of hazard or danger associated with the work eg work on oil-rigs or in biochemical laboratories requires special attention to safety procedures.

9.    A well-known example of a company which tried to take account of the variables at work in deciding spans of control is that of the Lockheed Company in the USA. In the 1960's they developed a method of span evaluation which allocated weightings and points to different degrees of key variables in delegation. These variables were as follows:

a. Similarity of functions – in a range from identical through similar to fundamentally distinct.

b. Geographic contiguity – together or dispersed.

c. Complexity of functions – in a range from simple repetitive to highly complex and varied.

d. Direction and control – from minimum supervision and training to constant close supervision.

e. Coordination – from minimum relation to others to extensive mutual non-recurring relationships.

f. Planning – from minimum scope and complexity to extensive effort in areas and policies not chartered.

Few organizations have gone to the lengths that Lockheed did, but the work provided some useful focal points for clarifying some of the vital aspects of managing people that have to be taken into account in establishing the levels of delegation which are possible in a given situation.

## SUMMARY

10. This short chapter has developed some further aspects of decentralization in organizations, by looking at the important management issue of delegation and its related issue of the span of control. Delegation was defined as the process by which an individual manager or supervisor transfers part of his authority, or power to act, to a subordinate, but without relinquishing the ultimate responsibility entrusted in him by his own superior.

11. A key issue in the process of delegation was seen to be the relationship between the responsibilities to be exercised and the amount of authority granted. Whilst authority to act has to be qualified in most cases, it should be sufficient to enable a person to fulfill his responsibilities.

12. The reasons for delegation are generally twofold: *practical* eg to relieve the burden on senior management, to speed up the decision-making processes etc, and *idealistic* eg as a contribution to individual growth and overall morale.

13. The span of control or the number of employees reporting directly to one person can vary considerably between one organization or unit and another. The most significant factors that affect the span include: the policy of top management towards the relative shape of the organization (flat or tall?), the degree of complexity of the work, and the capabilities of the management concerned. Other factors relate to issues such as cost, hazard and geographical location.

14. In terms of theory the most well-known contribution was made by V.A. Graicunas in 1933 when he showed the enormous increase in relationships that follows any increase in the number of subordinates supervised by an individual. In terms of practice, the Lockheed Company's exercise in the 1960's has been widely-quoted by many writers.

# 23

# ORGANIZATION DEVELOPMENT

## INTRODUCTION

1. So far we have looked at organizations in two principal ways in this manual:

   a. in terms of the theoretical choices of organizational type and structure (Chaps. 3–6 & 11–13), and

   b. in terms of alternative structures (Chaps. 21–22).

This chapter will now consider the problem of dealing with organizational change. The study of how organizations try to adapt to changing conditions, whether internal or external, is a development of the last decade or so. The phrase which has been coined to describe the conscious process of adapting to change is 'organization development'.

2. A working definition of organization development (or OD) is as follows:

> 'Organization development is a strategy for improving organizational effectiveness by means of behavioural science approaches, involving the application of diagnostic and problem-solving skills by an external consultant in collaboration with the organization's management.'

Several important points can be made about this definition. *Firstly*, OD is an organization-wide process; it takes an essentially systems view of the organization. *Secondly*, it utilizes the techniques and approaches of the behavioural sciences ie psychology, social psychology, and sociology, in so far as they relate to the study of people at work in organizations. *Thirdly*, OD involves the intervention of an external third party in the shape of a 'change agent' trained and experienced in behavioural science applications in the work situation. This person is usually an academic or experienced consultant, employed for a temporary period, or sometimes a member of a corporate department, seconded to a subsidiary unit or division. Last, but not least, OD is aimed at *organizational* effectiveness ie it is something more than *management* development; it is as concerned with changing structures and decision processes as it is with changing people's behaviour. OD, therefore, has something of the flavour of corporate planning about it, and would certainly be an important element in getting corporate plans implemented in times of change.

3.　A key feature of any OD process is the relationship built up between the change agent and his client group. It is essential that a collaborative relationship is developed, otherwise the process will never get off the ground. In practice, collaboration means being open with one another, having a high degree of trust, and being prepared to work through conflict in a constructive way. By definition, OD is about change, and change can be painful, especially when it involves people's attitudes, beliefs and self-image. Those involved in the process have to acknowledge the implications of collaboration, if they are genuine about improving their organization.

4.　The rest of this chapter considers some of the major questions surrounding OD – when is it utilized? what are the key stages in an OD programme? what is the role of the change agent? what are the major approaches which have been adopted so far? and finally, what are the benefits to organizations and individuals?

5.　When is OD utilized? The most likely answer is when the senior management of an organization come to recognize that the key components of the organizational system are not working harmoniously together. In other words, when the complex mix of objectives, people and structure is failing to produce the fruits of organizational activity, then is the time to consider re-vitalizing the entire enterprise. The diagnostic stage of the OD process, which will be described shortly, invariably commences with a review of the objectives and key tasks of the organization or sub-unit concerned. It continues with an assessment of the relationships between people (eg team-work, collaboration between sections/departments, leader-group relationships etc), and finally investigates the organizational structure itself. Such a searching self-analysis will not be undertaken lightly by an organization, but many business enterprises have embraced the risks involved in order to ensure their survival and growth in the face of significant change. This situation could be due to rapid expansion of the business, or radical changes in markets or technology, or to internal social pressures for change (eg demands for less autocratic or paternalistic styles in favour of more participation). Whatever the reason for adopting a programme of organization development, the answers it is expected to produce will be fundamental ones for the future of the organization.

## OD PROGRAMMES: THE KEY STAGES

6. There is no one best way of introducing and designing an OD programme. Nevertheless, certain patterns of treatment have developed over recent years, and the following sequence of events would not be untypical:

a. **Preliminary Stage**. The senior management team discuss the scope and implications of OD with the external third party (the 'change agent'). This will include discussion about the aims of a possible programme and the means by which it might be achieved. It will also include a consideration of the possible implications for the organization arising from the implementation of a programme. It will also define the nature of the relationships between the third party and the organization's management iewhether the third party is to play the role of an expert, a catalyst for new ideas, educator, or some other agreed role.

b. If agreement is reached about the idea of commencing an OD programme, the next stage is **Analysis and Diagnosis**. This is the stage where the third party usually takes the initiative by designing appropriate methods for obtaining relevant information (eg interviews, surveys etc) and by proposing a strategy for putting these into operation with the full backing of the management team. An example of the kind of questions which may be put to manage- ment staff, in particular, are shown in Figure 23.1. The information obtained should clarify the problems facing the organization, and build up a picture of staff attitudes and opinions, as well as supplying some important suggestions as to how the problems might be solved. On the basis of the information received, the management team aided by the third party agree their diagnosis of the situation.

**KEY TASKS**

(a)    List the four most important tasks in your Department/Section:

1.........................................................................

2.........................................................................

3.........................................................................

4.........................................................................

(b)    How do you know how well you are doing in relation to your most important key task?

☐    FORMAL FEEDBACK (Committees, reports, etc)

☐    INFORMAL FEEDBACK (calls,notes,gossip, etc)

☐    OTHER MEANS ...........................................

(c)    How long is it before you know how well you are doing in relation to this key task?

☐    IMMEDIATELY                    ☐    FEW WEEKS

☐    FEW MONTHS                     ☐    YEARS

☐    NEVER

(d)    If a wrong decision about the key task was to be made today, when would its effects be noticeable?

☐    ALMOST                         ☐    AFTER  A
       IMMEDIATELY                          FEW WEEKS

☐    MONTHS                         ☐    YEARS

☐    NEVER

**STRUCTURE-ENVIRONMENT**

(a)    How appropriate is the structure of your organization in terms of fulfilling its purpose?

☐    VERY APPROPRIATE             ☐    QUITE APPROPRIATE

☐    NOT VERY                      ☐    NOT SURE
       APPROPRIATE

If you don't think it appropriate, why? ...............................

.........................................................................

(b)    How is your organization basically divided? (Tick all that apply)

☐    PRODUCT                        ☐    REGION

☐    MARKET                         ☐    BUSINESS FUNCTION

☐    MANAGERIAL                     ☐    TECHNICAL

☐    NOT SURE

(c)    What are the three most important outside pressures to which your organization must respond?

1.........................................................................

2.........................................................................

3.........................................................................

## Figure 23.1 Part of an Organizational Diagnosis Questionnaire for Managers

(adapted with permission of Emas Group Ltd./MSC)

c. The third stage, is **Agreement about Aims of the Programme**. The management team, in close collaboration with the third party, agree what are to be the aims and objectives of the programme. These aims could be to improve profitability, secure a share of a new market, improve staff motivation or other desired improvement. To these ends, specific objectives would be required, such as 'to achieve the re-structuring of the company along matrix lines over a period of eighteen months' and 'to obtain the full commitment of all management staff to an open and democratic style of leadership' or 'to reduce substantially the number of customer complaints about after-sales service'. With aims and objectives firmly established, the next stage can be initiated – action plans.

d. **Action Planning**. The organization's problems have been analysed, a diagnosis of the overall situation has been made, agreement has been reached about the aims and objectives of the exercise. Now comes the moment for planning the content and the sequence of the activities designed to achieve the aims of the programme. Much of the tactics at this stage will be influenced by the third party, whose skills and expertise in behavioural matters will be brought to bear on the manner of introducing the various OD activities. These activities will be examined more closely in a moment. All that need be said now is that they are much wider in scope than management development or other forms of personnel development.

e. **Evaluation and Review**. Once the plans have been put into action, it is very important that they should be monitored at frequent intervals by the management team and their third party colleague. Difficulties and misunderstandings are bound to occur, and these must be registered as soon as possible and dealt with just as quickly. If a particular activity is having adverse results, it will have to be amended or even dropped from the programme From time to time, more substantial reviews of progress towards the aims and objectives of the exercise will be required, and this often leads on to a further and final stage as follows.

f. **Revised Aims and Plans**. In the light of a major review, it is possible that some important revisions of aims may be necessary, for which a further sequence of plans will be required. At the end of the programme, the third party leaves the scene and the management team get on with the task of running a more successful business.

## THE ROLE OF THE THIRD PARTY

7.   The success of any OD programme depends very largely on the part played by the external third party, or change agent. The change agent is at the centre of the entire OD process. If he is unable to build a firm relationship between himself and the management team concerned, or if he fails to establish his credibility with a range of other groups, his chances of obtaining the degree of commitment required will be slim. Conversely, if he gains trust and respect both as a person and as a skilled adviser, he has the best possible basis for achieving his own contribution to the aims and objectives of the programme.

8.   The role of the third party is, in practice, a multiple one. It would be more correct to speak of the *range* of roles required by the third party. These roles range from the highly directive, leader type of role to a non-directive counselling role. In the first mentioned role, the third party will tend to prescribe what is best for his clients; at the other extreme he will tend to reflect issues and problems back to his clients without offering any judgement himself. In between these extremes are several other possible roles, as indicated in Figure 23.2.

9.   Experience with OD programmes suggests that particular qualities, values and abilities are necessary for change agents. These can be summarised as follows:

Qualities of intellect and personality are important, in particular the ability to listen diagnostically, and to apply rational approaches to problems and situations; also a mature outlook in terms of an awareness, and acceptance, of personal strengths and weaknesses.

Values that include a preference for inter-personal relations based on mutual trust and liking, for team-work rather than competitiveness, and for conflict to be handled openly and constructively.

Abilities required are not only those associated with behavioural science knowledge, but more general skills such as interviewing skills, presentation skills and the ability to establish and maintain comfortable relationships with a wide cross-section of people.

THIRD PARTY – CENTRED ◄───────► CLIENT – CENTRED

DIRECTIVE ROLE ◄───────► NON-DIRECTIVE ROLE

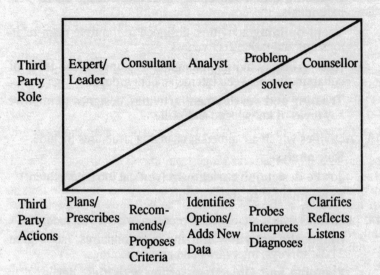

**Figure 23.2 Range of Roles for Third Party**

10. This combination of attributes suggests that OD change agents will not always be readily available. It takes a certain kind of person to be able to make the contribution to *joint* problem-solving and decision-making that is required in OD. Academics are not always suitable because many find it hard to apply theory to practice. Business consultants are often unsuitable because they feel that they must give *expert* guidance in order to justify their fee. What is really required is someone who can positively help a group of clients to help themselves and then fade gracefully into the background.

## MAJOR APPROACHES IN ORGANIZATION DEVELOPMENT

11. This part of the chapter considers the *means* by which OD programmes are carried out. Most of the activities in a programme can be classified in three ways – (a) those aimed at changing people's behaviour, (b) those aimed at changing organization structures, and (c) those aimed at problem-analysis. Examples of typical activities for each of these three classifications are briefly described below.

12.   Activities which are designed to change behaviour at work include the following.

- **Coaching and counselling** activities, designed to help individuals.
- **Team-building** activities, designed to improve team relationships and task effectiveness.
- **Inter-group activities**, designed to improve the level of collaboration between interdependent groups.
- **Training and development** activities, designed to improve key areas of knowledge and skill.

13.   Activities which are aimed at changing structures include:

- **Role analysis**
- **Job re-design/job enrichment** (vertical job enlargement)
- **Experimental re-structuring**

14.   Activities which are aimed at problem-analysis include:

- **Diagnostic activities** utilizing questionnaires, (see figure 21.3), surveys, interviews and group meetings.
- **Planning and Objectives-setting activities**, designed to improve planning and decision-making skills.
- **Process consultation**, where the third party helps clients to see and understand the human processes that are taking place around him (eg leadership, communication, competition, power struggles etc).

15.   Of the three groups of activities, those concerned with problem-analysis are the most frequently used, which is to be expected in the light of the need to assess the size and shape of the problems confronting the organization at the time. The other two groups of activities cannot usefully be activated before the initial diagnostic effort has taken place. Nevertheless, practically every OD programme highlights problems of human relations, if not of organization structure, and consequently there is invariably a need for two or three of the behaviour-changing exercises. As a whole, this is a developing field for all OD practitioners, and doubtless many new and imaginative methods will arise to enable organizations to achieve their programmes.

## Organizational Health Checklist

The twelve statements below describe various key aspects of an organization. The boxes alongside each statement contain four alternative responses.

You are asked to consider *your own organization* and select the response that, in your opinion, is the nearest to the truth. Circle the preferred response and enter the number in the Score column.

| Statement | Strongly agree | Partly agree | Slightly disagree | Strongly disagree | Score |
|---|---|---|---|---|---|
| Employees in this organization know what its objectives and aims are. | 1 | 2 | 3 | 4 | |
| The organization structure helps us achieve our objectives and aims. | 1 | 2 | 3 | 4 | |
| Communications in the organization are clear. | 1 | 2 | 3 | 4 | |
| Relations between managers and their staff are usually harmonious. | 1 | 2 | 3 | 4 | |
| People in this organization have a good team spirit. | 1 | 2 | 3 | 4 | |
| People are always encouraged to try out new ideas in the organization. | 1 | 2 | 3 | 4 | |
| | | | | | |

**Figure 23.3 Part of an Employee Opinion Questionnaire**

## BENEFITS OF ORGANIZATION DEVELOPMENT

16. The most significant benefits of an OD programme are as indicated below. The relative importance and relevance of any one benefit obviously depends on the needs of the organization at the commencement of the programme. Benefits of OD:

   a. Enables an organization to adapt to change in a way that obtains the full commitment of the employees concerned;

   b. Produces organization structures that facilitate employee cooperation and the achievement of tasks;

   c. Releases latent energy and creativity in the organization;

   d. Improves understanding of organization objectives by employees;

   e. Improves decision-making processes and skills;

   f. Provides opportunities for management development in the context of real organization problems;

   g. Stimulates a more creative approach to problem-solving throughout the organization;

   h. Increases the ability of management groups to work as teams.

## SUMMARY

17. Organization development is an organization-wide process designed to formulate and then implement a strategy for improving organizational effectiveness. The process hinges on the quality of the relationship developed between the management team concerned and the external third party, or change agent, who assists them in the diagnosis of problems and the design of appropriate forms of action. The techniques and approaches employed are rooted in the behavioural sciences (social psychology etc), and the dominant philosophy of OD is that organizations should be based on openness and trust and an overall sense of collaboration between the various groups in them.

18. The major approaches to action adopted in OD programmes are three-fold:

   a. those that aim to change behaviour, such as coaching, counselling and team-building activities,

b. those that aim to change organization structures, such as role analysis and job re-design, and

c. those that aim to assess and solve problems, such as diagnostic activities and process consultation.

19. There are numerous benefits arising from the implementation of an OD programme. In general terms, organizations benefit by being better able to cope with change as a result of a programme, and individuals benefit by being able to make a more creative contribution to their work.

# 24

# FORMAL COMMUNICATIONS IN ORGANIZATIONS

## INTRODUCTION

1.   The issue of communication is a vital one for any organization. It is worth considering for a moment what is the meaning of so important a concept. Communication is the process of creating, transmitting and interpreting ideas, facts, opinions and feelings. It is a process that is essentially a sharing one – a mutual interchange between two or more persons. In organizations, communication is generally thought of in terms of:

   a.   the *media* of communication eg memos, reports etc.

   b.   the *skills* of communication eg giving instructions, interviewing, chairing meetings etc and

   c.   the *organization* of communications eg the chain of command, briefing groups, committees etc.

2.   These three aspects sum up the *formal* communication present within the organization, and must be distinguished from the informal aspects of communication, such as the so-called 'grapevine' (rumour, gossip etc). The rest of this chapter is concerned with formal, or official, communication. Particular topics to be examined include communication flows, communication media, barriers to communication and the use of committees. In effect the chapter deals with the communications questions that face practically every organization:

   a.   What do we need to communicate?

   b.   When should we communicate?

   c.   To whom should we communicate?

   d.   How should we communicate?

## THE FLOW OF COMMUNICATIONS IN ORGANIZATIONS

3. Thecommunications network of most organizations consists of vertical lines of communication providing upwards and downwards means of transmitting information, with a few integrating mechanisms such as committees built across these lines. Some organizations also provide lateral lines of communication, which are seen as having equal importance with the vertical. As we saw in the discussion of the work of Burns and

Stalker (Chapter 13 paragraph 10), mechanistic (bureaucratic) organizations tended to adopt vertical lines of communication and interaction, whereas organic organizations tended to adopt lateral lines. We saw, also, that matrix-type structures contained both vertical and lateral lines of communication (Chapter 21 paragraph 9).

4.   **Vertical communication**. The greatest tendency in most organizations is for communication to be thought of in terms of vertical interaction. In particular, management communicates policies, plans, information and instructions *downwards*, and employees communicate ideas, suggestions, comments and complaints *upwards*. The downwards communication is achieved by means of the management chain, while the upwards communication is achieved by work-group meetings, by joint consultation machinery and by grievance procedures. Vertical communication tends to be dominated by what flows in the downward direction.

5.   **Lateral communication**. The flow of information *across* the organization is rarely comparable with the vertical flow. However, every organization has to make *some* arrangements for coordinating the efforts of more than one department or section, and this may be done by means of inter-departmental meetings or committees. This is a rational and controlled approach to the problem of integration. It represents about the least that organizations can do to set up lateral lines of communication. Where an organization is more organic in its operation, it tends to make greater use of lateral flows of information between people in the same specialisms or working on similar tasks, for example. Much of the information flowing between such groups is highly technical or task-orientated and facilitates cooperation between groups. Such information is only passed up the line if it is of particular significance, or where it comes under the category of 'need to know' for the manager concerned. Organizations which operate a system of 'management by exception' are able to make wider use of lateral forms of communication compared with organizations whose management insist on being kept fully in the picture all the time. Managing by exception implies a high degree of delegation, where, once responsibilities have been fixed and standards of performance agreed, the managers concerned will only ask for information if (a) there is a problem or (b) it is time for a periodic review of progress.

6.   Research work that has been carried out on groups at work suggests that, for simple problems, the quickest and most accurate

results will be obtained by means of centralized (leader-dominated) channels of communication. Conversely, for complex problems, the most acceptable results are likely to come from de-centralized communication channels, where there is greater encouragement to share facts, views and feelings. The most frequent channel-alternatives that have been tested are as follows:

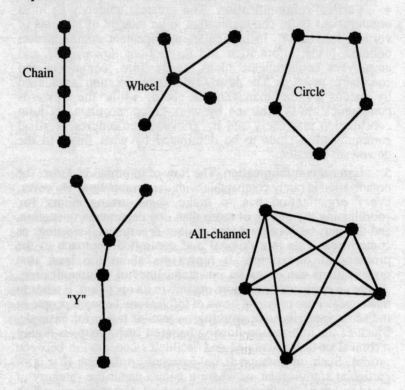

**Figure 24.1 Communication Networks**

In the above figure, the wheel represents the most centralized communication channel with its obvious leader or coordinator at the centre of relationships. By contrast, the circle and, especially, the all-channel networks rely on de-centralized channels with shared leadership. The chain and 'Y' networks are basically hierarchical and not de-centralized. Organic organizations would show a preference for all-channel networks, mechanistic organizations would tend to use the chain, the 'Y' and the wheel.

## COMMUNICATION MEDIA

7.   The media of communication help to answer the question *'how* should we communicate?' The media can be divided into two main groups: written methods and oral methods.

   **Written methods**. These are principally letters, memos, reports, notices and printouts. By comparison with oral methods, the written word is more permanent and less liable to misinterpretation. It also encourages the sender of a message to think about it before despatch. The disadvantages are that written communication takes longer to effect than oral methods, and is still liable to misinterpretation despite the efforts of the writer to be clear and logical.

   **Oral methods**. These are usually meetings of one kind or another, and telephone conversations. Oral communication may often lack the considered nature of written communication, but it does have the advantage of immediate feedback. In the case of face-to-face meetings, it has the added advantage of being reinforced by various forms of non-verbal behaviour such as facial expressions, gestures and body posture. One of the major difficulties associated with oral communication is its transience – the spoken word is a sound, and lasts only so long as it takes to pronounce it. Thus people are often able to deny, or to qualify what they have, in fact, said. This is one of the main reasons for the importance of minutes at a committee meeting – to provide a true and correct record. It also explains the growing use of audio-visual methods to capture spoken words and accompanying expressions every bit as much as the written word.

8.   In practical business there are two examples of communication methods which are especially widely used, and deserve further comment now: written reports and talks or presentations.   Meetings, and in particular committee meetings will be looked at later in the chapter.

9.   **Reports**. A written report is basically the outcome of a study of the facts and implications of a particular situation. It is intended to summarise the facts of the situation, relate them to what the organization is currently doing, draw appropriate conclusions and make useful recommendations.   Reports can range from the short one-page summary to the detailed work running into several thousand words. Whether long or short, a report is usually set out in the following format:

| | |
|---|---|
| Title of Report | Date |
| Terms of Reference | |
| Introductory Comments | |
| Findings | |
| Implications for the Organization | |
| Conclusions | |
| Recommendations or Proposals | |
| Name of author(s) | |
| Appendices (longer reports only) | |

## Figure 24.2 Typical Report Layout

Layouts such as the above enable report-writers to assemble their data and their ideas into a logical order. This is an important point for any report, as is clarity and conciseness of expression. A clear, well-argued report will stand a far higher possibility of acceptance than one which is rambling and verbose, however relevant its content.

10. **Presentations**. Most managers are called upon from time to time to make a presentation to their colleagues or their superiors. Presentations are widely used in selling situations, and in management planning exercises; they are also used when formally introducing major reports or when introducing new ideas or proposals to colleagues. There are three key elements in any presentation:

- Preparation
- Content
- Delivery

Preparation is a vital prerequisite for any presentation. The person making the presentation needs to consider the *content* of his talk and its *delivery*. So far as content is concerned, this is primarily a question of considering what to include and what to leave out, taking into account the needs and prior knowledge of the audience. Top management groups, for example, are mainly interested in the salient features of an idea or proposal, together with a summary of its principal benefits and disadvantages. Operational levels of management generally require more detailed information and will respond to a more technical approach than their senior counterparts.

The question of *how* to deliver the presentation, again depends largely on the nature of the audience. Some groups will not be satisfied with anything less than a brilliant display of wit and ingenuity, others will be quite satisfied with a low-key, but extremely relevant demonstration. One point that is always helpful, whatever, the audience, is the use of visual aids. There is hardly a presentation that does not benefit enormously from visual illustration. Visual aids that are most frequently employed include flipcharts, overhead transparencies, films (video and cine) and models or physical examples of an item.

11. A code of good practice in the making of presentations could be as follows:

   a. Consider your audience and their needs.

   b. Assemble your facts and ideas in the light of (a) above and taking account of the complexity of the material.

   c. Develop sufficient and suitable visual aids.

   d. Consider what other information should be made available (drawings, specifications, reports etc).

   e. Tell your audience what you are going to tell them, tell them, and then tell them what you have told them!

   f. Be enthusiastic about the subject (unless this would be completely inappropriate eg the announcement of a new redundancy plan).

   g. Be natural ie if you are a quiet person, then be *quietly* enthusiastic.

   h. Maintain eye contact with your audience.

   i. Be prepared for questions both during and at the end of your presentation.

## BARRIERS TO COMMUNICATION

12. There are numerous barriers to communication, and some of the most important ones are discussed briefly below:

   a. Individual bias and selectivity ie we hear or read what we want to hear or see. People are often unaware of their bias until it is brought to their attention. Much of the bias is to do with cultural background and personal value-systems.

   b. Status differences ie subordinates may well read more than was intended into a *superior's* message. By contrast, superiors may listen less carefully to information passed up the line by subordinates. People at all levels may be reserved about passing information upwards, in case they incur criticism. One of the reasons for the relative failure of the 'open door' policy of communication adopted by many managers is that it relies on subordinates overcoming both their natural reserve and the status barriers of the organization.

c. Fear and other emotional overtones can cloud the communication message. If a person has bad news to pass on, which is almost certain to upset the recipient, he will tend to avoid the whole truth and be content to pass on part of the message only. This issue of emotional barriers is particularly relevant in the handling of grievances. Angry people do not make good listeners, and thus any manager dealing with a deeply-felt grievance must allow for a period of 'cooling off' before expecting to make any headway with a solution. Indeed, it is now recognized that it is precisely in the area of the emotions that human beings appear to be worst at sharing ie communicating. Not surprisingly, this is an area of attention in Organization Development programmes, especially in relation to how conflict can be handled in a team.

d. Lack of trust is another important barrier to effective communication. If we are not sure of someone, we tend to hold back in our communication with that person. This mistrust may arise because of doubts about the recipient's motives or his ability to grasp what is being said.

e. Verbal difficulties are a frequent source of confusion and misunderstanding. These may arise because of the sheer lack of fluency on the part of the sender, or because of the use of jargon (specific application of words in technical and professional contexts), or perhaps because of pitching the message at too high a level of understanding. In terms of written words, the barriers are usually those associated with long-windedness ie a failure to get to the point quickly and concisely.

f. Other important barriers to communication include information overload (where a person is overloaded with memos, reports, letters, telephone messages etc), inadequate machinery for communication (committees, briefing groups, joint consultation meetings etc) and sheer lack of practice in the skills of communicating.

13. Overcoming, or at least reducing the effects of, barriers to communication mainly consists in finding answers to the issues raised in the paragraph above. Improvements in communication can be made by adopting a strategy of (i) ensuring that employees

are made aware of communication problems, (ii) setting up appropriate machinery for communication (upwards, downwards and laterally), and (iii) training employees in relevant techniques of communication. Particular mechanisms which have been widely adopted include:

**Downwards communication**

i.    Briefing Groups (where team leaders brief their immediate staff about events).

ii.    Staff Meetings (where all staff in one unit or from one site are brought together).

iii.    Bulletins, Notices and Circulars.

**Upwards communication**

i.    Joint Consultation committees (where management and staff meet to consult about issues).

ii.    Suggestions Schemes.

iii.    Trade union channels (via shop stewards, negotiating committees etc).

iv.    Grievance Procedure.

**Lateral communication**

i.    Inter-departmental Committees

ii.    Special Project Groups.

iii.    Coordinating Committees.

Note: The Employment Act, 1982, now requires companies of more than 250 employees to include in their Directors' Report a statement showing what arrangements have been made to encourage greater employee involvement in the affairs of the company by means of information, consultation, share ownership etc.

## COMMITTEES IN ORGANIZATIONS

14.   Committees abound in practically every kind of organization. They are an integral part of the operation of every public sector organization, and are almost as popular in the private sector. What are committees? The first thing that can be said about them is that they are *formal* groups with a chairman, an agenda and rules of conduct. Committees invariably have a specific task or set of tasks to achieve. These tasks are frequently, although not always, associated with decision-making. In fact, many committees are expressly forbidden from reaching decisions eg joint consultative committees and advisory committees. Some committees meet regularly eg monthly senior officers' committee in a public

authority or a quarterly planning committee in a manufacturing company. Others meet for ad hoc purposes only eg committees of enquiry set up by Parliament or steering committees set up to monitor short-term projects.

15. As was stated above, committees are formal groups. The formality of a committee is expressed by the following features:

**A chairman**, who is responsible for ensuring (a) that the committee is conducted in accordance with the rules, and (b) that it is supplied with the necessary resources, particularly with the written information it requires to carry out its work effectively.

**A secretary**, who is responsible for taking the minutes of meetings, sending out the agenda and other papers, and generally acting as the administrative link with the members.

**An agenda**, which sets out the agreed subject-matter of the meeting. Part of the chairman's job before the meeting is to approve the agenda, over which he usually has the final word. The agenda enables committee members to know what is to be discussed, and in what order, and this enables them in turn to prepare adequately before the meeting.

**The minutes of the meeting,** which are the official record of what has taken place. They serve to remind members of important issues or decisions that were debated at the time. Since they have to be agreed by the members as a true and correct record, they are a reliable source of information both to members and outsiders alike. In local authority committees and joint union-management committees, for example, the minutes are made public for the benefit of ratepayers or union members, as the case may be.

**Committee Papers and Reports**, which provide the committee with the quality of information, which will enable it to make well-informed decisions or proposals. Reports, for example, may be purely factual, or both factual and analytical. Yet others may be innovative and imaginative. Whatever their contents and presentation, their aim is the same ie to provide relevant information, ideas and suggestions as the focal points for the discussion of agenda items.

Rules of procedure, which are designed to promote the smooth-running of a committee and to ensure that consistency and fair-play are maintained. Such rules include procedures for:

a. speaking in a debate,
b. proposing motions,

  c. voting,

  d. adding emergency items to the agenda, and

  e. other issues relating to the operation of the committee as a communication medium.

The rules enable both sides in an argument to state their case, they help to minimise the effect of bullying tactics, and they ensure that a proper record of the proceedings is kept.

16. In the light of all this formality, what are the benefits and disadvantages of committees? The advantages can be summarised as follows:

## Advantages

  a. Precisely because they are *organized* groups, committees can undertake a larger volume of work than individuals or very small groups working in isolation.

  b. Decisions or proposals are based on a *group* assessment of facts and ideas, and not just on one powerful individual's preferences.

  c. Committees can encourage the pooling of special know-how and talents possessed by individual members.

  d. Committees are very useful for achieving coordination and collaboration between work groups.

  e. Committees act as a useful focal point for information and action within organizations.

These advantages are particularly important in two respects. *Firstly*, the sheer size and complexity of modern organizations make it increasingly impossible for isolated individuals or small groups to meet the decision-demands of their organizations. *Secondly*, the growing pressures from all sections of the workforce for a greater say in the decision- making processes of their organizations are creating expectations that decision-making will become more open and democratic. Committees are likely to be even more in demand as a result of these two factors.

17. However, it would be unrealistic to gloss over the disadvantages of committees as communication media. The main disadvantages are as follows:

## Disadvantages

  a. Decision-making is an altogether slower process when dominated by committees. It is also true that committee decisions may often represent compromise solutions rather than optimum solutions.

b. Managers may be tempted to hide behind committee decisions, where these have proved unpopular, and thus abdicate their personal responsibility.

c. Committees sometimes have a tendency to get bogged down in procedural matters, which reduces the time avail- able for the discussion of substantive issues.

d. Committee work demands certain skills. Members who are unsure of themselves or unskilled in committee practice tend to leave the initiative to the 'good committee-men'.

e. Committees do not exist between meetings, and thus cannot act quickly and flexibly to meet sudden changes in a situation.

On balance, committees are probably best suited to large- scale bureaucracies and organizations which have a high degree of public accountability. Smaller-scale enterprises, on the other hand, would probably benefit more from the greater flexibility obtainable from less formal, and perhaps less thorough, forms of decision-making, such as informal management meetings and temporary project groups.

## SUMMARY

18. The chapter has looked at the key features of formal communication in organizations in terms of the flows of communication, the media of communication, the barriers to communication, and the role of committees.

19. The flows of communication are mainly vertical, and sometimes lateral. Vertical flows are used to propagate management information *downwards* (plans, policies, instructions etc) and employee ideas and suggestions *upwards*. The major flow is downwards. Lateral flows are used to communicate across the organization structure. Committees are one means of integrating activities and decision-making *across* functions or departments. Organic organizations consistently make more use of lateral flows than mechanistic types.

20. Research into communication channels or networks suggests that relatively simple problems are most speedily and accurately dealt with by means of centralized networks, but that complex problems are best solved in de-centralized networks. Centralized networks are leader-dominated, but de-centralized networks encourage shared leadership and contribution.

21. The media of communication can be divided into two main groups: written methods and oral methods. Written methods

include letters, memos, reports and printouts. Reports were looked at in more detail, particularly in respect of their layout and clarity of expression. Oral methods include meetings and telephone conversations. Presentations, or talks, were examined more closely, especially in relation to their preparation, content and delivery. In making presentations it is important to consider the audience's needs and prepare the content in the light of those needs. A logical and interesting approach, backed up by appropriate visual aids, helps to make a presentation successful.

22. The barriers to communication arise more from inter-personal relationships than from lack of appropriate machinery for communication. Typical people-barriers are individual bias, status differences and lack of trust. Verbal difficulties are also significant, both oral and written. Several mechanisms for overcoming barriers to communication were mentioned. These included briefing groups, joint consultation committees, and special project groups. It would be important to ensure that such mechanisms were complemented by adequate training in communication skills.

23. Committees were considered in terms of their formal characteristics (chairman, agenda, minutes etc) and of their benefits and disadvantages. The main benefits were those arising from the volume of work undertaken by committees and from the democratic nature of their decision-making processes. The main disadvantages were the slowness of decision-making and the familiarisation problems associated with the procedures. These disadvantages may be felt particularly in smaller-scale enterprises, where informal management meetings and project groups would, in general, be more practicable. On balance committees seem better adapted to organizations which are bureaucratic in style, or which have a high degree of public accountability.

# 25

# TIME MANAGEMENT

## INTRODUCTION

1.   So far in this section on Organizing, we have been considering organizational and group issues. Ultimately, however, the effectiveness of organizations comes down to the effectiveness of individuals, which is the concern of this chapter. The management of time is an issue which is fundamental to job performance. In the past (see Scientific Management, Chap. 4) attention to the relationship between time and job performance was restricted to manual workers, and then, by means of Organization and Methods, to clerical workers. The consideration of time utilisation for managerial and professional grades has not received much attention until recently. Current approaches are based on the assumption that personal effectiveness at work is primarily a function of the individual's management of his or her time.

2.   Much of the subject-matter of this chapter overlaps with those dealing with such issues as leadership, delegation and communication. The interest in time management as a topic of attention in its own right has drawn together these other issues. The main factors affecting a person's use of time are set out in Figure 25.1 below.

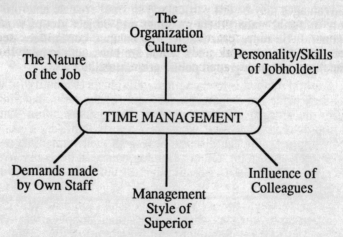

**Figure 25.1 Main Factors affecting Time Management**

These factors and the key issues arising from them form the subject of the rest of the chapter.

## KEY ISSUES IN THE USE OF TIME

3. The principal issues of time management can be grouped under three headings:

- those related to the nature of the job
- those related to the personality and attributes of the jobholder
- those related to the people who make up the jobholder's role-set (see Chapter 27).

## NATURE OF THE JOB

4.    The nature of a person's job is fundamental to the amount of control over time that is both desirable and necessary. For example, a person whose job involves regular contacts with others is always going to be under greater pressure from interruptions than someone whose work is of a solitary nature. Similarly, a person  who is employed in a new and developing job is more likely to suffer from conflicting priorities and unpredictable events than someone working in an established position, where predictability and routine are the order of the day.

5.    An important issue for any jobholder is the identification of the priorities in the job. In cases where Management by Objectives (see Chap. 18) or some form of target-setting is practised, then individuals will have had experience of identifying and working towards priorities, or key result areas, in the job. However, by far the great majority of managerial and professional employees do  not work under such systems, and are therefore unused to a  systematic approach to prioritising key tasks.

6.    A useful method is to encourage individuals to identify (a) the tasks they alone are responsible for, and (b) the tasks that either require the greatest effort, or produce the greatest return. Once individuals have identified what they see as their key tasks or responsibilities, they can discuss these with their immediate boss or with a job counsellor. Often a training course in the company of colleagues provides a useful stimulus to this form of diagnostic activity.

7.    It is not enough, however, just to consider job priorities. It is also important to consider what the individual jobholder has to do in order to fulfil them. Some jobs call for administrative skills and a sound knowledge of organization procedures, others demand

social skills and a sensitivity to people-needs, and yet others require technical and specialist knowledge and the ability to apply it. Individuals, therefore, need to examine the processes associated with their jobs.

8. A well-tried method of obtaining information about job processes is that of keeping a detailed time-diary, in which the individual records his or her work activities every day for a week or a month, for example. The simplest form is one listing the day in half-hour intervals alongside which are spaces for the jobholder to record what has happened, eg writing letters, conducting a meeting, travelling to a client, conducting an interview, answering the telephone etc. Jobholders are frequently surprised at how little time they have to themselves at work, as well as at the number of interruptions they accept.

## TYPICAL TIME-WASTERS AT WORK

9. Whilst a high level of interaction between people at work can normally be considered as a healthy phenomenon, there are nevertheless potential disadvantages for any one individual's personal effectiveness. These arise from the following:

- prolonged, or unnecessary, meetings with colleagues
- interruptions from own staff, colleagues or boss (however well-intentioned)
- idle conversations (in the sense of casual chit-chat)
- unnecessary memos and other paperwork

A further problem is that of time lost due to travelling between jobs. It is not easy to overcome such lost opportunities for effective working, but some ways will be discussed later.

## PERSONAL ATTRIBUTES OF THE JOBHOLDER

10. A person's ability to make best use of his time depends to a considerable extent on his personality and inclinations. For example, a naturally assertive person will be better equipped to deal with people who trespass on his time than someone who is naturally rather inoffensive. There are other important differences in personal attributes and styles, for example:

- some people work best early in the day, whilst others work best later in the day
- some people like to pace out their work effort, whilst others prefer to concentrate their efforts into short, intensive periods

- some people can only deal with one issue at a time, whereas others can juggle with several simultaneously
- some people are task-oriented whereas others are people-oriented
- some people like to delegate as much as possible, where others prefer to keep tasks to themselves
- some people are tidy and methodical, others are untidy and disorganized
- some individuals are more skilled or experienced than others

11. In the final analysis an individual will find that better use of time will probably come about by developing personal strengths and attempting to off-set weaknesses, in a word *self-discipline*.

## THE JOB CONTEXT

12. The context of a person's job consists of:
   a. the members of his role-set (boss, own staff, colleagues etc)
   b. the physical surroundings (office, location of others etc)
   c. the culture of the organization (the dominant values that prevail)

The implications of these three will be considered briefly.

13. The people who work alongside an individual are always an important influence on that person's use of time. An interfering boss, for example, can be very disrupting. By contrast a boss who is an effective delegator can be a positive source of help in identifying job priorities. Subordinates' abilities to work effectively on their own, rather than seeking advice from their manager all the time, can enable the latter to work on personal tasks without undue interruptions. Colleagues can be a frequent cause of wasted time, especially when they call into your office at a time when they themselves are less busy, or want a short break from what they are working on. Senior or experienced members of any group will find that they are regularly sought out by junior members wishing to clarify a point or discuss an immediate problem. All these activities have their benefits, but at the cost of any one individual's time.

14. Physical surroundings may help or hinder a person's efforts to make better use of his or her time. Clearly, if you do not have an office, then there are no real physical barriers that you can erect between you and all those who, however well intentioned, wish to interrupt your work. Those who do have an office of their own can always shut the door, even at the risk of a certain amount of

unpopularity. Whilst an 'open door' policy for staff communication is generally recommended, there are still occasions when it would be better to suspend this policy temporarily in the interests of personal work efficiency. The location of furniture and equipment can also affect the use of time. For example, if the photocopier and the computer terminal are on different floors to your office, or are at the opposite end of the building, then a good deal of time can be wasted walking to and from these machines. Currently, one of the most persuasive arguments for introducing computerised work-stations (see Chap. 30) is one of time-saving.

15. Another major physical influence on an individual's work pattern is that of travelling. The location of colleagues, customers and suppliers invariably means that an individual has to spend some time in travelling between appointments. This time can often be completely wasted, unless, for example, the individual travels by train or has a chauffeur-driven car, in which case it is possible to carry out work tasks whilst travelling.

16. The final aspect of the job context that we shall consider is the organization culture. Some cultures favour strict adherence to procedures and protocol, which discourages informal contacts and 'short cuts'. Others encourage an open access policy on all aspects of communications, which can be very stimulating but also very wasteful of individual time. Organizations that set great store by accuracy and quality are implicitly requiring their members to take more time over their work, compared with organizations who are always working to tight deadlines and thus have to risk the occasional error or inaccuracy. In yet other organizations, the speed with which decisions are reached is more important than the thoroughness of those decisions. Such an attitude clearly has considerable implications for an individual's personal work standards.

## IMPROVING THE USE OF TIME

17. There are several ways by which a manager may improve his use of time:
- personal planning
- target-setting
- negotiating with boss/clients/colleagues
- delegating tasks to own staff
- developing appropriate skills (faster reading/writing, assertiveness etc)

18. Personal planning implies developing personal priorities and the means for achieving them on the one hand. Whilst, on the other hand, it implies identifying time-wasting activities, considering how best to minimise them in the light of the job context, and devising methods for dealing with them in practice.

Clarifying work objectives and setting personal targets helps an individual to focus attention on the parts of the job that really matter. This process enables a manager to see more readily what ought to be delegated to someone else, what needs to be negotiated with a colleague or boss, and what priorities ought to be given to particular meetings and particular items of paperwork.

19. Useful skills that can be developed to enable individuals to make better use of their time include:

- delegation
- assertiveness
- faster reading
- report-writing
- handling meetings

## DELEGATION

20. The topic of delegation was looked at in general terms in Chapter 22. Here we are concerned with detailed aspects of the process. In delegating a task, a manager is to all intents and purposes sharing his workload with a subordinate. The extent of that sharing, especially in respect of the amount of authority granted to the subordinate, will depend on a number of factors, particularly on the level of confidence that exists between the two parties. The principal options open to the manager are as follows:

1. the subordinate is free to act and is not required to report back
2. action may be taken, but a report is required
3. the subordinate decides what action he would prefer, but consults with manager first (this implies the manager's right of veto)
4. the subordinate examines the problem/issue, outlines alternative solutions and makes recommendations
5. the subordinate examines the problem/issue, collects all the facts and presents them to manager for his decision

21. The delegation of tasks and responsibilities does not come easily to most people. One reason is that delegation takes time and effort, especially in the initial stages. As a result many managers

find it quicker to do the task themselves rather than delegate it. Another reason for not delegating work is because the manager concerned is worried about the risks involved. For example, can the subordinate be trusted to carry out the task properly? Managers who feel insecure in their role worry about delegation because they know that if anything goes wrong, they will be held accountable to their own superiors. What a manager delegates, and to whom, is his own responsibility, for delegation is not abdication, which is a refusal to accept responsibility.

22. Given the doubts many managers have about delegation, what steps can be taken to minimise the likelihood of failure on the part of the subordinate? A 'code of good practice' in delegation is likely to include the following points:

The manager should:

    a. set objectives to be achieved

    b. indicate the standards of performance expected

    c. allocate sufficient resources to the subordinate, especially by defining the level of authority granted for the purposes of the task (authority here means the power to act)

    d. establish a control mechanism in order to (i) check progress, and (ii) enable subordinate to raise any questions ordifficulties

    e. provide any training or counselling, as necessary

    f. ensure that the task is completed

23. The first step is to explain what is required of the employee concerned, both in terms of what is to be achieved and to what standard. Unless the person concerned is extremely inexperienced or the task truly warrants it, the manager should not normally explain in detail *how* the job should be done. It will be enough to give general guidance initially and then be available to assist if necessary, otherwise the subordinate loses an opportunity to learn from the experience. Part of the help that the manager must supply is to define the limits of the person's authority to commit the organization's resources (eg people, materials and money). Obviously, any authority delegated can only be within the authority of the manager himself. The next stage is for the manager to devise a simple control procedure for ensuring that progress is being made and that any difficulties are identified and dealt with. Part of this control procedure will embrace an opportunity for counselling or coaching the subordinate. In some cases special training may be required as part of the resourcing involved.

Finally, in order that the delegation is seen to be taken seriously, the manager should ensure that the task is completed, or the responsibility fulfilled, to an acceptable standard. If a task is delegated, but then forgotten by the manager, the credibility of the process comes into question.

## ASSERTIVENESS

24. Assertiveness can contribute to the better use of a person's time by enabling him to deal more effectively with interruptions. Turner (Developing Interpersonal Skills, 1983) defines assertion as 'the capacity to express our ideas, opinions or feelings openly and directly without putting down ourselves or others.'

Recently, attention has been given not only to identifying assertive rights, but also to training people in assertiveness. Assertive rights are based on the fundamental notion that each individual adult is the ultimate judge of his or her own behaviour. It implies taking personal responsibility for one's actions. Other rights include two which are particularly relevant to the effective use of time:

   a. the right to say 'no!'

   b. the right not to take responsibility for other people's problems

25. The right to say 'no' is difficult for most people to accept. They feel that they ought not to say 'no' because it is uncooperative, selfish etc. Assertiveness training attempts to emphasise the importance for individual rights of the capacity to say 'no' without feeling guilty about it, and points out that in saying 'no' we are rejecting the *request* not the person. Making better use of one's personal rights can enable a manager to fend off certain of the interruptions inflicted on him by others, and thus create more space for himself at work. Similar considerations apply to the right not to feel obliged to take responsibility for other people's problems. In this case the manager can learn by assertiveness training to improve his ability to tactfully, but firmly, pass back to colleagues, subordinates and even boss, problems which are the other person's responsibility.

## PERSONAL COMMUNICATIONS SKILLS

26. A manager's use of time can be made more productive if personal communication skills are improved. In paragraph 19 above, we mentioned three particular aspects: faster reading, report-writing and handling meetings. We shall look at these briefly in turn.

27. **Reading skills** – being selective in reading is probably as important as being able to read faster. Managers need to be able to identify:

- what is essential reading?
- what is of marginal use/interest?
- what is essential and urgent?
- what is essential but not immediate?

If a manager has to do a lot of reading in his job, then there are specific courses aimed at improving a person's speed in reading.

**Report-writing** – one of the key tasks of every manager is to present ideas, impressions and proposals in writing. A knowledge of the basic strategy involved in drawing up a report will help a manager to make better use of the time incurred.

**Handling meetings** – many managers find themselves at a meeting of one kind or another several times a day. To use the time spent on meetings more effectively a number of simple questions can be asked:

- is a meeting necessary to deal with this issue? (ie could a telephone call or a memo suffice?)
- how can we prepare for this meeting?
- how can we ensure that the meeting is going to be worthwhile to those attending?
- how long should the meeting last?
- who should be invited to attend?
- how will action points be captured and dealt with?

## CONCLUSION

28. The first step in improving one's personal use of time is to become aware that there is a problem, then it is possible to isolate the time-wasting activities, and finally to tackle them in a systematic way by improving the planning of daily activities and by improving communication and assertiveness skills to achieve results.

## SECTION SUMMARY – ORGANIZING

1. The five chapters in this Section have described key aspects of the process of organizing. This process was described mainly in terms of (a) organization structures, (b) delegation, (c) coping with organizational change, and (d) communication within organizations.

2.    Organization structures were looked at mainly from the point of view of the choices available to modern organizations. Key issues in this discussion were as follows:

a. **Specialization**. The advantages and disadvantages of different approaches to specialization, or the grouping of activities, were discussed. The principal options described were grouping by function, grouping by product, grouping by geographical location, grouping by division and grouping by means of a matrix structure.

b. **Centralization versus de-centralization**. This is concerned with the degree to which authority to act can be dispersed throughout an organization. Some functions, such as production and sales, are more easily de-centralized to advantage than others, such as planning and research and development. De-centralization helps to free senior managers from less important tasks, and speeds up decision-making. However, its main disadvantage is that it requires more controlling than a centralized system.

c. **The number of levels in an organization.** The profile of an organization can be flat or tall. Flat organizations have few authority levels and tend to be centralized with wide spans of control. Tall organizations have numerous authority levels, but tend to be de-centralized with narrow spans of control. The major factors determining the number of levels in an organization are: organization size; complexity or otherwise of production; and management style.

d. **Line and staff functions, or relationships**. The concepts of line and staff can be understood as I functions contributing to organization objectives (eg production and personnel), *or* relationships of authority (eg line relationships TELL and staff relationships SELL). It was argued that it is better to think of line and staff in terms of authority relationships. Line authority can be defined as direct authority over others, regardless of function. Thus specialist managers exercise line authority over their own staff just as much as so-called 'line' managers over theirs. Staff authority can be a misleading term, since it encompasses functional authority as well as the idea of service. A service relationship is only an advisory, or selling, relationship. A functional relationship, however, has the power to prescribe to other groups what shall be done *in respect of its specialist function.*

e. **Concepts of Authority, Responsibility and Power.** Authority can be defined as legitimate power, which can be delegated to others. Responsibility can be defined as the obligation to perform certain functions on behalf of the organization, and this obligation cannot be delegated. Power can be defined as the ability to implement actions, regardless of authority and responsibility.

3. Delegation was considered in terms of managing people, as opposed to diffusing authority throughout an organization structure. It can be defined as the process by which an individual manager, or supervisor, transfers part of his legitimate authority to a subordinate, but without relinquishing the ultimate responsibility entrusted to him by his own superior. Delegation is necessary to provide employees with sufficient authority, or power to act, to enable them to fulfill their responsibilities. The amount of authority delegated has to be prescribed in some way, so that subordinates know the limits of their authority. Delegation is primarily a matter of practicalities ie it shares out the decision-making process amongst managerial and supervisory staff, enabling decisions to be made more swiftly and more flexibly. However, it is also a matter of ideals – delegation is regarded by many as being 'a good thing' for people at work.

4. An aspect of delegation, which has received a great deal of interest, is the span of control, or the number of subordinates reporting directly to one superior. There has been considerable speculation about the optimum number of subordinates that can be effectively supervised by any one individual. A French- man, V.A. Graicunas, produced in the 1930's a formula claiming to show the dramatic increase in possible relationships as the number of persons supervised exceeded three. The idea of an optimum span of control was a key feature in the principles advocated by the classical theorists of management, such as L.F. Urwick, who personally suggested that no manager's span should exceed five or six, where their work was interlocked. Wide spans of control are a feature of flat organizations, and narrow spans are to be found in tall organizations.

5. Principal factors affecting the size of the span of control include the abilities of the managers, the level of skills and experience of the employees and the relative complexity of the work. An example of a practical attempt to measure the span of control in the light of such factors was given, based on an experiment by the Lockheed Company of the USA in the 1960's.

6.   The issue of organizational change, utilizing Organization Development, was dealt with in Chapter 23. Organization Development (OD) can be defined as 'a strategy for improving organizational effectiveness by means of behavioural science approaches, involving the application of diagnostic and problem-solving skills by an external consultant in collaboration with the management of the organization.' OD is:–

a.   an organization-wide process.

b.   a process utilizing behavioural science techniques.

c.   a process involving the intervention of an external third party, or 'change agent', experienced in the application of behavioural science techniques.

d.   a process aimed primarily at improving organizational effectiveness rather than just changing people's behaviour.

7.   The key Stages of an OD programme are as follows:

a.   Preliminary Stage – discussion of aims and implications of programme and role of third party.

b.   Analysis & Diagnosis – obtaining and analysing data to identify and clarify problems.

c.   Agreement about Aims – management and third party agree on aims and objectives of programme.

d.   Action Planning – planning the sequence of activities designed to improve the organization in the light of problems diagnosed.

e.   Evaluation and Review – evaluating and reviewing progress.

f.   Revised Aims and Plans – resulting from a major review, new plans may be required.

8.   The role of the third party is important. To be a change agent requires particular qualities and abilities. These include the ability to listen diagnostically, to establish and maintain comfortable relationships with people, and to be aware of personal strengths and weaknesses. It is also important for the change agent to accept underlying OD values, such as the need for trust, openness and teamwork in organizations.

9.   Typical OD activities fall under three main headings:

a.   Behaviour-changing activities – coaching, counselling, team-building etc.

b.   Structural changes – role analysis, job re-design etc.

c.   Problem-analysis – diagnostic questionnaires, process consultation etc.

Of the three groupings, the one concerned with problem-analysis is the most frequently utilized, as this provides much of the data on which further decisions can be made about the rest of the programme.

10. The primary benefits of Organization Development programmes are: they enable organizations to adapt better to change, they help to create structures that facilitate employee cooperation as well as the achievement of tasks, and they contribute to the better use of management, both as individuals and as teams.

11. Chapter 24 dealt with the topic of formal communication in organizations and referred to communication flows, to the media of communication, to communication barriers and to the work and role of committees in organizations. Communication flows may be vertical or lateral. Vertical flows are employed to pass management information downwards and employee views upwards. Lateral flows are employed for communication across internal boundaries. The media of communication can be grouped according to whether they are written or oral. Written methods include memos, letters and reports. In comparison with the spoken word, these methods are more permanent and less liable to misinterpretation, but take more time to put into effect. Oral methods include meetings and telephone conversations. These methods may lack the considered nature of written methods, but are more immediate and have the advantage of verbal and non-verbal feedback.

12. The barriers to communication are mainly those put up by people themselves as a result of personal bias, status differences, lack of trust and fear, for example. Some barriers are created by the lack of adequate machinery for communication, and a number of typical solutions, such as briefing groups and joint consultative committees, have been attempted to overcome these.

13. Finally, key aspects of committees were described. Committees are formal groups, having a defined leadership (chairman) and rules of conduct. The output of committees is slow, but thorough, in comparison with other, less formal approaches to decision-making and problem-solving. Nevertheless, committees enable a wider and more representative participation in decision-making, and are able to handle a larger volume of work than individuals or very small groups.

14. Chapter 25 concluded this Section by considering key aspects of *personal* organization, or 'managing time'. In organizing his own time an individual needs to be aware of:–

a. his job priorities
b. time-wasting activities
c. his personal work rhythms
d. the need for proper delegation
e. the need to improve personal communication skills.

## QUESTIONS FOR DISCUSSION/HOMEWORK

*1.    A national, single-product manufacturing company is about to take over a smaller, but more diversified, rival, which has one third of its productive capacity overseas Advise the managing director of the new group about the alternative organization structures which could best serve the company's increased size and scope. State the pros and cons of each alternative.*

*2.    In what ways are line and functional authority similar, and in what ways are they different? What is the basic difference between line and functional authority and so-called staff authority? Give examples of each of the different kinds of authority.*

*3.    What differences would you expect to find in the spans of control in the following situations:*

*a    routine mass-production process?*

*b.    central research department of an electronics company?*

*and   c.    large tax and financial planning consultancy?*

*4.    Taking an overall view of Organization Development, how would you describe its salient features to the top management team of either a commercial enterprise, or a public sector undertaking?*

*5.    What are the most frequent barriers to communication, and how can they be overcome?*

*6.    How would you describe the benefits of more effective time-management for persons in management positions?*

## EXAMINATION QUESTIONS – ORGANIZING

*The subject-matter of this Section is extremely popular with examiners in most of the professional examinations. The following examples are very typical of the questions asked. Outline answers may be found at Appendix 2.*

*EQ 19   Describe the phases of a typical Organization Development programme.              (ICMA OMM)*

*EQ 20    What would you expect to be the results of a mismatch between delegated authority and responsibility?*

*(ACCA Business Mgt.)*

**EQ 21**   What do you understand by the phrase 'matrix organization'? In what kinds of organizations and situations would you expect matrix organization to apply? Give reasons for your answer.                              *(ICSA MPP)*

**EQ 22**   What factors would influence your decision to delegate work to a subordinate? What are the major barriers to delegation?

*(IOB NOM)*

# LEADERSHIP AND GROUPS

The crux of every management job lies in the job-holder's capacity to obtain the commitment of people to the objectives of the organization, which is another way of saying 'to exercise appropriate leadership'. Leadership is a concept which has fascinated Man for centuries, but only in recent years has any kind of *theory* of leadership emerged. The following chapter (Chapter 26) describes and discusses some of the major issues associated with leadership in the context of work. Leadership is a function of groups and their behaviour, and Chapter 27 examines key aspects of formal and informal groups.

# 26

# LEADERSHIP: THEORY AND PRACTICE

## INTRODUCTION

1.   This chapter describes and comments on a number of the theoretical and practical aspects of leadership in the work situation. A review of the main theories of leadership is followed by a discussion of the alternative styles of leadership available, in practice, to a person in a management or supervisory position.

2.   Before attempting a working definition of 'leadership', it would be appropriate to reflect briefly on the various types of leader which have been identified, and to consider some of the practical difficulties arising from these. The most important types of leader are as follows:

a. the **Charismatic** leader, whose influence springs mainly from personality eg Napoleon, Hitler, Churchill, Billy Graham and others. The difficulty with charismatic leadership is that few people possess the exceptional qualities required to transform all around them into willing followers! Another issue is that personal qualities, or traits, of leadership cannot be acquired by training, they can only be modified by it.

b. the **Traditional** leader, whose position is assured by birth eg kings, queens and tribal chieftains. This is another category to which few people can aspire. Except in the small family business, there are few opportunities for traditional leadership at work.

c. the **Situational** leader, whose influence can only be effective by being in the right place at the right time eg the butler in J.M. Barrie's 'The Admirable Crichton'. This kind of leadership is too temporary in nature to be of much value in a business. What is looked for is someone who is capable of assuming a leadership role in a variety of situations over a period of time.

d. the **Appointed** leader, whose influence arises directly out of his position eg most managers and supervisors. This is the bureaucratic type of leadership, where legitimate power springs from the nature and scope of the position within the hierarchy. The problem here is that, although the powers of

214

the *position* may be defined, the job-holder may not be able to implement them because of weak personality, lack of adequate training or other factors.

e. the **Functional** leader, who secures his leadership position by what he does, rather than by what he is. In other words, a functional leader adapts his behaviour to meet the competing needs of his situation. This particular type will be looked at more closely later on in the chapter.

3. Leadership, then, is something more than just personality or accident or appointment. It is intimately linked with *behaviour*. It is essentially a human process at work in organizations. As a working definition, leadership can be described as a dynamic process in a group whereby one individual influences the others to contribute voluntarily to the achievement of group tasks in a given situation.' There are several points which can be made about this definition. *Firstly*, leadership is a dynamic process, not a static one. This implies that a *range* of leadership styles is preferable to any one 'best style'. *Secondly*, the role of the leader is to direct the group towards group goals. In an informal, or unofficial, group these roles will have been agreed by the group itself; in a formal group, the goals will have been set mainly, if not exclusively, by senior managers outside the group. *Thirdly*, the style of leadership and the reactions of the group will be determined considerably by the situation concerned (the task, external pressures etc).

4. The basic elements of the above definition of leadership are four in number as illustrated in Figure 26.1 .

| LEADER<br>● Skills<br>● Knowledge<br>● Personality | TASKS/GOALS |
|---|---|
| SUBORDINATES<br>● Skills<br>● Motivation | ENVIRONMENT/<br>SITUATION |

**Figure 26.1. The Key Leadership Variables**

The key variables are:
  (1)   the leader,
  (2)   tasks/goals,
  (3)   the group members (subordinates), and
  (4)   the environment/ situation.

Taken together these variables form the total leadership situation, and the art of leadership is to find the best balance between them in the light of the total situation.

## THEORIES OF LEADERSHIP

5.    Ideas about leadership in management range from the 'ideal' approaches of the Scientific Managers and the Human Relations School to the pragmatic, or adaptive, approaches of the Contingency theorists. The theories which have been put forward are generally classified under 'Trait theories', 'Style theories' and 'Contingency theories'. These will be looked at in turn.

6.    **Trait Theories**. As we saw earlier in the Manual, in the discussion of classical management ideas, the debate was usually led by practising managers who were strong characters in their own right. Part of their success was undoubtedly due to personal qualities, and it is perhaps not surprising that the earliest studies that were undertaken into leadership focussed their attention on the *qualities* required for effective leaders. Handy (Understanding Organizations, 1976) mentions that by 1950 over 100 studies of this kind had been undertaken, but that the number of common traits or characteristics identified by the researchers was only 5% of the total! It has proved an impossible task to identify the particular traits or characteristics that separate leaders from non-leaders. Of those traits which do appear more frequently, intelligence, energy and resourcefulness are perhaps the most representative.

7.    **Style Theories**. The interest in the human factor at work which was stimulated by the researchers of Human Relations, and taken up by the social psychologists who followed them, led logically to an interest in leadership as an aspect of *behaviour* at work, rather than of personal characteristics Since the 1950's, in particular, several theories about leadership, or management, style have been put forward. These have tended to be expressed in terms of authoritarian versus democratic styles, or people-orientation versus task orientation. In some cases, despite acknowledged inconsistencies in the theories themselves, style theories have led

to quite useful devices for improving training for leadership. A selection of the best-known style theories is discussed below.

8.  **Authoritarian-Democratic**. Three examples of this approach to management style are as follows:

  a.  D. McGregor's Theory X manager – tough, autocratic and supporting tight controls with punishment-reward systems – the authoritarian. The contrasting style is that of the Theory Y manager - benevolent, participative and believing in self-controls – the democrat. These styles flow from the assumptions about people that are the original basis of Theory X and Theory Y (see Chapter 9.7 et seq.)

  b.  Rensis Likert's four management systems:

     System 1   the exploitive-authoritative system, which is the epitome of the authoritarian style.

     System 2   the benevolent-authoritative system, which is basically a paternalistic style.

     System 3   the consultative system, which moves towards greater democracy and teamwork.

     System 4   the participative-group system, which is the ultimate democratic style.

  Likert's ideas were discussed in Chapter 9.20.

  c.  Tannenbaum and Schmidt's model of a continuum of leadership styles, ranging from authoritarian behaviour at one end to democratic behaviour at the other, as illustrated in Figure 26.2 below

9.    The implication behind the three approaches is that managers have a basic choice between being either authoritarian or democratic, and that the best style – the ideal – is a democratic one. In practice, the either/or choice proposed by the theorists may be somewhat artificial. Much will depend on the other elements of the leadership situation, as in Figure 26.1 above. In some circumstances an authoritarian style could be more effective than a democratic style, and vice versa. The suggestion that a democratic style is generally preferable to an authoritarian one has been criticised on the grounds that whilst this may apply to current trends in Western industrialised nations, it need not apply at all in other cultures. The main weakness of these approaches is that they place too much emphasis on the *leader's* behaviour to the exclusion of the other elements or variables of leadership.

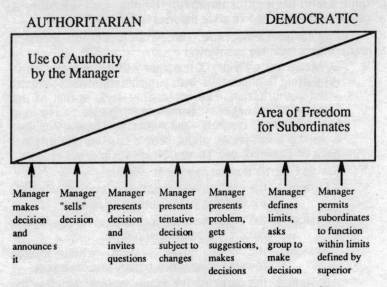

AUTHORITARIAN                                    DEMOCRATIC

Use of Authority
by the Manager

Area of Freedom
for Subordinates

| Manager makes decision and announces it | Manager "sells" decision | Manager presents decision and invites questions | Manager presents tentative decision subject to changes | Manager presents problem, gets suggestions, makes decisions | Manager defines limits, asks group to make decision | Manager permits subordinates to function within limits defined by superior |

**Figure 26.2  A continuum of leadership styles**

(adapted from Tannenbaum and Schmidt, Harvard Business Review, 1957)

10.  People-Task Orientations. Examples of approaches utilising *two* of the leadership variables – subordinates and tasks – are as follows:

a. **The Michigan Studies** – these studies, which were first reported in 1950, analysed a number of variables between managers of high-productivity groups and managers of low-productivity groups. The object was to see if any significant differences could be identified, thus providing some clues to leadership behaviour. In many respects (age, marital status etc) there were no such differences between the two groups. However, one significant difference was noticed, and this was that the supervisors in charge of the high-producing groups tended to be employee-orientated while their opposite numbers in the low-producing groups tended, ironically, to be production-centred. The employee-orientated supervisors paid more attention to relationships at work, exercised less direct supervision and encouraged employee participation in decision-making. Production-orientated supervisors were more directive and more concerned with task needs than people needs. The two different orientations appeared to represent different ends of the same continuum, as shown in Figure 26.3.

| High-producing groups | Low-producing groups |
|---|---|
| Employee-centred | Production-centred |

**Figure 26.3. The Michigan continuum.**

b. **The Ohio Studies** – these studies were conducted during the 1950's. Like the Michigan studies shortly before, they were concerned to describe leadership behaviour. The basis of the initial research was a Leader Behaviour Description Questionnaire of some 150 items. When the responses to this questionnaire were analysed two distinct groupings of behaviour emerged. These were defined as 'Consideration' and 'Initiating Structure'. Consideration described behaviour that was essentially relationships-orientated or considerate of employees feelings. Initiating structure referred to behaviour concerned with the organization of the work processes, including communication channels, allocating tasks etc. Unlike in the Michigan studies, the Ohio team's conclusion was that the two dimensions of Consideration and Initiating Structures were *separate dimensions*. It was shown to be possible for a supervisor to score high on both dimensions. This finding was developed by Robert Blake and Jane Mouton in their concept of the Managerial Grid (see Chapter 46).

c. **The 3-D Theory** – this approach, by Professor Reddin of New Brunswick University, Canada, takes the Blake-type grid a stage further and introduces a three-dimensional perspective. This adds considerably to the flexibility of leadership styles by including the factor of effectiveness in the dimensions. Reddin's Grid, as shown below, is able to consider aspects of the *situation* in which leadership is exercised, as well accounting for the concern for people (Relationship Orientated – RO) and the concern for production (Task Orientated – TO). The basic Grid together with the eight styles which spring from it are as follows:

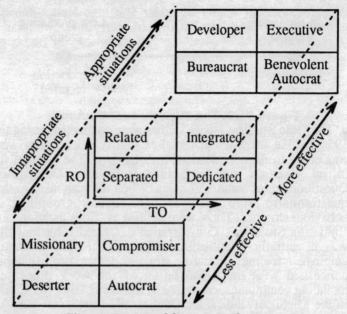

**Figure 26.4 Reddin's 3-D Theory**

Reddin describes the central grid as the set of basic styles available in the light of the Relationship and Task orientations. So, for example, a manager who is high on people and low on task has a *basic* style that is Related. However each basic style has two alternative *management* styles arising from it, depending on whether the style is appropriate to the leadership situation or not. Appropriate leadership tends to be more effective ie achieves the output requirements of that particular managerial job. Thus, a Related style that is used appropriately is called Developer, whilst an inappropriate style is called Missionary. The concept of effectiveness, added to the dimensions of relationships and task orientations, makes up the three dimensional perspective. Unlike the Blake Grid, which has only one effective style (9,9), the Reddin Grid has four effective styles. Like the Blake Grid, however, Reddin's ideas have not been validated by research, and whilst useful for the purposes of management development, are not an authoritative answer to the question of what is effective leadership.

d. **The Harvard Studies** – as a result of studying small-group behaviour, Hanard researchers identified two distinct groups of leaders: task leaders and socioemotional leaders, who were mutually exclusive. A person could not be a task leader and a socioemotional leader as well. The task leader showed a concern for the structuring of activities, whereas the socioemotional leader showed concern for supportive relationships. These two types of leader corresponded closely to the types defined by the Ohio studies ie Initiating Structure and Consideration, but, unlike those studies, the Harvard results suggested that the two dimensions were mutually exclusive.

## CONTINGENCY APPROACHES

11. Functional, or Action-centred Leadership. This concept of leadership was developed in the United Kingdom by Professor John Adair. It is based on the theory that leadership is more a question of appropriate behaviour than of personality or of being in the right place at the right time. Adair's model of leadership (Figure 26.5) incorporates the concern for task and concern for people that has featured in all the theories which we have just mentioned. The functional model, however, distinguishes the concern for *individuals* from the concern for *groups*, and stresses that effective leadership lies in what the leader *does* to meet the needs of task, group and individuals. This takes the functional model nearer to the contingency approaches of modern theorists, whose concern is with the variety of factors – task, people and situation – which have a direct bearing on leadership and leadership styles.

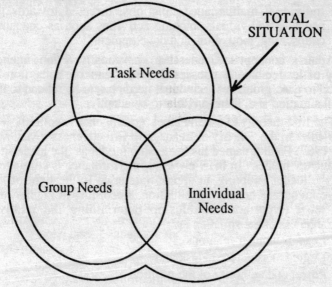

**Figure 26.5 Functional model of leadership**

12.  The key features of the functional model can be summarised
as follows:

   a.  Task, Group and Individual Needs are fulfilled in the
context of a total leadership situation. The circumstances of
each situation affect the priority which attaches to each area
of needs. An effective leader is one who is aware of these
priorities and who can act in accordance with them.  For
example, in a situation of great urgency, task needs must
predominate over group and individual needs. In another
situation, such as the re-building of a football team, it is
group needs which must come first, then individual needs
with task needs last. The model thus encourages a flexible
style of leadership, which may be relatively task-orientated
*or* group-orientated *or* individual-orientated, depending on
circumstances.

   b.  Task functions, directed towards task needs, include
activities such as the setting of objectives, the planning of
tasks, the allocation of responsibilities and the setting of
appropriate standards of performance.

   c.  Group maintenance functions, directed towards group
needs, include activities such as team-building and
motivation, communication, discipline, and acting as group
representative to others outside the boundaries of the unit.

   d.  Individual maintenance functions, directed towards the
needs of individuals, include activities such as coaching,
counselling, motivation and development.

13.  Adair's concept of leadership is basically a contingency
theory of leadership. It stresses that the leader's behaviour in
relation to task, group and individual needs has to be related to the
overall situation and, therefore, has to be adaptive.

14.  The first theorist to use the label 'contingency' explicitly was
F.E. Fiedler in the 'Theory of Leadership Effectiveness' (McGraw
- Hill 1967) Fiedler named his leadership model as 'the leadership
contingency model'. In his view group performance is contingent
upon the leader adopting an appropriate style in the light of the
relative favourableness of the situation. According to Fiedler, the
three most important variables in determining the relative
favourableness of the situation are:

   a.  Leader-member relations
   b.  Degree of structure in task and
   c.  Power and authority of the position

These three situational variables can produce eight possible combinations of situation, of which the most favourable to the leader is when (1) he has good leader-member relations, (2) the task is highly structured, and (3) he has a powerful position. By comparison, the least favourable conditions are when (1) he is disliked, (2) the task is relatively unstructured and (3) he has little position power.

15. On the topic of leadership style, Fiedler sees the two main choices as between 'relationship-motivated' and 'task- motivated'. Applying these styles to the range of situations possible, Fiedler found that task-motivated leaders tended to perform most effectively in situations which were either very favourable or very unfavourable. Relationship-motivated leaders tended to perform most effectively in situations that were intermediate in terms of favourableness. Fiedler's theory is another step towards the development of a comprehensive contingency theory of leadership. It is probably at its weakest on the issue of leadership style, but its greatest value lies in its attempt to distinguish and evaluate the key situational variables that influence the leader's role.

## SUMMARY

16. The principal leadership types to have been identified are:

| *Type* | *Based on:* |
|---|---|
| • Charismatic leadership | Personality |
| • Traditional leadership | Birth |
| • Situational leadership | The right place at the right time |
| • Appointed leader | Bureaucratic authority |
| • Functional leadership | Leader behaviour |

17. Leadership can be described as 'a dynamic process in a group whereby one individual influences the others to contribute voluntarily to the achievement of group tasks in a given situation.' The basic elements in the leadership equation are:
  • The leader (personality, skills etc)
  • The tasks/goals of the group
  • The subordinates (skills, motivation etc)
  • The environment/situation

18. Theories about leadership can be placed into three major categories as follows:

| Theory Category | Based on: |
|---|---|
| • Trait theories | Personal characteristics of leader |
| • Style theories | Leader behaviour |
| • Contingency theories | Adaptive leader behaviour in light of situation |

19. A comparative summary of the Style theories and Contingency theories referred to in this chapter is shown in Figure 26.6.

| Source | Title (if any) | Characteristics | Dimensions |
|---|---|---|---|
| D McGregor | Theory X/ Theory Y | authoritarian versus democratic | 'either/or' |
| R Likert | Systems 1-4 | authoritarian versus democratic | 'either/or' |
| Tannenbaum & Schmidt | Leadership Continuum | authoritarian versus democratic | 'either/or' |
| Michigan Studies | – | employee-centred v production-centred | 'either/or' |
| Ohio Studies | – | 'consideration' and 'initiating structure' | both |
| Blake & Mouton | Managerial Grid | 'concern for people' and 'concern for production' | both |
| W Reddin | 3-D Theory | relationships and task orientations; effectiveness | all three |
| Harvard Studies | – | 'task leaders' vs 'socioemotional leaders' | 'either/or' |
| J Adair | Functional Theory | task, group and individual needs; adaptive behaviour | multiple |
| F E Fiedler | Theory of Leadership Effectiveness | 'favourableness of the situation'; adaptive behaviour | multiple |

**Figure 26.6 Summary of Leadership Theories**

# 27
# GROUPS AT WORK

## INTRODUCTION

1.    The study of groups in work situations has been an important activity of behavioural scientists ever since the pioneering work of the Hawthorne Researchers over fifty years ago. The outcome of numerous studies into different aspects of the behaviour of groups is a considerable store of useful and practicable knowledge about the working of groups. Typical areas of research have included the study of group effectiveness, inter-group competition, and group cohesiveness.

2.    The most important factors in the behaviour of groups are as indicated in Figure 27.1 below.

**Figure 27.1 Key Factors in Group Behaviour**

Previous chapters have dealt with various aspects of leadership, tasks and environment, and whilst these factors cannot be ignored, this chapter focuses attention on the other factors such as group norms, group cohesiveness and roles within groups. It concludes with a summary of recent research into teams and team building.

3.    Groups at work are formed as a direct consequence of an organization's need to differentiate itself. Differentiation, or specialization, involves not only the breaking down of the organization into functions, but also the formation of groups to support the tasks assigned to those functions. A group is basically a collection of individuals, contributing to some common aim under the direction of a leader, and who share a sense of common identity. Thus, a group is more than an aimless crowd of people waiting in an airport lounge or at a bus-stop. A group has some central purpose, temporary or permanent, and a degree of self-awareness as a group. In the work situation, most tasks are in fact undertaken by groups and teams, rather than by individuals. Groups are also widely used for solving problems, creating new ideas, making decisions and coordinating tasks.

These group functions are what the organization itself needs to fulfil its purpose. However, individuals themselves need groups. Groups provide stimulus, protection, assistance and other social and psychological requirements. Groups, therefore, can work in the interests of organizations as a whole as well as in the interests of individual members.

4.    One of the earliest distinctions to be made between groups (arising from the Hawthorne investigations) was between formal and informal groups. Formal groups were those set up by the management of an organization to undertake duties in the pursuit of organization goals. Some writers have described formal groups as official groups, to avoid the confusion that can arise when describing groups operating in an informally structured organization (eg an organic type of organization). Such groups may be informal in the sense that they have few rules, enjoy participative leadership and have flexible roles. Nevertheless they are completely official. What is meant by informal organizations are those groupings which the employees themselves have developed in accordance with their own needs. These, of course, are unofficial. Every organization has these unofficial groups, and research has shown how important they are for organizational effectiveness.

## GROUP NORMS & GROUP COHESIVENESS

5.    A useful way of looking at the development of groups was made by B. Tuckman in 1965. He saw groups as moving through four key stages of development as follows.

Stage 1 – Forming. Finding out about the task, rules and methods; acquiring information and resources; relying on the leader.

Stage 2 – Storming. Internal conflict develops; members resist the task at the emotional level.

Stage 3 – Norming. Conflict is settled, cooperation develops; views are exchanged and new standards (norms) developed.

Stage 4 – Performing. Teamwork is achieved, roles are flexible; solutions are found and implemented.

6.    Group norms can be seen to develop at Stage 3 in the above analysis. Norms, in this context, are common standards of social and work behaviour which are expected of individuals in the group. Once such norms have been developed, there are strong pressures on people to conform to them. Norms are influenced by organizational factors such as policies, management style of superiors, and rules and procedures. They are also influenced by individual employees, whose standards may or may not be in line with those of the official organization. For example, a group norm for the young men in an engineering workshop could be to follow a fashion of wearing long hair. This could conflict with organizational norms concerning the safety of employees in the workplace. Another example of a conflict between official and unofficial group norms can be drawn from a situation where a group itself decides to operate a certain level of output over a given time, regardless of targets set by the management in their search for increased efficiency and productivity. The ideal situation, from an organization's point of view, is attained when the *unofficial* norms of the group are in harmony with the *official* norms of the organization. There is no doubt that part of the leadership role of a manager is to secure this harmony in his own section.

7.    Tuckman's analysis of group development can be compared with that of Woodcock (1979), who has made a particular study of teams and their development. Woodcock also sees a four-stage sequence of development as follows:

| 1. The Undeveloped Team – | Feelings are avoided, objectives are uncertain, the leader takes most of the decisions. |
|---|---|
| 2. The Experimenting Team – | Issues are faced more openly, listening takes place, the group may become temporarily introspective. |
| 3. The Consolidating Team – | Personal interaction is established on a cooperative basis, the task is clarified, objectives agreed and tentative procedures implemented. |
| 4. The Mature Team – | Feelings are open, a wide range of options considered, working methods are methodical, leadership style is contributory, individuals are flexible and the group recognises its responsibility to the rest of the organization. |

8.   The key point made by these analyses of team or group development is that effectiveness (see below) is an outcome which develops over time, as the group begin to understand what is required of them and how they can utilise the knowledge, skills and attributes of the individual members in fulfilling group and individual goals.   On the way to achieving effectiveness groups will undoubtedly face uncertainty, if not conflict, but these processes have to be seen as necessary costs of achieving both harmony and purposeful behaviour.

9.   Group cohesiveness refers to the ability of the group members to stick together. It also applies to the ability of a group to attract new members. A very cohesive group will demonstrate strong loyalty to its individual members and strong adherence to its established norms. Individuals who cannot accept these norms are cast out from the protection of the group. The sending of individuals 'to Coventry' as a result of some dispute within the group is an example of this behaviour. As Tuckman's analysis shows, cohesiveness develops over time. A newly-formed group has little cohesiveness.

10.   There are several factors which can help cohesiveness to develop in a group. These include the following:

a. similarity of work
b. physical proximity in the workplace
c. the work-flow system
d. structure of tasks
e. group size (smaller rather than larger)
f. threats from outside
g. the prospect of rewards
h. leadership style of the manager
i. common social factors (age, race, social status etc)

In general, the reasons why people do develop into closely knit groups are threefold: because of those things they have in common, because of pressures from outside the group, and because of their need to fulfill their social and affiliation needs.

## GROUP EFFECTIVENESS

11. Group effectiveness has to be considered in at least two dimensions – effectiveness in terms of task accomplishment, and effectiveness in terms of the satisfaction of group members. Clearly, the official organization-view of effectiveness is more concerned with output, efficiency and other benefits, than with satisfying the needs of individuals. By comparison, an individual's view of effectiveness is more concerned with personal success in his role and personal satisfaction from being a member of a team. Looking at the issue in ideal terms, effectiveness is achieved when the needs and expectations of the organization are one and the same as those of individuals.

12. In his classic work, 'The Human Side of Enterprise' (1960), Douglas McGregor provided a perceptive account of the differences between effective and ineffective groups. A summary of the most important features he noted appears below:

| Effective groups | Ineffective groups |
|---|---|
| 1. Informal, relaxed atmosphere. | 1. Bored or tense atmosphere. |
| 2. Much relevant discussion with high degree of participation. | 2. Discussion dominated by one or two people, and often irrelevant. |
| 3. Group task or objective clearly understood, and commitment to it obtained. | 3. No clear common objective. |
| 4. Members listen to each other. | 4. Members tend not to listen to each other. |

| Effective groups | Ineffective groups |
|---|---|
| 5. Conflict is not avoided, but brought into the open and dealt with constructively. | 5. Conflict is either avoided or is allowed to develop into open warfare. |
| 6. Most decisions are reached by general consensus with a minimum of formal voting. | 6. Simple majorities are seen as sufficient basis for group decisions, which the minority have to accept. |
| 7. Ideas are expressed freely and openly. | 7. Personal feelings are kept hidden and criticism is embarrassing. |
| 8. Leadership is not always with the chairman, but tends to be shared as appropriate. | 8. Leadership is provided by chairman. |
| 9. The group examines its own progress and behaviour. | 9. The group avoids any discussion about its own behaviour. |

McGregor's view of effective groups corresponds to Tuckman's Stages 3 and 4 ie Norming and Performing. The features of ineffective groups are closer to Tuckman's Stage 2 ie Storming. A difference between McGregor and Tuckman seems to be that the former sees some groups as fixed in their poor behaviour, whereas the latter implies that groups tend to move out of the ineffective stages into more effective behaviour.

13. The major influences on group effectiveness can be broken down into two main categories:

    a. Immediate constraints eg group size, nature of task, skills of members, and environmental factors.

    b. Group motivation and interaction.

The basic difference between the two categories is that (a) represents *things that cannot be changed in the short-term*, and that (b) represents *behaviour that (potentially) can be changed in the short-term*. Let us now look at key points in each of these categories.

14. Immediate constraints:

    a. Group size – small groups tend to be more cohesive than larger groups; small groups tend to encourage full participation; large groups contain greater diversity of talent.

b. Nature of task – in work-groups, the production system, including the type of technology used, has a major effect on groups eg high-technology plant often disperses employees into isolated couples incapable of forming satisfactory groups. Where group tasks are concerned with problem-solving, decision-making or creative thinking, different member talents may be required along with a variety of leadership styles. A further aspect of task is the time factor ie urgency tends to force groups to be task and action orientated.

c. Membership – the personalities concerned, the variety of knowledge and skills available cannot be changed over-night. A knowledgeable group, skilled at group working, are much more likely to succeed in their tasks, than an inexperienced group. Equally a group with a wider range of talents in its midst tends to be more effective than a group with a narrow range of talents.

d. Environmental factors – these include physical factors, such as working proximity, plant or office layout ie In general, close proximity aids group identity and loyalty, and distance reduces them. Other environmental issues include the traditions of the organization and leadership styles. Formal organizations tend to adopt formal group practices. Autocratic leadership styles prefer group activities to be directed. More participative styles prefer greater sharing in groups.

The important point about these immediate constraint is that they establish the scenario for the operation of the group. If the expectations and behaviour of the members match this scenario, then the group will tend to perform very effectively. By contrast, if there is a considerable mis-match, the chances of the group succeeding in its objectives will be slight.

15. Group motivation and interaction:

a. Group motivation – the level of motivation in the group will be a decisive factor in effectiveness. High motivation can result from members' perception of the task, and their role in it, as being of importance. Standards of performance are essential to motivation, together with adequate and are essential to motivation, together with adequate and timely feedback of results. Individuals also need to feel satisfied with membership of the group. Where these features are absent, motivation will tend to be low.

    b.  Group interaction – this depends mainly on factors such as leadership, individual and group motivation, and appropriate rules and procedures. As we saw in the previous chapter on Leadership, the key to success in leadership is to obtain the best 'mix' of attention to task and attention to people, taking the total situation into account. The ability of the leader in a group to obtain the commitment of his team to achieving the task (team spirit) will result in a high degree of collaboration. Where interaction is high people tend to be more open, and more comfortable with the pursuit of the task. All group need some modus operandi. This might consist of a few simple rules and procedure to control decision-making and conflict, for example. Alternatively, as in formal committees quite complex procedures may apply in order to encourage or control interaction.

The items under this category are essentially about actual behaviour in a group. This behaviour is part of a dynamic, or constantly changing process within the group, which can be influenced by individuals in response to issues that have occurred whilst undertaking the task. Thus, even where the immediate constraints impose tight restrictions on behaviour the group can still be effective if they can be motivated to work together to achieve their objectives.

## GROUP BEHAVIOUR & GROUP ROLES

16.  An area of considerable interest to behavioural scientists for many years has been the process of interaction within groups. This area of study was first opened up by Professor Kurt Lewin in the United States in the mid 1940's with the use of so-called 'T-groups' as a device for the study of inter-personal relations within groups. The T-group approach is based on unstructured, leader-less groups whose 'task' is to study their own behaviour and provide feedback to individual group members. The emphasis in such groups is on the 'here and now' situation and the thoughts and feelings generated by it. Each group is aided by a tutor or consultant, whose task it is to help the group with the feedback aspects. As a basis for developing information about the working of groups, the T-group method has been immensely useful. As a practical training method, however, the approach has proved less than popular on account of the threats posed to individuals by the exposure of their beliefs, attitudes and feelings to people with whom they have to work.

17.  Coverdale training is another approach aimed at throwing light on the behaviour of group members. The name is derived from the author of this approach, which is based on examining group processes during the progress of a series of practical tasks. Unlike T-groups, Coverdale exercises are structured events. Having discussed questions of how the initial task was planned and organized and how people felt about it, the experience is utilised to improve task effectiveness and member satisfaction for the next exercise, and so on until the series of tasks is completed. By using practical tasks as a vehicle for the real issue of assessing group interaction, much of the threatening nature of group process analysis disappears. Unlike in T-groups, the tutor, or trainer, plays a key role in briefing the group for its tasks and in directing the development of feed-back by means of questions and comments at the end of each exercise.

18.  Other approaches, designed to make people aware of their behaviour in groups, use questionnaires and rating scales to enable participants to record their feelings, perceptions and ideas about the group and its behaviour. Among such approaches is the Managerial Grid of Blake and Mouton, which is shown in Chapter 46.

19.  One of the most useful attempts to develop categories of behaviour, especially verbal behaviour, in groups was that of R.F. Bales in 1950. In several studies of small groups, Bales and his colleagues were able to generate a list of frequent behaviour categories to enable them to observe behaviour in a way that was relevant and consistent. Some examples of the categories were as follows:

- Shows solidarity
- Agrees
- Gives suggestion
- Gives opinion
- Asks for orientation
- Asks for suggestion
- Shows antagonism

These categories were grouped according to whether they furthered the task functions or whether they aided inter-personal relations, or socio-emotional functions, as Bales called them.

20.  Bales' ideas have been adapted by a number of British researchers, notably Rackham and Morgan (1977), who have used their version as the basis for improving skills in inter-personal

relationships. Their list utilises the following categories of possible behaviour in groups:

- Proposing (concepts, suggestions, actions)
- Building (developing another's proposal)
- Supporting (another person or his concepts)
- Disagreeing
- Defending/attacking
- Blocking/Difficulty Stating (with no alternative offered)
- Open behaviour (risking ridicule and loss of status)
- Testing understanding
- Summarising
- Seeking information
- Giving information
- Shutting out behaviour (eg interrupting, talking over)
- Bringing in behaviour (involving another member)

Experience in the use of such categories can enable observers of group behaviour to give constructive and relevant feedback to group members, instead of rather generalised or anecdotal descriptions of what has appeared to have taken place.

21. Categories of behaviour are a key element in distinguishing roles in groups. Feedback to groups can help the members to see what kind of role they played in the proceedings. Role is not quite the same as position (or job). The latter is concerned with the duties and rights attached to a particular job title. The former is concerned with *how* the job is performed, and is affected by the expectations of superiors, of organizational policies, of colleagues and subordinates as well as the expectations of the job-holder himself. This web of relationships has been called the role-set.

22. In any group activity a number of roles are likely to be performed – for example, the roles of leader, peacemaker, 'ideas man', 'humourist' and 'devil's advocate' to name but a few. In informal groups roles may emerge in line with individual personality and know-how. In formal groups many roles are already defined, such as chairman, secretary, visiting expert and others. Sometimes members of a group experience a conflict of roles. For example, a union representative may feel a conflict between his need to fulfill a spokesman role for his constituents, and his need to act responsibly as an employee of the company. Sometimes the chairman of a committee stands down temporarily from the chair in order to express a deeply felt personal view about

an issue in which he has an interest. This action prevents undue role conflict on the question of impartiality from the chair.

23. Roles are influenced considerably by organization cultures. In one organization managers may be expected to take a directive style in the management of their subordinates. Anything in the form of participation would be viewed as weak management. In another organization the dominant climate could well be democratic and participatory. In this kind of organization a directive style would be seen as quite out-of-place. Some organizations operate different cultures in different departments. Production departments, for example, tend to be task-orientated and directive in style, whereas research and development departments tend to be more considerate of people's needs, and less directive.

## COMPETITION BETWEEN GROUPS

24. So far we have been discussing behaviour *within* groups. Another important aspect of group behaviour is *intergroup* relations. Since every organization is made up of a number of different groups of employees, the question of collaboration between groups is vital for obtaining an overall balance in the social system. As Lawrence and Lorsch were at pains to point out (see Chapter 13) integration is as crucial to organizational success as differentiation. Breaking an organization down into smaller units (work groups) in order to cope adequately with the diversity of tasks that face it, creates opportunities to develop task interests and special know-how, but, at the same time it also creates rivalries and competing interests which can be damaging to the organization's mission. An understanding of the consequences, good and bad, of intergroup competition can, therefore, be of considerable help to an organization's management.

25. The first systematic study of intergroup competition was made about twenty years ago by Sherif and colleagues in the United States. They organized a boys' camp in such a way that two deliberately-created groups were formed for the experiment. Various devices were used to encourage the development of separate identities between the two groups. As the camp progressed, a number of interesting changes took place both within and between the groups.

  **Within groups** – collections of individuals, with no special ties with each other, grew into closely-knit groups; the group climate changed from being play-orientated to work-orientated, and leadership tended to become more autocratic; each group became more highly structured and put a much greater emphasis on loyalty and conformity.

**Between groups** – each group began to see the other group as 'the enemy', hostility between groups increased whilst communication between them decreased; stereotyped opinions of the other side began to emerge, especially negative stereotypes.

26. A further aspect of the Sherif study concerned the effects of winning or losing in an intergroup competition. This again provided some fascinating material for the researchers. Winning tended to maintain or even strengthen group cohesiveness, but reduced the motivation to fight; winning also caused a move away from task-orientation towards greater concern for individual needs. Losing tended to lead to a disintegration of the group, and the search for scapegoats both within and outside the group; tasks needs became even more important to the loser; losing, however, forced groups to re-evaluate their view of themselves and eventually come to a more realistic assessment of what changes were required to make the group effective.

27. Intergroup competition, as was noted above, has its advantages and disadvantages. The prime advantages are that a group develops a high level of cohesiveness and a high regard for its task functions. The main disadvantages are that groups develop competing or conflicting goals, and that inter-group communication and cooperation breaks down. Since the Sherif study several researchers have followed up with studies of conflict resolution between groups. The general conclusions are that to reduce the negative side-effects of intergroup competition, an organization would need to:

a. encourage and reward groups on the basis of their contribution to the organization as a whole, or at least, to large parts of it, rather than on individual group results;

b. stimulate high interaction and communication between groups, and provide rewards for intergroup collaboration;

c. encourage movement of staff across group boundaries for the purposes of increasing mutual understanding of problems; and

d. avoid putting neighbouring groups into a situation where they are competing on a win-lose basis for resources or status, for example.

28. Not all conflict is harmful. On the contrary, disagreement is an essential element in working through problems and overcoming

difficulties. The conflict of ideas when put to the service of organization or group goals is in fact the sign of a healthy organization. What is to be avoided is the point-scoring conflict that develops between groups who see their relative success and status vis-a-vis their neighbours as being more important than the pursuit of the common good.

## TEAMS &TEAM-BUILDING

29. A team, according to Adair (1986), is more than just a group with a common aim. It is a group in which the contributions of individuals are seen as complementary. Collaboration, working together, is the keynote of a team activity. Adair suggests that the test of a good (ie effective) team is:

> 'whether ... its members can work as a team while they are apart, contributing to a sequence of activities rather than to a common task, which requires their presence in one place and at one time.'

What we have described in this chapter are the key variables that determine the relative effectiveness of groups in achieving their goals and satisfying the needs of their members. These variables have to be addressed, if there is to be any chance of building a successful team.

30. What, then, are the characteristics of effective teamwork?

Research suggests that they are as follows:-
- clear objectives and agreed goals
- openess and confrontation
- support and trust
- cooperation and conflict
- sound procedures
- appropriate leadership
- regular review
- individual development
- sound inter-group relations

Adair emphasises the importance of careful selection of team members. They key factors here for individuals are not only technical or professional competence, but also the ability to work as a team member, and the possession of 'desirable personal attributes' such as willingness to listen, flexibility of outlook, and the capacity to give and accept trust.

31. Long-term research into management team-skills has been carried out by R.M. Belbin and colleagues (1981). The result

showed that a manager's team behaviour fell into one or more of eight fairly distinct team roles, as follows:

- **Chairman** An individual who can control and coordinate the other team members, who recognises their talents but is not threatened by them, and who is concerned with what is feasible rather than what is exciting or imaginative.
- **Shaper** This is another leader role, but one in which the role-holder acts much more directly to shape the decisions and thinking of the team.
- **Innovator** This type of person provides the creative thinking in a team, even if a concern for good ideas overshadows his ability to be sensitive to other people's needs.
- **Monitor/Evaluator** The strength of this role lies in the holder's ability to analyse issues and suggestions objectively.
- **Company Worker** Whilst the first four roles provide the major inspiration and leadership, this role provides for implementation of ideas by the roleholders' ability to translate general ideas and plans into practice.
- **Team Worker** This role meets the needs of the team for cohesiveness and collaboration, for role-holders tend to be perceptive of peoples' needs and adept at supporting individuals.
- **Resource Investigator** A person in this role looks for resources and ideas outside the team with the aim of supporting the team's efforts.
- **Completer** This is an individual whose energies are directly primarily to the completion of the task, and who harnesses anxiety and concern towards getting the job done on time and to a high standard.

32. Individual managers are likely to be predisposed to behaving in one predominant role, even though they may show tendencies towards others. The dominant role is closely linked to particular reasoning abilities and personality characteristics, but is also affected by the priorities and processes of a manager's job. An effective team is one that is likely to have a range of roles present in its make-up. Belbin concluded that the ideal team would be composed of one Chairman (or one Shaper), one Innovator, one Monitor Evaluator, and one or more Company Workers, Team Workers, Resource Investigators or Completers. Since ideal conditions are rarely present, managers have to build their teams from amongst the people they have, and encourage a greater

degree of role flexibility. However, a manager can benefit from understanding the distinctions between the roles and making an assessment of the role-strengths of his own staff. Knowing what to expect, as well as what *not* to expect, from colleagues enables the manager to head-off potential tensions or even group breakdown.

## SUMMARY

33. A group is more than just a random collection of individuals. It is a collection of individuals sharing some common purpose under a common leader, and seeing themselves as having a common identity.

34. The behaviour of groups is determined by a number of key factors, such as:

- Group leadership
- Group Norms (standards of behaviour)
- Group Cohesiveness (loyalty to the group)
- Roles played by members (leader, peacemaker etc)
- Nature and motivation of members
- Nature of the task (problem-solving, production etc)
- Size of group
- Environment (physical and social)

35. Group effectiveness has to be seen in two dimensions. Firstly, in terms of the ability to achieve organizational goals, and secondly, in terms of the ability to satisfy individual members' social and psychological needs. Groups tend to move through four different stages on their way to becoming effective in the sense described. These stages have been identified as follows:

(a) Forming → Storming → Norming → Performing

                                           (Tuckman, 1965)

(b) Undeveloped → Experimenting
      Team         Team
                              ↓

                   Consolidating → Mature
                   Team        Team

                                    (Woodcock, 1979)

The major factors influencing group effectiveness can be set under two headings:

- Immediate constraints ie the things that cannot be changed in the short-term (task, group size, members' knowhow etc)
- Group motivation and interaction ie the behaviour that (potentially) can be changed in the short-term (level of motivation and team-spirit)

36. Interaction within groups has been an important focus of study by behavioural scientists. Several notable developments have been as follows:

a. T-groups, in which participants study their interaction with each other in order to achieve greater awareness of, and skill in handling, interpersonal relations.

b. Coverdale training, where groups study their behaviour in the performance of a series of tasks.

c. The Managerial Grid, where the focus of attention is the leadership style of the individual.

d. Behaviour analysis, as developed by Bales in the United States and Rackham and Warr in Britain, in which a set of categories of behaviour is used for measuring individual and group performance, and for identifying roles in groups.

37. Behaviour between groups is as important as behaviour within groups. The subject of intergroup competition has been studied by several researchers, and in general the following conclusions have been reached:

a. Competition has both harmful and useful effects ongroups,

b. The most harmful effects are that groups develop competing or conflicting goals, and lose their ability to communicate and cooperate with one another,

c. The most useful effects are that groups develop strong ties of loyalty (cohesiveness) amongst their members, and that there is a high regard for the task.

In order to obtain the most benefit from intergroup competition, organizations need to reward groups on the basis of their contribution to the common good, encourage intergroup communication and collaboration, and avoid win-lose issues between groups.

38. Teams are collaborative groups, whose effectiveness depends considerably on the qualities, motivation and roles exercised by team members. To perform well a team needs a range of roles in its make-up.

## SECTION SUMMARY – LEADERSHIP AND GROUPS

1.  Leadership can be defined as 'a dynamic process in a group whereby one individual influences the others to contribute voluntarily to the achievement of group tasks in a given situation.' Several different types of leader have been identified as follows:
    a.  Charismatic ie based on personality,
    b.  Traditional ie based on birth,
    c.  Situational ie based on being in the right place at the right time,
    d.  Appointed ie based on bureaucratic authority,and
    e.  Functional ie based on behaviour/actions.

2.  Leadership depends for its success not only on the knowledge, skills and personality of the leader, but also on the task to be achieved, the skills and motivation of the team, and the environment or situation in which the leader has to operate.

3.  The three major categories of leadership, so far as theory is concerned are as follows:
    a.  Trait theories – based on personal qualities and attributes,
    b.  Style theories – based on leader behaviour, and
    c.  Contingency theories – based on adaptive behaviour by the leader in the light of the key variables in 2 above.

4.  Style theories were popularised in the 1950's–1960's by several American social scientists. The examples quoted in this Section were:
    a.  Douglas McGregor's Theory X and Theory Y
    b.  Rensis Likert's Systems 1 to 4
    c.  Tannenbaum & Schmidt's Continuum of Leadership Styles
    d.  The Michigan Studies – the 'employee-centred' versus 'production-centred' continuum
    e.  The Ohio Studies – a two-dimensional approach based on Consideration and Initiating Structure
    f.  Blake & Mouton's Managerial Grid, based on Concern for People and Concern for Production
    g.  Professor Reddin's 3-D Theory – a three-dimensional grid, which develops the ideas raised by the Blake & Mouton Grid and
    h.  The Harvard Studies – task leaders versus socio- emotional leaders.

Most of the above theories suggest that leadership style is a question of choosing between two or more mutually exclusive leadership alternatives eg *either* democratic *or* authoritarian. However, three of the examples quoted suggest that the alternatives are *not* mutually exclusive, and that it is quite possible for a person to be concerned both for people *and* for the task, for example.

5.    Contingency theories of leadership were exemplified by the work of Adair (Functional Leadership Model) and Fiedler (Theory of Leadership Effectiveness). Both of these writers stress the importance of assessing leadership in the light of the situation. Adair sees the leader's role as meeting the respective needs of the task, the group and individuals, within a given situation. Fiedler emphasises the importance of the relative favourableness of the situation for the leader. This favourableness depends not only on leader-member relations and the degree of structure in the task, but also on the power and authority of the position.

6.    The most important factors in group behaviour are as follows: nature of the task, size of the group, leadership, cohesiveness of the group, nature and motivation of the group members, group norms (standards), roles of individuals within the group, and, finally, nature of the environment.

7.    A group is a collection of individuals, who contribute to some common aim under the direction of a leader, and who share a sense of common identity. A group tends to pass through four major stages of development in its life. These stages are: Forming, Storming, Norming and Performing.

8.    Group norms are common standards of social and work behaviour expected of members of the group. These norms may be official (ie arising from the organization's rules and customs), or unofficial (ie arising from within the group itself. Part of the leadership role of a manager is to ensure, so far as possible, that official and unofficial norms are harmonised.

9.    Group cohesiveness is an important feature of groups. This refers to the ability of a group to retain the loyalty of its members and to attract new members. Highly cohesive groups display a strong loyalty to their members and a strong adherence to group norms. Factors which encourage cohesiveness include similarity of work, physical proximity of members, group size, leadership style of manager, and other factors.

10.    The effectiveness of groups is usually considered in terms of (a) accomplishment of the task, and (b) member-satisfaction.

The major determinants of effectiveness can be grouped under two headings: Immediate Constraints (ie things that cannot be changed in the short-term) and Group Motivation and Interaction. Examples of immediate constraints are group size, the nature of the task, and the personalities and other attributes of the members. Each of these may represent an opportunity or an obstacle to a group, and how well the group comes to terms with these constraints will, in turn, depend on the level of motivation possessed by the members, and on the degree to which they are able to work together. Leadership plays a key role in the overall levels of motivation and collaboration.

11.   Interaction within groups has been the subject of study by social scientists, and a number of different behaviour categories have been isolated. These include proposing behaviour, disagreeing, blocking behaviour, seeking information, shutting out behaviour and others. These behaviour categories are helpful in identifying roles within groups eg 'ideas man', 'humourist' and 'devil's advocate'. A role is concerned with *how* a person carries out his job, especially in terms of his own and others' expectations of the job. It is much more than just the duties of the job. Related groups of roles form a role-set.

12.   Competition between groups is an important issue in the study of groups. Such competition has both benefits and drawbacks. The benefits are a high degree of group cohesiveness and attention to task. The drawbacks are that inter-group cooperation breaks down and competing goals develop.

13.   Teams are essentially collaborative groups.  They tend to work effectively when a balance of roles is present in their composition.

## QUESTIONS FOR DISCUSSION/HOMEWORK

*1.   Why is it unhelpful to talk of leadership in terms of qualities? What would supply a more practicable answer to the question 'what is leadership?'?*

*2.   In what ways might the following influence a leader's style of leadership:*

   *a. his subordinates?*

   *b.the tasks to be performed?*

*and   c. he situation?*

*3.   What do you see as the advantages of Reddin's 3-D Theory over the Managerial Grid of Blake and Mouton?*

**4.** Discuss the concept of 'dimensions of leadership' with reference to the work of McGregor, Likert, Reddin and the studies made by the researchers at Michigan and Ohio.

**5.** What are the most important factors to take into account when assessing the behaviour of groups in an industrial or commercial setting?

**6.** How are group norms established, and why are they sometimes in conflict with the norms of the organization as a whole?

**7.** What roles would you expect to see played in:

a. effective groups?

b. ineffective groups?

**8.** What are the implication of Belbin's research for team development or team building?

## EXAMINATION QUESTIONS – LEADERSHIP AND GROUPS

Three representative questions follow below. Outline answers may be found at Appendix 2.

*EQ 23* The word leadership is sometimes used as if it were an attribute of personality, sometimes as if it were a characteristic of certain positions within an organization, and sometimes as an aspect of behaviour. Discuss. *(ICSA MPP)*

*EQ 24* Discuss the evidence which suggests that in order to be effective, a manager can and should be flexible in the choice of his managerial style. *(ICMA OMM)*

*EQ 25* List the factors influencing effective teamwork. Take four of the factors and write a short paragraph on each.
*(IOB Nature of Mgt.)*

# CONTROL IN MANAGEMENT

The POMC approach to the grouping of managerial activities, which was introduced in Chapter 15, commences by considering the Planning activities of management, continues with Organizing and Motivating activities and ends with Controlling activities – the subject of this Section. The control function of management, therefore, rounds off the total process of managing the human, material and financial resources of an organization. Its primary aim is to measure performance against standards with a view to enabling corrective action to be taken to keep plans on course. Controlling activities are so closely linked to Planning and Decision-making activities that it would be advisable to study the next two chapters in conjunction with Chapters 16 and 17. The three chapters in this Section describe the nature and methods of control (Chapter 28) and outline some of the most important techniques used to provide control information (Chapters 29 and 30).

# 28

# CONTROL: NATURE
# AND METHODS

## INTRODUCTION

1. It was noted in the introduction to Chapter 21 that, if planning represented the route map for the journey, then organizing represented the means by which one could arrive at the chosen destination. We can now add that controlling ensures that the travellers know how well they are progressing along the route, how correct their map is, and what deviations, if any, they need to make to stay on course.

2. The basic elements of control are as follows:
   a. Establish standards of performance
   b. Measure performance
   c. Compare actual results against standards
   d. Take corrective action where required

This sequence of events can be demonstrated diagramatically in a simplified form, as in Figure 28.1, which shows how each element is linked to form a continuous process ending *either* in the achievement of targets *or* the modification of plans as a result of feedback (see Figure 28.2).

3. Several comments can be made about the above diagram. *Firstly*, standards of performance need to be verifiable and clearly stated, for example in units of production or sales volumes. Where standards are qualitative rather than quantitative, it is preferable for them to be expressed in terms of end-results rather than of methods. Budgets are a particularly useful vehicle for the expression of quantifiable results, and will be looked at more closely later in the chapter. *Secondly*, the measurement of performance depends heavily on the relevance, adequacy and timeliness of information. The supply of such information comes from a variety of sources within the organization. The single most important source is the Management Accounting department, which is responsible for the regular production of operating statements, expenditure analyses, profit forecasts, cash flow statements and other relevant control information. *Thirdly*, when

comparing actual against target performance, most organizations only require action to be taken when the deviation against standards is significant. Otherwise no action is taken and no reference upwards is asked for. This is sometimes called the 'management by exception' principle. *Fourthly*, control is not just a matter of identifying progress, it is also a matter of putting right what may have gone wrong. Hence the importance of directing part of the control process to the implementation of appropriate corrective action.

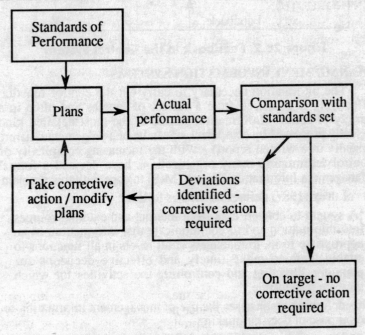

**Figure 28.1. The Control Sequence**

4.    The information generated by control systems is known as feedback. Feedback is usually produced on results ie on the outputs of the system. Actual performance is recorded and the information fed back to the managers responsible for achieving the target performance. Early feedback is essential for accurate control, especially where unexpected deviations have occurred. Where deviations occur, feedback may indicate the need for a change in the process or its inputs, or, possibly, a change in the basic plans or original standards. See Figure 28.2.

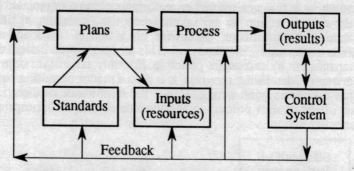

**Figure 28.2. Feedback in the Control System**

## MANAGEMENT INFORMATION SYSTEMS

5.    The information necessary to carry out the control function effectively is produced from a variety of sources and often in a variety of forms.  Information can be of the most detailed kind (usually processed by computer), or can be of a judgemental nature (usually in a written report).  With the increasing complexity of control information many organizations have devised a formal Management Information System (MIS) to cope with this problem.

6.    Lucey (1987) defines an MIS as follows:

'A system to convert data from internal and external sources into information and to communicate that information, in an appropriate form, to managers at all levels in all functions to enable them to make timely and effective decisions for planning, directing and controlling the activities for which they are responsible.'

This definition emphasises the use of management information for the purpose of decision-making.

7.    The model implied by this definition is basically as follows.

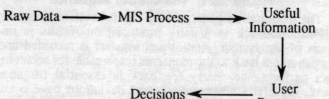

**Figure 28.3**

The raw data are the basic facts and figures of operational life, such as output figures, hours worked, invoice values, part numbers etc. These data may be stored on manual or computer systems. In themselves they may not have great meaning. Taken together and assembled into relevant groupings, they become *information*, which is basically data that has been analysed, summarised and interpreted for the benefit of the potential user, in this case a manager. The MIS processes are the various procedures and methods used to convert the data into useful information. This can be acted upon, for example to produce comparisons with expected standards and then take appropriate corrective actions (decision-making).

8.   It is possible to identify four types of formal MIS which are useful to management concerned with control at the tactical level. These are briefly:

1.  Control systems which monitor the organization's activities and report on them, eg production output, sales revenue etc.
2.  Database systems which process and store information, which can be drawn upon as a kind of organizational memory-bank.
3.  Enquiry systems, based on either internal or external databases, for carrying out investigations into the performance of departments, product lines, competitors etc.
4.  Decision support systems, providing computer-based facilities for conducting analyses, simulations etc.

9.   The application of an MIS to key management functions assists control in a variety of ways, as the following examples suggest.

Marketing/Sales
-   Clarify current order position
-   Identify profitability of particular products
-   Identify selling costs
-   Produce customer analyses
-   Provide surveys of markets

Personnel
-   Provide Wage & Salary analyses
-   Identify sickness absence trends
-   Analysis of manpower statistics
-   Production of labour turnover reports

Management Accounting
-   Production of operating and budget statements
-   Analyses of costs/expenditure etc

- Investment appraisal analysis
- Profit forecasts
- Cash flow projections/statements

Ideally the MIS should be operated on the basis of 'management by exception', ie it should enable managers to delegate confidently in the sure knowledge that significant variances in actual performance compared with standard performance will be highlighted in timely fashion by the system.

## CONTROL METHODS

10. The two major approaches to control are (a) those that focus on financial values, such as budgetary control, and (b) those that focus on physical values, such as quality control. By far the most widespread method of control is that of budgetary control, which will be considered first.

## BUDGETS

11. A budget is a statement, usually expressed in financial terms, of the desired performance of an organization in the pursuit of its objectives in the short-term (one year). It is an action plan for the immediate future, representing the operational and tactical end of the corporate planning chain. Budgetary control takes the targets of desired performance as its standards, then systematically collates information relating to actual performance (usually on a monthly or four-weekly period basis) and identifies the variances between target and actual performance. Thus, whereas budgets in themselves are primarily tools of planning, the process of budgetary control is both a planning device and a control device. The primary aims of a budgetary control system are to:

a. establish short-term business plans (N.B. Budgets are sometimes referred to as business plans or profit plans),

b. determine progress towards the achievement of short-term plans,

c. ensure coordination between key areas of the organization (eg between marketing and production),

d. delegate measurable responsibilities to managers, with-out loss of control,

e. provide a controlled flexibility for meeting change in the short-term.

12. The steps by which a budgetary control system is built up are basically as follows:

i.   **Forecasts** for key aspects of the business are pre- pared. These are statements of probable sales, costs and other relevant financial and quantitative data.

ii.  A **Sales Budget** is prepared based on an analysis of past sales and a forecast of future sales in the light of a number of assumptions about market trends. The resulting budget is an estimate of sales for a given budget period.

iii. A **Production Budget** is prepared on the basis of the Sales Budget. This involves an assessment of the productive capacity of the enterprise in the light of the estimates of sales, and a consequential adjustment of either, or both, to ensure a reasonable balance between demand and potential supply. Production budgets will include output targets, and cost estimates relating to labour and materials.

iv.  A **Capital Expenditure Budget** is drawn up to cover estimated expenditure on capital items (fixed assets) during the budget period.

v.   A **Cash Budget** is prepared by the accountant to ensure that the organization has sufficient cash to meet the on-going needs of the business. This budget reduces the organization's transactions to movements of cash and indicates shortfalls or excesses of cash at particular periods of time.

vi.  **Departmental Budgets** are drawn up in the wake of the Sales and Production Budgets.

vii. Finally, the budgets are collected into one **Master Budget**, which is effectively a statement of budgetted Profit and Loss together with a projected Balance Sheet.

viii. Production of **Period Budget Statements**, which inform management about their performance against budget in the immediately preceding period, and indicate any variances.

ix.  **Action by management**, as appropriate.

13.  In developing a system such as the one above, a number of points of good practice need to be considered. These are as follows:

a. Budgets should be sufficiently detailed to set clear targets for the managers responsible for carrying them out, but should not be so complex that they defeat their purpose of providing planning and control aids at the operating levels of the enterprise;

b. Budgets should not be kept to rigidly if conditions change significantly, but should permit reasonable flexibility. *They are a means to an end, not an end in themselves;*

c. The responsibility for a particular budget should be clearly defined;

d. Budgets should show variances between actual and budgetted performance (ideally in quantitative as well as financial terms, whenever possible);

e. Managers responsible for carrying out budgets should participate in their formulation.

## BREAK-EVEN ANALYSIS

14. Not all control information is expressed in statements and computer printouts. Some useful information can be made available in chart form, such as a 'break-even chart'. This is a chart which shows how costs and profits vary with the volume of production. The name is taken from the point on the chart where the total costs line crosses the sales revenue line ie at the point where neither a loss nor a profit is being made. An example of a simple break-even chart appears below (Figure 28.4).

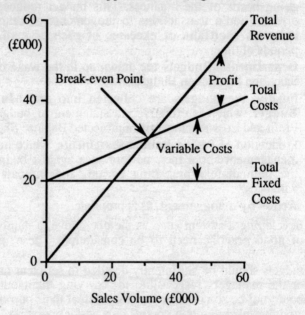

**Figure 28.4 Simple Break-even Chart**

In the above example, total cost (ie total fixed costs plus variable costs) range from £20,000 to about £38,000. Total revenue ranges from nil to about £55,000. The break-even point is achieved when a sales volume of about £32,000 is reached. Sales in excess of this figure begin to produce a profit.

15.  Break-even charts are useful for their indication of the effects of marginal changes in sales volume or costs on profit figures. They are also useful for converting profit targets into production targets or sales targets. The major criticism of such charts is that they assume linear relationships between costs and output, and sales and revenue, whereas this is not always true. The straight lines on the charts may be over-simplified, therefore, and would need to be treated with some caution. Like many other information sources, break-even analysis should preferably be used as one of several devices for obtaining an accurate picture of the business.

## RATIOS

16.  A key feature of all planning and control activities is the analysis of performance data. We have mentioned budgets and break-even charts above, but another useful form of analysis is by the use of financial (and other) ratios. Financial ratios are relationships that exist between accounting figures, and which are usually expressed in percentage terms. Such ratios can be grouped under a number of different categories, such as assessment of profitability, for example. Examples of typical financial ratios are as follows:

a.  Return on Capital Employed =
$$\frac{\text{Net Profit before Tax}}{\text{Net Capital Employed}} \times 100$$

b.  Net Profit Margin =
$$\frac{\text{Net Profit}}{\text{Sales}} \times 100$$

The above are tests of profitability. Other ratios include tests of liquidity, cost ratios and Stock Exchange tests. Examples of each of these in turn are:

c.  Current ratio (liquidity) =
$$\frac{\text{current Assets}}{\text{current Liabilities}}$$

This should usually be a 2 :1 ratio.

d. Selling/Distribution Costs to Sales =
$$\frac{\text{Selling \& Distribution Cost}}{\text{Sales}} \times 100$$

e. Earnings per share and Price-Earnings ratio.

17. Non-financial ratios indicate the relationship between quantifiable pieces of information, and may or may not be expressed in percentages. Examples of non-financial ratios are:

a. Labour Turnover Index =
$$\frac{\text{No. of leavers in period}}{\text{Average No.employed during period}} \times 100$$

b. Days lost through Strikes =
$$\frac{\text{No. of Working Days lost}}{1000 \text{ Employees}}$$

c. Sales/Volume of space =
$$\frac{\text{Total Sales of unit}}{\text{Square foot/metre}}$$

13. Ratios can provide useful summaries of relative efficiency or progress. Single figures on their own can mean very little but compared with other sets of figures, they can take on greater significance. Nevertheless, ratios themselves require standards of comparison if an organization is to compare its performance with its competitors, and these standards are not always available. Also some ratios are fairly crude eg Index of Labour Turnover, which shows the position in gross terms and gives no indication as to whether turnover is spread throughout the organization or is heavily concentrated in one department or in one occupation. As with break-even analysis, ratios need to be treated cautiously, and should preferably be used in conjunction with other forms of performance analysis.

## QUALITY CONTROL

19. In the physical world of production, numerous control systems are in operation. One example is that of Quality Control The control of quality rests on the assumption that in mass-production no two units are exactly identical, but that it is possible to mass produce vast quantities of *almost* identical units. These last-mentioned can be produced within certain tolerances, and a customer will accept variations between these tolerances, but not outside them. The role of Quality Control is to ensure that appropriate standards of quality are set and that variances beyond the tolerances are rejected. Thus Quality Control is basically a system for setting quality standards, measuring performance

against those standards and taking appropriate action to deal with deviations outside permitted tolerances. Quality Control activities can be very costly, and since they represent an overhead cost in the production area, the degree of time and resources spent on them must be related to factors such as price, consistency, safety and legal requirements, for example. Products such as highly-priced porcelain will be subject to far higher quality controls than run-of-the-mill household earthenware. Pharmaceutical products are subject to health controls, backed by legislation, and thus require the highest standards of quality. By contrast, the solid fuel merchant can afford to vary the content of what goes into pre-packed bags of household fuel, provided the weight is correct.

20. Inspection is an important part of Quality Control. Usually a choice has to be made whether to carry out 100% inspection or some lesser amount on a sampling basis. Where perfect quality is required, for example in the construction of nuclear reactor plant, then 100% inspection will be applied. In batch or mass-production (for definitions, see Chapter 39),100% inspection is not always necessary, nor is it always effective. Inspectors usually have to carry out their inspections in noisy and busy surroundings, which may affect their ability to concentrate. In fact several recent studies have shown that up to 15% of defective items have passed unnoticed in a 100% inspection. Better results than this can be achieved by sampling techniques in these circumstances. The most widely used techniques of inspection apart from 100% inspection are random sampling, where batches are concerned, or continuous sampling, in mass-production. Random sampling means that a batch is accepted or rejected on the basis of the number of rejects found after taking a random sample from the batch. Continuous sampling is used in mass-production systems, and entails an initial 100% inspection until a pre-determined number of correct items have passed in succession; then random sampling begins and continues until a further reject appears; 100% inspection is recommenced and the cycle is repeated if necessary. Further points relating to Inspection can be found in Chapter 38 (Production Planning & Control).

21. The benefits of Quality Control are primarily as follows:
   a. Reduction in costs of scrap or re-working
   b. Reduction in complaints from customers
   c. Enhanced reputation for company's products
   d. Feedback to designers and engineering staff about performance of products and the machines required to produce them.

## SUMMARY

**22.** The control function of management is closely linked to the planning function. Plans give rise to actions (performance), and actions have to be monitored to ensure that they reflect the aims and intentions of the plans. This monitoring of performance is the central core of the control function. Control establishes standards of performance, measures performance against the appropriate standards and identifies corrective action where required.

This chapter looked at systems and methods of control. A representative cross-section of systems and methods was outlined, including budgetary control as an example of a financial control, and Quality Control as an example of a control of physical standards. Two important methods of obtaining control information in a more specialised way were Break-even Analysis and the use of Ratios. A common feature of all these systems and methods of control is that they contribute to the setting of standards, as well as to the measuring of performance against standards. They also provide much useful information about performance generally, enabling managers to be better informed about the relative strengths and weaknesses of their operations.

# 29
# TECHNIQUES FOR CONTROL

## INTRODUCTION

1.   The scope for detailed questions on quantitative techniques in the examinations covered by this manual is very limited. However, in general questions about control in management, some reference ought to be made to the increasing number of mathematical and other techniques which are now available to management in the execution of their planning and controlling activities. This chapter provides a summary of the principal techniques which examiners could reasonably ask of candidates. The object in this chapter is to convey something of the nature and application of these techniques without going into detailed descriptions. For those wishing to enquire further into the field of quantitative techniques, an extremely useful book is 'Quantitative Techniques' – T. Lucey published in this series.

2.   The techniques which will be outlined in this chapter are Network Analysis (especially Critical Path Method and Programme Evaluation and Review Technique), Simulation and Inventory Control. Before going on to describe the basic features of these techniques, a few words are necessary about the general field of quantitative techniques.

3.   The label given to such techniques varies considerably. Sometimes they are referred to as Management Science, sometimes as O.R. or Operational Research, and sometimes as Quantitative Techniques. In this Manual the expression O.R. will be utilised. The purpose of these techniques is to make quantitative data available to managers in order to aid decision-making, planning and control. The basic approach of O.R. techniques was referred to briefly in Chapter 16 (para. 9), dealing with the topic of decision-making. The approach, this time in slightly more detail, can be stated as follows:

- Analyse Data and Define Problem
- Develop a Mathematical Model of the Situation
- Select Inputs/Data required
- Develop Optimum Solution
- Test/Modify Solution
- Provide Controls/Feedback Mechanism

257

- Obtain Management Support for Solution
- Implement, Maintain and Review

4.    The distinctive approach of O.R., according to the UK O.R. Society, is that it develops 'a scientific model of the system, incorporating measurements of factors, such as chance and risk, with which to predict and compare the outcomes of alternative decisions, strategies or controls. The purpose is to help management determine its policy and action scientifically. ' The models of O.R. are symbolic, or abstract, representations of real life problems. They are usually expressed in mathematical terms (symbols, equations and formulae), and can be contrasted with other models in common use in business, such as budgets, profit and loss statements, sales charts, and numerous others.

5.    The main advantage of O.R. models is that they provide a basis for the solution of *complex* problems in static or dynamic situations. Such models can be designed to take a large number of factors into account at any one time. They can reduce these factors to mathematical terms and experiment with them by introducing a variety of inputs to assess what effects they have. All this can be done without interfering with the operational or planning processes currently under way in the organization. Thus the risks of a particular strategy can be evaluated in a relatively safe manner before being put to the test in a real life context.

6.    The disadvantages of O.R. models are: (a) they take time to be developed, and are thus less useful for producing quick answers, (b) they can represent an over-simplified picture of a particular set of conditions, and therefore may suggest only partial solutions, and (c) they may be resisted by line managers on the grounds that such models are too theoretical to be put into practice. To some extent these criticisms are being offset by (a) the wider use of computers to handle complex calculations, and (b) the development of O.R. teams made up of managers from a variety of disciplines, and not just mathematics.

## NETWORK ANALYSIS

7.    Network analysis is the term used to embrace a number of techniques for the planning and control of complex projects. The basis of network planning is the representation of *sequential* relationships between activities by means of a network of lines and circles. The idea is to link the various activities in such a way that the overall time spent on the project is kept to a minimum. The optimum linking of the various stages is called the critical path. The two most frequently used forms of network planning are CPM

– Critical Path Method – and PERT – Programme Evaluation and Review Technique. The major difference between these two forms is that CPM assumes that the time required to complete an activity can be predicted fairly accurately, and thus the costs involved can be quantified once the critical path has been identified, whereas PERT assumes that time has to be estimated in drawing up the critical path. CPM tends to be used in large or complex projects in construction and manufacturing. PERT tends to be applied to one-off projects of a complex nature or to projects where time or cost are of overriding importance.

8.    The basic network is a combination of *events, activities* and *dummy activities*, as illustrated in Figure 29.1.

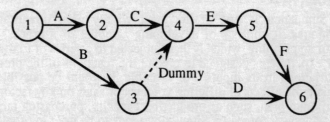

**Figure 29.1 A Simple Network**

Events are the start or the end of an activity eg kettle filled, tea poured out. Events are shown as a circle or node and are usually identified by a short description of the event or by a number (1, 2, 3 etc).

Activities are actions which take time eg filling kettle, pouring tea. They are shown as straight arrows, and are usually designated by letters (A, B, C etc).

Dummy activities are actions which do not incur time, but need to be shown to ensure the logic of the network. They are shown as a dotted arrow.

9.    Additional information can be added to the basic network as the exercise progresses. So, for example, times and costs can be included in the model which is being built up. The *critical path* through the network is the *longest* sequence of activities from the beginning of the network through to the end. In drawing up networks, estimating times and identifying critical paths, a number of rules and conventions have to be applied. Among these are that a complete network may have only one start event and only one finish event; that an event is not complete until all the activities

leading to it are themselves complete; and that a network must always move forwards in time.

10. The advantages of using networks are chiefly:
   a. they provide a logical picture of the layout and sequence of a complex project
   b. they help to identify the activities and events which are critical to the entire project
   c. they provide a basis for working out times, costs and resources involved in the project
   d. they act as a focal point for action and coordination
   e. they make an enormous contribution to both the planning and, especially, the control of complex projects.

## SIMULATION

11. Simulation is one of the most widely used quantitative techniques. It consists of developing a model of a process, eg corporate planning, which is then subjected to a series of trial-and-error experiments designed to predict the reactions of the process to variations in its inputs. For example, it would be possible to simulate the effects of differing volumes of sales on key factors in a corporate plan, such as production capacity, purchasing targets and manpower forecasts. Simulation tends to be used in problems where mathematical solutions are not possible, or where long time scales are involved (eg predicting – population changes over a 30 year period), or where there is no other way of tackling the problem (eg charting space-satellite trajectories).

12. The basic steps in a simulation are as follows:
   • Define problem to be simulated
   • Construct a model
   • Test the model
   • Gather relevant data for experiments
   • Run the simulation
   • Analyze the results
   • Re-run simulation in light of results
   • Repeat testing and simulation

For all practical purposes it is necessary to run simulations on a computer, on account of the number of times it is essential to re-run the model under different conditions.

13. The inputs to any model of a business operation will have to include probabilistic elements, if the model is to be a reason- able representation of reality. Every commercial business, in particular, is subject to chance or risk, and this is where probability comes in.

Probability is the quantification of chance (uncertainty). It is an important feature of every business simulation eg a corporate planning model or a production planning model. The rules of probability (p) state that the value of p ranges from 0 (zero) to 1 (one), where 0 indicates the lowest degree of probability and 1 indicates complete certainty. The values in between are usually expressed as decimals of 1. For example, the chances of your living to the age of 100 would be very small indeed, say .01. On the other hand your chance of dying before the age of 100 will be of the order of .99 ie a very high probability.

14. Probability is either objective or subjective. *Objective probability* applies to those events which have been tested previously and found to come up with consistent results. For example, if an ordinary coin is tossed, the probability that it will come down heads is .5. Where an estimate of probability has to rely on human judgement and experience, this is called *subjective probability,* and is the most widely used in business situations. An example of subjective probability is as follows: the Production Manager of a fast-growing microcomputer manufacturer, whose production has increased by 50% in the past year, without additional capital investment, now estimates the probability of repeating that 50% growth rate as .4, given no change in investment levels.

15. In the simulation of a corporate plan, for example, the probabilistic elements are selected on a random basis. This is sometimes known as a Monte Carlo simulation, due to the original gambling application of this approach. Random selection can be undertaken in several ways, but in this case the most likely methods will include the use of random number tables or computer-generated random numbers. A random number table consists of lists of randomly selected numbers in which there is no bias.

## INVENTORY CONTROL

16 . The final example of a quantitative technique in this chapter is that of Inventory, or Stock, Control. The inventory of an organization is its idle resources at any particular point in time. Taking a manufacturing organization as an example, its inventory can be described as:

    a. Raw materials and Purchased items

    b. Work in progress (partly-finished goods/sub-assemblies etc)

    c. Finished goods

In many organizations, the inventory figure is their largest current asset, and is a key factor in their ultimate profit situation.

17. The reasons for maintaining inventory levels are chiefly as follows:
    a. Raw materials
       – to take advantage of bulk-buying
       – to smooth out irregularities in supply
       – to ensure internal supply to production
    b. Work in progress
       – to act as buffer between production processes
    c. Finished goods
       – to ensure availability of goods to meet demand
       – to smooth out fluctuations in demand

18. The two basic questions of inventory control are:
    a. How much to order to replenish stocks?
    b. When to order?

Before these questions can be answered, organizations have to consider the costs involved. The two basic costs of inventory items are (i) *ordering costs* ie wages, administration and transport costs etc, and (ii) *carrying, or holding* costs ie interest on money invested in stock, storage costs, insurance costs etc. It is these two types of costs that inventory control aims to minimise in the light of the required inventory levels, referred to in the previous paragraph. The O.R. scientist applies mathematical and statistical formulae to models of an inventory so as to produce data on which buying and stockholding decisions can be taken. Inventory control is an important feature of Purchasing activities, and is referred to in more detail in Chapter 38 (paras. 16-12).

## SUMMARY

19. This chapter dealt briefly with a selection of management aids which come under the heading of Operational Research (OR) or Quantitative Techniques. OR techniques are a means to an end. They can help management to plan and control key business processes by developing mathematical models of problems or processes, which can be subjected to the influence of significant variables, including probability, and which can produce important data about the outcomes of such variables. This enables managers to assess both results and risks before taking major decisions relating to planning and control.

20. Three techniques were looked at in outline: Network Analysis, Simulation, and Inventory Control.

Network analysis was seen as important for the control of a wide range of complex projects. Its two most frequent forms are CPM (Critical Path Method) and PERT (Programme Evaluation and Review Technique). Networks are composed of three main elements: Events, Activities, and Dummy activities. These are represented by circles, arrows and dotted arrows respectively. Networks can be elaborated to show time and costs.

Simulation consists of a model-based exercise in which various changes are introduced and their effects recorded. Simulation is usually carried out on a computer, and tends to be utilised when mathematical or other measures are not practicable, eg in corporate planning exercises.

Inventory Control is used to ensure that the costs of buying and holding stock are minimised, taking into account the necessary inventory levels for operating the business and keeping the customer supplied.

# 30

# INFORMATION TECHNOLOGY

## INTRODUCTION

1. The advent of the silicon chip, or integrated circuit, as it is more properly called, has revolutionised the field of electronics. Today a tiny microelectronic processor less than a quarter-inch square can carry a hundred times more computing power than the massive Ferranti Mark 1 Star, Europe's first commercial computer produced in 1950. Integrated circuits are currently to be found in computers, pocket calculators, automatic bank tills, industrial robots and a host of other applications. The ability to harness electrical power in miniature form (ie microelectronics) is having a huge impact on modern life. In manufacturing we are drawing ever closer to completely automated production systems, and these will be examined in Chapter 41. However, the most likely way that people at work will come into contact with microelectronics' technology is in the area of 'information technology'.

## INFORMATION TECHNOLOGY

2. What is information technology (IT)? A useful working definition has been provided by the Department of Trade and Industry in Britain. This definition sees IT in terms of:

'the acquisition, processing, storage and dissemination of vocal, pictorial, textual and numeric information by a microelectronics based combination of computing and telecommunications'.

3. Whereas, in the past, information-handling involved massive dependence on paper, the emphasis now has shifted to the creation, storage and transmission of tiny electrical impulses. Today, the amount of information contained on a pair of floppy disks could fill an average-size book. Paper will doubtless continue to be important as a *tangible* product of the interchange of information between human beings ('hard copy'). However, when storage of information is the main consideration, then disks and magnetic tapes are likely to dominate the scene, until newer, even more compact devices are in common use.

4. There are three major components of information technology and these are as follows:

1. computers, ie electronic machines capable of making large sets of calculations very rapidly;
2. microelectronics, ie the design, application and production of very small-scale electronic devices containing densely-packed components;
3. telecommunications, ie the transmission of information by cable or radio waves.

We shall look at these components in turn.

## COMPUTERS

5.    The earliest attempts to process data by means of an electromechanical device were made in the United States by Herman Hollerith in the 1890's. In order to cope with the demands of recording and analysing the United States' census, Hollerith needed a way of automating the process. He took up an idea from a previous inventor, an Englishman named Charles Babbage, namely the punched card, but designed an electro-mechanical device called a tabulator to 'read' the information contained on the card. His tabulator worked successfully, reducing the number of man-hours for the task by two-thirds. Hollerith equipment formed the basis of commercial data processing for several decades.

6.    The first attempts at producing a problem-solving machine, or computer, were made during the Second World War as Allied scientists sought to break enemy codes. Shortly after the war the first commercial computers were developed. In Britain came the Ferranti Mark 1 and the Leo computer; in the United States the first Univac machine was produced. These electronic machines relied on valves (vacuum tubes) for their operation. They were large, costly, rather unreliable and required a dedicated data processing team to support them. Such machines were superseded in the late 1950's by so-called 'second generation' computers, utilising transistors for their operation. These computers were smaller than the first-generation machines, were cheaper to run, and were much more reliable. Nevertheless they still represented items of heavy capital expenditure, and still required a data processing department to be responsible for them.

7.    Large computers, usually referred to as 'mainframes', require to be housed in special, air-conditioned accommodation. Smaller desk-sized, machines are called mini-computers, and, like mainframes, require air-conditioning facilities. Microcomputers (see next page), by comparison, are altogether smaller and lighter, and do not require any special environment.

8. A typical data processing (DP) department of the 1960's would have been made up of the following components:

Equipment:

- mainframe computer (including central processing unit)
- input devices (keyboards, tapes, disks)
- storage devices (disks and tapes)
- output devices (printers and visual display units)
- telephone lines and modems (see note below)

Staff:

- Data Processing Manager
- Systems Analysts (to assess potential applications)
- Programmers (to write the instructions for the computer)
- Operators (to load, run and unload the computer)
- Data preparation staff (to convert raw data from documents into a form suitable for the computer)

(Note: A modem is a device for converting analogue signals to digital signals, and vice versa)

9. The existence of such a department encouraged the centralisation of data processing activities, and endowed its staff with considerable power within the organization. DP staff were seen as experts, and their function carried a valuable mystique. Users had to present their data in ways laid down by the DP department; they found themselves bound by the DP department's priorities rather than by their own; and, in addition, they had to compete with colleagues for use of the computer's facilities. This situation continued until the advent of the micro-computer, which has had the effect of placing considerable computing power in the hands of individual departmental managers and their staff, thus reducing their reliance on centralised computing facilities.

## THE MICROCOMPUTER

10. The micro-computer is essentially a microelectronic calculating system based on a microprocessor (see Fig. 30.1):

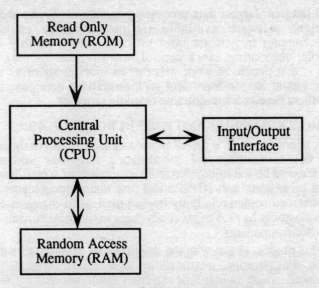

**Figure 30.1. Typical Microcomputer Layout**

Notes:

1. ROM refers to Read Only Memory. This is located on a permanent-memory chip, which can neither be added to, or altered, by an operator, nor erased when the machine is switched off. ROM contains the machine's operating codes.

2. RAM refers to Random Access Memory. This is located on a temporary-memory chip for storing information supplied to the machine by the user. Unlike ROM, the RAM chip does not retain information once the computer has been switched off. The difference between ROM and RAM is rather like that between a printed book, which can only be read, and a personal notepad written in erasable ink, and which can be used over and over again.

3. The Central Processor Unit is contained on a CPU chip, which controls all the calculating and coordinating functions of the computer.

4. The Input/Output Interface contains one or more chips for handling signals between the computer and other devices, such as disk drives, printers and visual display units (VDU'S).

11.  A microcomputer is small in size, but powerful and flexible in operation. Compared with a mainframe or a mini-computer, it is also vastly cheaper. It offers users the chance to be self-sufficient

for all but their largest data processing operations. Today there is sufficient software available (ie programs) to enable a microcomputer to perform most office functions reliably – for example, accounting, stock control, word processing etc). The result is that people at work, whether as individuals or as work teams, are no longer dependent on a centralised data processing department based on a mainframe or mini-computer.

## MICROELECTRONICS AND THE MICROPROCESSOR

12. A microprocessor is basically an integrated circuit designed to carry out calculating and coordinating functions. It can be considered to be the microelectronic equivalent of a mainframe's central processing unit (CPU). The first microprocessor as such was produced commercially by Intel in the United States in 1971. Its development has led to great advances in the miniaturisation of electronic components.

13. This process began with the development of transistors in the 1950's. Put simply, a transistor is a small, crystal-based component, which switches or amplifies small amounts of electric current between circuits. This kind of component is much smaller and more reliable than a valve, which was the earliest form of electronic switch. A valve, or vacuum tube, looks like a typical electric light bulb, it requires a large amount of power for its operation, generates a considerable amount of heat and is generally found to be unreliable in operation. By comparison, a transistor is smaller, more robust and requires much less power.

14. The biggest single leap in information technology, however, was the development in the 1960's of the first 'integrated circuits' (IC's) in the United States. Integrated circuits are so-called because they are manufactured as complete circuits. These circuits are built up by creating microscopic layers of metal and other components on small wafers of silicon, or 'chips', using a special photographic technique known a photolithography. These chips are the basis of modern electronics. The end result of the process is an immensely complex circuit contained on a minute slice of silicon crystal less than 1/4 inch in diameter and barely 15/1000th inch thick, and all achieved at a very cheap price, custom-built chips excepted.

15. Recently, methods have been devised of producing ever-more complex chips, and the modern trend is toward very large scale integration (VLSI) chips, on which there can be more than 10,000 components on a single chip.

16. Most integrated circuits are what are called 'general purpose chips' with circuits designed to handle one or more major functions of the host device (eg microcomputer, washing-machine programmer etc). There are currently three major classes of general purpose chips. These are:
   1) Memory chips (for storing information)
   2) CPU chips (ie microprocessors) (for carrying out all the calculating and coordinating functions of a computer)
   3) Interface chips (for handling the input/output requirements of a system)

Such chips are designed for varied use and tend to be mass-produced. They are usually extremely cheap.

17. Some integrated circuits are known as 'custom built chips'. These are designed and manufactured according to the requirements of a particular order. An example of a custom built chip might be one designed to monitor the pressure in some continuous process operation such as steelmaking or papermaking, where the processor would fit into a particular part of the host plant. Such a chip is usually very expensive for the purchaser.

18. The following diagram summarises the developments in electronic circuitry during this century (Fig. 30.2):

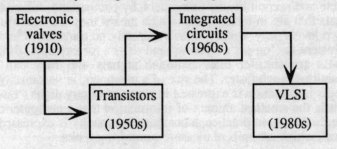

**Figure 30.2. Developments in Electronics**

19. The growth in the use of microcomputers in organizations means that people have become much less dependent on a central computer, which need only be used for large scale operations. Organization wide activities such as payroll processing will continue to be run on the organization's mainframe, but most applications relating to individual departments can now be handled comfortably on a microcomputer. If linking is required this can be achieved by creating networks of microcomputers linked to a mainframe or minicomputer, where necessary.

20. Computers are not only employed as tools for use within organizations. They can also be used for communications with the external world outside organizations. The key link here is telecommunications.

## TELECOMMUNICATIONS

21. The term 'telecommunications' means transmitting information by means of electric cables (telephone and telegraph) or by means of radio waves. Every nation in the world has some form of national network for transmitting information in these ways. Telephone links, for example, are used by businesses everywhere as an essential part of their communication with colleagues and clients. Because telephone links are based on electronics, they are an obvious resource to be used in the development of information technology.

22. Unfortunately, there is one major drawback to the closer integration of telecommunications with computers and microelectronics – telephones work in analogue form, but computers use digital signals. What this means is that telephones utilise variations in electrical current to *mirror* what is being fed into them, in this case the human voice. An analogue display on an electronic wristwatch would show a typical watch face with minute and second hands. Computers, by comparison, respond to signals that are in binary form, which means they are transmitted at two levels only. Binary signals can only be transmitted as the equivalent to 'on-off', 'yes-no' and '0-1', for example. Binary signals are simpler than analogue signals and they can be transmitted much faster. The size of a computer, ie its capacity to process information is expressed in terms of binary digits ('bits'). A bit is the smallest amount of information that a computer can store, ie 0 or 1. In practice, a computer's capacity is expressed in 'bytes', which are units of measure comprising 8 bits.

23. As information transmitted in binary form is so much faster than analogue signals, the full benefits of computer-based communication systems can only be gained when nations convert their existing telecommunications networks to digital operation. This is currently being undertaken in Britain, which has the fourth largest telephone system in the world. By the 1990's the whole network will be digitised. This situation has given a further boost to the microelectronics industry, which now has the incentive to apply its research and development programmes to telecommunications.

24. There are several developments which are enabling rapid change to take place in telecommunications. These are:
   a. fibre-optics – a fibre-optic cable is a finely drawn strand of glass of some tenth of a millimetre in diameter, which is capable of sending high-speed pulses of light in binary form. Telephone cables made of this material can transmit thousands more telephone calls than conventional copper cables.
   b. microwave transmissions – although such waves are used in land-based systems, they are now being developed to operate from geostationary (fixed-orbit) satellites.
   c. infra-red systems – these presently enable items such as television sets to be remotely controlled, that is without wires. Their future application is seen in terms of providing infra-red diffusers to act as cordless links between such machines as word-processors, telephones and computers, for example.

25. Telecommunications play a crucial role in information technology. Without them office communications would be entirely local, and the linking of office systems would be impossible. Fortunately, telecommunication technology is developing almost as fast as silicon chip technology and is expected to be able to meet the demands that will be made on it by computers and microelectronics over the next few years.

## INFORMATION TECHNOLOGY IN THE WORKPLACE

26. The impact of microelectronics technology on work practices and procedures is considerable. Slow, paper-based systems relying mainly on manual operations (eg typewritten reports and listings) are gradually being replaced by microelectronics-based systems relying mainly on telecommunications. Particularly important areas of microelectronics' applications are to be found in:-
   a. office automation
   b. industrial process control
   c. robotics
   d. computer-aided design and manufacture (CAD/CAM)
   e. worldwide electronic communication
   f. electronic funds transfer
   g. scientific measurement
   h. medical diagnosis

27. The industrial applications are dealt with in Chapter 41 (New Technology in Manufacturing). The other applications, especially

those relating to work carried out in offices will be considered in the remaining paragraphs.

## OFFICE AUTOMATION

28. The prime purpose of an office is to collect and process relevant information, which is subsequently stored or despatched to appropriate persons. Typical office activities include issuing invoices, handling purchases, dealing with customers' orders, preparing accounts and statistics, processing the payroll and other routine activities. Major activities of a non-routine type include the preparation and transmission of letters, memos, reports and various other documents.

29. Already the computer has made a significant contribution to the processing of much of the routine data generated by office staff. However, it is only within the last 10 years that it has become possible to process *text* electronically and thus improve the way non-routine information can be handled. Electronic text-processors are called word-processors, and are joint products of the computer and the electric typewriter. When we speak of the electronic office we are now referring to an administrative system based largely on computers, word processors and associated communication devices. Diagrammatically, this can be expressed as in Figure 30.3.

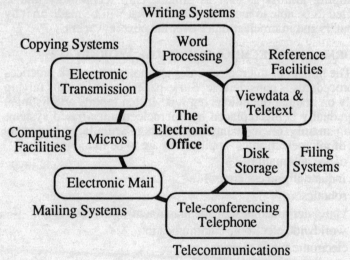

**Figure 30.3 The Electronic Office: Basic Features**

## WORD PROCESSORS

30. Word-processors can be classified broadly into three categories as follows:
- Stand-alones, or dedicated word-processors. These are independent machines used exclusively for text-processing. They comprise: keyboard, processor, memory, screen and printer.
- Shared-logic, or shared-facility, systems. These comprise a number of work-stations (keyboards and screens) connected to a central computer, which provides processing, storage and printing capabilities.
- General-purpose microcomputers, utilising a word processing program.

Dedicated word-processors, which are currently the most popular category with users, have special keys for formatting commands in addition to the usual QWERTY keys and Function keys associated with computer keyboards.

31. Benefits claimed from the use of word-processors include:
- improved productivity in processing documents, reports, letters etc
- increased job satisfaction among operators
- improved quality and consistency of final output
- staff savings (usually among copy typists)
- ease of editing and manipulating text
- ease of document recall from storage
- ability to integrate the word-processor with office computers

32. Disadvantages associated with the use of word-processors are as follows:
- they inevitably require changes to both the physical layout of the office and to existing procedures
- staff need time off-the-job to ensure adequate training
- eye-strain can be caused by excessive periods spent in front of the screen
- they may lead to staff redundancies
- they may reduce the scope of certain jobs, for example of secretarial posts

## OTHER OFFICE FACILITIES

33. In addition to microcomputers and word-processors, the automated office will have one or more of the following facilities:

- teletext
- viewdata
- electronic mail

34. The main features of these three facilities are as follows:

**Teletext** – this is a system for supplying commercial and other data via existing television networks. The system operates rather like an 'electronic reference book', whose data-filled pages can be read through by means of a hand-held signalling device pointed at, or linked to, a specially adapted television receiver. In the United Kingdom there are two competing systems – Ceefax (BBC) and Oracle (ITV).

**Viewdata** – this is somewhat similar to teletext in that it provides an up-to-date reference source on commercial matters. However, in contrast to teletext, the viewdata system is available only to subscribers and is an *interactive* system. An interactive system enables users to interrogate the database and to supply information, as well as drawing from it. The system is a combination of communication lines, accessed by telephone, computers (or terminals), and television. In the UK the public system is called Prestel, and there are a number of private systems.

**Electronic mail** – this is a system for communicating messages by electronic rather than physical means. One such system, telex, has been in use for many years. The difference between telex and the newer systems being developed (eg facsimile transmission) is that the latter enable electronic mail to be passed to and from a terminal on an individual's desk, instead of to a separately-located telex machine in another office. Recent improvements over the telex system include better editing facilities, more character sets, ability to send multiple letters as well as single letters, and, finally, the automatic filing of incoming and outgoing mail. The new systems are gradually being integrated into the other leading office systems (computer networks, word-processors etc). The latest developments in some offices include so-called 'work-stations' at each desk, comprising computer and word-processing facilities, electronic mail, and telephone facilities.

## ELECTRONIC FUNDS TRANSFER

35. Another fast-growing facility is 'electronic funds transfer'. This term describes the ability to effect cashless/paperless monetary exchanges by means of computers and telecommunications. Banks and other financial institutions are already heavy users of electronic funds transfer, and it is likely to be widely adopted by businesses handling large number of cash transactions, as in the retail trade, for example.

## EFFECTS OF INFORMATION TECHNOLOGY IN OFFICES

36. The principal point about information technology is that it serves *people* rather than things. Whereas robots, CNC machines and other industrial computers (see Chap. 41) serve *materials* and *components*, and data processing computers serve *clerical systems*, the new office technology serves *Man's needs to communicate* with his fellows. The availability of a wide range of information sources and transmission media gives management and professional staffs, in particular, the ability to make informed decisions based on an up-to-date picture of a situation, and an awareness of alternative responses and their likely consequences. Computers, for example, are now widely used to answer such questions as 'What is likely to happen, if we decide to take option A?' 'What is likely to be the result of changing X but not changing Y?'.

37. In assessing the effects of information technology in offices, there are several perspectives to be considered:
   • the general implications (economic, social etc)
   • the implications for employees
   • the implications for employers

38. The general implications of information technology in offices may be summarised as follows:
   1. investment in technology may lead to issues of work fragmentation, boredom, redundant skills and loss of job satisfaction
   2. office jobs will undergo significant changes
   3. fewer jobs may be required as routine work is taken over by machines
   4. the processing and transmission of information by offices will be speeded up considerably
   5. routine office work will become considerably more cost-effective

6. flexibility of services offered by offices can be greatly enhanced by the variety of equipment now available

7. international business communication will be readily accessible to even the smallest office

39. The main implications for office employees include several disadvantages as well as benefits.

**Benefits.**
- Learning new skills
- Tedious jobs can be delegated to machines
- Easier and quicker access to information
- Easier means of remedying typing errors
- More jobs for those who are skilled in maintenance
- More jobs for programmers and software designers
- Opportunities for shorter working day/week

**Disadvantages.**
- Fewer jobs will be required
- Office workers might become machine-minders
- Health problems associated with VDUs, printers, etc
- Strong competition between employees for available jobs
- Loss of personal contact as information is passed by machine instead of by more traditional methods

40. For employers there are few disadvantages and many advantages.

The disadvantages include:

- Time/disruption caused on transferring from manual to electronic systems
- Software may not necessarily meet operational needs, and may have to be custom-made
- Considerable upheaval amongst existing staff

The principal advantages are:

- Substantial savings on salaries due to fewer staff required
- Relative cheapness of new technology (eg a word processor may cost £3,500 compared with £10,000 plus benefits for a secretary)
- Substantial savings on overheads due to reduction in office space required as disk storage replaces filing cabinets etc
- Speed of obtaining, processing, storing and retrieving information aids decision-making
- Vastly improved productivity
- Flexibility of working due to variety of equipment available, all or most of which can be operated by existing staff
- Improved communications between individual executives and their offices.

## CONCLUSION

41. The availability of the new technology is likely to lead to two opposing tendencies in organizational behaviour.

Organizational structures will tend to favour decentralisation on account of the existence of powerful departmental computer facilities, whilst within *offices* the trend will be towards the integration of existing services, ie data processing, word processing, voice communication and electronic mail, along the lines suggested in Figure 30.3 in para 29 above. In these circumstances it will be important for organizations to plan for such a future, so as to ensure that:

a. facilities are compatible with one another, and

b. that the inevitable human and organizational consequences can be dealt wisely, fairly and economically.

Notes on further reading.

Readers may find the following texts helpful in learning more about information technology:

1. Birchall, D. & Hammond, V. (1981) Tomorrow's Office Today. *Business Books.*
2. Eaton, J. & Smithers, J. (1982) This is IT. *Philip Allan.*
3. APEX (1980) Automation and the Office Worker. *APEX.*
4. Kerridge, C. (1983) Microchip Technology. *J. Wiley & Sons.*

## SECTION SUMMARY – CONTROL IN MANAGEMENT

1.    The three chapters in this Section have looked briefly at the nature and methods of control, and some of the important techniques which aid control.

2.    Control means to establish standards of performance, measure performance against those standards, and take corrective action where required. Key factors in control are:

    a.   the ability to set clear and measurable standards,

    b.   the need to ensure the relevance, timeliness and adequacy of information,

    c.   the 'management by exception' principle, ie only take action if performance falls significantly against standards, and

    d.   the importance of taking corrective action, when required.

3.    An essential feature of most control systems is feedback, ie information generated by the control process. Feedback is usually produced from the results, or outputs, of the system.

4.    Important methods of control include budgetary control, break-even analysis, ratio analysis and Quality Control.

5.    Budgetary control. A budget is a statement of desired performance (ie a standard to be achieved), usually expressed in financial terms. A budgetary control system begins with business forecasts and the development of a sales budget; these are followed by the production budget, a capital expenditure budget, a cash budget and the various departmental budgets; finally these are all drawn up into one Master Budget; once in operation, period budget statements are produced to indicate performance against budget and the variances that have occurred; these variances provide the grounds for any necessary corrective action by management.

6.    Break-even analysis. This form of analysis of performance is based on a chart, showing monetary values on the vertical axis and sales volume or production on the horizontal axis. By charting in fixed and variable costs, and then showing revenue, it is possible to see the point at which total revenue equates with total costs ie the break-even point. Break-even charts are relatively simple to produce, but this simplicity itself may lead to an over-simplified statement of a situation, and needs to be treated with some caution.

7.    Ratio analysis. Financial ratios indicate the relationships between accounting figures. Common ratios include those for profitability eg

Return on Capital Employed =
$$\frac{\text{Net Profit before Tax}}{\text{Net Capital Employed}} = 100$$

and those for liquidity eg

$$\text{Current ratio (liquidity)} = \frac{\text{current Assets}}{\text{current Liabilities}}$$

Non-financial ratios indicate the relationship between quantifiable pieces of information eg

Labour Turnover =
$$\frac{\text{No. of leavers in period}}{\text{Average no. employed during period}} \times 100$$

Ratios are primarily useful for their ability to indicate relative efficiency.

8.    Quality Control. Quality Control is the term applied to a system of standards-setting, performance-measurement and action in relation to the quality of a product. It rests on the assumption that it is possible to produce large quantities of almost identical items in a modem industrial process, and therefore it is possible to establish certain tolerances within which quality is acceptable, and outside which it is not acceptable. Inspection is usually carried out on a sampling basis but 100% inspection is also common. Some techniques, especially in mass-production use a combination of sampling and 100% inspection.

9.    Important techniques which aid the establishment of control systems are Network Analysis, Simulation and Inventory Control. These techniques are often referred to as Operational Research, or Quantitative Techniques. Their object is to make *measurable* data available to managers in the areas of decision-making, planning and control especially.

10.   Network Analysis. This form of analysis is usually under-taken by the Critical Path Method (CPM) or the Programme Evaluation and Review Technique (PERT). The former is used widely in complex projects in the construction and manufacturing industries; the latter tends to be used in complex, one-off projects or in projects where time or cost are critical. Both techniques utilise networks to plot events and activities in sequence, with the object of identifying the optimum linking between them (the critical path).

11. Simulation. This technique develops a conceptual model of a process, subjects it to a number of experiments and studies the results with the aim of eventually predicting how the model will behave under certain conditions. It tends to be used for problems where probability is a key factor. Probability is the quantification of uncertainty, where zero probability is represented by the figure 0 and complete certainty is represented by the figure 1. Points in between these two are expressed as a decimal eg .5 for a one-in two chance. Simulation has been used to predict population changes over a long period of time and for charting space-satellite trajectories. The technique invariably involves the use of computers to handle the data.

12. Inventory Control. Inventory control is concerned with the control of an organization's idle resources in terms of raw materials, work-in-progress and finished goods, for example. It aims to answer two basic questions: How much should be ordered and when? Models of an inventory are developed, and subjected to various mathematical and statistical formulae, with the object of producing data to enable a considered answer to be given to the two questions mentioned.

13. Information Technology (IT). The advent of microelectronics has given a tremendous boost to Man's capacity to acquire, process, store and disseminate textual, numeric and other forms of information. The three major elements of IT are: computers, microelectronics and telecommunication.

14. Offices as centres of information – processing in organizations, are major beneficiaries of this new technology. The most significant benefits arise from the use of microcomputers and word- processors to handle a wide range of data in conjunction with telephones and other telecommunication media.

15. The overall benefits of IT lie in:
- faster, more efficient processing and transmission of information
- flexibility in office operations

## QUESTIONS FOR DISCUSSION/HOMEWORK
*1. What is the relationship between control and planning?*

*2. Discuss the role of feedback in a control system.*

*3. Write out a 'code of good practice' for an organization about to install a budgetary control system for the first time.*

*4. Why do firms need to pay attention to quality control?*

**5.** *In what ways can an Operational Research specialist contribute to the effectiveness of line managers?*

**6.** *What do you see as the advantages and disadvantages of the use of the following in the handling of routine office-work:*

    *a. microcomputers?*

    *b. word-processors?*

**7.** *How would you personally describe the term 'electronic office'?*

## EXAMINATIONS – CONTROL IN MANAGEMENT

*Questions on the control process in management are not among the most frequent questions in general management papers. Two fairly typical questions on this topic are included below. Outline answers may be found in Appendix 2.*

*EQ 26*   *In defining the basic principles of management, text-books often list Planning and Control as two separate and distinct functions. How far can they be regarded as independent of one another?*         **(IOM Business Organization)**

*EQ 27*   *What are the basic steps in the Control process? Identify and explain the key considerations in each step.*

                        **(IOB Nature of Mgt.)**

# FUNCTIONAL MANAGEMENT: MARKETING, PRODUCTION AND PERSONNEL

## INTRODUCTION

1.   The chapters which follow in this final part of the Manual focus on the key features and activities of the three functional areas of management which are the most frequent subjects of examination questions: marketing, production and personnel management.

2.   The term 'functional' is used to indicate a specialist area of management. Unlike the situation in our discussion of line, staff and functional authority in Chapter 21, these following chapters specifically do *not* refer to issues of authority, but only to the specialised role, or function, carried out by particular groups of employees, in this case in marketing, production or personnel departments. This point of view is in line with a systems approach to organizations, where the distinction between line and staff functions is rather academic, since *all* functions contribute to the success of the enterprise. Undoubtedly, certain functions, such as marketing and production, are of particular importance to business organizations, but they themselves rely heavily on other functions such as accounting and personnel in order to achieve their objectives.

3.   Each of the three functional areas is dealt with in terms of its salient features and its mainstream activities. Enough information is given to provide the reader with a grasp of the essentials of each area.

# MARKETING MANAGEMENT

## INTRODUCTION

1. Marketing is the one function of management which has to be more concerned with what is going on *outside* the organization than with what is happening internally. Marketing activities are conducted mainly across the *external* boundaries of the organizational system, and they are undertaken by managers of all kinds, not only by marketing specialists.

2. Marketing has been described in several different ways. A cross-section of definitions, which have appeared over the past twenty years or so, is as follows.

   a. 'Marketing is a human activity directed at satisfying needs and wants through exchange processes.'

      *(P. Kotler – Marketing Management, 4th Edition, 1980)*

     This definition emphasises marketing as an issue of social and economic exchange.

   b. (Marketing is). . . 'The management function which organizes and directs all those business activities involved in assessing and converting customer purchasing power into effective demand for a specific product or services and moving the product or service to the final consumer so as to achieve the profit target or other objectives of the company.'

      *(Institute of Marketing, 1966)*

     This definition is distinctly action-centred and managerial in approach.

   c. (Marketing is) ... 'the whole business seen from the point of view of its final result, that is from the customer's point of view.'

      *(P. Drucker, The Practice of Management, 1954)*

     This definition emphasises the *concept* of marketing and expresses a philosophical approach to marketing activities.

3. The idea of the 'marketing concept' is taken up in Chapter 31, and is compared with other approaches to marketing. The other chapters in the Section deal with those aspects of marketing, which are the most frequent topics of examination for non-marketing specialists. These are: the marketing mix, market research and the organization of a marketing department.

# 31

# THE MARKETING CONCEPT

1.   Every business or public organization has its market, that is to say the group of existing and potential buyers or users of its goods and services. A market may consist of a mere handful of people (eg specialist collectors of a certain type of antique porcelain), or it may consist of millions (eg consumers of breakfast cereals). Clearly, relationships with the market are an important ingredient of corporate planning and policy-making. Organizations have developed several different ways of regarding their existing and potential customers. The most notable options are as follows:

a.  **Production** orientation – in this situation, the organization concentrates its attention on production efficiency, distribution and cost in order to attract customers to its products. This works well when demand is well ahead of supply, and where lower costs will encourage people to buy. Japanese car manufacturers are examples of this kind of orientation.

b.  **Product** orientation – in this case the organization stands or falls by the quality of its products. The thinking behind this orientation is that customers buy products or services rather than solutions to problems. Examples of product orientation are to be found in education, the arts and journalism, where the inference often is that the supplier knows best what the customer needs.

c.  **Sales** orientation – here the dominant concept is that people will not buy until they are persuaded to buy by positive selling. Thus the focus of attention is more on the skills of selling, than on the needs of the buyer. Several life-insurance companies have adopted this approach over the years.

d.  **Market** orientation – a market-orientated organization is one which focuses on the needs of its customers. Its primary concern is to find out what its customers needs and wants are so as to meet them with the highest level of customer satisfaction. In this situation production responds to the demands of marketing rather than the other way round. This approach to marketing is called the 'marketing concept' and its perspective is radically different from the approaches of production, product and sales-orientated organizations.

Examples of market orientated attitudes can be found in some supermarket chains and in numbers of travel agency operations.

2.  The marketing concept takes the view that the most important stakeholders in the organization are the customers. This does not necessarily mean that the customer is always right, but it does mean that the customer forms the starting point for the organization's corporate strategy. Organizations that adopt the marketing concept also tend to see marketing as a very diffuse activity, shared by many, and not just the preserve of a specialist group called Marketing & Sales. This is a very important consideration, for, as we shall see shortly in the discussion of the marketing mix, there are certain key issues, such as pricing, which have to be considered and agreed on a *shared* basis.

3.  Reference was made earlier to customer needs and wants. What are the differences between these two? One way of distinguishing between them is to define *needs* as basic physical and psychological drives arising from being human (eg need for food, clothing, self-esteem etc), and to define *wants* as specific desires directed towards fulfilling the basic needs. A need for food, for example, could be transformed into a specific desire (want) for curried chicken, or for bread-and-cheese or countless other variations of food. The point is that human beings have relatively few needs, but can generate an enormous number of wants. Not surprisingly, therefore, most marketing efforts concentrate predominantly on satisfying people's *wants*. In addition to this, some marketing is directed specifically at creating or changing people's wants.

4.  The marketing role in an organization is carried out by numerous individuals. In the first place all those senior managers, and their advisers, contributing to the organization's corporate plan, are fulfilling, among other things, a definite marketing role ie examining the market-place and assessing the organization's ability to meet current and future demands on its resources. Many middle managers also carry out a marketing role when dealing with issues relating to their public. When a production manager for example, meets a customer to discuss a quality problem or a minor design change, he is fulfilling a marketing role; and so is a personnel manager when he negotiates an agreement with union representatives that a particular customer's goods may be moved from the premises during a strike. Finally, there is the Marketing department. Its staff are specifically charged with marketing duties – assessing customer wants, gathering market intelligence,

obtaining customer reactions, organizing sales and distribution, for example. The remaining chapters in this Section concentrate mainly on the activities of these Marketing specialists.

## SUMMARY

5.   A market is a group of existing and potential buyers or users of a product or service.

6.   Organizations can have a number of different orientations towards their markets. These are notably:
   a. Production orientation
   b. Product orientation
   c. Sales orientation
   d. Market orientation

7.   Organizations which have a market orientation are said to have adopted the 'marketing concept'. This implies that their organizational strategy commences by considering the needs and wants of the customers. It also implies that marketing is an activity carried out by numerous people in the organization, and not just by those called marketing/sales personnel.

8.   A distinction was made between needs and wants. Needs refer to basic physical and psychological drives. Wants are the specific desires that people seek to gratify in fulfilling their basic needs. Needs are few, but wants are many.

# 32

# THE MARKETING MIX: PRODUCT AND PRICE

## INTRODUCTION

1.   A vital element in every marketing strategy is the marketing mix. The concept was first expounded by Professor Neil Borden of Harvard University in the 1940's, when he identified twelve key variables in the typical marketing programme. These twelve variables have subsequently been reduced to four main headings by later writers. The mix may now be defined as 'the particular group of variables offered to the market at a particular point in time.' These variables are principally (1) product, (2) price, (3) promotion and (4) distribution. Each of these can be further sub-divided as illustrated in Figure 32.1 below.

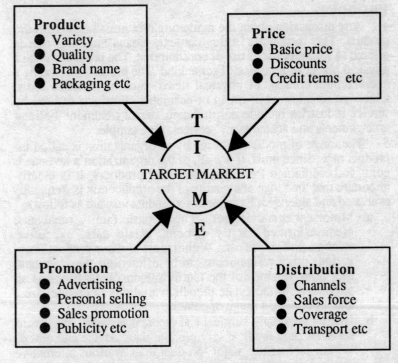

**Figure 32.1. The Marketing Mix**

2. The marketing mix as illustrated above is the central part of an organization's marketing tactics. Once the market situation (customers, competitors, suppliers, middlemen etc) has been identified and evaluated, and once the decision has been made to penetrate, or develop, a particular market, then the role of the marketing mix is crucial. This role will be amplified in the rest of this chapter, and in Chapters 33–34.

3. Before moving on to consider the different variables, the question of timing should not be overlooked.

The element of time is a vital factor in assessing the particular mix to be offered to a market. Any market situation can change rapidly over even a short period of time, as can be the case when a major competitor is suddenly declared bankrupt. By using the marketing mix as a tactical tool of an organization's marketing plans, it is possible to adapt speedily and profitably to changes in the marketing environment. Thus the development of the mix to meet conditions at a particular point or period in time is essentially a contingency approach to marketing management.

# PRODUCT

4. Any discussion about the marketing mix must begin with the product. The 'product', in this context, means anything that is offered to a market for its use or consumption. The product can be a physical object or a service of some kind. The product offered by a manufacturer consists of physical items, such as machine tools, television sets, loaves of bread or cosmetics. Products offered by service industries include hospital care, dental treatment, holiday arrangements and accountancy services, for example.

5. The range of products offered by an organization is called the product mix. Since most, if not all, of the organization's revenue is going to be obtained from the sale of its products, it is clearly important that the range and quality of the product mix is frequently evaluated and amended. Examples of a product mix are as follows:

   a. Motor car manufacturer – cheap, basic family runabouts, medium-priced family saloons, estate cars, executive saloons, and sports cars. Within most of these product lines, various other refinements can be offered eg two-door and four-door versions of the family saloons, hatchbacks as an alternative to the estate models, variations in engine sizes, and, of course, a range of colours.

   b. District hospital – surgical and medical services, diagnostic services, para-medical services, pre-natal advice and others. Within each of the major 'product lines' various alternative services are offered eg general surgical, accident services, coronary care, X-radiography, physiotherapy, pre-natal classes and so on.

6.  In considering products, it is important to note that people generally want to acquire the *benefits* of the product, rather than its *features*. For example, in buying a motor car a person is buying such things as luxury or speed or economy or status. The fact that these benefits are achieved by differences in engine size, suspension design or paintwork is really of secondary interest. Similarly, the reason why we want hospitals is for such aims as the preservation of life or the improvement of health or peace of mind. Whether these things are achieved by surgery, or by drugs, or by nursing care, or by modern diagnostic apparatus is, for many people, a matter of secondary importance.

7.  If we agree that customers are buying the benefits of a product, then equally organizations are *selling* the benefits of that product. The selling effort is not just confined to the Promotion element in the marketing mix. It begins by being designed into the product itself. So, for example, the very existence of a product range is, in itself, a selling point for a product. The same consideration applies to other aspects of the product, such as quality, brand, packaging and after-sales service, where applicable. Where quality is designed into a product, the benefits can be long product life, absence of faults and subsequent breakdowns, reliability, increase in value and many others. However, product quality may not be sought after at all. For example, the benefits of disposable goods are immediate and one-off. Such goods do not need to be durable or aesthetic, so long as they are hygienic and functional. Practically every airline traveller in the world has been introduced to plastic cutlery, and every nurse in training has been introduced to disposable syringes. Thus product quality may be high or low, depending on the wants or preferences of the market, and part of an organization's product strategy is to decide the level of quality to be aimed at.

8.  One important method used to sell benefits is by branding products. This means applying the organization's 'signature' to its product by the use of special names, signs or symbols. Branding has grown enormously during this century, and there is hardly a product in the Western world which does not have a brand name or designation of some kind. Famous brand names include Coca Cola, Biro and Hoover, all of which have become synonymous with certain categories of products, whether produced by them or by their competitors. A ball-point pen is a 'biro' to many people, regardless of whether it is a Biro, or a Parker, or a Papermate, for example. In Britain, the Marks & Spencer company market their products under the brand-name of St. Michael. These products are manufactured by

other reputable companies to a standard approved by Marks and Spencer and sold under the St. Michael label. By comparison, other retailers, such as Boots, John Lewis, and Sainsbury's market some goods under their own branding and some under the manufacturers label. Branding also occurs in certain consumer services, such as transport – Blue Riband, Economy, Four Star, Ambassador are all titles that are, or have been, used to differentiate between levels of service. In general, branding is a feature of consumer products. It is far less common in industrial products.

9.    Packaging is an important factor in the presentation of a product to the market. Not only does packaging provide protection for the product, but it can also reinforce the brand image and the point-of-sale attraction to the buyer. The protective aspect of packaging is vital in respect of items such as foodstuffs, dangerous liquids and delicate pieces of machinery. Goods such as soft toys and items of clothing may not need such protection, but here other considerations apply, such as the appearance of the goods on the shelf, or the possibility of seeing the contents through the packaging. Other aspects of packaging may emphasise the convenience of the pack, as for example in cigarette packets which may be opened and reopened several times, or beer cans, which can be opened safely by pulling a ring.

10.   Some products are sold with a very strong emphasis on after-sales service, warranties, guarantees, technical advice and similar benefits. Mail-order firms invariably have an arrangement whereby, if customers are not satisfied with the goods received, they may return them at the firm's expense without any questions being raised. Computer suppliers frequently provide customer training as an integral part of their total product package. Car retailers sell vehicles with various kinds of warranties concerning replacement of faulty parts at the suppliers expense. This facility applies as much, if not more to industrial and commercial buyers as it does to individual consumers. In recent years the growth of 'consumerism' or consumer protection lobbies has led to many organizations taking action to improve the service to the customer after the sale has been concluded.

11.   Emphasis on the make-up of the product is not only vital because of the need to sell benefits to potential customers, but also to take account of another key factor ie the 'product lifecycle'. Studies have shown that most products pass through a series of stages – their life-cycle – from the time they are introduced until the time they are withdrawn. A product will typically pass through five major stages in its life. These are shown in the diagram below (Figure 32.2).

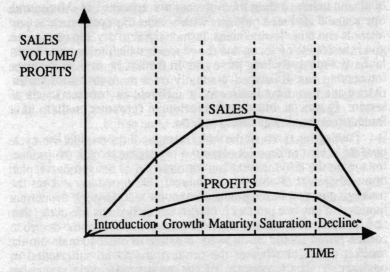

**Figure 32.2. Product Life-Cycle.**

12. The consequences of these stages of the product lifecycle are as follows:

**Introduction**   Costs are high (because they include the development costs), sales and profits are low. Few competitors. Price relatively high.

**Growth**   Sales rise rapidly. Profits at peak level. Price softens. Increasing competition. Unit costs decline. Mass market appears.

**Maturity**   Sales continue to rise, but more slowly. Profits level off. Competition at its peak. Prices soften further. Mass market.

**Saturation**   Sales stagnate. Profits shrink. Measures taken against remaining competition. Prices fiercely competitive. Mass market begins to evaporate.

**Decline**   Sales decline permanently. Profits low or even zero. Product is withdrawn from the market.

13. The total length of time over which a product may decline depends on a variety of factors, such as its relevance to basic needs, its adaptability in the light of economic trends and whether it is the focus of short-term fads or of longer-lasting fashions. A basic foodstuff, such as the common loaf of bread or a packet of ground coffee, will have a relatively long lifecycle. Conversely, in an economy where energy costs are high and fuel conservation is the fashion, the expensive motor car with a high petrol consumption

will tend to have a short lifecycle, but the economy car will continue for years. Fads breed products with a short life-cycle, such as pop records and other leisure items; fashions tend to develop or reappear over the course of years, and the products which follow them tend to have a relatively long life-cycle. In Britain the fashion for home ownership has developed gradually over three or four decades. Alongside this development have appeared key products such as estate agents services and mortgage facilities, which have established themselves firmly over the same period.

14. Taking into account the various stages of the product life-cycle and the period of time concerned, it is possible to plan the product mix, plan the development and introduction of new products, plan the withdrawal of obsolete or unprofitable products, and set the revenue targets for each product within the total range. If the current position of any one product is plotted correctly on its life-cycle, then it is possible to assess the potential growth of sales, or the degree to which prices should be allowed to soften in order to maintain the market share, or whether the product should be superseded by another. Thus the concept of the product lifecycle makes an important contribution to forecasting of sales and planning of products.

## PRICE

15. If product is the most important single element in the marketing mix, then price is usually next. Price is important because it is the only element of the mix which produces revenue; the others all represent costs. Sellers have to gear prices to a number of key factors, such as:

    a. the costs of production (and development),

    b. the ability to generate sufficient revenue and/or profits,

    c. the desired market share for the product,

    d. the prices being offered by the competition.

16. Price is especially important at certain times. For example:

    a. when introducing new products

    b. when placing existing products into new markets

    c. during periods of rising costs of production

    d. when competitors change their price structure

    e. when competitors change *other* elements in their marketing mix (eg improving quality or adding features without increasing prices)

    f. when balancing prices between individual products in a product line.

17. When a new product is introduced, such as a video-cassette recorder or a home computer, the price tends to be high on account of the initial development and marketing costs. This sort of product tends to be directed, initially, to higher-income groups or specialist-interest groups. As the product begins to attract increasing sales, and initial costs begin to be covered, then prices can be reduced and production volume stepped up. However, it is also possible to introduce a product with a very low price in order to obtain a foothold in a new market, or an increased share of an existing market. A bargain price may well attract considerable sales and at the same time discourage competitors. The cheap trans-Atlantic air travel pioneered by Laker Airways is an example of this kind of market penetration. The danger is, of course, that the price may be so low that the business fails to generate sufficient revenue to cover its operating and/or capital costs.

18. Few products stand still in terms of their costs. Labour costs increase from year to year; materials costs and energy costs may be subject to less regular, but sharper, increases; interest rates may be extremely variable, and hence the cost of financing products fluctuates. Many costs can be offset by productivity savings. Therefore, the costs which are the most crucial are those which represent sudden and massive increases, which cannot be absorbed by improving productivity. In this situation price increases are practically inevitable, and the question is 'by how much should we increase them?'. In certain situations, it may be possible to gain a temporary advantage over competitors by raising prices by the lowest possible margin, and offering some other advantage such as improved after-sales service or credit terms. Examples of this kind of approach are common in the motor car retail trade in times of low demand, when one-year warranties are extended to two years, and interest-free credit may be offered for a limited period.

19. The activities of competitors have an important bearing on pricing decisions. The most obvious example is when a competitor raises or lowers his prices. If your product can offer no particular advantages over his, then if he drops his price, you will have to follow suit. If, on the other hand, you can offer other advantages in your marketing mix, there may be no pressure at all to reduce your price. If a competitor raises his price, perhaps because of rising costs, it may be possible to hold yours steady, provided you can contain your own rising costs. Pricing is a very flexible element in the marketing mix and enables firms to react swiftly to competitive behaviour.

20. Competitors may throw out a challenge by improving the product and offering a better distribution service, for example. This kind of behaviour, too, can be countered by price changes – in this case by easing prices and/or improving credit terms. Much will depend on the sensitivity of the market to price changes. If price is the dominant issue for buyers, then they will prefer lower price to slightly higher quality or improved distribution arrangements. If price is not the major factor in the buyer's analysis, then marginal extra quality and delivery terms may prove the more attractive.

21. Finally, price is important in determining the relative standing of one product or product line vis-a-vis another within the product mix. This issue applies particularly in highly differentiated products in the consumer area. It is important, for example, that a motor car manufacturer establishes appropriate differentials between different models within a product-line eg between 1100cc and 1300cc models, between 2-door and 4-door versions, and between these and estate car versions. If 1100 cc models are selling well but 1300 cc models are not, it may be in the seller's interests to reduce the differential so as to attract more buyers to the 1300 cc models. Otherwise a reasonable differential will be expected in order to justify the enhanced engine rating of the larger model.

22. The concept of a loss leader is often applied to internal price-differentials. This means that one product in a line is reduced to below-cost levels with the aim of attracting attention to the product line or range as a whole. So, for example, a new fibre-tipped pen, in a range of such pens offered by a newcomer to the market, may be sold at a loss in order to draw attention to the range as a whole, and to establish a share of the total market. Loss leaders naturally represent very good value for money to the buyer, and can be a very useful way of establishing a range in the market-place.

# 33

# THE MARKETING MIX: PROMOTION

## INTRODUCTION

1.   Every product needs to be promoted, that is to say it needs to be drawn to the attention of the market-place, and its benefits identified. The principal methods of promotion are: advertising, personal selling, sales promotion and publicity. It is in these areas that Marketing departments come into their own. They provide the bulk of the expertise, and carry the biggest amount of responsibility, in respect of these aspects of the marketing mix. Each of these methods will be looked at shortly.

2.   The aim of an organization's promotional strategy is to bring existing or potential customers from a state of relative unawareness of the organization's products, to a state of actively adopting them. Several different stages of customer behaviour have been identified. These have been described in several different ways, but in summary can be stated as follows:

Stage 1   Unawareness of product

Stage 2   Awareness of product

Stage 3   Interest in product

Stage 4   Desire for product

Stage 5   Conviction about value of product

Stage 6   Adoption/Purchase of product

3.   The four different methods of promotion mentioned above are applied, where appropriate, to each of the stages of customer behaviour. Advertising and publicity have the broadest applications, since they can affect every stage. Personal selling and sales promotion activities, by contrast, tend to be more effective from Stage 3 onwards.

4.   Before describing each of the methods in greater detail, one further point can be made about them as a whole. This is that they have a different emphasis according to whether they are being applied to consumer markets or industrial markets. For example, whilst advertising is very important in reaching out to consumer markets, it is of relatively little significance to industrial markets, where personal selling is the most popular method. Publicity and

sales promotion activities appear to rank equally between both types of market.

## ADVERTISING

5. Advertising is the process of communicating persuasive information about a product to target markets by means of the written and spoken word, and by visual material. By definition the process excludes personal selling. There are five principal media of advertising as follows:

 a. the press – newspapers, magazines, journals etc
 b. commercial television
 c. direct mail
 d. commercial radio
 e. outdoor – hoardings, transport advertisements etc

6. By far the most important medium, in terms of total expenditure on advertising and sales promotion, is the press. In Britain this has averaged about 70% in recent years. The second most important medium is commercial television, which has consistently maintained about 25% of the total.

7. Whatever the medium a number of questions must be decided about an organization's advertising effort. These are basically as follows:

 a. How much should be spent on advertising?
 b. What message do we want to put across?
 c. What are the best media for our purposes?
 d. When should we time our advertisements?
 e. How can we monitor advertising effectiveness?

## ADVERTISING EXPENDITURE

8. Decisions about advertising expenditure will usually be made in conjunction with assessments about the position of the product in its life-cycle. If the product is at the introductory stage, a considerable amount of resources will be put into advertising. Conversely, if the product is in decline little or no expenditure on advertising will be permitted. If the product is at the saturation stage, advertising may well be used to score points off the competition eg 'our vehicle does more miles per gallon than theirs (naming specific competing models).'

9. There are various options open to an organization in deciding how much to spend on advertising its products. It could decide to adopt a 'percentage-of-sales' approach, where advertising

expenditure is related to sales revenue. This has the advantage of relating expenditure to sales, but it discourages innovative approaches to advertising expenditure and does not allow for distinctions to be made between products or sales territories. It is a relatively crude way of allocating such expenditure.

10. Another approach to advertising expenditure is to base it on what the competition is spending. Organizations such as Media Expenditure and Advertising Ltd. in the UK provide regular information on media expenditure for subscribers, and other sources provide information on other key facts such as competitors' market share. The important point to note about this approach is that it is vital to compare like with like, otherwise the value of the exercise is rather wasted.

11. The sales-task approach to advertising expenditure can be particularly useful in situations where it is possible to state clearly defined objectives for advertising eg 'to increase awareness of product X in Y market from present levels to (say) 70%.' This approach has the merit of allocating advertising expenditure to specific targets, but relies heavily on the organization's ability to define its objectives realistically.

## THE ADVERTISING MESSAGE

12. Probably the most important aspect of any advertising campaign is the decision about *what* to say to prospective customers, and *how* to say it. This is the message which aims to make people aware of the product and favourably inclined towards it. Advertising copy (ie the text) also aims to make people desire the product. The entire process is the fundamental one of turning customer needs into customer wants.

13. Advertising aims to achieve on or more of the following:
   a. increase customer familiarity with a product (or variations of it eg brand, product-range etc)
   b. inform customers about specific features of a product
   c. inform customers about the key benefits of a product
   d. indicate distinctive features and/or benefits of a product (implicitly or explicitly by comparison with competing product).
   e. establish the credibility of a product
   f. encourage potential customers to buy the product
   g. maintain loyalty of existing customers.

In setting out to achieve such aims, an advertiser usually has to abide by a number of laws and codes of practice. Most countries exert some degree of State control over the content and form of advertising. Issues such as obscenity, blasphemy, racial prejudice and sheer misrepresentation figure high on the list of proscriptions.

14. The content of an advertisement should not, therefore, contain anything offensive to particular groups in society; nor should it contain information or suggestions which are misleading. Most advertisements tend to select one or two features of their products for treatment and aim to sell the benefits of these. In some cases, no specific product is mentioned, but a key aspect of the organization's marketing policy is referred to eg 'We'll Take More Care of You . . . ' or 'Shop at X, where the customer comes first . . ' One way of drawing attention to a firm, or a brand, in general terms is to develop a symbol, or logo, by which everyone can recognise it. Well-known logos in the UK include those for ICI, Philips, and Lloyd's Bank (firms) and for Guinness, Anchor Butter and Birds Eye (specific products or brands).

15. What is the best way of putting a message across? This is an important question at this stage. The content and the form of the advertisement have been dealt with, and now the key point is to get the message over to the customers. The choice of media depends on the organization's requirements in terms of:

    a.  the extent of coverage sought to reach customers

    b.  the frequency of exposure to the message

    c.  the effectiveness of the advertisement ie is it making a relevant impact?

    d.  the timing of the advertisement

    e.  the costs involved

16. If wide coverage is sought (eg for a new Do-it-Yourself product or a new consumer banking service), then a television advertisement put out at a peak viewing time would be the most effective. However, cost would preclude very frequent advertising via this particular medium, so for frequency of exposure it would be preferable to consider hoardings and transport advertisements (eg as with the famous Guinness advertisements). For effectiveness, then, magazines and journals tend to reach the most relevant markets, provided they are selected carefully in the first place. For example, advertisements for camping enthusiasts will tend to produce better results in camping magazines than in national newspapers or magazines aimed at other interest groups, such as collectors of antique furniture. One of the problems with magazine advertisements, however, is their relatively long lead-

time before an advertisement appears. Newspapers are better media on this score. Direct mail scores high on relevance ie it can be directed very specifically at certain markets, but because of the personnel costs, it can be expensive. In the final analysis, organizations have to weigh up the anticipated benefits of particular media against the costs involved. This brings us on to the question of how do organizations assess the effectiveness of their advertising?

## ADVERTISING EFFECTIVENESS

17. There are two main ways of looking at the question of advertising effectiveness – the first is to consider the results of the advertising in achieving target improvements in specific tasks eg increasing brand awareness in a specific market; the second is to consider the impact of advertising on sales generally. It is extremely difficult to assess the impact of advertising on sales as a whole, because so many other factors, internal and external, are at work in the marketing process of an organization. It is easier to assess the impact of specific advertising campaigns on sales in specific product areas.

18. The evaluation aspect of advertising is an element of marketing which is remarkably short of measurement devices. The limited aids that are available are as follows:

    a. Television audience measurement figures

    b. Information on the circulation figures for printed media

    c. Information concerning the readership of newspapers and periodicals

    d. Information on specific campaigns obtained by interviews and/or questionnaires

The value of items (a)–(c) is restricted to quantifying or qualifying the market. They do not provide information about the effects of advertising, but point the way to relevant markets. Item (d) offers more genuine guidance about the effects of advertising. After a new series of newspaper advertisements, for example, a firm can test a sample of the readership to ascertain how many readers noticed the advertisement, how many recalled what it said and how many had actually bought the product since reading it.

19. Like any other aspect of management, if marketing activities can be made measurable, then it is much easier to assess their effectiveness in achieving their objectives. If they cannot be measured with any degree of objectivity, then effectiveness can only be judged in an incomplete way. At present the assessment of advertising effectiveness falls into the latter category.

## PERSONAL SELLING

20. However vivid the message put over by advertising, there is no substitute for the final face-to-face meeting between the buyer and the seller or his representative. Advertising creates the interest and the desire, but personal selling clinches the deal. In industrial markets, as was noted earlier, personal selling plays an even more extensive role. For the moment, let us consider the basic sales process. This is generally understood to mean:

    a. establishing customer contact
    b. arousing interest in the product
    c. creating a preference for product
    d. making a proposal for a sale
    e. closing the sale
    f. retaining the business

21. So far as *consumer* markets, and especially mass markets, are concerned, advertising must play a vital role in the first three stages of the process. After that, advertising becomes rapidly less important, and personal selling takes over. By comparison, advertising plays a much less important role in *industrial* markets, where even the first stage is dominated by personal selling.

22. Personal selling is the most expensive form of promotion. This is reflected in the marketing statistics, which show for example, that in the United States in 1976 about $100 billion were spent on personal selling compared with $33 billion on advertising. Such personal selling ranges from the mere taking of an order in a shop or a sales office, to the creation of new sales in a highly competitive market. Companies which utilize an aggressive sales policy, based on personal selling, are said to be adopting a *push* strategy. By comparison firms which rely more heavily on advertising are described as adopting a *pull* strategy.

23. The tasks of a sales representative, except in the routine order-taking role, include other duties than making sales. These other duties can comprise:

    a. after-sales servicing (dealing with technical queries, delivery matters etc)
    b. gathering information (feedback on customer reactions, competitors' activities etc)
    c. communicating regular information to customers and prospective buyers (new catalogues etc)
    d. prospecting (looking out for new selling opportunities)

24. In order to fulfil these duties a sales representative needs to have relevant information about:

   a. his own organization (Customer policies, resources available, organization structure etc)
   b. the products on offer (goods, services, ranges etc)
   c. sales and profit targets
   d. customers (size, type, location etc)
   e. sales plan for his territory
   f. promotional material (brochures, catalogues etc)
   g. techniques of selling (creating interest, dealing with objections, closing a sale etc)

25. Whilst many organizations still see the prime role of the sales representative as that of generating sales, there is an increasing trend which sees the representative in a wider marketing role, which emphasises the profit responsibility of the position. If sales are pursued regardless of costs and other limiting factors, such as reputation, the value of the sales volume obtained can be severely reduced, if costs have been excessive and/or the organization's image has been tarnished by over-zealous representatives. If, on the other hand, representatives are trained to put themselves in their customers' shoes ie develop a market-orientated approach, they are less likely to put immediate sales gains before the prospect of much larger market opportunities in the future. This, of course, assumes that they are rewarded on this basis as well. In a sales-orientated approach the sales representative is focussing on his needs as a seller. By comparison, a market-orientated approach to selling concentrates on the needs of the buyer.

26. In organizing their sales force, organizations usually have three basic options open to them:–

   a. they can organize their representatives on a geographical, or territory, basis
   b. they can organize on a product basis (eg where high technology products are involved)
   c. they can organize on a customer basis

The most frequent option is (a), and in some cases (a) plus one of the others. A *territory* is normally allocated on the basis of workload and/or potential sales. The aim is to ensure a fair balance of work and earnings potential amongst the representatives. The use of territories helps to reduce the costs of travel, accommodation and related expenses, and also eases some of the administrative burdens of controlling the sales-force.

Where the *product* provides the basis for allocating work, there are advantages in having specialist sales representatives who can deal with technical as well as general queries (eg as in computer sales). The main disadvantage is that there is a possibility, with large customers in particular, that several different representatives from the organization will each be calling on the same customer. This increases sales costs considerably, and may possibly outweigh the advantage of specialist representation.

Sales-forces organized on a *customer* basis have the advantage of a thorough knowledge of their customers' needs and sales records. They are thus in a good position to forecast potential needs as well. The drawback, as in the case of product centred sales-forces, is that of overlapping – in this case an overlapping of sales journeys. Here again organizations have to weigh up the relative gains of this approach against the extra costs.

27. The effectiveness of sales representatives can be measured in a number of different ways. Typical evaluation criteria include:

    a. Net sales achieved (per product, per customer etc)

    b. Call rate (number of calls in a given period)

    c. Value of sales per call

    d. Number of new sales/new customers (compared with colleagues or with last year's figures)

    e. Sales expenses in proportion to sales achieved.

In the total marketing effort of the organization, there are, of course, other activities than sales, and the performance of the sales-force cannot be taken in isolation. As was noted at the beginning of this chapter, personal selling is *one* part of the promotional activities of the organization, which brings us on to a consideration of the next item: sales promotion activities.

## SALES PROMOTION

28. Sales promotion activities are a form of indirect advertising designed to stimulate sales mainly by the use of incentives. Sales promotion is sometimes called 'below-the-line advertising' in contrast with above-the-line expenditure which is handled by an external advertising agency. Sales promotion activities are organized and funded by the organization's own resources. They can take a number of different forms, as, for example:

● Free samples
● Twin-pack bargains (two for the price of one)
● Temporary price reductions
● Point-of-sale demonstrations

] Promotions directed at consumers

● Special discounts
● Cooperative advertising
● Bonus/prizes for sales representatives
● Provision of display material

] Promotions directed at trade customers

29. Reference was made earlier to 'push' and 'pull' strategies. Sales promotion falls into the first category. It aims to push sales by offering various incentives at, or associated with, the point-of-sale. Its use is most frequent in the field of consumer products.

The objectives of a *promotion directed at consumers* could be to:

a. draw attention to a new product or line

b. encourage sales of slow-moving items

c. stimulate off-peak sales of selected items

d. achieve higher levels of customer acceptance/usage of a product or product-line

Objectives for a *trade-orientated promotion* could be to:

a. encourage dealer/retailer cooperation in pushing particular lines

b. persuade dealers/retailers to devote increased shelf space to organization's products

c. develop goodwill of dealers/retailers

30. The evaluation of a sales promotion is never a clear-cut matter, mainly on account of other variables in the overall marketing mix. The most popular method of evaluation is to measure sales and/or market share before, during and after the promotion period. The ideal result is one which shows a significant increase during the promotion, and a sustained, if somewhat smaller increase *after* the promotion. Other methods of evaluation could include interviewing a sample of consumers in the target market (eg to check if they had seen the promotion, changed their buying habits etc), and checking on dealers' stock-levels, shelf-space etc.

## PUBLICITY

31. Publicity differs from the other promotional devices mentioned in this chapter in that it often does not cost the

organization any money! Publicity is news about the organization or its products reported in the press and other media without charge to the organization. Of course, although the publicity itself may be free, there are obvious costs in setting up a publicity programme, but, pound for pound, these are considerably lower than for advertising, for example. Publicity usually comes under the heading of public relations, which is concerned with the mutual understanding between an organization and its public. In recent years several European football clubs have experienced acute problems of crowd behaviour at matches. One way of reassuring the thousands of well-behaved fans, who might well be turned away for ever, is to back up disciplinary action with a publicity campaign aimed at showing the better side of club football. Such a campaign could include articles and press releases about improvements in accommodation, the development of the Supporters Club and other club matters. It could also involve talks to youth groups and others by both players and staff.

32. Sponsorship events in the arts and sports are becoming an increasingly popular form of publicity. Concerts, both live and recorded, have been promoted jointly by the musical interests concerned and by industrial and commercial interests. Athletics meetings, tennis tournaments and horse-races have all been the subject of sponsorship. Again, although the publicity itself is free, the costs of sponsorship are not. Nevertheless, such activities can contribute significantly to an organization's public image. Organizations which are selling products that are the target of health or conservationist lobbies are often to be found sponsoring activities such as sporting events and animal welfare campaigns.

33. A final method of obtaining publicity, and one of the most costly, is by donating substantial sums of money towards an academic or research institution. In some cases the organization's name is included in the title of the project or position etc (eg as in the XYZ Chair of Industrial Relations at X University).

Thus patronage of sports, the arts and learning are all useful means of gaining publicity in a manner which casts a favourable light on the organization, and, ultimately, on its products.

## SUMMARY

34. This chapter has been concerned with outlining the principal methods by which suppliers of products bring their goods and services to the attention of their markets, with the object of increasing their sales or market share, or both. The most widely used methods are those of advertising and personal selling.

Advertising aims to attract attention and subsequent purchases by means of persuasively communicating product information *via the media* (the press, radio and television, direct mail and outdoor posters). Personal selling involves the use of *face-to-face exchanges* to achieve the same ends of attracting attention and achieving sales. Advertising is of greatest importance in consumer markets, while personal selling is the most popular method in serving industrial markets.

35. The two other methods included in the chapter were sales promotion activities and publicity. Sales promotion supports other sales efforts by providing incentives to both consumers and traders at the point-of-sale. Publicity is the free media coverage obtained by the reporting of the organization's activities/products in news items in the press and other media. Publicity provides a useful way of gaining a favourable public image for the organization and its products.

# 34

# THE MARKETING MIX: DISTRIBUTION

## INTRODUCTION

1.    Having looked at three major elements in the marketing mix – product, price and promotion – we can now turn to the fourth, and last, element: distribution. As the Institute of Marketing definition said earlier, one of the key functions of marketing is 'moving the product or service to the final consumer. . .' This is the purpose of distribution.

2.    Distribution is primarily concerned with (a) channels of distribution, and (b) physical distribution. We shall look at these in turn, commencing with channels of distribution. These channels are the marketing institutions which facilitate the movement of goods and services from their point of production to their point of consumption. Some channels are direct, as when a computer firm sells its products direct to the users. Others, the majority, are indirect. This means that there are a number of intermediaries between original producer and eventual buyer, as in the case of the box of foreign-made chocolates bought at a local retailer by a housewife.

3.    The choice of channels utilised by a producer is determined ultimately by the customer, and in recent years there has been a trend towards shorter channels, as customers, especially in consumer markets, realise that there are price advantages to be gained when middlemen, or retailers, are by-passed in the chain of distribution. Thus direct mail, cash and carry, and 'pick your own' (fruit, vegetables etc) operations are increasing in response to consumer interest in this approach.

4.    What are the most common channels of distribution, and what role is played by the various intermediaries in them? Figure 34.1 opposite illustrates the channel options, which are now described in greater detail .

5.    Channel A represents a direct marketing channel. This is to be found more in industrial markets than in consumer markets. Manufacturers of goods such as machine tools, computers, ships and other large or expensive items tend to move them direct to the buyer without involving middlemen or intermediaries. However,

this practice is becoming more frequent in consumer markets as well. For example, in mail order operations and in door-to-door selling (eg cosmetics, household wares and double glazing). The reasons for direct channels are basically as follows:

**Industrial markets** – Relatively small number of customers; need for technical advice and support after the sale; possible lengthy negotiations on price between manufacturer and customer; dialogue required where product is to be custom built.

**Consumer markets** – Lower costs incurred in moving product to consumer can lead to lower prices in comparison with other channels; manufacturers can exercise greater control over their sales effort when not relying on middlemen.

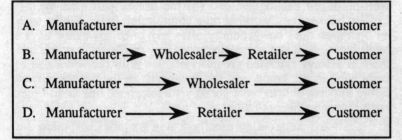

**Figure 34.1. Most Common Channels of Distribution.**

6. Channel B represents the typical chain for mass-marketed consumer goods. Manufacturers selling a wide range of products over a wide geographical area to a market numbered in millions would find it prohibitively expensive to set up their own Highstreet stores, even if they were permitted to proliferate in this way. For such manufacturers (eg of foodstuffs, confectionery, footwear, clothing and soaps, to name but a few), middlemen are important links in the chain. Wholesalers, for example, buy in bulk from the manufacturers, store the goods, break them down into smaller quantities, undertake advertising and promotional activities, deliver to other traders, usually retailers, and arrange credit and other services for them. Their role is important to both manufacturer and retailer. The role of the latter is to make products available at the point-of-sale. Individual consumers need accessibility and convenience from their local sources of consumable products. They also need to see what is available, and what alternatives are offered. A retail store, whether owned by an independent trader or a huge supermarket chain, offers various advantages to consumers: stocks of items, displays of goods,

opportunity to buy in *small* quantities, and convenient access to these services. So far as manufacturers and wholesalers are concerned the retailer is, above all, an outlet for their products, and an important source of market intelligence concerning customer buying habits and preferences.

7.    Channel C represents one of the shorter indirect channels, where the retailer is omitted. This kind of operation can be found in mail-order businesses, and in cash-and-carry outlets. The former are usually composed of the larger mail-order firms, offering a very wide range of goods (and some services, too). They buy from manufacturers, store and subsequently distribute direct to customers on a nation-wide basis. Their ability to attract custom in the first place relies heavily on (a) comprehensive, colourful and well-produced catalogues, and (b) the use of part-time agents, usually housewives, working on a commission basis. Whilst such an operation does not generally offer any price advantage over a retail business, it is a very convenient way of choosing goods and there is always extended credit available. With the wider use of computers in the home, and the prospects, in the not-too-distant future of being able to order goods via a telephone link, mail-order business seems likely to grow.

8.    Cash-and-carry outlets usually deal in groceries, and many are open only to trade customers. They tend to rely on a rapid turnover of stock, to keep down inventory levels. Their main advantages for buyers are (a) price, which is significantly lower than in a retail operation, and (b) the opportunity to buy small bulk quantities. Unlike mail-order businesses, they serve relatively local and specialised markets.

9.    Channel D is another version of a shorter, indirect channel. In this case, it is the wholesaler who is removed from the scene. Not surprisingly, the retailers who dominate this channel are powerful chains or multiples in their own right. Some such retailers, as in the footwear trade, concentrate on one range of goods only. They buy in bulk from manufacturers and importers, and distribute direct to their retail outlets. They usually offer a wide selection of lines, and are very competitively priced. Other large retail groups handle a diversity of goods, which are again competitively priced, and made available in prime shopping areas. The Woolworths chain was a pioneer in this field. Other examples include Marks and Spencer, and British Home Stores, two chains which based themselves originally on the clothing trade, but which between them have diversified into footwear, foodstuffs, toys and books, amongst other items. One of the important features of chains such

as Marks and Spencer is their use of private (ie own-name) branding, which is either used exclusively or at least predominantly. Other chains, such as Boots, supply a wide range of other brands in addition to their own. Invariably, the own-brand range is offered at lower prices than the competing brands. This is an advantage to the consumer, but not necessarily to the manufacturer, who may well have made both!

## MARKET SEGMENTATION

10. The above reference to large and powerful retail chains implies that they can exert a strong influence in the marketplace. This influence works in two directions:

    (a) it enables them to demand standards of quality, and ranges of goods which fit into *their* market strategy, rather than accepting what the manufacturer might prefer;

    (b) it enables them to cultivate a particular part, or segment, of a market. Some footwear chains are exclusively geared to meeting the demands of fashion conscious teenagers, for example. Others are aimed mainly at a middle-aged market, where comfort and quality are more important than the current fashion. In both examples, a conscious attempt has been made to segment the market.

11. The term 'market segmentation' is based on the concept that most, if not all, markets are made up of different types of customers ie within each total market, there exist sub-markets which express distinctive product preferences compared with each other. Market segmentation, therefore, can be defined as the sub-division of a market into identifiable buyer-groups, or sub-markets, with the aim of reaching such groups with a particular marketing mix. To take an example: in the private motor-car market as a whole there are several different sub-markets, ranging from buyers who are looking for sports cars, through those interested in family saloons and estate cars to those requiring a small, economical second car. A manufacturer may decide to attempt to meet the needs of the entire market or may decide to specialise in, say, sports cars. Either way such a manufacturer and his distributors have to vary their marketing mix, if they are to attract the 'right' kind of customer. The product offered, the price range, the manner of promotion and the distribution arrangements must all be considered carefully in the light of the differing requirements of the different market segments.

12. Market segmentation is especially important in consumer markets, where the numbers of potential buyers can be measured

in millions. The most frequent methods of segmenting a market are based on geographical, demographic and buyer-behaviour variables, as indicated in Figure 34.2 below:

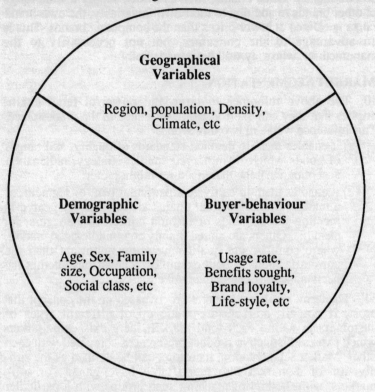

**Geographical Variables**

Region, population, Density, Climate, etc

**Demographic Variables**

Age, Sex, Family size, Occupation, Social class, etc

**Buyer-behaviour Variables**

Usage rate, Benefits sought, Brand loyalty, Life-style, etc

**Figure 34.2. Market Segmentation Variables.**

13. Geographical variables, such as regions and populations, may be of the utmost significance to suppliers of such goods as delicatessen foods or skiing equipment, for example. Such goods are attractive to specialised segments of the markets for food and sports equipment respectively. Attempts to achieve sales without segmenting these markets would result in a great deal of wasted effort. Large retail chains are usually only prepared to locate stores in areas of high population density, in order to gain the economies of scale that large local markets can stimulate. This is the result of a conscious decision to segment their markets in this way.

14. Demographic segmentation involves the sub-division of markets on the basis of variables such as age, sex, occupation and class, for example. Magazines and journals are examples of

products which are directed towards carefully segmented markets (readership). In addition to the basic reading material, the advertising contained in each edition reflects the segmentation. For example, a magazine aimed at mothers with young children will carry articles of interest to such mothers, and advertisements inserted by suppliers of mother-and-baby products. Age is a powerful basis for segmentation (a) because of the physical changes brought about by growth and ageing, and (b) because of frequently differing attitudes and preferences between age-groups. In retail operations, particular stores or chains will focus on particular segments of the market (eg Mothercare), whilst others will aim to attract a wide range of customers into their shops, but will organize their shelf-displays to cater for segment needs. Thus W.H. Smith's shops offer a wide range of magazines, books and records as well as fairly standard ranges of stationery and similar items, in order to meet the needs of a wide range of tastes from a variety of ages and social classes.

15. Segmentation by social class is aided, in Britain, by the use of a social grading structure based on the occupation of the head of each household. The grades which are used are as follows in Figure 32.3:

| Social Grade | Social Status | Occupation (Head of Household) |
|---|---|---|
| A | Upper Middle Class | Higher Managerial, administrative or professional |
| B | Middle Class | Intermediate Managerial, administrative or professional |
| C1 | Lower Middle Class | Supervisory, clerical or junior managerial etc |
| C2 | Skilled Working Class | Skilled manual workers |
| D | Working Class | Semi-skilled or unskilled manual workers |
| E | Subsistence Levels | Pensioners or widows on basic pension; casual and lowest paid workers |

**Figure 34.3. Social Class Grading Structure: UK.**

16. Whilst social class is a demographic factor, it is also a prime determinant of buyer-behaviour variables, since class background influences tastes, values and attitudes. For example, in beer advertisements there is a strong appeal to working class loyalty,

often to particular, local brews. By comparison, pre-Christmas television advertisements for liqueurs are openly aimed at those who are, or would like to be, middle and upper middle class. These appeals to distinctive class values are not hit-and-miss affairs, but are based on careful research into class preferences for particular goods and services.

17. An important variable in buyer behaviour is usage rate. Some buyers are very light users of a product, whereas others use the same product frequently. For example, there are regular readers of a particular Sunday newspaper, and these represent the core of its readership, but there are also occasional and casual readers, who may buy because of its coverage of particular events. Taking usage rate as a variable essentially means segmenting on the basis of volume purchased. If a supplier decides to increase his market share by attracting higher usage by occasional users, he must first attempt to find out whether they buy competitors' goods or not, or where there is something about the present marketing mix which dissuades them from buying more frequently. British Rail, for example, has conducted numerous surveys amongst the travelling public to enquire why they do not make more use of trains. Clearly, the family motorcar is the biggest competitor for seats on a journey, and price is probably the biggest disadvantage of rail travel. Therefore, to increase the usage rate for non-business travellers, some special price arrangements are needed to encourage people to leave their cars at home and travel by train instead. British Rail has offered a wide range of economy fares for off-peak periods as a result of its surveys. In their case, usage rate is an important aspect of marketing because of the high level of fixed costs involved in operating a railway network.

18. The approaches to market segmentation referred to above apply more naturally to consumer markets than to industrial markets, where an entire market may be made up of just a few customers. Industrial segmentation usually takes place on one or more of the following bases:

  a. Type of buyer – Government, public service, private firm etc.
  b. Customer size – Large, medium or small.
  c. Class of buyer – Insists on quality or economy or service, for example.
  d. Trade group – Standard Industrial Classification entry.
  e. End-use – Routine/non-routine, specialised/general etc.
  f. Usage rate – Regular or infrequent buyer.
  g. Location – Domestic or overseas, regional/national etc.

19. Industrial segmentation occurs when a micro-computer business applies differing marketing mixes to two markets, one of small private businesses, and the other of State secondary schools. The first market may be offered complete packages of equipment, including a printer and additional storage units in addition to the central processor and visual display unit. The package will be offered at a competitive rate in the medium price range for such a product. A regular follow-up servicing arrangement will be included as well as full training manuals. By comparison, the second market will be offered a cheaper price for a less comprehensive service. Instead of packages, it is more likely that options based on a central processor and visual display unit will be offered, to enable buyers to spend more on input and output devices rather than on storage and printing facilities. A key consideration in this example is the end-use to which the customer wishes to put the product. In the case of a small private business, the use is primarily aimed at invoicing, accounting and stock control activities. The school's use is primarily aimed at familiarisation training for pupils.

20. The principal benefits of market segmentation from the seller's point of view are that:
   a. he has a better idea of the total market picture, especially in relation to marketing opportunities between segments of that market,
   b. he can tailor his marketing mix to suit the needs of particular segments,
   c. by gaining familiarity with one or more segments, he is more likely to be able to assess the response from them, which is an invaluable asset for planning purposes.

21. The main benefit from the customer's point of view is that he is likely to have his needs met in a more appropriate way than if the market is not segmented ie where the same product range and price are offered regardless of geographical, demographic and buyer-behaviour considerations.

## PHYSICAL DISTRIBUTION

22. Whereas channels of distribution are marketing *institutions*, physical distribution is a *set of activities*. The former provide the managerial and administrative framework for moving products from supplier to customer. The latter provide the physical means of so doing. Physical distribution is concerned with order processing, warehousing, transport, packaging, stock/inventory levels and customer service. In recent years a number of attempts

to integrate and coordinate these functions has come to be called Physical Distribution Management. This aims to integrate the activities of marketing, production and other departments in this aspect of the organization's marketing task.

23. The degree of attention paid to physical distribution depends considerably on the proportion of total costs taken up by distribution costs. If the product is a high-quality, high-cost item, then distribution costs will probably represent a small proportion of total costs of manufacturing and marketing it, and so physical distribution may be considered very much a secondary issue. Where the product is offered at a very competitive price, and hence where profit margins may be tight, all overhead costs will be carefully examined. In this situation distribution costs will form an important issue for the supplier. An important feature of such costs is that they tend to increase rather than decrease with sales volume. Whereas unit production costs tend to benefit from increased volume of production, distribution costs tend to worsen. A high level of customer service also tends to greatly increase distribution costs. For example, if a customer requires 100% delivery from stock within two days, this means carrying extra stock levels as a buffer against any shortfall in supplies to the warehouse. If that customer could be persuaded to reduce his requirements to, say, 80% delivery within two days, this might effect useful savings in distribution costs.

## SUMMARY

24. Distribution is a key part of any marketing mix. It involves selecting the best channels by which to ensure the movement of goods and services from their original suppliers to their eventual consumers. The channels of distribution are marketing institutions such as wholesalers and retailers. A variety of channel options is available. A direct marketing channel moves goods directly from manufacturer to consumer. An indirect channel utilises intermediaries or middlemen, such as wholesalers.

25. Market segmentation is undertaken by suppliers in order to get a clearer picture of the market-place in order to offer a particular marketing mix to one or more segments. The concept assumes that within any single market there are invariably other sub-markets.

26. Consumer markets are usually segmented on the basis of geography, demography and buyer-behaviour. Industrial markets are segmented in a roughly similar fashion, but also include consideration of trade groups and end-use.

27.  Physical distribution is a term covering a set of activities aimed at achieving the physical movement of goods from supplier to consumer. It involves order processing, warehousing and transport and related activities. Physical distribution management aims to integrate the responsibilities of marketing, production and other departments engaged in aspects of distribution.

# 35

# MARKETING RESEARCH

## INTRODUCTION

1.   Marketing research is fundamentally about the acquisition and analysis of information required for the making of marketing decisions. The two basic areas in which the information is sought are (a) markets (existing and potential), and (b) marketing tactics and methods. The former is orientated towards what is happening *outside* the organization, in the market-place. The second is orientated towards the way in which the organization is responding *internally* to its customers, present and future.

2.   Kotler (op.cit.) sees an increasing need for marketing information, because of three important trends in marketing. These are:

   a.   the shift from purely local to wider national and international markets,
   b.   the changing emphasis from buyer needs to buyer wants,
   c.   the trend towards competition based on non-price weapons.

The implications of these points are that wider markets are not as familiar to suppliers as local markets, and they must therefore seek out sources of information about distant markets. The move away from relatively predictable needs towards much less predictable wants requires much more research into buyer behaviour. The trend towards non-price competition requires firms to evaluate their own methods of assembling the marketing mix for their markets. Ought a better after-sales service be offered to hold off competitors? How effective are our advertising campaigns compared with our competitors? Should we put more effort into sales promotions? These are examples of the kind of questions which firms have to face. In order to answer them they need marketing research.

3.   The data which forms the raw material of marketing research can be placed under two categories: primary and secondary. *Primary data* is gathered directly from the persons concerned, be they customers, wholesalers, or even competitors, for example. Such data is usually collected by means of surveys and other formalised methods. *Secondary data* is information available from published sources externally, and from company records. The use

of secondary material is cheaper than developing primary data, but may be less relevant or up-to-date.

4.   A marketing research study usually includes the following steps:

   a. Definition of problem and specification of information to be sought
   b. Design of study/project, with particular reference to data collection methods (surveys etc), instrumentation (questionnaires etc) and sample design (of target population)
   c. Field work (utilising questionnaires, structured interviews, consumer panels)
   d. Data analysis (using statistical and O.R. techniques)
   e. Presentation of report.

5.   As was noted earlier, marketing operates on the *external* boundaries of the organization. Its main object of attention is the customer (or market-place), and it is the customer's response, or non-response, that gives rise to most of the problems which marketing research is applied to. A typical problem could be that of a falling market share for one or more of the organization's product lines. In order to clarify the problem, and put it into perspective, a number of questions need to be asked. For example, 'Is the market expanding, declining or stable?'; 'What is the situation for competitors?'; 'Is the threat from UK competitors, or from overseas?'; 'What advantages, if any, are enjoyed by competitive products?'; 'What is the organization's reputation with its existing customers?'; and so on. Some of these questions can be answered by analysing secondary data and others by analysing primary data.

6.   Sources of secondary data are twofold: firstly, internal information from sales budgets, field sales reports and others; and secondly, external information from Government statistics, trade, banking and other reports, the press and marketing research agencies. The last-mentioned – marketing research agencies – play a significant role in the whole area of marketing research. They are employed not only by firms with no market research specialists of their own, but also by firms with large market research departments. Some agencies offer a comprehensive marketing research service, some offer a range of specialised services and others offer what is basically an information-selling service. Some well-known agencies include A.C. Nielsen which provides regular data on sales, brand shares and prices etc in the retail trade, Gallup, which specialises in opinion research, and AGB (Audits of Great

Britain), which is heavily involved in television audience measurement. Television and readership surveys in Britain are conducted under the umbrella of two national bodies – JICTAR (Joint Industry Committee for Television Advertising Research), which meters a representative sample of television sets throughout the nation, and JICNARS (Joint Industry Committee for National Readership Surveys), which conducts, and reports on, 30,000 interviews annually, covering over 100 different publications.

7. Primary data is most frequently collected by means of surveys, based on questionnaires or interviews. These surveys are invariably undertaken by specialist research organizations, since the construction and administration of questionnaires is a highly-skilled operation. Interviews are generally conducted in a structured form, so as to ensure consistency between interviewers. The agencies use trained interviewers, briefed about the objectives of each assignment. Both the questionnaires and the structured interviews tend to concentrate on *what* the customer likes and dislikes, rather than *why*. This last question is handled by means of a number of behavioural techniques, which form part of what has been called motivational research. The techniques include in-depth, and less-structured, interviews, discussion groups, role-playing and psychological tests. Motivation research is one of the newer aspects of marketing research, and since it concentrates on motives and attitudes, it relies heavily on the expertise of psychologists for the design of and interpretation of its surveys.

8. Some of the more important advantages and disadvantages of the three approaches described are as follows:

| | | Advantages | Disadvantages |
|---|---|---|---|
| a. | Questionn-aires | Wide coverage. Low cost. | Difficult to construct. Low return rate. |
| b. | Structured interviews | More flexible than questionnaires. Product etc can be shown to consumer. Target population can be controlled. | Costly and time-consuming. Permits interviewer and consumer bias. |
| c. | Motivational Research | Better understanding of consumer decisions. | Is only applied to small groups. Costly and time-consuming. Not easy to interpret results. |

9.    Some or all of the above approaches may be applied to consumer panels, which are permanent groups representing a cross-section of a particular market. These panels are used by individual companies and by specialised agencies, such as A.C. Nielsen. They receive regular samples of different products and lines, about which they complete questionnaires, diaries and similar records. They are usually well-disposed towards researchers and are good subjects for interview as well as questionnaires. The main advantage of panels is that they provide feedback over a period of time, which increases the reliability of their responses compared with people who may have been stopped for a brief interview outside their local supermarket, for example. The main disadvantage is that panels tend to be influenced in their buying behaviour by the role they are playing in consumer research. On balance, the advantages to be gained from panels outweigh the disadvantages.

10.    So far we have been concerned mainly with the *market* research aspects of marketing research. The other prime interest of marketing research, as was noted in paragraph 1 in this chapter, is the way in which the organization responds to the demands of the market-place. The most important method of evaluating the organization's total marketing effort is by employing a marketing audit. This is an independent examination of an organization's marketing objectives, marketing activities and marketing environment with the primary aims of assessing present effectiveness and of recommending future action. The audit needs to be carried out on a periodic rather than on an ad hoc basis, and, like any other rational evaluation, needs to be conducted in a systematic way. The audit may be carried out by the organization's own staff or by external consultants. The requirements of the task call for objectivity, independence and suitable experience. Many firms feel that these requirements can best be found in external rather than internal sources.

11.    A systematic audit would encompass the following aspects of the organization's marketing system:

| a.  The Marketing Environment | Economic and demographic trends<br>Technological change<br>Legal developments<br>Social change<br>Markets, Customers, Competitors, Suppliers, Middlemen, etc |
|---|---|

| | |
|---|---|
| b. Marketing Strategy | Corporate objectives<br>Marketing objectives<br>Marketing plan (strategy)<br>Marketing resources<br>Strengths and weaknesses |
| c. Marketing Plans and Control | Sales forecasting<br>Market plans<br>Product development<br>Control procedures<br>Marketing research |
| d. Marketing mix | Evaluation of products, pricing policies, advertising and sales promotion, channels of distribution and sales force |
| e. Profitability and Cost-effectiveness | Profitability of products and markets<br>Marketing costs |
| f. The Marketing Organization | Management structure<br>Staff motivation<br>Efficiency<br>Training<br>Relationships with other departments |

12. The advantage of such an audit lies in its ability to produce a critical assessment of the organization's marketing strengths and weaknesses, whilst at the same time weighing up the threats and opportunities posed by the external environment. This critical assessment is valuable to the organization's corporate planning process as well as to its marketing planning. The main disadvantages are those of time and cost. It takes a considerable amount of time to conduct an audit covering the points mentioned above, and this time is expensive in labour costs.

## SUMMARY

13. Marketing research is the title given to those activities which aim to provide information about markets and marketing methods for the purpose of facilitating decision-making in marketing.

14. Marketing research data comes in two basic forms: (a) primary data, which is obtained first-hand from customers, competitors and others in the market-place; and (b) secondary data, which is obtained from various internal and external sources, mainly company records and published reports and statistics.

15. A typical market research study encompasses the following steps: it defines the problem, specifies the information required, designs the methodology of the study, conducts the necessary fieldwork, analyses the data obtained and, finally, presents a report to the management.

16. Much of the secondary data available to marketing researchers originates from specialist marketing research agencies, which provide information on sales, prices, market shares, and other key factors. Such agencies utilise consumer panels, readership surveys and television audience measurement to generate their information.

17. Primary data is usually obtained by means of questionnaires and structured interviews, administered by trained personnel. A newer approach to gaining primary data, especially about consumer motives and attitudes, is called motivational research. This approach utilises interviews (unstructured), group discussions and psychological tests to gain the required information.

18. The assessment of an organization's marketing effectiveness is carried out by means of an audit. A marketing audit is a systematic evaluation, carried out by independent personnel, of the external marketing environment, the organization's own marketing strategy, its marketing plans, its marketing mix, its cost-effectiveness, and finally, its marketing organization (structure and personnel).

# 36

# MARKETING ORGANIZATION

## INTRODUCTION

1.   As was noted in Chapter 31, there are several ways of looking at marketing. Some organizations see it as an extension of their production process, others as the means by which their product or service is brought to the attention of the marketplace. Yet other organizations see marketing as essentially a selling activity, and finally, there are those who see marketing as an activity which begins and ends with the customer. Naturally, the particular group of values which are held will determine whether the organization will have a marketing department at all, and, if it does have one, what kind of department it will be.

2.   This chapter assumes that the organization sees some definite role for a marketing department, even if it is not a *comprehensive* marketing role. The next few paragraphs outline (a) the major structural alternatives that are available to a marketing department, (b) the principal objectives of a marketing department, and (c) the differing perspectives between the marketing department and other departments in the organization.

## MARKETING STRUCTURES

3.   Marketing grew out of sales activities. It eventually absorbed these activities into its own growth and development. This radical change of role for marketing led to a major change of organization structure, at least for those organizations that adopted the marketing concept.

4.   The early process of change was as follows (Figures 36.1–36.4)

**Figure 34. 1 – Stage One**

At this stage there is no specific marketing section or department. The Sales Manager is responsible for advertising and promotion as well as selling.

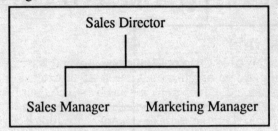

**Figure 36.2 - Stage Two**

Stage two introduces the first formal recognition of marketing as such, but places the marketing manager under the direction of the Sales Director. At this stage marketing is seen as an important provider of information to support the organization's sales effort. The marketing section will probably be concerned with advertising, sales promotion, product-development and marketing research.

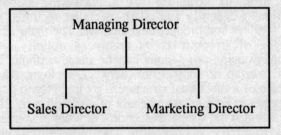

**Figure 36.3 - Stage Three**

By Stage three, marketing has moved up to a position of equality with sales. This situation probably produces the maximum amount of conflict between sales and marketing, as the former concentrate on their preocccupation with current sales and the latter concentrate on long-term market developments. Since marketing will see the sales effort as part of the total marketing mix, there will be a strong desire to tell sales what to do and why! The resolution of this built-in conflict has been achieved, in many companies, by giving predominance to marketing, as shown in Figure 36.4 below:

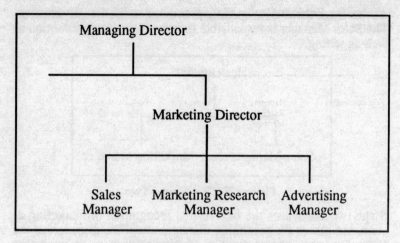

**Figure 36.4 - Stage Four**

5.  Stage four presents a functional view of the marketing department. The separate specialisms of sales, research and advertising/promotions each have their own manager. This is a common form of structure for a marketing department. Organizations frequently add other specialist sections, such as customer services and product development. The main advantage of this type of structure is its relative simplicity, whereby identifiable divisions of labour can be made without causing unwanted overlap or competition between sections. The main disadvantage of a functional structure is its inability to cope with multiple products or markets, because of difficulties in allocating priorities amongst the specialist sections. In order to cope with the increased diversity of decision-making required in these circumstances, several companies have introduced a matrix-type of structure, incorporating a number of operational roles, as in Figure 36.5 opposite.

This structure allocates specific responsibility for individual products/product groups and for specific markets, whilst retaining all the key functional posts. As in every matrix structure, the operational roles have reporting responsibilities to functional managers as well as to their immediate line managers. So, for example, a Brand Manager's freedom to act is not only prescribed by his immediate Product Group Manager, but also by any one of the functional managers, in respect of his own speciality. Thus, advertising programmes for a Brand would have to be agreed not only by the Product Group Manager, but also by the Advertising Manager.

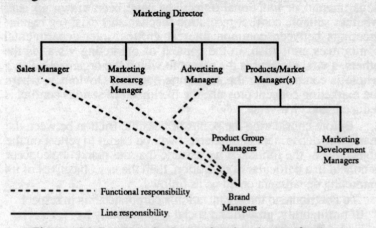

**Figure 36.5. - Matrix Organization in Marketing.**

6.   In very large organizations, where a divisionalized structure may have developed because of product or geographical reasons, for example, a decision has to be made about splitting the marketing activities between the divisions and corporate headquarters. Here the underlying values of the organization's top management come into operation. If the philosophy is to decentralise, in the way described in Chapter 21, that is to say by effectively delegating authority to the sub-units, then it is likely that little or no role will be available for a corporate marketing department. If, however, divisionalization is seen as a way of delegating part, but only part, of the organization's marketing effort, then a definite marketing role at corporate level will be established. A corporate role could just be confined to the provision of specialist services, such as marketing research and specialist advertising advice. Alternatively, there could be a strong corporate role, giving the staff concerned the right to direct key functional aspects of marketing in the divisions, eg in terms of product-design, corporate image, and marketing control information systems.

## THE MARKETING DEPARTMENT IN THE ORGANIZATION

7.   The question of conflict within the marketing function has already been touched on. We can now turn to the possible conflicts that can occur between the marketing department and other departments. In any organization it is natural for each sub-division to have its own perspective concerning the ultimate goals of the

organization, and the best way of achieving them. The degree of conflict which may occur depends largely on the way in which departmental or functional objectives have been drawn up, and whether suitable conflict-resolution mechanisms exist (eg regular meetings between common interest groups, inter-departmental committees etc). Also, in the context of marketing vis-a-vis the others, a vital element is the extent to which the organization as a whole is committed to the marketing concept. Obviously, where the marketing concept prevails, the likelihood of serious conflict is reduced, and vice-versa.

8.    Before considering the points of possible friction between the marketing department and others, it will be useful to reflect on the objectives of the former. If we assume that the marketing concept is upheld in a particular organization, then the key objectives of its marketing department could be as follows:

'To contribute to the organization's corporate aims in respect of profitability, growth and social responsibility by

a.  Proposing, and seeking acceptance for, improvements in the organization's marketing policies;
b.  Seeking out and identifying advantageous marketing opportunities;
c.  Preparing, in conjunction with other departments, suit-able marketing strategies to meet opportunities identified; d. Selling and distributing the organization's products;
e.  Developing new products in the market-place;
f.  Designing and implementing approved marketing plans;
g.  Acquiring sufficient and suitable information, both internal and external, concerning the organization's products, and their impact on customers, competitors, suppliers and others in the market-place;
h.  Ensuring that the organization's products are brought to the attention of existing and potential customers by means of suitable advertising and promotional methods;
i.  Promoting a reputable image for the organization in the market-place.'

9.    The opening sentence of the above list of objectives was included advisedly to indicate the contributive nature of the marketing department's efforts to corporate aims. Other departments, too, make their contribution to these overall aims. If the organization's strategy has been worked out in a thorough and

collaborative way, there should exist a mutual understanding of roles as between departments. This will affect the manner in which problems of misunderstanding and conflict are handled. However, there is no practical way in which it is possible to *avoid* all such misunderstandings and conflict. Even within the marketing department, there are potential conflicts. For example, the conflicts between current sales effort and market development and between short-term profits and long-term growth.

10. There are similar tensions between short- and long-term gains in other departments, and, of course, between departments. Some of the most important sources of friction between the marketing department and other departments are as indicated below.

| Marketing Preoccupations | Others' Preoccupations |
|---|---|
| *Production* | |
| a. Short production runs | Long production runs |
| Wide variety of models | Small range |
| Tailor-made orders | Standardisation |
| *Purchasing* | |
| b. Broad product line | Narrow product line |
| Ample stocks | Tight stocks |
| Quality of stock | Price of stock |
| *R & D* | |
| c. Applied research | Pure research |
| Sales benefits | Functional features |
| *Finance* | |
| d. Flexible budgets | Tight budgets |
| Pricing to promote market development | Pricing to cover costs |
| Easy credit terms | Tough credit terms |

11. The overall conclusion to be drawn from the above list is that the marketing department, in particular, disturbs the routines that other departments like to set for themselves in order to achieve efficiency in their own organization. This happens because marketing personnel are more concerned with what the customer desires, rather than whether it is practicable to give him what he desires. Marketing's task is to define the customer's needs and wants, but it is up to the other departments to convert those needs and wants into practical reality. In a truly market-orientated organization there will be a greater willingness to respond positively to the varied demands of marketing than in an organization whose orientation lies elsewhere, in production, for example.

## SUMMARY

12. Marketing departments grew out of the sales function in organizations. In many cases they are now wider in scope than the function which gave them birth; in others they are at least on a par with the sales function. Modern marketing departments usually encompass sales, marketing research, advertising and promotion, customer services and product development. They may also include product and/or market management, where these are diverse enough.

13. The principal structural options open to marketing departments are (a) a functional structure, based on individual specialisms eg sales etc, and (b) a matrix structure, based on functional roles eg sales managers, market research managers etc and groups of operational roles eg product managers, market managers etc. The matrix type of structure is more common in organizations with a diversity of products, brands or markets. In large de-centralised organizations, the marketing function may be split between sub-divisions and corporate headquarters.

14. The objectives of a marketing department are directed towards the attainment of corporate aims, such as profitability growth and social responsibility. Marketing contributes principally by identifying market opportunities for the organization, by designing a suitable strategy for meeting those opportunities, and then by implementing approved plans, in collaboration with other departments.

15. In pursuing its objectives, the marketing department will inevitably experience tensions between its aims and methods and those of its sister departments. This is mainly because it seeks, first of all, to satisfy the customer's needs and wants, whereas its colleagues seek rationality and efficiency of operations.

# 37

# CONSUMER PROTECTION

## INTRODUCTION

1. Commercial organizations spend a great deal of effort on assessing the needs and wants of their customers, and yet, as we saw in Chapter 31 (The Marketing Concept), there is a variety of possible orientations towards customers. Not all firms are 'market orientated' to the extent that they put the customers' needs and wants before all else. Even if firms were completely market orientated, they would still make errors of judgement from time to time. Therefore, even in the best-regulated circles, the customer may sometimes be badly treated. Over recent years consumers have become more vocal in reacting to shoddy products or poor service. As a result there are now Government, as well as private consumer organizations, whose purpose is to stand up for consumers' rights. The word 'consumerism' has been coined to describe the activities of pressure groups in this area, and the term 'consumer protection' used to describe the efforts made by Government and other bodies to provide rules and codes of conduct for relations between commercial organizations and their customers.

2. A consumer may be defined as 'any person (including a corporate body) who buys goods and services for money.' In the United Kingdom, there are several means by which consumer interests may be protected. These involve the application of one or more of the following:

   a. The Common Law
   b. Acts of Parliament
   c. Codes of 'Good Practice'
   d. Trade Marks
   e. Independent Consumer Groups

Each of these will be looked at briefly in this chapter, which will also examine some of the leading public and private pressure groups which help ordinary citizens to obtain redress against unfair trading in goods and services.

## COMMON LAW RIGHTS

3. Common law rights are acquired as a result of custom and practice over many years. In consumer matters these rights have

not stood the test of time, and in modern economic conditions, Britain and other Western nations have had to introduce numerous statutory regulations to clarify and indeed strengthen the rights of individual consumers. However, there are still general rules which apply to those who provide goods and services to the community. For example, a person offering a service must carry it out in a proper and workmanlike way, or to a standard agreed with the customer. Providers also have a duty of care in relation to any property (eg motor vehicle, television set etc) which a customer leaves with them.

## STATUTORY RIGHTS

4.   By far the greatest protection for consumers in Britain is provided by parliament, which in several important pieces of legislation has set up a framework in which the respective rights and duties of consumers and suppliers can be identified and clarified.

The most important statutes concerning consumer affairs include the following:

- Sale of Goods Act, 1979
- Trade Descriptions Act, 1968
- Consumer Safety Act, 1978
- Consumer Credit Act, 1974
- Unfair Contract Terms Act, 1977
- Fair Trading Act, 1973
- Supply of Goods and Services Act, 1982

The key features of these Acts will be described briefly below.

5.   So far as the sales of goods are concerned, the current law is consolidated in the *Sale of Goods Act, 1979*. This emphasises that goods must fulfil three basic conditions:

- a. they must be of merchantable quality
- b. they must be fit for the purpose and
- c. they must be as described

An example of how these conditions might be broken is as follows.

A person buys a new washing machine, and is unfortunate enough to discover that (a) the cabinet is badly scratched, and thus not of merchantable quality; (b) the machine ripped up the first batch of clothes and half-flooded the kitchen (ie it was not fit for the purpose); and (c) the model delivered by the suppliers was not the model agreed upon in the shop (ie the goods were not as described by the retailer). The remedies available to the consumer depend on the circumstances of the breach. For example, in the case of situation (b) above, there would be a right to a complete refund of the price paid together with compensation for loss and damage caused. In the case of (a) it is likely that the retailer would replace the machine, but his obligation would only be to offer a discount on the price in view of the damaged surface. In the case of (c), the customer is entitled to his money back. Note that suppliers are not obliged to offer anything more than cash compensation.

6.   The Sale of Goods Act, 1979 also contains provisions preventing consumers' rights from being eroded by exclusion clauses and special guarantees.

7.   Protection against being misled by false or inaccurate descriptions of goods on sale is provided by the *Trade Descriptions Act, 1968*. This Act has been used successfully by motorists, who have discovered that they had been deceived about the previous mileage covered by a second-hand car. The winding-back of car mileometers is a contravention of this Act. In such a case the dealer can be prosecuted and fined.

8.   The consumer's physical safety is considered in the *Consumer Safety Act, 1978*, which draws up regulations to minimise risks to consumers from potentially dangerous products, such as oil heaters, electric blankets and certain children's toys.

9.   Moneylenders have abounded in every society, and in recent years have achieved great importance in developed economies because of the stimulus that their services have given to trade. However, it has become increasingly important, too, that borrowers should not be exploited unknowingly. In Britain the *Consumer Credit Act, 1974* requires that borrowers should know the true rate of interest being charged, and, where an agreement is signed away from trade premises, the person is entitled to change his mind. There are also conditions preventing consumers from being unfairly penalised, if they get into arrears. The Act affects all transactions between £50 - £15000.

10.   Another protection for consumers in their dealings with commercial organizations is provided by the *Unfair Contract Terms Act, 1977*, which protects individuals against possible loss of rights from exclusion clauses and disclaimer notices on posters, tickets etc. Under the Act a contractor cannot 'contract out' of his liability for death or personal injury arising from his negligence, for example by supplying a vehicle with faulty brakes. Nor can he supply goods or services in a substantially different way from those ordered, for example by providing a 1Mb microcomputer

when a 10Mb version was what the customer ordered. The Act also stipulates that a *manufacturer's* guarantee cannot exclude liability for damage caused or loss suffered as a result of the manufacturer's negligence. Disclaimer notices, such as 'Articles left at owner's risk...etc' are not valid unless the firm concerned can show in court that they were reasonable in the circumstances, and in any case would not protect the firm against any claim arising out of the negligence in respect of the articles.

11. One of the growing practices in modern legislation is to set up supervisory bodies, or 'watchdogs', to monitor the effects of the law in society. In the consumer rights arena the central watchdog is provided by the Office of Fair Trading, set up by the *Fair Trading Act, 1973* to encourage voluntary codes of practice between sellers and their customers, and to provide a central reference point for doubtful cases and matters of principle. Currently codes of practice have been established in trades such as:

- motorcar servicing
- laundry services
- electrical repair work
- package holidays
- funeral services

12. The Fair Trading Act, 1973 also set up the Monopolies and Mergers Commission to:

a. investigate and report on references that relate to the existence of a monopoly situation, ie where 25% of a particular market is supplied by one supplier or supply group;

b. investigate mergers between business organizations. The intention of these investigations is to ascertain if there could be any adverse effect on the public interest as a result of a particular monopoly or merger situation. Adverse effects could include: a restricted choice of products/services, and a lack of responsiveness to consumer pressure.

13. The *Supply of Goods and Services Act, 1982*, was introduced to improve the consumers' rights in relation to poor service or workmanship. The Act was needed to make up for the shortcomings of the Sale of Goods Act, 1979, which applied only to the transfer of goods from a seller to a buyer and not to a situation where goods were being provided as part of a service, such as building work and car repairs, for example. The new Act adopts a similar approach to the Sale of Goods Act in respect of

description, merchantable quality and fitness for purpose of goods, but applies it to:

a. contracts for work and materials
b. part-exchange contracts (barter)
c. 'free gifts'
d. contracts for the hire of goods

The new Act also codifies the Common Law requirements relating to three key aspects of service, ie skill, time and price. The Act requires suppliers of services to act with reasonable care and skill, and to complete the work within a reasonable time. The purchaser is required to pay a reasonable price for the service. The Act also tightens up the application of the Unfair Contract Terms Act, 1977, in respect of services and disclaimer clauses.

## CODES OF PRACTICE

14. The Fair Trading Act, 1973, requires the Director General of Fair Trading to encourage Trade associations to draw up codes of practice for fair trading. Codes do not have the force of law in their own right, but are nevertheless very influential when a court is determining the rights and wrongs of a situation. Codes are less formal, more easily amended and less time-consuming to operate than legal provisions. Codes of practice have been developed by associations such as the Association of British Travel Agents, the Motor Agents Association and the Mail Order Traders' Association.

15. Since advertising and promotion play such a significant part in the marketing of consumer goods, it is not surprising that consumer protection applies to these activities. The *Trade Descriptions Act, 1968* has already been mentioned, but there are two very important voluntary bodies operating in this field - the *Advertising Standards Authority* and the *Independent Broadcasting Authority*.

16. The *Advertising Standards Authority* embraces press, poster, cinema advertising and direct mail. It has developed the *British Code of Advertising Practice* whose intentions are primarily to ensure that:

- advertisements are legal, decent, honest and truthful
- advertisements are prepared with a sense of responsibility to the consumer
- advertising conforms to the principle of fair competition
- advertisers do not bring the advertising industry into disrepute

17. An example of how the industry maintains its standards can be seen in the treatment of a complaint against a Japanese motor manufacturer by a member of the public (ASA Case Report 119, 1985). In this case the advertisement said 'Let us lead you into temptation' and described one of its models as having 'A decidedly illegal top speed.' The complainant considered that the advertisement was likely to encourage drivers to drive in excess of the legal speed limit. The complaint was upheld, and the advertisement was withdrawn.

18. Advertisements on commercial radio and television are controlled by the Independent Broadcasting Authority, which has produced a code of practice for advertisers to ensure, so far as possible, the legality, truthfulness and reputation of broadcast advertising.

## OTHER STANDARDS

19. Probably the most well-known body in Britain for establishing voluntary standards of quality and reliability is the *British Standards Institution*, whose famous Kitemark indicates that goods conform to the high standards set by the Institution. The BSI is an independent non-profit making body incorporated by Royal Charter in 1929. Its principal objectives include the promotion of health and safety, the protection of the environment and the establishment of quality standards. Domestic examples of items for which British Standards are available include pushchairs, cots and motor cycle crash helmets.

20. Another body somewhat similar to the BSI is the *Design Council*, set up in 1944 to improve design standards in a wide range of manufactured goods. The Council tests products to see if, in their opinion, they are well-designed, well-made and of practical value. In suitable cases they award their distinctive triangular logo as a mark of their approval. By their work they are promoting the idea that goods should be of merchantable quality and fit for their purpose.

## TRADE MARKS

21. Trade marks were originally established to protect manufacturers' products from being 'pirated' by their rivals. Once certain marks became well-known, they also provided an advantage to consumers, who were able to associate particular trade marks with a particular quality goods. Famous trade marks include Coca Cola, Guinness, Sellotape, IBM and WordStar.

Persons buying products bearing those names are entitled to expect the particular standards associated with them.

## MANUFACTURERS' LIABILITY

22. In England and Wales, a manufacturer has a common law duty of care to ensure that his products do not cause injury or damage to a person or to his property. Note that this duty does not extend to the *quality or performance* of the goods, but only to their causing injury or damage. In such a case, it is up to the complainant to show that the damage or injury was due to the manufacturer's negligence.

23. Statutory duties are imposed on manufacturers by the *Health and Safety at Work etc, Act 1974*. This Act, amongst other duties, requires designers, manufacturers and importers to ensure, so far as practicable, that any article is safe when properly used.

## INDEPENDENT PRESSURE GROUPS

24. There are a number of independent pressure groups in the United Kingdom working directly on behalf of consumers. These include:

- The Citizens' Advice Bureaux (incl. C.A.B. Consumer Advice Centres). These provide free advice for local citizens on a wide range of matters, including consumer affairs.
- The Consumers' Association This body carries out independent tests on a wide variety of consumer goods and services. The results are published in a monthly magazine ('Which').
- National Viewers' and Listeners' Association This organization monitors radio and television programmes with the aim of persuading programme planners to avoid excessive violence, sex and other issues which could be distasteful to family viewers.

## PUBLICLY-APPOINTED CONSUMER GROUPS

25. Publicly appointed bodies representing consumers' interests are considerably more numerous than private groups. Local authorities have established services such as Trading Standards Departments and Consumer Advice Centres, for example. There are also several bodies established by statute to represent the views of users of public services. Examples of such groups include:

- The Post Office Users Council
- The Transport Users' Consultative Committee

- Electricity Consultative Council
- Regional Gas Consumers' Councils
- Domestic Coal Consumers' Council
- National Consumer Council

These Councils are composed of representatives from various user-groups, including local authorities, Citizens Advice Bureaux, welfare groups etc. They are independent of the industry concerned.

## SECTION SUMMARY - MARKETING MANAGEMENT

1.    Chapters 31–37 have dealt with the salient features of marketing management in practice. The topics covered are those which occur the most frequently in the examinations of those bodies not principally concerned with the profession of marketing.

2.    Marketing has been defined in several ways – as an exchange activity, as a management activity, and as an attitude of mind. There are common threads running through each of the common definitions. These include the acknowledgement of groups of buyers (markets) in search of means to satisfy their needs, and the efforts made by producers to meet those needs in a profitable manner.

3.    The marketing concept considers the customer to be the prime reason for the existence of an organization, and therefore seeks to direct the organization's efforts towards identifying and meeting customer needs and wants. Organizations do not all subscribe to the marketing concept. They may instead opt for a production, product or sales-orientation.

4.    The marketing mix is a central feature of an organization's tactical plan for a particular market. It consists of the key marketing variables that are offered to a market at a particular point in time. These variables are primarily the product, its price structure, the way it is to be promoted, and how it is to be distributed. The product can be varied in terms of quality, number of versions, branding, packaging and after-sales service. A key aspect of this part of the mix is the life-cycle of the product. This requires adapting the mix to the appropriate stage of the cycle – Introduction, Growth, Maturity, Saturation, and, finally, Decline.

5.    The price element of the mix can be varied in terms of its basic price and by means of credit arrangements. Price is the most flexible element in the mix, and can be employed to ward off competitors, handle price-sensitive markets, and adapt to changes in the product life-cycle.

6.    Promotional variables include advertising, personal selling, sales promotion and publicity. They are all directed towards bringing potential customers from a state of unawareness of the product to a state where they are convinced of the value of the product and proceed to buy it. The promotion aspects of the marketing mix vary slightly between consumer markets and industrial markets. For example, advertising is used very heavily on consumer markets, and only lightly in industrial markets. Conversely, whereas personal selling is the single most important means of promoting industrial goods and services, it is rarely seen in consumer markets. Advertising is carried out via the following media – the press, commercial television, direct mail, commercial radio and hoardings/outdoor displays. Of these media the press is by far the most significant in terms of the expenditure by clients. Personal selling is carried out mainly by sales representatives and by sales assistants. Of the two groups the former are more biassed towards persuasive selling, whilst the latter tend to be order-takers.

7.    The role of the sales representative is extremely important in the organization's overall sales effort. The duties of representatives include the following – after-sales servicing, gathering market intelligence, communicating relevant information to customers, and prospecting for new business. These are in addition to straightforward selling activities. Representatives are usually organized on a territorial basis. They can also be organized on a product basis or a customer basis. Their results can be evaluated in several different ways, including the following – net sales, call rate, sales per call, number of new sales customers, and sales expenses as ratio of sales achieved.

8.    Sales promotion activities are particularly applicable to consumer products. These activities are directed at two main groups – customers (at the point of sale) and the trade (wholesalers and retailers). Sales promotion aims to act as a back-up to other forms of promotion, notably advertising, by offering incentives to customers and traders in order to push certain products or lines. For customers these incentives include free samples of the product and twin-pack bargains; for the trade they include special discounts and the provision of display material.

9.    Publicity was the final aspect of promotion to be considered. Publicity is part of the total public relations effort of the organization. It is concerned with the understanding between the organization and the public at large. Publicity itself is basically news material about the organization which is published in one or more of the media. Sponsorship of sporting events and patronage

of the arts are methods which are being used increasingly to promote an organization's reputation with the public.

10. Chapter 34 examined the issues of distribution, as part of the marketing mix, and of market segmentation. Distribution is primarily concerned with the task of moving the product to the consumer. This task is achieved via a number of channels of distribution. These are marketing institutions set up to facilitate the movement of goods and services from their point of production to their point of consumption. The most frequent elements to be found in a marketing channel are – manufacturers (or producers of services), wholesalers, retailers and customers. The middlemen may sometimes be excluded from a channel, as in most industrial marketing, where direct channels from manufacturer to customer are employed.

11. Market segmentation is one of the refinement processes of marketing. It is a tactical device for breaking down any one market into a number of separately identifiable sub-markets in order to be able to reach that sub-market (or segment) with a particular marketing mix. The market for private motor-cars, for example, can be broken down into several segments, depending on income levels, family commitments, benefits sought and many other preferences. Segmentation is usually undertaken on the basis of three major variables in target populations – geography, demography (age, sex, occupation etc), and buyer behaviour (brand loyalty, usage rate etc). These are the most important variables for consumer markets. For industrial markets, the variables have a different emphasis. They include the following examples – type of buyer (Government, private firm etc), trade group, and end-use (specialised application or general etc).

12. Physical distribution is concerned with the physical aspects of moving goods from the manufacturer or supplier to the customer ie transporting, warehousing, packaging etc. The attention paid to physical distribution is related to the relative proportion of distribution costs in total costs. If the proportion is high, then considerable efforts will be made to contain such costs.

13. Chapter 35 outlined the key features of marketing research. Marketing research consists of those activities which aim to provide information about markets and marketing methods for the purpose of facilitating decision-making in marketing matters. The object of the research is to enable the organization to find out what is going on in the market-place, and to evaluate the impact on customers, competitors and others, of the organization's own marketing activities. The raw material of marketing information

comes in two forms – primary data, which is obtained first hand, and secondary data, which is obtained from a variety of published sources, both within and external to the organization. The most frequent methods of gaining primary data are by the use of questionnaires and of interviews, usually carried out by trained agency staff.

14.  The most comprehensive way of assessing the organization's marketing performance is by means of a marketing audit. This is an independent examination of the marketing objectives, activities and environment of the organization, with the object of (a) assessing present effectiveness, and (b) recommending future action. Typical components of an audit would be – marketing environment, marketing strategy, marketing plans and controls, the marketing mix, profitability and costs, and the organization of marketing.

15.  This Section also looked at the organization of marketing. Marketing has developed out of sales. In some organizations it is still seen as the junior partner to sales, in others it has an equal status, in yet others it has a superior status. In market-orientated organizations, marketing encompasses all the marketing and sales functions. A typical marketing departments is organized either functionally or in a matrix-type of structure. The principal objectives of such a department are to identify market opportunities, design a strategy to meet them and then implement approved plans, in collaboration with other departments. The other departments will inevitably come into conflict with marketing from time to time because the latter's need to satisfy customers requires an adaptability that does not fit into their drive for efficiency of operations.

16.  Consumer protection has, in recent years, become more of a preoccupation for governments and pressure groups. In Britain the major contribution to consumer protection now lies in:

   a.  statutory rights
   b.  activities of voluntary bodies such as the British Standards Institution and the Consumers' Association.

17.  The principal purposes of legislation are to ensure, so far as practicable, that (i) goods and services fulfil basic standards of quality and fitness for for purpose, (ii) goods and services are fairly described in advertising etc, (iii) goods are safe, and (iv) any financial arrangements (esp. credit) are made clear to the purchaser.

# QUESTIONS FOR DISCUSSION/HOMEWORK

*1.     What are the implications for a business organization of adopting the marketing concept?*

*2      In what ways can marketing departments differ from other departments in terms of key objectives, main activities and system of values?*

*3.     'Promotion and Distribution are very much the second class members of the marketing mix.' Discuss this view of their role in the mix.*

*4.     How true is it to say that customers look for benefits, not for features when considering a product? Discuss in relation to some popular consumer item.*

*5.     What advice would you give a manufacturer of robots concerning the promotion of his products in Britain?*

*6.     How would you distinguish between 'push' and 'pull' strategies in selling?*

*7.     Why do so many suppliers of goods and services still rely on the services of middlemen? What factors do you think could change their reliance on such services?*

*8.     What is 'consumerism', what forms can it take, and how can marketing managers respond to it?*

*9.     In what ways might the following seek to segment their markets:*

*a. a manufacturer of beers and lagers.*

*b. an estate agent in a suburban area.*

*10.    Is marketing research a luxury? Discuss.*

*11.    How might an organization divide up the responsibility for marketing activities between its sub-divisions and head office?*

## EXAMINATION QUESTIONS - MARKETING MANAGEMENT

*Most of the questions selected below are taken from the examinations of bodies other than the Institute of Marketing. In most cases, therefore, what is required is a good general grasp of the topic. Detailed answers, showing an in-depth knowledge of the subject-matter, would not normally be expected.*

*EQ 28  'Without adopting the marketing concept a company cannot possibly hope to develop future plans.' Discuss this statement from the point of view of a manufacturer of capital goods*

*(ICMA OMM)*

*EQ 29*     In the concept of the 'marketing mix what is meant by the term 'below-the-line' activities? Discuss the range of objectives likely to be set in using such activities.

*(ICMA OMM)*

*EQ 30*     What is the importance of the concept of the 'product cycle' for business planning and budgeting?

*(ACCA Business Management)*

*EQ 31*     In the development of new products, the marketing, design and manufacturing departments have a contribution to make. Discuss the areas of potential conflict between these departments, in finalising new product design, and suggest ways in which these conflicts might be resolved.

*(IOM Business Organization)*

# PRODUCTION MANAGEMENT

## INTRODUCTION

1.   The production function of an organization exists in order to make available the goods or services required by the customer. Production management, in particular, is concerned with the provision of goods. It is the central part of the manufacturing process. Its responsibility is to plan, resource and control the processes involved in converting raw materials and components into the finished goods required to satisfy the needs and wants of the organization's existing and potential customers.

2.   In a market-orientated organization, production begins with the customer in the market-place. An idea for a new product is generated, or assessed in marketing terms, by the market research section. If the idea seems viable, it will be turned over to the Research and Development (R&D) section, where any necessary research, design and development work can be carried out. The next stage forward is for early prototypes to be produced. If the prototypes are satisfactory, then the pre-production stage can commence. This stage aims to simulate, as far as possible, the actual conditions on the production line. Thus at this stage the customer's needs are being set against the cost of materials and labour, the manufacturing capacity of the production department, and issues such as quality levels. In the case of a firm manufacturing industrial goods, it is likely that at this stage, if not earlier, samples of the new product will be sent to the customer for testing and approval. If the pre-production runs have been successful, then the product can move forward again, this time to the manufacturing stage.

3.   There are several key elements in the production process, and this Section looks at those that are the subject of examination questions for business and accountancy students. In particular, Chapter 38 sets out the main features of a production planning and control system, Chapter 39 briefly outlines the principal methods of production available to organizations, and Chapter 40 examines some of the leading aids to production, such as Work Study, and Chapter 41 outlines key features of new technology in manufacturing.

## PRODUCTION ORGANIZATION

4.   Before we proceed to these other chapters, it may be helpful to consider the likely organization structure of the Production function in a manufacturing organization. The organization chart below illustrates the principal divisions of labour within the

function and provides an example of the structural relationships between the different departments or sub-units.

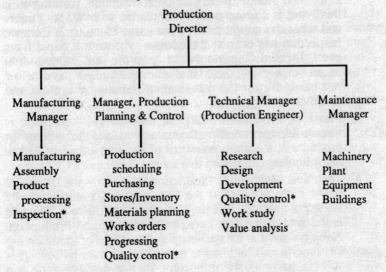

Production
Director

| Manufacturing Manager | Manager, Production Planning & Control | Technical Manager (Production Engineer) | Maintenance Manager |
|---|---|---|---|
| Manufacturing Assembly Product processing Inspection* | Production scheduling Purchasing Stores/Inventory Materials planning Works orders Progressing Quality control* | Research Design Development Quality control* Work study Value analysis | Machinery Plant Equipment Buildings |

\* See para 5 following

## Organization of the Production Function – Manufacturing Industry

5. The above organization chart represents just one of several ways in which production could be organized. Much depends on the type of production, the relative standing of groups such as Quality Control, Purchasing and Maintenance, and the extent to which sophisticated computerised systems are in operation. In the example shown above the asterisks indicate that Quality Control is shared among three sub-units: Manufacturing (as shopfloor Inspection), Production Planning & Control (as Quality Control of processes, materials and purchased items), and Production Engineering (responsible for quality of design and with overall responsibility for Quality Control standards in production).

6. In the example given, the production function has been divided up into four sub-units or departments. There could have been a greater degree of specialization, but this has been avoided here in order to emphasise the collaborative nature of many of the specialisms to be found in the production function. Brief observations that can be made about the four sub-unit management positions are as follows:

a. Manufacturing Manager – this person is responsible for the manufacturing and assembly processes, together with their associated product processes (heat treatment, painting etc); this work is carried out in accordance with Works Orders and schedules submitted by Production Planning & Control; Inspection has been included here, although it could have been located separately to provide an independent inspection service; the Manufacturing Manager has a heavy responsibility for the recruitment, training, rewarding and retention of employees.

b. Manager, Production Planning and Control – this role is responsible for providing the framework and the impetus for production; the main activities of the role are described in the following chapter on this topic.

c. Technical Manager or Production Engineer – the latter title is the more popular of the two, in practice, although the former is probably a better description of the role. The role is the first major link between Marketing and Production, being involved at the earliest possible stages of transforming customer needs and wants into practical possibilities. This role is particularly important in the development and application of computers in the production process.

d. Maintenance Manager – this role has been given considerable status in this example; it could have been placed in a subordinate position to the Manufacturing Manager, where it is frequently to be found.

The important point to remember is that all the sub-units are needed if the production function is to meet its aim of providing the goods required by its customers, and to do so in a way that meets the profit, growth and other objectives of the organization as a whole.

# 38

# PRODUCTION PLANNING AND CONTROL

## INTRODUCTION.

1. Modern production processes are complex and costly. Machines, computers, materials of all kinds, and labour all have to be blended together to enable the production system to carry out its operations in a cost-effective way. Thus production processes require careful planning and controlling.

2. The basic elements of a production planning and control system are as follows:

  a. Translate the customer's requirements, as defined by the final pre-production design and preliminary sales forecasts, into production instructions (Works orders).

  b. Prepare production schedules and programmes.

  c. Plan the supply of materials, parts, components etc.

  d. Plan availability of machines, specify jigs, tools etc.

  e. Ensure labour requirements.

  f. Set production targets.

  g. Maintain stock and purchasing records.

  h. Progress orders through the factory.

  i. Liaise with the marketing department.

  j. Raise final production documents (delivery notes, invoices etc).

3. There are several points arising from the above lists:

  a. The plans referred to are short-term plans for periods of from one week to one month. At the start of a new production process, these plans may be altered at frequent intervals.

  b. Production schedules are basically timetables. They are usually of a detailed nature, specifying the timetabled requirements for precise operations and jobs, and invariably set out the sequence of priorities. The major aims of scheduling are to ensure, so far as possible, that work is completed on time and within budgeted costs. Wide use is made of Gantt charts (see Figure 4.3) in production scheduling. These are particularly useful for the scheduling of relatively straight-forward, routine projects.

c. Plans for materials etc involve stock control and purchasing, which will be referred to later in the chapter.

d. Plans for machines include the availability, capacity and loading of machines. Capacity and loading may vary considerably between different types and models of machines, and these facts have to be taken into account in planning the overall production effort. Carefully — planned loading can reduce material waiting time, even out loads between machines and processes, reduce idle time and highlight machine utilisation.

e. Labour requirements are a vital part of the production process. As well as detailing the numbers and types of employees required, there are questions of pay and incentives to be agreed before production commences. If new machines or new processes are to be employed, it will be necessary to organize training in machine operations and safety.

f. All plans should set targets. In this case targets, based on sales forecasts, will be set in collaboration with marketing or sales staff, as representatives of the customer, and will take into account considerations such as planned maintenance, product quality control and machine breakdowns, for example.

g. The progressing of orders through the production process is essentially a monitoring and reporting task, which also involves some 'chasing-up' of progress in situations where orders have fallen behind schedule. The main job of a progress chaser is to watch out for, and report, any deviations from schedule, and provide help in sorting out delays in production.

h. Liaison with the marketing department is important to ensure that the productive effort is meeting the customer's needs, or, where there are difficulties in production, ensuring that the customer is informed and/or is prepared to accept a slightly different standard or quality of product, for example.

i. Finally, the outputs of the production system need to be accounted for, invoiced and delivered (to the customer or into stock). Thus the final step is to ensure that the appropriate paperwork is available and correctly completed.

4.   The process which has just been described is clearly a very complex affair, but most of the decisions involved in it are programmable types of decisions. It is possible, therefore, to apply the considerable power of a computer to the process. Computers have the ability to undertake masses of calculations very rapidly, they can perform a number of separate operations at one and the same time, and have the ability to store massive amounts of information.

5.   The use of computers in production is extending all the time, as fully-automated plants and robots can bear witness. However, in a more conventional way, computers can be employed to store and develop works orders, schedules, machine loading, stock levels, progress documents and many other related examples of production information. The prime benefits of computer applications in these circumstances are:

   a.  effective control over the processes concerned;
   b.  the ability to adapt quickly to avoid difficulties;
   c.  the ability to take advantage of opportunities arising from the speed and accuracy of feedback information received from the computer.

## PURCHASING

6.   A brief reference was made earlier to the subject of purchasing. This is an important aspect of production management and will be outlined below. Purchasing costs often represent a substantial part of the total costs of production, and they are costs which may be incurred by various sub-units of production. The purchasing function, therefore, has numerous links with other sections and departments internally, in addition to its links with external suppliers.

7.   The primary responsibility of the purchasing department is to secure sufficient and suitable raw materials, components, other goods, and services to ensure that the manufacturing process is fully supplied with all its materials, and to achieve this responsibility in a cost-effective manner. To this end the purchasing department can usually be expected to be responsible for the following:

   a.  Appraisal and selection of suppliers.
   b.  Collation of up-to-date information on suppliers, prices, distribution methods etc.
   c.  Purchasing goods and services at prices which represent the best value to the business in the long-term (ie not necessarily the lowest prices at a given time).

    d.  Maintenance of adequate stock/inventory levels.

    e.  Establishing and maintaining effective working relationships with relevant departments (Production, Marketing and Finance).

    f.  Developing effective links with existing suppliers, and maintaining good relationships with potential suppliers and with competitors.

8.   The above description clearly denotes an extremely important function. Purchasing ought not to be seen as mainly a question of routine paperwork. Purchasing decisions are often very risky, and can involve an organization in carrying considerable costs. It has been estimated that a 5% excess in purchasing costs can lead to a 25% reduction in profits. By contrast, a small saving in purchasing costs can be worth considerably more in terms of equivalent sales value.

9.   The Purchasing Manager in charge of a purchasing department exercises his responsibilities in close collaboration with other colleagues. For example, most purchasing decisions can only be taken after due agreement with financial, production or marketing colleagues. Where the Purchasing Manager's particular expertise comes into its own is in the presentation and evaluation of purchasing alternatives, or in the assessment of whether to make or buy a particular product or component. It is in these discussions that the knowledge of materials, their quality, prices, availability etc enables the Purchasing Manager to contribute significantly to the ultimate decision to buy, or not to buy.

10.  If a decision is made to proceed with a purchase, then the sequence of events could follow these lines:

    a.  Purchasing receives requisition from appropriate authority.

    b.  Purchasing approaches selected supplier to negotiate quantity, quality, price and delivery of goods.

    c.  If (b) proceeds satisfactorily, purchasing places an order with the supplier. This could be a one-off, or spot, order, or a contract order over a period of time.

    d.  Purchasing maintains records of orders made, orders fulfilled, delivery dates, invoices etc.

    e.  Purchasing arranges for originating requisition to be met, either directly from supplier or via stores, and amends stock/delivery records as appropriate.

11.  In the purchase of material goods, issues of quantity, quality, price and delivery are crucial in several respects. These could be described as the key elements of the 'purchasing mix'.

**Quantity.** The quantity of goods to be ordered, and the time at which they should be ordered are major considerations. On the one hand insufficient quantities at a particular point in time, will cause costly delays in production. On the other hand, the larger the quantity ordered, the more will have to go into stock as temporarily idle resources, also a costly business. The ideal to be aimed at is to find the optimum way of balancing the costs of insufficient stock against the costs of holding stock (tied-up capital, storage space, insurance, damage etc). Techniques have been devised by Operational Research scientists to enable organizations to work out the Economic Order Quantity (EOQ) for individual stock items, and to aid them in setting optimum re-order levels (ie the levels at which stock needs to be replaced). In some cases, the decision about quantity (and indeed time) may be dictated by considerations of future supply, particularly where these may be threatened by economic or political pressures. Decisions may also be influenced by favourable trends in short-term prices.

**Quality.** The quality of the goods purchased needs to be suitable (a) for the manufacturing process, and (b) for the customer's wants. In seeking decisions about quality, the purchasing department have to work closely with both production and marketing staff to arrive at a suitable compromise. Inspection of goods received is vital to check that the supplier is fulfilling the order to the correct specification.

**Price.** Purchasing should ideally aim for a price which gives the best value to the organization, taking quality, delivery and relative urgency into account. This may not always be the lowest price available, but the one which represents the best value over a period of time.

**Delivery.** One of the factors which needs to be considered by the purchasing department in the appraisal and selection of suppliers is the reliability of deliveries. The lead time between an order and a delivery is an important aspect of stock control. Where lead times are certain, they can be allowed for in stock calculations. Where they are uncertain, it makes stock control much more difficult. Not only is stock affected by the delivery situation, so is production. The latter is particularly vulnerable to delays in deliveries for items which are used continuously, and for which minimum buffer stocks are held. Buffer stocks are reserve stocks held for emergency shortages.

12. Several aspects of stock control have been mentioned in paragraph 11, and these can be drawn together in a simplified graph of stock-levels. Such graphs have a typically saw-tooth pattern, reflecting the outputs (usage) and the inputs (deliveries) to stock, as in Figure 38.1.

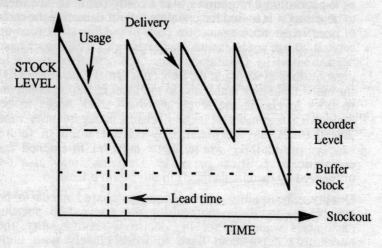

**Figure 38.1. Simple Stock Control Graph.**

Usage reduces stocks over a period of time. Such usage will invariably absorb some of the buffer stock unless planned deliveries are made on time. The lead time as shown is the time taken between the order being made and the delivery taking place. As soon as the delivery is made stocks shoot up again, until further usage reduces them, and this produces the saw-tooth effect on the graph. Should planned deliveries not take place, and should usage continue, then eventually a stockout situation will be reached, where, for the time being, the goods in question will be temporarily out-of-stock.

## INSPECTION

13. In addition to the purchasing and stock control aspects of production planning and control, there is the question of the control of quality. This control begins with inspection of the raw materials and other items purchased from suppliers, continues with inspection during production, and ends with a final inspection before delivery to the customer. The responsibility for checking quality on the shop-floor is usually that of the Inspection department, whose main task is to ensure adherence to the

organization's quality standards. These standards are normally set with several objectives in mind:

    a. to produce products which are satisfactory to the customer, (quality, reliability, variety etc).

    b. to produce products that are consistent with the organization's responsibility to its workforce, shareholders and other stakeholders, (safety of production, ethically acceptable etc).

    c. to attain (a) and (b) within agreed levels of inspection costs.

14. The costs of ensuring quality are twofold – *direct* costs, such as the wages and salaries of designers and inspectors, and *indirect* costs, such as the loss of orders, wastage and rectification costs. Some of these costs are directed towards preventing faults and errors, others are directed towards curing faults and errors.

15. In inspection there are basically three main reasons for inspecting work:

    a. to accept or reject items

    b. to control the process of producing the items

    c. to improve the process itself, if necessary.

There are two main methods of dealing with these issues:

Process control and acceptance sampling. These are examples of what has been called 'Statistical Quality Control'.

Process control consists of checking items as they progress through the production process, comparing them with the relevant standards, and taking any immediate corrective action to prevent further faults. Process control may be expedited by the use of control charts, which can show in graph form actual performance against standard performance, and the amount of any deviation. Another form of process control is automatic process control, where sensing and other measuring devices are built into the machine concerned to provide immediate information and immediate corrective action. Automatic inspection of this kind is more feasible than human inspection in cases where (a) accurate measurement is possible, (b) where continuous inspection is highly desirable and (c) where reliability of inspection is important. Objective measurement in inspection is called checking by variables, which contrasts with checking by attributes, which is a subjective method.

16. This leads us on to acceptance sampling. This is where the customer samples a batch of newly delivered goods, and either

rejects or accepts the batch on the basis of an acceptable quality level, usually a small percentage of rejects per batch. If the number of rejects in the sample is in excess of the agreed percentage, the whole batch is returned to the supplier. The sampling may be checked by variables, or by attributes (eg 'satisfactory' or 'unsatisfactory'). The latter calls for a human judgement instead of a 'scientifically' measured fact. Human inspection is most suited to instances where (a) objective standards are not available, and (b) where discretion is required in analysing and assessing faults and errors. This approach is most likely to apply to the more complex issues of quality control, and to the improvement of processes, where machine functioning and location, materials used and other factors need to be seen in context, if changes are to be made in the process.

## MAINTENANCE

17. The role of maintenance in a production planning and control system is to so organize maintenance activities that production has the optimum availability of plant and machinery in the conduct of its operations, and that, if an unexpected breakdown occurs, it will be dealt with in the minimum possible time.

18. According to the British Standards Institution, maintenance is 'work undertaken in order to keep or restore every facility.' There are several different kinds of maintenance, as follows:

   a. Preventive maintenance, which aims to prevent breakdowns.

   b. Corrective maintenance, to repair faults.

   c. Breakdown maintenance, to rectify breakdowns and prepare contingency plans for possible breakdowns (provision of important spare parts etc).

   d. Running maintenance, carried out whilst plant or machinery is operating.

   e. Shutdown maintenance, carried out when plant or machinery is taken out of service.

19. The above forms of maintenance can be combined into a planned programme of maintenance for each major piece of plant or machine. Planned maintenance means that routine servicing and overhaul arrangements are scheduled in advance and contingency plans drawn up for unexpected breakdowns. The effect of having planned maintenance is to minimise unforeseen faults or breakdowns. Thus maintenance can make an important contribution to containing machine running costs as well as ensuring optimum machine availability.

## SUMMARY

20. The role of production planning and control is to plan, acquire, schedule and control all the resources and facilities required to transform customer requirements into acceptable end-products. The process involves planning the supply of men, machines and materials and organizing all these elements into a coherent system of production. Several of these tasks require the collaboration of production with other departments, notably Marketing and Finance.

21. Purchasing plays an important role in production activities. Its key responsibility is to ensure that the manufacturing process is fully supplied with materials in a cost-effective way. This entails appraising and selecting appropriate suppliers, being well-informed about the purchasing market, purchasing goods at optimum prices in terms of value, and maintaining adequate stock/inventory supplies.

22. Purchasing involves important decisions about quality, price, quantity and delivery – the key elements of what can be called the 'purchasing mix'. The general principles to be followed in each of these elements are as follows.

Quality - this should represent the best compromise between the wishes of the customer and the limitations of production.

Price - ideally this should provide the best value over a period of time.

Quantity - this should be sufficient to ensure that items do not run out of stock, but not so much that unnecessary inventory costs are incurred through excessive stock-holding.

Delivery - here the key issues are timing and reliability and these are the features of the delivery service to be expected of suppliers.

23. Inspection is another important activity in the production process. The Inspection department's role is to ensure that quality standards are properly maintained, without incurring disproportionate costs. Inspection is undertaken primarily by (a) process control, and (b) acceptance sampling. Process control is conducted during the manufacturing process. It consists of checking items as they progress through the process, comparing them with relevant standards and taking corrective action, where required. Such control is often fully automatic. Acceptance sampling is usually carried out at the customer's premises and consists of examining samples of goods delivered, noting the number of reject, or unsatisfactory, items, comparing this number

with an agreed acceptable quality level. If the number of rejects exceeds the level, the batch is returned.

24. Maintenance comes in several different forms (preventive, corrective etc), all of which can be combined into a system of planned maintenance. Planned maintenance minimises unforeseen breakdowns, reduces machine running costs and ensures optimum machine availability.

# 39

# TYPES OF PRODUCTION

## INTRODUCTION

1. The most common method of distinguishing between production systems or types of production is to separate them into the three categories of jobbing, batch and mass production. This is the approach which will be used in this short chapter. The three categories are very broad, as Joan Woodward and her researchers discovered in the 1950's during their work on industrial organization in Essex (See Chapter 13 paras. 13–19 above). In the Essex research, written up in 'Industrial Organization: Theory and Practice, O.U.P., 1965 it was felt necessary to sub-divide these broad categories further so as to produce eleven. A comparison between the Woodward list and the three common categories will be made towards the end of this chapter.

2. The jobbing, batch and mass production categories each have their own distinctive systems of operation, and their own problems of production planning and control. Each will be examined in turn with the aim of highlighting the most important factors involved.

## JOBBING PRODUCTION

3. Jobbing production may also be called job production or unique production. The essential feature of jobbing production is that it produces single articles or 'one-off' items. These products may be small, tailor-made components, huge pieces of equipment or large single items, such as a ship. Most products are made for a particular customer or to a particular order. Jobbing production is to be found in industries such as heavy engineering (eg production of electricity generating plant), shipbuilding and civil engineering (eg bridge construction). It is also to be found in most other industries, where it is employed to produce prototype models, spare parts, modifications to existing plant and countless other 'one-off', tailor-made pieces. There is hardly a factory in existence which does not have a jobbing department somewhere or other.

4. Because of the unique or individual nature of each article or item to be produced, planning is not easy in jobbing production, neither is control. Efficiency of operations has to give way to inventiveness and creativity. This can be illustrated by considering

some of the key characteristics of jobbing production. These are as follows:

 a. A wide variety of different operations to be performed under varying circumstances ie no standardisation.

 b. Varying sequences of operations, also subject to varying circumstances.

 c. General-purpose machinery and equipment.

 d. Varied work layouts, depending on process and/or operation.

 e. Unpredictable demands on stores.

 f. Workforce skilled in wide range of skills.

 g. Adaptable and equally skilled supervision.

Many of the above conditions make it extremely difficult to plan, integrate and control the types, sequence and timing of operations. It is difficult to avoid idle time for both men and machines. Thus the entire manufacturing process tends to be relatively expensive compared with other forms of production. Against this can be weighed the advantages of producing an article or item which is made especially to the customer's own specification.

## BATCH PRODUCTION

5.  Batch production is the production of standardised units, or parts, in small or large lots (batches). It represents a halfway position between jobbing production and mass production, and is mostly to be found in the light engineering industry. The main distinction between batch and jobbing production lies in the standardised nature of the former. Unlike the varied operations and sequences of the unique 'one-off' products of jobbing production, the products of batch production are dealt with systematically in lots, or batches, only moving on to the next operation, when each lot has been machined or processed in the current operation.

6.  Batches may be produced to order and forwarded direct to the customer, as in the production of subcomponents for another manufacturer, or they may be made for stock. One of the major problems associated with batch production is to determine the optimum size of batches, particularly where a generalised, rather than specific, demand for a product exists. If too many units are produced, stocks will lie idle or go to waste; if too few are produced, the item will go out of stock, and it may be difficult to fit in further batches in the short-term.

7.  The key characteristics of batch production are as follows:

    a.  A standardised set of operations, carried out intermittently, as each batch moves from one operation to the next.

    b.  General purpose machinery and plant, but grouped in batteries of the same type.

    c.  Heavy shop-floor stores requirement.

    d.  Narrower range of skills required.

    e.  Emphasis on production planning and progressing.

    f.  Relatively short production runs.

These characteristics lead to a generally well-controlled and efficient method of production, whose main disadvantage is the time-delay caused by the queueing effect of individual units waiting for the batch to be completed before moving on to the next operation. This problem can be overcome by changing to an assembly line operation which is a prominent feature of flow production, or mass production, as it is commonly called.

## MASS PRODUCTION

8.    Mass production dates from the time of Henry Ford, who was the first man to adopt the principle of the production line, when he used this approach to produce a restricted range of motor cars put together in a flow-line process. In a unit mass production system, a small range of products is produced in large quantities by 'flowing' uninterruptedly from one operation, or process, to the next until completion. This type of production requires careful and lengthy planning of plant and processes. The capital costs are high on account of the specialised nature of the machines required for the production line. However once the line has been set up, control is relatively simple. Mass production systems are dependent on the high demand created by mass markets, for it is only by making the fullest use of the capital equipment involved that a manufacturing organization can achieve its target profit levels.

9.    The key features of mass production are as follows:

    a.  Rigid product specifications, previously tested.

    b.  Specialised machines and equipment, set out in a line formation.

    c.  Highly-standardised methods, tools and materials.

    d.  Long production runs for individual products.

    e.  Narrow range of skills, and specified range of operations required by workforce at any one point in the line.

In purely rational terms, mass-production is the most efficient way of producing large quantities of articles or items. Control can be exercised to a sophisticated level because of the standardised nature of the entire process. Its greatest drawback is that it requires human beings to adapt themselves to the production process, and in most Western countries, there has been a reaction against this requirement. Employees are seeking to counteract the tedium and monotony of the highly specialised work patterns in mass-production by pressing for more integrated roles, requiring a wider range of skills and operations. In some cases this has led to the complete break up of production lines into autonomous circuits, each operated by teams of employees using their skills on a shared or flexible basis.

10. Another form of mass production, usually called flow production or process production, can be seen in continuous process industries such as steel-making, paper-making and cement production. In such industries the products literally flow from one process to the next, but, unlike in the mass production of individual products, this process is continuous for weeks or months on end. In flow processes, the supply of raw materials has to be planned to the highest standards in order to avoid complete plant shutdown owing to unforeseen shortages. In these situations shortages have a much more serious effect than in unit mass-production. Fortunately, the control mechanisms and procedures for flow processes are usually so sophisticated that the processes become automatically selfregulating. Another important difference between this form of mass-production and unit mass-production is that the former invariably requires a lower labour force than the latter.

## SUB-DIVIDING THE CATEGORIES

11. As was noted above (in paragraph 1), the three common categories are very broad. Even our analysis has had to distinguish between two forms of mass production, and the use of batch methods was applied to small and medium sized lots, which omits the possibility of large batches. Clearly it would be better to have a more detailed picture, which more accurately represented the number of options available. This is all the more reasonable if one considers that very few, if any, manufacturing concerns engage solely in one type of production.

12. The list which follows compares the much more detailed analysis of Woodward's researchers with the broader one that has been applied above. The Woodward list is taken from the published account of the research.

| Broad Categories | Woodward Categories | |
|---|---|---|
| a. Jobbing Production | i. | Production of units to customer's requirements |
| | ii. | Production of prototypes |
| | iii. | Fabrication of large equipment in stages |
| b. Batch Production | i. | Production of small batches to customer's orders |
| | ii. | Production of large batches |
| | iii. | Production of large batches on assembly lines |
| | iv. | Intermittent production of chemicals in multi-purpose plant |
| c. Mass Production - Flow Production | i. | Mass production |
| | ii. | Continuous flow production of liquids, gases and crystalline substances |

13. It can be seen that the Woodward analysis of jobbing production corresponds to the description given in paragraph 3 above, but by giving each of the main types of jobbing production its own title, the Woodward analysis provides for a more accurate representation of the range of options. Where batch production is concerned, the Woodward analysis distinguishes four types of batch production compared with the one type we have described. The Woodward team not only distinguished between small and large batches, as described in paragraph 5 above, but also between large batches produced by single machines or batteries of machines and large batches produced on assembly lines. (The latter, in our definition, would fall under 'mass production'.) They also included the intermittent production of chemicals as a separate batch process. Thus their range of batch options is much more comprehensive and distinctive than the broad category we have used. Finally, the Woodward breakdown of mass production into two categories makes explicit the distinction made in our analysis between mass production and flow or process production.

14. On balance, it is probably helpful to think firstly in terms of the three broad categories, so as to separate the main production options available, and secondly in terms of the more detailed breakdown in order to draw up a truer picture of what may be possible in practice.

## SUMMARY

15. This brief chapter has sought to describe the main features of the basic types of production systems – jobbing, batch and mass production. Jobbing production refers to the production of unique or 'one-off' items, made to order. These items may be small or large, and they are produced under conditions of what is appropriate at a given time, rather than conditions which are standardised. Both planning and control are difficult to achieve in this form of production.

16. Batch production refers to the production of standardised units in batches, or lots. Only when a batch has completed one process can it be moved to the next. Batches may be produced to order, or for stock. Batch production can be relatively well planned and controlled, but queueing problems may arise when batches are ready to move on to the next operation. These problems can be overcome by utilising assembly lines ie moving over to a mass production method.

17. Mass production refers to the production of vast quantities of product units in a flow-line process, where each  smoothly from one operation, or process, to the next until completion. Where the mass-production of continuous processes is concerned, the method is called flow production or process production. Mass production methods call for detailed planning and sophisticated control procedures. There is very little scope for the exercise of skills by the workforce, and the flowline layout has been challenged in several quarters.

# 40

# AIDS TO PRODUCTION

## INTRODUCTION

1.  This chapter outlines the key features of three aids to production management – Work Study, Value Analysis or Value Engineering, and Quality Circles. They may all have applications elsewhere, but in the paragraphs which follow they are considered in terms of their contribution to production.

## WORK STUDY

2.  Work Study was developed in American industry in the 1920's. The first known attempts to make a rational assessment of work and tasks were made by F.W. Taylor and the other 'Scientific Managers', whose ideas were described earlier, in Chapter 4. Since their time, Work Study has become an established part of the industrial scene.

3.  Work Study has been defined in a British Standard (B.S. 3138) as follows:

'A generic term for those techniques, particularly method study and work measurement, which are used in the examination of human work in all its contexts, and which lead systematically to the investigation of all the factors which affect the efficiency and economy of the situation being reviewed, in order to effect improvement.'

The two basic techniques, Method Study and Work Measurement, are complementary to each other, and are rarely utilised in isolation from each other. The usual practice is for a method study of some kind to precede a work measurement activity. Each technique will be described in outline shortly.

4.  The reasons why Work Study techniques are utilised in production include the following:
    a.  To eliminate wasteful work.
    b.  To improve working methods.
    c.  To increase production.
    d.  To achieve cost-savings.
    e.  To improve productivity of men and machines.

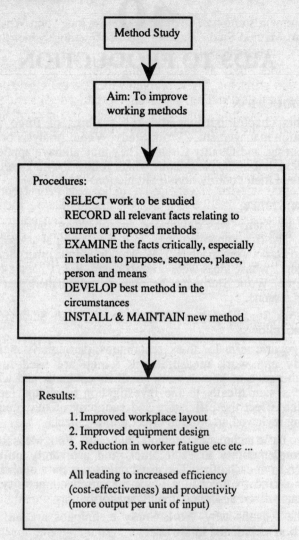

**Figure 40.1. Method Study: an Outline.**

5.   **Method Study.** This technique is itself composed of a collection of techniques, all of which systematically examine and record all the methods, existing and proposed, utilised in an operation or process, with a view to increasing efficiency. It could be said that Method Study attempts to answer the questions What? When? How? Who? and Where? in contrast to Work

Measurement's emphasis, which asks How long? and When? The scope of Method Study, therefore, is considerably wider than that of Work Measurement.

6. Method Study is used to aid solutions to a variety of production problems. These problems include those of workplace layout, materials handling, tool design, product design and process design~ for example. The basic approach of a method study is illustrated in the simplified diagram on the previous page (Figure 40.1).

7. The procedures noted in the above diagram are the vehicle for a rational analysis of working methods. Firstly, the target operation or process is selected. If a choice has to be made between priorities for attention, the likelihood is that the activity having the biggest impact on costs will be selected, since if this can be improved, some real savings will be achieved. Secondly, a thorough examination of all the pertinent facts is made. Much of the data collected for a method study is presented in a flow-chart form, which utilises a standard set of symbols for all the basic activities and operations. The symbols are as shown on the next page in Figure 40.2:

A simple flowchart records the activities in the order in which they occur, assigns the appropriate symbol to each activity, notes the elapsed time taken for each activity and adds any comments that may be useful. Thus the recording of facts for a method study is a very detailed business. The third step in the procedure is to examine critically the data obtained, even to the extent of questioning the very purpose of an activity. 'Is this activity necessary?' 'Is this the most economical sequence of events in the process?' 'What are the alternative ways of conducting this operation?' These and other questions can help the person conducting the study to eventually produce a best method of working, taking all the circumstances into account. If this new method is approved, the final stages are implementation and subsequent maintenance and review.

8. It was mentioned in the previous paragraph that much of the data for a method study is present in flowchart form. Other charts and diagrams used in method study are as follows:

    a. Multiple activity charts – these are charts where the activities of more than one subject (eg workers, machines etc) can be recorded against a common time-scale, and where Time is registered on the vertical axis, and Subjects on the horizontal;

| Symbol | Meaning |
|---|---|

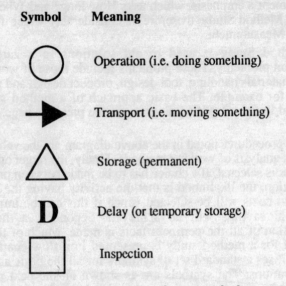

Operation (i.e. doing something)

Transport (i.e. moving something)

Storage (permanent)

Delay (or temporary storage)

Inspection

**Figure 40.2. Flowchart Symbols.**

b. Flow diagrams – these are scale drawings of the workplace which indicate where each activity takes place;

c. String diagrams – these are similar to flow diagrams, but where movements between activities are recorded by means of string, or thread, connecting pins inserted into all the activity points on the diagram; they enable the paths of all the movements taking place to be recorded with clarity, and can highlight short-cuts;

d. Chronocyclegraph – this is a photographic record, which traces the path of movement onto a photographic plate; in principle, it is similar to the string diagram, and is most effective when recording short, rapid movements.

e. Therbligs – these are the basic units of work activity, originated by Frank Gilbreth in the United States (see Chapter 4); they are used in so-called micromotion studies, which are detailed studies of repetitive work.

9. **Work Measurement.** This is a collection of techniques, particularly Time Study, aimed at establishing the time taken by a qualified worker to complete a specified job at a defined level of performance. As mentioned above, Work Measurement techniques set out to answer the questions How long? and When? They usually follow or overlap with a method study, and are employed

not only to improve methods of working, but also to develop costing systems, production schedules and incentive schemes, as well as to establish machine capacities and manning levels.

10.   Like Method Study, Work Measurement has a systematic set of procedures to be followed, and these are set out below. When work measurement is linked into a method study, it is introduced at the 'DEVELOP best method' stage, as shown in Figure 40.1. The basic steps in work measurement are as follows in Figure 40.3.

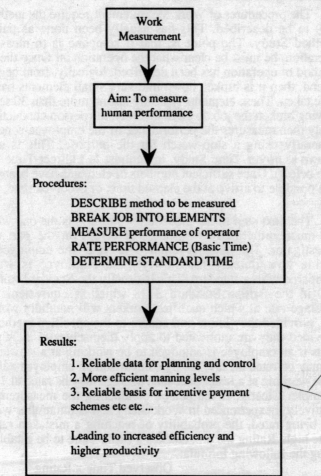

**Figure 40.3. Work Measurement - an Outline.**

11. It can be seen from the above diagram that the aim of Work Measurement is significantly different from that of Method Study. The latter aims to improve working methods; the former aims to measure, or assess, the performance of people. In pursuing its aim, Work Measurement has to rely on the exercise of a greater degree of *subjective* judgement than is required for Method Study. In particular, the rating of performance and the determination of the standard time rely heavily on the judgement of the person conducting the measurement.

12. The procedures of Work Measurement require the method (or job) to be described. This has usually been done as part of a Method Study. The point is, that if someone is to measure an operation, he must be clear what the operation is! Once the job or method of operation has been described, logically, from beginning to end, then it is broken down into very small elements based on time taken. These elements typically last no more than 30 seconds. Having broken the job down in this way, the person conducting the study then measures the performance of the employee concerned, generally using a stop-watch for the purpose. This is usually known as *direct* Time Study, in contrast to indirect Time Study (see below). Once sufficient numbers of elements have been timed, it is possible to arrive at the elapsed time, or observed time, for the job.

13. The next step in the procedure – rating – is the one which is the most vulnerable to mistakes or errors on the part of the investigator. The latter is required to 'rate' the employee ie to decide how quickly (or slowly!) the employee is working compared with a standard. This is usually the Standard Rating of 100 in the British Standard 3138 which is equivalent to the 'average rate at which qualified workers will naturally work at a job, provided they know and adhere to the specified method and provided they are motivated to apply themselves to their work.' Thus if an employee is adjudged to be working at a slower pace, he may be rated at, say, 80; by comparison an employee adjudged to be working at a faster pace than average may be rated at 115 for example. Clearly, if the person conducting the measurement is relatively inexperienced in Work Study and is unfamiliar with the job being rated, the probability of reaching a mistaken rating is quite high. Rating the job, enables a Basic Time to be established, using the following formula:–

$$\text{Basic Time} = \frac{\text{Observed Time x Rating}}{\text{Standard Rating}}$$

For example, if an employee's time for a particular element is observed to be 0.30 minutes, and he is rated as 115, then his Basic Time will be as follows:

$$\text{Basic Time} = \frac{0.30 \times 115 \text{ minutes}}{100}$$

$$= 0.345 \text{ minutes}$$

14. In order to reach a Standard Time for the job, a number of allowances are added to the Basic Time. These allowances are designed to accommodate such contingencies as relaxation, collection of materials or tools, and unavoidable delays, for example. This is another area of Work Measurement where subjective judgements have to be made, and where the person conducting the study may come under strong pressure from employees to allow more, rather than less, time for these allowances.

15. Where indirect time study is carried out – that is where times are worked out on paper without observing employees – the following techniques are the most commonly employed: Synthetic Timing, Predetermined Motion Time Study (PMTS), and Analytical Estimating. Briefly these may be described as follows.

**Synthetic Timing.** This is a technique for obtaining Basic Times for new jobs, which have not been time-studied previously and where it is impracticable (eg because of time constraints) to conduct direct Time Studies. In developing synthetic (or madeup) times, a job is broken down into elements, following a study of the drawings involved. Element times are assigned on the basis of past experience by utilising records from previous studies. The key to Synthetic Timing, therefore, is the existence of adequate past records of earlier *direct* studies. It has proved to be a reliable and consistent method for many businesses.

**Predetermined Motion Time Study (PMTS).** This is a technique which according to British Standard 3138, is one in which 'times established for basic human motions (classified according to the nature of the motion and the conditions under which it is made) are used to build up the time for a job at a defined level of performance'. PMTS differs from Synthetic Timing in that it is concerned not with job elements but with the basic motions that underlie every job element. PMTS is concerned with the lowest common denominators of work carried out by human beings. The most important method, to date, of PMTS is known as Methods Time Measurement (MTM). MTM is based on a small number of basic hand, eye and other movements, for which *universal* times have been established for skilled workers.

**Analytical Estimating.** As its title suggests, Analytical Estimating is a form of calculated guess-work. It is the most subjective technique employed in Work Measurement, and consequently the least reliable. It involves breaking a job into larger than usual elements and allocating Basic Times on the basis of the estimator's knowledge of the operations and skill in estimating times. This method tends to be used for one-off jobs.

## VALUE ANALYSIS (VALUE ENGINEERING)

16. This is another analytical technique which is widely used, especially in engineering, hence the alternative title. It is very like Method Study in its approach. The purpose of Value Analysis is to examine critically the function of a product with a view to fulfilling that function at the least cost consistent with reliability of the function. Thus Value Analysis is concerned with identifying the relationship between costs and reliability of function.

17. The stages of a value analysis are typically as follows:
   a. Select product to be studied.
   b. Determine function, design and cost of product (including components).
   c. Develop alternative designs for product in order to achieve same function at less cost ie designs of 'higher' value.
   d. Evaluate the alternative designs.
   e. Adopt optimum design ie the one able to perform the required function reliably but at least cost.
   f. Implement design and review results.

This process is usually carried out by a multi-disciplinary team composed of the following: value analyst/engineer, product designer, cost accountant, production representative and purchasing manager.

18. Value Analysis is applied most frequently in mass production or assembly line production processes, where large numbers of items are being produced, and where marginal cost savings can lead to substantial savings overall. Figure 40.4 provides an illustration of this point, indicating the effects, in terms of *quantity* savings, of unit savings of a few pence or even a fraction of a penny.

| | Cost per item | Best cost Saving | % | Volume per annum | Total Savings |
|---|---|---|---|---|---|
| Item A | £1.00 | £0.15 | 15 | 50,000 | £7,500 |
| Item B | £0.25 | £0.01 | 4 | 4 millions | £40,000 |

**Figure 40.4. Value Analysis - Examples of Cost Savings.**

19. The benefits of Value Analysis are that it encourages cost consciousness and the search for alternative designs and materials etc, and also permits more competitive pricing. However, it does tend to require large-scale production to show it off to the greatest advantage, and must, to a certain extent duplicate work carried out at the design stage of a product.

## QUALITY CIRCLES

20. The development of so-called 'Quality Circles' is a recent phenomenon. Quality Circles are small groups of about eight to ten employees, meeting together on a regular basis to discuss day-to-day issues such as quality, productivity and safety, with the object of (a) making improvements, and (b) organizing their implementation. The second object is significant, as it implies a degree of grass-roots decision-making which is new to most shop-floor situations. In the past employee involvement in initiating changes on the shop floor could only arise via formal productivity committees or via the firm's suggestion scheme. With Quality Circles, there is an attempt to delegate real power to ordinary employees not only to make suggestions regarding quality etc, but also to implement those suggestions.

21. Membership of Quality Circles is voluntary, but usually consists of a number of shop-floor employees and a foreman or supervisor, or may consist of a mixture of skilled and unskilled employees together with one or two shop-floor specialists such as Quality Engineers and Inspectors. Each Circle selects its own leader, and usually the organization concerned provides training for such leaders in appropriate subjects (discussion leading, quality control etc).

22. Typically, a Quality Circle will adopt the following approach to its task:

    a. Identify and clarify problems in the local work situation,

    b. Select a problem for solution (eg wastage rates),

   c.  Set realistic target for improvement (eg to reduce wastage rates by 15% over next 12 months),

   d.  Establish a plan, together with a timetable, for achievement of the target,

   e.  Propose plan to local management,

   f.  Implement and test plan,

   g.  Revise plan, where necessary, and monitor results.

23.  Those organizations which operate Quality Circles claim to see them as a practical means of achieving employee participation on the shop-floor. They are not primarily instruments of cost-reduction exercises, even though costs may well figure in their discussions. Surveys in Japan, for example, where Quality Circles are widely employed, indicate that whilst costs are one of the major topics of discussion in the Circles, there are several others of equal importance, such as quality, use of equipment, efficiency and safety.

24.  The benefits of Quality Circles are:

   a.  greater awareness of shop-floor problems by Circle members,

   b.  greater confidence in tackling problems and generating solutions on the part of Circle members,

   c.  improved productivity and/or quality, and

   d.  improved motivation on the shop-floor.

## SUMMARY

25.  Three types of aid to production management have been described briefly in this Chapter – Work Study, Value Analysis and Quality Circles.

26.  Work Study is the name given to what is, in effect, a collection of techniques. These are predominantly Method Study and Work Measurement. Their aim is to study work in all its contexts so as to highlight all those factors which affect efficiency and economy in a particular situation, and so as to bring about improvements. Examples of the kind of improvements which can be achieved following Work Study include the elimination of waste, and the improvement of productivity in both men and machines.

27.  Value Analysis, or Value Engineering as it is sometimes called, is a technique for examining the function of a product with the aim of providing that function reliably at the least possible cost. Value Analysis is applied in situations where large scale

production methods are in operation, since it is only where large quantities are being produced that marginal cost-reductions in unit costs can produce a worthwhile pay-off.

28.  Quality Circles are voluntary groups of employees working at the shop-floor level to identify problems of quality, productivity etc; to set targets to improve the situation caused by problems; and to implement required changes at shop-floor level. As well as being aids to production, Quality Circles may also be regarded as a form of employee participation.

# 41

# NEW TECHNOLOGY IN MANUFACTURING

## INTRODUCTION

1.   What is the new technology in manufacturing? It can best be summarised as 'the selective application of computing and microelectronics to the planning, resourcing and controlling of the manufacturing process, from the design stage to the completion of the product' . In practice this means the development and application of one or more of the following:
   a.   computers for production control
   b.   computer-aided design (CAD)
   c.   computer-aided manufacture (CAM)
   d.   robots;
   e.   process measurement and control devices

2.   The above applications can be combined in various ways to form:
   a.   computer-integrated manufacturing (CIM)
   b.   computer-aided engineering and
   c.   flexible manufacturing systems (FMS)

There is a certain amount of confusion currently as to what these integrated manufacturing systems should be called. In this chapter they will be taken to have the following relationship to each other (see Figure 41.1.).

Each of the items will be described briefly in the following paragraphs. The chapter will end with a summary of the overall impact of the new technology on industrial nations.

## COMPUTERS AND PRODUCTION CONTROL

3.   As in other businesses, manufacturing organizations have been quick to see the advantages of using computers in their day-today activities. Over 70% of the computers currently in use in Britain's factories are microcomputers, and several of their principal applications are described in this chapter. Perhaps the most orthodox use of computers in manufacturing is to be found in the processing of information for production planning and control. Typical production control programs handled by computers include stock control, sales orders, purchase orders, machine scheduling, capacity planning, tooling lists and work scheduling.

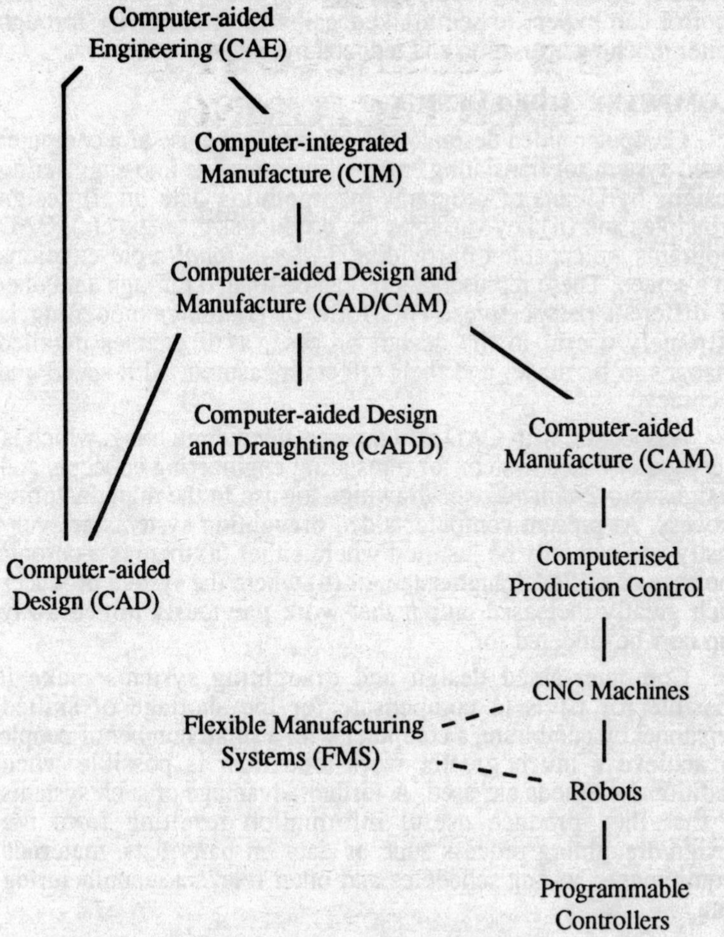

Computer-aided
Engineering (CAE)

Computer-integrated
Manufacture (CIM)

Computer-aided Design and
Manufacture (CAD/CAM)

Computer-aided Design
and Draughting (CADD)

Computer-aided
Manufacture (CAM)

Computer-aided
Design (CAD)

Computerised
Production Control

CNC Machines

Flexible Manufacturing
Systems (FMS)

Robots

Programmable
Controllers

## Figure 41.1. Hierarchy of Manufacturing Systems

4. The main benefits of these applications are:
   - they improve control of the production process
   - they enable more efficient utilisation of plant and equipment
   - they enable fewer items to be held as stock or as work-in progress
   - they reduce labour cost
   - they speed up deliveries by reducing the waiting time between processes

Overall, firms using computers for production planning and control can expect to see marked gains in productivity through better machine utilisation and reduced overheads.

## COMPUTER-AIDED DESIGN

5.    Computer-aided design (CAD) refers to the use of a computer based system for translating engineering concepts into engineering designs by means of programs incorporating data on (i) design principles and (ii) key variables (eg product size, shape etc). CAD programs are capable of providing *3-dimensional* representations on a screen. These representations can be rotated through a number of different perspectives. This form of computer modelling is extremely useful in the design process, as it enables detailed changes to be made, and their effects measured, with speed and accuracy.

6.    Associated with CAD is computer-aided draughting, which is a computer based system for translating engineering concepts and designs into *2-dimensional* drawings for use in the manufacturing process. At present computer-aided draughting systems are very costly and can only be justified where either (a) there is a chronic shortage of skilled draughtsmen, or (b) where the system produces such greatly increased output that work previously turned away can now be tendered for.

7.    Computer-aided design and draughting systems make it possible for firms to compensate for the shortage of skilled personnel by combining a computer with a small number of people to achieve a much greater work-load than is possible when traditional methods are used. A further advantage of such systems is that they produce useful information resulting from the design/draughting process such as data on parts lists, materials requirements, wiring schedules and other relevant manufacturing data.

## COMPUTER-AIDED MANUFACTURE

8.    Computer-aided manufacture (CAM) is a general term which refers to any production system in which manufacturing plant and test equipment are controlled by computer. CAM is more than just metal-cutting. It embraces important engineering processes such as welding, assembling and painting. CAM is particularly applicable to processes where parts are complex and accuracy is vital. A CAM system can be expected to achieve:

    a.  more speedy production of parts;
    b.  a consistently high level of product quality;

   c.  replication to within very close tolerances;

   d.  ability to achieve high production levels even when skilled craftsmen are in short supply.

9.   An important feature of CAM is that its software generates numerical control (NC) tapes for the computer-control of machines (CNC machines) and robots. Numerical control of machine tools is not new. What is new is the ability of a computer program to introduce far greater flexibility into the way the numerically-controlled machine can be operated. In the past this had to be done on a step-by-step process, but now several processes can be woven together by the computer. Another advantage is that programs can be amended very easily under a computer-controlled system. Typical work handled by CNC machines (Computerised Numerical Control) includes turning, drilling, milling and sheet metal working. The use of such machines has been found to lead to greatly improved productivity on account of the reduced requirement for toolsetting. One example of CAM is the Flexible Manufacturing System which we shall describe briefly.

## FLEXIBLE MANUFACTURING SYSTEMS

10.  A Flexible Manufacturing System (FMS) is one where a small group (or cell) of CNC machine-tools is used in a coordinated way for producing components without manual intervention in a small batch operation. The objective in this case is to mirror the productivity possible on large-scale, fully-automated systems. A typical FMS would consist of the following:

- a group of NC machines each with the capacity to manufacture a range of parts
- a number of robots and/or wire-controlled work-carriers
- a computer control station

11.  Such systems are costly to introduce, but where justified can lead to:

- reduced work-in-progress
- reduced stock-levels
- faster throughput times
- quicker change-over times
- lower unit costs

## ROBOTS

12.  The expression 'robot' derives from the Czech word for 'work'. In modern usage 'robot' means *a programmable machine that can replicate a limited range of human actions*. Most of the

robots in use in the world are so-called 'first generation' machines, which are basically mechanical arms used for such repetitive tasks as machine-loading, spot-welding, injection-moulding and paint spraying. Fig. 41.2 shows the most frequent applications of robots in the United Kingdom in 1984:

| Application | No. of Robots |
|---|---|
| Spot welding | 471 |
| Injection moulding | 412 |
| Arc welding | 341 |
| Machine loading | 213 |
| Assembly | 199 |
| Surface coating | 177 |
| Unspecified | 133 |
| Education/Research | 122 |
| Handling/Palletising | 102 |

**Figure 41.2. Robot Applications in U.K. (1984)**
(Source: British Robot Association, December 1984)

13. More sophisticated robots ('second generation' models) can be used for more complex operations than those mentioned above. This is because they are supplied with improved sensing abilities, especially 'sight', 'smell' and 'touch'. In the automotive industry, for example, such robots are deployed to fit windscreens on cars and to locate test leaks from completed vehicle bodies. Even more 'intelligent' machines are being developed in the laboratory, and will no doubt be employed in factories within the next ten years.

14. The principal reasons why firms introduce robots into their manufacturing plants are as follows:

- competitors are installing them;
- they can be employed on work which employees are reluctant to undertake, because it is repetitive or dirty or noisy;
- they can be employed on dangerous tasks such as handling radioactive materials or dangerous viruses;
- they help to reduce production costs, for, once programmed, they are tirelessly accurate and thus free skilled employees for other tasks;

- they are necessary prerequisite for any firm intending to work towards the adoption of highly-automated systems such as FMS and CIM (see below)

15. Figure 41.3 shows the latest estimates of world robots as supplied by the British Robot Association.

| Nation | No. of Robots | Robots per 10,000 workers |
|--------|---------------|---------------------------|
| Japan | 64,000 | 32.0 |
| USA | 13,000 | 4.3 |
| West Germany | 6,600 | 5.7 |
| France | 3,380 | 4.3 |
| Italy | 2,700 | 3.5 |
| UK | 2,623 | 4.8 |
| Sweden | 2,400 | 17.7 |
| Belgium | 859 | 6.4 |
| Spain | 518 | 3.8 |

**Figure 41.3 World Robot Population**

As the table shows, Japan is far ahead of other industrialised nations in her investment in robots.

## PROCESS MEASUREMENT AND CONTROL DEVICES

16. Microprocessor-based process measurement and control devices are used mainly in situations where the measurement and analysis of chemicals, gases, liquids and solids are important. The devices can monitor and record such variables as flow, pressure, temperature and constituent levels. In the cement-manufacturing process, for example, a controller known as a fluorescent spectrometer can analyse samples of the product and produce a complete chemical analysis of seven elemental oxide constituents of the material.

17. Process measurement devices tend to be relatively easy to use, do not require highly-qualified operators and can carry out a wide range of monitoring and testing activities. A new device for checking telephone equipment can automatically perform over 40 tests on the equipment in a few hours. Using earlier methods such a test would have taken several days.

## PROGRAMMABLE CONTROLLERS

18. Programmable controllers are microprocessor-based devices capable of performing a wide range of switching, monitoring and signalling functions. Fitted to a particular machine or part of a process plant, they are linked to a host computer and can carry out a variety of monitoring and reporting functions during operations. In a large plant several such controllers may be fitted to control various stages of the process. These controllers are frequently to be found in such industries as petrochemicals, brick-making and food processing.

## CAD/CAM SYSTEMS

19. The computer-aided manufacturing systems that have just been described have close links with the computer-aided design and draughting referred to in paragraphs 5 and 6 above. Where such systems are combined they are usually referred to as a CAD/CAM system, and undoubtedly this will become the standard for the future.

20. The benefits of CAD/CAM can be summarised as follows:
    a. greatly improved productivity of designers and draughtsmen (eg drawings produced in a quarter of the time previously taken using traditional methods);
    b. reduction in waiting list of projects to be tackled by the design department;
    c. ability to tender for work which previously would have been turned away for lack of skilled personnel;
    d. development of uniform design standards throughout the organization;
    e. consistency of specifications, and the elimination of inconsistencies between drawings;
    f. ability to amend designs/drawings to take account of modifications or improvements;
    g. shorter production times leading to lower optimum batch sizes and more rapid changes of product lines;
    h. improved quality and consistency of finished products;
    i. simplified quality control through automatic testing and inspection using the specification already held in a computer.

21. Given the substantial benefits of CAD/CAM, it is surprising that many British firms have not yet taken it up. The answer

appears to lie in one or more of the following reasons given by firms as to why they have not introduced CAD/CAM:

   a. such systems are extremely costly to install, and may not produce enough sizeable benefits for small and medium-sized companies;

   b. many firms are unaware of the advantages of CAD/CAM;

   c. industrial managements often lack the confidence to incorporate such sophisticated systems into their production areas;

   d. the personnel implications of introducing CAD/CAM can be daunting, requiring firms to recruit additional, qualified staff, retrain many grades of existing staff and develop new payments systems to cope with all the job changes.

## COMPUTER-INTEGRATED MANUFACTURE

22. Computer-integrated manufacture (CIM) refers to the integration and coordination of all aspects of manufacturing from the design and layout of plant, product and component design, through processing and production control to quality assurance and final despatch. Currently examples may be seen in modern motor manufacturing plants, where dealer-orders for specific models are fed into a master-computer, and subsequently passed down to production for manufacturing in accordance with the dealers' requirements as to colour, engine size and so on. Such a system incorporates despatch and delivery procedures, as well as monitoring stock levels and a host of other production and marketing data. CAD/CAM systems, in themselves, are advanced systems, but on an altogether smaller scale than CIM. CAD/CAM equipment could be used in a piecemeal way and fail to reap the full benefits of the new technology. By integration of the total manufacturing system the greatest result will be possible, and for large-scale manufacturing will probably become the norm in future.

## COMPUTER-AIDED ENGINEERING

23. This is another general term which encompasses not only computer-integrated manufacture but also the analysis of design and other software used in computer-aided systems. In our original Figure (Fig. 41.1) this item comes at the head of the hierarchy of computer-based manufacturing systems.

## THE IMPACT OF THE NEW TECHNOLOGY

24.  In sheer economic terms, the impact on manufacturing of the new microelectronic technology is likely to produce as many threats as it does opportunities, especially for advanced industrial nations. There are several reasons why this may be so:

- microelectronic technology is as available to the emergent economies of the East as it is to the powerful economies of the USA, Japan and Western Europe

- the emergent economies have far lower labour costs than the advanced nations and will therefore be able to compete more keenly for world trade in a wide range of manufactured goods

- whereas in the emergent economies new technology is likely to lead to greater employment opportunities, the reverse is likely in the advanced nations, where employment levels in manufacturing are falling in any case

- yet any nation that does not adopt the new technology will fail to compete in world markets for manufactured goods, and is likely to end up as a museum of industrial history

- generally speaking the biggest gains from the new technology will come from increased productivity and improved product quality

25.  The application of microelectronics technology to the economic life of advanced industrial nations is more likely to be successful in the exploitation of information processing. Figure 41.4 illustrates the declining role of industry and the increasing role of information processing in an advanced economy, in this case the United States.

26.  As Figure 41.4 shows, since the 1950's industry has been in decline in the USA, whereas by contrast information processing activities have been increasing sharply since the 1940's (the advent of the computer). The challenge for advanced nations will undoubtedly be to maintain a viable, though much smaller, manufacturing industry based on the best of the new technology.

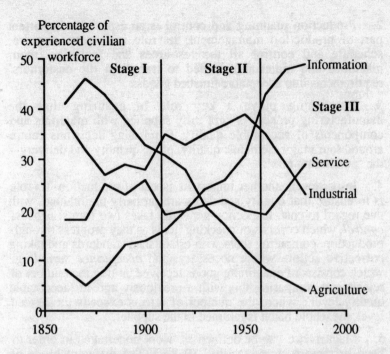

The chart shows that almost half of America's civilian workforce are already employed in the information field. Things are similar in Western Europe, where a considerable proportion of the service sector's workforce are also involved in generating, recording, processing and transmitting information in one form or another.

Stage I has been described as the agricultural economy;
Stage II the industrial economy.
Stage III the information economy.

**Source: Bureau of Labor Statistics - USA**

**Figure 41.4. Towards the information economy.**
*The changing pattern of employment in the USA, 1860-1980.*

## SECTION SUMMARY - PRODUCTION MANAGEMENT

1.   Production management is central to the manufacturing process. Its task is to plan, resource and control the process of converting raw materials and components into finished goods that meet the customers' specifications. Key functions in production management are: manufacturing, production planning and control, production engineering, maintenance, purchasing and quality control.

2. Production planning and control is an especially important part of production management. Its role is to plan, acquire, schedule and control all the resources and facilities (men, machines and materials) needed to transform the customers' requirements into acceptable finished goods.

3. Purchasing plays a key role in ensuring that the manufacturing process is kept fully supplied with materials and components of acceptable quality. Purchasing decisions centre around four major elements: quality, price, quantity and delivery – the 'purchasing mix'.

4. Inspection is another important aspect of production. Its role is to ensure that quality standards are properly maintained, with due regard to cost. Inspection generally takes two forms: *process control,* which consists of checking items as they progress through production, comparing them with established standards and taking corrective action, where necessary; and *acceptance sampling*, which consists of examining goods received, noting the number of rejects and comparing this with a previously agreed 'acceptable quality level'; where the number of rejects exceeds the agreed level, the whole batch is returned to the supplier.

5. Maintenance can be defined as 'work undertaken in order to keep or restore every facility' (B.S.I.). The different kinds of maintenance are: preventive, corrective, breakdown, running and shutdown maintenance. Planned maintenance involves planning ahead for routine servicing and overhauling, and preparing contingency plans for emergency breakdowns.

6. The most commonly-used categories for distinguishing different types of production are as follows:

| | | |
|---|---|---|
| a. | Jobbing production | – the production of unique 'one-off' items (large or small), made to the customer's order. |
| b. | Batch production | – the production of standardised items in lots (or batches), where each batch must complete one process before it moves on to the next process. |

c.  Mass production  – the production of goods in large quantities by means of assembly lines or continuous flow processes, in which the individual items move from one operation or process to the next in an uninterruptable fashion (assembly line), or in which the materials in transit literally flow from one process to the next until completion (continuous flow process).

7.    Work Study is the name for a number of techniques, but notably Method Study and Work Measurement, used to examine human work in a systematic manner with a view to achieving improved economy and efficiency. When Work Study is applied in a production situation, it is directed towards the elimination of wasteful effort and the improvement of working methods, so as to improve the productivity of men and machines.

8.    Method Study systematically examines and records all the methods used in an operation or process with a view to increasing efficiency (cost-effectiveness) and productivity (output per unit of input). Method Study makes wide use of flowcharts to record data about methods of operation. Flowcharts record activities in the order in which they occur, utilising a standard set of five symbols to denote Operation, Transport, Storage, Delay and Inspection. Elapsed times are also noted, and comments may be made on the charts. A variety of other forms of data collection are used eg multiple activity charts, flow diagrams etc. All such data allows the Method Study engineer to examine methods critically with a view to improving them.

9.    Work Measurement aims to establish the time taken by an operator to complete a specified task, and to assess this time against a standard. The most widely-employed method of Work Measurement is Time Study (direct and indirect). Direct Time Study involves observing an operator and timing his efforts with a stop-watch. The initial purpose is to obtain an 'elapsed time' or 'observed time' for the task concerned. Next the Time Study engineer has to rate the observed performance against the British Standard Rating of 100, which is the 'average rate at which qualified workers will naturally work at a job, provided they know and adhere to the specified method and provided they are motivated to apply themselves to their work.' (B.S.I. 3138). Rating clearly depends heavily on the subjective assessment of the observer. Once a job has been rated it is possible to arrive at a

Basic Time for the operator. To this Basic Time is added an allowance for rest periods, unavoidable delays etc to give a Standard Time for the work. Indirect Time Study uses past data and pre-determined times as the basis for arriving at Standard Times. Examples of indirect Time Study include Synthetic Timing (based on past data) and Predetermined Motion Time Study (based on predetermined times for basic human movements).

10. Value Analysis is the term used to describe the critical examination of the function of a product with a view to providing that function at the least cost, consistent with reliability of the function. It is most widely used in mass production environments, where even quite marginal cost savings can lead to substantial savings overall.

11. Quality Circles are small groups of employees, meeting regularly on a voluntary basis to discuss day-to-day problems of quality, productivity, safety and others, with a view to making improvements and implementing them. The difference between Quality Circles and other forms of employee participation at shop-floor level (eg productivity committees) is that the former permit the *employees themselves* to implement changes agreed by the management. The benefits of Quality Circles include a greater awareness of, and confidence in tackling, shop-floor problems by ordinary employees; and also increased productivity/quality.

12. New technology in manufacturing is based on two major developments:
   a. the computer
   b. microelectronics

These two developments have enabled design, draughting, manufacturing and control functions to be employed more speedily, flexibly and cost-effectively than conventional design and manufacturing systems.

13. Practical applications of the computer and microelectronics can be seen in:
   a. computer-aided design and draughting
   b. computer-aided manufacture (especially by means of CNC machines)
   c. robot machines capable of replicating basic human actions
   d. wire-controlled work-carriers
   e. devices for controlling and measuring manufacturing processes (eg in chemicals and gases)

14. The overall benefits of the new technology lie in increased productivity and improved product quality.

# QUESTIONS FOR DISCUSSION/HOMEWORK

*1.     In what ways can the use of computers be advantageous in the production planning and control process?*

*2.     It could be said that a typical Purchasing Manager is under pressure from suppliers to order to the maximum, and under pressure from colleagues to keep prices to the minimum. Discuss to what extent this is a fair view of the Purchasing Manager's role?*

*3.     What is the role of Inspection in Quality Control?*

*4.     How far can maintenance be planned? What kinds of maintenance would you expect to find in a planned maintenance programme for a continuous process plant?*

*5.     How can batch production be distinguished from mass production? Give an example of each type of production.*

*6.     What, basically, is Work Study and what benefits are claimed for it?*

*7.     What alternative ways exist for collecting or presenting Method Study data?*

*8.     What is a Standard Rating and what significance can this have for Work Measurement?*

*9.     Where is the value in Value Analysis?*

*10.    How do Quality Circles approach shop-floor problems, and what is considered to be distinctive in this approach?*

*11.    What problems do you foresee for production managers considering the introduction of an integrated manufacturing system in a mass-production plant?*

*12.    What, in your opinion, are the most convincing arguments for extending the application of microelectronics to manufacturing processes?*

# EXAMINATION QUESTIONS - PRODUCTION MANAGEMENT

*The subject of Production Management only appears infrequently in the examination papers at which the main emphasis of this manual is directed. However it is a frequent enough topic in the Business Organization paper of the Institute of Marketing, so the majority of questions selected are taken from that particular paper. It should be sufficient to show that you have grasped the essentials of the subject-matter of the questions concerned. Suggested answers appear in Appendix 2.*

*EQ 31*    *Describe briefly the main activities within a Production Planning and Control system.*

                                    *(IOM Business Organization)*

*EQ 32*    *Describe the circumstances which would justify the adoption of (a) jobbing, (b) batch, and (c) flow/mass patterns of production.*

                                    *(ACCA Business Management)*

*EQ 33*    *Briefly describe the sequence of necessary activities for the purchasing department of a manufacturing company to carry out, in purchasing a raw material not previously required.*

                                    *(IOM Business Organization)*

# PERSONNEL MANAGEMENT

## INTRODUCTION

The chapters in this section describe the main features of the specialist Personnel function in organizations. Particular aspects of Personnel Management which are dealt with are as follows: the role of Personnel (Chapter 42), recruitment and selection (Chapter 43), training and development (Chapter 44), Employee Performance Appraisal (Chapter 45), Management Development Chapter 46), job evaluation (Chapter 47), Employee Relations (Chapter 48), and Employment Law (Chapter 49). The selection is based primarily on the scope of previous examination questions in this field, and partly because several aspects of Personnel have already been dealt with in earlier chapters eg manpower planning (Chapter 19), organization development (Chapter 23).

# 42

# THE ROLE OF PERSONNEL

1.   Personnel management, in the sense of managing people, can be said to be part of the role of every person who is responsible for the work of others. This is a very broad meaning of 'personnel management' and does not tell us anything about the particular areas of work in which personnel specialists make a distinctive contribution to an organization. In the context of this Manual, the expression 'Personnel Management' will refer to the duties and activities of personnel specialists.

2.   What then is Personnel Management? It is that specialist function of management which has the prime responsibility for the following:

   a. formulating, proposing and gaining acceptance for the personnel policies and strategies of the organization,

   b. advising and guiding the organization's managers on the implementation of personnel policies and strategies,

   c. providing adequate personnel services for the organi- zation to enable it to recruit, motivate and develop sufficient and suitable employees at all levels,

   d. advising the organization's managers of the human consequences of change.

3.   The policy-making and strategic responsibilities are carried out by senior Personnel Managers; advisory and guidance responsibilities are carried out both by senior and middle ranking Personnel Managers; the provision of personnel services is very much a middle-management responsibility; finally, the management of change is primarily a senior Personnel role.

4.   By virtue of their specialist function, all Personnel Managers, regardless of seniority, are able to concentrate exclusively on personnel matters, unlike their colleagues in other departments (line or functional) who are only able to give a proportion of their time to such matters. How other managers see their personnel colleagues depends on several factors such as the organizational climate, the managerial styles of the managers concerned and the extent to which Personnel is able to be helpful. Personnel Managers, in particular, have to tread a delicate path between offering constructive, and sometimes unpopular, advice to their

colleagues and appearing to tell them how to handle their own staff. Under modern conditions of employment, the needs and wishes of staff have never been so well protected, and, as a result, many issues which, formerly, could have been dealt with solely by a manager acting on his own, now have to tackled jointly with the Personnel department.

5.    Personnel policies, like any other corporate policies, are not just the preserve of a particular group of Managers. Such policies have to be agreed by the top management team as a whole, and approved by the Board. The role of the senior personnel staff is to formulate draft personnel policies and to argue the case for their acceptance. In many instances it will be the personnel department which provides the initiative for the introduction of new policies and the revision or rejection of existing policies. Key areas of personnel policy can include the following:

Recruitment and Selection

Pay and Benefits (Pensions etc)

Relations with Trade Unions or Staff Associations

Career Development

Training

Safety and Health

Employment Legislation

As in other policy areas, personnel policies are guidelines for behaviour stating what the organization will do, or positively will not do, in relation to its employees and employee affairs.

6.    Examples of personnel policies are as follows:

a.    Every job vacancy will be advertised within the organization before any external advertising takes place,

b.    The Company will encourage employees to pursue training and education opportunities, where this might qualify them for promotion or career development moves within the organization,

c.    The organization will always negotiate in good faith with the representatives of recognised independent trade unions,

d.    The Company will always endeavour to obey the spirit as well as the letter of laws relating to employment; it will actively discourage any activities which might cause a breach of the law.

7.    Strategic advice on personnel matters is directed towards the fulfilment of the organization's corporate plan, and covers issues such as the manpower plan, the development of harmonious and

mutually respectful relationships with trade union representatives, the maintenance of employee motivation by means of fair and equitable payment systems and of adequate personal and career development opportunities, and, finally, the organization's actions in relation to new developments in employment legislation.

8.    Personnel services represent the operational or production aspect of Personnel Management. Personnel services include the following:

a.  recruitment services (eg advertising, preparing candidate specifications, shortlisting candidates, arranging interviews and handling the correspondence)

b.  pay procedures and associated procedures, such as the provision of job evaluation services

c.  appraisal procedures (ie appraisal forms, timetable for appraisals, maintenance of records etc)

d.  employment services (ie conditions of service procedures – informing managers and employees, recording employee details, handling enquiries etc)

e.  employee relations – especially, organizing arrangements for management-union meetings, taking records, providing relevant information on pay rates, recent agreements, legal aspects etc; monitoring grievance and disciplinary procedures etc

f.  training services (ie. providing information about training, handling arrangements for courses, maintaining training records etc)

g.  safety, health and welfare services (eg organizing safety committees, maintaining safety records, provision of welfare and canteen facilities etc)

9.    In addition to the policy-making, strategic and personnel services roles, most modern Personnel departments are expected to have something useful to say about the implications of change for the employees of the organization. In some organizations this is specifically referred to as the Organization Development function of Personnel. Whether it has a title or not, the activity itself is directed towards the recognition of change, from whichever quarter, and the assessment of the likely impact of that change on personnel affairs in the organization. The introduction of new technology, for example could reduce the demand for certain categories of employee, whilst increasing the demand for other categories. This, in turn, could lead to difficult negotiations with unions over redundancies, re-training opportunities, pay

arrangements for the introduction of the new technology and other personnel issues.

10. Ultimately the role of Personnel will be determined by the attitudes of the top management of the organization. Where Personnel is recognised as having a major part to play in the renewal and maturation processes of the organizational system, then the Personnel Manager will be given a key role in the corporate development of the organization. Where, by contrast, Personnel is seen mainly as a provider of services to other managers, then the Personnel Manager will be given a routine administrative role, enlivened at intervals by 'fire-fighting' responsibilities whenever there is a crisis.

## THE ORGANIZATION OF PERSONNEL

11. The type of structure which may be found in a Personnel department will be a reflection of the role it is expected to play in the organization. For example, in an organization where Personnel is held to be of vital importance to the future of the organization as well as to its present, the Personnel department is likely to be structured along the lines of the example shown in Figure 42.1. Some junior posts have been ignored in the interests of simplicity.

12. In the example, the senior Personnel Manager is shown as an executive director, to emphasise the Board level role which is expected of Personnel in this organization. The Personnel Services' Manager is responsible for recruitment and personnel administration, and would also have other responsibilities not indicated on the chart (eg welfare, canteen, office services etc). The Employee Relations Manager is responsible for industrial relations matters, including job evaluation, job grading and industrial relations intelligence. The Training & Development Manager is responsible for all aspects of training, including job training, management development and related matters. The Organization Planning Manager is responsible for assessing manpower requirements, organization design projects, management succession planning and career planning. He would probably share some of the responsibility for appraisals with the Training & Development Manager. Several options are open to the Personnel Director concerning the allocation of responsibilities between the Training Manager and the manager responsible for organization planning. In the final analysis, the decision would probably be made on the basis of experience and personality.

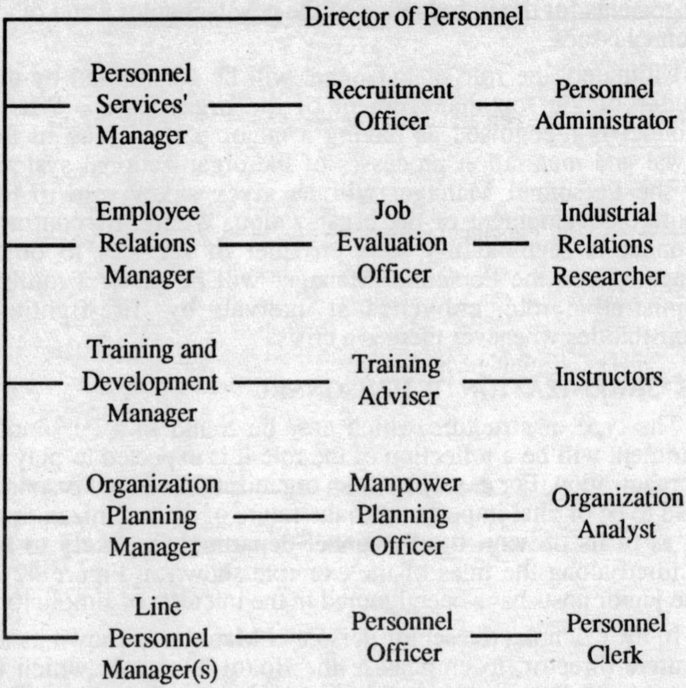

Director of Personnel

| | | |
|---|---|---|
| Personnel Services' Manager | Recruitment Officer | Personnel Administrator |
| Employee Relations Manager | Job Evaluation Officer | Industrial Relations Researcher |
| Training and Development Manager | Training Adviser | Instructors |
| Organization Planning Manager | Manpower Planning Officer | Organization Analyst |
| Line Personnel Manager(s) | Personnel Officer | Personnel Clerk |

**Figure 42.1. Personnel Function with Wide-ranging Role.**

13. In an organization, where little is expected of Personnel apart from the provision of services, and where line managers are expected to bear the brunt of dealing with the personnel matters raised by their own employees, then the structure shown in Figure 42.2 is likely to be met.

14. In the structure described above, the emphasis is entirely on the provision of services. Each of the jobs referred to is intended to pursue a routine, here-and-now path. There is no intention of including Personnel in any strategic activity, nor in any corporate advice-giving, except for routine information.

15. In between the two structures illustrated are many other options, as Personnel departments grow or wane in stature, as top management attitudes to Personnel change, and as external conditions (especially legislation) make labour more, or less, important. The rest of this Section assumes an organization which has the full range of Personnel activities, and which assumes a corporate role for the Personnel function.

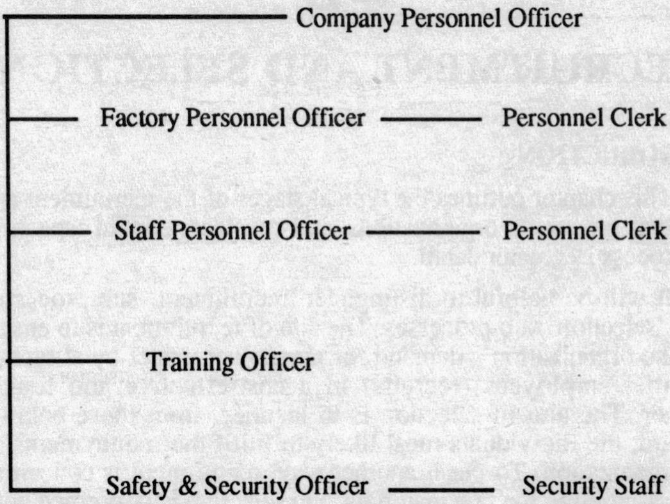

```
┌──────────────────── Company Personnel Officer
│
├────── Factory Personnel Officer ──────── Personnel Clerk
│
├────── Staff Personnel Officer ──────── Personnel Clerk
│
├────── Training Officer
│
└────── Safety & Security Officer ──────── Security Staff
```

**Figure 42.2. Routine-orientated Personnel Department.**

# 43

# RECRUITMENT AND SELECTION

## INTRODUCTION

1.   This chapter outlines the typical stages of the recruitment and selection process in organizations, and considers certain aspects of the process in greater detail.

2.   It will be helpful to distinguish 'recruitment' sub-processes from 'selection' sub-processes. The aim of recruitment is to ensure that the organization's demand for manpower is met by attracting potential employees (recruits) in a cost-effective and timely manner. The aim of selection is to identify, from those coming forward, the individuals most likely to fulfil the requirements of the organization. To put it another way, recruitment is concerned with assembling the raw materials, and selection is concerned with producing the right blend for the organization, at a particular point in time.

## RECRUITMENT: POLICIES AND PROCEDURES

3.   Recruitment policies constitute the code of conduct which the organization is prepared to follow in its search for possible recruits in the market-place. Some examples of reputable policies in this field are as follows.

'In matters of recruitment, this Company *will*:

a.   advertise all vacancies internally before making use of external sources,

b.   always advertise under the Company name when advertising externally,

c.   endeavour to ensure that every applicant for a position in the Company is informed in advance about the basic details of the vacancy, and the basic conditions of employment attached to it,

d.   endeavour to ensure that applicants are kept informed of their progress through the recruitment procedures,

e.   seek possible candidates on the basis of their ability to perform the job required.'

'In matters of recruitment, this Company *will not*:
   a. knowingly make exaggerated or misleading claims in recruitment literature or job advertisements,
   b. discriminate unfairly against possible candidates on the grounds of sex, race, age, religion or physical disablement.'

4.   The recruitment activities of an organization are carried out mainly by Personnel staff. These activities represent the marketing role of Personnel, reaching out across the organization's external boundaries into the labour market. It is important, therefore, that such activities are conducted in a manner that sustains or enhances the good reputation of the organization. People who are treated well when they seek employment with the organization are potential ambassadors for the organization, whether they are successful in their application or not. Conversely, those who are treated badly in this situation are quick to spread their criticism. Examples of bad treatment of applicants include omitting to reply to a letter or form of application, keeping applicants waiting for an interview, and failing to inform applicants who have been unsuccessful.

5.   Well-organized Personnel departments work to a checklist of recruitment procedures designed to minimise errors and thus avoid marring the organization's image externally and Personnel's reputation internally. A typical checklist is shown overleaf (Figure 43.1). It helps to ensure a rational and logical approach to the recruitment of employees throughout the organization.

6.   The job description referred to in item 2 would usually contain at least the following information about the job concerned:

- Title of Job
- Grade/Salary Level of Job
- Title of Immediate Superior's Job
- Number of Subordinates
- Overall Purpose of the Job
- Principal Responsibilities of the Job
- Limits of Authority
- Location of Job

In most organizations this information is contained in a formal document, completed following an analysis of the job. In some cases it may be less formally expressed, but nevertheless covers the points noted above.

| Item | Question to be considered |
|------|---------------------------|
| 1 | Has the vacancy been agreed by the responsible manager? |
| 2 | Is there an up-to-date job description for the vacant position? |
| 3 | What are the conditions of employment (salary, hours, holidays etc) for the vacant position? |
| 4 | Has a candidate specification been prepared? |
| 5 | Has a notice of the vacancy been circulated internally? |
| 6 | Has a job advertisement been agreed? Have details of the vacancy been forwarded to relevant agencies? |
| 7 | Do all potential candidates (internal or external) know where to apply and in what form? |
| 8 | What arrangements have been made for drawing up a shortlist of candidates? |
| 9 | Have the interviewing arrangements been agreed, and have shortlisted candidates been informed? |
| 10 | Have unsuitable candidates, or candidates held in reserve, been informed of their position? |
| 11 | Have offer letters been agreed and despatched to successful candidates? Have references been taken up, where necessary? |
| 12 | Have suitable rejection letters been sent to unsuccessful shortlisted candidates, thanking them for their attendance? |
| 13 | Have all replies to offer letters been accounted for? |
| 14 | Have the necessary procedures for placement, induction and follow-up of successful candidates been put into effect? |

**Figure 43.1. Recruitment Checklist.**

7. The candidate specification, or personnel specification, as it is frequently called, is a summary of the knowledge, skills and personal characteristics required of the jobholder to carry out the job to an acceptable standard of performance. This is an extremely important feature of the recruitment process, because it sets down a standard by which candidates for interview may be tested. There

are two very well-known classifications for personal requirements: the Seven-Point Plan, developed by Professor Rodger of the National Institute of Industrial Psychology in the 1950's, and the Five-point Plan produced by J. Munro Fraser at about the same time. These two attempts to produce general profiles of candidates for selection are compared in Figure 43.2 below.

| Seven-Point Plan (A. Rodger) | Five-Point Plan (J. Munro Fraser) |
|---|---|
| 1. Physical make-up | 1. Impact on others |
| 2. Attainments | 2. Acquired Qualifications |
| 3. General intelligence | 3. Innate abilities |
| 4. Specialised aptitudes | 4. Motivation |
| 5. Interests | 5. Adjustment |
| 6. Disposition | |
| 7. Circumstances | |

**Figure 43.2. Personal Classifications.**

8.   It can be seen that are many common features between the two classifications. In practice, the Seven-Point plan tends to be the most popular, and individual firms often model their own personnel specifications on it. A formal layout for a specification is shown in Figure 43.3. Note that the form enables a distinction to be drawn between points that are essential in order to fulfil the job requirements, and those that are desirable, but not essential for adequate performance.

| | Essential | Desirable |
|---|---|---|
| Formal Qualifications | | |
| Knowledge | | |
| Experience | | |
| Skills<br>  – Manual<br>  – Social<br>  – Other | | |
| Personality/Motivation | | |
| Physical Requirements | | |
| Interests | | |
| Circumstances | | |

**Figure 43.3. Personnel Specification.**

9. In cases where a tight specification is drawn up ie where the emphasis is on the essential requirements of the job, the job market is being effectively segmented, and the response will be specialised. Where a loose specification is drawn up, the emphasis will be more on what is desirable than on what is essential, and the response will tend to be proportionately larger. When skilled manpower is plentiful, specifications will tend to be tight, and vice versa in times of manpower shortages.

10. To illustrate the use of such a document as shown in Figure 43.3, we could take the example of a Chief Accountant's position in a medium-sized engineering company employing, say, 1500 people. In this case a formal accountancy qualification would be regarded as essential, as would a practical knowledge of the accounting systems used in engineering companies. Experience of deputising for the chief accountant in an accountancy department would be desirable. Any reference to skills would tend to relate to social skills (eg ability to work with line colleagues) and intellectual skills (eg ability to see opportunities for developing computer-based control systems).

The requirements for personality/motivation would probably include an ability to work under pressure and a willingness to adapt accountancy procedures to meet the needs of marketing and production, where existing systems are not working effectively enough. Physical requirements would probably be omitted, and interests might be related only to work interests. The circumstances of the position might require the Chief Accountant to live within a reasonable travelling distance of the company's head office, and might require him to be away from home for short periods on company business.

11. The job advertisement referred to in item 6 in Figure 43.1 is the external advertisement in the Press and trade or professional journals. The basic principles of an effective job advertisement (ie one that attracts sufficient numbers of the right kind of candidates) can be summarised as follows:

An effective job advertisement, should, ideally, contain the following features.

It should:

    a. Provide brief, but succinct details about the position to be filled,

    b. Provide similar details about the employing organization,

    c. Provide details of all *essential* personal requirements,

    d. Make reference to any *desirable* personal requirements,

   e.  State the main conditions of employment, especially the salary indicator for the position,

   f.  State to whom the application or enquiry should be directed,

   g.  Present the above information in an attractive form.

12.  Short-listing arrangements are necessary to select, from the total number of applicants, those who appear, from their application form, to be worthy of an interview. If an external advertisement has hit the target segment correctly, then only relatively small numbers of applications will be forthcoming, and most of these will be strong candidates for interview, and the difficulty will be to decide who *not* to invite. If the advertisement has been drawn up rather loosely, or has deliberately sought to tap a large segment of the labour market, then large numbers of applications can be expected, many of whom will be quite unsuitable. In drawing up a short-list, it is common practice to divide the applications into three groups as follows:

1. **Very suitable** – must be interviewed.
2. **Quite suitable** – call for interview, if insufficient numbers in category (1), or send holding letter.
3. **Not suitable** – send polite refusal letter, thanking them for their interest in applying.

If there are numbers of very suitable candidates, then it may be necessary to have two or more sequential interviews, until only the best two or three candidates remain. This whole procedure may sound quite long-winded, but when purchasing the *human* assets of the organization it is worthwhile spending time over the selection of these the most valuable assets of all.

## SELECTION PROCESSES

13.  In the overall process of tapping the labour market for suitable skills and experience, recruitment comes first and is followed by selection. Recruitment's task is to locate possible applicants and attract them to the organization. Selection's task is to cream off the most appropriate applicants, turn them into candidates and persuade them that it is in their interests to join the organization, for, even in times of high unemployment, selection is very much a two-way process – the candidate is assessing the organization, just as much as the organization is assessing him. The main objective of selection, therefore, is to be able to make an acceptable offer to the candidate who appears, from the evidence obtained, to be the most suitable for the job in question.

14. The most widely-used technique in the selection process is the interview. Well behind the interview, in terms of popularity, comes psychological testing, and both interviews and tests will be considered shortly. However, before turning to them, it is important to reflect on the role of application forms, and letters of application, in the selection process.

## APPLICATION FORMS

15. An application form or a letter of application tells an organization whether or not an applicant is worthy of an interview or a test of some kind. This initial information constitutes the bedrock of the selection process ie prima facie evidence of an applicant's suitability or unsuitability for the position in question. An applicant who is deemed suitable on this evidence, then becomes a candidate for interview. Many organizations require applicants to write a letter explaining why they are interested in the vacant post and how they propose to justify the role they think they could play in it. This approach enables the organization to see how well applicants can argue a case for themselves in a letter, but it has the disadvantage that the information provided is controlled by the applicant – he can leave out points which may not help his case, and build on those which do. Thus most organizations prefer to design their own application forms, so as to require applicants to set out the information about themselves in a standardised way.

16. Application forms vary considerably in the way they are set out. Some, for example, as in Figure 43.4, require prospective candidates to answer routine questions in a form that gives them no opportunity to discuss their motives for applying or to talk about themselves in a general way. Others, as in Figure 43.5, are very open-ended in their format, and require applicants to expand at some length on themselves and on how they see the job. In between the two forms illustrated are several com promise versions, which aim to establish some kind of balance between closed and open questions. The answers to the closed questions supply the organization with routine information in a standardised form; the answers to the open questions provide a clue to the motives, personality and communication skills of the applicants.

17. The two contrasting approaches to application form layout are as follows:

| Post Applied For: |
| --- |

| Surname: | First Names: |
| --- | --- |
| Address: | Telephone No.: |
| Date of Birth: | Place of Birth |
| Marital Status: | Children: |

| Education: | Examinations Passed: |
| --- | --- |
|   School: | |
|   College: | |
|   University: | |
| Training: | |
|   Courses Attended/Qualifications Obtained: | |

Work Experience:
  Present Post (Title, length of service, current salary):


  Previous Posts Held:


| Employer | Job Title | Dates | Reasons for Leaving |
| --- | --- | --- | --- |

Interests/Hobbies

Referees :   (One from current employer
               one from personal referee)
   1.

   2.

| Notice Required by Current Employer: | weeks/months |
| --- | --- |
| **Signed:** | **Date:** |

**Figure 43.4. Form to Obtain Routine Information.**

| |
|---|
| **Post Applied For:** |
| Surname:                          First Names: |
| Address:                          Telephone No.: |
| Date of Birth:                    Marital Status: |
| Details of Examinations Passed / Qualifications Obtained |
| Current Post: |
| Last Three Posts (starting with the latest): |
| Principal Interests / Hobbies |
| What attracts you to this post? |
| How do you think you can contribute to the post? |
| What has given you the greatest satisfaction, to date, in your current or previous employment? |
| How do you see your career developing over the next ten years or so? |
| How soon could you start work if appointed? |
| Please supply the names of two persons who could speak on your behalf. |
| Signed:                          Date: |

**Figure 43.5. Open-ended Application Form.**

## THE SELECTION INTERVIEW

18. The selection interview is far and away the most common technique used for selection purposes. Unlike most other management techniques, it is employed as much by amateurs as by professionals. Whereas in Work Study, for example, only a trained work study analyst will generally be permitted to conduct method studies and work measurement exercises, in the selection of staff everybody is deemed capable ! Few managers and supervisors carry out selection interviews regularly; many of them have received no formal training in the technique either, so it is not surprising to learn that research has shown that such interviews are frequently neither reliable nor valid. The measure of the reliability of an interview is the extent to which conclusions about candidates are shared by different interviewers; the measure of the validity of an inter view is the extent to which it does measure what it is supposed to measure ie the suitability of a particular candidate for a particular job.

19. The main reasons why so many poor interviews are carried out are two-fold:

  i.    lack of training in interviewing technique, and
  ii.   lack of adequate preparation for an interview.

Training designed to enable appropriate staff to conduct competent interviews generally involves two major learning methods: firstly, an illustrated talk/discussion; and, secondly, practical interviewing exercises. The first method enables trainees to *understand the process* that is taking place during an interview, and to acquire a method for harnessing that process (ie an interview plan). The second method helps trainees to *experience the process* by means of role-playing exercises, and to understand how they may need to adapt their behaviour in order to meet the aims of this kind of interview.

20. Much has been written about selection interviewing, but most of the points made can be condensed into the following guide to good practice (Figure 43.6). This highlights the sort of issues which busy managers need to know about if they are to make optimum use of their own, and the candidates', time in the short period available for the interview.

| | |
|---|---|
| Be Prepared | Obtain available information eg job details, candidate specification & application form.<br>Arrange interview room. Ensure no interruptions.<br>Plan the interview. |
| Welcome the Candidate | After initial courtesies, thank candidate for coming.<br>Explain **briefly** what procedure you propose to adopt for the interview<br>Commence by asking relatively easy and non-threatening question. |
| Encourage Candidate to talk | Ask open-ended questions.<br>Prompt where necessary.<br>Indicate that you are listening.<br>**Briefly** develop points of interest raised by candidate. |
| Control the Interview | Direct your questions along the lines that will achieve your objectives.<br>Tactfully, but firmly, clamp down on the over-talkative candidate .<br>Do not get too involved in particular issues just because of your own interests.<br>Keep an eye on the time. |
| Supply Necessary Information | **Briefly** add to information already made available to candidate.<br>Answer candidate's questions. Inform candidate of the next steps in the selection procedure. |
| Close Interview | Thank candidate for his/her responses to your questions.<br>Exchange final courtesies. |
| Final Steps | Write up your notes about the candidate.<br>Grade, or rank, him/her for suitability.<br>Operate administrative procedures regarding notifications etc. |

**Figure 43.6    Selection Interviewing – Guide to Good Practice**

21. There are a few points arising from the above guide, which particularly ought to be stressed. The first is the question of preparation. As with so many tasks, the better the preparation, the

better the final result. It is very important to be properly prepared before an interview. It enables the interviewer to feel confident in himself about his key role in the process, and enables him to exploit to the full the information provided by the candidate. It also helps to minimise embarrassment caused by constant interruptions, inadequate accommodation and other practical difficulties.

22. Questioning plays a vital role in a selection interview, as it is the primary means by which information is obtained from the candidate at the time. Questions have been categorised in a number of different ways. For our purposes, it is enough to distinguish between *closed questions* and *open questions*. The major differences between them are as follows:

   Closed questions – These are questions which require a *specific* answer or a Yes/No response. For example: 'What course of study led to your qualification?' (specific); 'How many people were you responsible for in your previous job?' (specific); 'Were you personally authorised to sign purchase orders?' (Yes/No); 'Have you had experience of..?' (Yes/No).

   Open questions – These are questions that require a person to reflect on, or elaborate upon, a particular point in his own way. Examples of open questions are: 'What is it that attracts you about this job?' 'Why did you leave... Company?' 'How would you tackle a problem of this kind, if you were the manager?' Open questions invariably begin with What? or How? or Why?

23. It is usual to ask closed questions to check information which the candidate has already partly supplied on his application form, and to re-direct the interview if the candidate is talking too much and/or getting off the point. Open questions tend to be employed once the interview has got under way, with the object of getting the candidate to demonstrate his knowledge and skills to the interviewer.

24. Controlling the interview is sometimes a problem for interviewers. Lack of control can be manifested in the following ways:
   a. the candidate takes over the interview, dominating the talking, following his own interests and interrupting the interviewer,
   b. the candidate is allowed to spend too long over his replies, and to repeat things he has already mentioned,

    c.  the interviewer appears to be tentative in asking questions, and appears to accept whatever the candidate says,

    d.  the candidate patronises the interviewer.

25.  Interviewers can help themselves to maintain control in a firm, but diplomatic way by:

    a.  proper preparation, especially the preparation of key questions to be put to the candidate,

    b.  returning to questions which they feel have not been adequately answered by the candidate ie they are showing that they will not be fobbed off by a plausible non answer,

    c.  politely, but firmly, cutting short a response which has gone on too long,

    d.  taking an opportunity themselves to supply information to the candidate, thus requiring him to listen,

    e.  using the application form as a map of the interview, on which progress can be plotted,

    f.  resisting the temptation to get involved in an interesting, but time-consuming, issue raised by the candidate,

    g.  allocating the time available for the interview between the key phases to be covered.

26.  It is usual for interviewers to supply a certain amount of information to candidates. It is better not to treat the candidate to a ten-minute account of the job and its conditions right at the beginning of the interview, when he or she is feeling tense and wants to get started. If possible, it is better to feed in information as the interview progresses and to round off the final stage of the interview with any routine information about conditions of service. Candidates' questions may be left to the end or dealt with during the course of the interview. In general, the more information that can be supplied *before* the interview, the better.

27.  Ideally, the time available for the interview should be spent in assessing the candidate as a person, and adding a feedback dimension to the information obtained from the application form, references and any other previous data about the candidate. Thus the hallmark of a good interview is a lively exchange of relevant facts and impressions between the interviewer and the candidate, which enables the interviewer to decide if the candidate is suitable, and which enables the candidate to decide if he or she still wants the job.

28.  Interviews are usually conducted on a one-to-one basis, but a two-to-one situation is also widely favoured, and there is still a lot of support for panel interviews, especially in the public services. In a two-to-one situation, the two interviewers usually agree amongst

themselves as to how they will share the questioning and information – supplying during the interview Frequently, in medium and large organizations, one of the two organization-representatives is a Personnel specialist, and the other is the 'client', seeking to fill the vacancy in question. The advantages of this type of interview are that whilst one interviewer is asking a question, or pursuing a point, the other can observe the candidate's reactions and make an independent evaluation of this response; and that each interviewer can specialise in his own areas of interest in the selection process, the 'client' concentrating on technical capability and the ability to fit into his team and the Personnel member concentrating on the wider aspects of having such a person as an employee of the organization. The slight disadvantage of this approach is that the candidate may be less forthcoming if there are two people present to interview him.

29. The panel interview is an altogether different prospect for a candidate. In this case the individual candidate is faced by several interviewers – at least three and possibly as many as eight or ten. In the case of a panel interview, it is of greatest importance to decide who is going to ask which questions, and how the panel is to be chaired. In some public sector panels, there are members who do not ask any questions and who do not comment either – they are there simply as observers, until after the interviewing process is over, when they contribute their impressions to the final decision-making discussion. Generally, however, panel members agree beforehand how they will allocate questions, and then they rely on the discretion of the chairman to deal with the allocation of supplementary issues. The advantage of this type of interview is that it ensures the fairness of the proceedings. There are several disadvantages, however – the candidate will find it difficult to feel at ease in such a formal atmosphere; the individual panel members may be more concerned about being cued for their questions than being concerned to listen to what the candidate is saying; and there is also the problem that the interviewers are often not able to follow up points with the candidate because they are under pressure from their chairman or their colleagues to move on to the next question.

30. Taken as a whole, interviews are most useful for assessing the personal qualities of an individual. They help to answer questions such as 'Is this candidate likely to be able to fit into our team or our environment?' and 'Has this particular candidate any special personal characteristics which give him an advantage over his rivals?' Interviews are not so useful for assessing technical ability or the value of *past* experience. This is one of the reasons why

organizations may consider using psychological tests to supplement information gained during interviews.

## PSYCHOLOGICAL TESTS

31. Psychological tests, or selection tests as they are often called, are standardised tests designed to provide a relatively objective measure of certain human characteristics by sampling human behaviour. Such tests tend to fall into four categories as follows:

    i.   intelligence tests

    ii.  aptitude tests

    iii. attainment tests and

    iv. personality tests

32. Intelligence tests and others are standardised in the sense that the same set of tasks have been given to many other people over a period of many years, and bands of typical results have been developed to provide standards against which subsequent results can usefully be compared. Publishers of tests invariably insist that only trained personnel should administer their material so that the standard conditions of each test are adhered to strictly, and so that the scoring of tests can be relied upon. All reputable tests have been carefully checked for their validity and their reliability. Checks for validity are designed to ensure that any given test measures what it sets out to measure eg an intelligence test should be able to measure intelligence, and a manual dexterity test should be able to measure manual dexterity. Checks for reliability are designed to ensure that tests produce consistent results in terms of what they set out to measure. Thus, if a test which is carried out on an individual at a particular point in time is repeated, the results should be similar.

33. The different categories of tests are as follows:

    **Intelligence tests**: These tests are designed to measure thinking abilities. The word 'intelligence' has no generally accepted definition, as yet, and has to be defined in terms of a number of different interpretations of its meaning. It is enough for our purposes to understand that general intelligence can be manifested by verbal ability, or spatial ability, or numerical ability or a combination of these. Popular tests in use for personnel selection are often composed of several different sections, each of which aims to test candidates on the key ability areas just referred to.

    **Aptitude tests**: These are basically tests of innate skills. They are widely used to obtain information about such skills as mechanical ability, clerical and numerical ability, and manual dexterity. Several standard tests are available for the use of organizations, and it is also possible to have tests specially devised, although this is a much more expensive business, since the tests have to be validated before they can be implemented with any confidence.

**Attainment tests**: These tests measure the depth of knowledge or grasp of skills which has been learned in the past – usually at school or college. Typical attainment tests are those which measure typing abilities, spelling ability and mental arithmetic, for example.

**Personality tests**: The use of personality tests derives from clinical situations. Their application to personnel selection is rather restricted, because of the problems associated with the validity of such tests. Where they are employed in work situations, they usually take the form of personality inventories – lists of multiple choice questions in response to theoretical situations posed by the test designers – or of projection tests – where the candidate is required to describe a series of vague pictures or a series of inkblots. The aim of personality tests is to identify an individual's principal personality traits or dimensions eg introverted or extroverted, sociable or isolate etc.

34. Psychological tests can provide useful additional or confirming information about a candidate for a position. They can supplement the information obtained from application forms and from interviews, and are particularly useful where objective information would be illuminating. They are probably most economically applied in situations where reasonably large numbers of recruits are needed every year eg school-leavers, college-leavers and other younger employees. Apart from attainment tests, most of the categories still remain relatively unpopular with employers, and there is no question of psycho logical tests ousting the need for application forms and interviews.

## SUMMARY

35. Recruitment and selection activities are part of the on-going activitities of practically every business and public service organization. Recruitment activities are those which are aimed at attracting sufficient numbers of potential recruits to the organization in a cost-effective and timely manner. Recruitment is conducted mainly by Personnel specialists, who are in touch with the organization's labour market and who endeavour to interpret the labour demands of their colleagues.

36. Recruitment involves the preparation of job descriptions, and personnel specifications, which supply the basic information

required to notify the job vacancy – internally via notice-boards, externally via advertisements and/or job agencies. The initial selection of candidates on the basis of their application form is called shortlisting. This aims to identify those applicants who are deemed worthy of an interview.

37. Selection activities are designed, firstly, to identify those candidates who, on the evidence available, appear to be the most suitable for the vacancies concerned; and, secondly, to persuade these candidates to join the organization by making acceptable offers of employment to them.

38. Selection activities are dominated by application procedures and by interviews. Letters or forms of application provide the basic information of the selection process. This information is built on by means of interviews, tests and references. An effective interview should produce a lively and relevant exchange of information between the interviewer and the candidate, which enables both parties to make up their minds about each other. The achievement of this situation depends mainly on the competence of the interviewer in terms of how well prepared he is, and how well he handles the progress of the interview. Most interviews are conducted on a one-to-one basis or a two-to-one basis. These structures facilitate the flow of information between the candidate and the interviewer(s). Panel interviews, where three or more persons may be facing the candidate, are an altogether more formal affair, and may restrict the flow of information between the two sides.

39. Selection procedures in a number of organizations are supplemented by the use of psychological tests. These are basically tests to obtain relatively objective measures of various dimensions of human behaviour. The most common types of test are:

a. intelligence tests, which attempt to measure an individual's ability to think (understand relationships between things, solve problems etc),

b. aptitude tests, which aim to measure abilities and skills, which are innate,

c. attainment tests, which aim to measure acquired skills ie assessing previous learning, and

d. personality tests, which attempt to measure an individual's personal traits or characteristics.

Tests need to be employed with care, but can provide useful information which adds to, or confirms, other information arising from application forms or interviews.

# 44

# TRAINING AND DEVELOPMENT

## INTRODUCTION

1. Human resources are the most dynamic of all the organization's resources. They need considerable attention from the organization's management, if they are to realise their full potential in their work. Thus motivation, leadership, communication, work re-structuring, payments systems and training/development may all be included in the issues which have to be faced by management today. Most of these issues have already been considered in this Manual, but now it is time to consider the role of training and development activities in the organization. This short chapter highlights the principal features of a training and development sub-system within the Personnel function.

2. A question frequently raised by examiners is 'what is the difference, if any, between 'training' and 'development'?' Another question which is sometimes asked is 'what is the difference between 'education' and 'training'?' It will be useful to examine these three terms and compare their meanings. The principal meanings of each are as follows:

Education – this is usually intended to mean basic instruction in knowledge and skills designed to enable people to make the most of life in general; it is personal and broadly-based.

Training – this usually implies preparation for an occupation or for specific skills; it is more narrow in conception than either education or development; it is job-orientated rather than personal.

Development – this usually suggests a broader view of knowledge and skills acquisition than training; it is less job-orientated than career-orientated; it is concerned more with employee potential than with immediate skill; it sees employees as adaptable resources.

3. Generally, education is a matter for the community to sort out. Training.and development, however, are matters for individual organizations to sort out. The rest of this chapter looks at how organizations set about meeting their training and development needs.

## TRAINING AND DEVELOPMENT: BASIC FRAMEWORK

4.    The scope of training and development activities, as in most other activities in an organization, depends on the policy and strategies of the organization. There are many organizations in the commercial field that carry out the minimum of staff training and development, because, as a matter of policy, they prefer to recruit staff who are already trained or professionally qualified. These organizations are prepared to pay the top market-rates for skilled staff, and what they put into recruitment, selection and pay and benefits, they do not put into training and development. In fact, one of the reasons for the establishment of Industrial Training Boards in Britain was precisely to ensure that *all* organizations in their scope contributed to total training costs, even if they carried out little or no training themselves.

5.    The majority of organizations, however, do have a positive policy on training and development. In some cases, this may be no more than to state that 'The Company will provide resources to ensure that key skills are maintained within the organizations'; in other cases, the policy may refer comprehensively to the various actions it will take to ensure not only a regular supply of skills, but also a high degree of personal motivation through development opportunities provided by the Company. For the purposes of this chapter, it will be assumed that organizations see an important role for training and development in the provision of skills and the improvement of employee motivation.

6.    A term frequently used to describe well-organized training (and development) is 'systematic training'. This can be illustrated diagramatically as a cycle of events, which is initiated by the organization's policy, and sustained by its training organization as shown on the facing page (Figure 44.1).

7.    Once the training organization has been set up, the first priority is to establish what the training and development needs of the organization are. This will involve the use of job descriptions, employee appraisal records and other data which may indicate such needs. The next step is to plan the training required to meet the needs identified. This entails such matters as setting budgets and timetables, and deciding on the objectives, content and methods of training to be employed. The implementation of plans is usually a joint affair between the training specialists and their line and functional colleagues. Having implemented the required training, it is important to evaluate the results, so far as possible, so that subsequent changes to content and methods can be made, if necessary. Events then move on to the identification of new needs, which re-starts the cycle afresh.

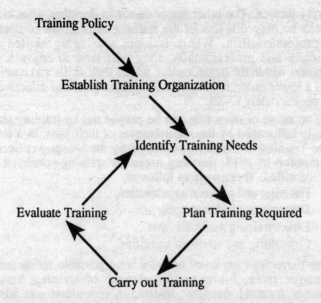

**Figure 44.1. Systematic Training: The Basic Cycle.**

8.   The benefits of systematic training include:
   a. the provision of a pool of skilled manpower for the organization,
   b. the improvement of existing skills,
   c. an increase in the knowledge and experience of employees,
   d. improvements in job performance with resulting improvement in productivity overall,
   e. improved service to customers,
   f. greater commitment of staff (ie increased motivation),
   g. increased value of individual employees' knowledge and skills, and
   h. personal growth opportunities for employees.

## THE ROLE OF THE TRAINER

9.   The role of training staff in the organization ie the part they are expected to play, as well as the part they themselves expect to play, depends considerably on the style or culture of the organization. If the organization actively encourages training and development activities, then trainers will have an exciting and important role to play; if, however, the organization wishes only to pay lip-service to training, then the role for trainers will be

severely limited. The other major factor in deciding what kind of role can be played is that of the training staff's own competence and professionalism. Where trainers are highly skilled both politically and professionally, they will tend to enjoy a good reputation within the organization; where their skills and ambitions are of a lower order, then so will their reputation and effectiveness be proportionately lower.

10. The range of roles that can be played out by training staff is strongly influenced by the requirements of their jobs. In a Report on the Training of Trainers, published by the Manpower Services Commission in 1978, four key areas for training-specialist jobs were identified. These were as follows:

    a. Planning and organizing activities,

    b. Determining and managing activities,

    c. Direct training activities, and

    d. Consulting and advisory activities.

From these four areas of activity it is possible to see several alternative roles, for example: planner of training, training organizer, training manager, instructor, consultant and adviser. Clearly, the more senior the job, the wider the range of possible roles, and vice versa for less senior jobs. A Training Manager, for example, would encompass all the above mentioned roles, although with an emphasis on determining, managing, consultancy and advisory activities. By comparison, a Job Instructor would only be concerned with direct training or instructional activities, and with some organizing.

11. In performing their direct training roles, training specialists are intimately concerned with (a) the identification or assessment of training needs, and (b) the design, content and methods of training to be employed, and (c) the evaluation of training. These three key aspects of training will be looked at in the next few paragraphs.

## IDENTIFYING TRAINING NEEDS

12. A training need is any shortfall in terms of employee knowledge, understanding, skill and attitudes against what is required by the job, or the demands of organizational change. In diagramatic form this can be expressed as shown in Figure 44.2.

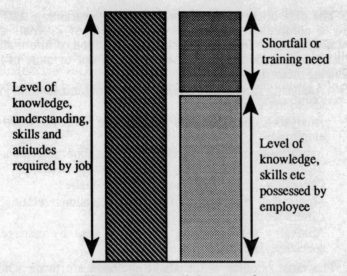

**Figure 44.2. Training Need.**

13. All jobs make some demands on their job-holders. Simple jobs will require only a little knowledge with no need for any deeper understanding of what is involved; such jobs will also require little in the way of skill, but may demand more in terms of attitude ie attention to detail, acceptance of routine and lack of discretion etc. Complex jobs, by comparison, will demand not only a specialist knowledge, but also a real understanding of the basic principles or underlying concepts of the work involved; such jobs will probably require a high level of specialist skill, and attitudes that foster an awareness of the importance of teamwork and the necessity for first-rate quality, for example.

14. When training staff conduct a comprehensive training needs analysis in their organization, they may seek the basic data for this process at three different levels as follows:

**Organization level:** data about the organization as a whole eg its structure, markets, products or services, manpower requirements etc,

**Job level:** data concerning jobs and activities eg job descriptions, personnel specifications, on the one hand, and leadership and communication activities on the other.

**Individual level:** data about individuals eg appraisal records, personal training records, test results, notes made at counselling interviews and results of attitude surveys.

15. The data obtained in this way enables the training staff to draw a comprehensive picture of the areas of current, and potential, shortfall in requirements. The collection of information for a training needs analysis is carried out by one or more of the following methods:

- Analysing recorded data relating to the organization, to jobs and to individuals.
- Analysing questionnaires and attitude surveys issued to employees.
- Interviewing managers and supervisors about their own or their subordinates' training and development needs.
- Observing the job performance of individuals.
- Monitoring the results of group discussions relating to current work-problems etc.
- Analysing self-recording diaries etc kept by managers, specialists and others.

16. The most popular of the above methods are those which utilise *existing* records, and those which involve interviewing managerial and supervisory staff. One particularly important document which contributes to the analysis of training needs is the appraisal form. This is the record of an employee's job performance, usually completed following an annual interview with his superior. Appraisal interviews, and the documentation which accompanies them, are the formal mechanisms by which organizations can assess or evaluate their human assets. In a well-managed organization, this formal appraisal merely rounds off, in a relatively standardised way, the frequent informal appraisals carried out regularly by the organization's managers as a normal part of their job.

17. The objectives of the formal system of appraisals are various. They include some or all of the following:
   a. To identify the current level of job performance,
   b. To identify employee strengths and weaknesses,
   c. To enable employees to improve on current performance,
   d. To identify training and development needs,
   e. To identify potential performance,
   f. To provide the basis for salary reviews,
   g. To encourage and motivate employees,
   h. To provide information for manpower planning purposes.

18. The document on which formal appraisal records are held may take one of several forms. A simple appraisal form is

illustrated in Figure 44.3. This example could be used with junior retail staff, for example.

| Name: | Job Title: | | |
|-------|-----------|--|--|
| Department: | Appraised by: | | |
| | Date: | | |
| Present Performance: | Unacceptable | Barely acceptable | Perfectly acceptable |
| Appearance and Manner | | | |
| Relationships with Customers | | | |
| Relationships with Staff | | | |
| Cash Handling | | | |
| Documentation Handling | | | |
| Enthusiasm | | | |
| Reliability | | | |
| Timekeeping | | | |

**Figure 44.3. Simple Appraisal Form.**

The above document is relatively easy to complete, and does cause the manager or supervisor concerned to consider the employee's performance in a number of different work areas. Such a document can provide the basis for a constructive appraisal interview between the employee and his superior.

19. An example of a more complex appraisal form is provided in Figure 44.4. In this case the document asks the employee's superior to assess performance against previously agreed targets or objectives, and is the kind of appraisal one would expect to find in an organization where Management by Objectives was installed.

417

| Name:<br>Department: | | | | Job Title:<br>Appraised by:<br>Date: | |
|---|---|---|---|---|---|
| **Current Performance** | | | | | |
| Objectives set for the period | Achieved? | | | Reasons for any shortfall | Comments |
| | Yes | No | Partly | | |
| 1. | | | | | |
| 2. | | | | | |
| 3. | | | | | |
| 4. | | | | | |
| Overall Assessment: Outstanding / Fully Satisfactory / Satisfactory / Unsatisfactory | | | | | |
| Training, Development or Guidance Needs | | | | | |
| Potential Performance | | Ready for Promotion Now<br>Ready for Promotion in One / Two Years<br>No Promotion Potential<br>Move to another Department | | | |

**Figure 44.4. Objective Appraisal Form.**

20. A document such as the one illustrated in Figure 44.4 can provide a substantial amount of relevant information about training and development needs. Not only is current performance assessed, in terms of specific and measurable parts of the employee's job, but also potential performance is considered. Thus it is possible to consider training and development needs in terms of future job performance as well as in terms of improving current performance.

## PLANNING TRAINING

21. Once training needs have been identified by means of the training needs analysis, the training staff can begin the tasks of sorting training priorities, drawing up initial plans, costing them and then submitting their draft plans for approval by the senior management. These draft plans spell out the key areas for training, the numbers and categories of employees concerned, the nature of

the training proposed, the preliminary time-tabling of the training programmes contained in the proposals, and an estimate of the costs which are likely to be incurred.

| On-the-job Training Methods | Advantages | Disadvantages |
|---|---|---|
| On-the-job instruction | Relevant; develops trainee-supervisor links | Noise, bustle and pressure of workplace |
| Coaching | Job-related; develops boss-subordinate relationship | Subject to work pressures; may be done piecemeal |
| Counselling | Employee needs help and boss provides it | Counselling skills have to be developed |
| Delegation by boss | Increases scope of job; provides greater motivation | Employees may make mistakes or may fail to achieve task |
| Secondment | Increases experience of employee; creates new interest | Employee may not succeed in new position |
| Guided Projects / Action Learning | Increases knowledge and skills in work situation, but under guidance | Finding suitable guides and mentors |
| Off-the-job Training Methods | Advantages | Disadvantages |
| **(a) In-company** | | |
| Lectures / Talks | Useful for factual information | One-way emphasis; little participation |
| Group discussions | Useful for generating ideas and solutions | Requires adequate leadership |
| Role-playing Exercises | Useful for developing social skills | Requires careful organizing; giving tactful feedback is not easy |
| Skills development exercises eg: manual operations, communication skills etc | A safe way to practise key skills | Careful organization required |
| **(b) External** | | |
| College courses (long) | Leads to qualification; comprehensive coverage of theory; wide range of teaching methods | Length of training time; not enough practical work |
| College courses (short) | Supplement in-company training; independent of internal politics | May not meet client's needs precisely enough |
| Consultants / Other Training Organizations | Clients' needs given high priority; fills gaps in company provision; good range of teaching methods | Can be expensive; may rely heavily on 'packages' |

**Figure 44.5. Summary of Training Methods.**

22. Training programmes can be formal or informal, and can take place on-the-job or off-the-job. The latter can mean in-company, or in-service, training or it can refer to externally-provided training. Figure 44.5 illustrates some of the different methods of on-the-job and off-the-job training, and indicates some of the advantages and disadvantages of each approach:

23. Training plans are designed to encompass the following:
  a. *what* training is to be provided,
  b. *how* it is to be provided,
  c. *when* it is to be provided,
  d. *by whom* it is to be provided,
  e. *where* it is to be provided, and
  f. at *what* cost it is to be provided.

For many companies the resources put into training and development represent a considerable investment in time, money and manpower. This investment needs to be evaluated from time to time to ensure, so far as possible, that it is being deployed wisely.

## EVALUATION OF TRAINING

24. The evaluation of training is part of the control process of training. Evaluation methods aim to obtain feedback about the results or outputs of training, and to use this feedback to assess the value of the training, with a view to improvement, where necessary. Like any other control process, training evaluation is firstly concerned with setting appropriate standards of training. These may take the form of policies, objectives, adherence to external standards, and standards of trainer-training and qualifications. Clearly, the more precise the standards set, the easier it is to evaluate the success of training. This brings us on to the next key point, which is the collection of relevant feedback data about training.

25. Two British contributions to this important issue are those of Hamblin (1970) and of Warr, Bird & Rackham (1970). Hamblin takes the view that evaluation can take place at a number of different levels, ranging from immediate to long-term results. Each level requires a different evaluation strategy, as indicated in Figure 44.6, which is based on Hamblin's ideas.

26. *Training-centred* evaluation aims to assess the inputs to training ie whether we are using the right tools for training. *Reactions-centred* evaluation, which is probably the most widely-used strategy for evaluation, seeks to obtain and assess the reactions of trainees to the learning experiences they have been put through.

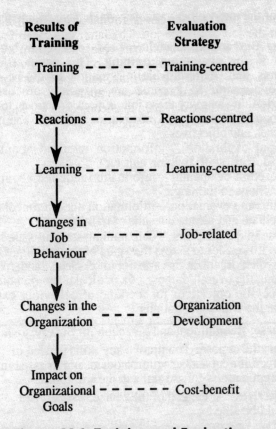

| Results of Training | Evaluation Strategy |
| --- | --- |
| Training | Training-centred |
| Reactions | Reactions-centred |
| Learning | Learning-centred |
| Changes in Job Behaviour | Job-related |
| Changes in the Organization | Organization Development |
| Impact on Organizational Goals | Cost-benefit |

**Figure 44.6. Training and Evaluation.**

*Learning-centred* evaluation seeks to measure the degree of learning that has been achieved. This is usually achieved by testing trainees following the training, as in a driving test. *Job-related* evaluation is aimed at assessing the degree of behaviour change which has taken place on-the-job after returning from a period of training. It is, of course, a measure of learning, but learning which has been applied in the workplace. It is not an easy task to evaluate the degree to which learning has been applied, especially in cases where training in social skills, such as leadership, is concerned. Organization changes can be brought about by training, and here the evaluation strategy is linked to an *Organization Development* programme. Finally, there is the impact on organizational goals to be considered ie what has training done for profitability or company image, for example? This is a favourite question asked by top management, but is extremely difficult to evaluate on account of the many other variables which have an impact on these goals.

27. Warr, Bird and Rackham have produced a somewhat different framework for evaluating training. This takes four major dimensions, and suggests what information should be sought to enable evaluation to become an on-going process in the organization. In summary these four dimensions are as follows:

a. Context evaluation – information required about training needs and objectives.
b. Input evaluation – information required about training resources (staff, training aids etc).
c. Reaction evaluation – information required about trainees' reactions to training.
d. Outcome evaluation – information about immediate, intermediate and ultimate results of training.

28. It was said earlier that, where training standards are laid down precisely, it is easier to assess the value of the training. One of the ways in which organizations attempt to set clear standards is by (a) establishing the overall purpose of a particular programme, and (b) setting specific objectives for the kind of behaviour expected of trainees at the end of the training.

---

**Course:** Recruitment and Selection for Supervisors.

**Overall Purpose:** To improve key skills needed in the recruitment and selection process, and to assist in the application of these skills in the workplace.

**Objectives:** At the end of the course, a supervisor should be able to:

i. Describe the key stages in the recruitment and selection process,

ii. Prepare acceptable job descriptions and personnel specifications,

iii. State the role of the Personnel department in recruitment and selection,

iv. Apply the Seven-point Plan as an assessment tool in an interview,

v. Conduct a systematic interview of a prospective employee,

vi. Complete correctly all the Company's selection documents, which apply to his/her role as a supervisor.

---

**Figure 44.7. Training Objectives.**

It is obviously easier to set specific objectives for measurable features of behaviour, than it is for those features which are difficult to measure. A typical example of an attempt to set standards for a training programme is set out in Figure 44.7 below:

29. The overall purpose stated above is put in rather general terms eg 'improve key skills ...' What the objectives try to do is to specify *how* a supervisor can indicate that he has gained an improved grasp of this topic. In each case, the objective aims to describe *behaviour* (ie what the trainee is expected to do) at the end of the course. If few members of a supervisory course were able to demonstrate that they *could* now do the things that the course had set out to achieve, the organizers would know that they had failed to achieve their training objectives, and would have to change any further courses in the light of this feedback. This approach is sometimes known as training validation ie assessing if training achieves what it is supposed to achieve. Validation is one facet of the overall evaluation process.

## SUMMARY

30. Training can be distinguished from education and development as follows:

> *Training* is concerned with imparting knowledge, and improving skills, *in relation to a job* or occupation, whereas *education* is a personal *preparation for life*, and *development*, so far as the work setting is concerned, is aimed at personal growth and *realisation of potential* as an employee.

31. Systematic training is the term used to describe a rational approach to training and development based on the following: a training policy, a training organization, the identification of training needs, the planning and execution of training, and, finally, the evaluation of training.

32. Training specialists undertake activities such as the planning and organizing of training, the determining of training needs, the management of the training function, the provision of direct training activities, and the provision of consultancy and advisory services. The exact scope of a particular training department will depend heavily on the culture of its parent organization.

33. A training need is the shortfall, in terms of knowledge, understanding, skills and attitudes, between what the organization requires of its employees, and what the employees are able to supply. Information about training needs can be obtained by

analysing written records, conducting interviews, and observing job performance, for example. These activities can be conducted at the level of the organization, or the job or the individual employee. One especially important source of training and development needs is the appraisal form, which provides a record of employee performance in the job, and often includes information about employee potential too.

34. Training plans follow on from the analysis of needs. They are intended to make clear what training is to be provided, and how, when, by whom, where, and at what cost. Training programmes may take place on-the-job (eg job instruction, coaching, counselling etc) or off-the-job (eg attendance at lectures, role-playing and other practical exercises located in-company; or attendance at external courses run by colleges, consultants and other training organizations).

35. The evaluation of training activities is an important part of the training function. Evaluation aims to obtain, and act on, information (ie feedback) about the results of training. The focus of evaluation can be the training input, trainee reactions, trainee learning, job behaviour, organization change or the impact of training on organizational goals. A popular method for setting precise standards for training is to set specific objectives, couched in terms of behaviour expected at the end of training. This method is sometimes called training validation.

# 45

# EMPLOYEE PERFORMANCE APPRAISAL

## INTRODUCTION

1.   Only a minority of activities in personnel management are concerned with evaluating employees as individuals. These activities are primarily selection and appraisal, but also include grievance and disciplinary matters. In all other cases, the focus of attention is not on individuals but on jobs, structures, procedures. or people in groups. Thus, for example, job evaluation focuses on jobs, not on job-holders; job design and organization development focus on job/task structures; wage and salary administration focus on procedures; whilst manpower planning and collective bargaining focus 'on people in groups.

2.   This chapter considers the evaluation of individuals in terms of their job performance. This is a task requiring a quality of managerial judgement which places a considerable responsibility on the managers involved. It is a task that is delicate as well as complex. This chapter examines the key features of performance appraisal and suggests a code of good practice in this area.

## PERFORMANCE APPRAISAL

3.   At its simplest, the appraisal process can be depicted as in Figure 45.1.

Any systematic approach to performance appraisal will commence with the completion of an appropriate appraisal form. This preparatory stage will be followed by an interview, in which the manager discusses progress with the member of staff. The result of the interview is some form of agreed action, either by the staff member alone, or jointly with his manager. The action generally materialises in the shape of a job improvement plan, promotion to another job or to a salary increase, for example.

4.   The expression 'performance appraisal' usually relates to the assessment of staff or managerial performance, and not to that of manual workers. There are two main categories of appraisal:

(i)   informal, and

(ii)   formal.

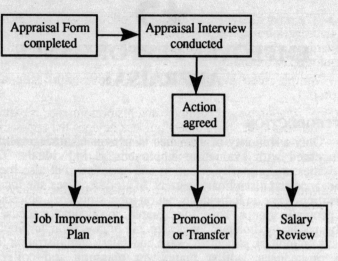

**Figure 45.1 The Appraisal Process**

Informal appraisal is the continuing assessment of an individual's performance by his manager in the normal course of work. This kind of assessment is of an ad hoc nature and is as much determined by intuitive feelings as by factual evidence of results. It is a natural by-product of the day-to-day relationship between manager and subordinate. Formal appraisal is altogether more rational and orderly than informal appraisal. In this chapter, when we refer to performance appraisal we mean formal appraisal, that is an assessment of employee performance in some systematic and planned way.

## REASONS FOR APPRAISAL

5.    There are several reasons why appraisals are carried out in organizations. These may be summarised as follows:
- to identify an individual's current level of job performance
- to identify employee strengths and weaknesses
- to enable employees to improve their performance
- to provide a basis for rewarding employees in relation to their contribution to organization goals
- to motivate individuals
- to identify training and development needs
- to identify potential performance
- to provide information for succession planning

6.     The most likely reason for the adoption of staff appraisal is to draw attention to present performance in the job in order to (a) reward people fairly, and (b) to identify those with potential for promotion or transfer.

7.     Writers such as Drucker (1954) are enthusiastic about appraisal:

> 'To appraise a subordinate and his performance is part of the manager's job. Indeed, unless he does the appraising himself he cannot adequately discharge his responsibility for assisting and teaching his subordinates.'

Drucker's view as a whole is that managers are responsible for achieving results. These results are obtained from the management of human, material and financial resources, all of which should be monitored. Monitoring means setting standards, measuring performance and taking appropriate action. In respect of people this entails taking action to improve performance by means of training and help, ie 'management development' (see Chap.46)

8.     Other writers such as McGregor (1960) are critical of formal appraisals:

> 'Appraisal programs are designed not only to provide more systematic control of the behaviour of subordinates. but also to control the behaviour of superiors...'

He thus sees them as promoting the cause of Theory X, ie a management style that assumes that people are unreliable, unable to take responsibility and therefore require close supervision and control .

9.     Whenever the argument is more about practicalities than managerial philosophy, the main issue is not whether performance appraisal, in itself, is justified but whether it is fair and accurate. McBeath & Rands (1976), in discussing salary administration, comment:

> '...equitable salary relationships depend on sound job classification, periodic salary surveys of competitive levels, employee appraisal and effective salary planning.'

For them appraisal is part and parcel of an important personnel activity-salary planning and administration. They are keen to acknowledge, however, that 'it is clearly essential to make some attempt at accurate measurement of performance if the appraisal is to be taken seriously into account as a factor which will influence salaries.'

10. If we accept that staff performance appraisal *is* a legitimate activity in organizations, what are the difficulties concerning both accuracy and fairness? Briefly, they boil down to:

- the construction of the appraisal documents
- the style in which the appraisal is approached
- the culture of the organization

Taking the last point first, the 'culture', or value-system, of the organization will act as the major determinant of both the appraisal scheme adopted and the way it is introduced. For example, if the culture is one which favours control and measurement of people then it is likely that a system will be imposed on the participants, but that it will at least contain some measurable criteria against which to judge performance. In another situation, where openness and participation are encouraged, any system will be discussed first with those involved, with the result that appraisals are more likely to be joint problem-solving affairs rather than a 'calling to account' by a superior.

## APPRAISAL FORMS

11. There are various ways in which appraisal forms can be devised. The key elements, however, are the following:

(1) the focus of the appraisal, ie the job or the person
(2) the performance criteria selected
(3) the performance ratings used

Where the appraisal focuses on the job. the appraisal form is more likely to ask the appraiser to look for success in achieving job targets or objectives than to comment on the job-holder's personal attributes. Where the focus is on the person rather than on the job, the reverse is true, ie the appraiser is expected to give an account of the jobholder's qualities and attitudes rather than of his or her relative success in achieving results. Thus, the focus of the appraisal will determine the nature of the criteria against which individual performance will be judged, as well as of the ratings or measures to be used.

12. Forms which seek information about the person rather than about his performance in the job are typified by an emphasis on:

(a) generalised criteria
(b) generalised ratings of performance
(c) individual qualities rather than results
(d) box-ticking as method of describing performance.

Figure 45.2 provides an illustration of such a form, employed originally by a medium-sized manufacturing company:

| Personal Attributes | | |
|---|---|---|
| Leadership | 1 | Always at the centre of activity |
| | 2 | Capable of leading smallish groups |
| | 3 | Has no real leadership qualities |
| Initiative | 1 | Always acts on own initiative |
| | 2 | Will act on own initiative in minor ways |
| | 3 | Never acts unless instructed |
| Judgement | 1 | Assesses a situation with cool discernment |
| | 2 | Sometimes confused by strong counter arguments, but generally makes sound assessment |
| | 3 | Totally lacks any critical faculty |
| Decision-making Ability | 1 | Makes sound decisions at all times |
| | 2 | Cannot always foresee the outcome of his decisions |
| | 3 | Decisions are more like guesses |
| Customer Awareness | 1 | Aware of need for quality, timeliness and price |
| | 2 | Only partially aware of the importance of the customer during the working day |
| | 3 | Customers' needs are seen as secondary to his own |
| Self-discipline | 1 | Has well-balanced attitude towards work and leisure |
| | 2 | Concentrates on work he prefers |
| | 3 | Needs constant instruction and supervision |

| Technical Attributes | | |
|---|---|---|
| Technical Knowledge | 1 | Wide technical knowledge of Company's products with specialist knowledge of some |
| | 2 | Limited technical knowledge but useful practical ability |
| | 3 | Very little required knowledge |
| Quality of Work | 1 | Always careful, rarely makes mistakes |
| | 2 | Sometimes makes mistakes |
| | 3 | Work characterised by carelessness |
| Dilligence | 1 | Consistently hard worker |
| | 2 | Occasionally needs reminding about time-wasting |
| | 3 | Makes no great effort when working |
| Cost Consciousness | 1 | Fully appreciates the importance of cost control |
| | 2 | Give some thought to costs |
| | 3 | Tends to be wasteful, rarely considers costs |

**Figure 45.2   Appraisal Form Emphasising Individual Qualities**

13. The first difficulty with the above approach is that of measurement. How can a manager fairly assess qualities of leadership or judgement, for example? The second difficulty is that of relevance. How central to success are diligence and cost consciousness, for example? Hard work is not synonymous with *effective* work; awareness of costs may be disadvantageous if it discourages initiative or decision-making. The third difficulty is that the managers completing the form have to rely on subjective impressions instead of concrete evidence. Fortunately, the senior management of the company concerned found it too difficult to operate such a generalised instrument and eventually substituted a results-orientated system.

14. The approach just described does not provide a sound basis on which to take decisions about pay and promotion, for example. It clearly deserves the comment made by McGregor (1960) that:

> 'If we then take these somewhat questionable data and attempt to use them to make fine discriminations between people for purposes of salary administration and promotion, we can create a pretty picture, but one which has little relation to reality.'

The way forward to reality for many organizations is to take the *job* duties and responsibilities as the focal point of appraisal. In this approach the emphasis is placed on results achieved against standards set, and after taking circumstances into account.

15. In any situation what is 'real' depends partly on the perceptions of those concerned, ie how they 'see' things, and partly on objective evidence, ie information that can be verified by a third party. To build such elements into an appraisal form requires a document such as the one illustrated in Figure.45.3 opposite.

16. In an appraisal form set out as the above, it is possible to identify the relevant aspects of the job and to set measurable targets against which to assess the individual jobholder's performance in a fair and accurate manner. Humble (1967) sees a performance standard as 'a statement of the conditions which exist when the required result is

- Quantity (How much?)
- Quality (How well?)
- Time (By what time?)
- Cost (At what cost?)

| Company: **Office Equipment Sales** | | | | |
|---|---|---|---|---|
| Position: **Managing Director** | | | | |
| Key Result Areas | Targets set for the period* | Achieved ? | Evidence | Notes |
| Profitability | Increase profit:sales ratio by 5% | Yes | Annual accounts | |
| Market Share | Maintain present market share at 15% | No (13%) | Industry statistics | Price-cutting by all competitors |
| Sales | Achieve gross sales of £150m | No (£148m) | Annual accounts | |
| Delivery | Reduce average delivery time to four weeks | Yes | Customer accounts | |
| Staff Performance | Ensure staff costs do not exceed 55% of total expenditure | Yes | Annual Budget Summary | |
| * Financial year | | | | |

### Figure 45.3 Results-orientated Appraisal Form

17. The example in Fig. 45.3 illustrates the kind of approach suggested by Humble and other advocates of Management by Objectives. In the example all the potential criteria of performance are measurable in quantitative terms. Qualitative standards can also be utilised. Indeed theorist-managers such as Wilfred Brown (1960) insist that they are inescapable – 'I cannot wholly assess the work of a general manager... on figures of output... etc. I must come to difficult intuitive judgements on the relationship of actual to optimum performance.' When such judgements have to be made, they should be based on criteria which, though general, are sufficiently assessable to enable a reasonable manager to measure the extent to which due standards of performance had been met.

18. An example of a general criterion of managerial behaviour could be:

'To achieve a major shift in employee attitudes regarding labour flexibility .'

Reddin (1970) dislikes this latter example: 'If no measurement method is available... some expression such as 'subjective judgement' is added. Try and avoid this.' Brown's (1960) rebuff to this advice is to comment '...the results obtained in any manager's command are a function not only of his own decisions but also of those of his superior manager, and of the policy operated by the Company..' Thus, to return to the example above, to achieve a major shift in employee attitudes requires the joint efforts of various managers. It also requires meshing together such factors as pay structures, job design, redundancy arrangements and shop-floor supervision in order to achieve any real prospects of change.

## RATING SCALES IN PERFORMANCE APPRAISAL

19. We have just seen that appraisal criteria are generally either personality orientated or results orientated. Within each of these orientations appraisers still have to 'measure' individual performance. They do so by using one or more scales for rating performance. The principal options available are:

a) Linear or Graphic Rating Scales, in which the appraiser is faced with a list of characteristics or job duties and is required to tick or circle an appropriate point on a numerical, alphabetical or other simple scale. Examples are:

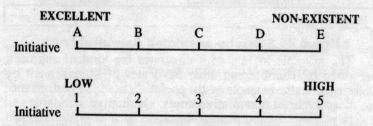

b) Behavioural Scales, in which the appraiser has a list of key job items against which are ranged a number of descriptors, or just two extreme statements of anticipated behaviour. One example is shown in Figure 45.3 above. Another scale, dealing with customer relations, could demonstrate a range of possible behaviour from the *best* eg 'Deals politely and efficiently with customers at all time' to the *worst* 'is barely civil to customers, is inefficient.'

c) Results/Targets Set, as in Figure 45.3 above.

d) Free Written Reports, in which appraisers write essay-type answers to a number of questions set on the appraisal document.

20. The most common scales currently in use are linear scales although both results-orientated measures and written reports also have their advocates among several companies. One other approach, which has not been mentioned so far, is that of self-appraisal. where the employee concerned either writes an 'annual report' on his work or answers questions set out in an appraisal document. In a survey carried out by the IPM in 1977, over a quarter of firms questioned mentioned that they were making use of self-appraisal forms as part of their appraisal procedures.

21. We noted in paragraph 9 above that one of the difficulties in achieving accuracy and fairness in appraisals concerns the style in which the appraisal is approached. Having considered the effects of (a) the organization culture, and (b) the appraisal documentation, we can now turn to the appraisal interview conducted by the jobholder's manager.

22. The appraisal interview is the formal face-to-face meeting between the jobholder and his manager at which the information on the appraisal form is discussed and after which certain key decisions are made concerning salary, promotion and training, for example. Judging from research studies into appraisal, the majority of managers do not like conducting annual appraisals of their staff. McGregor (1957) in an article on appraisal interviews commented that 'Managers are uncomfortable when they are put in the position of playing God'.

23. In a study of six British firms,it was found that:

a) appraisers were reluctant to conduct appraisals, finding ways of evading full completion of the appraisal forms

b) appraisers were extremely reluctant to carry out face-to-face interviews

c) there was inadequate follow-up to the appraisals, in terms of their effect on transfers etc.

Thomason (1981) summarises the situation as follows:

> '...the appraiser feels...put on the spot in carrying out plans of this type. He is required, whatever his own perception of the subordinate's expectations, to confront the individual in an authoritarian setting and to prescribe courses of action on the basis of judgements which he may or may not understand or accept.'

24. The manner in which a manager approaches an appraisal interview will be strongly influenced by his understanding of the purpose of the interview. Appraisal interviews can serve several purposes:

1) to evaluate the subordinate's recent performance
2) to formulate job improvement plans
3) to identify problems and/or examine possible opportunities related to the job
4) to improve communication between superior and subordinate
5) to provide feedback on job performance to the employee
6) to provide a rationale for salary reviews
7) to identify potential performance/possibilities for promotion or transfer
8) to identify training and development needs

Clearly some of the above purposes involve the manager and his subordinate in joint discussion of common issues, with only a hint of remedial work for the appraisee. A few involve a 'top-down' emphasis in which the manager as representative of the senior hierarchy passes judgement on those lower down the pyramid. Others fall somewhere between these two extremes.

## APPRAISAL STYLES

25. Maier (1958) identified three basic approaches to the appraisal interview. These were as follows:

a) TELL AND SELL approach, in which the manager tells his subordinate how he is doing, and endeavours to persuade him to accept what has been decided for him in terms of improvement.
b) TELL AND LISTEN approach, where the manager tells his subordinate how he is doing, but then sits back and listens to the individual's point of view both about the appraisal and about any follow-up action required.
c) PROBLEM-SOLVING approach, in which the manager effectively puts aside the role of judge in order to join the subordinate in mutual reflection on progress and mutual discussion about required action.

Maier has in effect described a continuum of interviewer behaviour ranging from a relatively autocratic style to one that is fully participative. The continuum may be described graphically as in Figure 45.4 opposite.

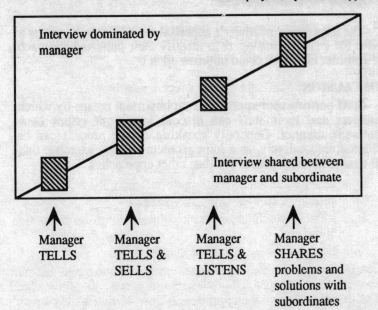

Interview dominated by manager

Interview shared between manager and subordinate

↑ Manager TELLS

↑ Manager TELLS & SELLS

↑ Manager TELLS & LISTENS

↑ Manager SHARES problems and solutions with subordinates

**Figure 45.4    A Continuum of Appraisal Interview Styles (after Maier)**

26. The likely success of the varying styles, judging from research into appraisals, can be summarised as follows:

'TELLING' can be counter-productive. It has been found that praise has little effect one way or the other on appraisees. Criticism, however, has a *negative* effect on subsequent achievement. At least this approach does give the employee some idea of his or her progress.

'TELLING/SELLING' unless the manager is very persuasive, it is unlikely that the employee will accept his version of what is required to be done.

'TELLING/LISTENING' this approach has the merit of informing the employee of his progress, but then goes further by actively involving him in the process of deciding what ought to be done, which is much more likely to produce a positive response.

'SHARING' this is generally considered to provide the best basis for an appraisal owing to its joint problem-solving approach, in which the manager and his subordinate work together more or less as equals. This approach is closer to coaching than anything else.

27. The importance of Maier's appraisal model lies in its use as a device for enabling managers to identify their preferred approach and consider how they could improve upon it.

## CONCLUSION

28. Staff performance appraisal is an important means by which managers and their staff can discuss key work issues in a systematic manner. Generally speaking, if the process can be tackled collaboratively, as a joint problem-solving exercise, this will tend to be more productive than other approaches.

# 46

# MANAGEMENT DEVELOPMENT

## INTRODUCTION

1. In the field of training and development, management development has become an important activity in its own right. It has developed its own techniques, practices and literature. This chapter reviews the subject of management development, commencing with some definitions, continuing with an assessment of typical management development techniques and practices, and concluding with a consideration of the relationship between management development and corporate policies and culture.

## MANAGEMENT DEVELOPMENTS – SOME DEFINITIONS

2. The following definitions of management development indicate some of the differences of emphasis that exist:

   a. '... manager development must embrace *all* managers in the enterprise. It must aim at challenging all to growth and self development. It must focus on performance rather than on promise, and on tomorrow's requirements rather than those of today.'

   *Drucker (1955) The Practice of Management*

   In this statement Drucker was well ahead of his time, especially in terms of seeing management development as self-development within the total management structure, and of recognising the importance of preparing for change in the organization.

   b. '...any attempt to improve managerial effectiveness through a planned and deliberate learning process.'

   *MSC (1978) Policy paper on Management Development.*

   This general statement emphasises the wide range of options facing organizations wishing to undertake management development, and stresses the need for a systematic approach.

   c. '...development is a continuing improvement of effectiveness within a particular system, which may be a person, but in the case of management development is within the management function of an organization...'

   *Morris (1978)*
   *Management Development and Development Management*

Professor Morris sees management development as part of the process of organizational renewal, with the implication that a variety of approaches are possible.

d. 'In some organizations the focus of management development will primarily be upon the training and education of managers. In other(s)...(it)..may be seen to be aiming to change the managerial style... In yet others...the main focus will be on formalised systems...associated with performance appraisal and career planning... '

*Easterby-Smith et al (1980)*
*Auditing Management Development*

Easterby Smith and colleagues found a variety of approaches to management development in their studies of several hundred managers' experience of management development.

3.  Although by no means the majority of management development systems are formalised, the structure of activities implicit in such an approach can be illuminating. Figure 46.1 opposite indicates the range of features likely to be present in a formal system.

In a formal system, management development arises from needs expressed in plans and manpower reviews, as influenced by the corporate culture, or value-system. Present and future needs for managers imply recruitment and succession planning measures. Performance of managers is formally appraised. in terms of present and potential level of achievement. Improvements in performance are dealt with by a variety of training and development activities, which are evaluated individually, and, in some cases, may also be subjected to a management development audit as a whole.

4.  Three underlying trends can be discerned in the variety of possible approaches to management development, and these are as follows:

a) the improvement of individual manager effectiveness (ie 'The extent to which a manager achieves the output requirements of his position.' Reddin, 1970)

b) the improvement of management performance as a whole

c) the improvement of organizational effectiveness (ie the achievement of corporate objectives by means of collaborative efforts throughout the enterprise)

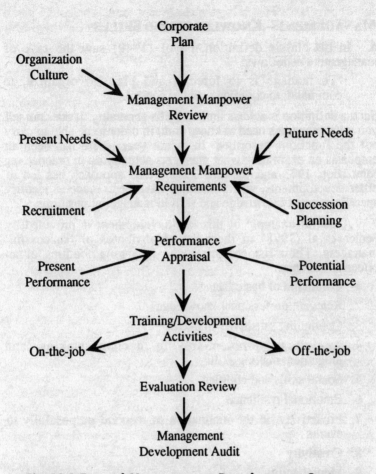

**Fig 46.1 Formal Management Development System**

5.    In practice the first of these three trends results in specific educational and training activities provided to meet individuals immediate and short-term needs. The second trend is directed more towards common, medium-term needs of *groups* of managers. The third trend emphasises the medium and long-term needs of the organization as a whole in adapting to the pressures of its environment. If we take the first two trends, a key question is 'What do managers need to know and need to perform to be effective?' This question will be considered in the next few paragraphs. The third trend will be considered towards the end of the chapter.

## MANAGEMENT – KNOWLEDGE AND SKILLS

6. In his classic definition, Fayol (1949) saw the task of management as follows:

> 'To manage is to forecast and plan, to organize, to command, to coordinate and to control.'

Such a definition is always limited by its generality. It does not tell you what managers need to know or do in order to be able to carry out the functions described. In recent years there has been an emphasis on examining what managers actually do in practice (eg Mintzberg, 1973 and Stewart, 1982). This approach has led to other developments, where attempts have been made to identify specific areas of knowledge and skill in managerial positions.

7. A useful example of this last development is provided by Pedler et al (1978) in their list of attributes of 'successful' managers. Their list comprises the following features of an effective manager:

1. Command of basic facts
2. Relevant professional knowledge
3. Continuing sensitivity to events
4. Analytical, problem-solving decision-making and judgement making skills
5. Social skills and abilities
6. Emotional resilience
7. Proactivity, ie the inclination to respond purposefully to events
8. Creativity
9. Mental agility
10. Balanced learning habits and skills
11. Self-knowledge

Whilst the list reads rather like a prosaic version of Kipling's 'If', nevertheless it does provoke other questions, as the authors themselves are aware, and these questions can help to direct managers' thinking about their effectiveness as managers.

8. Pedler and colleagues raise several questions under each of their eleven features to enable managers to assess themselves at the start of a series of self-development exercises built around their list. Rosemary Stewart (1982) takes a rather different approach to

analysing manager's jobs. She looks at managers' jobs in terms of the demands. constraints – and choices that are present. Jobs were described along these lines. and , then managers were encouraged to consider how they could extend – their range of choices, as well as learning to cope with those aspects that could not be changed.

9. Another view of managerial jobs was expressed by Simmons & Brennan (1981)

> '...managing well means:
>
> 1. Having frequent reviews of performance as a group...
>
> 2. ...listening to each individual's views on the situation and how things can be improved...
>
> 3. Proposing and getting commitment to a solution ... which is in line with the goals ... of the system.'

This particular viewpoint emphasises the team-leadership aspects of a managerial position.

10. Taking all these views about the nature of managerial jobs as a whole, four key elements can be discerned in terms of what managers might need to know or be able to do. These are as follows:

- Managerial knowledge - what the manager needs to know about the organization, the job, the procedures involved etc

- Managerial skills - what problem-solving, social and other skills the manager needs to be able to practise

- Managerial attitudes - what the manager is required to accept in terms of coping with stress, dealing with clients etc

- Managerial style - the expectations that people have concerning the way the manager exercises leadership.

These four elements can be found in most management development programmes, whether for individuals or for groups.

## MANAGEMENT DEVELOPMENT METHODS

11. The various methods employed in management development can be placed into three main categories, as follows:

a. Management education: qualification-bearing courses run by universities or public-sector colleges, for example MBA degrees, Diplomas in Management Studies, and various professional examinations, such as the Institute of Personnel Management; the level of work is regarded as post experience, and the emphasis is on acquiring knowledge and theory.

b. Management training: internal and external courses, off the job and focussing on acquiring specific knowledge and relevant job skills; some experimental learning via course exercises.

c. Experiential learning: 'learning by doing'; on-the-job experience usually with guidance from superior or colleague.

12. Of these three categories, the first two have been discredited in many respects. Writers such as Humble (1967) and Hague (1974) have criticised off-the-job methods on grounds of their lack of relevance to 'real' needs. Humble proposes the alternative of Management by Objectives (MBO), which in essence is a jointly-planned target-setting exercise, in which a manager and his superior identify job priorities, agree targets to be attained, and set up a system for (a) monitoring the manager's progress and (b) providing help when necessary. Such an approach can be an extremely effective way of developing management skills and experience. Hague, on his part, favours what he calls 'executive' self-development, which, in practice, means on-the-job guided experience.

Most modern approaches to management development concentrate on experiential learning on the job, and relegate courses to a secondary role.

## EXPERIENTIAL APPROACHES TO MANAGEMENT DEVELOPMENT

13. The most widely-used experiential methods are as follows: coaching / guided experience, delegation, projects, secondments / job rotation. In Figure 46.2, we briefly examine each of these, and highlight their key points and advantages.

14. The emphasis in these experiential approaches is on learning whilst doing the job. In some cases off-the-job training will be required to enable the manager concerned to understand important concepts or to carry out initial practice in a 'safe' environment. Such off-the-job training, however, is only employed in a supporting role. Nevertheless, there are several well-tried methods for employing experiential learning in a 'safe' off-the-job environment. Some of the leading methods will be described below.

| METHOD | SALIENT FEATURES | ADVANTAGES |
|---|---|---|
| • Coaching / Guided Experience | Planned involvement of the manager in advising and aiding subordinate manager to develop effective job performance. Involves discovery learning with support. | Relevant to learner. Improves boss-subordinate collaboration. Good feedback for subordinate. |
| • Delegation | Boss gives subordinate specific responsibility, authority and resources. Performance is monitored. | Individual able to exercise real responsibility for results. |
| • Projects | A specific problem or opportunity is worked on by an individual or a team with the object of producing concrete proposals in a given time span. | May generate a high degree of commitment. Utilises problem-solving, negotiating skills. |
| • Secondments / Job Rotation | A manager is assigned to a post in another department / unit for a limited period. | Valuable experience based on doing the job assigned. Tests individual. |

**Fig. 46.2    Experiential Methods in Management Development**

## OFF-THE-JOB METHODS AND EXPERIENTIAL LEARNING

15.  The majority of experiential methods used in management courses are directed at social skills development, eg leadership, influencing skills, negotiating, assertiveness etc. A few are directed at cognitive skills development, eg problem-identification, problem-analysis etc. Perceptive use of such methods by trainers can overcome many of the problems of lack of relevance to the job levelled at off-the-job training by its critics. The point here is that skills development in these particular areas extends the range of an individual's competence in his whole life, not just in his present job. These particular skills are in fact 'context-free', that is they do not depend on any one situation in order to be of use to the learner, unlike the on-the-job activities mentioned in para. 13 above. An example of one such method is the use of the so-called 'Managerial Grid'. The Grid (see Figure 46.3) represents a matrix

of potential management styles of leadership, and was first devised as an aid to management development. Using the basic Grid model, managers can identify their current style and, if appropriate learn what to do to achieve a 'better' style. Learning is achieved by means of structured questionnaires and a combination of group discussion and practical exercises. The basic Grid is set out as:

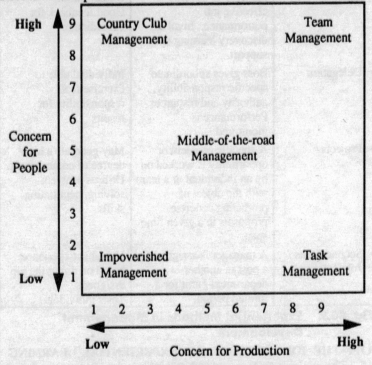

**Fig. 46.3   The Managerial Grid (after Blake & Mouton, 1964)**

The Grid uses two dimensions: *concern for people* and *concern for production (or task)*. *By* measuring responses to questionnaires, for example, managers can identify what preferences they have when faced with certain 'context-free' situations. They can then plot their initial positions on the Grid, and begin to see a picture of themselves emerging. The Country Club style is very considerate to people, but shows little concern for the task. *By* comparison, the Task Management style emphasises getting the task completed, more or less regardless of people's feelings or views. Of the five styles, the Team Management style is seen to he the 'best' style, in that it emphasises both the task and people's needs. As a

management development device, the Grid has proved very useful.
(As a theory of leadership, it has not received much support.)
16. Typical methods used in courses are described briefly in
figure 46.4 below:

| METHOD | SALIENT FEATURES | ADVANTAGE |
|---|---|---|
| Group exercise | Group are given a task and certain limits; the results achieved and the process by which they were achieved are examined by the group and a tutor | Definable focus for activities; task provides peg on which discussion can take place; useful for leadership and team-building |
| Role-playing | Individuals take on a role and experience the nature of an interpersonal encounter; may be tightly or loosely-scripted | Participants learn to think on their feet; experience genuine emotions so long as role is authentic |
| Sensitivity training | Group exercises in which processes taking place in the group are examined; the focus is on the 'here and now' interactions; requires careful guidance by trainer | Enables groups to explore interpersonal relations and to share feelings |
| Case study | A real or imaginary account of an organizational problem is studied by an individual or a small group with a view to diagnosing a situation or proposing solutions | Provides focal point for developing analytical and problem-solving skills |
| Brainstorming | A group are asked to suggest ways of dealing with an issue/problem; no discussion or criticism of suggestions is made until after the list has been completed | Has proved to be an effective means of stimulating new ideas and creative suggestions |
| Simulation exercise | This is a combination of a case-study with role-play; participants are given a fairly detailed scenario and are asked to undertake a number of decisions within a time limit | As a kind of enlarged role-play, this can reproduce many real-life situations; useful for developing negotiating and decision-making skills |
| Workshops | These are practical exercises in which participants work on particular work-based problems as a group | Provide opportunity to share ideas on real day-to-day problems; useful when devising plans/systems |

**Fig 46.4 Experiential Methods in (Courses)**

17. These methods try to overcome the problem stated by Schein (1970) that:

> 'The typical training effort therefore faces the problem not only of how to teach a new employee the specifics of a complex job for today, but also how to create a learning situation in which that employee can develop his other capacities by way of preparing for an uncertain future. In management training the latter factor is paramount.'

Whilst it is by no means easy to measure the effects of management training courses and on-the-job development, the outcomes that senior management might expect from 'successful' management development activities will include:

a) individual managers performing at a fully-satisfactory level

b) improved performance from work-teams as a result of better leadership

c) pool of managers ready and able to take up promotion or stand in for absentees

d) managers working collaboratively together

e) improved communication between managers and their staff and between managers and colleagues

f) improved problem-solving capacity throughout the organization

## SUCCESSION PLANNING

18. One of the key features of a structured management development system is a succession plan. This is basically a plan for identifying who is currently in post and who is available and qualified to take over in the event of retirement, voluntary leaving, dismissal or sickness, for example. As Figure 46.5 )on the page opposite) indicates, a typical succession chart includes details of key management jobholders and brief references to their possible successors.

## AUDITING MANAGEMENT DEVELOPMENT

19. Some important outcomes of management development were referred to in paragraph 17 above. However, the assessment of the effects of management development activities is a complex matter, as the Durham University Business School team discovered when conducting their study into management development in a number of British companies.

| Department: | | | Manager: | Date: | |
|---|---|---|---|---|---|
| Present Management Jobholders | | | | Possible Successors | Ready |
| Post | Jobholder | Age | Performance | First choice:<br>Second choice: | |
| | | | | | |
| | | | | | |
| | | | | | |
| | | | | | |
| | | | | | |
| | | | | | |

**Fig. 46.5 Management Succession Chart**

Part of the Durham remit was to produce an instrument for evaluating management development, and this is described in Easterby-Smith et al (1980). The so-called Management Development Audit aims 'to ensure that the provisions adopted by any organization for developing its managers do produce the intended results.' The essence of the Audit approach is 'to ask individual managers to describe their own experiences of, and views about, management development, and then to reflect the collective view back to those responsible for making decisions about the development of managers.'

20. The Audit, which is intended to be a neutral instrument, not preferring any particular approach to management development, attempts to portray a picture which contrasts:

a) the formal view of what is intended to happen

b) managers' perceptions of what is happening in fact

c) what managers would like to see happening in management development

The Audit seeks answers to questions such as the following:

• What are the main objectives of Management development, and how well are they being achieved?

• What are the main forms of training available for managers, and what emphasis is placed on them?

• How is self-development encouraged?

• What discussion takes place before a manager goes on a course, and what happens on his return?

- What kind of appraisal system exists?
- Is there a formal system of career development, and is this related to appraisal?
- For what levels of management is succession planning carried out?
- What internal and external resources are made available for management development?
- What are the main problems confronting management development in the organization at the present time?

21. The Audit represents a thorough review of management development activities, enabling senior management to pinpoint strengths and weaknesses of the current system as well as obtaining a 'feel' for the way the system is operating. Many of the responses to the audit will undoubtedly reflect the various cultural influences at work in the organization, and these will be considered briefly next.

## MANAGEMENT DEVELOPMENT AND CORPORATE CULTURE

22. The approach to management development in an organization will tend to reflect the dominant value-system of the senior management. They are the persons who, above all, are charged with building a management team and developing their successors. If the top management is centralist and bureaucratic, for example, then its view of management development is likely to produce a logically structured system such as that shown in Figure 46.1. above. In such a system, job descriptions, appraisal forms, succession charts and the like are vital items in the analysis of needs and in decisions about how they are to be met. Such a system would probably favour structured efforts, both on and off-the-job. to supply individual manager needs. Where top management believes in delegation and devolution, then the emphasis in management development is on self-development on-the-job. Where management is considered an elite group, then features such as 'accelerated promotion' and graduate trainee programmes tend to predominate. Such systems provide selective support for manager development by concentrating on so-called 'high fliers', ie persons with outstanding potential.

## CONCLUSION

23. The current mood among writers and researchers on management development suggests that a contingency approach to management development is preferable. A contingency approach

in essence adapts to the dominant culture of the organization concerned, but takes into account a number of forces for change, such as the influence of new technology. The most successful attempts at management development are likely to be those relying on an appropriate mix of on-the-job experience and off-the-job courses offered in a variety of ways to meet different individual requirements and learning styles.

# 47

# JOB EVALUATION

## INTRODUCTION

1.    Job evaluation is the name given to a set of methods designed to compare jobs systematically with a view to assessing their relative worth. Job evaluation produces a rank order of jobs based on a rational, and reasonably objective, assessment of a number of key factors taken from a representative cross-section of all the jobs in a particular job hierarchy. Job evaluation sets out to answer such questions as 'Is the Company Secretary's job as demanding as the Chief Accountant's?' and 'Should specialised, but in-depth jobs, be placed in the same grade as broader, but shallower jobs?'

2.    The purpose of job evaluation is to produce a defensible ranking of jobs which can be used as the basis for a rational pay structure. Following job evaluation, pay can be based on a rational estimate of the contribution made by individual jobs to the organization in terms of skill, responsibility, length of training and other factors. There are several key points which need to be noted about job evaluation. These are as follows:

    a.  Job evaluation deals in relative positions, not in absolutes,

    b.  Job evaluation assesses *jobs*, not the individuals in them, (ie it is not a performance appraisal exercise),

    c.  The evaluation process is usually carried out by groups (job evaluation committees) rather than by individuals,

    d.  Job evaluation committees utilise concepts such as logic, fairness and consistency in their assessment of jobs,

    e.  There will always be *some* element of subjective judgement in job evaluation,

    f.  Job evaluation by itself cannot determine pay scales or pay levels, it can only provide the basic data on which decisions about pay can be taken.

3.    Job evaluation is clearly not the only basis for settling pay. Collective bargaining between unions and management is often the dominant method of determining pay, and this, in the final analysis, boils down to who has the strongest bargaining position at a particular point in time. 'Custom and practice' is another common method for arriving at pay structures and pay levels. This tends to produce a haphazard structure derived from a variety of ad hoc and often conflicting pressures from employee groups at the grass-roots. In other cases, management attempt to determine pay

in the light of the 'going rate' for their industry or their local market. Whilst this may work reasonably well for the overall level of pay, it does nothing to sort out differentials in pay between different groups of employees. The advantage of a job-evaluated pay structure is that it does provide a defensible basis for allocating pay differentials between groups. Where such a structure is developed in a unionised situation, the job evaluation results enable both management *and* trade union representatives to defend the gradings which are drawn up. The major effect of collective bargaining in this situation is to maintain or increase the *overall* level of earnings, but without interfering with differentials.

## JOB EVALUATION METHODS

4.   Most job evaluation methods can be divided into two categories:
   a.  Non-analytical methods, and
   b.  Analytical methods.

Non-analytical methods take whole jobs, compare them and then rank them. The two most common examples of such methods are:

   a.  **Job Ranking** – in this method, basic job descriptions are written up for a representative sample of jobs in the total population; evaluators compare the descriptions and then make an initial ranking of the jobs in order of perceived importance, ie this is their subjective view of relative importance; the rankings are discussed in an evaluation committee, and eventually a final rank order is agreed; the remaining jobs in the population are then slotted in to the rank order. The advantage of this method lies in its simplicity; the main disadvantage is that, because of the high degree of subjective judgement required, it can only be effective in a relatively simple and clear-cut organization structure.

   b.  **Job Grading/Job Classification** – in this case, the usual procedure is reversed, for in job grading the pay/salary grades are worked out first, then the broad characteristics of each grade are defined (eg in terms of knowledge, skill etc expected for each grade); a representative sample of jobs, known as benchmark jobs, is selected as typical of each grade; full job descriptions are written for these jobs; the remaining jobs (usually written up in outline) are then compared with the benchmarks and allocated to the appropriate grade. Like Job Ranking, this is also a simple method to operate, but it relies heavily on the credibility of the initial salary grades, and does not permit sufficient distinctions to be made between jobs, especially in a relatively complex organization with a wide variety of specialist roles.

5.   In a phrase, non-analytical methods are simple, but crude. In complex organizations it is essential to use analytical methods, as these are the only way of discriminating fairly between jobs which are not at all similar. For example, they could be used to distinguish the relative importance of a systems analyst compared with, say, a management accountant, or of a chief architect compared with a head brewer.

6.   Analytical methods break jobs down into their component tasks, responsibilities and other factors, and assess the jobs factor by factor, sometimes allocating points for each factor and sometimes allocating monetary sums to them. A group of benchmark jobs is evaluated in this way, and ranked according to the scores. The remaining jobs in the population are slotted in to this benchmark rank order. Then all the jobs are either allocated to a salary grade, or, if monetary sums were allocated, are allotted a specified total salary. The most commonly used analytical method is *Points Rating*, where points are allocated to job factors; the method where monetary sums are allocated to the factors is known as *Factor Comparison*, and is not widely used nowadays.

7.   The most commonly used factors in analytical methods are as indicated in Figure 47.1.

---

**SKILL**
- Education and training required
- Experience
- Initiative and creativity

**RESPONSIBILITY/DECISION-MAKING**
- Complexity of work
- Supervising work of others
- Equipment or process
- Material or product

**EFFORT**
- Mental demands of job
- Physical demands of job

**WORKING CONDITIONS**
- Pressures in the job
- Difficult or hazardous conditions

---

**Figure 47.1 Analytical Methods - Typical Job Factors.**

8.    In a Points Rating Method, each factor is broken down into degrees or levels, which are allocated points in accordance with an agreed weighting. In evaluating manual jobs, a greater weighting may be given to factors such as Effort and Working Conditions, whereas in evaluating white-collar jobs, the greater weighting will tend to be given to Skill and Responsibility. In a situation where trade unions are involved, the weightings given to each factor are usually a matter for negotiation. The important point to be borne in mind is that, whatever is eventually agreed, the same treatment will be applied to every job. There is no question of applying different criteria to different jobs in the same population, apart, that is, from the manual/ white-collar differential. An example of a possible Points Rating matrix for the evaluation of manual jobs is shown in a simplified form in Figure 47.2. In terms of degrees of each factor, 1 represents a *minor* requirement in the job, whilst 8 represents a *major* requirement.

| Job Factor | Degree | | | | | | | |
|---|---|---|---|---|---|---|---|---|
| | 1 | 2 | 3 | 4 | 5 | 6 | 7 | 8 |
| **SKILL** | | | | | | | | |
|    1. Education | 15 | 30 | 45 | 60 | 75 | 90 | – | – |
|    2. Experience | 20 | 40 | 60 | 80 | 90 | 100 | – | – |
|    3. Initiative | 15 | 30 | 45 | 60 | 75 | 90 | 105 | 120 |
| **EFFORT** | | | | | | | | |
|    4. Physical | 10 | 20 | 30 | 40 | 50 | – | – | - |
|    5. Mental | 5 | 10 | 15 | 20 | 25 | 30 | 35 | 40 |
| **RESPONSIBILITY** | | | | | | | | |
|    6. Supervisory | 5 | 10 | 15 | 20 | 25 | 30 | 35 | 40 |
|    7. Equipment | 5 | 10 | 15 | 20 | 25 | – | – | – |
|    8. Safety | 5 | 10 | 15 | 20 | 25 | – | – | – |
| **WORK CONDITIONS** | | | | | | | | |
|    9. Hazards | 5 | 10 | 15 | 20 | – | – | – | – |
|    10. Noise/dirt | 10 | 20 | 30 | 40 | 50 | – | – | – |

**Figure 47.2 Manual Jobs - Points Rating Matrix.**

9.    The matrix shown above weights the points in favour of the skill factors, physical effort and noisy/dirty working conditions.

These are typically the most important factors to be considered in establishing the comparative value of manual jobs. If an example for managerial or senior white-collar jobs had been chosen, there would still have been an emphasis on skill factors, but then responsibility factors would have outweighed effort and working conditions. To help make evaluations as consistent as possible, the various degrees of each factor are described in an accompanying document. For example, if we take Education: 1st degree could equate to 'basic secondary education', 3rd degree could equate to 'GCSE in 4 subjects' and 6th, degree could equate to 'HNC equivalent'; the other two degrees are not required for manual jobs.

10. Some points rating methods are available in proprietary form. A notable example is the Hay-MSL Guide-chart System, which is particularly popular with organizations composed of a wide variety of specialist, professional and managerial occupations, although it can also be applied to junior clerical and to manual grades of work. The Hay-MSL system is a points system based on three key factors – Know-how, Problem-solving and Accountability – all of which can be broken down into several important sub-factors or dimensions as follows:

  a. Know-how: can be scored in terms of *depth* as well as *breadth* of Knowledge and Skills required; it can also be scored in terms of Human Relations Skills.
  b. Problem-solving: can be scored in terms of the thinking *environment* (eg routine or broadly defined etc) and in terms of the thinking *challenge* (eg repetitive, variable or creative etc).
  c. Accountability: can be scored in terms of *freedom to act, impact* on the organization/department (ie remote, contributory, shared or prime) and in terms of the money involved in the business (eg turnover of business, size of annual budget etc).

Clients pay for the use of the Hay-MSL Guide-charts, the services of their consultants, and for a salary guidance service which enables them to keep up-to-date in the market-place for labour. The Guide-charts form a standardised system of job evaluation, and it is thus possible to see what other organizations are paying for jobs of a particular points total. This feature overcomes one of the major drawbacks of most points methods, which is that whilst they can solve the problem of internal differentials, they cannot link the results into the external labour market or the 'going rate' for the jobs they have evaluated.

11. Taking a broad view of job evaluation, as a technique for facilitating management decision-making in an important area of personnel relations, namely pay, the advantages are:
   a. it provides a rational and defensible basis on which to decide pay in general, and differentials, in particular, because it focuses on *job content*,
   b. it provides a rational basis for devising, or improving, grading structures,
   c. it reduces the effects of ad hoc or traditional arrangements for pay or grading,
   d. it encourages management and employees alike to think of jobs in terms of key components.

The full range of advantages can only come from the use of analytical methods, nevertheless there are certain disadvantages of job evaluation. These are:
   a. implementation of even quite simple methods can be a costly and time-consuming business,
   b. analytical methods, in particular can give the impression that they are completely objective and scientific, but they still rely considerably on human judgement ie subjective influences cannot be ruled out,
   c. whilst job evaluation can provide a rational basis for grade differentials based on job content, it is usually unable to link the resulting pay grades into the labour market itself.

## SUMMARY

12. This chapter has looked briefly at the subject of job evaluation. Job evaluation can be defined as a management technique in which a number of different methods are available to compare jobs systematically with other jobs with a view to assessing their relative worth and placing them into a rank order based on this assessment. The rank order provides a basis for the establishment of appropriate wage or salary grades.

13. Job evaluation methods can be divided into
   a. non-analytical methods, which compare whole jobs, such as in job ranking and job classification, and
   b. analytical methods, which compare jobs in terms of certain common factors, such as skill, responsibility and others. Examples of analytical methods are Points Rating, Factor Comparison and Hay-MSL Guide-charts.

14. The main strength of job evaluation lies in its ability to provide a rational basis for establishing job differentials. Its major disadvantage is that it is costly and time-consuming.

# 48

# EMPLOYEE RELATIONS

## INTRODUCTION

1.   'Employee relations' is a term used to describe the regulation of management-employee relationships. It encompasses a variety of such relationships and not just the formal relationships arising from collective bargaining between management and trade unions, which is generally referred to as 'industrial relations'. The major parties involved in employee relations are as follows:

   a.   Managers (representing employers),
   b.   Employers' associations' representatives,
   c.   Individual employees,
   d.   Trade union representatives,
   e.   Government representatives,
   f.   Representatives of the law.

2.   The contractual relationship between an individual employee and his employer is still the cornerstone of employee relations, even though this relationship has been affected by collective relationships, and the results of collective bargaining. The reason for the continued existence of the individual employment contract lies in its great flexibility. It can, and does, contain matters which are implied in the relationship, just as much as it contains matters which are expressly agreed upon; it can, and does, include unwritten as well as written terms of agreement; it includes matters which are decided informally as well as those decided formally; and it still represents an *individual* contract, however much this may be influenced by *collective* agreements.

3.   In broad terms, the key issues of employee relations are those of conflict, cooperation, rule-making, authority and power, information and communication, and motivation. For managers and individual employees all these issues are part and parcel of their working lives; for other parties, involvement focuses around specific issues, usually for a specific period of time. This chapter considers some of these issues, and provides an outline of the respective roles of the parties concerned . The emphasis in the chapter is influenced considerably by the nature of questions on this topic in the examinations of the professional bodies.

## PERSPECTIVES IN EMPLOYEE RELATIONS

4. In view of the number of groups having an interest in employee relations, it is not surprising that differences of viewpoint should arise concerning both the subject-matter and the ultimate goals of this major element of relationships at work. The subject-matter of employee relations can be seen quite differently by the parties concerned, as the following examples can illustrate: Managers may see employee relations as one or more of the following:

   a. creating and maintaining employee motivation,
   b. establishing workable and credible channels of communication with employees,
   c. negotiating with trade union representatives,
   d. sharing power with employee representatives (not necessarily trade unions) in an organized way,
   e. achieving higher levels of efficiency and service by cooperation with employees and their representatives.

Employees may see employee relations as one or more of the following:

   a. management's efforts to win them round to their way of thinking,
   b. a genuine attempt by management to adopt a benevolent approach to employees,
   c. a 'them-and-us' situation involving management-union meetings and frequent wranglings,
   d. an opportunity to participate in shop-floor decision making, and possibly even at Board level.

Third Parties, such as Government ministers, conciliators, arbitrators and judges may see employee relations as one or more of the following:

   a. attempting to achieve mutually harmonious relationships between employers and employees,
   b. Laying down rules of conduct (ie fair play) for employer-employee relations,
   c. regulating the power struggle between owners and managers on the one side, and employees and organized labour on the other,
   d. establishing peace-making arrangements between the two sides referred to above, and the protection of the interests of the rest of the community.

5.   In situations where managers see their role as motivating employees by means of 'good human relations' and thus adopt a collaborative, if not paternalistic, style of management, their approach to employee relations is described as a *unitary approach*. This basically assumes that the organization is one large, happy family with a generally agreed sense of its common purpose. There are organizations which take this approach, and, where the employees are happy to accept it, the end-result seems to be harmony and success. Where, however, employees begin to feel dissatisfied with a paternalistic management (ie in Argyris's terms, they want to become more mature, more independent, at work), then conflict is likely to ensue, unless management can adapt its style. Where the existence of separate interests is openly admitted, and where arrangements are made to resolve the conflict that is seen to be inevitable, then this is called a *pluralistic approach* to employee relations. In situations where managers see their role as exercising 'managerial prerogatives' and where the employees and their representatives see their role as opposing this exercise of power, we are in a classical confrontation situation. In this last case, there is less room for negotiation, but a solution can be found eventually.

## RULES AND AGREEMENTS

6.   In the rest of this chapter, the assumption will be made that a pluralist view is closest to the facts, at least in the United Kingdom, and the discussion will reflect this perspective. An important implication of accepting a pluralist view of employee relations is that rule-making is essential if the parties concerned are to contain their conflict within manageable bounds. The main body of rules in employee relations is drawn from the following:

   a.   company/organization rules – these are usually generated by, and enforced by, managers;

   b.   union rule-books – these are drawn up by the members and enforced by union officers;

   c.   collective agreements – jointly agreed rules or practices made by management representatives and employee representatives;

   d.   custom and practice – these are the informal rules which arise from the behaviour of managers and employees over a period of time; unlike the other rules just mentioned, these rules are not usually written down;

   e.  the Law – these are the rules arising from statute, from judicial precedent, and from the Common Law insofar as they relate to employee relations;

   f  codes of practice – these may be the codes of professional bodies or those of bodies such as ACAS (the Advisory, Conciliation and Arbitration Service, set up under the Employment Protection Act, 1975).

7.   From the point of view of employee relations the rules of greatest importance are:

   a.  those made by Parliament (ie statutes) which are dealt with in the next, and final chapter, of the Manual, and

   b.  those made as a result of collective bargaining (ie collective agreements).

The latter are usually divided into two major categories: *procedural* agreements and *substantive* agreements. The aims and contents of these are as follows:

**Procedural agreements** – these constitute the foundation stones of collective bargaining, for they lay down the rules of behaviour, which the parties should adhere to in their relationships with each other; examples of matters covered by such agreements include:

   a.  negotiating rights for unions,

   b.  union membership (eg. categories of employees to be covered),

   c.  numbers and rights of union representatives,

   d.  procedure to be followed in the case of a dispute between the parties,

   e.  grievance and disciplinary procedures.

The concluding of an initial procedure agreement is the first union aim in a situation where it has just been recognised by the employer for bargaining purposes.

**Substantive agreements** – these are the agreements which deal with the substance of employee relations ie terms and conditions of employment; examples of topics normally to be found in such agreements include:

   a.  pay ie wages and salaries,

   b.  hours of work, including shift work etc,

   c.  holiday entitlements,

   d.  manning arrangements, establishments etc.

Substantive agreements are usually negotiated annually – the so-called 'annual pay round' – but procedural agreements are negotiated only as and when the parties feel the need to change or clarify the rules. Most procedural agreements require either side to give several months' notice of variation or termination of the agreement, whereas most annual agreements run out automatically at the end of the period concerned.

8.   In conducting a negotiation both sides engage in a considerable amount of prior preparation. This invariably includes:

   a. Deciding objectives,
   b. Assessing relative bargaining power,
   c. Deciding tactics to be employed, and
   d. Assessing the impact of external influences (eg. cost-of-living, legal requirements etc)

An objective for the management side could be 'to obtain acceptance of flexible rostering/shift-working at minimum cost to the organization'; an objective for the trade union side could be 'to achieve pay parity with XYZ group of workers in the industry'. The relative bargaining power depends on several issues, including the economic situation and the strength of union organization. For example, when the demand for particular skills is high, the union has the advantage; when the demand for labour is low, then management have the stronger position. This latter situation can be offset to a certain extent by a union that is well-organized and not afraid to employ sanctions (ie strikes, overtime bans etc). The immediacy of the impact of possible sanctions is an important factor here. For example, where the use of sanctions by a union can bring immediate chaos or disruption of a service, then clearly that union is in a stronger bargaining position than one whose sanctions have no immediate effect whatsoever.

9.   The tactics to be employed by each side are those actions which, in the course of the negotiations, can contribute to the achievement of their respective objectives. The issue of tactics can be illustrated by considering a substantive matter - the negotiation of a pay increase. As Figure 48.1 shows, each side in the negotiation has its idea of the ideal settlement ie the lowest possible increase from management's side, and the maximum possible increase from the trade union side. Recognising the relative bargaining strength of the other side, plus the influence of external factors, each side also has its fall-back position. This represents the point beyond which each side is not prepared to retreat. In cases where this point is reached, but is not recognised until it is too late, the likelihood of a breakdown in negotiations is very great. Experienced negotiators hope to be able to recognise when the other side is close to its fall-back position, and settle

before it is too late, hopefully somewhere near the realistic solution. In the example shown below, the likely increase will be in the 7% – 9% range.

**Trade Union's Claim**

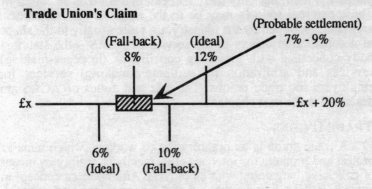

**Management's Response**

### Figure 48.1. Tactics in Pay Negotiations.

10. In assessing the external influences on a negotiation, the management side normally have to consider:

  a. the organization's ability to pay (ie the budget available for pay increases and improved benefits):

  b. the organization's policy on pay and conditions;

  c. comparable rates of pay/trends in pay elsewhere in the industry/economy;

  d. any legal restraints (eg. equal pay for women employees);

  e. any incomes policy set by Government.

The union side will have to consider the above points also, but will add topics such as the cost-of-living index, trade union policy, and successful results of comparable negotiations elsewhere.

11. A key feature of any comprehensive procedure agreement is the disputes procedure, which in a few cases, such as in the engineering industry, is a separate agreement. The aim of every disputes procedure is to settle disputes speedily and as near to the original source as possible. Disputes can arise from a failure to agree during the course of negotiations, or from a differing interpretation of an existing agreement, or from an issue which has arisen as the result of the implementation of an agreement. Disputes can, of course, also arise from issues not covered in any existing agreement. However they arise, disputes have to be tackled at once, for it is generally in everyone's interests that

disputes should be short-lived. Most organizations have two or three stages of an internal procedure, involving progressively more senior managers and union officers: if the dispute cannot be solved internally, then, but only then, can external sources be called in. These external sources may be in the shape of an independent arbitrator appointed by the industry, or, more usually in the shape of a conciliation officer in the service of ACAS – the statutory body concerned with providing conciliation (ie peace-making) services and arbitration (ie settlement-making) services for employers and trade unions. The role and duties of ACAS are described in the next chapter.

## TRADE UNIONS

12. A trade union is an organization of workers, which aims to protect and promote the interests of its members, mainly by means of collective bargaining with employers. An important concept in current British law is that of the 'independent trade union'. Independent, in this context, means that the union concerned is not dependent on an employer for funds, facilities or organization it also means that the union must show that it can provide adequate services to its members, and is able, where necessary to sustain the effects of collective disputes. Trade Union rules and organizations are monitored by a Certification Officer who is required to maintain records and ensure that statutory procedures are followed.

13. At the year ending 31 December 1988, the Certification Officer reported that there were 354 trade unions listed in the U.K. This represented a net fall of 13 unions, mainly as a result of mergers. There were 24 unions with a membership in excess of 100,000 members, and those made up 81% of total union membership.

14. Unions can be divided into a number of different categories as follows:

**Manual Workers' Unions**

    a. Craft Unions – based on skills obtained following an apprenticeship; examples are NGA (National Graphical Association – a print union), and ASLEF (Associated Society of Locomotive Engineers and Firemen – the train drivers' union).

    b. Industrial Unions – based on entire industries; examples are NUM (National Union of Mineworkers), and UCATT (Construction and Allied Trades).

    c. General Unions – broadly-based on unskilled and semi-skilled workers across a variety of industries; examples are

TGWU (Transport and General Workers), NUPE (National Union of Public Employees) and GMBAT (General and Municipal Boilermakers and Allied Trades).

## White-collar Unions

a. Open white-collar – based on clerical, administrative and technical employees from a wide range of employers and occupations; examples are MSF (Manufacturing Science and Finance Union), and APEX (Association of Professional, Executive, Clerical and Computer Staffs).

b. Closed white-collar – based on specific occupations; examples are NALGO (National and Local Government Officers) and CPSA (Civil and Public Services Association).

## Managerial/Professional Unions

a. TUC-affiliated – based on managerial occupations or professional qualifications; these unions, like those already referred to above, are members of the TUC (Trades Union Congress); examples are NATFHE (National Association of Teachers in Further and Higher Education – College lecturers), BALPA (British Airline Pilots Association) and EMA (Engineers and Managers' Association).

b. Non-affiliated – based on managerial or professional qualifications; not affiliated to the TUC; eg RCN (Royal College of Nursing).

## Staff Associations

a. TUC-affiliated – based on the employees of a single employer, but not an industrial union; an example is the Inland Revenue Staff Federation.

b. Non-affiliated – based on the employees of a single employer and usually with origins in the firm itself ie the staff association was set up originally by the employer; now fully independent; examples are the various staff associations in banking and insurance.

(Note: A few staff associations have been refused a certificate of independence by the Certification Officer).

15. The number of employees in Britain who are members of an independent trade union is about 10.5 million, that is to say almost one half of the working population. Union density (ie the proportion of union members in a total population) is about 60% in manual occupations and about 40% in whitecollar occupations. Union density tends to be high in such industries as coalmining, transport, public utilities and central and local government; it tends

to be low in such industries as agriculture, construction, distribution and hotels and catering. Density is high in the industries where trade unionism began – mining, transport, engineering and pottery, for example; it is also high in the public sector, as a result of encouragement by the employers. Density is low in industries which are difficult for unions to organize on account of their scattered nature; examples are agriculture, construction and distribution (especially retail). It is also low in banking, insurance, finance and professional services, probably because trade union protection has not been seen as important by such employees.

16. Of the 10.5 million union members, about 10 million are in unions affiliated to the central trades union confederation, the Trade Union Congress (TUC). Membership of the TUC gives unions access to Governments, employers' confederations, national bodies (eg. National Economic Development Council) and to the media. The annual congress of the TUC, which has been held since 1868, debates issues of industrial, economic, social and political importance to the unions. The results of these debates at the centre of the trade union structure are resolutions which define broad policies for all the affiliated unions. Such policies are not at all mandatory, for each union maintains its own independence during membership, but there are strong moral pressures to abide by them. In between congresses, the General Council is responsible for the implementation of policies, and for coordinating union action on important issues which arise from political decisions and economic changes. The General Council is currently composed of 41 members from 19 different trade groups, representing a cross-section of all trade unions. The members, mostly General Secretaries of individual unions, are elected by Congress every year.

## EMPLOYERS' ASSOCIATIONS

17. The employers' equivalent of the TUC is the Confederation of British Industry (the CBI). This body represents the major industries and their associations. Its aims include acting as a national reference point for those seeking industry's views (ie Governments), and providing a means for British industry to influence general policy on industrial, economic, commercial and social matters. Like the TUC, the CBI has access to Governments and important public bodies.

18. Employers' associations, which are not the same as *trade* associations, are primarily instruments of employee relations. Their main objectives are:

a. to represent employers in collective bargaining,
b. to develop machinery for the avoidance of industrial disputes,
c. to provide information and advice to members on employee affairs, and
d. to represent members on national issues.

These aims are very different from those of trade associations, which are essentially commercial organizations. Examples of employers' associations are the EEF (Engineering employers), the BPIF (Printing Industries) and the Newspaper Society.

## WORKPLACE REPRESENTATIVES

19. Whilst many important issues are dealt with by the national or central bodies, which have just been mentioned, it is at the workplace level that employee relations are ultimately decided. At this level, the organization is represented formally by managers, part of whose task is to deal with individual and collective issues raised by their subordinates. In some cases, these issues can be solved quite naturally and easily as part of the normal superior-subordinate relationship. In other cases, however, a more formal approach is required, either because the rules demand this, or because the employee representatives are insisting on it. In these formal cases, the employees are represented by other employees, who are unpaid union officers with defined roles, agreed by both the management and the trade union concerned as part of a procedure agreement. These other employees are usually called 'shop stewards' – the term most frequently used in industry – but may be known as 'union or grade representatives' – especially in white-collar employment – or as 'Fathers-of-the-Chapel' – a term peculiar to the printing industry.

20. The work of these unpaid officers of the union includes such matters as:
a. monitoring the implementation of agreements,
b. handling members' pay problems,
c. negotiating local (ie plant or office) agreements, where permissible,
d. communicating union policy to membership,
e. acting as a communications link between the management and the employee on matters raised collectively,
f. handling grievances on behalf of members, g. recruiting new members for the union.

21. Despite the adverse publicity given to a few notorious cases, the average shop steward or representative is not there to cause trouble for his employer. On the contrary,research studies have shown that the shop steward spends considerably more time in a peace-making role than he does in the role of a belligerent. The fact is that shop stewards operate within a framework of rules, union as well as company rules, and this has a great influence on their power and authority. The shop steward's authority derives principally from collective agreements and from his union rule-book. Whether a shop steward has the *power* to exercise the authority granted to him depends on several factors such as:

   a. the degree of personal support he can command from the members,

   b. the degree of support he can expect from other union officers,

   c. the labour market situation ie if labour is in short supply, he is in a stronger position than if labour is plentiful,

   d. the level of decision-making in the organization, ie if decisions affecting conditions of employment are generally taken at local level, his position is stronger than if they are taken at company level,

   e. the wages structure in the plant (office), ie if wages can be determined, or at least influenced by, local agreements, as opposed to company or industry-wide agreements, then he has greater power. .

## DISCIPLINARY AND GRIEVANCE PROCEDURES

22. An important part of any employee relations policy is to set out the broad standards of conduct which the organization intends to follow in respect of:

   a. unacceptable behaviour on the part of employees (ie disciplinary matters), and

   b. grievances raised by the employees.

A policy statement on discipline could be as follows:

> 'In matters of alleged employee misconduct, the Company will ensure that each case is thoroughly and fairly investigated before any action may be taken against the employee concerned. Every employee in a disciplinary situation will be given ample opportunity to state his case. Any disciplinary action that may be taken will be applied fairly and consistently, in accordance with the Company's disciplinary procedure.'

23. Good practice in disciplinary matters is represented by an ACAS Code of Practice on disciplinary procedures. In summary this proposes that disciplinary procedures should:

    a. be in written form,

    b. specify to whom they apply (ie all, or some of the employees?),

    c. be capable of dealing speedily with disciplinary matters,

    d. indicate the forms of disciplinary action which may be taken (eg. dismissal, suspension or warning),

    e. specify the appropriate levels of authority for the exercise of disciplinary actions,

    f. provide for individuals to be informed of the nature of their alleged misconduct,

    g. allow individuals to state their case, and to be accompanied by a fellow employee (or union representative),

    h. ensure that every case is properly investigated before any disciplinary action is taken,

    i. ensure that employees are informed of the reasons for any penalty they receive,

    j. state that no employee will be dismissed for a first offence, except in cases of gross misconduct,

    k. provide for a right of appeal against any disciplinary action, and specify the appeals procedure.

24. A model disciplinary procedure should aim to *correct* unsatisfactory behaviour, rather than to *punish* it. It should specify as fully as possible what constitutes 'misconduct' and what constitutes 'gross misconduct'. It should then state what is the most likely penalty for each of these categories. In cases of proven 'gross misconduct', this is most likely to be immediate (or summary) dismissal, or suspension, followed by dismissal. In cases of less serious misconduct, the most likely consequence is that a formal warning will be given. For *repeated* acts of misconduct, it is likely that the employee concerned will be dismissed. So far as appeals are concerned, a model procedure should aim to ensure that these are dealt with quickly, so that the employee involved can be informed of the final decision without undue delay.

25. Because of the serious implications of disciplinary action, only senior managers are normally permitted to carry out suspensions, demotions or dismissals. Other managers are normally restricted to giving warnings of one kind or another, and

the same applies to supervisors. However, when it comes to handling grievances, all managers and supervisors have an important role to play, for one of the key features of every effective grievance procedure is that it should aim to settle the grievance as near as possible to the point of origin. In Britain the Employment Protection (Consolidation) Act 1978, requires employees to be informed, within 13 weeks of commencing employment, about the main terms and conditions of their employment, including a reference to disciplinary and grievance procedures.

26. What is a typical grievance procedure? It usually follows the stages set out below:

> **Preamble**. Management recognises the right of every employee to seek redress for any grievances they may have relating to their conditions of employment. The procedure which follows aims to provide a fair and speedy settlement of grievances, as near as possible to their point of origin.

> **Stage 1**. The employee should first raise the matter with his immediate supervisor or manager, and may be accompanied by a fellow employee. The manager or supervisor will endeavour to resolve the grievance without delay.

> **Stage 2**. If the employee is not satisfied with the response of his immediate manager or supervisor, he may refer the grievance to his departmental manager or other appropriate senior manager, who will hear the grievance within five working days of it being referred to him. At the meeting the employee may be accompanied by a fellow employee, and the Company Personnel Manager will be present.

> **Appeal**. If the employee is still dissatisfied after the second stage, he may appeal to a director, who will arrange to hear the appeal within five working days. The employee, any accompanying employee, and the Company Personnel Manager will be present at the appeal hearing. The results of the appeal will be recorded in writing and distributed to all the parties concerned.

27. When dealing with a grievance interview, a manager or supervisor is usually unable to prepare in advance for it. An employee, however, may have been storing up a particular grievance for weeks. In order, therefore, to help them cope with the demands of what is often an extremely emotional situation, many managers and supervisors are trained in the tactics of grievance interviewing. These can be summarised as follows in Figure 48.2.

| Objectives | 1. Obtain the facts |
| | 2. Arrive at an acceptable solution |
| Strategy | Aim for a 'win/win' conclusion |
| Tactics | a. Listen carefully to the employee's side of the story |
| | b. Ask probing questions to elicit relevant facts and feelings |
| | c. Summarise from time to time to ensure mutual understanding |
| | d. Attempt to unravel cause(s) of grievance |
| | e. Check facts obtained and meet any other parties involved |
| | f. Consider actions that could be taken and assess their consequences |
| | g. Reply to the aggrieved employee and record actions taken |

**Figure 48.2. Planning a Grievance Interview.**

28. Whether a grievance turns out to have any substance or not, after due investigation, it has still been a source of upset feelings for an employee. It is important, therefore, that managers and supervisors aim for a mutually beneficial result at the end of a grievance interview. The employee concerned should be able to go away feeling reassured that, either he has no problem, or, if he has, it is being tackled constructively by his immediate superior. The manager or supervisor concerned should be able to feel that the grievance has been handled correctly, and that both parties have 'won'.

## EMPLOYEE PARTICIPATION AT WORK

29. The term 'participation' means different things to different people. At one extreme, there are those who see it as nothing more than consultation with employees; at the other extreme, there are those who see it as nothing less than workers' control of industry. In between these two extremes are several other viewpoints, as illustrated in Figure 48.3 below, which demonstrates a continuum of choices. At the bottom of the continuum, management dominates decision-making, but as one moves upwards the control

of decision-making passes away from management and becomes joint control or, ultimately, workers' control.

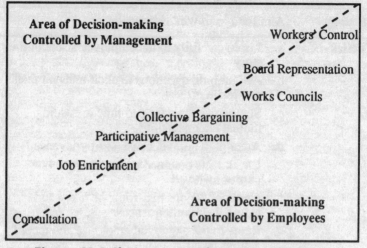

**Figure 48.3 Choices in Employee Participation.**

30. Each of the possible choices shown in Figure 48.3 will be considered further as follows:

    a. **Consultation:** This is 'participation' only in the sense that employees are consulted about decisions affecting their working lives. It may take the form of joint management-employee consultative committees or of briefing groups, for example. The former enable representatives of management and of employees to discuss matters of mutual interest and concern: the latter are regular briefing meetings held by managers to keep their staff informed about matters of interest. Many people do not regard these measures as 'participation' in any way.

    b. **Job enrichment:** This is 'participation' at the level of the job, when the employee is given greater discretion to make his own work decisions in relation to his job duties. Clearly, this kind of participation is extremely relevant to an employee, but it does not involve him in any way in strategic decisions affecting his total employment situation.

    c. **Participative management style:** In this case, the initiative for participation rests firmly with the management – a moderately participative style could involve merely a more 'open' approach to managing people; a radically participative style could involve the establishment of plant and company-level councils. At these the senior management representatives and a cross-section of employee representatives could discuss, and jointly decide, a wide range of important strategic and tactical decisions.

d. **Collective bargaining:** There are many people – trade unionists in particular – who think that the answer to increased 'participation' lies in the extension of collective bargaining between employers and trade unions. At the present time, there are numerous issues connected with planning, for example, which are considered to be the prerogative of management. However, under the umbrella of increased collective bargaining, even planning would become the subject of joint negotiations. There are major problems with this suggestion, mainly because bargaining is essentially about reaching *compromises* in the face of *conflicting* interests, whereas 'participation' is about reaching *optimum decisions* on matters of *common interest* (ie the growth or survival of the enterprise, no less! ) .

e. **Works Councils:** This choice is based primarily on the West German experience of the 'Betriebsrat' or Works Council. In the German situation, the Betriebsrat, which is composed *only* of employee representatives, has legal rights of access to information from management on a wide range of matters, and has the right to co-determination, ie joint decision-making, on all personnel-related matters. Such councils are not permitted to engage in trade union activities and vice versa. This choice would not be an easy one to adopt in the United Kingdom, because of the pervasiveness of collective bargaining. However some larger firms have developed such councils with considerable success alongside their negotiating committees.

f. **Board representation:** This is 'participation' at the policy-making and strategic level where employees are permitted to elect representatives to sit as directors. The thinking behind such an approach to participation is that major corporate decisions, and attitudes, can be influenced by the presence of employee-directors on the Board. The degree of influence, of course, depends considerably on the *proportion* of employee-directors to other directors, as well as on the *personal* influence of individual employee directors. In West Germany, where Board-level representation on a Supervisory Board complements participation at lower levels via Works Councils, the ratio of employee-directors to shareholders' directors can be as. high as 50:50 in companies with more than 2000 employees.

The balance of voting power, however, is still with the shareholders' side, and in any case, there are no employee-directors on the Management Board (Executive Board) in what is a two-tier system. In Britain, Board-level representation has been seen, at the most, as including a small number of employee representatives to bring a shop-floor influence to bear on Board decisions. A few experiments have been tried (eg. in the Post Office and in the British Steel Corporation) but these have not attracted much enthusiasm from either employers or from trade unions. The Bullock Committee proposals, made in 1977, were for the establishment of equal numbers of employee and shareholder representatives plus a smaller, unequal, number of independent directors (the famous 2x + y formula), all sitting on a single (unitary) Board. These proposals are not in line with EEC thinking on employee participations, and have more critics than supporters in the U.K. For the future, some kind of employee representation at Board level is likely in the U.K., but it will probably follow the European model of between half and one-third employee-directors sitting on a supervisory board in a two-tier system.

g. **Workers' control:** The thinking behind proposals for workers' control is that workers should be the shareholders of the enterprise, and that workers' committees should exercise the policy-making and strategic functions over appointed managers, who would be held responsible for the day-to-day running of the business. This system has been adopted in Yugoslavia, but studies have suggested that, even in this apparently democratic arrangement, it is not easy to make a reality of shop-floor participation. It is as difficult for employee-shareholders to gain more than a limited control of the enterprise as it is for shareholder-representatives in a capitalist system. Probably the most successful example of this form of participation is that of the workers' cooperatives at Mondragon, in the Basque region of Spain.

31. Having outlined some of the options available in arriving at a meaning for the term 'participation', let us consider where the most likely consensus of agreement might be found, and what are the most important questions to be faced in reaching this consensus. The middle ground viewpoint, which almost certainly represents a majority, is that 'participation' is about the sharing of decision-making between management and employees, and that

this can, and ought to, take place at the level of the workplace and at some strategic level. Participation, therefore is considerably more than mere consultation; it is considerably less than workers' control: but it does represent a real challenge to previously-held ideas about management prerogatives.

32. The key questions in the debate about 'participation' are briefly as follows:

    a. At what level, or levels, should participation be developed, ie at Board-level, some other strategic level, at plant-level or on the shop-floor?

    b. Should all, or only some, topics be the subject of shared decision-making?

    c. Does participation imply the introduction of a two-tier Board?

    d. What should be the proportion of employee-directors on Boards?

    e. In the elections for employee-directors should all employees be entitled to vote ie even managers?

    f. To what extent should trade unions be involved in the work of participative bodies below Board level?

33. Experience on the Continent of Europe suggests that if 'participation', in the sense of genuine joint decision-making, is to have any chance of success, then the following conditions need to be observed:

    a. employee involvement in decision-making should take place at plant-level as well as at Board level;

    b. elections for employee representatives at any level should be open to all permanent, full-time employees, regardless of position or trade union membership;

    c. candidates for such elections should be representative of all main sections of the organization below Board level, ie manager, supervisors, white-collar and manual workers;

    d. the day-to-day management of the organization should be entrusted to professional managers, who are responsible to the Board;

    e. participation machinery should be kept separate from negotiating machinery, even though union representatives (ie shop stewards) may be active members in both;

    f. the scope of topics which are to be the subject of shared or joint decision-making needs to be sufficiently important to retain the interests of the employee representatives;

    g. lastly, an extensive programme of training of employee representatives should be carried out.

## SUMMARY

34. Employee relations is primarily concerned with the regulation of relationships between employers on the one hand, and employees on the other. These relationships involve other parties such as trade unions, employers' associations, Government representatives and representatives of the law. Employee relations is as concerned with the individual relationship between employer and employee, as it is with collective relationships between them.

35. Employee relations is an area of work relationships where conflicting points of view are inevitable. All the major parties involved – managers, employees and representatives of third parties – have their differing perspectives about the relationships. Managers, for example can approach their role in at least three different ways:

    a. from a unitary perspective ie the one, happy family; or

    b. from a pluralistic perspective ie accepting the existence of differing interests; or

    c. from a confrontation perspective ie 'them and us.'

36. In the United Kingdom the pluralistic approach is the most usual one in practice. A key feature of this approach is the importance of rules to enable conflict to be contained within manageable bounds. These rules include company rules, union rules, collective agreements, custom and practice, the law, and, finally, codes of practice. Where collective bargaining is carried out, the most important source of rules is the procedural agreement, which lays down the framework of behaviour between the parties. Procedural agreements differ from substantive agreements, which are agreements about the outcomes of collective bargaining ie changes in terms and conditions of employment.

37. Collective bargaining, ie the making of collective agreements, is carried out by employers and trade unions. In Britain there are numerous such unions in several different categories. These are principally as follows: craft, industrial and general unions (manual employees); open and closed (white-collar unions); managerial/professional unions; staff associations. Current membership of trade unions in Britain is running at about 50% of the working population. Most unions are affiliated to the Trades Union Congress, which acts as a focus for trade union issues on a national scale.

38. The employers' side of collective bargaining is conducted not only by individual employers, but also by employers' associations,

who provide employee relations services to their member organizations. They have to be distinguished from trade associations which are specifically charged with trade and commercial matters, and not employee affairs.

39.  Workplace representatives are an important feature of British trade unionism. These are the unpaid officers of the union, who are elected by their members to represent them in local negotiations and consultations with management. Representatives are most frequently known as 'shop stewards' or 'union representatives' or, in printing, as 'Fathers-of-the-Chapel.' Workplace representatives deal with a wide range of shop-floor issues, and generally play a major role in maintaining industrial peace.

40.  Two particularly important aspects of employee relations are disciplinary and grievance procedures. In the case of the former, the objective should be to correct unsatisfactory behaviour rather than punish it. A good disciplinary procedure should be clearly stated, in writing, and should enable employees to feel assured of fairness and consistency of treatment if ever they should become subject to the procedure. Grievance procedures should provide a speedy means by which employees can seek redress for any grievances they may have at work. A good procedure aims to achieve a solution to a grievance as near to the point of origin as possible, and where this is not possible, it aims to process the grievance without delay to a higher level in the management chain. In a grievance situation, the manager or supervisor concerned should aim to establish the facts relating to the grievance, and eventually reach a mutually acceptable solution.

41.  'Employee participation' is an expression with several, often contrasting, meanings such as improved consultation with employees, job enrichment, a participative management style, or extended collective bargaining, works councils, workers on the Board and workers' control of industry. The meaning that probably commands the greatest support is one which agrees that 'participation' is about the sharing of decision-making between management and employees, ie it is considerably more than mere consultation, but is considerably less than anything as radical as workers' control. Implementing participation in this form requires consideration of questions relating to the level at which participation should be developed, to the subject-matter of shared decision-making, to the introduction of a two-tier Board, to the proportion of employee-directors, to the extent of the franchise for elections, and, finally, to the degree of involvement of trade unions in the work of participative bodies.

# 49

# LEGAL ASPECTS OF EMPLOYMENT

## INTRODUCTION

1.   There are very few direct questions about employment law in the Management papers of the principal professional bodies. Nevertheless, some understanding of the current legal situation relating to employment is clearly implied in many of the questions relating to personnel management in general, and to specific issues such as discipline, in particular. This chapter sets out to provide a brief guide to employment law looked at from the point of view of a practising manager.

2.   The chapter begins with a short consideration of the nature of employment, and then considers some of the most important statutes currently affecting the employment scene in Britain. The statutes will be analysed in terms of:

   a.   individual rights at work,

   b.   trade union (ie collective) rights,

   c.   discrimination at work.

## EMPLOYMENT

3.   A person employed by an organization is either employed under a *contract of service*, as an employee, or under a *contract for services*, as an independent contractor. It is only the former which is referred to as the contract of employment. The distinction is important because legal rights granted to individuals under current legislation, such as the right not to be unfairly dismissed, are only applicable to employees, and not to independent contractors.

4.   Several legal cases have helped to clarify what is, and what is not, a contract of employment. At the present time there are three main tests applied by the Courts to establish whether a contract of employment exists in a given situation. These are as follows:

   i.   The control test  – this asks where the control lies in the situation; if the individual is told *what* to do and how to do it, he is an employee; if not, then he is an independent contractor;

ii.   The organization test – this asks whether the individual is integrated into the organization; if he is, then he is an employee; if not, he is an independent contractor;

iii.   The multiple test – this takes several circumstantial factors into account as well as both the control and organization factors; this is the most comprehensive test to date; where an individual appears, in all the circumstances, to be carrying out the role of an employee, then he is an employee; where there is sufficient doubt about the role being performed, it is more likely that he is an independent contractor.

5.   As mentioned above, the difference is important. For example if a person is an employee, his employer is liable vicariously for any civil wrongs he himself may commit in the course of his employment, whereas an employer bears no such responsibility in respect of independent contractors. Another reason why the difference is important is that only *employees* are granted certain rights or protection in recent legislation, such as rights to minimum periods of notice, and to a written statement of the main terms and conditions of employment, and to protection such as the right not to be unfairly dismissed, and the right to pursue trade union activities without being penalised. Another distinction between employees and independent contractors is made in matters relating to benefits. For example only *employees* are permitted to claim unemployment benefit and industrial injuries benefit.

6.   Where an individual *is* employed under a contract of employment this need not necessarily be written, except in the case of an apprenticeship. Most employment contracts are in fact a mixture of written and unwritten terms, and of express and implied conditions. The written elements of the contract can be contained in a formal document, in a letter of appointment and in the statement of main terms of employment required by statute (Employment Protection (Consolidation) Act, 1978); these written terms constitute the express conditions of the contract. The unwritten, and therefore implied, terms of the contract arise from the common law duties of the parties, from custom and practice in the organization, and from the operation of collective agreements.

Variations to a contract should normally be subject to a period of notice not less than that to which the employee is entitled by virtue of his length of service, unless, of course, the employee agrees to a shorter period.

7.   The common law duties of the respective parties can be summarised briefly as follows:

The Employer has an obligation to:
  a. pay wages,
  b. provide work (but only for those who are paid by results eg salesmen on commission),
  c. take reasonable care of the employee,
  d. indemnify the employee where he necessarily incurs expenses and liabilities in the performance of his duties,
  e. treat the employee with courtesy,

The Employee has an obligation to:
  a. render a personal service, and be willing and able to do so,
  b. take reasonable care in the performance of his duties,
  c. obey reasonable and lawful instructions from his employer,
  d. act in good faith towards the employer eg not to work for two employers at one and the same time,
  e. not to impede his employer's business,

As can be seen from the above lists, the common law duties of the parties to each other are set out very generally, and have to be related to the circumstances of each situation in order, for example, to assess what is reasonable. Where statute law and common law appear to conflict, then it is the statute which prevails. Where aspects of a contract are not clear, and where no statutory rule applies, then the common law rules are applied.

## EMPLOYMENT LEGISLATION – INDIVIDUAL RIGHTS

8.     Until the last decade or so, employment legislation was directed at *collective* rights arising out of the bargaining between employers and trade unions, and was contained principally in a number of Trade Union Acts passed between 1871 and 1927. It was not until the 1960's that statutes dealing with individual rights began to appear on the scene. The trend towards individual rights received a massive boost in 1971, with the passing of the Industrial Relations Act, and since that time numerous statutes defining individual rights have been passed. These statutes have covered issues such as redundancy payments, notice periods, unfair dismissal and maternity rights. In 1978, all these individual rights were assembled, with a few minor changes, under the Employment Protection (Consolidation) Act. This Act is mainly concerned with the legal situation of persons who are *not* in work – those for example who are dismissed, redundant or on maternity leave. So far as protection *in* work is concerned, the law has little

involvement outside the common law duties referred to earlier, and the main protection is generally provided by means of collective agreements.

9.   One recent development in individual rights is to grant individual employees greater protection against arbitrary action taken by trade unions. The relevant provisions are contained in the Employment Acts, 1980, 1982 and 1988, and in the Trade Union Act, 1984. These provisions and those arising from the Employment Protection (Consolidation) Act, 1978, will be outlined in the following paragraphs.

## WRITTEN PARTICULARS OF EMPLOYMENT

10. The opening sections of the Employment Protection (Consolidation) Act, 1978 deal with particulars of terms of employment, especially the requirement on employers to provide a written statement of specified particulars of employment. These particulars should include the following:

a.  the scale or rate of remuneration, or the method of calculating remuneration (eg piece-rates, over-time rates etc),

b.  the intervals at which remuneration is paid, ie weekly, monthly etc,

c.  the hours of work,

d.  holiday entitlement, holiday pay, sickness arrangements and sick pay, pensions arrangements,

e.  the length of notice to be given on either side,

f.  the title of the job the employee is employed to do,

g.  the disciplinary rules which apply to the employee, or a reference to a reasonably accessible document (eg a Company handbook) which specifies the disciplinary rules and procedure,

h.  the grievance procedure applicable to the employee.

The above particulars have to be given to the employee within 13 weeks of the commencement of his employment. These terms originated in the Contracts of Employment Act, 1972, a piece of legislation with a misleading title since only part of the contract is represented by the details required in the written statement. The intention of the legislation is to provide employees with a written statement of their main terms of employment, and not to provide them with a written contract.

## RIGHT TO MINIMUM PERIOD OF NOTICE

11. The EPCA, 1978, as amended by the Employment Act, 1982, gives employees the right to a minimum period of notice of termination of employment. Currently, these minima are as follows:

- at least one weeks' notice if employed for between one month and two years
- at least two weeks' if employed for two years
- one additional weeks' notice for each further complete year of service up to a maximum of twelve weeks' notice

These rights may be extended or waived by agreement, and an employer may offer pay in lieu of notice. Contracts can, of course, be terminated without notice, if the conduct of either parties justifies it (see unfair dismissal notes below).

## REDUNDANCY PAYMENTS

12. The provisions in the Consolidation Act relating to redundancy originated in the Redundancy Payments Act, 1965. The current position is that an employee, with at least two years continuous service with an employer, is entitled to a redundancy payment from the latter, if his services are no longer required as a result of the cessation or diminution of the business at the place where he works. This right does not apply to those over the normal retiring age at the time of the redundancy.

13. The provisions for redundancy pay represent the minimum standard, and many organizations pay substantially more mainly as a result of collective agreements. The legal minima are as follows:

- For each year of service from age 41

..... *1½ weeks' pay* (up to 65 for a man / 60 for a woman)

- For each year of service from age 22 to age 40

..... *1 weeks' pay*

- For each year of service from age 18 to age 21

..... *½ weeks' pay*

The maximum number of weeks' pay that can be claimed is 30 weeks, and there is a statutory limit on weekly pay (currently £155 a week).

## RIGHT NOT TO BE UNFAIRLY DISMISSED

14. Since 1971, the concept of unfair dismissal has probably been the most celebrated aspect of labour law. It was introduced by the

Industrial Relations Act, 1971, and has remained firmly entrenched in subsequent legislation. It now forms an integral part of the Consolidation Act. Its main provisions are set out below. They commence as follows:

> ' ... every employee shall have the right not to be unfairly dismissed by his employer.'

15.  Dismissal occurs when an employee has had his contract of employment terminated by his employer, with or without notice; it also refers to the non-renewal of a fixed term contract; and it applies in a situation when, because of the employer's conduct, the employee himself terminates the contract, with or without notice, in circumstances where he is entitled to terminate it without notices (known as 'constructive dismissal'); finally, dismissal also applies in the case of a woman employee who is not permitted to return to work after maternity leave (provided she has exercised her rights concerning her return, ie, notification etc, and provided she has not been employed by a firm employing less than 5 employees).

16.  A dismissal may be justified on the following grounds:
- for reasons of the capability or qualifications of the employee
- for reasons relating to the employee's conduct
- redundancy
- where continuation of the employment would contravene a legal duty or restriction
- some other substantial reason which could justify dismissal

17.  A dismissal for reasons of lack of capability usually revolves around questions of ill-health or incompetence, and the Courts will invariably want to know whether other, more suitable, work has been offered to an employee in one of these situations, for, even if the grounds for dismissal are considered as fair, the employer must still show that it was reasonable to dismiss in the circumstances. A dismissal for reasons of (mis) conduct is very much an issue where 'reasonableness' must be taken into account. The ACAS Code on this topic (see Chapter 48) provides useful guidance as to how misconduct should be dealt with. It especially advises against dismissal for a first offence, except in cases of gross misconduct. What constitutes 'reasonable behaviour' by the employer depends on how tribunals interpret the difference between 'misconduct', 'repeated misconduct' and 'gross misconduct'; it also depends on what is stated in Company rule-books, how previous cases have been dealt with by the Company, and the extent to which the

ACAS Code has been adhered to. A dismissal on the grounds of redundancy requires the employer to show that there is no longer any need for that job in the organization. The job becomes redundant and the employee is dismissed—this at least is the logic of the situation. Such a dismissal can be unfair, however, if the employee is unfairly selected for redundancy in a situation where some jobs are redundant, but other similar jobs are not.

18. The grounds on which a dismissal will usually considered to be *unfair* have been extended by the Employment Acts, 1980, 1982 and 1988 and can be summarised as follows:

- if the employee was dismissed solely or mainly for reasons of pregnancy
- if dismissal was on grounds of taking part in trade union activities
- if the dismissal is for non-membership of a trade union
- where the dismissal was on grounds of redundancy, but where usual selection-for-redundancy procedures were not followed, and/or where the employer failed to provide adequate warning or consider providing alternative employment
- where dismissal took place during an industrial dispute, but where other employees in the dispute were treated differently

It is up to the individual employee to show that he was dismissed, but if he is able to do so, then the employer must show that the reason for the dismissal was an admissible reasons (see para. 16).

19. The remedies for unfair dismissal are as follows: (a) an award for compensation, (b) reinstatement (ie in the employee's original post), (c) re-engagement (ie in some other post).

Most applications relating to unfair dismissal do not reach a tribunal for decision. About two-thirds are conciliated ie withdrawn or settled out of court. Of the one-third which do reach a tribunal, the results are generally as follows:

- about two-thirds are dismissed
- a little over ten percent are upheld
- the remainder are referred back for further conciliation The conclusion to all this is that, despite the apparent legal safeguards against dismissal, the employee continues to be extremely vulnerable to the unilateral termination of the employment contract by his employer.

## MATERNITY RIGHTS

20. Maternity rights included in the Consolidation Act stem directly from the Employment Protection Act, 1975, which was the first British attempt to make provisions for women employees who are pregnant, who wish to carry on working during their pregnancy and who wish to exercise the right to return to their work after their confinement. The basic rights are as follows:

a. an employee who is absent from work on the grounds of her pregnancy or confinement is entitled to maternity pay for up to six weeks of her absence, and is entitled to return to work, subject to a number of conditions (mainly concerned with the woman's length of service and notification to the employer of her intentions to leave, seek re-employment etc);

b. an employee who is dismissed on the grounds of her pregnancy is *automatically* considered to be unfairly dismissed unless
   i. she was incapable of adequately doing her work as a result of her pregnancy, or
   ii. she would be contravening another law (possibly some Health and Safety at Work provision).

Recently, the Employment Act, 1980, added a further right, that of paid time off work to attend for ante-natal care.

## DISCRIMINATION AT WORK

21. Discrimination, in the sense of deciding, for example, which of two or more individuals should be appointed to a post, or allocated to certain work, or recommended for a merit award, is part and parcel of every manager's duties. Discrimination implies selection between alternatives, and this is an important feature of every managerial job. In recent years, the word 'discrimination' has come to have a pejorative meaning which implies that discrimination is always unfair. It is important to recognise, therefore, that the law on discrimination is concerned with *arbitrary* or *unfair* discrimination only. In Britain, the statutes dealing with such discrimination are basically the Equal Pay Act, 1970, the Sex Discrimination Act, 1975 and the Race Relations Act, 1976. Between them these statutes prohibit discrimination on the grounds of sex, marital status, colour, race, nationality, ethnic or national origin. In other words, if a person is refused a job, and can show that he or she has been treated less favourably than other applicants by reason of sex, race or marital status, then there is a

prima facie case against the employer concerned of unfair discrimination.

22.  The remedies which can be sought under these laws are:
    a.  complaints to a tribunal by individuals, usually followed by an award for compensation, if successful and
    b.  notices of 'non-discrimination' served by the relevant Commission (Equal Opportunities Commission or Commission for Racial Equality), which may be enforced by injunction through the County Courts, if ignored by an employer.

23.  The Equal Pay Act, 1970 applies to all the main contractual terms and conditions of employment, not just pay. It applies as much to men as to women, although its effect has been primarily to improve the relative position of women at work. The Act establishes the right of an individual woman (man) to equal treatment in respect of the terms of her (his) contract of employment when employed
    i.    on work of the same or broadly similar nature to that of a man (woman), and
    ii.   in a job, which although different from that of a man (woman) has been rated as equivalent under job evaluation.
    iii.  on work of equal value to that of a man (woman) in the same employment in terms of the demands made (this amendment was brought into effect on 1 January 1984)

The implications of item iii are firstly, that women (or men) who feel that the demands of their job are equal in value to other jobs in the organization may claim equal pay, and secondly, that any employer intending to rebut such a claim will have to utilise an analytical method of job evaluation, since only such methods are considered as 'proper' job evaluation.

It is worth noting that 'equal pay' does not mean the same as 'identical pay', which can depend on many other factors such as age, length of service and performance. What is important is that the same terms or opportunities apply regardless of sex.

24.  The Sex Discrimination Act, 1975 and the Race Relations Act, 1976 can be considered in tandem, since the latter is shaped on the former. Whereas the Equal Pay Act is concerned with the contractual terms of employment (pay, hours, holidays etc), these two Acts are concerned with the context of the employment (promotion, training etc). The Acts define two kinds of discrimination: *direct* discrimination and *indirect* discrimination. The former occurs in situations where an employer treats a person

less favourably than others on the grounds of sex, marital status or race. The latter occurs where the effect of a condition of employment is discriminatory, even though on the surface it appears to apply equally to all employees. For example, in a leading case on sex discrimination, it was held that a Civil Service requirement, that applicants for a post should be under 28 years of age, operated indirectly against women, because in practice fewer of them would be able to meet this requirement than men. It is important to notice that whereas direct discrimination is intentional, indirect discrimination is usually not so.

25. Each of the two Acts under consideration makes exceptions to general rules. So, for example, in the Race Relations Act, it is not unlawful for a Chinese restaurant to recruit only Chinese waiters! In a similar way, under the Sex Discrimination Act, it is not unlawful to discriminate in favour of women in respect of pregnancy or childbirth, nor to discriminate on grounds of 'genuine occupational qualification' eg where acting or modelling calls for men (or women) for reasons of physiology or credibility!

26. The general intention behind the anti-discrimination laws is to create a framework which can deal with the worst abuses of employers, but without being particularly punitive, and which can educate employers to adopt a more genuinely fair approach to those who are liable to be discriminated against unfairly because they are women, or married, or racially distinctive.

## RIGHTS TO TIME OFF WORK

27. Employees have a number of rights to time off work to fulfil particular duties or tasks. Most of these rights, but not all, carry with them the right to receive payment during their absence. The basic rights are as follows:

- the right to paid time off to look for another job when under notice of redundancy
- the right to paid time off to pursue trade union duties/ receive training (applies only to union officials of recognised trade unions) (eg shop stewards, safety representatives etc)
- the right to agreed (unpaid) time off for ordinary union members to participate in union activities
- the right to reasonable time off to undertake certain public duties (eg as magistrates, members of local authorities etc)
- the right to paid time off work to undertake duties or receive training as a safety representative
- the right to have reasonable time off (paid) to receive antenatal care

## INDUSTRIAL TRIBUNALS

28. Industrial tribunals were established, originally, under the Industrial Training Act, 1964 to determine appeals by employers against levies imposed on them by Industrial Training Boards. Since then their role has been increased by subsequent legislation, in particular the Industrial Relations Act, 1971 and the Acts that replaced it.

29. The tribunals were set up to provide a cheaper and less complex approach to legal issues. Each tribunal is made up of a Chairman (who has to be legally – qualified) and two other persons (usually representing an employer and employee viewpoint respectively). The procedures are considerably less formal than in other courts of law, and neither side need necessarily be represented by a lawyer. An individual bringing a case before a tribunal does not incur court costs, as he will do in other courts.

30. The jurisdiction of industrial tribunals now includes a whole range of items under the label of 'employment protection'. In particular, this jurisdiction extends to claims for unfair dismissal and complaints relating to maternity provisions, to questions of equal opportunity and to unfair discrimination on grounds of race.

## EMPLOYMENT APPEAL TRIBUNAL

31. Appeals from industrial tribunals on a 'point of law' are made to the Employment Appeal Tribunal (EAT). The EAT is presided over by a High court judge, who is supported by two lay-members, one representing employers and the other trade unions. Further appeal lies to the Court of Appeal and, ultimately, to the House of Lords.

## EMPLOYMENT LEGISLATION – COLLECTIVE ISSUES

32. The next few paragraphs deal with what is essentially trade union law, that is to say with the collective issues arising from the purpose and activities of trade unions in their regulation of relationships with employers and employers' associations. In the last ten years or so, considerable attention has been focussed on the role and power of trade unions by successive Governments. In 1971, the Industrial Relations Act attempted to introduce some radical changes into British industrial relations law. Most of these changes were repealed by the Trade Union and Labour Relations Act, 1974 (TULRA) and its Amendment Act of 1976. At the present time, these two TULRA statutes from the basis of trade

union law in Britain. However, in the present decade collective activities of trade unions and employers have been qualified by the Employment Acts, 1980 and 1982, and the Trade Union Act, 1984. The general effect of these new pieces of legislation is (a) to place restrictions on certain trade union activities, such as strikes and membership recruitment, and (b) to strengthen the ability of individual employees to resist certain collective pressures exerted by trade unions. The Employment Act, 1975, also contains some measures affecting collective issues. The essential features of trade union law will be looked at briefly statute by statute, commencing, with TULRA.

33. Trade Union and Labour Relations Act, 1974. There are several important legal definitions contained in this Act. Some of the most important are as follows:

a. Definition of a trade union: '................. 'trade union' means an organization .............. which either (a) consists wholly or mainly of workers of one or more descriptions and is an organization whose principal purposes include the regulation of relationships between workers ...... and employers or employers' associations; or (b) consists wholly or mainly of (1) constituent or affiliated organizations which fulfil the conditions specified above ...... or (2) representatives of such ......organizations.'

b. Definition of 'independent trade union': ' .... means a trade union which (a) is not under the domination or control of any employer .... and (b) is not liable to interference by an employer ....' Under the Employment Protection Act, 1975, a Certification Officer (similar to the former Chief Registrar of Trade Unions) is responsible for examining unions with the object of granting them, or of with-holding, a certificate of independence. The Certification Officer is also responsible for the custody of all trade union documents (annual reports, accounts etc) submitted in accordance with various trade union laws.

c. Definition of a closed shop (union membership agreement): 'Union membership agreement' means an agreement or arrangement which –

   i. is made by or on behalf of .... one or more independent trade unions and one or more employers or employers' associations; and

   ii. relates to employees of an identifiable class; and

     iii.  has the effect in practice of requiring the employees for the time being .............to be or become a member of the union or one of the unions which .... are parties to the agreement or arrangement .... ' This definition is the current one, that is as amended by the TULRA Amendment Act, 1976.

  d. Definition of 'trade dispute': This has been amended by E Act, 1982, so as to narrow the interpretation of a dispute. In effect the current legal position is that (i) the dispute must be between employers and their *own* employees, and (ii) must be wholly or mainly about terms and conditions of employment (eg pay, allocation of work, discipline, trade union membership etc). The importance of the definition lies in the protection against civil actions granted to trade unions in furtherance of a trade dispute. It should be noted that political motives are not included in the definition, and therefore not given the protection just referred to.

## EMPLOYMENT PROTECTION ACT, 1975

34.  Employment Protection Act, 1975. Most of this Act has either been repealed or transferred to the Consolidation Act 1978. However some significant elements still remain. Briefly these are as follows:

  a. The establishment of ACAS: The Advisory, Conciliation and Arbitration Service is the central body for promoting improved industrial relations. ACAS is an independent organization working under the direction of a Council comprising a Chairman and nine members – three CBI (Confederation of British Industry) nominees, representing employers, three TUC (Trades Union Congress) nominees, representing the unions, and three independent members. The principal functions of ACAS are:

- to conciliate in trade disputes,
- to refer disputed matters to arbitration,
- to refer disputes to mediation,
- to provide advice to employers and trade, unions on employee relations matters,
- to issue Codes of Practice,
- to conduct inquiries into any aspect of industrial relations,

In relation to the above, *conciliation* means helping the disputants to reach a mutually acceptable agreement; *arbitration* means making the decision for the disputants; *mediation* means making formal proposals to the disputants as the basis for an eventual settlement (ie it is a kind of 'half-way house' means between the other two options). As a general rule, ACAS insists that conciliation shall always be attempted before other measures.

b. Disclosure of information to trade unions: the Act imposes a general duty on employers to disclose to independent trade unions, on request, information which is important for the smooth-running of collective bargaining; an ACAS Code suggests that such information should include details of pay and benefits, conditions of service, manpower plans, financial results etc; there are several restrictions on the duty to disclose, for example the employer is not obliged to disclose information against the interests of national security or information obtained in confidence; also there must be a reasonable relationship between the information sought by the union(s) and the effort required by the employer to obtain it.

c. Procedure for handling redundancies: the *individual's* rights in relation to redundancy were considered briefly in paragraphs 11-13 above; the rights of trade unions to be warned of, and consulted about, impending redundancies are contained in the Employment Protection Act. Where an employer proposes to dismiss employees as redundant in a situation where an independent trade union is recognised, he is obliged to consult with trade union representatives (eg shop stewards as well as full-time union officials); this consultation has to begin at least 90 days before any dismissals in cases where 100 or more redundancies are planned within a period of 90 days, and at least 60 days before any dismissals involving 10 or more employees within a period of 30 days; for the purposes of this consultation, the employer is obliged to disclose the following information in writing: the reasons for the proposals, the numbers and descriptions of employees concerned, the proposed method of selecting employees for redundancy, the period over which the dismissals are to take place, and certain other relevant information; if the above procedure is not carried out, the trade union(s) concerned may complain to an industrial tribunal, which, if the complaint is upheld will make a 'protective award' in respect of the employees involved – this requires the employer to pay remuneration to the employees during a protected period on the basis of a week's pay for each week of the period.

## LEGAL IMMUNITIES FOR TRADE UNIONS

35. The reason why the legal definition of a 'trade dispute' is so important to trade unions is that, so long as certain conditions are fulfilled, the law will provide protection against civil actions for those organizing strike action or other forms of industrial action on behalf of a trade union in furtherance of a trade dispute. If immunity was *not* provided, the officials concerned would be liable to civil action for inducing employees to break their contracts of employment by going on strike, for example. In the 1970's in Britain, the legal immunities provided for trade unions (in particular) and their officials were extremely wide-ranging. In the current decade, these immunities have been closely-restricted. Now, if a union or an official organizes industrial action which interferes with contracts, including the employer's contracts with his customers, there will only be immunity from civil action if the following conditions apply:

1. there is a trade dispute, and the action is in furtherance of that dispute

2. the trade union concerned has previously held a secret ballot of members, and a majority have agreed to support the action

3. the action does not constitute secondary action or lead to secondary picketing (ie the action does not involve an employer who is not a party to a trade dispute)

4. the action is not designed to prevent employers from employing non-union labour

36. Where immunity is not provided, or where it does not apply (eg in the case of other civil wrongs committed by strikers), the persons who have suffered loss as a result may sue the union or the officials concerned for damages. The damages that may be awarded are limited by the current legislation (Employment Act, 1982), but could amount to £250,000 for a union with more than 100,000 members. Other action that may be taken is for persons affected to seek an injunction (an order restraining somebody from doing something) from the courts. If an injunction is disobeyed, the union concerned may be declared to be in contempt of court and face heavy fines. If the fines are not paid, as happened in the case of the Miners' dispute 1984–5, then the union's funds may be liable to seizure by the courts. The law, therefore, is playing an increasing role in disputes. However, as ACAS (1985) puts it in its Annual Report for 1984:

'Changes in the law, and the growing willingness of employers, trade unions and individual workers to consider... applying to the courts in situations where a dispute has arisen may... encourage the parties to exercise greater caution in the conduct of industrial action.'

ACAS still considers that 'industrial relations in general continue to rely on the voluntary efforts and cooperation of all those involved'.

## PICKETING

37. Picketing is a tactic that has been employed by trade unions for a century or more. Basically it consists of an attempt to enforce a strike and its effects by placing union members at the gates of the employer's premises in order to persuade fellow employees and others (e. g. suppliers' employees) not to cross the picket line and go into work. There has never been any legal right to picket, but the practice has not been considered as unlawful in the pursuit of a trade dispute, so long as the picketing did not cause a breach of the peace. Whereas most picketing has been conducted in a peaceful manner, there have been a few notorious case in recent years of mass picketing involving considerable violence to persons and damage to property.

38. An indication of the change in the law can be judged by comparing the definition of picketing contained in the Trade Union & Labour Relations Act, 1974 (TULRA) with the current definition contained in the Employment Act, 1980. The TULRA definition can be summarised as follows:

'It shall be lawful for one or more persons in contemplation or furtherance of a trade dispute to attend at or near

a. a place where another person works or carries on business; or

b. any other place where another person happens to be, not being a place where he resides, for the purposes only of peacefully obtaining or communicating information, or peacefully persuading any person to work or abstain from working.'

(TULRA, S.15)

39. This definition permits picketing to be carried on at several possible sites, the only exception is at an individual's private house. Note that the picketing is only lawful if in connection with a trade dispute and if it is carried out peacefully.

491

The new definition is more restrictive in that immunity will only be granted to a person picketing near or at his own place of work. This means that if a group of pickets travel from one site to another in order to boost a picket line, they may be liable to civil actions being taken against them. There are exceptions to the general rule for special cases, such as trade union officials, and employees who have no normal place of work.

40. The new law has been supported by a Code of Practice on Picketing (1980), which though not binding in its own right may be taken into account by the courts when considering actions taken against pickets or their union. Among its guidelines the Code includes:

- organizers should ensure that in general the number of pickets does not exceed six at any entrance to a workplace
- an experienced person, preferably a trade union official should be in charge of the picket line
- pickets should be properly identified by means of badges or armbands
- organizers should maintain close contact with the police during the picketing
- union members who cross a picket line should not have disciplinary action taken against them by the union
- essential supplies and services (eg to hospitals, schools and public health etc) should not be impeded

## BALLOTS

41. The recent legislation has placed considerable emphasis on the necessity for trade unions to ballot their members on key issues such as industrial action, union membership and election of officials. The Employment Act, 1980, provides for public funds to be made available to trade unions, via the Certification Officer, for the conduct of postal ballots for specified purposes. Also, where a ballot takes place at work, and where more than 20 persons are employed, the employer is under an obligation, if the union so requests, to provide a place for the ballot to be held.

42. The Trade Union Act 1984, is especially concerned with ballots. The focus of its attentions is mainly as follows:

a. strike ballots;

b. election of senior officials;

c. political funds.

**43.** The Act aims to ensure that all trade unions follow the practice of organizing a secret ballot of their members when they wish to test the degree of support for strike action. The question on the ballot paper must be put so that it merely requires a 'Yes' or 'No' answer from the respondent. Thus there will be an end to the 'show-of-hands' type of ballot, which has been the normal procedure in many unions.

**44.** The Act also extends the balloting procedure to the election of key union officials, and especially the national executives. Unions must now make arrangements to organize a national ballot of their members when such posts are to be filled. Further regulations governing the election of senior officers have been introduced by the Employment Act 1988. The most important is the requirement to 'hold a secret postal ballot of members'. This Act also gives individual union members greater power to complain if they think a ballot has not been conducted properly or fairly.

**45.** The Trade Union Act 1984 also introduces certain.changes to the Trade Union Act, 1913, concerning the political activities of unions. The law has been amended so as to include a wider range of activities in the definition of what is 'political', and which therefore must be met out of the political fund of a union and not out of its general funds. Additionally, unions are now required to ballot their members every 10 years on whether to continue with their political fund.

**46.** The overall effect of the Act is to strengthen the role of the individual members in a union by ensuring that the leadership consult with them individually on all major issues.

## SECTION SUMMARY – PERSONNEL MANAGEMENT

**1.** The role of the specialist function of Personnel was examined in Chapter 42. The key features of the role of Personnel are: the formulation of personnel policies, the implementation of agreed policies, the provision of adequate personnel services and the provision of advice and assistance in relation to organizational change.

**2.** The particular aspects of Personnel Management dealt with in the Section (Chapters 43 - 49) were as follows:

**Recruitment and Selection:** this is the activity which ensures that the organization has the skills and the supporting procedures to enable it to meet its need for sufficient and suitable staff at all levels.

**Training and Development:** this activity is designed to ensure that the organization has a competent and skilled workforce to meet present needs, and is taking steps to ensure that fresh skills and knowledge are being developed to meet future needs; the basis of this activity is systematic training involving the establishment of a policy, the setting up of a training organization, the analysis of training and development needs, the planning and execution of training, and, finally, the evaluation of training and development activities.

**Job Evaluation:** this activity enables the organization to develop a pay structure based on the systematic comparison of jobs, which is made either between whole jobs or between common job factors.

**Employee Relations:** this activity is undertaken in order to ensure harmonious and productive relationships between the organization and its employees; it includes issues such as employee motivation, joint consultation, fair treatment of individuals, and collective bargaining between employers and employee representatives.

**Legal aspects of Employment:** the Personnel department has an important role in deciding how the organization shall meet its numerous legal obligations to its employees; in addition to the basic contract of employment that exists between each employee and his employer, there are several important Acts of Parliament which have to be implemented; these include legislation on individual rights, on collectives issues and on discrimination at work.

## QUESTIONS FOR DISCUSSION/HOMEWORK

*1.* '*The role of the Personnel department is mainly to provide routine personnel services to line managers.' Discuss this assertion.*

*2. Devise a personnel classification plan of your own, but based on the Seven-Point Plan. Under each heading write one question you might ask a potential applicant for a job of your choice.*

*3. In a selection interview, what are the marks of an effective interviewer?*

*4. Using your own words, distinguish between the terms 'training' and 'development'.*

*5. What sources of information are likely to prove the most fruitful for a person undertaking a training needs analysis in an office environment?*

*6. What are the essential features of an analytical method of job evaluation?*

**7.** How might **managers** view employee relations in a different light from other employees in the same organization?

**8.** What rules operate at the place of work? Comment on the most important of these.

**9.** Why is the role of the workplace representative, or shop steward, important in employee relations?

**10.** In what ways in the past decade has legislation granted additional rights to employees? Do you see any groups who may appear to have benefitted more than others from these additions?

**11.** What are the principal changes that have taken place in trade union immunities since the Trade Union & Labour Relations Act, 1974?

## EXAMINATION QUESTIONS – PERSONNEL MANAGEMENT
*The following are a cross-section of questions about various aspects of Personnel Management which have been asked during the last three years (19 79 onwards). Suggested answers are given in Appendix 2.*

*EQ35 Comment on the usefulness of the Seven-Point Plan as a framework for the preparation of person specifications in the selection process To what extent are alternative frameworks available, and how do they compare with the Seven-Point Plan?*

*(ICSA PPP)*

*EQ36 Identify the essential features of. a. an ideal disciplinary procedure; b. an ideal grievance procedure. Evaluate the role of each in industrial conflict.*

*(IOB Nature of Management)*

*EQ37 What is the difference between 'training' and 'development'? To what extent can these processes occur through the medium of courses?*

*(ICSA PPP)*

*EQ38 Discuss the possible ways in which employees can participate in decision-making at work.*

*(ACCA Business Management)*

*EQ39 What do you understand by the term 'collective bargaining'? How far may it be considered a problem solving, decision-making process?*

*(IOB Human Aspects of Management)*

# 1

# EXAMINATION TECHNIQUE

## INTRODUCTION

1.   It is rarely easy to write a good narrative answer to an examination question. This is particularly true in the field of Management studies where the *quality* of your discussion of a topic is as important, if not more important, than the *quantity* of facts you can raise to support your arguments. It is also worth recognising that in most cases there is no one correct answer. The important thing for you is to convince the examiner of the reasonableness of your own particular solution.

2.   Nevertheless, it is possible with practice to develop a technique to enable you to improve the way *you* tackle the more popular questions that occur in examinations.

3.   Part of the aim of this Manual is to help you with both the technique and the practice.

## AT THE START OF THE EXAMINATION

4.   Read the instructions on the paper and follow them. Make quite sure how many questions you must answer.

5.   Mark off the questions that seem to be the easiest ie those which trigger off plenty of ideas the moment you look at them.

6.   Make an appropriate allocation of time for each question. Then select your first question.

## TACKLING THE QUESTIONS

7.   Read each question carefully. It will be worth it! Ask yourself, 'Is there more than one question?' 'What is the examiner getting at?' 'What issues are raised by the question?'

8.   Now make a rough answer plan, jotting down key points that come to mind, and rearranging them into some kind of order. This will take perhaps five minutes, but will enable you to proceed with confidence to write a satisfactory answer. If the question is set out in a particular sequence, answer it in the same sequence.

9.   Where opinion or comment is asked for by the examiner, don't be afraid to say what you think, *so long* as you can point to

some evidence or other source of opinion to back up your assertions.

10. Remember that neat writing and tidy layout always create a good impression with examiners. It helps them in their task, and may earn you an extra mark or two.

11. Your final task is to read quickly through your answer and make any amendments or last-minute additions.

## TOWARDS THE END OF THE EXAMINATION

12. Make sure you have moved on to your final question even if the previous one is incomplete. You will tend to earn more marks at the beginning of an answer than towards the end, so it is wise to make a start, however brief. If you are desperately short of time (as a result of bad planning) then write down brief notes or headings for the examiner.

13. If you do have time to spare at the end of the examination, it is worth looking to see if you can add any further relevant points to your completed answers.

## AT THE END OF THE EXAMINATION

14. Check that your answer sheets are correctly numbered and collated.

## FINAL NOTES

15. The above techniques can be thoroughly practised in this Manual by working through the Practice Questions, making use of the Outline Answer-guides and getting your tutor or lecturer to comment on what you have written.

16. One final mark of good practice is to keep to the point. Identify the issues raised in each question and build your answer around them. Do not go off at a tangent, for there will be precious few marks awaiting you at the end.

# 2

# OUTLINE ANSWERS TO EXAMINATION QUESTIONS AT SECTION ENDS

## EQ1

**Comments:**

*This is a general question which can be handled in a general way. Note that there are two parts to the question ie to first discuss the role and then to assess it.*

**Key points:**

i.   Fayol's definition (to manage is to forecast and plan, to organize etc).

ii.   More up-to-date variations of Fayol eg Drucker's inclusion of motivation, staff development etc.

iii.   Management the dynamic element of organizations, enabling (a) the processing of resources and inputs to provide goods and services to clients in efficient and profitable way, and (b) the development of appropriate change.

iv.   The discussion so far could be summed up by reference to Mintzberg's managerial roles (entrepreneur, resource-allocator etc).

v.   The importance of management as a resource itself can be illustrated in terms of organizational control, efficient use of materials and manpower, level of employee morale, ability to promote and control change (innovation).

## EQ2

**Comments:**

*This question requires some explanation of the terms management and scientific methods before commencing any discussion of the topic.*

**Key points:**

i.   Management is a process of planning, coordinating, motivating and controlling.

ii. The use of scientific methods involves searching systematically for evidence to prove or disprove some theoretical proposition.

iii. Early examples of attempts to apply the methods of science to management were provided by F.W. Taylor and the Scientific Managers, who observed and measured work in order to establish more efficient ways of working.

iv. Those such as Fayol, Urwick and Brech who attempted to define certain laws or principles of management also may be included amongst the users of scientific or rational methods.

v. In more recent times the scientists are generally social scientists, interested in the study of human behaviour in organizations. Their methods are based on observation and analysis of people as individuals and in groups.

vi. Management has also been described as 'getting things done through people'. The application of scientific methods has shown that it is easier to record, measure and evaluate information about things, and much more difficult to make consistent sense of human behaviour.

vii. Scientific methods have made management more exact in terms of measuring and predicting things, but have done much less to prove that management is a science rather than an art.

## EQ3
**Comments:**
*The first step here is to identify who were the classical/traditional school and what their ideas were, before proceeding to assess their contribution to organization theory.*

**Key points:**
i. The leading exponents of classical theory were Henri Fayol, F.W. Taylor (and the scientific managers), L.F. Urwick and E.F.L. Brech.

ii. The scientific managers concentrated on improving the organization and efficiency of work at the workplace.

iii. Fayol, Urwick and Brech were concerned with the organization as a whole, especially in terms of its structure and the principles required to maintain that structure.

iv. Important principles were the Principle of Specialization or Division of Work, the Principle of Authority, the Span of Control etc.

v.   The classical theorists showed that it was possible to study management and organizations and to isolate key aspects of them. They provided us with a basic definition of management which has proved useful as a general guide to the scope of the function. They showed that attention to organization structures was a vital element in establishing healthy operations.

vi.   They also demonstrated that an organizational hierarchy is almost unavoidable for most enterprises. Their ideas illustrated the bureaucratic type of organization as described by Max Weber.

vii.   Overall they have indicated the importance of considering structure as one of several factors in developing a successful organization.

## EQ4

**Comments:**

*Firstly give an outline of Taylor's approach to the study of work and then apply it to a marketing context .*

**Key points:**

i.   Taylor's approach to work was essentially as follows: study the job, determine a time and a method for it, set up a management organization to plan and control it, select and train the worker to perform it. The pay-off for management was to be increased productivity and profits; for the workers it was to be increased pay.

ii.   Taylor's ideas have given rise to Work Study ie work measurement and method study techniques. Work measurement is concerned with the time taken by a qualified (trained) worker to complete a particular task at a specified level of performance. Method Study involves the systematic recording and critical examination of job methods with the aim of improving them.

iii.   These ideas can be applied to modern marketing management in the following ways: applying clerical work study (O & M) to sales office etc to improve form design, office procedures etc; using work measurement to establish performance standards for field sales staff; set up training programmes to enable staff to achieve/exceed measured standards of performance.

## EQ5

**Comments:**

*Most of the answer will be taken up with a description of the major features of the Studies. The Examiner is also looking for some evaluation and comment from you concerning the impact of Hawthorne on social psychology.*

**Key points:**

i.   The Hawthorne experiments were conducted at the Western Electric Company's Chicago plant during the period 1927–1932. The researchers consisted of company personnel and members of Professor Elton Mayo's Industrial Research Department at Harvard Business School.

ii.   The first stage of the experiments was to study the effects of lighting on output. Two groups of workers were selected for study – one group had no variations in its level of lighting, whilst the other had several variations from better to worse. The significant result was that the output of *both* groups increased. Obviously some factor other than purely physical conditions was at work in the situation. At this stage Mayo's staff were invited in by the company.

iii.   The next stage was called the Relay Assembly Test Room. A group of women were made the subject of various studies into the effects of changes in working conditions, especially in relation to rest periods, meal breaks etc. As before, regardless of whether the conditions were improved or worsened, productivity always increased. The women were responding to the attention of the researchers, and saw themselves as a special group. This form of behaviour has been called the Hawthorne Effect. Awareness of this effect has helped subsequent researchers to make allowance for it, or obviate it, in the design of their programmes.

iv.   The third stage consisted of a major interview programme to establish employee attitudes towards working conditions, jobs and supervision. This recognition of the importance of work attitudes represented a complete break from the ideas of scientific management, and laid the foundation for later developments in understanding employee motivation at work.

v.   Stage three established the importance of social relationships in the work situation. The findings led to a greatly increased interest in 'human relations' at work. This idea was furthered by the results of the fourth stage – the Bank Wiring Observation Room. In this case the group concerned set their own standards of work and work behaviour. The importance of *groups* with their informal or unofficial standards was seen to be a key factor in workplace productivity.

vi.   The final stage took the form of personnel counselling, in which employees were able to discuss their work problems. The result was an improvement in personal relationships, especially with supervisors. Here again the importance of taking account of employee needs as individuals was recognised by the Company.

vii. The main significance of the Hawthorne Studies was in its impact on subsequent social research methods. For managers it indicated the vital importance of groups and social relationships at work.

## EQ6

**Comments:**

*First it is necessary to establish who were the respective theorists and what were they saying. In this question the Examiner has referred to alternative descriptions for both groups. The important point is that the reference to human resources theorists means discussing the work of later social psychologists as well as that of the human relations school.*

*The second step is to compare the approaches of the two groups.*

**Key points:**

i.     The classical/traditional theorists focussed their attentions on the structure and activities of the formal organization at work. By contrast, the human relations/ resources theorists focussed on people in organizations.

ii.    The major theorists of the classical/traditional school were Fayol, Taylor, Urwick and Brech. Each of these attempted to lay down principles of organizational behaviour, which, if adopted, would open the way to 'effective' organization ie capable of achieving its goals and objectives. For example Fayol's Principles of Management referred to the importance of the division of work, the scalar chain (or chain of command), and unity of direction etc. Urwick's principles referred to issues such as the importance of the overall purpose or objective of the organization, and the clear definition of duties, the span of control etc.

iii.   F.W. Taylor focussed his attention on organization at the workplace with his ideas of scientific management ie the application of rational and systematic methods to tasks. His emphasis was on work rather than on the worker.

iv.    The theorists of human relations/resources originated with the Hawthorne experiments and the writings of Elton Mayo in the mid-1920's. They were initially concerned at the effects of scientific management on the worker in terms of fatigue and absenteeism, for example. However, their researches took them into a study of people as part of the *social* fabric of the organization. At first, social relationships and the importance of groups were the focus of attention. Subsequently, from the 1940's onwards, interest broadened into factors other than physical conditions, pay and social needs to questions of personal growth and fulfilment at work.

v.    The label 'human resources' has been applied to the social psychologists who took up these self-fulfilment needs. This line of approach relies considerably on the work of Maslow in identifying an hierarchy of needs in which a person moves up from satisfying basic needs to situations where higher needs are activated. Theorists who have utilised this approach include Frederick Herzberg, Douglas McGregor and Rensis Likert. Herzberg's motivation-hygiene theory, for example, has become well-known for its distinction between intrinsic job factors such as achievement possibilities, recognition and job interest, and external factors such as pay, company policy and administration etc. The former tend to produce high motivation, the latter can only serve to prevent de-motivation.

vi.    The two approaches described are different in their emphasis, but they have one thing in common – neither is sufficient to explain fully the complex nature of organizations.

## EQ7

**Comments:**

*This question is about the motivation to work, and invites you to discuss the truth or otherwise of the assertion which has been made.*

**Key points:**

i.    People do come to work for money ie they have economic motives. It is unlikely that they come *only* for money. The reasons why people work have been studied by various writers and researchers. In several cases, assumptions about people's behaviour have been considered as important as research evidence.

ii.    In the first twenty-five years of this century the assumptions made by owners and managers were that Man comes to work primarily to fulfill economic needs. Therefore pay and monetary incentives are the key to employee motivation. Examples of this concept are F.W. Taylor and the Scientific Managers.

iii.    By the 1930's it was becoming evident, on the basis of research studies such as the Hawthorne experiments, that Man has other needs, especially needs relating to personal relationships. In other words, whilst money is still an important factor, it is by no means an over-riding one.

iv.    Since the period following World War II, a number of theorists and research workers have concluded that Man has a variety of needs at work. In particular, there is strong evidence, from the work of social scientists such as Herzberg and Likert, that people seek self-actualization at work, ie they seek to realise their full potential.

v. The implications of self-actualization are that people seek more than financial returns from work. They seek more than friendly relationships. What they are looking for are opportunities to exercise responsibility, to obtain a sense of achievement and to develop new ways of doing things.

vi. In the final analysis people come to work for a variety of motives. Each person has his or her own set of priorities. The challenge for modern management is to be aware of these needs and to meet them in an adaptable manner.

## EQ8
### Comments:
*This is a question of practical motivation. It does not require lengthy statements of motivation theory, but a practical approach, especially to the second part.*

### Key points:
i. Most people are motivated by money to the extent that they come to work to fulfill economic needs. It is very debatable whether people are motivated to work harder by the lure of money. Even where money is seen as a real incentive, the evidence seems to be that it is not a lasting form of motivation.

ii. Most people are also motivated by the social contacts they make at work. There is plenty of evidence to suggest that the formation of social relationships and the need to belong to groups, is a very important motivator. The building of supportive work-teams can therefore be a powerful motivator to people.

iii. A person's standing or reputation at work are important motivators, whether he receives then from his peers or from the organization. Opportunities to achieve and to receive recognition for that achievement are also significant factors in the work needs of most people. On balance, the evidence seems to suggest that motives associated with the job itself are the most likely to encourage people at work. Nothing succeeds like success!

iv. A manager could take the following steps to motivate his subordinates:
    a. ensure adequate level of pay etc.
    b. train the individual so as to enable him to master the job, and eventually move to a bigger one.

c. develop a team-spirit in which the members feel that they can support the others and yet be supported by them as well.

d. provide means whereby the employee can measure his progress in the job.

e. take an interest in the person as an individual, and thank him when he has worked well.

f. ensure that the person's job was a challenging one, however modest the level.

g. keep the employee well-informed about matters that may concern him.

# EQ9

**Comments:**

*This question is in two parts. The first part seeks a description of the major features of the Trist-Bamforth studies, while the second part requires some comment about the significance of these studies.*

**Key points:**

i. The main purpose of the research carried out by Trist and Bamforth of the Tavistock Institute was to assess the effects of mechanization upon social and work organization at the coalface.

ii. Prior to mechanization the coal had been extracted by small, closely knit teams of men, working at their own pace and in their own way. Loyalty to the group was intense, both during and after work. Conflict between groups was settled in ways determined by the men themselves. The control of work was basically in the hands of the teams.

iii. The introduction of a mechanized coalface required a different social system. The small teams were broken up and replaced by much larger groups, each with their own supervisor. More than that, the larger groups were no longer responsible for the whole operation, but only for a specialized part of it.

iv. The outcome of these changes in production methods was that the men were unhappy, petty disputes persisted, absenteeism increased and productivity fell.

v. Eventually, a compromise situation was arrived at, where the working arrangements were altered to enable groups to tackle a range of tasks, and to do so by agreement within their groups. The revised situation improved employee morale and productivity.

vi.   The prime significance of the research was that it identified the inter-dependence between technical factors and social factors at work. Changes in either set of factors would inevitably bring about changes in the other.

vii.   Effective work organization, therefore, depended on attention to social as well as technological needs in the workplace.

viii. The description 'socio-technical system' was given to the situation described above. This concept helped to advance the ideas of theorists about organizing for change.

## EQ10, EQ11

**Comments:**

*These two questions are seeking the same answer ie comment on the contingency approach to organization structures. Allowing for the slightly different emphasis in each question, the following points should be noted.*

**Key points:**

i.   The contingency approach to organization structures is based on the concept that there is no one best way to design an organization. It all depends on a variety of circumstances, or contingencies.

ii.   For many years theorists held the view that an organization could be structured according to certain principles, and the implication was that the principles applied to most, if not all, situations. In recent years, researches such as those of Joan Woodward have shed considerable doubt on the validity of such 'principles'.

iii.   In the 1960's/70's other theorists felt that the most important factor in considering how to structure an organization was to take account of the needs of people. The main focus of their attention was on issues such as group behaviour, individual motivation, leadership and self-fulfilment. This approach has been criticized on the grounds that it does not pay sufficient attention to the realities of other key factors, such as technology, environmental conditions and the handling of conflict.

iv.   The conclusion to be drawn from the most recent research is that organization design depends not on one or two major variables, but on several. Structures may be relatively mechanistic (highly structured) or relatively organic (less structured) depending on the kind of environment in which the organization exists, the technology it has to utilize, the size of the organization and the nature of its personnel.

v. The contingency approach suggests that all these variables must be considered in attempting to find the optimum form of organization structure. Burns and Stalker, for example, found that firms facing a situation of change were better adapted if they took on an organic structure. Firms in situations of stability tended to benefit more from a mechanistic type of structure.

vi. Lawrence and Lorsch, in another study, found that successful firms were those that adapted best to their environment in terms of coping with (a) issues of specialization, and (b) issues of integration. A key point in this study was that even where less specialization was required, there was always a need for *integrating* activities.

vii. The net result of the influence of the 'no one best way' approach is that organizations in future can only be studied in various dimensions. No other way can make adequate sense.

## EQ12

**Comments:**

*Note that this question does not ask for discussion or comment. It would be reasonable to infer, therefore, that the examiner is looking for a full rather than partial description of the principal factors.*

**Key points:**

i. The most important factors that have a bearing on the design of the structure of an organization are as follows: size, technology, environment, people, tasks, goals and values.

ii. Size is one of the most significant factors in determining structure. Small organizations require little or no formal structure. As organizations grow, they have to differentiate or specialize, and the more they differentiate, the more pressure there is for integration. The end-result is a high degree of formal structuring.

iii. Technology refers not just to machines, but also to production or operational methods. The degree of sophistication of machinery is not as significant in itself as the impact it makes on the organization of work activities. Studies carried out by the Tavistock group in British coalmines, and by Joan Woodward's team in Essex, showed that there was an important relationship between technology and structure.

iv. The environment of an organization is made up of a variety of social, economic and political elements, all of which may have some bearing on the way an organization is structured. Research studies have suggested that where the environment is relatively stable, a more formalized structure is advantageous. By contrast, turbulent environments require a less formalized and more flexible structure.

v.    A further point is that the environment may affect one part of an organization differently from another part. In such cases, part of the organization, eg production, could be formally structured while another part, eg research and development, could be organized much less formally.

vi.   People's needs and aspirations are also influential in the design of organizations. As the Tavistock studies in the mines showed very clearly, it is not enough to just consider production issues. People have their views about how their work should be organized, and this has to be taken into account when designing the structure. Argyris's views concerning people's needs to move towards maturity are relevant here. Formal organization, he says, treats people as being immature by prescribing their duties and controlling their activities. People who wish to take an active, less dependent role will rebel against formality.

vii.  Tasks are important in that complex tasks have to be broken down into sub-tasks and the higher the degree of differentiation, the greater the need to integrate activities. Goals and values will often be associated, as part of the philosophy or culture of the organization. A market-orientated firm, for example, will adopt a more flexible structure in order to be responsive to customer needs.

## EQ13

**Comments:**

*The issue of bureaucracy has been looked at earlier. This particular question, however, asks you to assess the response to change in the environment, which is an extremely relevant issue for this Section.*

**Key points:**

i.    The main features of a bureaucratic organization are as follows:
    a.  a high degree of specialization of jobs.
    b.  an hierarchical arrangement of jobs where one level is controlled by the next higher level.
    c.  a system of rules and procedures.
    d.  impersonal roles filled by professional managers and administrators.

ii.   These features have been developed in response to the increasing size and complexity of organizations ie to *internal* considerations. In a bureaucracy the structure itself becomes all-important. Other factors, such as technology and environment, have to comply with the demands of a bureaucratic structure.

iii.  Bureaucracy, therefore, is adapted to stable conditions. It is not adapted to changing conditions, least of all in its environment. Research such as that carried out by Burns and Stalker indicated that formal ie 'mechanistic' structures appeared unsuited to conditions of change.

iv.   The existence of formal rules of conduct both in relation to internal staff as well as customers and clients, means that there is insufficient discretion in the power of employees to amend their behaviour towards colleagues or members of the public. Rules are fine for achieving consistency and fairness in routine situations, but they are frequently ineffective for dealing with new needs and new demands.

v.    The hierarchical structure of a typical bureaucracy is another obstacle to adaptability. Decisions have to be referred to higher levels in the hierarchy before new precedents may be set to meet changing conditions externally.

vi.   Finally, the very fact that jobs are highly specialized means that they must automatically become redundant in the face of radical change. People with broad roles encompassing a variety of skill and knowledge requirements will invariably be better able to cope with the effects of change in the environment of their organization.

## EQ14

**Comments:**

*The question is looking for an understanding of some of the pros and cons of typical business enterprises, ie limited companies, partnerships, sole traders and cooperatives.*

**Key Points:**

i.   Recognised types of business enterprise include:
   a.  public limited companies
   b.  private limited companies
   c.  partnerships
   d.  sole traders
   e.  cooperatives

ii.  All to a greater or less degree are in business for profit.

iii.   State-owned enterprises in industries such as steel,. rail transport and coal-mining have not usually had to meet profit targets, and are excluded from this analysis.

iv.   Limited companies are endowed with separate corporate status and thus exist independently of the members and directors. The key advantage to managers who are investors is that they are only liable for the debts of the company up to the level of their share-holding. Managers employed by limited companies are able to check on company progress as reports have to be made regularly by the directors to shareholders. Details of companies have to be made available to a central Registrar, where they are open to public inspection. There are few disadvantages to managers. Perhaps the most import ant are the legal requirements to set up and operate a business.

v.   Partnerships, usually two but not more than twenty people, have the advanta ge to the partners (proprietors) of relatively little legal fuss to start trading, no obligation to publish accounts, and the chance of sharing talents and stresses with others. The disadvantages are that the partners may not get on well personally, and that each partner is personally liable for the debts of other partners.

vi.   A sole trader is a person working on his own. The main benefits are freedom to run the business as he wishes, few legal restrictions and the opportunity to retain all the profits of the business. The disadvantages are mainly that he is responsible for all the debts of the business, works in isolation and has to carry out all the usual management roles.

vii.   Cooperatives are set up on the basis of one person – one vote and operate on an openly democratic basis. The advantages to managers are that they do have limited liability and they share in the decision-making process as well as sharing profits. The disadvantages are that profits are normally modest, decision-making processes can be frustratingly slow, and that long term progress depends heavily on members' ability to work together.

## EQ15

**Comments:**

*This is a straightforward question designed to test your understanding of the basic decision-making process.*

**Key points:**

i.   The major steps in the decision-making process are as follows:

a. Define the problem.
b. Collect relevant data.
c. Develop alternative solutions.
d. Assess the consequences of proposed solutions.
e. Select optimum solution and implement.
f. Measure results.

ii. Key considerations in each step include the following:

**Defining the problem:** this is a matter of asking the right questions, and of isolating the *crucial* problem from subsidiary issues; it is important to identify underlying problems and not to confuse them with the overt effects of such problems.

**Collecting data:** the important point here is to collect information which is relevant to the problem concerned, and which involves the staff associated with the problem; seeking information and points of view from the staff concerned helps decisions to be accepted in a positive spirit.

**Developing solutions and assessing their consequences:** solutions depend not only on their technical ability to solve a problem, but also on their acceptability to the parties involved and other factors (cost, legality etc); the use of quantitative techniques may help to develop solutions and assess some of the consequences; assessing consequences is vital because most decisions can produce negative as well as positive results.

**Selecting and implementing optimum solution:** the final selection of a solution will be based on a number of factors, ie optimum implies the best solution *in the circumstances;* the implementation of the solution is the responsibility of management.

**Measuring results:** this step implies some ability to monitor and evaluate the end-results of a decision; this final step also enables decisions to be modified or even revoked in the light of experience.

# EQ16

**Comments:**

*Although it is not stated in the question, it is reasonable to assume that the weight of the answer should be given to the second part of the question, ie to setting out the objectives of a business.*

**Key points:**

i. The main reasons why it is necessary for companies to establish and periodically review their objectives are as follows:

a. a statement of objectives gives substance to the overall goals of the organization, which are usually stated in very general terms eg 'meet customer requirements for high-quality goods in a profitable and cost-effective way'; objectives can clarify how the organization intends to achieve profitability etc;

b. a statement of objectives gives managers and other employees a focal point for their efforts;

c. a review of objectives helps to ensure that existing objectives are still relevant, and that new objectives are added as required in response to changing conditions.

ii. In addition to the overall goals, which are objectives in themselves, companies need to set long-term, or strategic, objectives and short-term, or tactical, objectives.

iii. Strategic objectives are usually set for five years or so ahead in all the major functional areas of the business, ie marketing, sales, production, research and development, manpower, finance and other resourcing functions. Examples of strategic objectives are:

Marketing: 'to develop export sales to Third World nations so that 25% of total sales is represented by these markets five years from now';

Personnel: 'to ensure that the company's needs for skilled and professionally qualified manpower are met over the next five years'.

iv. Other strategic objectives are set with stakeholder groups in mind, eg customers, employees, suppliers etc. Examples are:

Customers: 'to introduce measures designed to reduce customer complaints, about the level of service provided, by at least two-thirds over the course of the next three years'.

Employees: 'to develop, in close collaboration with employees and employee representatives, a system of employee participation in decision-making, which can be installed throughout the company in the next three to four years'.

v. In setting strategic objectives, companies have to make some statements about the manner in which these objectives shall be pursued, ie they must develop policy guidelines for the guidance of management and other employees.

vi. In achieving strategic objectives, companies have to set short-term, or tactical, objectives. These are usually prepared by individual departments for endorsement by senior management and set out in specific and quantifiable terms the particular targets to be aimed at in pursuit of strategic aims.

# EQ17

## Comments:

*The question seeks to establish your familiarity with the concept of MBO by asking for a description of the system and some appraisal of its advantages and disadvantages. The answer can be divided neatly into (i) the description, (ii) the advantages, and (iii) the disadvantages.*

## Key points:

i. Management by objectives (MBO) is a system of management which attempts to integrate individual goals, such as job satisfaction and personal growth, with organizational goals, such as profitability and expansion.

ii. The vehicle of this integration is the organization's strategic plan, from which are developed operating or tactical plans, unit objectives and individual manager objectives. Thus MBO is operated at the tactical end of the business, where detailed results are expected in pursuit of organizational goals.

iii. MBO assumes that managers have personal objectives or goals which are closely linked to success at work. Thus if a job can be seen as challenging, as providing responsibility and as relevant to organizational aims, then managers will be motivated to cooperate in achieving these aims in a purposeful manner.

iv. In keeping with these assumptions, MBO assumes that knowledge of results is an important factor in managerial motivation, and as such concentrates on the outputs or end-results of management activities.

v. A typical MBO programme begins with establishing management job descriptions, isolating key task areas and setting mutually agreed performance standards for the key tasks. It continues with the development of a job improvement plan, which is essentially a list of short-term targets to be achieved in a three or six month period. Control data are identified for both Key Tasks and Targets to enable progress to be monitored by the individual manager and his superior. The programme concludes with reviews of performance – current performance and, frequently, potential performance. Where MBO is part of a management development programme, succession planning may also be a feature of MBO.

vi. The advantages of MBO are mainly that:
    a. it enables managers to see their priorities clearly,
    b. it provides specific targets to work for,

     c.  it keeps managers and their superiors informed of progress in the job,

     d.  it can help to identify obstacles in the way of effective performance,

     e.  it provides a sound basis for measuring management performance,

     f   it provides useful material for assessing the training and development needs of managers.

vii.  The disadvantages are mainly that:

     a.  it can become an end in itself, with individuals going through the motions to satisfy the company's bureaucrats,

     b.  it requires time, effort and a considerable amount of inevitable paperwork to be successful,

     c.  it can be used by superiors to exert pressure on their subordinates to accept targets which are not fully acceptable ie it is just another way of increasing managerial productivity.

viii.  On balance, the advantages would seem to outweigh the disadvantages considerably.

## EQ18

**Comments:**

*The major part of this answer will need to be taken up with a description of manpower planning, leaving the second part of the answer in a subsidiary role.*

**Key points:**

i.    Manpower planning is the name given to the systematic approach to the recruitment, retention, utilization, improvement and disposal of an organization's human resources.

ii.   Manpower planning is not just a matter of obtaining the right numbers of particular categories of employee; it is also a matter of obtaining the right blend of skills and experience in the organization's current and planned workforce.

iii.  The major stages of the manpower planning process are as follows:

     a.  analysis of existing manpower situation

     b.  forecast of future demands for manpower,

     c.  assessment of external labour market, (ie external manpower supply)

     d.  establishment of manpower plans in detail.

iv.   Activities involved in (a) above include: an analysis of current employment categories and the numbers of employees currently in post; an analysis of the knowledge and skills available; an analysis of the employee turnover rate; an assessment of the training/ development potential of existing employees.

v.   The forecast of future demands for labour is closely linked with the organization's long-term corporate plans ie the quantity and quality of employees required will depend on marketing intentions, new product development, new production processes (technology, robotics etc) and other key variables in the organization's total plans.

vi.   The assessment of the external labour market has to take account of questions such as what changes in the national employment situation are forecast and how these might affect the organization.

vii.   Detailed manpower plans are laid with time-horizons of about one year. These plans encompass intentions in respect of recruitment, internal promotion, training and development, pay and productivity, and retirement and redundancy.

viii.   As in the case of every other planning activity, the final stage of all is the review. Manpower reviews may be carried out monthly (in line with budgets) or annually (or any suitable review period).

ix.   The reasons why manpower planning is necessary are:
- a. to ensure that the organization can fulfil its *existing* commitments to customers,
- b. to ensure that suitable manpower is available *in the future* to meet changes in the organization's circumstances,
- c. to enable the organization to audit its human resources,
- d. to enable the organization to develop an *integrated* approach to the recruitment, retention, development and disposal of its human resources.

# EQ19

## Comments:
*This is a very straight-forward question, which does not even ask for any comment on O.D.*

## Key points:
i.   Organization Development (O.D.) is the name given to any strategy for improving organizational effectiveness by means of behavioural science approaches involving the diagnostic and problem-solving skills of an external consultant or change-agent.

ii.   An O.D. programme is directed towards improving an organization's effectiveness, ie its ability to achieve its various corporate objectives. It is designed to enable the organization to become sufficiently adaptable in the face of changing circumstances.

iii.   The phases of a typical O.D. programme are as follows:

**Preliminary**: Discussion of aims of programme between top management and the external consultant(s), and the respective roles of the parties concerned.

**Analysis and Diagnosis**: The consultant designs and implements appropriate methods for obtaining relevant information about the organization – problems, employee attitudes etc. The information obtained is used to diagnose problem areas and to confirm certain facts about the organization.

**Agreement about Aims**: With a clear picture of the organization and its problems in front of them, the top management team and the consultant agree the objectives of the programme eg 'to introduce and maintain an open and participative style of management in all departments' and 'to re-structure the production departments to permit greater delegation by senior management'.

**Action Planning**: Planning the content and sequence of the activities designed to put agreed changes into effect. Such activities could include briefing meetings, training programmes, job analysis, organization-planning committees and so on.

**Evaluation and Review**: Once action plans have been put into operation, measures must be taken to check their progress, obtain feedback, and make preparations for corrective actions, if required.

**Completion**: The third party – the consultant – leaves the scene, and the management team continue with the task of leading a more effective organization.

# EQ20

## Comments:

*The danger in a question such as this is that you will not be able to include sufficient material in your answer. It is very much a 'thinking' question. A useful way to start the thinking process is to define what you understand by delegated authority and responsibility.*

## Key points:

i.    Delegated authority usually refers to the power to act which is conferred on managers by other, more senior managers, or by shareholders. All authority of this kind is prescribed in some way, ie limits are set over the power to act.

ii.    Responsibility refers to a person's accountability for certain tasks or duties. The degree of responsibility is usually prescribed by written job duties, custom and practice, and rules of various kinds.

iii.    Ideally an individual manager should be given sufficient delegated authority to enable him to execute his responsibilities fully. Authority, as the classical writers put it, should be commensurate with responsibility.

However, the ideal situation does not always obtain, and there is a mis-match between delegated authority and responsibility.

iv.    The results of this mis-match can be as follows:

a.   managers are unable to fulfll their responsibilities because they have insufficient authority to effect changes or improvements,

b.   managers who have insufficient power to act feel demotivated by their powerlessness,

c.   in cases where too *much* authority is granted, an individual manager may find that he has exceeded his responsibilities, and this means someone else has to bear the consequences of his actions,

d.   in bargaining or negotiating situations, a mismatch between delegated authority and responsibility can easily lead to a loss of credibility on the part of the manager concerned on the grounds that he is unable to substantiate his side of the bargain,

e.   managers are unable to delegate authority to their own subordinates, if they have insufficient to carry out their own personal responsibilities.

## EQ21

### Comments:

*This question can be answered in three parts: (i) definition of matrix organization, (ii) description of where such organization structures are to be found, and (iii) why they are found there. The first part of the question is probably the most important. An illustration is helpful in this answer.*

## Key points:

i.    A matrix organization is one whose structure is based on a combination of lateral as well as vertical lines of communication and authority. The lateral lines enable a project-based organization to be formed; the vertical lines enable this project-based organization to be superimposed on the functional organization. This can be illustrated as follows:

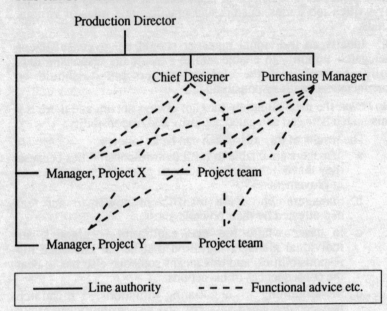

ii.    In this situation the functional managers and the Production Director provide technical expertise and organizational stability, whilst the Project Managers provide leadership and control of the individual, and rather temporary, projects. While a project is under way, the client has only to deal with one manager – the Project Manager – for routine monitoring of progress instead of having to deal with several specialist and line managers.

iii.    A distinct advantage of a matrix organization is that it enables individual project managers to identify strongly with their projects their clients and their project teams in a way that is not always possible in a typical functional organization. A further advantage is that the matrix approach helps to put functional specialisms in perspective ie they are there to provide line managers with advice, guidance and expertise. This is especially highlighted in the role of specialist members of a project team. Their first priority is to put their knowledge and skills at the disposal of their team, rather than to beat them over the head with functional rules and procedures. Nevertheless, this situation does cause conflicts of loyalty for some team members, who may be torn between adhering to their own functional standards and cutting corners in order to satisfy the demands of their project manager.

iv.   Matrix organizations are most likely to be found in complex industries, such as aerospace and electronics, which are often widely differentiated in terms of processes, skills and production methods, but which require careful coordination in order to meet customer requirements and to ensure adequate resourcing from corporate funds etc. They are not always applied to the entire organization, but may be limited to certain complex units within it.

v.   The reasons for adopting a matrix organization are mainly that:

    a.  the matrix approach enables a high degree of collaboration between line managers and functional specialists,

    b.  it is possible to hold one person – the project manager – responsible for the success of the project, for the link with the customer and for the motivation of the project team,

    c.  it enables complex contracts to be broken down into a number of separate projects without losing overall control, and without losing the benefits of considerable functional involvement.

## EQ22
**Comments:**
*This question is about the reasons for delegating work, and about some of the difficulties involved.*
**Key points:**

i.   The factors that would influence my decision to delegate work to a subordinate would be as follows:

    a.  The degree to which I was under pressure in carrying out my duties, as a result of volume of work or of complexity of work,

    b.  the degree to which I felt able to cope with the risks associated with delegation,

    c.  the capabilities and experience of the subordinate,

    d.  my assessment of how much benefit he might obtain from being given increased responsibilities,

      e.  the degree of cost involved in the work to be delegated (financial cost, reputation with customer etc),

      f.  the amount of help available to the subordinate from colleagues,

      g.  my intention to use the opportunity to delegate as part of his planned development at work.

ii.   The major barriers to delegation are:

      a.  Unwillingness on the part of superiors to delegate work through desire to retain personal control over work or through fear that subordinates may be so successful that the superior's own job may be threatened,

      b.  inability of busy superiors to (i) see the need to delegate, or (ii), if they do see the need, the inability to make time to brief subordinates, allocate additional tasks and provide some form of feedback ie planned delegation,

      c.  unreadiness of subordinates to carry additional responsibilities,

      d.  insufficient training available to enable subordinates to be adequately prepared to accept greater responsibilities,

      e.  complexity of work, which limits the number of people who are able to carry it out safely and correctly,

      f.  uncertain nature of work, eg in technical or scientific research and development, requires experienced staff.

## EQ23

**Comments:**

*This question is about the meaning and nature of leadership. The examiner has provided a few prompts to stimulate the discussion.*

**Key points:**

i.   The concept of 'leadership' is open to several different meanings – there is no ideal definition, as yet.

ii.   Among the various definitions that have been attempted are:

      a.  those that see leadership mainly as a matter of personal qualities – the so-called 'trait theories' of leadership;

      b.  those that identify leadership with the tenure of a particular position (eg manager) in an organization – the bureaucratic-type of leader; and

      c.  those that see leadership in terms of behaviour, ie what the person *does* to fulfil a leadership role.

iii.   Research has shown that there are difficulties in attempting to rely on trait theories. The main difficulty is that remarkably few *common* characteristics of personality have been identified. Reliance on personal qualities, therefore, is no sound foundation for an analysis of what constitutes leadership.

iv.   There are situations where leadership is identified with position-power, ie appointed leaders such as managers and supervisors. In these cases, job-holders receive delegated authority commensurate with their position. Their leadership responsibilities are thus built into their work-roles. However, it is quite obvious that, whilst many such appointed leaders are able to respond to the demands of team-management, there are many others who fail in this respect. The appointment clearly does not make the leader – being a leader must imply other factors.

v.   The most promising research into leadership suggests that leadership consists of performing certain functions in relation to tasks and to people. Leadership is seen as an aspect of human behaviour, and human behaviour can be observed and, to some extent, measured.

vi.   Important contributions to a behavioural analysis of leadership have been made by so-called 'style theories'. These have attempted to define key dimensions of leadership behaviour such as:

    a.   Authoritarian versus Democratic styles of management; (eg D. McGregor and R. Likert). These suggest that a democratic style is more productive in terms of team commitment, but more recent studies suggest that this is not necessarily so, and there will be times when an authoritarian approach represents the optimum style.

    b.   Task-orientation versus People-orientation; examples of these dimensions have been provided by the Ohio Studies, the Michigan Studies and by the so called 'Managerial Grid'. The Ohio studies identified two distinct forms of leader-behaviour: 'consideration' (ie considerate of employees' feelings) and 'initiating structure' (ie organizing task processes). It was possible for a manager to score high on *both* dimensions. By contrast the Michigan Studies concluded that leader-behaviour was an either/or matter viz. either employee-centred *or* production-centred. The Managerial Grid devised by Blake & Monton followed the Ohio view by concluding that it was possible for leaders to behave in two dimensions at once – in this case the variables were 'concern for people' and 'concern for production'. The optimum style according to Blake & Monton is one which is high on both dimensions.

vii. Another important contribution to behavioural theories of leadership is Adair's functional model of leadership. This sees leadership as behaviour designed to balance the needs of people (as groups and as individuals) and the needs of the task in pursuit of team goals. The clear implication of this model is that effective leadership depends on the leader's ability to adapt his behaviour in the light of circumstances ie essentially a contingency view of leadership. This latter approach is the one most likely to provide the best definition of leadership.

## EQ24

**Comments:**

*Note that the question asks you to discuss the evidence concerning a flexible managerial style. To date there is more speculation than evidence available to answer such a question.*

**Key points:**

i. There is not a great deal of evidence on this issue, although there is considerably more untested speculation.

ii. An early attempt to suggest a range of leadership styles, as opposed to one or two mutually exclusive styles, was made by Tannenbaum and Schmidt in the 1950's. Their continuum of leadership styles ranged from authoritarian behaviour at one extreme to democratic behaviour at the other with several alternative styles in between. Like most of their contemporaries, Tannenbaum and Schmidt were more concerned with identifying a 'best' style rather than an 'appropriate' style (ie the best *in the circumstances*).

iii. Professor John Adair's functional model of leadership goes some way towards an appropriate style by suggesting that a leader's aim is to achieve the task set for him by paying sufficient attention to task needs, group needs and the needs of individuals within the group. Depending on the circumstances, the leader may need to pay more or less attention to each of the three variables, but he must direct some attention to all of them. The approach suggested by Adair has been used as the basis for training leaders.

iv. The most influential theory on the issue of flexible leadership style, however, is that of F E. Fiedler. His researches were first written up in 1967 in a volume entitled 'Theory of Leadership

Effectiveness', in which Fiedler referred to a 'contingency' approach to leadership. His conclusions were that group performance was dependent, or contingent upon, the leader adopting an appropriate style in the light of the relative favourableness of the situation. Fiedler found that the most important variables in determining the relative favourableness of the situation were as follows:

    a.  the quality of leader-member relationships,

    b.  the degree of structure in the task, and

    c.  the power and authority of the leader's position.

v.   The most favourable combination of variables for the leader appeared to be when (i) he had good leader-member relations, (ii) the task was highly structured, and (iii) his position was powerful. By comparison, the least favourable combination was when (i) the leader was disliked by the members, (ii) the task was relatively unstructured, and (iii) the leader had little position power. vi. In considering the issue of style flexibility, a number of important factors appear to be emerging from the theories and researches carried out so far. These factors are as follows:

    a.  there is no 'one best way' of arriving at an optimum leadership style,

    b.  the most practicable approach is to aim for the 'best fit' between the leader and his situation,

    c.  the situation usually comprises the following variables:

        •  the requirements of the task

        •  the needs of the team

        •  the needs of individuals within the team

        •  the relations between the leader and the team

        •  the authority granted to the leader as part of his appointed role

        •  the power of the leader to act

    d.  meeting the demands of the situation requires leaders to select an appropriate style from a range of styles, depending on the circumstances.

## EQ25
**Comments:**
*This is the sort of question which lends itself to a neat and concise answer.*

## Key points:

i.　The principal factors which influence effective teamwork are as follows:

    a.　Leadership.

    b.　Nature of tasks required to be performed.

    c.　The knowledge, skills and motivation of the team-members.

    d.　The size of the group.

    e.　The group's stage of development.

    f.　Extent to which group sticks together (group cohesiveness).

    g.　Group norms and organization norms.

    h.　The roles played by individuals.

    i.　The environment in which the group has to work.

ii.　**Leadership**: Every group needs adequate leadership. An effective leader can meet the team-needs of the group (eg fair treatment, adequate resourcing, development of team-spirit etc). He can also meet the needs of individuals (eg counselling, practical assistance etc) and of the task (eg allocating work, arranging resources, scheduling events etc). Ideally, an effective leader will have a dominant style which suits his team for most of the time, but which can be adapted to meet contingencies arising from outside task pressures or from within the group (ie conflict). Conflict is not a bad thing in itself but it does require carefully handling by the leader to prevent the team from disintegrating.

iii.　**Stage of development**: The effectiveness of a team, ie its ability to fulfil its tasks competently and with satisfaction, depends considerably on the relative state of development of the group who make up the team. A newly formed team will spend a good deal of their time in finding out what is expected of them, what the rules are, and where they can obtain information and resources. In other words, they will be inward looking during this formative stage. As the team begins to settle down, the first conflicts and doubts tend to appear. Here again a good deal of the team's energy will be taken up resolving these internal issues. As internal conflicts and doubts are settled, the team will find new levels of cooperation and standards of operation. At this stage team-spirit will be very high, and the group will be outward looking. As success with the task is experienced, and individual collaboration is achieved in practice, the team will be performing at about its optimum level.

iv.   **Group cohesiveness**: This is the extent to which the members of a team stick together, and also the extent to which they can attract new members. Highly cohesive groups demonstrate a strong loyalty to individual members and a strong adherence to group norms (standards of behaviour). Cohesiveness tends to be high in groups where there is similarity of work, close physical proximity, common social factors (eg age, sex, social status etc) and where the group size is smaller rather than bigger than average. Cohesiveness is important in the development of teams as collaborative groups of workers, but it does have the disadvantage that it puts the needs of the group before all else.

v.   **Roles in groups**: In a team, as in any other human group, a variety of roles can be played out by the members. Roles are an aspect of the way in which jobs are performed by the job-holders. Roles are affected considerably by the expectations of job-holders, their colleagues and others, concerning the way the jobs should be carried out. Typical roles in a team are as follows: spokesman, expert, ideas person, willing helper, humourist and devil's advocate. Some of these roles are defined by the work, others by the group itself and others by the organization's rules.

## EQ26

**Comments:**

*In this case an early explanation of terms is necessary before going on to discuss the links between the two functions.*

**Key points:**

i.   In management the term planning is given to those activities which define the various objectives of the organization and the means by which they are to be achieved. Planning encompasses policy-making, for policies are the behavioural guidelines which must be followed in seeking to achieve objectives. Plans lead to actions, and these actions need to be monitored to check if they are in accordance with the results expected. This is where the control function of management comes in.

ii.   Control rounds off the process of managing the organization's resources by measuring results, checking them against previously agreed standards of performance, and then indicating any corrective action that may be required. Planning and control are inextricably linked together, even though, for the purposes of analysis, they are often treated separately.

iii.   One of the major distinctions that can be drawn between the two is that planning is a decision-making activity, while control is a monitoring process which depends on the existence of the former – control serves no useful purpose in its own right.

iv.  Another distinction, arising from the first, is that planning is concerned with ends and means, whereas control is concerned with results and feedback.

v.  Common features between planning and control include the following:
- a. they are both concerned with identifying and quantifying standards of performance.
- b. the measures used for planning purposes are frequently the same as those used for control purposes (eg budget targets, financial and other ratios etc.)
- c. they both make use of quantitative techniques such as Network Analysis and Inventory Control.

vi.  To sum up, planning and control cannot be regarded as independent functions of management. Some distinctions can be made between them, but in reality they are intimately linked together with control following planning in a cyclical fashion.

## EQ27

**Comments:**

*This is a straightforward question with a definite focal point, ie the steps in the Control process.*

**Key points:**

i.  The basic steps in the Control process are as follows:
- a. Set standards of performance.
- b. Measure performance.
- c. Compare results obtained with standards.
- d. Initiate corrective action, where required.

ii.  The key considerations to be taken into account in setting performance standards are:
- a. standards need to be demanding, but not out of reach, otherwise the employees involved become disheartened;
- b. standards should be clear and measurable, preferably quantitatively, but if not, then qualitatively;
- c. qualitative standards should ideally be expressed in terms of end-results, otherwise standards may become confused with methods;

    d.  quantitative techniques may help in the establishment of suitable standards, and managers should be aware of appropriate techniques.

iii.  The key considerations in respect of measuring performance are:

    a.  to ensure that performance is rated against the appropriate standards;

    b.  to ensure the flow of information about results to the management; this is crucial if the control process is to act as a feedback mechanism;

    c.  to ensure that the information obtained is relevant, adequate for the purpose and timely, otherwise inappropriate action may be taken – or – worse still action may be too late to be effective;

    d.  budgetary systems are probably the single most important source of information about performance results, and should play the key role in any control system.

iv.  The key points to be considered when comparing actual performance with standard performance are:

    a.  the process must allow for variances to be identified and notified without delay to the appropriate manager, for this – after all – is the raison d'etre of the Control Process;

    b.  action should only be taken on the 'exception principle', ie only significant variances should be dealt with, otherwise managers can spend fruitless hours reviewing systems which are working perfectly well.

v.  The key considerations in respect of corrective action are:

    a.  the responsibility for taking corrective action should be clearly allocated to the appropriate managers; the control process is only a tool of management and, to be effective, its results must be put into effect in a systematic way by those in authority;

    b.  as the control process is essential a regulatory process, corrective action should be taken without delay, otherwise the system concerned will continue to malfunction until attended to.

## EQ28

**Comments:**

*The answer needs to explain what is the marketing concept and then to illustrate its significance for planning, using a manufacturer of capital goods as an example.*

**Key points:**

i.   The marketing concept is an approach to business which looks at the needs and wants of the customer before all else, and then directs the energies of the business towards the fulfilment of those needs and wants.

ii.   Other approaches to business are those which concentrate firstly on production efficiency or product quality, before the needs of the customer. This is not to say that the customer is ignored, but only that he has a somewhat lower priority than these other issues.

iii.   A manufacturer of capital goods, ie goods for use by other manufacturers, could use any one of the three alternative approaches mentioned. The best approach for the development of future plans would almost certainly be the adoption of the marketing concept, but the others would also have considerable relevance too.

iv.   The advantages of utilising the marketing concept are that the manufacturer would:

   a.   be aware of his existing customers' needs in the short-term, and possibly further ahead;

   b.   be developing new or revised products with customer-requirements firmly in mind;

   c.   be consulting with existing customers about new developments in the field concerned, eg computer controls, robots etc;

   d.   be flexible about adapting his products to compete with new features offered by competitors;

   e.   be sensitive to the needs of potential customers, and able to discuss their requirements with them;

   f.   be able to produce goods to a specification agreed by an individual customer to meet particular needs;

   g.   generally be able to offer a marketing mix which was closely geared to customers' requirements.

v.   The adoption of the marketing concept would give the manufacturer a very good idea of what his customers – existing and potential – are seeking from him, and his competitors. This would certainly provide him with a confident base on which to build his future plans. Nevertheless, he could still plan ahead with a fair degree of confidence, if he used one of the other alternative approaches.

vi. For example, if he were to adopt a production-orientated approach, he would certainly be concerned to ensure that every modern facility was available to support the production of his goods. He would be concerned with developing a high reputation for his goods, on the assumption that if his goods are reputable, customers will buy them. He would also be concerned with efficiency of production with a view to offering his goods at a more competitive price than his competitors. All these contingencies could be planned for, and there is no question of the marketing concept being the only way to develop future plans in this situation.

vii. If he adopted a product-orientation, much of what was mentioned in paragraph vi would also apply. In this case, however, it would be the products themselves which would be the centre of attention for the future. The aim would be to develop a range of products which were so technically brilliant that potential customers would be bound to be attracted by them. This approach implies a considerable degree of confidence in the products and their future prospects in terms of sales. However, this is a risky approach since, if customers do change their minds, the manufacturer is left high and dry with excellent products that nobody wants! Nevertheless, many firms successfully adopt this approach in planning for the future.

viii. If the manufacturer was producing fast-moving consumer goods in a competitive market, then it would be easier to demonstrate that the marketing concept was the best approach. In this case, however, the issue is not at all so clear-cut.

# EQ29

**Comments:**

*This is a two-part question, requiring an introductory definition of the term 'below-the-line' activities followed by some discussion of the objectives of such activities. A brief description of the 'marketing mix' should also be included.*

**Key points:**

i.    The term 'below-the-line' activities refers to sales promotion activities which are organized by a firm's own staff out of its general marketing budget. Such activities can be contrasted with 'above-the-line' activities, which are those undertaken by external advertising agencies on behalf of the firm, and separately accounted for.

ii.    Below-the-line activities form part of the Promotion element in the marketing mix, which is the group of variables assembled by the firm for presentation to its customers at a particular point in time. The other variables are the Product, the Price and the Distribution arrangements.

iii.    Below-the-line activities may be directed at consumers or to the trade. They usually consist of measures such as special offers, free samples, point-of-sale demonstrations, (for consumers) and special discounts and the provision of display material (for trade customers).

iv.    The objectives likely to be set for sales promotion activities directed at consumers include the following:

    a.    to draw customers' attention to a new product,

    b.    to encourage sales of slow-moving items,

    c.    to stimulate off-peak sales of seasonal items,

    d.    to achieve higher level of customer acceptance of a product.

v.    The objectives mentioned fall into two main categories: firstly, those aimed at encouraging sales among items that are stagnating; and, secondly, those aimed at promoting new or recently-introduced items. In each case, incentives of one kind or another are being offered to consumers to tempt them into buying.

vi.    Objectives likely to be set for a promotion aimed at trade customers could include the following:

    a.    to stimulate retailer or dealer cooperation in pushing selected items,

    b.    to persuade retailers to increase shelf-space devoted to the company's products,

    c.    develop goodwill amongst retailers and dealers.

vii.    These objectives fall into the categories of (i) those that are designed to encourage retailers and dealers to play their part in pushing sales of particular items; and (ii) those that are designed to promote good relationships between the suppliers or manufacturers and the dealers or retailers selling their products to the consumer. As in the case of consumer-orientated promotions, those directed at dealers and retailers also contain incentives.

viii. The particular objectives set in any one sales promotion campaign will depend mainly on whether the supplier wants to shift old stock or encourage new products. The principal overall purpose will always remain to increase sales by positively pushing, or promoting, them.

# EQ30

## Comments:

*The first step is to describe the concept of the 'product cycle' before relating it to planning and budgeting.*

## Key points:

i. The concept of the 'product cycle' has been developed from studies of the life-cycles of individual products. These studies suggest that any product tends to pass through a number of common stages, which are as follows: Product introduction, Growth, Maturity, Saturation and Decline.

ii. Each of the stages has its dominant features, for example:

**Product introduction**: Production costs are high, partly as a result of development costs; price is also high; competitors are few, if any, but sales and profits are low at this stage.

**Growth**: Sales rise rapidly; prices ease; unit costs decline and profits are at their peak; mass market appears but competition increases.

**Maturity**: Sales continue to rise, but less rapidly; competition is fierce and prices ease further; profits begin to level off.

**Saturation**: Sales stagnate; prices become very competitive and profits begin to shrink; mass market begins to evaporate.

**Decline**: Sales take a permanent downturn; profits low or non-existent; product is eventually withdrawn.

iii. The implications for business planning and budgeting are various, as the following examples indicate:

   a. At the introductory stage pricing can be geared at least to the recovery of costs, and possibly to what the market will bear. As there is little or no competition, this is a time to be bold about prices.

   b. From the budgeting point of view, targets for sales and profits should not be set too high at the introductory stage, but need to set at a demanding level for the subsequent stage of growth.

   c. When the product reaches the growth stage, production needs to be planned at peak levels to meet increasing sales; distribution needs to be geared up to moving goods to the point-of-sale as efficiently as possible. From the planning point of view, this is the period of peak activity to ensure that the product realises the benefits of maximum availability to the consumer at a time of minimum competition from rival products.

d. As sales increase, and competition begins to appear this is the time to take advantage of the flexibility of pricing, by reducing prices just at the moment when competitors are having to bear their own development costs. Budgets at this stage can set maximum profit targets with confidence.

e. During the maturity stage competition will tend to be at its highest, and this is a time for utilising advertising to help beat off the worst effects of this competition. It is also a time to consider further reductions in prices. At this stage both sales and profits will need to be budgeted at a lower level.

f. At the saturation stage, as sales begin to stagnate, efforts can be directed towards a variety of sales promotion activities to boost flagging sales and demoralise competitors by offering special offers to both consumers and dealers etc. At this stage, earnings from the growth period can be used to support some of the costs incurred in subsidising sales. Profit targets should continue to be set, but at a nominal level. By now production resources should be curtailed considerably in the face of the slow-down in sales.

g. As the decline stage approaches, budgeted costs should be set at the lowest possible levels, as the whole product cycle begins to wind down for good. By now replacement products should be well under way and another cycle about to begin.

# EQ31

## Comments:

*This is an interesting question which raises the important issue of how business organizations can cope with the conflicting priorities between key departments such as marketing, design and production. The question is looking for some explanation of these different priorities, together with some suggestions as to how conflict may be resolved.*

## Key points:

i. In organizations which have adopted the marketing concept, there will tend to be a lesser chance of serious conflict since every department's priorities will include some direct reference to the needs of the customer. The reverse will apply in organizations that have not adopted the marketing concept, but have opted for another approach eg product-orientation.

ii.   Nevertheless, whatever approach is adopted certain underlying causes of conflict will be present. These arise out of the differing priorities of the three departments concerned. These priorities include the following:

**Product design**: Marketing departments seek primarily the designs that meet the customers expressed wishes, whereas design departments are primarily motivated to produce designs that are technically satisfying and/or innovatory, and production departments prefer designs that can be translated readily into production terms.

**Product costs**: Marketing departments usually want the costs to be low enough to enable attractive prices to be quoted, whereas design departments may not be interested in costs so much as product quality. Production departments may well prefer costs to be kept to a minimum consistent with product reliability.

**Product features**: Marketing departments usually look for a variety of product features as a way of boosting sales, whereas design departments look for purely functional features and production departments look for simplicity of production, ie the maximum amount of standardisation.

**Pricing**: Marketing departments look for prices that are flexible and have the effect of stimulating sales. Design departments are not usually so sensitive to price, since they are more interested in assembling the most suitable product in the light of their interpretation of marketing's wishes. Production departments are traditionally concerned with pricing only to the extent that it covers the costs of production.

iii.   Given these underlying differences of priorities between the groups in question, what are the ways in which potential conflict may be resolved or at least contained within reasonable limits? Possible answers are as follows:

   a.   by establishing regular review meetings between the three departments concerned to build up mutual understanding and ensure a regular flow of information between them;

   b.   by ensuring that regular meetings are held during the product development stage of any product to enable potential problems to be ironed out as soon as possible;

   c.   by ensuring that each department's objectives refer to their contributory role in relation to other key departments ie as opposed to a competitive role;

    d.  by endeavouring to achieve acceptance throughout the organization of the marketing concept, ie ensuring that every department is market orientated so far as practicable.

## EQ32

**Comments:**

*This is a straight-forward question requiring a descriptive answer.*

**Key points:**

i.    The role of production planning and control is central to the production process, and consists of planning, acquiring, scheduling and controlling all the resources and facilities required to transform customer requirements into acceptable end-products.

ii.    In fulfilling this role, production planning and control can be divided up into a number of different activities. These are described below.

iii.    The first activity is to translate the final preproduction design into production instructions, so that those responsible for the manufacturing know what they are expected to make and how.

Secondly, production schedules, or timetables, need to be prepared in some detail, using Gantt charts among other devices.

This step is followed by the planning of the various resources (labour, materials, parts etc) and facilities (machine tools etc). Labour requirements have to be discussed with the Personnel department, who will be responsible for the initial recruitment; materials supply and parts etc, have to be discussed with the Purchasing department, who have the responsibility of purchasing at prices, and in quantities, that represent the best interests of the organization. Plans for facilities include the allocation of machines and plant in accordance with technical requirements, machine availability and capacity, and machine loading.

The next step is to set production targets for the various work groups involved, and this has to be done in conjunction with either marketing or sales, as representatives of the customer.

Once production is under way, part of the control function will be to ensure that work is progressing as scheduled and in accordance with job standards. This aspect of production planning and control is usually called 'progress chasing'.

Another aspect of control is that all appropriate records are maintained, eg work completed, work delayed, stock levels etc.

The final step is to ensure that the outputs of production are properly accounted for, invoiced and delivered – either to the customer or into stock.

iv. Today computers are utilised to handle the complex paperwork of the production planning and control process. Their advantage is that they can cope with vast amounts of record-keeping and at great speed, which are important factors in the control process.

## EQ33

**Comments:**
*The answer requires a brief definition of each of the production patterns referred to in the question, before going on to discuss the circumstances that would justify them.*

**Key points:**

i.   **Jobbing production** is the production of single items usually to order. The circumstances which would justify the adoption of jobbing patterns of production include the following:

    a.   where large items such as ships are to be built;

    b.   where single large pieces of equipment such as electricity generating plant are to be manufactured;

    c.   where large individual items such as a major bridge are to be constructed;

    d.   where small one-off parts or components are to be produced to the order of the production department in a factory;

    e.   where prototype models are required for design and/or planning processes in a manufacturing or construction organization.

ii.   **Batch production** is the production of standardised units in lots, where each lot has to be processed at each operation before moving forward to the next operation. The circumstances which would justify the adoption of batch patterns of production include the following:

    a.   where items such as standard components are to be produced for stock, eg to support production in due course;

    b.   where standardised items are being manufactured on a sub-contracted basis for another manufacturer;

    c.   where production requires a variety of quantities and types of items, which cannot be produced under a flow-production process, because of the interruptions to the flow of operations.

iii. **Flow/mass production** is the continuous production of items which move, or flow, from one operation to the next until completion without break. The circumstances which would justify the adoption of flow or mass patterns of production include the following:

   a. where large quantities of a narrow range of goods are required to meet the demands of mass-markets;
   b. where standardised units can be moved *individually* from one operation or process to the next without requiring any break in operations;
   c. where the returns from mass-production are more than able to meet the expensive start-up costs of an assembly-line form of production;
   d. where large quantities of liquids, powders or gases are to be processed, as in the case of paper production, the manufacture of cement or the production of petroleum spirit, for example.

# EQ34

**Comments:**

*The question is seeking no more than a brief set of descriptive statements about the key steps in a purchasing operation.*

**Key points:**

i.  The necessary activities which the purchasing department would need to carry out in purchasing a raw material not previously required would be as follows

   a. seek out suppliers of the new raw material;
   b. appraise suppliers' in terms of how they propose to meet the potential purchase order in respect of quantity, quality, price and delivery;
   c. select supplier who appears on the evidence to represent the most cost-effective source of the raw material;
   d. negotiate contract with supplier, so as to achieve sufficient quantities of a suitable quality of the material required for the manufacturing process; and so as to obtain price and delivery arrangements which are acceptable;
   e. prior to negotiating (d) above, the purchasing department would need to know the details of quantity, quality and delivery times from the user departments (production, stores, and inspection etc);

f. place order with supplier and maintain all necessary records (purchase orders, delivery notes, invoices etc);

g. arrange routine follow-up checks with user departments to ensure that the order is being met satisfactorily, and to iron out with the supplier any problems that may arise;

h. review the contract, as necessary, after a suitable period, and be prepared to either submit further orders or to change supplier.

## EQ35

**Comments:**

*This question is in three parts – first you are asked to comment on the Seven-Point Plan, (having previously described it;) next you are asked to discuss what alternatives are available; and, finally, you are asked to compare these alternatives with the original Plan.*

**Key points:**

i. The Seven-Point Plan is the name given to a classification of personal requirements produced by Prof. Alec Rodger of the National Institute for Industrial Psychology (NIIP) in the 1950's in Britain. The classification is as follows:

• Physical make-up (Build, height, colouring etc)

• Attainments (Exams passed etc)

• General Intelligence

• Specialised aptitudes (particular skills)

• Interests

• Disposition (Character or personality)

• Circumstances (Domestic and personal situation).

ii. The usefulness of this Plan lies in its application to employee assessment, especially in the area of selection. The range of factors in the Plan covers most of the attributes that could be looked for in an employee. If it is applied to an individual employee or candidate, then at least the right sort of questions are going to be asked about that person's suitability for a particular job. Such a Plan also enables personnel specifications to be written up for job vacancies in order to clarify what kind of person is to be sought.

iii. The Plan is not intended to be a tightly-drawn measuring device able to identify an ideal candidate with precision, and this it could not do in any case. Nevertheless it can and does provide a useful frame of reference for those seeking to describe the 'ideal' candidate in a general way.

iv.   Alternative frameworks are available mainly as versions of the Seven-Point Plan. However, there is one well-known alternative, which was produced in its own right. This is the so-called Five-Point Plan of J. Munro Fraser, which also dates back to the 1950's. v.   The Munro Fraser Plan consists of five points, and is rather more condensed than the Rodger Plan in that it does not refer to General Intelligence and specialised aptitudes, which can hardly be measured in an interview, but refers instead to Innate abilities, which places the emphasis on skills generally rather than on reasoning power. The full Munro Fraser list is as follows:

- Impact on others (Presence, dress etc)
- Acquired qualifications (Exams etc)
- Innate abilities (What the person can do)
- Motivation (Personal drive)
- Adjustment (Temperament)

This list does not take specific account of circumstances, although these can be covered under the item of Adjustment, which seeks among other things to assess how well a person might adjust to a new situation.

vi. Organizations frequently use their own versions of one or other of the above-mentioned Plans. The Seven-Point plan seems to be generally more attractive as a starting-point, since it enables personnel selectors to specify a more narrowly-defined set of standards for potential candidates. A typical example of such a personnel specification could include the following:

- Formal qualifications
- Manual skills
- Physical requirements
- Personality requirements
- Interests/Hobbies
- Experience (work)
- Social skills
- Personal circumstances
- Motivation
- Experience (other than work)

vii.   The list in paragraph vi. above could be incorporated into an interview plan to ensure that all interviewers covered approximately the same ground, and that each candidate had to prove himself against each of the items.

viii.  Greatly reduced versions of these Plans can be found in job advertisements under the title of 'The Person Sought' or some similar wording.

ix.   To sum up, the use of the Seven-Point Plan, and its derivatives, is an extremely important means for assessing personnel, especially in an employment interview situation.

# EQ36

**Comments:**

*The first two parts of the question are straightforward, but the third part requires some reflection before answering.*

**Key points:**

i.    The essential features of an ideal disciplinary procedure are as follows:

    a.  it should be written down and made known to all those involved;

    b.  it should specify clearly to whom the procedure applies, ie *all* employees or only some?

    c.  it should be capable of dealing swiftly with disciplinary matters;

    d.  it should indicate what is meant by misconduct and gross misconduct, and what are the likely forms of disciplinary actions which may be taken against those found guilty;

    e.  it should clearly specify who has the authority to enforce disciplinary actions, and to what extent, eg power of dismissal etc;

    f.  it should ensure that every disciplinary case is fully investigated, and that the employees concerned are given every opportunity to state their case and to be accompanied by a fellow employee if they wish;

    g.  it should ensure that employees are informed of the reasons for any action taken against them, permit them the right of appeal and ensure that no person is dismissed for a first offence, except in cases of gross misconduct.

ii.    The essential features of an ideal grievance procedure are as follows:

    a.  it should recognise the right of every employee to seek redress for grievances at work;

    b.  it should aim to provide for the fair and speedy settlement of grievances as near to the source as possible;

    c.  it should provide, initially, for the employee to raise the grievance with his immediate superior; if this does not produce a satisfactory conclusion, the employee should be permitted to refer the issue to the next higher level of management, and if he is still dissatisfied, to a senior manager or director, on appeal;

    d.   at each stage the employee should be allowed to take a fellow employee with him;

    e.   it should provide for time limits to be set for each stage, so as to ensure that no delays occur;

    f.   it should make arrangements for the results of grievances to be recorded in writing and distributed to the parties concerned.

iii.   The aim of the two procedures described above is to ensure, so far as possible, that employees will receive fair and just treatment if ever they are involved with these procedures. The effect of this overall aim is to minimise conflict. After all, employees do not seek confrontations with their employers if they feel well treated at work.

iv.   Of course, the aim of a particular procedure may not be realised because of some misunderstanding about it. For example, if a manager believes, incorrectly, that he has the power to suspend an employee without pay in a situation of alleged gross misconduct, he is likely to spark off a major conflict with employee representatives if he proceeds to enforce his supposed power. To avoid such conflict, it is essential to make every manager and supervisor absolutely clear about the extent of his authority to impose disciplinary action on employees.

v.   So far as grievances are concerned, the most likely cause of conflict with employees is delay on the part of management in dealing with the issues raised by the person with the grievance. Time limits are an important means of ensuring that such delays do not occur, and open conflict is avoided.

vi.   Provided the above procedures are clear, and are fairly operated, there is no reason at all why they should not be supported by employees just as much as by managers, as a means of reducing conflict and ensuring fair treatment for all, regardless of position.

## EQ37

**Comments:**

*This is a question that is popular with examiners. It is in two parts, the second of which asks you to consider how much training and development takes place in training courses.*

**Key points:**

i.   Training usually implies preparation for a specific occupation or for specific skills, and aims primarily to ensure that organizations have sufficient skills and experience available to fulfil their business objectives. Training is thus job-orientated rather then aimed primarily at the personal development of individuals.

ii. Development, by contrast, is more concerned with enabling individuals to grow in skills and experience in order to be of greater potential use to the organization at some later date. Development is broader in scope than training and is career-orientated rather than job-orientated. Development tends to contribute to personal growth as much as it does to securing future resources for the organization. Development may include activities such as management by objectives and succession planning as well as traditional training type activities, such as courses.

iii. Courses are an important feature of most training and development activities. In some respects, courses lend themselves more to training than to development. A course can provide a few hours or a few days of instruction and/or practice opportunities in closely specified skills, such as learning how to operate a till or learning how to conduct an employment interview. At the end of the course, whether it was organized internally or arranged by an external provider, the organization can expect to see some noticeable improvement in the way knowledge or skill is applied in the workplace. However, this assumes that the course was appropriate for the trainee, and that the trainee was thought to be capable of benefitting from the training. If these conditions are not met, no effective training will have taken place.

iv. Some courses, a minority, are not designed with specific skills or knowledge in mind. These are the more broadly developmental courses that key employees are sent on to widen their horizons, increase their self-confidence and improve their ability to think in strategic terms. On such courses what takes place is development rather than training. Organizations that send their key personnel on such courses are always faced with the risk that these employees will make use of their more marketable position by moving to a competitor before making any further contribution to the business. The pay-off in developmental courses is medium to long-term, rather than immediate as in the case of most training events.

# EQ38
**Comments:**
*This is a general question about employee participation, and allows scope for a wide-ranging answer to take in the various options available at different levels in the organization.*

## Key points:

i.    There are several different ways of enabling employees to participate in the decision-making processes of their organization. In some organizations the senior management regard employee participation in decision-making as no more than allowing employees, or their representatives, access to a number of joint consultative bodies. Many organizations utilise their collective bargaining machinery to provide employee participation in decision-making. In such cases, joint negotiations between management and trade unions produce compromises which are jointly agreed and implemented.

ii.    The drawbacks of the first two options referred to above are that, in the case of joint consultation, there is no real employee participation in the sense of joint decision-making; and that, in the case of collective bargaining, this involves only union members and excludes non-members and managerial staff.

iii.    Another option which is currently much in favour is that of job enrichment, ie restructuring an individual's job so that he is able to exercise greater discretion over the way the job is done. This is a genuine form of employee participation, but only at the level of the individual job. Naturally, this may have an enormous impact on employee motivation, but it is stretching a point to suggest that this can ever be considered to represent employee participation in the sense of joint decision-making with management.

iv.    An extremely important and significant form of employee participation is that installed in many German companies, ie the works council system. This system, which in the Federal Republic, is supported by the force of law, produces one or more workers' councils which have certain rights to co-determination (joint decision making) on matters affecting a wide range of employment conditions. A few organizations in Britain have experimented with this form of participation on a voluntary basis. In these cases, the council is usually at company level and is a *joint* council but which has a majority of employee-representatives on it. Decisions are usually taken by consensus, rather than by a vote, and can include vital strategic decisions as well as routine and local decisions. This is a genuine form of participation in the sense of joint decision-making.

v.    Another important option is that of appointing or electing employee directors to the boards of companies. This is another feature of the German system mentioned above. In Germany the law requires most organizations to arrange for the election of employee directors onto Boards. In some situations the employee directors are only entitled to a one-third of the Board seats; in others, half the members must be employee representatives. So far, in Britain, only a few attempts have been made to put workers on the Board. The difficulty in Britain is that, unlike German companies, which have a two-tier Board (a Supervisory Board and a much smaller Executive Board), British companies have only one Board – the unitary Board. In this situation it is difficult to reconcile the conflicts inherent in having day-to-day executive decisions mixed up with long-term and/or strategic decisions. In the Federal Republic, day-to-day decisions are left firmly with the Executive Board and the works councils, while strategic decisions are left with the Supervisory Board.

vi. The final option which is available is that of workers' control. This way suggests that workers should take over the ownership and general management of organizations. The experiment has been tried successfully in Spain, at Mondragon, for example, where workers are shareholders in their companies, and elect the Board, but where the day-to-day task of running the business is left to a professional manager reporting to the Board. A key feature of the Mondragon experiment is that all organizations have to be less than 400 strong. Small size, therefore, is seen as crucial to the success of this kind of partnership.

## EQ39

**Comments:**

*This is a two-part question. The first part is straight forward: the second part requires some thinking about the extent to which collective bargaining is a problem-solving, decision-making exercise.*

**Key points:**

i. The term 'collective bargaining' means, principally, bargaining between employers and employee organizations about terms *and* conditions of employment and about the nature of the relationship that shall exist between the two parties.

ii. Collective bargaining is more than just the collective version of individual bargaining between an employee and his employer; it is also a mechanism for regulating relationships between employees and their employers.

iii. The products of collective bargaining are collective agreements – procedural agreements and substantive agreements. The former deal with the rules of behaviour that shall be applied to the consenting parties, and cover such issues as:

- trade union membership and recognition.
- facilities for union representatives (shop stewards etc).
- negotiating machinery (number and composition of committees etc).
- grievance procedures (individuals' disputes).
- disputes procedures (collective disputes).

iv.   Substantive agreements deal with terms and conditions of employment, and cover such issues as pay, hours of work, holidays and job grading. These agreements usually operate for one year and then are re-negotiated, unlike procedural agreements which are intended to be relatively permanent. Where one party wishes to amend or revoke a procedural agreement, they are obliged to give due notice, eg six months, one year etc.

v.   There are several grounds for stating that collective bargaining is a problem-solving, decision-making process. These include the following:

   a.   collective bargaining helps to solve the problem about how much of the organization's income should be made available to employees in the form of wages and other employee benefits;

   b.   it helps to produce decisions relating to employee product-ivity, which are acceptable to both employees and

   c.   it helps to deal with potential sources of conflict between employers and employees over issues such as pay, changes in working arrangements and discipline by establishing jointly agreed rules and conditions;

   d.   it provides a framework for the regulation of collective representation of the employees by establishing procedure agreements designed to control the extent of bargaining and the behaviour of people within it;

   e.   it helps to solve many of the problems arising from the need for organizational change, and produces jointly agreed decisions which can enable changes to be put into effect without either side resorting to punitive action.

vi.   Collective bargaining may also be considered as part of a power struggle between management and workers, and in this sense it is not primarily a problem-solving, decision-making process. However, in practice, this is not the attitude of the parties concerned in the majority of organizations in Britain. There are differences of aims, but collective bargaining sets out to find acceptable compromises between the parties.

vii. There is also a sense in which collective bargaining can be considered more of a bureaucratic process to organize the collective relationships between employers and employees. In the public sector, the machinery which has been set up ensures that there is a well organized structure of collective bargaining and consultation. Too much emphasis on machinery, however, can lead to a neglect of many of the problems and decisions which it is intended to deal with.

# 3

# EXAMINATION QUESTIONS FOR ADDITIONAL PRACTICE

**PQ1** List some advantages and disadvantages of decentralising decision-making in large organizations. *(ICSA MPP)*

**PQ2** How might the practical assistance of a psychologist help a group of people to work together effectively as a team?

*(ICMA OMM)*

**PQ3** Describe what you understand by the phrase 'matrix management'. *(ICSA MPP)*

**PQ4** 'Marketing does not merely take over where production leaves off, but is concerned with determining the nature and scale of production....' (L.W. Rodger). Discuss this view of the marketing concept for:–

    a. a large manufacturer of breakfast cereals, and

    b. a small commercial printer.

*(ICMA OMM)*

**PQ5** Identify and discuss the distribution alternatives available to a manufacturing company in the distribution of its products to consumer markets. Illustrate by reference to any particular industry with which you may be familiar. *(ACCA)*

**PQ6** a. What are the objectives of sales promotion activities?

    b. At whom are the sales promotion activities aimed, what forms can they take and how can their success be evaluated?

*(ICMA OMM)*

**PQ7** Assess the role of pricing as an element in the marketing mix. *(ICMA OMM)*

**PQ8** Traditionally, your organization has been non-unionised but you are becoming increasingly aware of pressure from the employees to gain union recognition. From your management view point, what are likely to be advantages and disadvantages of recognising trade union representation?

*(ICSA MPP)*

**PQ9** *'Management always gets the shop stewards it deserves.'
To what extent do you regard this as an adequate analysis of the
industrial relations climate in an organization?* (ICSA PPP)

**PQ10** *Discuss the role of a formal committee structure within an
organization. Make particular reference to the importance and
content of written records as an integral part of committee
activity.* (ACCA)

**PQ11** *'The reliability and validity of the selection interview is
usually so low as to render it practically useless as a selection
technique.' To what extent is this true?* (ICSA PPP)

**PQ12** *To what extent is the Points Method of job evaluation
useful in establishing the basis for factory pay scales?* (ACCA)

**PQ13** *Examine and assess the problems you see for the
personnel manager in devising, implementing and controlling a
dismissals procedure.* (ICSA PPP)

**PQ14** *In what major ways has British legislation attempted to
pursue social fairness in employment over the past twelve years?*
(ACCA)

**PQ15** *What are the likely consequences of a manager
introducing an element of competition*
> a. *between individuals, and*
> b. *between work groups, in order to increase
> organizational efficiency?*

(ICMA OMM)

**PQ16** *Describe and discuss the requirements for an effective
grievance procedure.* (ICSA PPP)

**PQ17** a. *State the different types of pricing policy open to a
manufacturer.*
> b. *Discuss the reasons why the pricing policy of a
> manufacturer of pet foods should be different from that
> of a manufacturer of scientific measuring equipment.*

(ICMA OMM)

**PQ18** *What do you understand by the term 'market
segmentation'? Select two from the following:–*
> i. *a manufacturer of machine tools;*
> ii. *a supplier of office cleaning services;*
> iii. *a manufacturer of PVC pipes; and describe the likely
> bases on which each might segment his market.*

(ICMA OMM)

# 4

# SUGGESTED ANSWERS TO ADDITIONAL PRACTICE QUESTIONS

*PQ1    List some advantages and disadvantages of decentralising decision-making in large organizations.(ICSA MPP)*

*ANSWER*

**Advantages of decentralisation:**

Prevents top-management overload. Where selected major decisions are delegated, top management are free to concentrate on corporate priorities instead of taking responsibility for *all* important decisions.

Speeds up operational decisions. Line units, ie those actually producing the organization's goods or services, can take major decisions about local matters without further reference. This is especially relevant for diverse product-groups or those who are geographically dispersed.

Enables real delegation. Middle-management in particular can exercise far greater authority in a decentralised situation. This may well enhance their feeling of responsibility for their actions and a willingness to live with their decisions, ie there *has* to be less buck-passing!

Encourages initiative. Organizations that pass decision making down the line stimulate managers and supervisors to use their own initiative.

Attracts lively staff. Organizations that delegate decision making tend to attract more imaginative and resourceful types of managers.

Copes better with change. Organizations that are operating in a highly flexible market or in conditions of rapidly-changing technology, can cope more easily if they decentralise decisions to those in touch with the immediate problems of adaptation.

Easier to identify cost and profit-centres. Decentralisation encourages top-management to look at large chunks of the organization with a view to breaking them down into manageable and *measurable* units. This enables functional managers to be as aware of their costs as line managers are of their revenue.

## Disadvantages of decentralisation:

More difficult to control. Once authority has been delegated, top-management must live with the results. This means *knowing* less as well as making fewer decisions. It means having to accept that things may get out of hand if a more junior manager makes a bad error of judgement.

More difficult to achieve consistency. This is a major disadvantage for a service industry, and especially a public sector one. Decentralised decision-making by local social security staff, for example, could lead to justifiable complaints of unfairness between one office and another.

Makes co-ordination difficult. Where, for example, a multiproduct company is selling to the same consumer market, it will be difficult for the company to ensure a co-ordinated sales policy without a great deal of voluntary commitment by the various product managements.

Encourages parochialism. Decentralised units can become cosy little operations of their own, well removed from the corporate objectives of the organization's top-management. Local agreements with a large trade union, for example, could drive a wedge between different units, and lead to leap-frogging claims completely contrary to overall pay policy.

Requires good supply of middle-management. If an organization decentralises, it must be capable of staffing the lower units with sufficient and suitable management. In many developing countries, for example, it has been shown that decentralisation is not possible, however desirable, precisely because there is not the reservoir of management talent to call upon.

More difficult to obtain company-wide decisions. There are times when a commercial enterprise, in particular, has to react strongly on a corporate basis to a major threat from outside, eg collapse of a market or warnings of nationalization. At such times it may be considerably more difficult to obtain an acceptable company-wide decision about the action to be taken.

Extended lines of communication. Decentralisation inevitably leads to more complex lines of communication as well as more skill in their operation. This requires more time and effort to be devoted to internal communications rather than to other priorities.

*PQ2*     *How might the practical assistance of a psychologist help a group of people to work together effectively as a team?*

*(ICMA OMM)*

## ANSWER

The first two advantages of employing a psychologist are, firstly, that he is not a member of the team, and secondly, that he is a trained observer of people in groups. By being detached from the team, the psychologist is not involved in status or emotional considerations with the individual members; by being trained to analyse behaviour in groups, the psychologist can act as a social interpreter to the team, and advise on ways behaviour can be modified to enable individuals, and the team, to achieve what they have to do.

Assuming that the team is already clear about its purpose, the first factor the psychologist is likely to consider is the leadership situation. The person responsible for providing leadership in a work situation is usually a nominated leader. He or she may have little idea about the requirements of good leadership. The psychologist can help such a person to clarify the key issues of leadership, such as task needs, individual and group needs, leadership styles and organizational constraints. The outsider's contribution here can create confidence in both the leader and the team, enabling the leader to discuss the leadership situation with the team, and highlight their respective needs. Leadership is intimately linked with considerations of motivation, commitment and job satisfaction. On these matters the psychologist can help the leader and the individual team members to discover what their motivation needs are, and to suggest ways of supplying them. For example, the psychologist could outline the technique of job enrichment, and help the group to apply it in their own context. This could be an extremely valuable exercise both in terms of morale and productivity.

Another important factor the psychologist might consider is the role played out by each team-member. After observing a team discussion the psychologist can identify the different responses played out by individuals. For example, criticising, questioning, suggesting ideas, peacemaking or just being passive! By feeding this information back to the team, the psychologist helps each member to become aware of his or her role at that time, and to see how it contributes to, or obstructs, the work of the team. It is quite possible that the intervention of the psychologist could lead to a number of team changes!

Of major importance in any team is the level of interpersonal communication between the members. A trained psychologist can help make individuals more aware of the nonverbal aspects of communication and their importance in teamwork. This is especially important in teams where morale is high and individuals may not wish to state disagreements or doubts openly. In such cases they may well show something of their views by a facial expression or a meaningful glance across the table. Socially-skilled groups will bring these signs out into the open and ensure their implications are discussed. An unskilled group could well learn from observation exercises under the psychologist's guidance.

The presence of the psychologist can make a team very conscious of its obligations to its members, to its leader, and to itself as a group. A very cohesive group may well find itself in conflict with another group or an outsider from management. A criticism of just one member of the team may be taken as an attack on all. The psychologist may be able to help the team to turn the conflict into a source of fruitful collaboration, or, failing that, to help them to contain it.

Conflict *within* the group can also be lessened by the psychologist giving the leader an early warning of a possible clash. Conflict may arise because of overlapping job roles not previously recognised, or because of stress or insecurity felt by individuals as they develop in the group. A trained observer can spot underlying tensions and frustrations before the parties themselves have become aware of them. He can communicate these potential problems to the leader and the group and give them the opportunity to tackle the causes before the trouble escalates.

Two remaining services that a psychologist might give to the team are the provision of selection tests for potential newcomers to the team, and the undertaking of performance assessment of existing team members, including the leader.

The above examples show how a psychologist can help a team to be aware of its own social processes, and can provide it with a means for enabling it to handle those processes with the maximum effectiveness in terms of tasks achieved, individual and group satisfaction.

***PQ3*** *Describe what you understand by the phrase 'matrix management'.* *(ICSA MPP)*

### ANSWER

'Matrix management' means that management is organized laterally as well as vertically. The basic idea behind a matrix organization is to combine the stability and relative efficiency of an hierarchical structure with the flexibility and informality of an organic structure.

A typical hierarchy provides for vertical lines of authority and communication; its organization is founded on functional or departmental groups; it may be centralised or decentralised, but control is still exercised from the top downwards.

A so-called organic organization is very loosely structured; its lines of communication are generally horizontal rather than vertical; its idea of authority is based more on the possession of knowledge and skills than on rank or status; its roles are flexible rather than pre-determined.

Most large organizations are structured along hierarchical lines to enable them to control and direct their numerous activities, but increasingly such organizations are unable to respond quickly enough to changes in their environments. This is especially true of business enterprises in highly competitive markets.

A matrix structure seems to combine the benefits of both hierarchical and organic forms, thus making for flexibility in decision-making whilst enjoying stability of structure.

In a matrix structure an individual belongs to two workgroups; one of these would be a functional department, the other would be a project team or product group, for example; the functional department provides the vertical link, while the project group forms a horizontal link; rank/status are preserved, if necessary, through the functional line, and peer-group collaboration is maintained through the project group.

To sum up, matrix management can be understood to be the process of operating and adapting a combined vertical and horizontal structure to achieve the organization's objectives more effectively.

*PQ4*     *'Marketing does not merely take over where production leaves off, but is concerned with determining the nature and scale of production....' (L.W. Rodger). Discuss this view of the marketing concept for:–*

    *a. a large manufacturer of breakfast cereals, and*

    *b. a small commercial printer.*          *(ICMA OMM)*

### ANSWER

The marketing concept is founded on the notion that the primary task of a business enterprise is to satisfy the needs of its customers, or markets. Thus every part of the business should be geared to meet these needs. As Rodger's comment suggests, individual functions such as production must take their cue from marketing, and not the other way around. For example, the production departments of a business will inevitably have their own ideas about a product. They will tend to prefer longer production runs, a smaller range of models, and a high degree of standardization. The marketing situation, however, may well demand short runs with a wide range of models, and a facility for producing custom-made items. If firms are to stay in business and be successful, they must remain tuned to the needs – present and future – of the markets they are serving, and adapt their productive effort accordingly. We can apply this concept firstly to the large manufacturer of breakfast cereals. The first essential here would be to segment the market and focus attention on any variations in buyer-behaviour between different parts of the country or between different social classes, for example. Once the needs of each market segment have been satisfactorily identified, they can be supplied in accordance with the buyers' preferences. For example, certain market segments may show definite loyalty to the company's own brand-name, and they can be supplied on that basis. Other market segments may reveal a demand for 'good value', ie where price is more important than packaging, for example. In these cases the need could be met be selling cereals more cheaply in a simple plastic bag under the name of a supermarket chain.

The packaging of cereals causes many problems for manufacturers. It is essential to maintain the freshness and crispness of most types of cereal, both in transit and after they have been opened by the consumer. This has led to demands for changes in the internal packaging of cereals, which could hardly have been welcomed by the production personnel! But consumers have made it quite clear to manufacturers that they just will not buy less-than-crisp products.

In a highly competitive field such as breakfast cereals, it would be vital for the manufacturer to carry out almost continuous market research to assess consumer demand, and keep and eye on the competition. Firms who are alive to their markets will respond quickly to change by varying their marketing mix (product, price etc). A cereals manufacturer could seize an opportunity to increase his market share, at least temporarily, by being the first in the field to supply 'family-sized' packs, and by selling these in areas of population growth. This is the kind of behaviour which keeps firms in step with, and sometimes ahead of, their markets.

The small commercial printer may well be in a less competitive and volatile market than the cereals manufacturer, but even he must make some attempt to analyse his customers. Some will demand high quality work before all else, others may be more concerned with speedy and reliable delivery, yet others will be attracted by lower-than-average prices. The printer must therefore ensure that his production personnel understand what is important to which customer, and supply the work accordingly. He can ensure that those responsible for deliveries and invoicing, for example, are aware of the special needs of the various customer-groups and the arrangements that must be made to ensure their continued patronage. This level of attention to the marketing aspect of the business puts a heavy stress on those responsible for carrying out the wishes of the customer. Nevertheless, it is one of the most vital factors in the continued existence of *all* businesses, be they large manufacturers of breakfast cereals or small commercial printers.

**PQ5** *Identify and discuss the distribution alternatives available to a manufacturing company in the distribution of its products to consumer markets. Illustrate by reference to any particular industry with which you may be familiar.* (ACCA)

**ANSWER**

The main distribution alternatives available to a manufacturing company in the distribution of its products to consumer markets are as follows:

- i. direct from factory to consumer
- ii. indirect to consumer via wholesalers and/or retailers
- iii. a mixture of direct and indirect channels.

The particular alternatives chosen by a manufacturing organization will be decided ultimately by success in achieving planned levels of sales and profits. Such success can only come about by satisfying the needs of the consumer. How this may be done, can be seen from the example of the manufacturer of soap and detergents. The widespread and regular consumption of soap and detergents by consumers effectively precludes *direct* selling by the manufacturer on the grounds of cost alone. The mass market for such products requires an enormous number of outlets to satisfy the consumer's need for the convenience of purchasing these everyday items. These outlets can best be provided by middlemen of one kind or another, that is to say by using *indirect* channels.

A major indirect channel in this case would be a large supermarket chain. Supermarkets represent huge retail operations. They are able to buy soaps and detergents in bulk direct from the manufacturer and sell them conveniently in single packets off-the-shelf. The manufacturer only has to arrange to deliver in quantity to the individual supermarket. Naturally, he will continue to be responsible for his own national advertising (TV, newspapers etc), but does not have to concern himself with the final retailing to the individual consumer. It will be sufficient to have salesmen calling at the supermarkets to take orders, arrange displays and pick up any useful market intelligence.

Other large retail outlets would also be important channels to the manufacturer. Here again delivery would be direct from the factory, and no wholesaler would be involved. Selling direct to large retailers and supermarkets is particularly beneficial to the manufacturer in terms of the turnover of his products. The relative size, shopping location and pricing policy of supermarkets and large retailers makes them an attractive channel of distribution to a manufacturer of such widely-used products as soaps and detergents.

Many consumers nevertheless are still served by small independent traders, and it would be unwise for the manufacturer to ignore this large, albeit diminishing, section of the market. In this case the manufacturer will sell to wholesalers, who in turn will supply the retailers. Wholesalers are able to buy in bulk from the manufacturer, thus reducing his stocks in store. They can also relieve the manufacturer of the tasks of delivery, arranging terms, organizing promotions etc.

By using the services of middlemen as described above, the manufacturer of soaps and detergents is able to reach his consumer markets efficiently and profitably. The middlemen concerned are experienced in their operations, and just as concerned with profitability as the manufacturer. By using them as part of his own marketing mix the manufacturer is ensuring the most cost-effective way of getting his products through to the mass consumer. Middlemen enable the products to move on towards the ultimate point of sale, using their own advertising and their own distribution network. This service provides the manufacturer with a cheaper means of distributing his products to the consumer, than if he was to do so from his own resources.

*PQ6*   a.   *What are the objectives of sales promotion activities?*

   b.   *At whom are the sales promotion activities aimed, what forms can they take and how can their success be evaluated?*

*(ICMA OMM)*

## ANSWER

a.   Sales promotion activities are undertaken in support of wider advertising and publicity campaigns. The basic tactics of such activities involve the provision of immediate and short-term incentives to buyers of the product. The overall aim is to bring about increased sales and/or acceptance of a product. Subsidiary objectives can be divided between those aimed at traders and those aimed at consumers, ie the two target populations for sales promotion. Objectives in respect of the trade might be:–

–  encourage dealers, retailers etc, to participate in the campaign.
–  achieve maximum testing opportunities for new or improved products.
–  achieve increased dealer-stocking, increased shelf-space etc.
–  encourage movement of slow-moving lines.

Objectives so far as the consumer is concerned could be as follows:–

–  direct attention to the specific product or line.
–  obtain consumer evaluation of new or trial products.
–  achieve high level of sales and/or acceptance of a product or line.

b.   The various forms of sales promotion depend principally on whether they are intended for the *trade* or for consumers. Typical forms of trade promotion include:–

–  the provision of display materials by the manufacturer.
–   assistance with special advertising for the campaign.
–  special limited-term discounts/payment terms.
–  competitions for sales staff with provision of gifts, prizes etc.

Promotions aimed at consumers directly will usually include one or more of the following:–

–  temporary price reductions, ie 'special' offers.
–  coupon offers, enabling price reduction on the item and/or next purchase of the same.
–  premium offers, where consumer sends off for gift or other benefit.
–  bargain packs, eg two for the price of one.
–  free gifts attached to item purchased.
–  free trial offers on the product or line itself (for new products).

Other forms of sales promotion may involve consumer contests or the provision of trading stamps, for example.

It is difficult for firms to evaluate the relative success of their sales promotion campaigns, primarily because there are so many other factors involved. Price, quality, suitability, packaging, for example will all be relevant factors. Nevertheless, provided reasonably quantifiable criteria can be set for promotional activities, it should be possible to get a fair idea of their relative contribution to the total sales effort. Taking trade promotions, for example, it should be relatively easy to see if a campaign at least achieved the involvement of dealers etc, by checking the percentage of those participating. Indicators of increased stocking by retailers, for example, could be assessed in terms of percentage increases over existing stock-levels, or if it were a new product, in terms of some target set at the commencement of the campaign. The best overall indicator of success would be the level of sales to dealers, retailers etc. Success in terms of the consumer must also be evaluated by reference to sales levels in the short term, but would also include indicators such as the proportion of coupons redeemed, competition forms returned etc. On a longer term basis it would be possible to obtain some estimate of consumer loyalty to a new product or brand from the continued level of sales/market share figures.

In summary, therefore, it would be fair to say that it is possible to obtain some picture of the effects of sales promotion activities, but that the results will be inevitably blurred by the presence of several other closely related factors in the marketing mix.

**PQ7**    *Assess the role of pricing as an element in the marketing mix.*    *(ICMA OMM)*

**ANSWER**

The marketing mix is the particular package of variables offered to a market at any point in time in terms of the product, price, promotion and distribution. The role of pricing has to be seen in relation to these other key elements of the mix.

Traditional views of pricing were based on the assumption that a consumer's decision to buy is determined mainly by the cost of the product. Current thinking disputes this viewpoint as being too narrow an explanation. Modern experience indicates that other factors in the marketing mix can be more influential than price. At any particular time factors such as product image, after-sales service and product availability may be much more decisive than price in influencing buyer-behaviour. To take one example, where the product image is one of high quality or social-respectability, the buyer will expect to pay a high price. Conversely, for utilitarian products a relatively low price will be expected.

From the seller's point of view pricing has several important roles:
  a. to generate an acceptable level of revenue and/or profit
  b. to secure, maintain or increase his share of the market
  c. to respond to the pricing policies of competitors
  d. to cover the costs of production

These roles have to be played out in association with the other elements of the marketing mix. In some cases price will play the key role, in others it will play a minor role.

Where production methods and distribution channels are geared to high-production and fast turnover of products, it is possible to generate sufficient profits with relatively low, bargain, prices. In this case the marketing mix depends more on product and distribution than on price.

Price also plays a less important role where products are highly differentiated eg convenience foods. Here considerations of advertising, sales promotion and product branding are more important in achieving marketing objectives. Prices tend to be based on product-ranges rather than on individual items, some of which may be deliberately under-priced (loss-leaders).

Where relatively undifferentiated products, such as petroleum are concerned, price becomes extremely important. Such products are vulnerable to violent swings in demand, and in order to protect price levels, and to ensure adequate returns, the oil-exporting countries have banded together into groups such as the Organization of Petroleum Exporting Countries, which agree production levels and prices. In products such as steel, it is governments who take action, through subsidies to support prices.

To sum up, pricing plays an essentially flexible role in the marketing mix, enabling sellers to arrive at the best possible combination of variables for tempting their markets.

*PQ8     Traditionally, your organization has been non-unionised but you are becoming increasingly aware of pressure from the employees to gain union recognition. From your management view point, what are likely to be advantages and disadvantages of recognising trade union representation?     (ICSA MPP)*

### ANSWER

When an employer considers the issue of whether or not to recognise a trade union for his employees, he is about to take a decision which will have far-reaching effects on the total labour force. The advantages of recognition are principally as follows.

1. It indicates to the employees that management at least recognises their need to be independently represented whatever else may be available within the organization already, ie consultative committees.

2. By conceding the idea of union representation at an earlier rather than later stage, the employer is in a much better position to influence the kind of trade unionism that will exist in his organization. In other words unionism will start off in an atmosphere of relative goodwill, with the employer responding positively to his employees needs, rather than fighting some rearguard action based on an instinctive dislike of trade unionism.

3. One firm advantage is that proper recognition means drawing up an agreement with the employees about the methods and procedures to be applied to this new form of management employee relationship, ie a procedure agreement.

4. Where management is willing to grasp the nettle of union recognition, it is also in a better position to prevent multi-unionism from developing by stating right at the outset that it will only be prepared to negotiate with *one* union for the group of employees concerned. This helps to prevent future interunion conflicts.

5. Once a union is recognised, it is then possible to get down to the business of negotiating improvements in pay and conditions in an orderly manner. This provides both employer and employees with a vehicle for introducing changes in working conditions. It also enables change to be brought about on a mutually acceptable basis.

6. Recognition also brings greatly improved opportunities for communication between the organization and its employees. The details of a procedure agreement will also include arrangements for union representatives (or shop stewards) and joint management-union meetings. These are invariably in addition to rather than instead of existing internal communication methods.

However, in spite of these advantages, there are several reasons why employers may feel wary about acknowledging the existence of a trade union in their own organization. Most of the disadvantages are based on the feeling, no doubt correct, that 'things will never be the same again!' These disadvantages are principally as follows.

1. From henceforth management will have less discretion to act. It will have to negotiate actions which previously could have been put into effect quite unilaterally. Instead of just consulting employees, management must gain acceptance for change. This has been called 'management by consent'.

2. Another major disadvantage lies in the formality that inevitably attends management-union discussions. Issues that were once dealt with rather casually will now have to be tackled in a more open and collaborative manner. This may well lead to delays in decision-making as well as inflexibility in the carrying out of decisions.

3. Another disadvantage is that management will find that it has to make more concessions to staff than in a non-unionised situation. These concessions may arise not only from internal negotiations but also from agreements made nationally by the recognised union.

4. Where disagreement ensues, the management may find itself in a position of confrontation with the union, and this could lead to strike action or some other form of union sanction, which would otherwise have been absent in a non-union situation.

On balance, it is probably best to recognise a trade union in the circumstances described in the question. This will enable the management to manage the new situation instead of being sucked into it, like it or not. If management can retain the initiative in the early stages, it can lay down a firm foundation for future employee relations in the organization.

*PQ9*     *'Management always gets the shop stewards it deserves.' To what extent do you regard this as an adequate analysis of the industrial relations climate in an organization?*     *(ICSA PPP)*

*ANSWER*

The quotation implies that the determining factor in management-union relations is the attitude of management towards the trade unions.

Whilst management's attitude towards the unions is clearly one important factor in the industrial relations climate of an organization, it is by no means the only factor. An adequate analysis would need to take several factors into account. These factors can broadly be divided into two main groups: those concerned with *attitudes* and those concerned with *behaviour*.

In terms of *attitudes*, a number of variables may be analysed. For example:

a. Management's attitudes towards trade unions
b. Management's attitudes towards the employees
c. The employees' attitudes towards management
d. The employees' attitudes towards the unions

This list emphasises the point that even in terms of attitudes there is more to this question than just management attitudes.

There are three major alternatives available to management in facing up to a trade union:

a. to be *negative* ie to confront or obstruct the union on the grounds that it challenges the legitimate power of management to manage the organization.

b. to be *neutral* ie to adopt the view that the union is neither good nor bad, and generally to play down its importance in the organization.

c. to be *positive* ie to accept that the union has a real role to play, in partnership with management, in creating a harmonious and productive workforce.

The first alternative leads either to hardened attitudes on both sides, or an early withdrawal by the union – an unlikely possibility. Where the union has consolidated its representative role, its shop stewards will tend to be people who are capable of looking after themselves in an argument. In such a situation it could be argued that negative management deserved negative shop stewards.

The second alternative could lead to a situation where management's shortsightedness results in control by the union of the industrial relations climate. If management does not make decisions, then the union representatives surely will. Many examples of restrictive practices and union fragmentation have arisen from such a policy of neutrality, even in firms whose attitudes to employees have been based on generous paternalism.

The third alternative is likely to produce the most beneficial results for both management and union, since both sides will accept the legitimate role of the other and behave accordingly. Management will have a clear industrial relations policy; there will be agreed procedures for negotiations and disputes; and the shop stewards will be *expected* to play their part in dealing with day-to-day problems and grievances. In this situation management-union relations are based on mutual respect and co-operation.

The above points give some indication of the real importance of management attitudes in determining the industrial relations climate in the organization. There are other attitudes that can be usefully explored, however. For example, the attitudes of the employees towards their trade union. If the employees themselves are apathetic, they may find themselves controlled by militant shop stewards who have pushed themselves to the forefront of management-union relations without ever really being opposed. Conversely, where employees take their trade unionism seriously, they will tend to act with responsibility. This does not mean that management can look forward to a quiet life, but it does mean that negotiations or problems will be dealt with in a constitutional manner.

Also important is the general attitude of the employees to their own management. Where an atmosphere of loyalty and trust has been built up, it is unlikely that this will suddenly be affected by trade union membership. In contrast, where employees have grown cynical of their management, it will be their cynicism rather than trade union activities which will determine the industrial relations climate.

Other, perhaps more measurable, factors which could be used to analyse the industrial relations climate include: levels of absenteeism and labour turnover, productivity ratios, number of disputes and grievances etc. These are some of the more obvious *behavioural* signs of employee dissatisfaction. They only represent the tip of the iceberg. What lies beneath the surface is invariably an issue of deeply-held attitudes. In the final analysis, it is these attitudes that hold the key to the problems posed by the question.

**PQ10**    *Discuss the role of a formal committee structure within an organization. Make particular reference to the importance and content of written records as an integral part of committee activity.*

(ACCA)

**ANSWER**

A formal committee structure may be used by an organization as the mainstay of its communications system.

Committees can be used to co-ordinate the ideas, plans and activities of the different sections or departments. They can enable things to be discussed and shared *across* the organization as well as vertically within departments.

Committees may also be used for their effectiveness in handling a number of different issues at once, and sharing out the resulting tasks amongst the members. Where committees form part of a rational and formal structure, the issues they discuss are subject to open, democratic discussion and to review by a higher committee in many instances. The formal structure, whilst slow, is nevertheless thorough and open.

Typically, the more formal committee structures are to be found in the public services, although even in the private sector, areas such as industrial relations are controlled chiefly through formal committees for consultation and negotiation.

It seems we prefer formal committees where a high degree of public accountability is required. An important element of this accountability lies in the ability to produce *written* records of matters discussed and conclusions reached.

The principal written records are the agenda, the minutes and the committee reports.

The agenda is important because it defines the subject matter of a meeting. It enables committee members to know what is going to be discussed, and with what degree of priority. It enables them to prepare for the meeting.

The minutes of a meeting are even more important, for they are the official record of what takes place. They provide committee members with continuity from one meeting to the next. They serve to remind members of important points which arose at the time (resolutions passed, tasks delegated to individuals etc).

As minutes have to be agreed as a true and correct record of a meeting, they are a reliable source of information both to committee members and outsiders who may have access to them, as in local authorities, for example.

The essentially thorough approach of formal committees requires that the important items on an agenda shall only be discussed after a suitable report has been made by an individual or a sub-committee. Reports should provide a committee with the kind of information that will enable it to take a well-informed decision. Some reports are purely factual, others may be analytical, suggesting alternatives and weighing up arguments, yet others may be innovative and imaginative. Whatever the contents of a report, its purpose is the same: to provide relevant information and ideas as the focal point for the discussion of an important agenda item.

*PQ11    'The reliability and validity of the selection interview is usually so low as to render it practically useless as a selection technique.' To what extent is this true?        (ICSA PPP)*

# Appendix 4. Suggested Answers to Additional Practice Questions

## ANSWER

The interview has never been more popular as a technique for selection. Even where other techniques, such as aptitude tests or intelligence tests, have been employed, the selection process has been rounded off by an interview. Yet, despite its popularity, the interview has been strongly criticised for its lack of reliability and validity. Research studies in Britain, Canada and the United States have demonstrated that certain types of interview, such as the unstructured interview, are practically useless for successful employee selection. They have also shown that some interviews do have a greater degree of reliability and/or validity.

The *reliability* of an interview is a measure of the degree of agreement among interviewers concerning the same candidates. Where agreement about the candidates is consistent, a high degree of reliability has been obtained. Conversely, inconsistent judgements between interviewers indicate a low level of reliability. The *validity* of an interview is a measure of the extent to which it measures what it is supposed to measure, that is the suitability of a candidate for a particular job.

It has been shown that unstructured interviews, with no specific plans for questions, produce very inconsistent results under research conditions. With such poor reliability, it is unlikely that such interviews will correctly predict the best person for the job, which means that validity is also poor.

On the other hand, better results have been achieved where interviews have been structured. That is to say, where questions have been standardised and where the interviewer has focussed his attention on a few specific attributes. One particular research study in the United States showed that when interviews each used three different interview strategies on a set of candidates, it was only from the structured interview that they were able to achieve any consistency of agreement.

Other studies have indicated that where specific behavioural objectives have been set for an interview, the interviewer will focus on questions that will enable a more valid assessment of the candidate's suitability. The interviewer will know what to ask and, more important still, he will know what to do with the answers received. These interviews have been found to be valid for predicting such attributes as motivation and inter-personal skills.

The assertion contained in the question clearly has a great deal of truth in it. It is equally clear that our use of the interview as a selection technique can be improved. However, with improvement there is no reason why the interview should not continue to play a useful part in the selection process. After all, most interviews are conducted against a background of other selection devices, such as application forms, candidate specifications, selection tests and references. What is perhaps needed is for us to forget the interview as a technique for assessing the *overall* suitability of candidates, and to use it instead as a device for measuring fairly specific attributes only. That is to say the interview should be seen as a supplement to other selection techniques rather than as the core of the process. The conclusions of the researchers seem to be that we have expected too much from the interview in the past, and hence its poor reputation as an accurate tool of selection. By using it more selectively to evaluate *specific* information rather than to acquire general impressions, we can use it as a more valid and reliable part of the selection process. There is no reason for dispensing with the technique altogether.

**PQ12**    *To what extent is the Points Method of job evaluation useful in establishing the basis for factory pay scales?*    (ACCA)

**ANSWER**

Factory pay scales may come to be established in several ways. They may be the result of collective bargaining, of local labour market pressures, of custom and practice or of job evaluation. In some cases these scales are incorporated into some kind of pay structure, but in others there is no structure at all – just a collection of arbitrary and haphazard pay scales. The ideal structure would be one containing the minimum number of grades consistent with the different levels of skill and responsibility existing within the factory. Such a structure would probably contain five to seven grades with adequate differentials between them.

The most fruitful way of achieving the ideal structure would be by use of an analytical method of job evaluation such as the Points Method. However, before looking at the usefulness of this particular method, it would be relevant to turn briefly to the other major alternatives and comment on them. Collective bargaining may contribute some rational elements to a factory pay structure, but inevitably the outcomes are based on the relative bargaining strength of particular unions or sectional interests. Might rather than right is the dominant factor. Use of local labour market rates is a notoriously unreliable method for establishing pay scales mainly because of the difficulty of finding an adequate answer to the question 'what is the market rate?' An additional drawback is that market rates are not much help in sorting out internal differentials. The custom and practice method produces a haphazard structure derived from various ad hoc pressures, especially from the shop-floor employees. Both pay scales and differentials are decided on a fairly arbitrary basis.

In contrast to the methods just described, job evaluation provides a much more objective and rational approach to the establishment of a pay structure. The Points Method, in particular, is useful in the context of a factory pay structure because of its ability to distinguish the relative degrees of difference between selected factors which are common to all the jobs in the factory. The evaluation of jobs by common factors, such as knowledge or skills required, responsibility and job conditions, enables the differences between jobs to be justified on rational grounds instead of on arbitrary or political grounds. A further advantage of using a points system is that the resulting evaluations are expressed in quantifiable terms: a points total. Once evaluated, jobs can be ranked in accordance with their points totals. In practice these points totals tend to form clusters in the rank order. Groups of skilled jobs would probably be found clustered together a clear distance above a group of semi-skilled jobs. These clusters usually provide the basis for pay-grades since they are indicative of clear points differentials between groups of jobs.

Many of the differences between jobs are already acknowledged by employees and management alike. For example there would be no disagreement about the seniority of a time-served toolmaker over an unskilled process worker. In these cases job evaluation provides no surprises – it merely confirms a self-evident situation.

However, where the differences between jobs are in doubt or in dispute, then job evaluation using the Points Method can help to settle any arguments by quantifying the differences, if any. This is one of the great advantages of the Method – it can clarify the doubtful areas in an existing job hierarchy. In a factory situation, for example, it can help to identify the relative importance of a work study officer's job compared with that of a production foreman. Such distinctions are vital if a pay structure is to be both fair and credible.

The Points Method of job evaluation can be extremely useful in establishing the basis for factory pay scales because of the rational way it distinguishes job differences. Such differences need no longer be decided by union pressures or custom and practice or other arbitrary forces, but by fully defensible arguments. The actual sums of money to be allocated to the grades resulting from Points evaluation will of course be decided by procedures outside the scope of job evaluation.

**PQ13**   *Examine and assess the problems you see for the personnel manager in devising, implementing and controlling a dismissals procedure.*                    *(ICSA PPP)*

## ANSWER

The purpose of a dismissals procedure is to ensure that an organization administers its own form of internal justice with openness, fairness and consistency. This purpose is not easy to realise.

Typical problems which may arise when *devising* a procedure are:

a. defining terms such as 'misconduct' and 'gross misconduct'
b. agreeing appropriate forms of punishment
c. establishing a procedure that is both simple and fair to operate
d. deciding how to allocate authority for disciplinary action
e. ensuring that the procedure complies with any legal requirements.

The above problems are extremely important. The credibility of the entire procedure depends on how they are tackled. Distinctions between what constitutes 'gross misconduct' as opposed to other forms of misconduct are vital to enable management to apply the correct punishment, and to enable employees to know where the line is drawn.

The traditional view of punishment is that it should fit the crime, and there is no reason why this view should not apply in a business. It is important, therefore, that where an offence is agreed to be very grave, the punishment should be equally grave – instant dismissal, for example. On the other hand, it would be entirely inappropriate to permit dismissal for relatively minor offences.

The procedure must make it absolutely clear who has what powers to carry out punishment. If the rules are not crystal clear someone will eventually administer the incorrect punishment for his level of authority, which is unfair to the employee and most embarrassing for the firm.

An uncomplicated procedure which is clear about the rules and simple to put into operation will minimise confusion over interpretation or implementation.

The problems of *implementing* a procedure are:

a. ensuring adequate communication of the procedure
b. ensuring consistency of treatment
c. deciding how to deal with precedents
d. devising suitable training for managers/supervisors

Adequate communication is vital. No procedure can hope to be fair if those affected by it are ill-informed about it. It would be ideal to have the procedure *explained* to all employees, as well as having it properly circulated.

Ensuring consistency of treatment is a major problem in the early days of a new procedure. The personnel manager would need to fulfil a vital role in this respect in guiding and advising his management colleagues. Employees will expect consistency of treatment and the law will expect it too.

Precedents should be dealt with so that the punishment is fair, and consistency is maintained, otherwise every new precedent throws the system into doubt and confusion.

Most of the points concerning implementation can be aided by a suitable training programme aimed at supplying knowledge and developing skills related to discipline.

The problems of *controlling* a procedure are: a. ensuring that authority levels are not exceeded b. devising a suitable system of records c. allocating roles for the overall control of the procedure

Once authority levels have been set, they must be strictly adhered to, so that no manager or supervisor acts beyond his powers. Most procedures include a proviso that any punishment handed out at one level of authority must be endorsed by the next highest level. The Personnel Manager needs to have the support of both superiors and colleagues to ensure that these controls are effective.

Records are necessary to ensure that evidence is collected in a consistent manner, and that adequate notes are made of decisions taken. Records may need to be produced later on appeal or at a tribunal. Most organizations will turn to their Personnel department for assistance with this aspect of control.

Finally, there is the question of who should have the overall responsibility for control of the procedure. This again usually falls to the Personnel department, since they are well placed to co-ordinate the operation of the procedure and to insist that its standards are enforced.

*PQ14     In what major ways has British legislation attempted to pursue social fairness in employment over the past twelve years?*
*(ACCA)*

## ANSWER

The individual employee will always be at a considerable disadvantage in respect of his employer. An employer has many more options open to him if he comes into conflict with his employees. Increasingly, in recent years, the law has recognised this unequal relationship and has taken steps to adjust the balance. Initially, the law has concentrated on protecting the average fulltime employee, but in the last five years or so it has also turned its attention to what might be described as the disadvantaged employee: the immigrant worker and the female employee, for example.

The first protection the law can give is against arbitrary or unfair dismissal. Ever since the Industrial Relations Act, 1971, employees have been protected against 'unfair dismissal' – a statutory concept which considerably extends the common law rights arising out of 'wrongful dismissal'. If an employee feels he has been unfairly dismissed, he may pursue a claim through an industrial tribunal which has the power to order reinstatement or re-engagement or to make compensatory award.

Not only is the employee protected against dismissal, he may also be protected against action short of dismissal, for example where he wishes to engage in trade union activities in a business that is anti-union. This right was introduced into the Industrial Relations Act, and now resides in the Employment Protection (Consolidation) Act, 1978, which contains the bulk of the individual rights now in force.

Further important protection against arbitrary behaviour by the employer is provided by the various requirements to make information available to employees. So, for example, employees must receive basic details of their employment (rate of pay, hours of work, length of notice etc) during the first thirteen weeks of their employment. Other examples include the right to a written statement of the reasons for dismissal (in dismissal cases) and the right to an itemised pay statement. The well-informed employee is less likely to be taken advantage of by an unscrupulous employer. This issue of information has been extended to trade unions when acting in their representational role. Employers are bound, therefore, to disclose information to trade unions concerning planned redundancies, and, if requested must supply certain information to the unions prior to collective bargaining. These points all help to ensure that employees have a fair and reasonable chance to keep informed about vital matters affecting their employment.

Apart from being unfairly dismissed, the average employee's greatest worry is to find that his job is no longer required, that is to say redundant. The main assistance given to employees whose jobs become redundant is provided by the Employment Protection

(Consolidation) Act, 1978 which incorporates the earlier provisions of the Redundancy Payments Act, 1965. The Act provides for the payment of a service-based lump sum to all employees with more than two years' service. This at least has the effect of cushioning the immediate hardship of unemployment. The Act also includes such benefits as time off to seek other employment and the right to a trial period in any alternative job the employer may offer him.

The situation of women at work has been affected considerably in the last few years by changing social attitudes. Today it is not accepted as fair that a woman should be paid less than a man when doing work of equal value. It is also felt that women have been less than fairly treated in terms of promotion and career growth compared with men. These issues have been dealt with by such legislation as the Equal Pay Act, 1970, the Sex Discrimination Act, 1975, and the Employment Protection (Consolidation) Act, 1978. These Acts combine to improve the relative position of women in terms of pay, training, promotion and maternity leave for example.

The law also acts to prevent immigrants from being unfairly treated. The most recent law on this is the Race Relations Act, 1976, which makes it unlawful for an employer to discriminate against a person on grounds of colour, race or nationality in respect of recruitment, training or promotion, for example. In this way the law protects minority groups in our society.

The overall effect of the above-mentioned legislation has been to protect both majority groups and minority groups of employees from the worst effects of unfairness arising either from arbitrary actions on behalf of employers or from adverse economic conditions.

*PQ15   What are the likely consequences of a manager introducing an element of competition*
  a.   *between individuals, and*
  b.   *between work groups, in order to increase organizational efficiency?*                          *(ICMA OMM)*

## ANSWER
The likely consequences of introducing an element of competition between individuals and between work groups can be analysed by reference to both the positive and the negative aspects. To take competition between individuals first, we could identify the following positive responses:-

- increased motivation indicated by enthusiasm for the task, and greater concentration on it
- higher output and/or better quality of work
- increased earnings (where related to an incentive scheme) and/or job satisfaction
- a minority of individuals will thrive under such conditions

These benefits of healthy rivalry can, however, be outweighed by the negative responses that may occur. For example, these could include:–

- selfish 'every-man-for-himself!' attitudes with no commitment to co-operative behaviour
- the development of mistrust and tension between colleagues
- increased willingness to 'cut corners' by ignoring procedural or safety rules, for example
- excessive stress on certain individuals leading to emotional conflicts or illness.

In addition to these disadvantages is the probable need to introduce further departmental rules in order to deal with the conflict that may arise as a direct result of the competition.

Groups will also display both positive and negative reactions to competition. Positive reactions could include:–

- a closing of the ranks, and the development of greater group self-consciousness
- increased commitment by individuals to the work of the group, ie a real sense of co-operation
- willingness to achieve higher output if the incentive is there
- increased demands on the group leader to achieve success, which minimises weak or complacent leadership
- establishment of high standards of working for the group

On the other hand, negative reactions could include:–

- arguing over 'territorial' claims for accommodation, typing services and other disputed items
- pressures on the leader to break established rules or customs where this could lead to beating rival groups
- aggressive behaviour towards the other groups, including accusations of cheating, and refusal to share equipment or people
- setting group standards regardless of the goals of the unit as a whole and possibly detrimental to it.

As with individuals, there would also be a need for additional machinery for, (a) reducing conflict, and (b) arbitrating in cases where conflict has escalated.

In the final analysis, it will be the way in which the manager introduces the element of competition which will have the greatest effect in determining whether the outcome will be positive or negative.

***PQ16*** *Describe and discuss the requirements for an effective grievance procedure.* *(ICSA PPP)*

**ANSWER**

There are three basic features which should be the cornerstone of any acceptable grievance procedure:–

   i.    it should be fair and seen to be fair,

   ii.   it should aim to settle the grievance as near as possible to its point of origin,

   iii.  its details should be simple to understand and should be well-communicated.

A typical grievance procedure will have the following stages:–

   i.    the employee raises the issue with his immediate superior, and may be accompanied by a colleague or union representative if he wishes.

   ii.   if the employee is not satisfied with the result of this first meeting, he may meet a more senior person to discuss his case.

   iii.  if the employee is still not satisfied after the second stage, he may appeal to a director or other appropriate senior manager for a final decision.

   iv.  where a trade union is involved, a procedure agreement may permit an individual grievance to be taken up as a collective dispute following stage three.

If the requirements for an effective procedure are to be met, organizations must allow for:–

   i.    representation at every level of the procedure, if requested by the employee.

   ii.   speedy replies by the supervisor/managers involved.

   iii.  adequate training of managers and supervisors in the handling of grievances.

   iv.  sufficient delegation of authority to lower levels of management to enable decisions to be made properly but quickly in respect of grievances.

   v.   clearly-written, easily-understandable procedure.

vi.   thorough dissemination of the procedure, eg by individual letters, posters etc.

**PQ17**   a.   *State the different types of pricing policy open to a manufacturer.*

b.   *Discuss the reasons by the pricing policy of a manufacturer of pet foods should be different from that of a manufacturer of scientific measuring equipment.*

*(ICMA OMM)*

**ANSWER**

a.   Different types of pricing policy for manufacturer:–

–   Market Penetration: low prices to gain major market share in short time-span.

–   Short-term Profit Maximisation: High prices for unique or revolutionary product in the short term.

–   Cost-plus Pricing: prices based on estimated production costs plus a margin related to return on investment, capital or similar ratio.

–   Product-line Pricing: prices based on *total* contribution of a range of products, which could include 'loss-leaders' to stimulate sales of more profitable lines.

–   Variable Pricing: prices carried according to peaks and troughs of the business cycle, eg as in off-peak rates for hotels, travel etc.

–   Competitive Pricing: prices set very much with an eye on the competition. Famous example here is the John Lewis policy of 'Never Knowingly Undersold'.

–   Bid Pricing: specialised form of pricing for large-scale contracts, relying heavily on estimates of contract costs and likely bids by competitors.

b.   Pricing policy of petfood manufacturer should differ from manufacturer of scientific equipment on grounds of:–

–   The market for petfoods is highly segmented and very competitive, which tends to cause swift reactions to any price changes. The market for scientific measuring equipment is less volatile and less price-sensitive.

–   There is a high degree of elasticity of demand in the petfood market. Buyers will look for alternatives at once if prices were to increase significantly. The buyers of scientific equipment will be looking for quality and reliability as much as any other factor. Demand will be less elastic and less influenced by price increases.

- Petfood manufacturer could consider product-line pricing because of his wide range of products. It is most unlikely that this could apply to the manufacturers of scientific equipment where the product range would be quite small. Some products would almost certainly be unique.

- The manufacturer of scientific equipment could always consider a profit-maximisation policy for a new and much sought-after invention. At the very least he would need to cover high research and development costs by some form of cost-plus pricing. In the kind of market described for petfoods, there is no way these pricing policies could be maintained for any length of time.

**PQ18** *What do you understand by the term 'market segmentation'? Select two from the following:–*

*i.    a manufacturer of machine tools;*

*ii.   a supplier of office cleaning services;*

*iii.  a manufacturer of PVC pipes;*

*and describe the likely bases on which each might segment his market.* (ICMA OMM)

**ANSWER**

'Market segmentation' means sub-dividing a market into identifiable buyer-groups, with the object of reaching such groups with a distinctive marketing mix. Markets are chiefly segmented by reference to geographical, demographic or buyer behaviour variables. The various market segments for the three examples in the question could be analysed as follows:–

(NB You only need to write about *two* of them. The answer-guide covers all three examples).

*Machine-tool manufacturer:*

Geographical
- Industrial towns/cities
- New towns
- UK/EEC/Commonwealth/Other overseas

Demographic
- Customer size (large, medium and small)
- Customer class (economy buyer, quality seeker?)
- Use of Standard Industrial Classification (SIC)

Buyer-Behaviour
- Regular/infrequent buyer?
- Large/small-scale buyer?

*Supplier of Office Cleaning Services:*

Geographical
- Conurbations/towns/cities
- Local/regional/nation-wide clients

Demographic
- Customer size (single office? several?)
- Customer class (basic service only? de luxe service?)

Buyer-Behaviour
- Weekday users only (evenings/days?)
- All day – every day users

*Manufacturer of PVC pipes:*

Geographical
- Urban/agricultural/construction users
- Local/regional/national customers
- UK/EEC/other export customers

Demographic
- Customer size
- Customer type (public utility? Private construction firm? builders' merchants etc?)
- Use of the SIC

Buyer-Behaviour
- Customer size
- Regular/infrequent buyers
- Large/small-scale buyers

# 5

# LIST OF FURTHER EXAMINATION QUESTIONS

There are suggested answers for Lecturers/Tutors only, available separately on application.

Well over 50 previous examination questions have been supplied with either outline or fuller suggested answers in this Manual. These should provide ample scope for students to practise their examination technique and to apply the knowledge they have gained to authentic examination questions. It also seems sensible to include a number of such questions without answers in the Manual, in order to provide lecturers and tutors with an opportunity to test students in situations where no ready answer-guide is available. The following selection of questions aims to fill this need for unseen answers. The guides which have been prepared are available only to staff, on application, in writing, to the publishers.

*FEQ1    Comment critically on the contribution made to contemporary personnel policies by any one of the following behavioural theorists:*

*Abraham Maslow*

*Frederick Herzberg*

*Douglas McGregor*

*Rensis Likert*

*(ICSA PPP)*

*FEQ2    You have been appointed as the first manager of a new department. Your first task is to establish the objectives of the department, to establish the departmental organization structure and to decide on staffing levels. What steps will you take and what information will you require? The new department can be any ONE of the following: (a) production; (b) personnel; (c) accounts; (d) marketing.    (ICSA MPP)*

*FEQ3    Outline and comment on the stages involved in managerial decision-making.    (IAM Dipl.)*

***FEQ4*** *What would be the major factors you would wish to consider when drawing up the corporate plan for ONE of the following organizations:*
   *a. a nationalised industry;*
   *b. a manufacturing company;*
   *c. a college or university;*
   *d. a water authority.*

*(ICSA MPP)*

***FEQ5*** *What difference in structure would you expect to find between:–*
   *a. a company manufacturing and selling chemical plant worldwide,*
   *b. a company manufacturing and distributing fastmoving domestic appliances in its home market,*
   *c. a company operating a chain of retail supermarkets?*

*(IOM Business Orgn.)*

***FEQ6*** *Outline the role of committees and examine their importance as part of an organization's management structure.*

*(IAM Dipl.)*

***FEQ7*** *What do you understand by the term 'functional relationship' in an organization? Choose one example of a functional executive and describe his work and method of operation.* *(ICMA Orgn. of Production)*

***FEQ8*** *Outline the main theories relating to individual motivation to work and show how leadership styles may be adapted to accommodate the aspirations of employees.*

*(IOB Human Aspects of Mgt.)*

***FEQ9*** *Explain the phrase 'leadership style'. Discuss the strengths and weaknesses of the various types of leadership style, illustrating your answer by reference to any banking organization with which you are familiar.* *(IOB Nature of Mgt.)*

***FEQ10*** *How might the organization of production into work teams: (a) help, and (b) hinder the efficient running of the enterprise?* *(ICMA OMM)*

***FEQ11*** *You have been asked to investigate the effectiveness of the use of 'budgetary control' in your organization. Set out and discuss the problem areas you would expect to find.*

*(IAM Approach to Office Admin.)*

**FEQ12**   a.   What is advertising?

b.   What range of objectives might be set for an advertising campaign?

c.   How might their success be evaluated?

*(ICMA OMM)*

**FEQ13**   Outline the main sequence of events of a Work Study programme. In what ways have recent changes in the attitude of workers and management towards the working environment affected the usefulness of this technique?

*(IOM Business Orgn.)*

**FEQ14**   What factors determine the maximum number of subordinates who can be effectively managed by one person?

*(ACCA Business Mgt.)*

**FEQ15**   Identify the similarities and differences between 'organization development' and 'management development' programmes.

*(ICMA OMM)*

**FEQ16**   How can the role of the personnel manager be distinguished from that of any manager with responsibility for the supervision of personnel?

*(ICSA PPP)*

**FEQ17**   a.   What is meant by Job Evaluation, and for what purpose is it used?

b.   Briefly describe-three methods of Job Evaluation.

*(IOM Business Orgn.)*

**FEQ18**   What are the main features of the Employment Protection Act, 1975?

*(ACCA Business Mgt.)*

**FEQ19**   How far, in your view, can industrial relations be regulated or improved by means of legislation?

*(ICSA PPP)*

**FEQ20**   Discuss what is meant by the term 'two-tier Board of Directors', and suggest plausible functions for each tier.

*(ACCA Business Mgt.)*

# APPENDIX

# 6

# GUIDE TO FURTHER READING

The following alphabetical list of authors comprises a fair cross-section of writers on the subject of Management. Most of the works referred to in the list have been mentioned in the text of the Manual. Several others are included to provide readers with a range of writings that will enable them to follow up any particular areas of personal interest.

| Adair, J. | Training for Leadership | MacDonald |
| Ansoff, H.I. | Corporate Strategy | Penguin |
| Argenti, J. | Corporate Planning | Allen & Unwin |
| Argyris, C. | Understanding Organizational Behaviour | Tavistock |
| Argyris, C. | Integrating the Individual and the Organization | Wiley |
| Armstrong, M. | Handbook of Personnel Management Practice | Kogan Page |
| Bales, R.F. | Personality and Interpersonal Behaviour | Holt, Rinehart & Winston, |
| Belbin, R.M. | Management Teams | Heinemann |
| Blake, R. & Mouton, J. | The Managerial Grid | Gulf |
| Brech, E.F.L. (ed.) | The Principles & Practice of Management | Longman |
| Brech, E.F.L. | Organization – the Framework of Management | Longman |
| Brown, W. | Exploration in Management | Heinemann |
| Burns & Stalker | The Management of Innovation | Tavistock |
| Child, J. | Organization | Harper & Row |
| Drucker, P. | The Practice of Management | Heinemann |
| Easterby-Smith, M. | Auditing Management Development | Gower Press |

| | | |
|---|---|---|
| Fayol, H. | General and Industrial Management | Pitman |
| Fiedler, F.E. | A Theory of Leadership Effectiveness | McGraw Hill |
| Hamblin, A.C. | Evaluation and Control of Training | McGraw-Hill |
| Handy, C.B. | Understanding Organizations | Penguin |
| Hawkins, K. | Handbook of Industrial Relations Practice | Kogan Page |
| Herzberg, F. | Work and the Nature of Man | World Publishing |
| Humble, J.W. | Improving Business Results | McGraw Hill |
| Katz & Kahn | Social Psychology of Organizations | Wiley |
| Kotler, P. | Marketing Management (4th edn.) | Prentice Hill |
| Lawrence & Lorsch | Organization and Environment | Harvard U.P. |
| Likert, R. | New Patterns of Management | McGraw Hill |
| Lucey, T. | Quantitative Techniques | DP Publications |
| Lupton, T. | Management and the Social Sciences | Penguin |
| Maier, N. | The Appraisal Interview | Wiley |
| Maslow, A. | Motivation and Personality | Harper & Row |
| Mayo, E. | The Human Problems of an Industrial Civilization | MacMillan, N.Y. |
| McClelland, D.C. | The Achieving Society | Van Nostrand |
| McGregor, D. | The Human Side of Enterprise | McGraw Hill |
| McMillan, C.J. | The Japanese Industrial System | de Gruyter |
| Miller & Rice | Systems of Organization | Tavistock |
| Mintzberg, H. | The Nature of Managerial Work | Harper & Row |
| Ouchi, W.G. | Theory Z | Addison-Wesley |

| | | |
|---|---|---|
| Pedler, M. | A Manager's Guide to Self-development | McGraw-Hill |
| Porter, Lawler & Hackman | Behaviour in Organizations | McGraw Hill |
| Pugh, D. & Hickson, D. | The Comparative Study of Organizations (from Industrial Society) | Penguin |
| Pugh et al | Writers on Organizations | Penguin |
| Rackham, Honey & Colbert | Developing Interactive Skills | Wellens |
| Reddin, W. | Managerial Effectiveness | McGraw Hill |
| Roethlisberger & Dickson | Management and the Worker | Harvard U.P. |
| Schein, E.H. | Organizational Psychology | Prentice Hall |
| Simmons, J. & Brennan, R. | New Approaches to Management Development | Gower/ATM |
| Stewart, R. | Managerial Choice | McGraw Hill |
| Tannenbaum & Schmidt | How to Choose a Leadership Pattern | Harvard Business Review,1958 |
| Taylor, F.W. | Scientific Management | Harper & Row |
| Thomason, G. | A Textbook of Personnel Management | IPM |
| Trist & Bamforth | Some Social and Psychological Consequences of the Longwall Method of Coal-getting | Human Relations Vol.4 No.1, 1951 |
| Trist, E.L.et al | Organizational Choice | Tavistock |
| Urwick, L.F. | The Elements of Administration | Pitman |
| Vroom,V.H. | Work and Motivation | Wiley |
| Weber, M. | Theory of Social and Economic Organization | The Free Press |
| Woodcock, M. | Team Development Manual | Gower Press |
| Woodward, J. | Industrial Organization – Theory & Practice | Oxford,U.P. |

# INDEX

# Index